# OUT OF ACTIONS:
### between performance and the object, 1949-1979

COL⟩

# OUT OF ACTIONS:
## between performance and the object, 1949-1979

with essays by
Kristine Stiles
Guy Brett
Hubert Klocker
Shinichiro Osaki
Paul Schimmel

Thames and Hudson

This book was published on the occaision of the exhibition
**"Out of Actions: Between Performance and the Object 1949-1979,"**
organized by Paul Schimmel and presented at
The Geffen Contemporary at The Museum of Contemporary Art, Los Angeles,
February 8 - May 10,1998.

"Out of Actions:
Between Performance and the Object, 1949-1979"
is dedicated to the memory
of Sydney Irmas,
and is made possible by a generous gift
from The Audrey and Sydney Irmas
Charitable Foundation.

The exhibition has also received
significant support from the National Endowment
for the Arts, a federal agency;
The Japan Foundation; the Japan-United States
Friendship Commission;
the Austrian Cultural Institute, New York;
the Austrian Federal Chancellery - Arts;
the Austrian Consulate General in Los Angeles;
The British Council; Merrill Lynch;
Service Culturel du Consulat Général de France
à Los Angeles; and *Association Française
d'Action Artistique* A -A A
*Ministère des Affaires Étrangères*

**Exhibition Tour**

The Museum of Contemporary Art
at The Geffen Contemporary, Los Angeles
8 February - 10 May 1998

MAK - Austrian Museum of Applied Arts,
Vienna
17 June - 6 September 1998

Museu d'Art Contemporani, Barcelona
15 October 1998 - 6 January 1999

Museum of Contemporary Art, Tokyo
11 February - 11 April 1999

Editor: Russell Ferguson
Assistant Editor: Stephanie Emerson
Editorial Assistant: Jane Hyun
Design and production:
Lorraine Wild, Amanda Washburn, Yuki Nishinaka
Separations:
DeskTopProduction Bucher GmbH, Stuttgart
Printed at Cantz in Germany
Bound in Germany

First published in the United States of America
in paperback in 1998 by Thames and Hudson, Inc.
500 Fifth Avenue, New York, New York 10010.

First published in Great Britain in 1998
by Thames and Hudson Ltd, London

Library of Congress Catalog Card
Number 97-62054

British Library Cataloguing-in-Publication data
A catalogue record for this book is available from
the British Library

ISBN 0-500-28050-9

# CONTENTS

**Carolee Schneemann**, *Eye Body*, 1963 (detail). Collection of the artist.

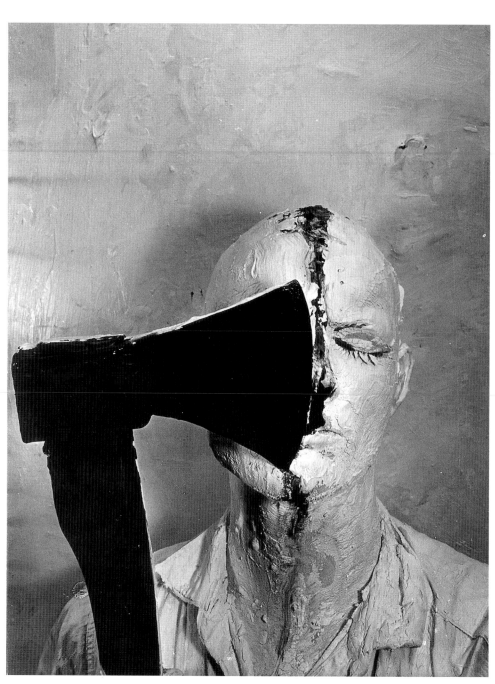

**Günther Brus**, *Selbstbemalung*, 1964. Archiv Conz, Verona

# LENDERS TO THE EXHIBITION

## Institutions

Arts Council Collection, Hayward Gallery, London
The Ashiya City Museum of Art & History
Greenville County Museum of Art
Solomon R. Guggenheim Museum, New York
Hyogo Prefectural Museum of Modern Art, Kobe
Kunstmuseum Bonn
The Menil Collection, Houston
Museum of Contemporary Art, Tokyo
The Museum of Modern Art, New York
Museum moderner Kunst Stiftung Ludwig, Vienna
Museum Wiesbaden
Nagoya City Museum
Rose Art Museum, Brandeis University, Waltham
San Francisco Museum of Modern Art
Staatsgalerie Stuttgart, Archiv Sohm
Takamatsu City Museum of Art
Tate Gallery, London
Toyota Municipal Museum of Art
University of California, Berkeley Art Museum
Walker Art Center, Minneapolis
Wexner Center for the Arts, The Ohio State University
Whitney Museum of American Art, New York

## Artists, private collectors and foundations

Marina Abramović
Vito Acconci
Genpei Akasegawa
Laurie Anderson
Eleanor Antin
Rasheed Araeen
Mowry Baden
Artur Barrio
Alberto Bassi
Gerard Beaufour
Ole Bjornsdal Archive, Denmark
Block Collection
Mark Boyle and Joan Hills
Stuart Brisley
Robert Delford Brown
Günter Brus
Chris Burden
Mercedes Casanegra
Richard Castellane, Esq.
Shashi Caudill and Alan Cravitz
Lygia Clark Estate
William Claxton
Pinchas Cohen Gan
Houston Conwill
W.L. Conwill and F.V. Harrison
Archiv Conz, Verona
Paul Cotton
Jane Crawford and Gordon Matta-Clark Estate
Guy de Cointet Estate
Niki de Saint Phalle
Gino di Maggio, Fondazione Mudima, Milan
Jim Dine
John Duncan
Felipe Ehrenberg
Thomas Erben
Roberto Evangelista
Valie Export
Sante Falconèr
Wolfgang Feelisch
Frayda and Ronald Feldman
Robert Filliou Estate
Rose Finn-Kelcey
Sherman Fleming

Fondazione Lucio Fontana, Milan
Arnold and Marie Forde
Terry Fox
Howard Fried
Barry Friedman
Sammlung Friedrichshof, Zurndorf
Gideon Gechtman
Jochen Gerz
Eva Geyer
The Carol and Arthur Goldberg Collection
Alberto Greco Estate
Ion Grigorescu
Victor Grippo
Bibbe Hansen
Maren Hassinger
Eléanore Hendricks
Jon and Joanne Hendricks
Lynn Hershman
Hess Collection
Susan Hiller
Sammlung Hoffmann
A.C. Hudgins
Pontus Hulten
Julius Hummel
Jasper Johns
Kim Jones
Donald Judd Estate
Allan Kaprow
Mike Kelley
Jurgen Klauke
Yves Klein Archives
Milan Knížák
Alison Knowles
Eustachy Kossakowski
Jannis Kounellis
Yayoi Kusama
Suzanne Lacy
Phyllis Lambert
John Latham
Uwe Laysiepen
Jean-Jacques Lebel
Lea Lublin
Ronald Maker
Leopoldo Maler
Archivio Opera Piero Manzoni
Anne Marchand and the Estate of Gina Pane
Tom Marioni
Cusi Masuda
Georges Mathieu
Paul McCarthy
Robert McElroy
Bruce McLean
Cildo Meireles
Gustav Metzger
Jacques Miège
Marta Minujin
Jan Mlčoch
Andrej Monastyrskij
Linda Montano
Makiko Murakami
Natsuyuki Nakanishi
Peter Namuth and Hans Namuth Estate
Bruce Nauman
Paul Neagu
Senga Nengudi
Joshua Neustein
Hermann Nitsch
Peter and Eileen Norton
Projeto Helío Oiticica, Rio de Janeiro
Claes Oldenburg and Coosje van Bruggen
Reinhard Onnasch
Yoko Ono
Orlan
Raphael Montañez Ortiz
Lorenzo Pace
Lygia Pape
Tom Patchett
Hubert Peeters
Adrian Piper
Michelangelo Pistoletto
William Pope L.

Alison Radovanović and the Kerry Trengove Estate
Agnès and Jean-Pierre Rammant
Robert Rauschenberg
Carlyle Reedy
Klaus Rinke
Sergej Romaschko
Ulrike Rosenbach
Hans Ruepp
Lia Rumma
Zorka Ságlová
Vanni Scheiwiller
Alfons Schilling
Carolee Schneemann
Arturo Schwarz Collection, Milan
Bonnie Sherk
Ushio Shinohara
Kazuo Shiraga
Harry Shunk
Gilbert and Lila Silverman Collection
Gilbert and Lila Silverman Fluxus Collection Foundation
Barbara T. Smith
Sonnabend Sundell/Methodact Ltd.
The Rainer Speck Collection, Cologne
Stelarc
Petr Štembera
Jirō Takamatsu
Atsuko Tanaka
Fundacio Antoni Tàpies, Barcelona
Tatsumi Hijikata Memorial Archives, Theatre Asbestos
Mark Thompson
Raša Todosijević
Cosey Fanni Tutti
Dorine van der Klei
Daniel Varenne
Ben Vautier
Wolf Vostell
Franz Erhard Walther
Julian Wasser
Peter Weibel
Franz West
Estate of Hannah Wilke
Emmett Williams
Zaj Group Archives

## Galleries

Gallery Paule Anglim, San Francisco
Bugdahn und Kaimer Gallery, Düsseldorf
Galeria Cohn Edelstein, Rio de Janeiro
Galerie Chantal Crousel, Paris
D'Amelio Terras Gallery, New York
Anne de Villepoix, Paris
Anthony d'Offay Gallery, London
Thomas Erben Gallery, New York
Ronald Feldman Fine Arts, New York
Lance Fung Gallery, New York
Gagosian Gallery, New York
Barbara Gladstone Gallery, New York
Galerie der Haupstadt Prag, Prague
Hulton Getty Picture Gallery, London
Akira Ikeda Gallery, Tokyo
Sean Kelly, New York
Galerie Rudolf Kicken, Cologne
Galerie Krinzinger, Vienna
Galerie Lelong, New York
Lisson Gallery, London
Galleria Martano, Turin
Robert Miller Gallery, New York
Galerie Nelson, Paris
Galerie Georg Nothelfer, Berlin
Margarete Roeder Gallery, New York
Wendy Shafir Gallery, New York
Sonnabend Gallery, New York
Christian Stein Gallery, Milan
John Weber Gallery, New York
Michael Werner Gallery, New York & Cologne
David Zwirner Gallery, New York

## FOREWORD

Contemporary art—roughly defined as art from 1940 to the present—is a vast ferment, a shifting sea of currents that rise to the surface, fall from sight, re-emerge intertwined. The task of any museum grappling with contemporary art is to convey the richness of this sea, and to continually examine the effects of the various currents on subsequent artistic output. Unlike historical museums, which can rely heavily on solo exhibitions of artists whose reputations are firmly secured, contemporary museums' relevance rests on thematic exhibitions that shed light on art seen in new contexts.

"Out of Actions: Between Performance and the Object, 1949-1979" is a splendid addition to a series of thematic explorations that have defined the character of The Museum of Contemporary Art since its inception. In its brief history, MOCA has undertaken, as part of its mission, an ambitious program designed to reexamine the pivotal events and junctures in the evolution of contemporary art. Such exhibitions as "A Forest of Signs" (1989), "Reconsidering the Object of Art: 1965-1975" (1995), and "Helter Skelter: L.A. Art in the 1990s" (1992), to name just a few, have made invaluable contributions to the understanding of contemporary art and its place in the larger world. Similarly, "Out of Actions" breaks new ground in revealing the complex international web of connections that produced a truly new kind of art based on elements of process and time. Although each of the movements and groups in the exhibition—such as the New York School, Fluxus, performance art, and the Gutai Group, among others — has been individually explored, "Out of Actions" will be the first major exhibition to link a seemingly disparate series of artists and trends worldwide, and will reveal the indelible stamp of three crucial decades on contemporary output since then.

Even among MOCA's other large-scale programs to date, "Out of Actions" stands out as one of the museum's more ambitious efforts, and reflects the perseverance, vision, and passionate commitment of Paul Schimmel, our Chief Curator. His extraordinary work in organizing the exhibition over many years has not only produced remarkable results, but has enhanced the international reach and stature of the museum overall. His efforts have also been aided by an exceptional staff team, and we extend kudos to Kim Cooper, Linda Genereux, Susan Jenkins, and Denise Spampinato in particular.

The presentation of this exhibition is also a tribute to two peerless individuals without whom the museum would not be what it is today: Audrey and Sydney Irmas. "Out of Actions" is dedicated to Syd's memory through a major gift from The Audrey and Sydney Irmas Charitable Foundation, and as such strikes a poignant note: All of us at MOCA will always miss Syd, with his incomparable vigor and capacity for friendship. We are incredibly fortunate to be graced by Audrey's continuing presence at the museum, and it is impossible to overstate her contributions on every level—as Chair of our Board of Trustees, through magnificent gifts to the museum's collection and permanent endowment, through support of numerous exhibitions in addition to "Out of Actions," and as our matchless advocate on every front.

This exhibition has also been supported by a remarkable "coalition" of nations whose artists are represented in the show. Our appreciation in particular to the following agencies and staff whose efforts made additional funding possible: Jennifer Dowley at the National Endowment for the Arts; Shin'ichiro Asao and Isao Tsujimoto of The Japan Foundation; Eric Gangloff of the Japan-United States Friendship Commission; Peter Wittmann and Andreas Mailath-Pokorny of the Austrian Federal Chancellery; Wolfgang Waldner and Thomas Stelzer of the Austrian Cultural Institute; Consul General Werner Brandstetter of the Austrian Consulate General in Los Angeles; Andrea Rose of The British Council; Rod Hagenbuch of Merrill Lynch; Juliette Salzmann at the Service Culturel du Consulat Général de France, Los Angeles, and Jean Digne, Director, Française d'Action Artistique, Ministère des Affaires Étrangèrs.

Our thanks to all, and we look forward to celebrating "Out of Actions" with them and enthusiastic audiences throughout the exhibition's international presentation.

Richard Koshalek
Director

## INTRODUCTION AND ACKNOWLEDGMENTS

This exhibition brings together a very specific group of works to represent that crucial period in which performance both informed and altered the nature of artists' practice. "Out of Actions: Between Performance and the Object, 1949-1979" — the exhibition and the accompanying catalogue — make no attempt to survey performance, per se. In that respect, extraordinary work made by dancers, musicians, playwrights, authors, architects, and social scientists (all of whom had a profound effect on and an interaction with the visual arts and performance) are not explored. Instead, a very specific collection of the material culture of art has been brought together. It represents an exploration into the visual arts, and the paintings, sculptures, installations, objects, and documentation that form the residue, the work of art, that resulted from their performance work. This is not an illustrated history of performance art. It is, however, an international survey that brings together artists of the 1950s, 1960s and 1970s whose work was undeniably altered by their association with performative actions. Although there are aspects of this tendency to be found in many important earlier movements (especially in Dada), the era following World War II saw a veritable explosion of activity which brought process and performance directly to bear as the subject of works themselves. The line between action, performance and a work of art became increasingly indistinguishable and irrelevant. Works in this exhibition have been selected because they demonstrate both a critical period in the artists' career, and because they embody that fragile quality where the object itself is imbued with the performance that created it. I have attempted to at least erode nationalist boundaries in both the selection of the work and in the interaction that is encouraged in their primarily chronological representation. Today we are far enough removed from this period to understand and appreciate the international relationships, broad cultural exchanges and multigenerational interactions during this extraordinarily protean period. The necessity of travel associated with performance work allowed and encouraged an extraordinary degree of interaction that brought the studio into the world arena.

"Out of Actions: Between Performance and the Object, 1949-1979" takes as its model the kind of exhibition that was, for example, a hallmark of The Museum of Modern Art, New York during the 1960s. In "The Art of Assemblage" (1961), organized by William C. Seitz, well over a half-century of assemblage was surveyed through individual works by virtually unknown artists, or well over a dozen by some of the leading practitioners. Similarly structured but even more ambitious, was Pontus Hulten's "The Machine as Seen at the End of the Mechanical Age" (1968). In recent years the large-scale thematic exhibition has been increasingly in decline. To a significant degree, we have given up broad associative interactions between individual objects by different artists in favor of a more monographic approach. Unfortunately, because of this respect for individual achievement, the significant thematic, iconographic and formal associations that illuminate the artistic practice of an era have not been regularly surveyed in recent years. Under the leadership of Richard Koshalek, MOCA has in recent exhibitions such as "Hall of Mirrors: Art and Film Since 1945" and "1965-1975: Reconsidering the Object of Art" attempted to fill some of this significant void. I have Richard to thank for creating a supportive climate for a project such as "Out of Actions." In a time when museums are increasingly concerned with the bottom line and formulas that "work", Richard has allowed, and even encouraged, experimentation and speculative investigation.

MOCA's staff in its entirety is extraordinary in their appreciation of demanding and creative adventures. I wish to thank Kathleen Bartels, Assistant Director, for her administrative guidance and help with the exhibition tour; Erica Clark, Director of Development, for the leadership she provides towards the significant demands of funding the exhibition; Dawn Setzer, Assistant Director of Communications, Media Relations, for her great sensitivity and enthusiasm to bringing a wider coverage and audience to the exhibition; Sharla Barrett, Manager Special Events, for orchestrating the opening dinner; Alma Ruiz, Assistant Curator, for the endless details in coordinating the tour and her assistance to me in developing a budget for the exhibition; Jack Wiant, Chief Financial Officer, for his appreciation of both the financial responsibilities and creative opportunities in financing and controlling the expenses associated with such a large-scale exhibition. John Bowsher, Exhibitions Production Manager, and his incredible staff along with David Bradshaw, Media Arts Technical Manager, have done a remarkable job of transforming The Geffen Contemporary from an open warehouse to a tightly sequenced series of rooms that allow the viewer to take a chronological walk through the history of art made out of performance. The Registrarial department — with the leadership of Robert Hollister, Registrar, and the resourcefulness of Portland McCormick, Assistant Registrar — has worked tirelessly and tenaciously to bring works from the four corners of the earth to Los Angeles, and for inclusion in the exhibition's subsequent tour.

This book is in many ways the most lasting product of the exhibition, and we hope that it will make a significant contribution to the literature of performance-based art. It has been the result of the contributions of MOCA's Editor, Russell Ferguson, and the vision of him and his staff, including most importantly, Stephanie Emerson, Assistant Editor, who has done an extraordinary job to bring the catalogue to completion, with the assistance of Jane Hyun, Editorial Secretary. The catalogue has benefitted from the deft design and a sense of grace under fire (necessitated by a short design period) of Lorraine Wild. She is a brilliant and original designer who deserves more time than she ever gets. My essay benefitted tremendously from the editorial assistance of both Sue Henger and John Farmer.

This exhibition has benefitted enormously from the contributions of Guy Brett, Hubert Klocker, Shinichiro Osaki, and Kristine Stiles. I traveled through both Germany and Austria with Hubert Klocker. Guy Brett and I spent important time together in London. Shinichiro Osaki singlehandedly organized my visits to Osaka and Tokyo. Kristine Stiles worked with me on several occasions here in Los Angeles. Over the past years, Ferguson and I have met with the authors and benefitted enormously from their contributions, both in the development of the checklist and in their significant contribution to the catalogue. They have contributed more than just essays — they have helped to shape and define the exhibition itself. A special thanks is due to Kristine Stiles, who, given the breadth of her interests, wrote

an essay and worked with me in the sequencing of the exhibition — ultimately giving her a role which can only be described as critical for the exhibition and of singular importance in the catalogue. Kristine and all of the essayists have been extraordinarily generous in the time they have spent talking with me, guiding me, and most importantly, in the development of their own scholarship, making a lasting contribution on this subject. In the creation of this exhibition, I owe them a tremendous debt of gratitude.

In the organization of all the travel related to the exhibition, the hundreds of letters that have gone out in my preliminary investigations, for the exhibition itself, the tour and a myriad of other details, I have to thank my trusted and ever optimistic assistant, Diane Aldrich. The assistant who has toiled the longest in putting this exhibition together is Kim Cooper, Project Coordinator, who for the last three years has tirelessly focused first on the research, then on the execution of a tremendously complex task, and she has created a thorough timeline for the catalogue. She has been joined by Denise Spampinato, first in research and then in the development of an extraordinary reading room, with accompanying rare manuscripts and documents associated with these artists and this period. Susan Jenkins has brought her extraordinary organizational skill and her exemplary standards of accuracy and art historical research to the finalization of the exhibition's checklist and bibliography. Linda Genereux has, with grace and humor, chased down photographs for the catalogue from all over the world, in a time frame which was simply impossible. Thanks also go to Jeanette Roan, who assisted with early research on the show.

Over the years I have gained enormously from the inspiration and guidance of many colleagues. Early on, when I called my exhibition "When Performance Became Art," Harald Szeemann's exhibition "When Attitudes Became Form: 1969-1970" was an obvious inspiration. More personally appreciated was the early guidance and encouragement of James Harithas, of whom I was a student while he was the Director of the Everson Museum in the early 1970s, who hired me at the Contemporary Arts Museum, Houston, and created a foundation on which this exhibition was built. His introduction to me of artists such as Nam June Paik, Hermann Nitsch, and Yoko Ono, among others, was critical in shaping my interests and future development. I would also like to acknowledge Kevin Consey's support, while he was the director of the Newport Harbor Art Museum, for an early investigation into these ideas. Other colleagues I would like to acknowledge include: Bernard Blisténe, Gary Garrels, Michael Govan, Yuko Hasegawa, Madoka Moriguchi, Sadamasa Motonaga, Suzanne Pagé, David Ross, Didier Semin, Kirk Varnedoe, Sohei Yoshino, and especially Jean de Loisy, for his important work with the exhibition "Hors Limites, l'art et la vie 1952-1994" and his much appreciated invitation for me to speak about this project.

Over the years, I've had the opportunity to meet with dozens of artists. The time they have spent with me and the generosity they have provided to me is greatly appreciated. I would especially like to thank the following artists for their help: Marina Abramović, Vito Acconci, Stuart Brisley, James Lee Byars, Paul Cotton, Jim Dine, Valie Export, Terry Fox, Howard Fried, Gilbert & George, Jon Hendricks, Lynn Hershman, Rebecca Horn, Akira Kanayama, Allan Kaprow, Jannis Kounellis, Yayoi Kusama, John Latham, Uwe Laysiepen, Jean-Jacques Lebel, Lea Lublin, Tom Marioni, Georges Mathieu, David Medalla, Gustav Metzger, Robert Morris, Otto Muehl, Bruce Nauman, Hermann Nitsch, Claes Oldenburg, Yoko Ono, Raphael Ortiz, Nam June Paik, Lygia Pape, Michelangelo Pistoletto, Niki de Saint Phalle, Carolee Schneemann, Bonnie Sherk, Shōzō Shimamoto, Kazuo Shiraga, Daniel Spoerri, Atsuko Tanaka, Mark Thompson, Ben Vautier, Wolf Vostell, Peter Weibel, and Emmett Williams. Several artists have agreed to remake works for this exhibition, and I deeply appreciate their willingness to revisit works going back in some cases almost forty years. All of the artists, however, made important contributions of time and effort. In some cases, my discussions with them go back for more than ten years, and their willingness to participate is deeply appreciated. This is particularly true for Chris Burden, who, since the time of his retrospective in 1988 has provided me with special guidance and support.

Mike Kelley and Paul McCarthy deserve a special thanks for their contribution in an artist-organized "exhibition within an exhibition" as an orientation to the show. Paul McCarthy has also made a significant contribution in the organization of an accompanying symposium being held at UCLA under the leadership of Mary Kelly, Chair of the Art Department there. We appreciate Mary's enthusiastic support. I would also like to thank the Education department at MOCA — Kim Kanatani, Director, for her organization of both the Paul McCarthy/Mike Kelley collaboration in the Gil Friesen Visitors' Gallery, and her assistance in the organization of the symposium, and Caroline Blackburn for her great efforts with the art talks and symposium.

Certain institutions have been extraordinarily generous in making significant loans from their collections. I would like to thank their staff for their generosity in allowing important works to remain away for extended periods of time. They include: Isobel Johnstone of the Arts Council Collection, Hayward Gallery; Seiichiro Matsunaga at Ashiya City Museum of Art and History; Jacquelynn Bass at the Berkeley Art Museum; Thomas W. Styron at the Greenville County Museum of Art; Thomas Krens and Lisa Dennison at the Solomon R. Guggenheim Museum; Hirohiko Hino, Toshitami Kaihara, and Yutaka Hayami of the Hyogo Prefectural Museum; Dieter Ronte at the Kunstmuseum Bonn; Paul Winkler and Walter Hopps at The Menil Collection; Lóránd Hegyi of Museum moderner Kunst Stiftung Ludwig; Yasuo Kamon of the Museum of Contemporary Art, Tokyo; Kirk Varnedoe, Margit Rowell, and Cathy Magdalena of The Museum of Modern Art, New York; Volker Rattemeyer of the Museum Wiesbaden; Ichiro Kemmochi of Nagoya City Museum; Carl Belz of the Rose Art Museum; John R. Lane of the San Francisco Museum of Modern Art; Karin van Maur of Staatsgalerie Stuttgart; Ryoichi Yamaguchi of Takamatsu City Museum of Art; Nicholas Serota of the Tate Gallery; Masahiro Aoki of Toyota Municipal Museum of Art; Kathy Halbreich of the Walker Art Center; Sherri Geldin of the Wexner Center for the Arts; and David Ross of the Whitney Museum of American Art.

I'd also like to thank the following artists, private collectors, and foundations for their loans to the exhibition: Marina Abramović , Vito Acconci, Genpei Akasegawa, Laurie Anderson, Eleanor Antin, Rasheed Araeen, Mowry Baden, Artur Barrio, Alberto

Bassi, Gerard Beaufour, Ole Bjornsdal Archive, René Block, Mark Boyle and Joan Hills, Stuart Brisley, Robert Delford Brown, Günther Brus, Chris Burden, Mercedes Casanegra, Richard Castellane, William Claxton, Houston Conwill, William Conwill, Francesco Conz, Paul Cotton, Shashi Caudill and Alan Cravitz, Jane Crawford and the Gordon Matta-Clark Estate, Jim Dine, John Duncan, Felipe Ehrenberg, Thomas Erben, Roberto Evangelista, Valie Export, Sante Falconèr, Wolfgang Feelisch, Frayda and Ronald Feldman, Marianne Filliou, Rose Finn-Kelcey, Luciano Figueiredo of the Oiticica Foundation and the Clark Estate, Sherman Fleming, Mario Bardini at Fondazione Lucio Fontana, Terry Fox, Howard Fried, Barry Friedman, Magdalena Stumpf of Sammlung Friedrichshof, Fundacio Antoni Tàpies, Pinchas Cohen Gan, Gideon Gechtman, Jochen Gerz, Eva Geyer, Hal Glicksman from the Guy de Cointet Estate, Carol and Arthur Goldberg, the Greco Estate, Ion Grigorescu, Victor Grippo, Bibbe Hansen, Maren Hassinger, Jon, Joanne and Eléanore Hendricks, Lynn Hershman, Hess Collection, Susan Hiller, Sabrina van der Ley of Sammlung Hoffmann, A.C. Hudgins, Pontus Hulten, Julius Hummel of Kunsthandlung, Jasper Johns, Kim Jones, Bettina Landgrebe at the Donald Judd Estate, Allan Kaprow, Mike Kelley, Jurgen Klauke, Milan Knížák, Alison Knowles, Eustachy Kossakowski, Yayoi Kusama and her assistant, Kho Takakura, Suzanne Lacy, Phyllis Lambert, John Latham, Uwe Laysiepen, Jean-Jacques Lebel, Ronald Maker, Leopoldo Maler, Elena Manzoni at the Archivio Opera Piero Manzoni, Anne Marchand and the Estate of Gina Pane, Tom Marioni, Cusi Masuda, Georges Mathieu, Paul McCarthy, Robert McElroy, Bruce McLean, Cildo Meireles, Gustav Metzger, Jacques Miège, Marta Minujin, Jan Mlčoch, Andrej Monastyrskij, Linda Montano, Daniel Moquay of the Yves Klein Archives, Gino di Maggio of Fondazione Mudima, Makiko Murakami, Natsuyuki Nakanishi, Peter Namuth, Bruce Nauman, Paul Neagu, Senga Nengudi, Joshua Neustein, Hermann Nitsch, Peter and Eileen Norton, Claes Oldenburg and Coosje van Bruggen, Reinhard Onnasch, Yoko Ono, Orlan, Raphael Montañez Ortiz, Lorenzo Pace, Lygia Pape, Tom Patchett, Hubert Peeters, Adrian Piper and her assistant, Scott Walden, Michelangelo Pistoletto, William Pope L., Agnès and Jean-Pierre Rammant, Robert Rauschenberg and David White of his studio, Klaus Rinke, Sergej Romaschko, Hans Ruepp, Lia Rumma, Zorka Ságlová·, Niki de Saint Phalle and her assistants Janice Parente, Valérie Villeglé, and Chappell Howard, Vanni Scheiwiller, Alfons Schilling, Carolee Schneemann, Arturo Schwarz, Bonnie Sherk, Ushio Shinohara, Kazuo Shiraga, Harry Shunk, Gilbert and Lila Silverman, Barbara T. Smith, Rainer Speck, Daniel Spoerri, Stelarc, Petr Štembera, Kristine Stiles, Jirō Takamatsu, Atsuko Tanaka, Tatsumi Hijikata Memorial Archives, Mark Thompson, Raša Todosijević, Alison Radovanović of the Kerry Trengove Estate, Cosey Fanni Tutti, Dorine van der Klei, Ben Vautier, Wolf Vostell, Franz Erhard Walther, Julian Wasser, Peter Weibel, Franz West, Estate of Hannah Wilke, Emmett Williams, and Zaj Group Archives.

Many galleries have been instrumental in both facilitating and making individual loans, and I'd like to thank the following: Paule Anglim and Ed Gilbert at Paule Anglim Gallery, Bugdahn und Kaimer Gallery, Galleria Cohn Edelstein, Galerie Chantal Crousel, D'Amelio Terras, Thomas Erben Gallery, Anne de Villepoix, Ronald Feldman Fine Arts, Lance Fung Gallery, Gagosian Gallery, Barbara Gladstone Gallery, Karel Srp of Galerie der Haupstadt Prag, Hulton Getty Picture Gallery, Akira Ikeda Gallery, Sean Kelly, Rudolf Kicken, Ursula Krinzinger at Galerie Krinzinger, Mary Sabbatino and Raquelin Mendieta at Galerie Lelong, Lisson Gallery, Galleria Martano di Liliana Dematteis, Robert and Peter Miller at Robert Miller Gallery, Galerie Philip Nelson, Galerie Georg Nothelfer, Anthony d'Offay Gallery, Margarete Roeder, Wendy Shafir, Illeana Sonnabend and Antonio Homem of Sonnabend Gallery, Gianfranco Benedetti of the Christian Stein Gallery, Galerie Daniel Varenne, John Weber Gallery, Gallery Michael Werner, and David Zwirner Gallery.

Special thanks go to Peter Kirby, as the Media Coordinator for the exhibition, who formulated an important part of the exhibition. Also my thanks to Jon Hendricks, Allan Kaprow, and Steven Leiber for making so much of their archives available to us for the reading room. I want to thank Juliette Salzmann, Cultural Attaché of the Consulate of France, for her kind assistance with AFAA's partici-pation in the exhibition and her overall support.

We also give our great appreciation to Randy Roth of Lakin Tire of California, Inc. for their kind donation. We must give our thanks to those who helped us with the remaking of the Wolf Vostell piece — Jim and Jan Clark of James Clark & Co., Santa Clarita Railway; our Trustee, Councilman Joel Wachs; Joan A. de Bruin, Director, Folk & Traditional Arts Division and Adolfo V. Nodal, General Manager, both of the Cultural Affairs Department of the City of Los Angeles; Fred Hoffman; and Richard Stanger, Executive Director of Metrolink. Thanks go to Bob Tuttle and his assistant Maureen Molloy for their special assistance. Thanks also go to Merrick Baker-Bates, Consul General of the British Counsulate General. Our appreciation and thanks for the assistance of Wayne Baerwaldt, Barbara Bertozzi, Mitchell Clark, Jean-Marie Cusinberche, Simon Ford, Adrian Glew, Deborah Irmas, Fred McDarrah, Claudia Mesch, Otto Rosenberger, Donna de Salvo, Patrizia Sandretto Re Rebaudengo, Alan Scarritt, Bob Smith, and Philippe Vergne.

This exhibition has benefitted enormously from the participation of a prestigious group of international venues. Their support in bringing a complex, thematic exhibition to their institution is greatly appreciated. I would like to thank Peter Noever, Director, and Daniela Zyman, Curator, at MAK-Austrian Museum of Applied Arts, Vienna; Miquel Molins, Director, Jose Lebrero Stals, Head of Exhibitions, and John S. Zvereff, CEO, of MAC Barcelona; and, Yasuo Kamon, Director, Junichi Shioda, Chief Curator, Kunio Yaguchi, Chief Curator, and Keiko Okamura, Curator, at the Museum of Contemporary Art, Tokyo.

I am deeply grateful to my wife Yvonne, who has for the past twenty-five years created an environment and a foundation in which I felt supported to explore contemporary art within a museum environment, and to my two children, Max and Dean — their genuine love and appreciation of my work has made bearable the time I have spent away from them in the process of organizing the exhibition.

My final thanks go to the funders of the exhibition, an extraordinary group of international and national agencies and individuals who provided the initial and much appreciated support for the exhibition. They include Jane Alexander, Chairman and Jennifer Dowley, Director of Museum Programs of the National Endowment for the Arts; Shin'ichiro Asao, President, and Isao Tsujimoto, Director General, Los Angeles Office of The Japan Foundation; Eric J. Gangloff, Executive Director of the Japan-United States Friendship Commission; Wolfgang Waldner, Director and Thomas Stelzer, Deputy Director of Programming, of the Austrian Cultural Institute, New York; Peter Wittmann, Minister of State and Andreas Mailath-Pokorny, Director General for Cultural Affairs, of the Republic of Austria Federal Chancellery; Werner E. Brandstetter, Consul General, of the Austrian Consulate General in Los Angeles; Andrea Rose, Head of Visual Arts, David Evans, Director, USA, and Joanna Tudge, Cultural Affairs Officer, USA, at The British Council; Rod Hagenbuch, Senior Resident Vice President of Merrill Lynch; Juliette Salzmann, Attaché Culturel of the Service Culturel du Consulat Général de France à Los Angeles; and Jean Digne, Director and Marie-Paule Serre, Head of the Department of Visual Arts Association Française d' Action Artistique, Ministère des Affaires Étrangères.

My final and most heartfelt thanks go to Audrey Irmas, who, in a singular act of generosity ensured that this exhibition could and would be organized. She is a dear personal friend, and as the Chairman of the Board of Trustees of The Museum of Contemporary Art, Los Angeles, has provided extraordinary leadership. Her choice to honor the memory of her late husband, Syd Irmas — a generous and dynamic man who was indeed someone who embodied action — by choosing this exhibition to support is, in fact, the greatest honor. I believe that Syd would have appreciated the youthful energy, political awareness, and most importantly, the creative spirit which these artists have brought to making their work.

Paul Schimmel

**Jackson Pollock**, painting in his studio, photographed by Hans Namuth

Paul Schimmel

# LEAP INTO THE VOID:
## PERFORMANCE AND THE OBJECT

After World War II, the Holocaust, and the atomic bomb, a change of consciousness occurred in the world at large. The possibility of global annihilation made human beings more aware than ever before of the fragility of creation, subject as it was to forces of destruction of unprecedented magnitude. In this regard, it also made them more cognizant of the primacy of the act, which would become one of the central concerns of existentialism, the most influential philosophical movement to emerge in the postwar period. This social, political, and philosophical legacy stimulated a pervasive movement in the visual arts in the United States, Europe, and Japan.

There is a tendency in the history of art to see movements as discrete and to think of national frontiers as borders that art cannot cross. Increasingly, it is evident that neither concept is true. In fact, because of the economic and political changes that occurred during and after World War II, artists had the ability to travel internationally to a historically unprecedented degree. Coterminous with this increased mobility was the dramatic growth of the mass media, whose ravenousness extended to the visual arts. The experiments of the avant-garde in New York would thus have immediate implications in Europe and Japan, and vice versa. The popular magazine *Life*, for example, published numerous articles, always accompanied by dramatic photographs, about artists of the New York School, the Gutai group in Japan, and the Destruction in Art Symposium in Europe, allowing both the general public and artists themselves to rapidly learn of the latest developments in regions of the world other than their own. By examining the periods between movements and the works of artists who transcended the places in which they lived, a more complex representation of art in the postwar period can be sketched out.

During this period, an overwhelming number of artists from the United States, Europe, and Japan increasingly began to define their production in terms of the dialectic of creation and destruction. Whether manifested as a studied Zen line, a heroic but fleeting painterly gesture, or an explosively destructive act, beginning and end became their subject — a subject driven by an overriding preoccupation with the temporal dimension of the act. The exhibition "Out of Actions" is a comprehensive examination of the work produced through this new focus on the act in the period ranging from 1949 to 1979. International in scope, it begins with the generation of artists that came of age in the fallout of the postatomic age and reached maturity during the Cold War and ends with the generation that matured during the aftermath of the Vietnam War and its legacy of global cynicism.

Modernism's march from the heroic gestures of Abstract Expressionism, through Minimalism's reductive tendencies, to Conceptual art's objectlessness is paralleled in the action-based works in this exhibition. The activities, actions, and performances of artists during this period were successively realized as paintings, sculptures, and installations; objects, props, relics, photographs, films, and videotapes that documented ephemeral events; and finally, in some cases, nothing but the ever changing perceptions of the audience. Thus, this exhibition traces in the thirty-year span bracketed by modernism at its height and at its end the reversal of the traditional precedence of the object over the act. Actions performed with the goal of producing objects gave rise to the execution of performative actions whose primary goal was the process of creation rather than the production of objects, which gave rise to the creation of performances that often involved audience participation, from which no resulting object was produced. Although there are instances of lighthearted irreverence, joy, and laughter in this work, there is always an underlying darkness, informed by the recognition of humanity's seemingly relentless drive toward self-annihilation. From the outwardly explosive character of the work of the early 1950s to the inwardly self-destructive work of the late 1970s, one finds an emphatic questioning of the experience of living in a global village perched on the brink of self-destruction. This exhibition is neither a history of performance art in the postwar period nor a history of painting and sculpture in those decades. Instead, it is a specific slice through the history of art that has at its center the conviction that performances, actions, Happenings, events, and activities associated with the act of creation had an enormous impact on the objects that emerged from them. The following essay presents just such a slice by surveying works by selected artists in the exhibition associated with the most important nodes of activity in the vast network of practices that constitute postwar action-based art. These nodes, which include Gutai, Nouveau Réalisme, Happenings, Fluxus, Viennese Actionism, 1960s performative sculpture, and 1970s performance, will be examined in greater detail in the other essays in this volume. The objective of this essay is to provide a road map through the exceedingly complex, yet still underexplored, territory that is the subject of "Out of Actions."

**Origins: Pollock, Cage, Fontana, Shimamoto** Although the end of World War II was greeted with relief throughout the world, any optimism that may have resulted was tempered by a certain hollowness, in light of the extraordinarily unprecedented destruction wrought by the war and the realization that the possibility of global annihilation was real. This split in consciousness encouraged and incubated activities that broke the traditional relationship between the artist and the object, and the subject of art increasingly became its own making. In the United States, Europe, and Japan, four artists who would exert a tremendous influence on the development of postwar art began to place a new emphasis on the role of the act in the creation of the object. Jackson Pollock danced over canvases laid horizontally on the floor, dripping and pouring paint to create fields of color; John Cage used the principles of chance and indeterminacy to create compositions that were realized differently every time they were performed; Lucio Fontana punctured and slashed the pictorial surface in violent, though elegant, gestures; and Shōzō Shimamoto created abstract paintings through increasingly destructive acts. Through their pioneering investigations of the primacy of the act in the production of the object, these four figures left a lasting legacy that would be of enormous importance to subsequent artists who sought to liberate their work from the bonds of objecthood.

Pollock's significance as the sole perpetrator of the concept that a painting was the material embodiment of an action has been overstated to such a degree that other less dramatic and less fully resolved experiments have received little recognition. Nevertheless, his works, as objects whose process of making is recorded in the paintings themselves and in

widely seen photographs, did have a singular impact on the direction of both Color Field painting and performance art. The myth that has been made of Pollock's life emphasizes his method. While this emphasis captured the imagination of innumerable postwar artists, it has limited the appreciation of his paintings.

Pollock's primary impact was as an archetypal painter caught in the arena of a ritualized — yet uncontrolled, brutally direct, and explosive — creative activity. However, the most celebrated exemplars of this activity, the pure drip paintings, constitute a brief period in his oeuvre. Moreover, from a more measured regard, the most orthodox of these paintings, such as *No. 1* (1949), have begun to be recognized as having been carefully constructed. Visual evidence suggests that Pollock applied his drips and pours with labored and painterly care and even used brushwork to achieve coherently constructed compositions. This view runs counter to the spectacularly theatrical photographs by Hans Namuth that capture an image of the artist as a caged animal in a high-contrast, black-and-white trance of creative, mythmaking action. Were these photographs real evidence of Pollock's working method? Certainly. Have they been given attention beyond their singular ability to explain Pollock's work? Undoubtedly. Pollock became a unique central figure against which other artists would gauge themselves.

With Pollock, and to a lesser degree with Franz Kline and the other action painters, a shift took place in painting. With some notable exceptions, painters had tended to conceal the fact that their works were the result of a process, in favor of the creation of equilibrated compositions that displayed carefully selected segments of the world that could be appreciated as *pictures*. With action painting in general, and the work of Pollock in particular, each gesture "animates" the subsequent moves, producing a non-narrative linearity that focuses the viewer's attention on the performative dimension of the act of painting. Although Pollock may have questioned this dimension of his work, his desire to maintain "contact" (his word) with the canvas essentially transformed the artist's role from that of a bystander outside of the canvas to that of an actor whose very actions were its subject.[1]

**Jackson Pollock**, *No. 1*, 1949. The Museum of Contemporary Art, Los Angeles. The Rita and Taft Schreiber Collection. Given in loving memory of her husband, Taft Schreiber, by Rita Schreiber

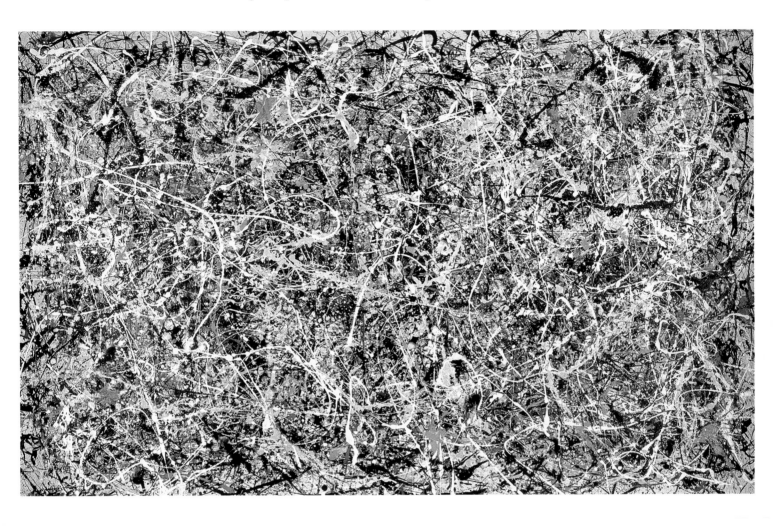

Although the Surrealists had experimented with the concept of automatic painting, they had never emphasized the primacy of the act to the degree that Pollock and the action painters did. The move from an uncontrolled action of the wrist to the more dramatic sweep or gesture of the arm, which required the artist to move around a canvas rolled out flat on the floor, altered both the traditional conception of what a painting was and the perception of how one could be made. Pollock's action portended the dissolution of the boundaries between the object and the activity of its making. The very pictorial qualities that painting had had prior to Pollock were now relegated to the realm of "the merely aesthetic."[2]

With Pollock in mind, the influential critic Harold Rosenberg famously declared in 1952 that "at a certain moment the canvas began to appear to one American painter after another as an arena in which to act — rather than as a space in which to reproduce, re-design, analyze or 'express' an object, actual or imagined. What was to go on the canvas was not a picture but an event."[3] In overstating the case for the performative qualities of Pollock's painting, action painting, and the New York School in general, Rosenberg encouraged a myth that has been more protean for subsequent generations of artists than the canvases themselves. His words, coupled with Namuth's famous photographs, mightily enforced a monocular view of Pollock's contribution.

In a now legendary leap of imagination, Allan Kaprow prophetically proposed, two years after Pollock's death in 1956, that the performative quality of the artist's work would be most significant for the generation of the 1960s and, further, that Pollock's paintings themselves heralded the end of the tradition of two-dimensional representation. While it is

1. Wayne J. Froman, "Action Painting and the World-As-Picture," Journal of Aesthetics and Art Criticism 46, no. 4 (Summer 1988): 472–73.

2. Ibid., 474.

3. Harold Rosenberg, "The American Action Painters," in Tradition of the New (New York: Horizon Press, 1959), 25. Originally published as "The American Action Painters," Art News 51, no. 8 (December 1952).

true that the mural-like scale of Pollock's canvases, laid on the floor of his studio, literally forced him to be "inside" his work, this was a far cry from Kaprow's claim that because of their scale, they "became *environments*."[4] Kaprow's own work attained this state in 1958; Pollock's never did, but such was the tendency of artists to apply their own aspirations to Pollock's inclusive vision. Again anticipating his own Happenings, Kaprow states in his discussion of Pollock that "What we have then, is a type of art which tends to lose itself out of bounds, tends to fill our world with itself, an art which, in meaning, looks, impulse, seems to break fairly sharply with traditions of painters back to at least the Greeks. Pollock's near destruction of this tradition may well be a return to the point where art was more actively involved in ritual, magic and life than we have known it in our recent past."[5] Finally, in a dazzling assumption, Kaprow assigns to Pollock responsibility for the end of painting: "The other [alternative] is to give up the making of paintings entirely, I mean the single, flat rectangle or oval as we know it."[6]

This prophetic declaration represented a more informed reading of Pollock's legacy than the more commonly acceptable alternative in the late 1950s — Color Field painting. Although Pollock probably would have rejected Kaprow's assessment, Kaprow's closing speculation in this legendary article would prove to be visionary. "Pollock, as I see him," Kaprow writes:

> left us at the point where we must become preoccupied with and even dazzled by the space and objects of our everyday life, either our bodies, clothes, rooms, or, if need be, the vastness of Forty-Second Street. Not satisfied with the *suggestion* through paint of our other senses, we shall utilize the specific substances of sight, sound, movements, people, odors, touch. Objects of every sort are materials for the new art: paint, chairs, food, electric and neon lights, smoke, water, old socks, a dog, movies, a thousand other

things which will be discovered by the present generation of artists. Not only will these bold creators show us, as if for the first time, the world we have always had about us, but ignored, but they will disclose entirely unheard of happenings and events, found in garbage cans, police files, hotel lobbies, seen in store windows and on the streets, and sensed in dreams and horrible accidents.[7]

In this passage, Happenings and events are defined for the first time as legacies of Pollock's pioneering achievements.

Over two decades later, in 1979, nearly thirty years after Namuth's first photographs of Pollock appeared, the art historian and critic Barbara Rose addressed the significance of the *documents* of Pollock's painting process. Appreciating the mythmaking effect that Namuth's photographs had had on both critics and artists, she recalls that "Namuth's photographs of Pollock at work received broader circulation in May of that year [1951] when *ArtNews* published a series of black and white photographs illustrating "Pollock Paints a Picture" by Robert Goodnough. On June 14, 1951, The Museum of Modern Art screened the color film of Pollock painting. From that moment, the images of Pollock in action attached themselves as additional meanings to his works to a degree that they began to color the perception of his paintings."[8]

Regarding Kaprow's article, Rose notes that "What Kaprow saw . . . and I suspect he saw it in Namuth's photographs and not in Pollock's deliberately controlled paintings, was the liberating possibility of uninhibited acting out — catharsis through art."[9] She goes on to remark that "Namuth's Pollock photographs and film affected a far larger audience than the paintings had" (the same is true for many other artists in this exhibition, whose work is informed through photographic documentation of the process by which it was created).[10] Rose concludes: "Moreover, because the paintings deliver so little of themselves in reproduction, the photographs of the

4. Allan Kaprow, "The Legacy of Jackson Pollock," Art News 57, no. 6 (October 1958): 56.

5. Ibid.

6. Ibid.

7. Ibid., 57.

8. Barbara Rose, "Hans Namuth's Photograph and the Jackson Pollock Myth: Part One: Media Impact and the Failure of Criticism," Arts Magazine 53, no. 7 (March 1979): 112.

9. Ibid., 114.

10. Ibid., 115.

artist, which are ideally reproduced, had a fullness of informational content which reproductions of the work lacked, and it was through reproduction that most people experienced Pollock."[11] In a slam against much of the performance-based work of the two decades after Pollock's death, Rose claims that "As a result of the popularity of Namuth's film and photographs of Pollock, the persona of the artist took on a dimension greater than his works. This could not help but have a devastating effect on the generation of artists who matured in the late Sixties and Seventies, who relieved of the burden of Pollock's art have focused their energy on projecting a persona or self-image that could be as compelling as Pollock's media image."[12] In spite of this appraisal, this very legacy of "devastation" would constitute an extraordinarily protean influence on certain performance artists, and even on artists of the 1990s, who have explored persona and self-image as a significant and appropriate subject.

For subsequent generations, the step from the arena of the painting to more visceral, body-oriented work was a logical one. It is inconceivable that the Gutai phenomenon would have occurred without Pollock's breakthrough; for example, Kazuo Shiraga's foot paintings are undoubtedly a direct extension of Pollock's technique of working on the floor. Similarly, Yves Klein's *anthropométries* and the even more theatrical experiments of the Viennese Actionists owe a great debt to Pollock for both content and form. This tendency can also be traced to the late 1960s, to the work of process artists such as Richard Serra and Barry Le Va. Finally, an enormous number of artists working in the decades bracketed by this exhibition credit Pollock, after Cage, as the most significant figure in their artistic development.

The composer and artist John Cage, an American not specifically known for his visual art, was to prove as influential and liberating to artists of the postwar period as Pollock. Cage's open-ended, conceptually derived, performative activities stimulated a sense of freedom among artists, including Robert Rauschenberg, Jasper Johns, and the dancer Merce Cunningham. Through his work and his teaching,

Cage's influence extended to the vast array of artists who came to be affiliated with such movements as Neo-Dada, Happenings, Fluxus, Arte Povera, and an entire generation of new-music artists that emerged in the late 1960s and early 1970s.

Cage began his career as a musician and composer in the 1930s; his study of Eastern philosophy in the late 1940s stimulated him to radically rethink the conventions of traditional Western music by incorporating chance and then indeterminacy into the process of composition and performance. By relinquishing complete control over the final realization of a composition, Cage placed a new emphasis on the primacy of performance in the constitution of the work. His use of the "prepared piano" — an ordinary piano transformed into a percussion instrument of diverse timbres through the insertion of various objects between the strings — influenced the work of artists including Nam June Paik and Raphael Montañez Ortiz, among many others.

At Black Mountain College near Asheville, North Carolina, in 1952, Cage organized an event considered to be a key precedent for the development of Happenings and Fluxus. This "concerted action," later entitled *Theater Piece No. 1*, involved a "multifocus" presentation that included the simultaneous performance of music for piano by David Tudor, improvised dancing by Cunningham, the exhibition of four of Rauschenberg's White Paintings (which were hung from the rafters of the ceiling), the reading of poetry from a ladder by M. C. Richards, the projection of slides and films, and the delivery of a lecture by Cage himself. With no rehearsals, scripts, or costumes, each performer was given a randomly chosen time bracket in which he or she was to enact a particular activity. Knowing the personalities of the participants, Cage had an idea of what each would do, but he made no assignments. In addition, this legendary performance took place not on a stage, but among the audience, thus dissolving the hierarchical relationship between performers and audience members.[13]

The cultivation of the visual dimension of an aural work, so crucial to *Theater Piece No. 1*, is also

11. *Ibid.*

12. *Ibid.*

13. *Mary Emma Harris,* The Arts at Black Mountain College *(Cambridge: MIT Press, 1987),* 228–29.

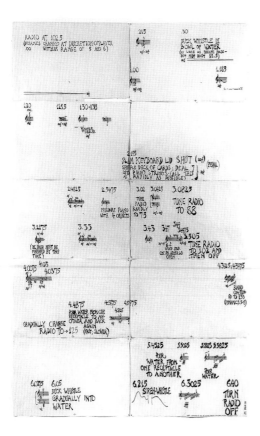

manifested in Cage's other works of the early 1950s. The score of one of his most engaging compositions, *Water Music* (1952), called for a pianist to pour water from pots, prepare the piano by inserting objects between the strings, blow whistles underwater, use a radio and a pack of cards, and perform other nonmusical actions to engage the eye. These activities were charted on ten sheets joined to make a single score large enough for the audience to follow if they so chose. Similarly, Cage's composition *4'33"* (1952), inspired in part by Rauschenberg's White Paintings, was distinguished by its visual dimension, in that the performer remained completely silent.[14] Through these and other compositions Cage sought to (1) dissolve the opposition between art and life; (2) contest the hierarchical relationships between composers and performers (by writing compositions in which the latter did not simply execute the formers' instructions but made their own compositional decisions as they performed) and between performers and audience members (by permitting the latter's participation in the performance of certain works); and (3) invest greater significance in the process of creation than in the production of objects. This legacy would prove to have a tremendously liberating effect on the many artists who came under his influence.

Simultaneous with Pollock's development of the drip paintings and Cage's experiments with chance and indeterminacy, Lucio Fontana, who was born in Argentina but moved to Italy in 1947, was questioning the traditional status of a painting as a static two-dimensional surface in his own way. In his *Buchi* (Holes) and *Tagli* (Cuts) Fontana challenged the claims of painting to create the illusion of three-dimensional space on a two-dimensional surface. By respectively perforating and lacerating the monochomatic planes of his painted canvases to reveal the existence of a void-like space, produced by a layer of black gauze, behind the pictorial surface, Fontana created, rather than simply represented, space. This violation of the canvas was perhaps more revolutionary than the work of Pollock and the action painters, which was emerging in the United States at the same time, in that it was more radically destructive. Its very destructiveness would prove to have profound consequences for subsequent artists.

Fontana's *Concetti spaziali* (Spatial Concepts), as he called his paintings, were a direct result of theoretical concepts he addressed in the *Manifiesto blanco* (White Manifesto), which he wrote in 1946 with ten of his students at the Academia d'Altamira in Buenos Aires. In this manifesto, which advocated "integral art" (art defined as a "gesture," not merely as an object), Fontana abandoned the myth of the tradition of object making and the immortality of the painted canvas in favor of "the act of the spirit freed from all matter." By breaking into the canvas, he no longer represented space but created it. At the time of the composition of the manifesto, Fontana had also already encouraged a proto-Happening on an abandoned building site, in which his students threw paint and various objects. In addition, he also created a "spatialist" window display for a clothing store on Buenos Aires's most fashionable street. These activities directly led to the subsequent creation of a "rain" of rapid dashes with pens or brushes that perforated the flatness of the canvas — the *Holes* and the *Cuts*.[15]

Fontana emphatically insisted on the primacy of his over Pollock's development of a new type of pictorial space, both of which were contingent on dramatic actions. As he stated in 1968 in his last interview, "I make a hole in the canvas in order to leave behind me the old pictorial formulae, the painting and the traditional view of art as I escape symbolically, but also materially, from the prison of

14. See David Revill, The Roaring Silence: John Cage, a Life *(New York: Arcade Publishing, 1992),160.*

15. See Erika Billeter, "Lucio Fontana: Between Tradition and Avant-Garde," in Lucio Fontana, 1899–1968: A Retrospective, *exh. cat. (New York:* Solomon R. Guggenheim Museum, and San Francisco Museum of Modern Art, 1994), 87.

**Lucio Fontana**, *Concetto spaziale* (Spacial Concept) (49 B 2), 1949
Fondazione Lucio Fontana, Milan

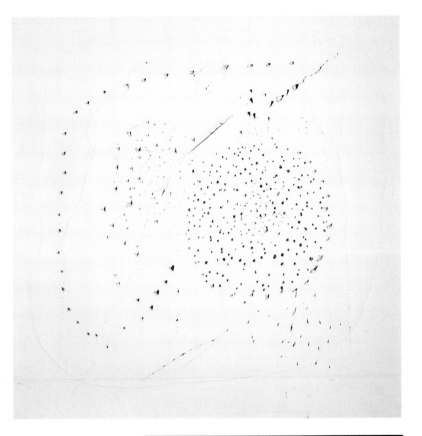

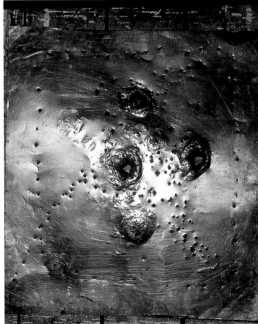

**Lucio Fontana**, *Concetto spaziale* (Spacial Concept) (50 B 4), 1950
Fondazione Lucio Fontana, Milan

**Lucio Fontana**, *Concetto spaziale* (Spacial Concept) (50 B 9), 1950
Fondazione Lucio Fontana, Milan

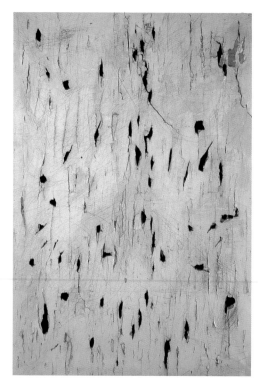

**Shōzō Shimamoto**, *Work (Holes)*, c. 1950
Museum of Contemporary Art, Tokyo

the flat surface. . . . Pollock, then, threw paint on the canvas. He was looking for a new dimension of space, but all he could produce was post-impressionism because he threw paint *onto* the canvas, although he wanted to go *beyond* the canvas. . . . So, the 'hole' is free space and is way in advance of Pollock." Indeed, Fontana's punctured and lacerated surfaces proved to be an enormously versatile resource for artists such as La Monte Young and Peter Weibel, and his quiet marks were closer to the more ephemeral spirit of Fluxus than the grand gesture that constituted Pollock's contribution.

Simultaneous with Fontana's experiments in Italy, Shōzō Shimamoto in Japan created the pioneering collage paintings of his own *Holes* series (c. 1949–52). Shimamoto began this series tentatively and modestly by gluing together layer upon layer of newspaper. This process bore some resemblance to the tradition of Japanese paper stretching by which *shōji* screens are constructed. After painting and then drawing into the delicate, papered surface, Shimamoto would then make dozens of holes — first accidentally and then with greater authority.[16] Like many artistic experiments that began as chance operations, such as Fontana's first cuts, the accident was repeated until it became a formal device that eroded the picture plane and left a record of the artist's physical action. Though not as gestural as Fontana's works, Shimamoto's cracked and fissured surfaces do exhibit certain affinities. Yet, by his own account, he was unaware of parallel trends in European art at that time, specifically of Fontana. In fact, he has stated that he did not discover Fontana's work until a decade later. The fact that the dates of the newspapers he used, which preceded Fontana's *Holes* and *Cuts*, are still visible in some of the works gives credence to this assertion.

From these modest and subtle beginnings, Shimamoto developed *A Work to Be Walked On* (1956). Casually constructed and under-engineered, this work was a rocking, creaking catwalk fabricated from a series of foot-size squares of wood mounted to springs, on which people were encouraged to attempt to walk; it had to be experienced actively, rather than observed in a passive manner.[17] The par-

ticipatory nature of this work not only emphasized the primacy of its performative dimension over its material status but also provided opportunities for extensive media coverage. It is fascinating to note the significance of media coverage for Shimamoto (no doubt taking a cue from Namuth's photographs and film of Pollock painting), whose next most important technique was the execution of paintings through the explosive contact of paint with the pictorial surface. In April 1956, for a Gutai exhibition organized expressly for the photographers of *Life*, Shimamoto and his colleagues re-enacted for just one day their previous performative work. At this special exhibition held on the banks of the Muko River in Hyogo Prefecture, Shimamoto re-created *Work (Created by Cannon)* (1956) by putting paint into a cylinder and shooting it from a cannon onto the canvas. (Only one work from this series remains because of their fragility and because many were destroyed as they were created.) These randomly executed, high-velocity, explosive paintings took "action" to a level of theatricality never imagined by the New York School and incorporated mechanical means precluding the artist's specific control over the results, a method that ran counter to Pollock's controlled linearity.

By the late 1950s and continuing into the 1960s, Shimamoto had all but abandoned the use of the cannon and instead filled jars with paint, which he threw against unstretched canvases laid horizontally on the floor. Whereas Pollock left cigarette butts as traces of the process of creation, as seen in *No. 1*, Shimamoto left glass-encrusted surfaces. In these deliberately explosive works, he achieved a level of proficiency through the repetition of the most uncontrollable actions in both his choice of colors — oranges, reds, and blacks that alluded to fire and destruction — and in his increasingly predetermined actions. As his technique developed, so did the theatricality of their creation. Working close to the

16. See Alexandra Munroe, Japanese Art After 1945: Scream Against the Sky, *exh.* cat. *(New York: Solomon R. Guggenheim Museum, 1977), 13.*   17. Ibid., 90.

**24**

**Kazuo Shiraga**, *Challenging Mud*, 1955

canvas, wrapped from head to toe, and wearing goggles, Shimamoto's blasts created waterfalls of paint. For "The First Gutai On-Stage Art Show" in 1957, reviewed in the 8 September issue of *The New York Times*, Shimamoto had a huge white cylinder slowly lowered from the rafters and then smashed it with a stick, caused a great explosion of falling balls.

Pollock, Cage, Fontana, and Shimamoto shared a common desire to disrupt or pierce the pictorial surface, to question the authority of the picture plane, and to introduce chance, randomness, and the unconscious into creative activity — in short, to leap into the void. Simultaneously in the United States, Europe, and Japan, these artists were creating a temporally based and disruptive vision as a direct response to World War II's destruction and the accompanying awareness of humanity's fragility in a post-Holocaust, post-bomb world. This vision would become pervasive among the legions of artists receptive to their influence.

**Gutai** Founded in Japan in 1954 by Jirō Yoshihara, the Gutai Bijutsu Kyōkai (Gutai Art Association) was composed of diverse artists who had lived through the devastating experience of World War II, which culminated for the Japanese with the explosions of atomic bombs in Hiroshima and Nagasaki. Emerging from this historical context, their works exhibit striking affinities with action painting and *art informel*, a mode of gestural abstraction that became prevalent in Europe during the postwar period. Yoshihara's understanding of group activity, coordinated effort, and the growing international importance of abstraction, along with his general enthusiasm for organizing large exhibitions, inspired Shimamoto and other younger Japanese artists who supported Yoshihara's pursuit of an artistic language liberated from the constraints of tradition. Although he remained committed to the legacy of calligraphy and other traditional genres, Yoshihara encouraged his students to transform painting into a more process-oriented and theatrically inspired improvisational medium. Yet art historians have tended to address the paintings and the performative activities of the Gutai group as separate — a tendency that resulted from the split between Michel Tapié, an influential French critic who strongly supported their work, and Kaprow. While Tapié pursued a painterly reading of the Gutai group's works on canvas, based on his desire to stress their affinities to *art informel* and to his commercial interests, Kaprow embraced its works as proto-Happenings. At their very best, the most richly evocative Gutai works are both objects and actions.

If Pollock is the mythic embodiment of action painting, Kazuo Shiraga is the most complete and multifaceted embodiment of Gutai. The specificity and pointed clarity of his actions and paintings truly anticipate the visual gesturality of Happenings. The clearest link between Pollock and action painting, Yves Klein and the Nouveaux Réalistes, and the Viennese Actionists, Shiraga engaged in actions that transferred dramatically to film. For him, unlike for Pollock, the camera was an integral part of his activity from the beginning. The media could cavalierly embody Shiraga, like Pollock, in a single phrase: while Pollock was christened "Jack the Dripper," Shiraga was the artist who "painted with his feet." In each case, dripping and sliding, no one was able to touch the singularity of their techniques again.

Shiraga's *Making a Work with One's Body* and *Doru ni idomu* (Challenging Mud, 1955) were the most viscerally gestural activities associated with Gutai. Under the watchful gaze of cameras and with photographers and film-makers literally entering the

Kazuo Shiraga, *Kotei*, 1963. Hyogo Prefectural Museum of Modern Art, Kobe

**Akira Kanayama**, *Work*, 1957. Collection Kitakyushu Municipal Museum of Art

**Saburō Murakami**,
*Breaking through Many Screens of Paper*, 1956

mud circle, Shiraga performed for posterity a writhing, violent, gestural act. He fought the mud like action painters fought their compositions; in it he squeezed, wrestled, submerged, crawled, and gesticulated. The result was essentially a two-dimensional painting made from mud that exhibited figurative qualities similar to those that would appear in Klein's *anthropométries* and Stuart Brisley's and David Hammons's work of the 1970s. The photographic documentation is preserved in the Gutai archive at the Ashiya City Museum of Art and History.

This action led directly to Shiraga's signature paintings, which were executed with his feet. Covering his feet in paint, he would suspend himself from a rope and swing over a canvas rolled flat on the ground, applying the paint in the process. He explained the origin of this technique in "Only Action," an article published in the 20 October 1955 issue of the journal *Gutai*: "When I first discovered what seemed to be my own talent — when I decided to be 'naked,' to shed all conventional ideas — forms flew out the window and techniques slipped off my painting knife and shattered. In front of me lay an austere road to originality. Run forward, I thought, run and run, it won't matter if I fall down. Before I knew it, my knife had changed into a piece of wood, which I then impatiently threw away. Let me do it with my hands, with my fingers. Then, as I ran, thinking that I was moving forward, it occurred to me: Why not feet? Why don't I paint with my feet?"[18]

Like Shimamoto's palette of explosive oranges and reds, Shiraga's feet paintings tend toward the same supersaturated colors and, secondarily, blues and purples. But the act of swinging allowed the artist to move in a circular dance of figure eights, swirls, and arabesques, which would seem to run counter to the brutally forceful manner in which he applied the paint, a technique he still uses. When asked how he could have developed such a convulsive activity in the context of traditional Japanese art,

he replied that there was more freedom to experiment in Japan in the first half of the 1950s than is the case today. In losing the war, the divine singularity of the Japanese empire was completely dismantled by a new political and economic formula established by the United States under General Douglas MacArthur's direction. This radically changed religious and cultural landscape was a void into which such anarchic acts as making a work with one's own feet could reign.[19]

Another Gutai artist, Akira Kanayama, produced works that were, as he stated, "intentionally opposite Shiraga's. I'm interested in concept."[20] Less than a decade after Pollock's first drip paintings, Kanayama constructed what he considered to be an objective means for creating paintings through mechanical intervention. Instead of the intuitive dance of Pollock's pours and drips, Kanayama made a remote-controlled toy car that carried a container filled with paint. Under the watchful eye of photographers and film-makers, he created paintings by directing the car over the vinyl-coated canvas. Rather than being *in* the painting as Pollock had been, Kanayama was outside of it. His use of a mechanical action, with its obvious similarity to Jean Tinguely's *méta-matics* of two years later, proved to be prophetic not only for the mechanically based work of the 1960s but even more directly for 1990s works such as Tatsuo Miajima's *Running Time*, which used motorized cars with digital diodes, and Yukinori Yanagi's *Wandering Position*, in which the paths of ants were traced in chalk on the floor. Like Cage, Kanayama investigated chance within specific and confined probabilities.

A scant five years from the time Fontana punctured and lacerated and Shimamoto first eroded the picture plane, Saburō Murakami dramatically ruptured it in a series of works. He created picture planes and environments made of paper, which he hurled himself through in skilled reference to the Japanese

18. Kazuo Shiraga, "Only Action," *Gutai*, no. 3 (20 October 1955): 22, cited in ibid., 372–73.

19. Conversation with artist.

20. Akira Kanayama, cited in Munroe, 89.

**27**

**Saburō Murakami**, *Work: Box (Sakuhin: Hako)*, 1956/1981
Museum of Contemporary Art, Tokyo

martial-arts tradition. These performative actions resulted in a residue (ripped paper) that would remain on view for the duration of the exhibition in which they were presented, after which this residue was destroyed. Instead of producing objects for posterity, Murakami thus chose to create works anew for each exhibition. In fact, his specifications for these works were so precise that others could perform them. This, of course, gave the works a life beyond the artist and undermined their monetary value.[21]

For the "First Gutai Art Exhibition," presented at the Ohara Kaikan Hall in Tokyo in October 1955, Murakami performed *Isshun ni shite rokko no ana o akeru* (At One Moment Opening Six Holes). Enlarging to a heroic scale the traditions of *shōji* and *fusuma* paper and wood partitions, this work consisted of a series of three 6-by-12-foot paper panels that Murakami burst through six times. The work's scale was similar to the mural-sized paintings of Pollock and the action painters, although its performative component was more important than the production of a permanent object, which was always the action painters' ultimate objective. Murakami exploded his laboriously constructed wood-and-paper screens, taut with the tension of their craft, in one gestural moment. The artist hurling himself through the picture plane was an assault on the traditions of both

Western and Eastern art, as well as a metaphor of the atomic bomb's rupture of the fabric of humanity.

Simultaneous with his gestural performances, Murakami created a participatory work in the form of a handmade wooden cube. Before Piero Manzoni's *Base magica* (Magic Base) and Yoko Ono's *Painting to Be Stepped On*, he instructed his viewers "to please sit on the box," thus transforming the viewer into an active participant in the completion of the work. For the "Second Gutai Art Exhibition," presented at the Ohara Kaikan Hall in October 1956, Murakami made another box on which he wrote the instruction, "Please put your ear to the circular mark on top of the box." Inside was a clock that would ring different bells at unpredictable moments. The conceptual nature of such works underscores the equally conceptual nature of Murakami's more gestural and theatrical work. Finally, in the same period, Murakami made works, such as *Peeling Off Painting* (1957), whose delicate and permeated surfaces related to his performance works. More conservative than the conceptual or performative works, however, these paintings refer to Shimamoto's experiments of the early 1950s.

One of the most richly metaphorical works created by a Gutai artist is Atsuko Tanaka's *Electric Dress* of 1956, a powerful conflation of the tradition

*21. Munroe, 91.*

**28**

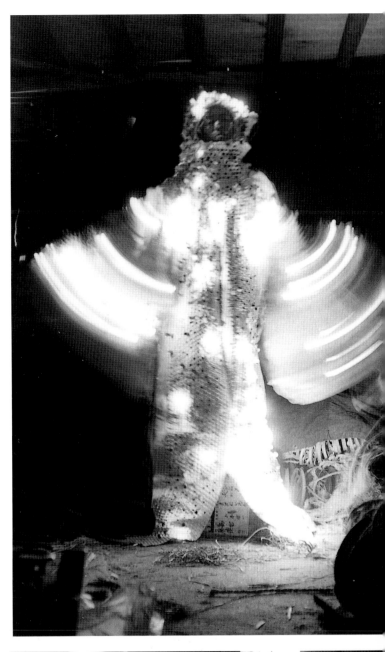

(right) **Atsuko Tanaka**, *Electric Dress*, 1956
(below) **Atsuko Tanaka**, at the studio in theatre costume
with many electric bulbs, April 1957

of the Japanese kimono with modern industrial technology. Prior to her conception of this work, Tanaka
had appeared in a larger-than-life paper dress that
was peeled away layer by layer, not unlike the peeling away of Murakami's paintings; she was ultimately
disrobed to a leotard fitted with blinking lights. Tanaka
began to envision *Electric Dress* in 1954, when she
outlined in a small notebook a remarkably prophetic
connection between electrical wiring and the physio-
logical systems that make up the human body. Using
the armature of the human figure, she created dozens
of small drawings that formed the plans for the
wiring, which would constitute a garment reflecting
the nervous and vascular systems. She also made a
group of twenty large drawings, which, in schematic
form, created a diagram for *Electric Dress* and
implied its relationship to the human figure. After fabricating the actual sculpture, she costumed herself in
it in the tradition of the Japanese marriage ceremony.
Hundreds of light bulbs painted in primary colors lit
up along the circulatory and nerve pathways of her
body. When *Electric Dress* and the drawings for it
were exhibited together in the late 1950s, one could
understand how Tanaka's pseudoscientific and conceptual underpinnings separated her activities from
those of the other members of Gutai. Clearly, this
work anticipated 1970s feminist art and artists' use
of their own bodies in dangerous situations.

What had begun for the Gutai artists in the
mid-1950s with the utter assault on the tradition of
painting was, by the end of the decade, transformed
into a more traditional commercial disposition of the
artists' creative activities. The fact that, for most of
these artists, a great deal more work exists from the
late 1950s and early 1960s than from the critical
period of their first innovations five years earlier
attests to their changed relationship to the object of
art itself. It is particularly poignant to note that after
the first Gutai exhibition closed, the participating
artists elected to build a bonfire and burn their works.
In spite of the practical reasons that may have motivated this act (which obviated the expense of
transporting and storing the work), it refocused the
public's attention on the creative primacy of the
action over the object.

**Nouveau Réalisme** In 1954, one year prior

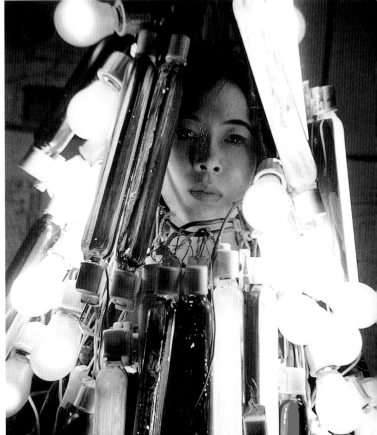

**Georges Mathieu**, *Hommage au Connetable de Bourbon*, 1959

to the Gutai artists' critical breakthroughs, the French artist Georges Mathieu, who would subsequently have a direct relationship with and influence on these artists, created his first completely realized performative painting, *La Bataille de Bouvines* (The Battle of Bouvines). Theatrically garbed in artist's working clothes, with a cloth helmet and strips of cloth wrapped around his pants to keep them from interfering, the media-conscious Mathieu created a monumental gestural frieze about an undistinguished battle in European history. In a series of strokes, gestures, marks, and diagrammatic traces, the paintings record a remarkably formal and controlled texture and weave of contrasting reds, blacks, and yellows, similar to the Gutai artists' palette. Positioning the canvas upright on an extended easel, in contrast to Pollock's floor paintings, Mathieu staged a history lesson in which the canvas was used as a blackboard, a full generation before Beuys's more somber and socially responsible investigations. He subsequently became well-known for his performances, in which he would create large paintings in front of audiences.

Mathieu had had considerable experience in the art of promotion. In 1947 he became director of the public relations department of United States Lines, an American company in Paris. In addition, he had promoted one of the twentieth century's most publicity-driven and theatrical artists, Salvador Dalí, whose own performative action paintings in the 1930s provided a precedent for several of the artists in this exhibition. It was therefore natural that Mathieu himself would gravitate toward staged paintings elaborately documented in photographs and films. His over-the-top performances, which included actions for *Life* and other mass-circulation periodicals, have blurred the important contribution that Mathieu made. Although he remains vested primarily in the formal attributes of his work, he was the forerunner of the self-promotional aesthetic of such artists as Andy Warhol and Jeff Koons, who expertly manipulated the mass media.

Another one of those artists was Yves Klein. Klein was perhaps the most famous artist associated with *Nouveau Réalisme* (New Realism), a movement mostly of French artists that emerged in the early 1960s. It was officially inaugurated with the release of a manifesto dated 27 October 1960, written by the influential critic Pierre Restany and signed by a select group of artists. Most of the artists affiliated with *Nouveau Réalisme*, including Jean Tinguely, Niki de Saint Phalle, and Daniel Spoerri, among others, reacted against the tradition of *art informel* epitomized by artists such as Mathieu. With the notable exception of Klein, they generally abandoned painting for the creation of assemblages made from everyday objects. Nevertheless, they revealed their continuity with *art informel* — specifically with Mathieu — through the primacy they placed on the act, both in the production of objects for exhibition and in the execution of performative actions, as well as in their sophisticated use of the mass media.

Like Mathieu, Klein traveled to Japan in the early 1950s (a journey largely motivated by his desire to study judo, which was then one of his passions). However, when he arrived there in September 1952, it would have been impossible for the Gutai, who did not form a group until 1954, to have had any direct impact on his artistic development. Although there had been proto-Gutai experiments around that time, the remarkable breakthroughs of 1954–55 had not yet occurred. While visiting Hiroshima in 1953, however, Klein did see the preserved silhouette of a man burned into a rock by the atomic flash, a phenomenon of terror with a visual analogy to the cave paintings at Lascaux. Both of these sources stimulated his interest in prehistoric rituals, even though the Hiroshima image was a shadowy remnant of a catastrophic human event rather than an intentional act of drawing. The fact that a human shadow could remain after death deeply inspired Klein; in 1956, when he saw Fumio Kamei's film *Ikite-iteyokata* (The Shadow on the Stone), he wrote, "Hiroshima, the shadows of Hiroshima. In the desert of the atomic catastrophe, they were a witness, without doubt terrible, but nevertheless a witness, both for the hope of survival and for permanence — albeit immaterial — of the flesh."[22] Created by the permanent imprint of the human figure on a surface, this image foreshadowed the *anthropométries* (body paintings) that Klein began to produce at the end of the decade.

By this time, the Gutai artists had achieved

22. *Yves Klein, in Sidra Stich,* Yves Klein *(Stuttgart: Cantz Verlag, 1994), 179.*

**31**

(above and right) **Yves Klein**, "the living paintbrushes," 5 June 1958

significant international attention. Yet, Klein was more willing to acknowledge the Hiroshima experience as an artistic source than the influences of the Gutai artists and Mathieu. Certainly by the late 1950s he was keenly aware of the variety of the Gutai artists' experiments; moreover, given their precedence, it was clearly impossible that they had borrowed from him, as he claimed: "With great ardor [Gutai artists] used my method in a strange way. These painters simply transformed themselves into living brushes. By diving into color and then rolling on their canvases, they became representatives of 'ultra-action-painting!'"[23] Some five years prior to Klein's *anthropométries* and his first experiments with the living brushes, the Gutai were well into their second wave of experimentation. This clearly was a sensitive issue for Klein, who attacked the "deformed ideas spread by the international press" that implied a connection between the Gutai group and his own work.[24] It is unfortunate that Klein did not acknowledge this relationship, which would in fact have clarified the profound differences between their work and his. Most notably, the Gutai artists, reflecting Pollock's influence, sought to put the artist *into* the canvas, whereas the more conceptually oriented Klein repositioned the artist as a conductor whose role was to orchestrate and compose the individuals who would make his paintings for him. As he stated in his 1960 essay *Le vraie devient réalité* (Truth Becomes Reality),

[My models] became living brushes!

I had rejected the brush long before. It was too psychological. I painted with the more anonymous roller, trying to create a "distance" — at the very least an intellectual, unvarying distance — between the canvas and me during the execution. Now, like a miracle, the brush returned, but this time alive. Under my direction, the flesh itself applied the color to the surface, and with perfect precision. I was able to remain constantly at the exact distance "X" from my canvas and thus I could dominate my creation continuously throughout the entire execution.

In this way I stayed clean. I no longer dirtied myself with color, not even the tips of my fingers. The work finished itself there in front of me, under my direction, in absolute collaboration with the model. And I could salute its birth into the tangible world in a dignified manner, dressed in a tuxedo. . . .[25]

Klein's first use of the human figure as a living brush took place, at least in the public arena, at a dinner party at the home of his friend and fellow Judo master, Robert Godet, in June 1958. His first tentative experiment with a "flesh brush" was to cover a nude model with his signature ultramarine blue paint, which he named International Klein Blue (I.K.B.), and have her crawl over a gigantic piece of white paper that, like Pollock's canvas, was laid on the floor. The model used her hands and body to spread the paint across the paper, giving the surface a fleshlike texture distinct from the blue monochromes Klein had painted by brush up to that time. As the art historian Sidra Stich has commented, "Given the context of a dinner party, and Godet's penchant for eroticism, the event took on an aura of folly and lascivious entertainment, much to Klein's displeasure. He might have expected this, since he knew that Godet envisioned the performance as a captivating, collective, sexual, existential experience, but he did not take the precautions to affect an alternative ambience."[26]

This dichotomy between the conceptual underpinnings of Klein's work and the obvious theatrical and sensational means employed to execute it naturally created a misunderstanding of the artist's intention. On the one hand, he wanted to create a distance between himself and what he considered the formal, theatrical trickery used by artists such as Mathieu. On the other, he chose to create a spectacle out of the execution of the work, which he could very well have staged in private in a studio rather than in public at a dinner party. Clearly, Klein wanted it both ways, and on 9 March 1960 he created a performance that was even more contrived, theatrical, sexually titillating, and more spectacular than anything Mathieu or the Gutai artists had previously conceived. This performance was presented at the Galerie Internationale d'Art Contemporain in Paris —

23. *Ibid.*, 189.

24. *Ibid.*,188.

25. *Ibid.*, 176–77. Essay written in March 1960 and originally published in Zero, no. 3 (July 1961).

26. Stich, 172–73.

**33**

**Yves Klein**, *Untitled Anthropometry (ANT 106)*, 1960. Yves Klein Archives

**Yves Klein**, Rehearsal. Practice canvas later cut into several paintings

**Yves Klein**, *L'Étoile (ANT 73)*, 1960. Yves Klein Archives

a prestigious, but not especially cutting edge, gallery that also represented Mathieu. The affluent patrons arrived and were seated on gilded chairs. A large portion of the floor was covered with sheets of paper, and along the front wall hung a twenty-foot-long sheet in front of which were pedestals of varying height. With a formal seriousness, an ensemble consisting of three violinists, three cellists, and three choristers entered and took their place on the stage area on the far side of the gallery. Klein, dressed in a tuxedo and white tie like the musicians, entered as the conductor and bowed to his orchestra, which began playing his *Symphonie monotone* (Monotone Symphony), which consists of a cycle of twenty minutes of one musical note followed by twenty minutes of silence. Of this reductive, Cage-inspired composition Klein observed in a lecture delivered at the Sorbonne: "No longer having either beginning or end, even imperceptibly, this symphony escaped the phenomenology of time. It lived outside the past, the present, the future since it never was born and never died."[27] The symphony contrasted starkly with the entrance of three completely nude women carrying pails of I.K.B. paint. Under the artist's quiet direction, these models sponged the paint onto themselves and imprinted their bodies onto the paper. This part of the

performance had been carefully choreographed the day before in an exacting rehearsal. The practice painting that was produced was subsequently cut into a series of individual *anthropométries* almost indistinguishable from the large-scale composition made during the performance. This extraordinary degree of control over a seemingly playful, even frivolous, event was a characteristic of Klein's work.

After the performance, which was attended by over one hundred guests, most of whom were mature art patrons rather than critics and artists of the avant-garde, there was a discussion with the audience. Mathieu, recognizing Klein's embrace and mockery of his own work, asked the younger artist, "What is art for you?" Klein, whose thinking was more conceptually advanced than Mathieu's formalistic approach, responded, "Art, it is health!" This remark was not just an off-the-cuff remark but a reflection of Klein's focus on the body, whose well-being is necessary for its spiritual transcendence. "This health makes us exist," Klein stated. "[It is] the nature of life itself. [It is] all that we are."[28]

The eight imprints of varying height, depending on the height of the pedestals, were created by two of the models pressing their breasts, abdomens, thighs, and shoulders against the surface. Each fig-

27. Klein, in Stich, 177.       28. Ibid., 175.

ure differed because of the careful composition of the model's application of the body to the paper. The wall painting is a more static composition than the one on the floor, which was created by the third model, who was doused with paint and dragged across the surface of the paper in a gestural evocation with similarities to Shiraga's work. The wall painting, in fact, evokes the blueprints that Robert Rauschenberg and Susan Weil had collaboratively produced in New York a decade earlier.

Klein's ability to control and contrive seemingly spontaneous actions was dramatically exemplified by the infamous photograph *Leap into the Void* of October 1960. Like the void the Gutai artists sought to fill with anarchy, and the homogeneous surface that Fontana chose to break through, Klein's leap served as a powerful metaphor for the creative act, both in its uncontrolled, visceral manifestation and in the highly contrived conceptual theory that created it. The first, and possibly the only *real*, "leap into the void" took place on 12 January 1960, when Klein jumped from the second story of the gallery owner Colette Allendy's home in Paris. Bernadette Allain witnessed the private performance and confirmed that there was no support to break the artist's fall. (The house from which he later leapt was across the street from a judo club, where he was able to enlist the help of friends to catch him in a tarpaulin.) While a twisted ankle offered proof of Klein's leap, many of his colleagues doubted the validity of his claims, in view of their skepticism about his self-professed quest to train himself to levitate.

In October 1960 the photographer Harry Shunk made a series of photographs collaged together to create the impression of Klein leaping unaided out of another second-story window, fifteen feet above the street, with no tarpaulin to break his fall — a fictionalized photographic document that was clearly the product of careful manipulation. This myth-making image, on a par with Namuth's photographs of Pollock, would solidify Klein's extraordinary place in the annals of heroic gestures. Although the photograph ironically undermined his claim to have made the leap unassisted the previous January, the visual

document, fictionalized though it may have been, had an extraordinary impact on the self-endangering body work of the Viennese Actionists and on much of the performance-based body work of the 1970s. It is difficult to imagine the work of the French artist Gina Pane or the American Chris Burden occurring without the precedent of Klein's leap. And it is all the more fascinating to know that through photographic manipulation Klein was able to construct the perception of a life-threatening action, which obviated the need to actually execute one. As Stich has noted, "the final depiction is a composite that invisibly merges separate photographs taken of the jump and the setting into a seamless, dumbfounding 'document.' It is a photograph that suggests superhuman aeronautic power, though it also conveys the image of someone who has put his life at risk to prove the irrepressible idea that humans can fly. Thus, as is typical of most of Klein's art, it's not only an image with a mystical, awesome component but also an endeavor that is hyperbolic and precocious."[29]

One of Klein's closest friends was Jean Tinguely. During their formative years, their relationship was exceptionally important to their artistic development. While Tinguely brought speed, motion, and energy, Klein brought a more conceptual and expansive notion of the parameters of art. In November 1958 they presented a joint exhibition entitled *Vitesse pure et stabilité monochrome: Yves Klein et Jean Tinguely* (Pure Speed and Monochrome Stability: Yves Klein and Jean Tinguely) at Galerie Iris Clert in Paris — the artists' alternative to the more commercial Galerie Internationale d'Art Contemporain. For this exhibition, Klein and Tinguely created six monochromatic blue discs of various sizes fixed to the wall, which were motorized to spin at different speeds. They also produced two freestanding structures: *Excavatrice d'espace* (Space Excavatress) and *Perforateur monochrome* (Monochrome Perforator). The former featured a white disc eight inches in diameter; the latter, a tiny red one spinning at 10,000 rpm.[30]

Tinguely's *méta-matics*, or drawing machines, which he began to produce in 1959, were a series of

29. Stich, 220.

30. See K. G. Pontus Hulten, Tinguely, exh. cat. (Paris: Centre Georges

Pompidou, Musée National d'Art Moderne, 1989), 47.

Jean Tinguely, *Baluba*, 1964. The Menil Collection, Houston
Gift of Jean Tinguely

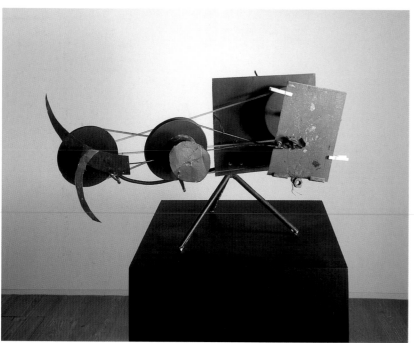

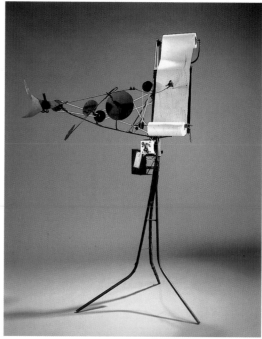

elegant, spindly, awkward, and energetically dynamic mechanical sculptures that, when activated, would create childlike drawings. In their early manifestations they moved lyrically; however, they became increasingly violent, vigorous, and spectacular, until they turned into monstrous and foreboding sculptures that exploded, destroying themselves. To promote his exhibition of *méta-matics* presented in July 1959 at Galerie Iris Clert, Tinguely distributed announcements all over Paris. These announcements invited the public to "Do it yourself and create your own abstract painting with Tinguely's *méta-matics*. A prize of 50,000 francs is offered by the gallery to the best painting made on Tinguely's *méta-matics*"; the jurors included the most influential personalities in the Paris art world. The artist also hired men wearing sandwich boards to parade in front of the gallery. Advertising the exhibition like a business, Tinguely anticipated the consumer aesthetic that would appear more clearly and unequivocally in Claes Oldenburg's *The Store* and Ben Vautier's *Le magasin*.[31]

This *super-manifestation-spectacle-exposition* was a tremendous success; five to six thousand visitors made four thousand machine drawings. The large attendance was as much the result of sophisticated advertising as it was of interest in Tinguely's work, and the controversial exhibition was both acclaimed and condemned in the media. The controversy, however, may have been due less to the fact that machines made the art than to the accompanying promotional campaign. The following October Tinguely stole the show at the first Biennale des Jeunes in Paris with his *Méta-matic No. 17*, which drew on a continuous roll of paper and exhausted its fumes into a balloon until it burst.

The next presentation of Tinguely's mechanical drawings took place at the Cyclo-matic Evening at the Institute of Contemporary Arts in London on 12 November 1959 — a lecture-demonstration entitled "Art, machines et mouvement: Une conférence de Tinguely" (Art, Machines, and Motion: A Lecture by Tinguely.)[32] Although this event has been wrongly

31. Ibid., 55.

32. For the text of Tinguely's lecture, see ibid., 67.

Tir by Niki de Saint Phalle, target of real flowers by Jasper Johns,
Robert Rauschenberg painting as Jean Tinguely looks through stage curtain, 1961

Entre-acte by Jasper Johns, Robert Rauschenberg painting onstage, sharpshooter aiming at Niki de Saint Phalle's tir. 1961

called one of the first Happenings in Europe, it certainly can be credited with blurring the distinction between demonstration, performance, and sculpture. Over the next several years, and with increasing resources, Tinguely, in works such as *Hommage à New York* (Homage to New York, presented at the Museum of Modern Art in New York on 17 March 1960) and *Étude pour une fin du monde* (Study for the End of the World, presented at the Louisiana Museum in Humlebaek, Denmark, on 22 September 1961) created machines with complex pyrotechnic self-destructive properties that began to take on environmental proportions. The cataclysmic conclusions of these mechanical sculptures were consistent with the investigations of many of the aforementioned artists and show a continuing trend toward violence and self-annihilation.

On 20 June 1961, Tinguely, Rauschenberg, Johns, and Niki de Saint Phalle participated in a performance entitled *Homage to David Tudor* at the Théâtre de l'Ambassade des États-Unis in Paris. While the renowned pianist David Tudor played

**39**

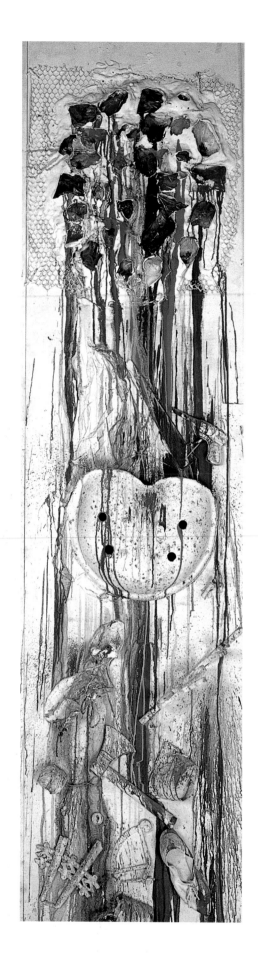

Cage's music, the four artists simultaneously presented actions within predetermined brackets of time. Tinguely coordinated a mechanical sculpture with feathers that destroyed itself; Rauschenberg painted *First Time Painting* on stage, with the back of the canvas facing the audience, which never saw the front; Johns provided a target painting made of flowers; and Saint Phalle created one of her notorious shooting paintings, which she termed *tirs*.

In a letter to Pontus Hulten, Saint Phalle stated that in the early 1960s she had begun to sublimate the intense aggression she felt into her work, which became increasingly violent. She produced her first assemblages incorporating actual pistols in 1960, she made a work entitled *Portrait of My Lover* in which the figure's head was a target pierced by darts in 1961, and she created her first *tirs* that same year.[33] To create these works, Saint Phalle would cover assemblages with balloons containing paint. With precision, she would place each color strategically. Then, wearing an all-white shooting uniform of her own design, she would aim and fire. The act of making a painting through a violent gesture is reminiscent of Shimamoto's performances, in which he exploded bottles of paint or shot it from a cannon. However, in contrast to Shimamoto, Saint Phalle would occasionally invite others to shoot, as in her first one-person exhibition at Gallery J in Paris in June 1961, the same gallery that sponsored Daniel Spoerri's first restaurant.

Saint Phalle presented more than twelve *tirs* in 1961–62. In a manner reminiscent of the splash Tinguely had made in the media, more than fifty international magazines and journals published reports about her during this period. This visibility led to her invitation to the Malibu beach house of gallery owner Virginia Dwan, where she staged the first of two *tirs* in the United States with the assistance of Ed Kienholz. Rauschenberg, who had participated in a *tir* presented at the Staket sandpit near Värmdö, Sweden, on 23 May 1961, during an exhibition entitled "Rörelse I Konsten," organized by Stockholm's

33. Niki de Saint Phalle, letter to Pontus Hulten, in Hulten, Niki de Saint Phalle, exh. cat. (Stuttgart: Kunst-und Ausstellungshalle der Bundesrepublik Deutschland and G. Hatje, 1992).

**Niki de Saint Phalle** sitting on floor,
Robert Rauschenberg standing, 1961

**Niki de Saint Phalle** with tir at the opening of her solo exhibition,
"feu à volonté," Gallerie J, Paris, 28 June 1961

**Daniel Spoerri**, *Le lieu de repos de la famille Delbeck*, 1960
Collection of Daniel Varenne, Genève

**Daniel Spoerri**, in the *Restaurant*, 1966-1968

**42**

**Daniel Spoerri**, *Le coin du Restaurant Spoerri*, c. 1968

Moderna Museet, helped create the construction for Saint Phalle's other American *tir*, presented in the parking lot of the Renaissance Club on Sunset Boulevard in Los Angeles in March 1962. Saint Phalle's celebrity also led to a 1962 exhibition of her work at Iolas Gallery in New York, and her behavior became the model for an artist portrayed by Shirley MacLaine in the Hollywood movie *What a Way to Go*.

Another important artist affiliated with *Nouveau Réalisme* was Daniel Spoerri. In the early 1960s, Spoerri created a series of assemblages — his *tableaux pièges* (trap paintings) — that trapped and froze the last moment of a diner's meal. The section of the table or support where the meal occurred was fixed in place and then oriented vertically and hung like a painting. Although seemingly part of the junk aesthetic then prevalent in the United States and France, these works were more like photographs capturing a moment in time, a "portrait" of the person who had dined. The identity of the diners and the circumstances under which the meals had been eaten became an evolving aspect of traps, manifesting Spoerri's interest in the phenomenon of celebrity.

In March 1963 Spoerri opened his Restaurant Gallery J in Paris for twelve days, followed by an exhibition of 723 cooking utensils. He included the following information on the invitation to the restaurant and the subsequent exhibition: "The gastronomic activities of 'Chef Daniel' Spoerri bear immediate aesthetic consequence (within the purity of the most orthodox traditions of *Nouveau Réalisme*) and will result in works which the public is invited to view on the day immediately following the closing of the restaurant, March 14, starting at 5:00 p.m." Although Spoerri had once managed an actual restaurant, this one was perhaps more closely related to his snare-pictures. The waiters included such art world notables as Restany and the poet John Ashbery. Within the restaurant, Spoerri took pride that foodstuffs would be exhibited as works of art without being incorporated into assemblages and that the sense of taste was added to the visual and tactile dimensions of the works on view.

In June 1968, Spoerri founded Restaurant Spoerri in Düsseldorf, which enjoyed great success. In this restaurant he offered conventional items such as steaks, in addition to such specialties as omelets with roasted termites, chicken embryos, bear paws, rattlesnake ragu, sliced elephant trunks, and so forth. Eventually, Spoerri cut the corner out of the restaurant and moved it from Dusseldorf to Milan, where he prepared a meal for each sign of the zodiac; sixteen guests ate meals corresponding to their respective signs. The final relic of both the restaurant and the

**43**

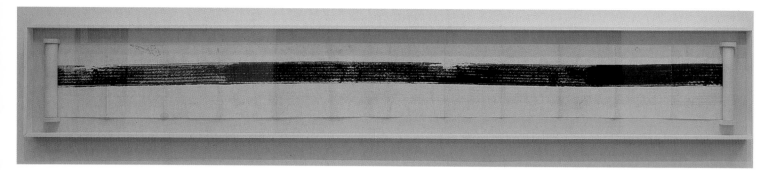

**Robert Rauschenberg** with John Cage, *Automobile Tire Print*, 1953
Collection of the artist

dinner performance in Milan was entitled *The Corner of the Restaurant Spoerri*. The artist had turned life into art.

Robert Rauschenberg was another artist who sought to redefine the relationship between art and life through the performative act. Rauschenberg first investigated the role of the act in the creation of an object in his works of the early 1950s. These works included the blueprints, such as *Female Figure* (c. 1950), that he made with Weil by imprinting the silhouettes of human beings and objects onto photosensitive blueprint paper. Another work in which Rauschenberg captured the indexical trace of an action was *Automobile Tire Print* (1953), which he created by laying a twenty-two-foot-long strip of paper, formed from twenty separate sheets, on the street outside of his studio. He then instructed Cage to drive the inked back wheel of his Model A Ford over the strip's entire length. The resulting imprint was the visual equivalent of a sustained single note, as well as an important precedent for the use of the line by other artists, including Piero Manzoni, James Lee Byars, and Nam June Paik.

Rauschenberg's interest in investigating the performative act is also evident in his participation in the performance at the Théâtre de l'Ambassade des États-Unis in Paris with Johns, Saint Phalle, and Tinguely in 1961. In contrast to Mathieu, Rauschenberg painted his canvas, which he titled *First Time Painting*, with its back facing the members of the audience, who never saw the completed work. The painting was finished when an alarm clock attached to it rang (at this signal, Rauschenberg wrapped the painting in paper and gave it to a bellhop from the Hôtel du Pont Royale, where he was staying). With this gesture, he implied that the act of painting was more important than what was painted — an interpretation underscored by his incorporation of the clock into the work. *Second Time Painting*, which he created later that year, also incorporates a working clock. Moreover, most of his major works from the mid-1960s through the end of the decade incorporated sound, motion, and light-sensitive devices. The most technologically complex of these works were produced with the assistance of Billy Klüver, a Bell Systems electronics engineer who had worked with Tinguely on *Homage to New York* and assisted other

**Robert Rauschenberg**, *Second Time Painting*, c. 1961
Rose Art Museum, Brandeis University, Waltham, Massachusetts
Gevirtz-Mnuchin Purchase Fund, 1962

**Robert Rauschenberg**, *Trophy III (For Jean Tinguely)*, 1961
The Museum of Contemporary Art, Los Angeles. The Panza Collection

**45**

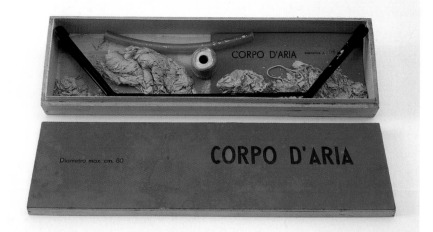

**Piero Manzoni**, *Corpo d'aria*, 1961. Block Collection

artists who worked with technology.

During the same period that Rauschenberg produced these works, he became increasingly interested in performance. On 4 May 1962 he participated in another performance with Saint Phalle and Tinguely — a fifteen-minute play by the poet Kenneth Cox entitled *The Construction of Boston*, presented at the Maidman Playhouse in New York. For this production, Rauschenberg designed the set and served as stage manager, lighting director, and a performer. In the last capacity, he operated a machine made by Tinguely that projected balls onto audience members and poured rain onto the performers; presenting one of her *tirs*, Saint Phalle shot a rifle at a statue of the Venus de Milo, which seemed to bleed; and Tinguely built a wall between the performers and the audience. This collaboration reopened the arena of performance to creative and imaginative play.

Since 1954 Rauschenberg had designed sets, costumes, and lighting for Cunningham. By 1963 his interest in performance stimulated him to choreograph a work of his own, entitled *Pelican* — the first of eleven works that he choreographed through 1968.[34] The dancer Steve Paxton and the director of the Jewish Museum Alan Solomon called these works *Theater Pieces*. Inspired by the location of *Pelican* — a Washington roller-skating rink called America on Wheels — Rauschenberg designed for himself and his co-performer Per Olof Ultvedt parachute-like wings that metaphorically took flight as the skaters increased their speed. Speculating on the origin of Rauschenberg's interest in performance, Paxton writes in his 1997 essay "Rauschenberg for Cunningham and Three of His Own,"

> I have wondered how Rauschenberg made the mental transition from painting to choreography. A performance is, of course, experienced sequentially, but so might a painting be. Even the boldest simple image — a work by Frank Stella, for example, or an early Jasper Johns — allows a second look. My experience of Rauschenberg's flat(ish) painting *Rebus* (1955) was sequential.

*Monogram* (1955–59) was a spiral sequential experience, as I walked around it, circling closer. Like other painters, Rauschenberg often faces empty stretched canvases and envisions how he might populate and color them. In the *White Paintings* (1951–52), he just left them white and let the shadows play. Time and movement entered his more material paintings too, in the form of clocks and radios. His work was animated to a degree before he began his own theatrical ventures.[35]

Rauschenberg's influence on younger artists dedicated to investigating the role of the act both in creation of objects and actions would prove to be extremely significant.

**From Manzoni to Arte Povera** Like Klein, Tinguely, Saint Phalle, and Spoerri, the Italian artist Piero Manzoni accentuated the performative dimension of the objects he created in the late 1950s and early 1960s; however, his work was distinctly different in character. Seeing Klein's work in January 1957 and meeting the artist at the Galerie Apollonaire stimulated Manzoni to produce his first *Achromes* in October of that year, which he continued to make until his death in 1963. Describing the difference between his paintings and *art informel*, Manzoni questioned the validity of paintings that had been "reduced to a sort of receptacle into which unnatural colors and artificial meanings are shoved and pressed. Why not empty this receptacle, free the surface, try to discover the unlimited meaning of total space, and pure and absolute light?"

Manzoni later became particularly interested in investigating the philosophical implications of the straight line. In the early 1950s Fontana had introduced the line into the repertoire of postwar art through his lacerated canvases, and in 1953 Rauschenberg had created *Automobile Tire Print*. However, Manzoni was to become the most rigorous advocate of the line, his only potential rival being the

34. On Rauschenberg's performances see the following essays in Rauschenberg: A Retrospective, *exh. cat. (New York: Solomon R. Guggenheim Foundation, 1997): Nancy Spector,* "Rauschenberg and Performance, 1963–67: A 'Poetry of Infinite Possibilities,'" 226–45; Steve Paxton, "Rauschenberg for Cunningham and Three of His Own," 260–67; Trisha Brown, "Collaboration: Life and Death in the Aesthetic Zone," 268–74.

35. Paxton, 264.

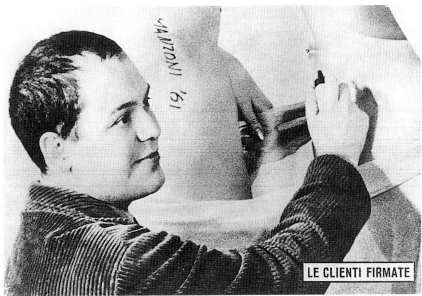

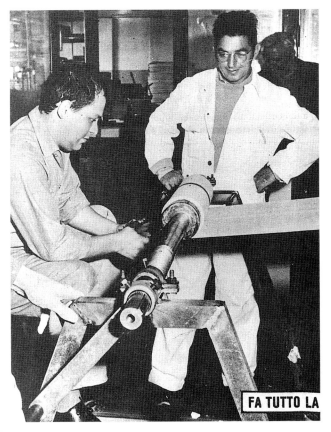

**Piero Manzoni**, photographs from
*Gente* magazine, 1961

composer La Monte Young. Regarding the line from a temporal perspective, he stated that "the line develops only in length, it runs to infinity: its only dimension is time." From the spring of 1959 onward, he produced numerous drawings of lines executed on sheets and rolls of paper, which he termed his *Lineas* (Lines), often encasing the rolls in metal cylinders so that they were invisible. He executed the Lines both in the privacy of his studio and in public. On 4 July 1960 he created his longest Line, *Linea m. 7,200* (Line 7,200 Meters Long) in the printing facility of the Danish newspaper *Herning Avis* by pressing the tip of a bottle of India ink against a large roll of white paper; after this "performance," he encased the roll in a zinc container and displayed it in a park in front of a local shirt factory.

As measurements of the time necessary to make them, Manzoni's Lines represent fragments of existence measured, sealed, and contained. In the 6 July 1960 issue of the Danish newspaper *Herning Folkeblad*, he points to their relationship not only to temporality, but to infinity: "Time is something different from what the hands of a clock measure, and the 'Line' does not measure metres or kilometres, but is zero, not zero as the end but as the beginning of an infinite series."[36] Indeed, the Lines' potential extension into infinity signified the fragmentary nature of

life, in that no matter how long they were, they were only fractions of the nondimensionality of timelessness — indexes of actions disappeared into the void of being. As Alma Ruiz observes in her 1995 essay "Piero Manzoni: Line Drawings," "Each Line functions as the index of an action, just as Manzoni's *Fiato d'artista* (Artist's Breath) — a balloon inflated with the artist's breath — and *Merda d'artista* (Artist's Shit) — a tin packed with his feces — do. In fact, the act of making a Line can be defined as a performance, whether conducted in the solitude of the studio or before an audience in the street or a printing house, where the production of the Lines was collaborative — Happenings or Fluxus events, of a sort."[37]

As this passage implies, Manzoni's activities increasingly centered on his own body. With his *Artist's Breath* (1960) and *Artist's Shit* (1961), he respectively transformed an exhalation and an excretion into a work of art. The latter, canned in thirty-gram tins, was sold by the gram at a price fixed to that of gold. His related *Corpi d'aria* (Bodies of Air, 1959–60) were pneumatic sculptures consisting of a container enclosing an air pump and a balloon that could be inflated by the purchaser. If the purchaser wished, Manzoni himself would inflate the balloon, at 200 lire a liter, and the work would be retitled *Artist's*

36. Piero Manzoni, cited in Freddy Battino and Luca Palazzoli, Piero Manzoni: Catalogue raisonné (Milan: Edizioni di Vanni Schweiwiller, 1991), 100.

37. Alma Ruiz, "Piero Manzoni: Line Drawings," in Piero Manzoni: Line Drawings, exh. cat. (Los Angeles: The Museum of Contemporary Art and

Ravenna: Danilo Montanari Editore, 1995), 14.

**Piero Manzoni**, *Base Magica*, 1961
Archivo Opera Piero Manzoni

**Giueseppe Pinot Gallizio**, *Industrial Painting*, 1958
Galleria Martano, Torino

**Piero Manzoni**, with cans of *Merda d'artista*
(Artist's shit), 1961

*Breath.* For the artist, these works were an expression of "being in reality and in the void," as well as "being reality and being void."

Manzoni also incorporated the bodies of his public into his art. In 1960 he boiled eggs, stamped them with his thumbprint, and distributed them to the public to eat. In 1961 at Galleria La Tartaruga in Rome he presented his *Base magica* (Magic Base). This simple pedestal, on top of which were affixed two felt footprints, allowed members of the public, at the artist's invitation, to be transformed into works of art. The structure and audience participation that Murakami had initiated in *Sakuhin: Hako* (Work: Box, 1956) was brought to an elegant and obvious resolution, as Manzoni generously signed the bodies of his participants and handed them certificates of authenticity. Like his Lines, the *Magic Base* works formed a measurement of time in which the transformative aspects of art could be appreciated. Given Manzoni's obsession with the measurement and demarcation of time and his embrace of the life, it is all the more profound that he should have died at such a young age in 1963.

In 1958 Giuseppe Pinot Gallizio, a chemist-turned-industrialist and then painter, invented a machine to produce his first *Pittura industriale* (Industrial Painting) — a year before Tinguely's first drawing machine. Using fast-drying resins, spray guns, and long rolls of canvas, Pinot Gallizio intended to engulf entire cities with his art. In his 1959 *Manifesto della pittura industriale* (Manifesto for Industrial Painting), he stated that "Artistic production by these machines, bent docilely to our will, [will] be so great that we will not even have time to fix it in our minds: the machines remember for us. Other machines will intervene to destroy it all determining situations of *no-value*: there were will no longer be *specimen-works of art* but exchanges of *ecstatic-artistic-air* among populations. The world will be the stage and the counter-stage for a continual performance; the earth will be transformed into an immense funfair, creating new emotions and passions." The manifesto ends with the following challenge: "The long days of atomic creation have begun like this. Now it is up to us artists, scientists and poets to create the earth, oceans, animals, sun and other stars, airs, waters and things all over again. And it will be up to us to breathe into the clay in order to create the *new-man* fitted for resting on the *seventh* day."

Pinot Gallizio's industrial paintings were often up to ninety meters long. For an exhibition in 1959 he lined the entire space — floor, walls, and ceiling — with a selection of these paintings, into which he had incorporated the corrosive effects of gunpowder, as well as the sun, wind, and rain. He titled the resulting installation *la caverna dell'antimateria* (Cave of Antimatter) and described it as "the uterus of the world." In a manner reminiscent of the strategies of the media-savvy Gutai group, and anticipating those of the *Nouveaux Réalistes* and Happenings artists, Pinot Gallizio arranged for fashion models dressed in his paintings to attend the exhibition's opening.

**49**

**Jannis Kounellis**, *Untitled*, 1960. The Reiner Speck Collection, Cologne

**Michelangelo Pistoletto**, performance *Globe*, 1966-68

**Jannis Kounellis**, *Untitled (Da inventare sul posto)*, 1972. The Reiner Speck Collection, Cologne

These models interacted with an environment altered by the use of lights, colors, mirrors, perfumes, and sounds, whose intensity would vary according to the movements of visitors.

Jannis Kounellis, the Greek artist most often associated with Arte Povera, a movement that emerged in Italy during the mid-1960s, produced a series of conceptual, performative paintings in the late 1950s coterminous with Manzoni's and Pinot Gallizio's experiments. These paintings inaugurated his longstanding practice of introducing temporal, performative, and living elements into his work.

From the late 1950s through the mid-1960s, Kounellis focused on letters, numbers, and signs, which, like Johns's number paintings, were literal representations of abstractions. Underscoring the performative dimension of these paintings, he once observed: "Around 1958–59 I began to paint my letter pictures. Soon after, the number paintings followed. Many of these were also conceived to be sung . . . . All this, the act of painting, took place while singing. I sang my paintings. This was, if you will, my contribution to the overcoming of Informel, and it also was, at the same time, my first performances." Kounellis showed a selection of these works while he was still a student in his first one-person exhibition, entitled *L'alfabeto di Kounellis* (Kounellis's Alphabet), presented at Galleria La Tartaruga in Rome in 1960. Further underscoring their performative dimension,

later that year he wore one of his letter paintings as a garment, mimicking the Dadaist Hugo Ball's famous costume from the Cabaret Voltaire in Zurich, and performed an action in his studio in which he became part of one of the works. He documented this performance in photographs.

After receiving international acclaim as one of the founding members of Arte Povera in the mid-1960s, Kounellis began to reanimate his work by including performative elements. In 1969 he concentrated on a series of bedframe sculptures, which incorporated fire in a disturbingly manner.[38] The bedframe was a metaphorical object that suggested birth and the creation of new form. In an untitled performance work from 1970, Kounellis positioned a woman on an iron base the size of a bed or coffin. She was wrapped completely, with one foot protruding; to this foot was attached a propane torch with a hissing gas flame.

In 1972 Kounellis completed three "note" paintings, each in a different color: green, brown, and pink. Each work was presented along with a ballet performance accompanied by cello and cello bass. With these works, which included the representation of a fragment from *La Pucinella* by Igor Stravinsky on a large pink canvas, Kounellis briefly returned to his days as a painter of musical notes. During this period, he created many performance-based paintings and installation works, including a notorious performance,

38. For documentation of these and other works, see Mary Jane Jacob, *Jannis* Kounellis, *exh. cat. (Chicago: Museum of Contemporary Art, 1986).*

**John Latham**, *Shaun II*, 1958. Arts Council Collection, Hayward Gallery, London

which he describes as a painting, in which he dragged a horse up the stairs to the third floor of 420 West Broadway in New York, where Sonnabend Gallery was located. The act of sitting on the horse signaled the conclusion of the "painting."

Another artist associated with the Arte Povera movement was Michelangelo Pistoletto. In 1966 Pistoletto created a large globe out of mulched paper. He drove around with this sphere in a convertible, and

it became a prop for actions he would perform. As documented in the film *Good Morning Michelangelo*, he used the sphere — the world globe of the artist — in a series of performances-actions that took place on the streets of the city and in nontraditional exhibition spaces, including restaurants and bars. Half the size of a human, Pistoletto's sculpture allowed the artist to redirect social interaction. In addition, as a vehicle for visual insurrection, it served as a humorous inter-

**52**

**John Latham,** *Soft Skoob*, 1964. Courtesy Lisson Gallery, London

vention into Pistoletto's daily life. The fact that this globe still exists in its original form is a lasting testament to the importance that it held for Pistoletto during the period of his public performances.

Prior to 1967 Pistoletto had also made mirror paintings, which contained images of the human figure and were completed by the viewer's reflection. The viewer's participation in these works, reminiscent of *Nouveau Réalisme* and Pop paintings, distinguishes them from the majority of work being produced by artists of the preceding generation. However, in that year he abandoned painting for real-life actions. His theater group, called "The Zoo," had a deliberately unrefined and direct quality, and its presentations were designed for streets and public squares, rather than for more traditional theatrical venues. Although the process-oriented work of other artists associated with Arte Povera, including Mario Merz, Alighiero Boetti, and Pier Paolo Calzolari exhibited the temporal component of both Kounellis's and Pistoletto's, these two artists investigated the role of the performative act in greater depth.

**Two Artists between the Cracks** In spite of the pioneering works that the English artist John Latham and the American James Lee Byars began to produce independently in the early 1960s, the achievements of neither have been fully recognized, in part because they fell through the cracks of the stylistic categories in which postwar art was commonly divided. The centerpiece of Latham's work was the book. His singleminded obsession with using, reusing, and reformulating books — through which the history of humanity is recorded — radically differentiated him from the other American and French assemblage artists with whom he was often associated. Latham referred to the sculptures, assemblages, and actions he produced from books with the term *skoob* (*books* spelled backward). Although this oddly exhibitionistic hermit was identified with assemblage, *Nouveau Réalisme*, and Pop, and even participated in some of the most important exhibitions of these currents in the 1960s, his works eluded each of these stylistic categories. It is perhaps for this reason that Latham — in spite of the breadth of his artistic ambitions and influences, especially in

England, where he is revered — has been deeply under-recognized.

Latham's conceptually motivated book works emerged from his sophisticated theoretical posturings. In the early 1950s he had met two scientists — the astronomers Clive Gregory and Anita Kohsen, who had graduated from Oxford with a degree in animal ethology — who sought to integrate the various disciplines of knowledge into a new science they christened psychophysical cosmology. In 1958 they founded, and made Latham an honorary founding member of, the Institute for the Study of Mental Images. In 1959 the institute published a book entitled *The O-Structure: An Introduction to Psychophysical Cosmology*, and in 1960 it began to publish a journal entitled *Cosmos*. The theories generated under the auspices of the ISMI had a profound effect on Latham's artistic development.

In the late 1950s Latham used a spray gun to develop what he called the *quantum-of-mark* approach to form, which reflected the influence of Gregory and Kohsen. In 1958 he began to make works using books. As John A. Walker has stated, "Disregarding the meaning of the words on the page, Latham was struck by the similarity of form — black marks on a white surface — between printed text and his 'dust-cloud,' spray-gun paintings. Initially, the choice of books appears to have been fortuitous. However, it was not long before the multiple possibil-

**John Latham**, *Soft Skoob as Dress*,
late 1960s. Courtesy Lisson Gallery, London

**John Latham,** *Skoob Tower*, 1964/1988
Courtesy of the artist and Lisson Gallery, London

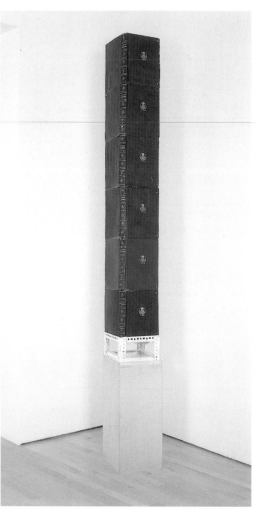

**John Latham**, burning of *Skoob Tower*, 31 May 1996
Courtesy of the Mattress Factory, Pittsburgh

ities and implications of his decision became clear to him."[39] In 1960 Latham's work was exhibited in the United States for the first time in the exhibition "New Forms, New Media," presented at Martha Jackson Gallery. At the same time, he was making films with such titles as *Unclassified Material* and *Unedited Material from the Star* (1960). Latham's interest in film-making, quantum physics, and mathematics invested his work with a dense, even incomprehensible quality, which was also reflected in his assemblages and his later performance *Skoob Towers*.

The years 1961 and 1962 were extremely productive for Latham. In the former year he included his book works in the important exhibition "The Art of Assemblage," organized by William C. Seitz for The Museum of Modern Art in New York. In the latter, he participated in the exhibition "The New Realists," presented at Sidney Janis Gallery, and in an exhibition at the Galerie Internationale d'Art Contemporain, to which he contributed several of his book works, including *Skoob Box*. As Walker writes, this work was "an environmental sculpture consisting of a cube, large enough to contain a standing human being, made from hardboard lined with canvas. It had three relief masses extending from the walls and ceiling positioned where a right-hand spiral would intersect them. The work was completed when someone stood inside the box and contributed their attention. Above the head of the viewer, embedded in the ceiling, was a single book plus two lights — one white, one 'black' (that is, ultraviolet) — operating with a dimmer to produce a three-phase sequence of 'black,' white and twilight (each phase lasted fifteen seconds."[40] Latham created numerous other works in 1962, including *Skoob Dress*, which consisted of a spray-painted canvas, into which books had been stitched, worn by his wife Barbara, and *Kinetic Sculpture*, which consisted of three battered suitcases, a connecting rod, and two electric motors that rocked the suitcases in nine- and eleven-second cycles. The suitcase, shaped like an enlarged book, was an awkward and decidedly unsophisticated response to Tinguely's more elegant and refined mechanical devices.

By 1963 Latham had received significant critical attention for his assemblages. In a review of his and other works entitled "Sculpture — Inside and Outside," published in the venerable English periodical *Apollo* in June of that year, worth quoting at length, the critic Edwin Mullins writes:

John Latham (Kasmin), it can be claimed, is one of the few living artists capable of extending the boundaries of visual experience. When looking at Latham's constructions with books and metal there is a feeling that the responses to which twentieth-century art has so far conditioned us — even our responses to Schwitters and Duchamp — are altogether inappropriate. On the easiest level they can be appreciated in the manner of an abstract expressionist painting: as impulsive gestures which convey a host of immediate sensations of destruction, desolation, metamorphosis, of the movement and concentration of objects in space, and so on. But this is not enough; otherwise why the use of books . . . , of actual machines, and why the tacit invitation to tinker with them? This intellectual appeal in his work — almost a philosophical message — is outside the scope of purely abstract art, if not of visual art altogether. What with Kitaj, New Realist art generally, and now Latham, the spectator is increasingly being asked to consider intellectual, often literary, references as a legitimate part of our enjoyment of art.[41]

Nevertheless, the fact that this critic also termed him a "misguided intellectual," that his dealer believed that he had become "too theoretical," and that his exhibition that year at Bear Lane Gallery in Oxford turned out to be extremely controversial and resulted in part in his departure from John Kasmin Gallery contributed to deep personal despair.

Out of this despair, and no doubt bullied by the maverick growth of the destruction-in-art movement (legitimated by the strong, if eccentric, history of violence among English artists from Francis Bacon to Gustav Metzger), in July 1964 Latham transformed his time-based film-making experiments into a series

39. John A. Walker, John Latham: The Incidental Person—His Art and Ideas (Middlesex: Middlesex University Press, 1995), 35.

40. Ibid., 52.

41. Edwin Mullins, "Sculpture—Inside and Outside," Apollo 77, no. 16 (n.s.) (June 1963): 504.

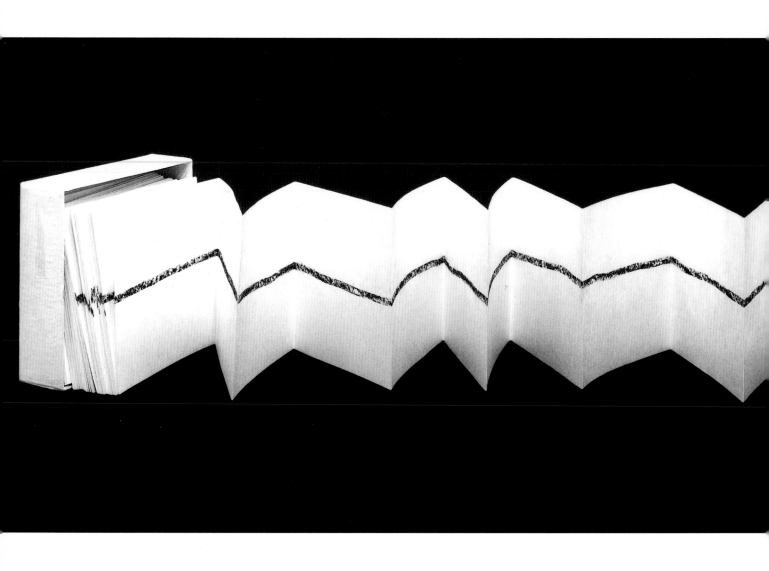

**James Lee Byars**, *Untitled Object*, 1962-64. The Museum of Modern Art, New York.
Gift of the artist

of public events in which he burned skyscraper-like towers of books — *Skoob Towers*. With Metzger's South Bank demonstration as a precedent, he created biographically pointed works that were also connected with the broader postwar political context of the legacy of Nazi Germany and the emergence of the Holocaust. As Latham recalled in 1994, "The towers were a solution to the problem of the constitutional anomaly whereby the right to free speech and silent constructs can be covertly run into the sea by the use of crown charters."[42]

Specifically framing each of the burnings he conducted over the next several years, Latham burnt art books near the British Museum and law books at the Courts. Echoing the words of Dine, Metzger, Shiraga, and Tinguely, he responded to a question about the meaning of these destructive actions by stating that "It was not in any degree a gesture of contempt for books or literature. What it did intend was to put the proposition into mind that perhaps the cultural base had been burnt out."[43] Using James Joyce's *Finnegan's Wake* as a model, Latham became convinced that what he termed event-structure theory was the new model of thinking that would replace the "burnt out" intellectual traditions of the West.

In 1966 Latham participated in the Destruction in Art Symposium in London. That same year he created the pointedly outrageous *Still and Chew* with his students from St. Martin's School of Art. Using a library copy of Clement Greenberg's 1961 collection of essays, *Art and Culture*, Latham had his students chew the pages of the formalist critic's book, distilled the pulp, poured it into a flask, and labeled it "essence of Greenberg." He used this demonstration to focus on the primacy of process over object, continuing his own tradition of rendering useless the organs of printed knowledge. Upon returning the book to the library in liquid form, he was dismissed from his teaching position. Although destruction had been a significant ingredient of action-based art since the end of World War II, no artist with such a global vision of its impact has remained as obscure as Latham.

If Latham was a distinctively English artist, James Lee Byars was the embodiment of the internationalism that characterized the postwar period. Raised in Detroit, Byars lived in Japan for most of the period from 1958 to 1967 and then became an artist of the world, spending time in Los Angeles, New York, Germany, Santa Fe, New Mexico, and Egypt, where he died in 1996. While living in Kyoto, he studied traditional Japanese ceramics and papermaking with various master craftsmen. On one of his trips to New York Byars somehow convinced Dorothy Miller, an influential curator at The Museum of Modern Art, to allow him to install his large paper works in the museum's five-story emergency stairwell. This installation-performance inaugurated Byars's lifelong pursuit of interventions that involved himself and objects he made.

Byars's first group action in 1960 consisted of one hundred students reciting one hundred lines from Gertrude Stein while positioned in a circle at the Yukawa Center for Theoretical Physics in Kyoto. Two years later Byars created "several giant, performable paper works in Japan made of many sheets of Japanese flax paper connected by paper hinges. These works are folded into solid geometric shapes and intended to be exhibited in stylized, gestural presentations in which a performer, sometimes Byars, sometimes an individual he had invited, deliberately unfolds the paper over the course of as much as an hour. While these works were conceived as performable pieces, it appears that they were seldom performed immediately; rather they were shown months later."[44] Although it is unlikely that Byars was aware of Manzoni's Lines of a year earlier, it is probable, given his location in Kyoto and involvement with the visual arts of that community, that he was aware of Kanayama's performance action for an outdoor Gutai exhibition of 1958, in which he left imprints of his footsteps on hundreds of feet of paper that formed a ribbon. Nevertheless, Byars's work had none of the theatricality and participatory spirit that characterized Gutai; instead, the artist drew from the legacies of Zen Buddhism and Noh theater to create a reductive action that was respectful of the contem-

42. Walker, 65.

43. John Latham, in ibid., 80.

44. James Elliott, The Perfect Thought: Works by James Lee Byars, exh. cat.

(Berkeley: University Art Museum, 1990), 75.

**Allan Kaprow**, *Rearrangeable Panels*, 1957-59

**Allan Kaprow**, *18 Happenings in 6 Parts*, 1959. Collection of the artist

plative aspects of traditional Japanese performance.

One of Byars's 1962 works, a 1 x 200–foot drawing, was exhibited at the Shokokuji Temple in Kyoto in 1963–64. On this long sheet of Japanese flax paper, Byars drew with charcoal a single line running the length of the sheet, folded it in an accordion shape, then unfolded it and stood it on its edge. Using the paper as a performative object, he transformed Manzoni's line of infinite length from a conceptual object into an explicitly performative one. This work was consistent with another work of the same period, exhibited at the same monastery, that consisted of a 1,000-foot-long sheet of white Chinese paper also folded like an accordion; this drawing was unfolded into an oval shape by a Japanese woman in traditional ceremonial dress.

After leaving Japan in 1967, Byars first moved to Los Angeles, where he exhibited the white version of *Four in a Dress* at the Eugenia Butler Gallery at the same time that he exhibited the black version at the Green Gallery in New York. This performative costume, as the title implies, involved four people wearing a dress the size of a pup tent. Byars's per-

formable clothing works, which included pants for three, hats for one hundred, and a dress for five hundred, had connections with a tradition that includes Lygia Clark, Pinot Gallizio, Milan Knížák, Yayoi Kusama, Hélio Oiticica, and many others.

**Happenings** In 1959, at the Reuben Gallery in New York, Allan Kaprow presented the first Happening. Although Happenings were pioneered by New York artists such as Kaprow, Jim Dine, Red Grooms, Claes Oldenburg, and Robert Whitman, they were soon embraced by artists internationally. Initially presented in limited spaces for limited audiences (except when they were presented outdoors), Happenings were performances that differed from traditional theatrical productions in that they did not follow conventional narratives, they typically invited the active participation of audience members, and they were characterized by their strong visual dimension. Indeed, the frequent presentation of Happenings in art galleries underscored their emergence from the tradition of modern painting and sculpture — specif-

Allan Kaprow, *Self-Portrait*, from *18 Happenings in 6 Parts*, 1959
Collection of the artist

Allan Kaprow, *18 Happenings in 6 Parts*, 1959
Collection of the artist

ically, from action painting and assemblage. These traditions, however, were filtered through the precedent of Cage, who exerted a tremendous influence on many of the artists who became associated with the movement through his teaching. (Cage taught his class in experimental composition at the New School for Social Research in New York from fall 1956 through summer 1960; his students included George Brecht, Al Hansen, Dick Higgins, Kaprow, Jackson Mac Low, and La Monte Young).

Kaprow's openness to other artists, his ability to articulate his philosophy verbally, and his missionary zeal for Happenings put him in the spotlight as an unprecedented advocate for the new art. Specifically, he played a pivotal role in positioning himself and his colleagues in the lineage of Pollock, Gutai, and the assemblagists. Emerging as a painter at the same time as the second-generation Abstract Expressionists, Kaprow rigorously thought his way through the medium of painting, taking it in a new direction that assumed installational, environmental, and performative qualities. After studying painting and theories of *push-pull* with Hans Hoffman and

musical composition with Cage, Kaprow moved from action painting into the collage-assemblage works that led directly to his first Happenings. This transition took place between 1957 and 1959. Regarding this period, Kaprow has recalled:

I developed a kind of action-collage technique, following my interest in Pollock. These actions-collages, unlike my constructions, were done as rapidly as possible by grasping up great hunks of varied matter: tinfoil, straw, canvas, photos, newspaper, etc. . . . Their placement in the ritual of my own rapid action was an acting-out of the drama of tin soldiers, stories and musical structures, that I once had tried to embody in paint alone. The action-collage then became bigger, and I introduced flashing lights and thicker hunks of matter. These parts projected further and further from the walls and into the room, and included more and more audible elements: sounds of ringing buzzers, bells, toys, etc., until I had accumulated nearly all the sensory elements I was to work for during the following years. . . . Now I just simply filled the whole gallery up, starting

**59**

Allan Kaprow, *Yard*, 1961. Collection Feelisch, Remscheid

from one wall and ending with the other. When you opened the door, you found yourself in the midst of an entire Environment . . . . I immediately saw that every visitor to the Environment was part of it. I had not really thought of it before. And so I gave him opportunities like moving something, turning switches on — just a few things. Increasingly during 1957 and 1958, this suggested a more "scored" responsibility for the visitor. I offered him more and more to do until there developed the Happening.[45]

In his groundbreaking *18 Happenings in 6 Parts*, presented at the Reuben Gallery in New York in the fall of 1959, Kaprow synthesized his training in action painting with his study of Cage's scored and performed events. Working from a carefully conceived and tightly scripted score, he created an interactive environment that manipulated the audience to a degree virtually unprecedented in twentieth-century art. Audience members were sent

information about the Happening in advance in invitations that consisted of "plastic envelopes containing bits of paper, photographs, wood, painted fragments, and cut-out figures," as RoseLee Goldberg has written.[46] On the evening of the Happening, they were given programs and three stapled cards, which provided instructions for their participation: "The performance is divided into six parts. . . . Each part contains three happenings which occur at once. The beginning and end of each will be signaled by a bell. At the end of the performance two strokes of the bell will be heard. . . . There will be no applause after each set, but you may applaud after the sixth set if you wish."[47] These instructions also stipulated when audience members were required to change seats and move to the next of the three rooms into which the gallery was divided.

These rooms were formed by semitransparent plastic sheets painted and collaged with references to Kaprow's earlier work; by panels on which words

45. *Allan Kaprow, cited in Adrian Henri, "Allan Kaprow," in* Total Art: Environments, Happenings,

and Performance *(New York: Oxford University Press, 1974), 90-91.*

46. *RoseLee Goldberg,* Performance Art:

From Futurism to the Present *(New York: Harry N. Abrams, 1988), 128.*

47. *Allan Kaprow, cited in ibid., 129.*

**Red Grooms**, advertisement for *A Play Called Fire*, August 1958

**Red Grooms**, painting from *A Play Called Fire*, 1958. Greenville County Museum of Art
Museum purchase with funds from the Arthur and Holly Magill Purchase Fund

were roughly painted, in anticipation of his *Words* (1962); and by rows of plastic fruit. Aspects of previous works by Kaprow, such as the collage *Hysteria* (c. 1956), were also incorporated into the environment. *Rearrangeable Panels* (1957–59), a wall panel unfolded, was another element of this Happening. An important remnant that indicated that, at least at the time, Kaprow had not yet abandoned objecthood in favor of pure event, this work was later altered with the addition of carnival-like lights along the upper edge. In addition to such objects, slides and films were projected on the walls, and various musical and nonmusical sounds were incorporated into the action, which included a girl squeezing oranges and an orchestra for toy instruments. No artist in New York or elsewhere had defined the performative environment of his or her work to such an extreme degree.

Although Kaprow took from Pollock whatever served his evolving conception of the boundaries of art, it was Cage who provided him with the means to expand beyond the medium of painting. For example, in its cacophonous layering of various aural and visual effects and its nonlinearity, *18 Happenings in 6 Parts* remained close to Cage's 1952 experiments at Black Mountain College and *Water Music*. Like Cage, Kaprow had developed a series of simultaneous actions, activities, and tasks, none of which seemed to be related to one another, at least in the traditional narrative sense. In addition, Kaprow attempted to transform audience members into active participants in the realization of the work. However, in contrast to Cage, whose encouragement of the participation of audience members was motivated by his desire to relinquish authorial control, audience members in many of Kaprow's Happenings became props through which the artist's vision was executed. For example, in *Yard*, first presented at the Martha Jackson Gallery in New York as part of the groundbreaking group exhibition "Environments, Situations, Spaces," Kaprow created an allover field of used tires in the tight confines of the backyard of a Manhattan townhouse; the work existed as an entity only when audience members activated it by walking through the piece. Although these audience members were encouraged

to believe that they were playing, Kaprow had in fact established very controlled parameters within which they had to act. As his work continued to evolve away from Cage in the early 1960s, it drew closer to the broad, gestural, physical quality of the action painters. This tendency is evident in pre-Happening works such as *Hysteria,* in *Rearrangeable Panels*, and eventually in the allover environment of Happenings such as *The Apple Shrine* (1961) and *Words*.

Kaprow's large-scale and richly textured Happenings quickly opened up the space between installation and performance that one might term the *performative environment*. Independent of his initial contact with Kaprow in 1959, Grooms had created such an environment by creating a painting before an audience in a twenty-five-minute performance entitled *A Play Called Fire*, presented at the Sun Gallery in Provincetown, Massachusetts, in August 1958. Mathieu's highly theatrical executions of paintings before live audiences, with which Grooms had become familiar through television broadcasts and photographs published in *Life*, were clear precedents for this play. Working in a palette of red and black, like the Gutai, Grooms created before his audience a childlike and raucously jubilant painting featuring the images of a burning man and several firefighters. His childlike theatrics and improvisations were a cross between graffiti and second-generation Abstract Expressionist figurative painting, and his audience included individuals well-schooled in the latter. Subsequent performances thematically related to *A Play Called Fire* include a play entitled *The Burning Building*, performed nine times from 4 to 11 December 1959 at a studio he called the Delancey Street Museum, and *The Magic Train Ride* (originally entitled *Fireman's Dream*), presented at the Reuben Gallery in 1960. In contrast to Kaprow, Grooms did not encourage audience participation in such works. Instead, he called his performances plays, reflecting his desire to create a more literary type of theater than that of his colleagues.[48]

Jim Dine first ventured into Happenings with such performative environments as *The House*, presented in conjunction with an environment by

48. For more information on these works, see Judith E. Stein, "Red Grooms: The Early Years (1937-1960)", in Red Grooms: A Retrospective, exh. cat. (Philadelphia: Pennsylvania Academy of the Fine Arts, 1985), 29-38.

**63**

**Jim Dine**, *Crash Drawing with White Cross #2*, 1959
Collection of the artist

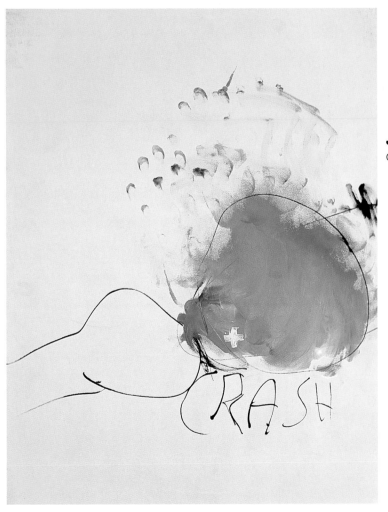

**Jim Dine**, *Crash Drawing with White Cross #1*, 1959
Collection of the artist

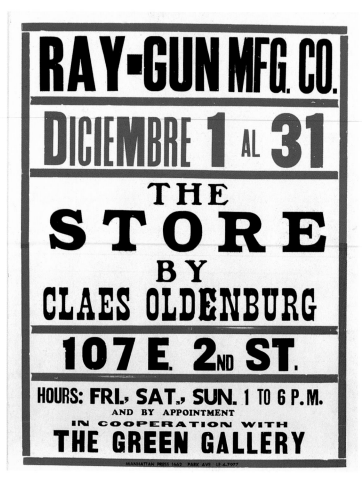

surrounding the automobile was a common theme in American popular culture in the late 1950s and early 1960s. Wearing a silver jumpsuit, his face whitened and his head bandaged, Dine began a drawing demonstration in which he described the crash repetitively in an agitated manner while continuously pleading for help. The related paintings, drawings, and lithographs were displayed in an area that led into the main room of the Reuben Gallery, where the performance took place. Throughout the early 1960s, Dine's work in performance informed, inspired, and coexisted with his work in the traditional mediums of painting and sculpture, and vice versa.

Dine moved quickly from the alternative scene downtown, including exhibitions at the Reuben Gallery and Martha Jackson Gallery, to the very bastion of the New York School, the Sidney Janis Gallery, following a trajectory similar to that of his friend Claes Oldenburg. For their joint "Ray Gun Show," Oldenburg created *The Street*, a ragged tableau of cardboard figures and an automobile — a fragmented, Dubuffet-inspired reportage of life in the Lower East Side slums, about which he wrote: "The show will consist of 1) an epic construction in the form of a Street, 2) & 3) drawings and small sculptures and constructions also having to do with The Street. The material will be mostly paper and wood, glued paper, torn paper, paper over wire, on wooden frames, paper hanging down, paper jumping up, paper lying etc. etc. The scale will vary from heroic to very very small. . . . (all components of the Street can be purchased separately)."[49] Having illustrated scenes of daily life for the popular press in Chicago, Oldenburg was sensitive to the dark, rich detritus of living, and in a Kaprow-like move, he encouraged the public to contribute to the scene.

In conjunction with the "Ray Gun Show," Oldenburg also organized a series of performances entitled *Ray Gun Spex* (as in spectaculars), which included himself, Dine, Higgins, Kaprow, and Whitman. In a manner that anticipated his *Store* of a year later, he created a currency that allowed ticket buyers to purchase the junk objects and debris on display in the lobby of the Judson Gallery. The per-

Oldenburg at Judson Gallery in New York in February–March 1960 as the "Ray Gun Show." For this exhibition, the gallery was transformed into a three-dimensional environment completely encrusted with accumulations of objects, furnishings, painted scraps, rags, and paper. *Bedspring*, originally made for *The House*, is one of several junk sculptures that has survived.

In his thirty-second performance, *The Smiling Workman*, presented at Judson Memorial Church in 1960, Dine, his face painted red, wore a floor-length smock and stood behind a table that supported buckets of paint. Behind him was a large sheet of paper stretched Murakami-style to look like a canvas. On this surface he very rapidly scrawled in orange and blue paint, "I love what I'm doing." As he finished, he drank a bucket of red paint (actually tomato juice), poured two other buckets of paint over his head, and then jumped through the painting (no doubt in homage to Murakami). With this brief performance, Dine simultaneously parodied the angst-driven actions of the New York School, by literally jumping into the "painting," and anticipated the liberal and dramatic use and consumption of paint by the Viennese Actionists and such artists as Paul McCarthy and Christian Boltanski.

In another performance of 1960, Dine staged a car crash in which he reenacted the personal experience of a real accident. The danger and excitement

49. Claes Oldenburg, "Brief Description of the Show" (1960), in Claes Oldenburg: An Anthology, exh. cat. (New York: Solomon R. Guggenheim Museum, 1995), 50.

**Claes Oldenburg**, Interior view of *The Store*, 107 East Second Street, New York, December 1961

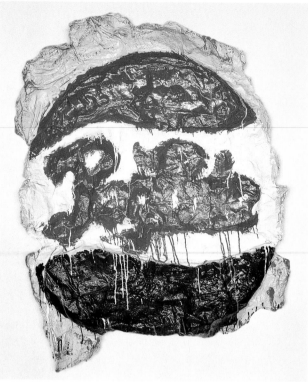

**Claes Oldenburg**, *Blue and Pink Panties*, 1961
The Museum of Contemporary Art, Los Angeles. The Panza Collection

formances presented as *Ray Gun Spex* were, as the gallery's press release stated "paintings in the shape of theater." But the connection to theater, with its narrative implications, was a bit too tradition-bound for Oldenburg, who made a naively cynical breakthrough by turning his studio into a store.

From 1 December 1961 to 31 January 1962, Oldenburg operated a gallery-studio-performance-environment in a storefront at 107 East Second Street. The store was operated under the auspices of Oldenburg's Ray Gun Manufacturing Co., which had its own stationery, a ledger, business cards, and a modest, primarily word-of-mouth, advertising strategy. In a brief text entitled "The Store Described & Budget for the Store" (1960), Oldenburg states: "In the front half [of the store], it is my intention to create the environment of a store, by painting and placing (hanging, projecting, lying) objects after the spirit and in the form of popular objects of merchandise, such as may be seen in stores and store windows of the city, especially in the area where the store is."[50] An inventory dated December 1961 lists well over a hundred items, including paintings and objects in the form of consumer products, such as foodstuffs, clothing, jewelry, and printed matter; the most expensive item, at $899.95, was *Bride Mannikin*, while the least expensive, at $24.98, was *Cube Pastries*. Keeping tight controls on supply and demand, Oldenburg replenished items (which he would make in a studio in the back room) only after sales were made, and he negotiated a special arrangement with the Green Gallery to handle public relations. In his conflations of studio-gallery and artist-dealer, Oldenburg undermined the processes of "museumification" and "collectionization" that threatened the creative purity of his work. *The Store* was a shrewd conceptual project that demonstrated the extent to which the art object functioned as a commodity in consumer capitalist society. Although some of the objects for sale, such as the plaster hamburgers and pies, were humorous, other objects — such as the howling *Bride Mannikin*, as well as other figures with fetishistic emphases on body parts — expressed a darker vision reminiscent of *The Street*.

50. Claes Oldenburg, "The Store Described & Budget for the Store" (1960), in ibid., 104.

**Claes Oldenburg**, *Store Cross*, 1961
The Museum of Contemporary Art, Los Angeles. The Panza Collection

**Claes Oldenburg**, *Bride Mannikin*, 1961
The Museum of Contemporary Art, Los Angeles. The Panza Collection

Not surprisingly, *The Store*'s success was limited to the art world. In spite of its strategic positioning as a direct conduit between the artist and the general public, most vistors were artists, critics, curators, and collectors. In a preliminary report presented to Dick Bellamy, the Green Gallery's director, Oldenburg reported that,

> the store was open to the public from December 1 through January 31, two months rather than one month which was planned. Sales in the period totaled to $1,655 as itemized. Of this amount, $300 is still owed. I will bill for this. No sales tax was computed in the sales. The expense for the store, excluding electric bills, not yet received, a total of $368. This as itemized includes construction, telephone, photos, utilities, publicity and printing but not the cost of addressing and mailing, additions of which ought to bring the amount near to the anticipated $400. The gallery agreed to pay half the expenses and take a commission of 1/3 of all sales above $200 or my share of expenses. Thus, sales of $1,655 minus $200 equals $1,455. One third of $1,455 is $485 minus the $200 leaves $285. I owe the gallery $285. The tax on the sales above to be paid $49.65.

After *The Store* closed, Oldenburg organized a series of ten Happenings, entitled *Ray Gun Theater*, presented in the same storefront. These Happenings included *Store Days I* and *II* (23–24 February; 2–3 March), *Nekropolis I* and *II* (9–10 March; 16–17 March), *Injun (N.Y.C.) I* and *II* (20–21 April; 27–28 April), *Voyages I* and *II* (4–5 May; 11–12 May) and *World's Fair I* and *II* (18–19 May; 25–26 May). In a brief text he wrote that year, entitled "Residual Objects," Oldenburg poses questions and suggests answers to the vexing question of the relationship between the residual object and the situation in which it was created. As he writes,

> Love objects. Respect objects. Objectivity high state of feeling.
>
> Residual objects are created in the course of making the performance and during the repeated performances. The performance is the main thing but when it's over there are a number of subordinate pieces which may be isolated, souvenirs, or residual objects.
>
> To pick up after a performance, to be very careful about what is to be discarded and what still survives by itself. Slow study & respect for small things. Ones own created "found objects." The floor of the stage like the street. Picking up after is creative. Also their particular life must be respected. Where they had their place, each area of activity combed separately and with respect for where it begins & ends.[51]

To this declaration was attached a list of residual objects from *Store Days*, including chairs, beds, tables, wall pieces, wood, magazines, costumes, and

51. Claes Oldenburg, "Residual Objects" (1962), in ibid., 143.

**George Brecht**, *Coat Rack (Clothes Tree)*, 1962-63. Collection Onnasch

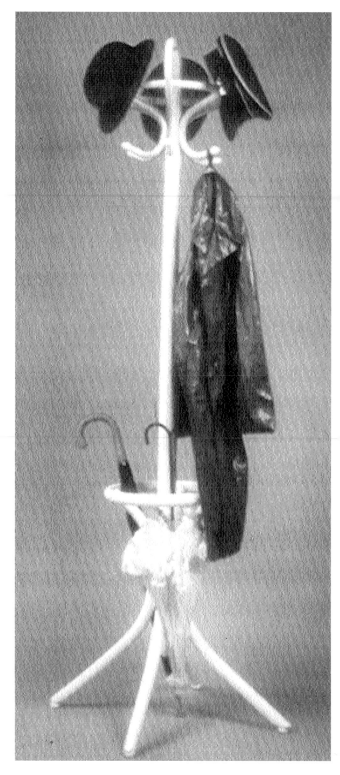

**George Brecht**, *Table with Rainbowleg*, 1962-63. Collection Onnasch

**70**

**Ben Vautier**, *Le magasin de Ben*, 1962. Collection of the artist

boxes of leftover supplies and materials. What had started as a lark with the printing of money at Judson Memorial Church had become a living tableau that inspired a moving meditation on the changing status of the object.

**Fluxus** Whereas Happenings developed primarily in response to second-generation action painting and only secondarily in response to Cage, Fluxus was much more closely identified with the avant-garde composer and with new music in general. International in scope, it encompassed a diverse range of artists and composers who began to emerge in the early 1960s. The term itself was coined in 1961 by George Maciunas, the most influential promoter of the tendency. As Owen F. Smith states in his 1993 essay "Fluxus: A Brief History," "Maciunas used the actual dictionary definition of *flux* as part of the definition of Fluxus: 'Act of flowing: a continuous moving on or passing by, as of a flowing stream; a continuous succession of changes.' Defined in this way, as a continually shifting process, contradictions that were inherent to all Fluxus activities and ideology became a natural part of its impulse."[52]

George Brecht, one of the most important artists associated with Fluxus, attended Cage's class

in experimental composition at the New School for Social Research. Brecht became well-known for his events, which consisted of instructions written as musical scores that could be performed by anyone. One of his most well-known events, *Three Aqueous Events* (1961), is also one of his most evocative. The score is simply a column consisting of the words *ice*, *water*, and *steam*. Yet, many of Brecht's events involved the manipulation of objects. For example, the score of *Ladder*, included in a boxed collection of scores entitled *Water Yam* (1963), reads: "Paint a single straight ladder white. Paint the bottom rung black. Distribute spectral colors on the rungs between." Advertisements for specially painted ladders, available for $150, were published in the third issue of Fluxus's newspaper in March 1964, but it is not known whether they were ever produced as one of Maciunas's Fluxus Editions.[53] Brecht also produced objects expressly in conjunction with his events; his games and puzzles, for example, were available through Fluxus. In many respects, such objects were the most archetypal Fluxus performance sculptures of the period.

Another Fluxus artist who made works that could be termed performance sculptures was Ben Vautier. Prior to Oldenburg's *The Store*, Vautier, commonly known as Ben, who was a close friend of Klein's, created *Le magasin* (The Shop, begun 1960), directly out of his activities as a purveyor of records and other youth-oriented materials. In a desperate move to draw attention to his shop, which he misguidedly believed offered the opportunity to support his other art activities, Vautier began a series of events and Happenings intended at the very least to draw attention to his commercial business. This venture would subsequently inform the artist's future activities in a blur of creative art and entrepreneurial activities.

Vautier's work had very strong conceptual underpinnings from the beginning. In a manner with obvious parallels to both Klein and Manzoni, he used the process of certification to proclaim himself as an anointer of actions of daily life as works of art, as in

52. Owen F. Smith, "Fluxus: A Brief History" in In the Spirit of Fluxus, *exh. cat. (Minneapolis: Walker Art Center, 1993), 24.*

53. See Jon Hendricks, Fluxus Codex *(New York: Gilbert and Lila Silverman Fluxus Collection in association with Harry N. Abrams, Inc., 1995), 202-203.*

**Ben Vautier**, *Le magasin de Ben*, Nice, n. d.

*Everything Is Art* (1960–61). This process extended to Vautier's audience: in a Faustian move, he created certificates with which he purchased the soul of willing participants; in *Announcement of My Funeral* he created certificates in which he signed off on his own and Klein's deaths; and in 1961 he created a sculpture mobile in Vivon, France, that required the body of a willing participant. Like Oldenburg, Vautier thus placed himself at the center of his living tableaux, offering his body as the intermediary between the environment and the viewer. As Kristine Stiles observes in her 1993 essay "Between Water and Stone: Fluxus Performance: A Metaphysics of Acts," "By situating himself physically at the signifying center of verbal and visual communication, Vautier commented on how artists function as intermediaries between viewer and viewed as they point to things in the world and negotiate their meanings through symbolic productions. But in calling attention to himself, Vautier also isolated the problem of ego with respect to the social reception of art. His actual presence illustrated the interconnection between careerism, artistic signature, the economies of art, and the art historical market for personalities — all written in corporeal textuality."[54] At the same time, it is important to acknowledge that a certain attitude of frivolity and humor accompanied Vautier's activities, especially his role as the artist-shopkeeper.

Unlike the projects of the more orthodox Fluxus artists, Vautier's *Le magasin* took on the characteristics of the total environment that were hallmarks of Kaprow, Oldenburg, and the *Nouveaux Réalistes*, as well as certain Pop artists. Much like Spoerri, Vautier developed a richly textured environment that became a lifestyle: if for Oldenburg *The Store* was conceived with a beginning and an end, for Vautier *Le magasin* was simply how he lived and what he did. Vautier first photographed the shop in 1958, nominated it as a work of art in 1960, and by 1972 had transformed it into a large-scale, three-dimensional tableau that incorporated much of the original material accumulated over a decade of transactions. It was not until almost a decade after its initial creation that the curator and museum director Pontus Hulten encouraged the artist to freeze *Le magasin*

and allow it to be acquired by an institution.

When asked to participate in the Festival of Misfits, presented at Gallery One in London from 23 October to 8 November 1962, Vautier installed himself as a fixture in the window. This wry conceptual strategy was more than an opportunity to get publicity. In fact, for Vautier, as for Oldenburg, Spoerri, and Wolf Vostell, such actions were serious efforts to support their art-making activities through commercial businesses — to make financially viable work while retaining control over its representation and integrity. For these artists, this objective could best be accomplished metaphorically, through performative actions that eliminated the distinction between action and object. If Oldenburg had sold his objects through his presence, Ben sold his presence through his objects. For the viewing public, the macabre gallows humor of this situation was mediated by the comfort of seeing a person living in a shop window as an extension of his home, with bed, tables, chairs, modest cooking facilities, and even a television set for entertainment.

The Korean-born Nam June Paik's work emerged from the cross-pollination of a variety of sources, including classical and avant-garde music, Dada and Neo-Dada manifestations such as Fluxus, radical politics, and electronic technology. Paik studied music and art history at the University of Tokyo, where he graduated in 1956 with a degree in aesthetics after completing his thesis on the composer Arnold Schoenberg. That year he traveled to West Germany to study modern music. He matriculated at the Universität München and became thoroughly conversant with serialism, then the dominant tendency in experimental music in Europe. In 1958 Paik moved to Cologne to work at the *Studio für elektronische Musik des Westdeutsches Rundfunk* (Studio for Electronic Music of West German Radio), with which the serialist composer Karlheinz Stockhausen was affiliated. That summer he met Cage, who was in residence at the prestigious *Internationale Ferienkurse für neue Musik* (International Vacation Course for New Music) in Darmstadt. His meeting with the elder composer revolutionalized his artistic development.

Paik subsequently began to compose and per-

54. Kristine Stiles, "Between Water and Stone: Fluxus Performance: A

Metaphysics of Acts," in In the Spirit of Fluxus, 67.

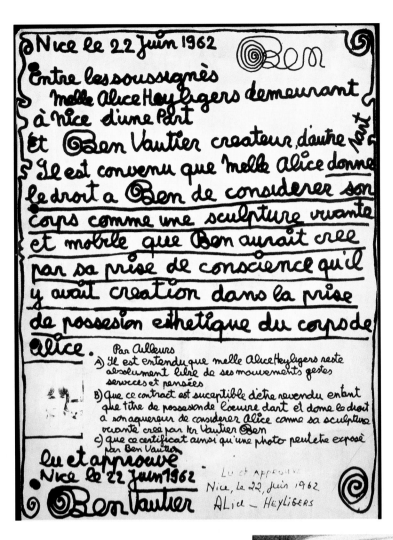

**Ben Vautier**, *Human Sculpture Certificate*, 1962

**Ben Vautier**, *Living Sculpture*
at the Festival of Misfits, London, 1962

**Nam June Paik**, *Zen for Head (I)*, 1962. Museum Wiesbaden

**Nam June Paik**, *Klavier K* (Piano K), 1962-63. Block Collection

**Nam June Paik**, *Zen for Head (II)*, 1962. Museum Wiesbaden

form action music — antimusic in the Dada tradition designed to draw audience members out of the state of passive distraction. For example, in his *Hommage à John Cage: Musik für Tonbänder und Klavier* (Homage to John Cage: Music for Tape Player and Piano), first presented at Galerie 22 in Dusseldorf on 13 November 1959, Paik played a tape collage while he performed a series of violent actions, which involved "screaming, toys, tin boxes full of stones, eggs, smashed glass, a live hen and a motorcycle."[55] On 6 October he performed *Étude für Piano* (Study for Piano) in the studio of the artist Mary Bauermeister in Cologne. Paik concluded this performance by exiting the stage, approaching Cage, who was sitting in the audience, cutting off his tie, pouring shampoo on him and pianist David Tudor, and then leaving the building. And at the *Fluxus Internationale Festspiele Neuester Musik* (Fluxus International Festival of Very New Music), the first official Fluxus festival, presented at the Städtisches Museum in Wiesbaden in September 1962, Paik performed *Zen for Head*, a 1960 composition by La Monte Young that consisted of the score "Draw a straight line and follow it." Paik interpreted this composition by inking the top of his head and using it to brush a line onto a piece of scroll-like paper laid on the floor.

A year later Paik presented his most ambitious project in West Germany — the "Exposition of Music Electronic Television," which opened at Rolf Jährling's Galerie Parnass in Wuppertal on 10 March 1963.[56] For this exhibition, his first, Paik took Cage's invention of the prepared piano to a new level of complexity by presenting three prepared pianos and thirteen prepared television sets. In these works, he subjected the piano and the television set, two of the most culturally revered objects in the middle-class home, to a series of destructive acts so that they no longer functioned as intended. In a massive assault on bourgeois sensibilities, the one piano that has survived, *Klavier Intégral* (Integral Piano, 1958–63) was covered with a brassiere, a feather duster, a padlock, coins, barbed wire, and other objects. During the opening of the exhibition, one of the guests, Joseph Beuys, hacked apart one of the pianos with an ax.

In 1964 Paik moved to New York, reuniting with the Fluxus artists he had associated with in Europe, including his longtime collaborator, the cellist Charlotte Moorman. That year he performed at Judson Hall in Stockhausen's *Originale*, presented as part of the Second Annual Avant-Garde Festival, which Moorman organized. In 1965 he presented his first one-person exhibition in the United States at Galeria Bonino. Entitled "Electronic Art," this exhibition featured his prepared television sets;

55. Michael Nyman, "Nam June Paik, Composer," in John G. Hanhardt, Nam June Paik, exh. cat. (New York: Whitney Museum of American Art in association with W .W .Norton and Co., 1982), 82.

56. For a detailed description and interpretation of this exhibition, see John Alan Farmer, "Circuits/Nam June Paik," in "Art into Television, 1960-65" (Ph.D. diss., Columbia University, 1998), chap. 4.

**Yoko Ono**, *Painting for the Wind*, 1961/1993. Collection of the artist

**Yoko Ono**, *Painting to be Stepped On*, 1960/1997. Collection of the artist

**Yoko Ono**, *Painting to Hammer a Nail*, 1961/1998. Collection of the artist

demonstrating his continuing respect for Paik's work, Cage wrote an essay for the catalogue. This exhibition was to have a profound effect on the generation of video artists that emerged in the late 1960s and early 1970s.

Yoko Ono, like Paik, made the transition from music to the visual arts through her study of the work of Cage. Born in Japan, Ono moved to the United States in the 1950s. She studied poetry and music at Sarah Lawrence College in New York and lived in San Francisco during the latter half of the decade, when the Gutai group was in its ascendancy; however, she has stated that she was not aware of its performance activities at this point. In 1960 Ono began a series of instructional works similar to Brecht's that were remarkable for their simplicity, generosity, and participatory nature. By focusing on the single gesture, rather than combining many, as in Cage's complex, multifaceted events, Ono unknowingly returned to the simplicity of such works by Murakami as *Work: Box*. Ono exhibited these works at Maciunas's AG Gallery in New York with accompanying objects in July 1961. As the art historian Alexandra Munroe has noted, "When visitors entered the gallery, Ono led them one by one to each piece and recited the action or participation that was to take place. For *Smoke Painting*, the viewer was asked to burn the canvas with a cigarette and watch the smoke; the piece was completed when the canvas turned to ashes. *Time Painting* and *Painting to See in the Dark* required the viewer's imagination to complete, and *Painting in Three Stanzas*, which presented a vine growing out of a burned hole in the canvas, suggested concepts of organic growth, death, and eternity."[57] For the exhibition "Instructions for Painting" at the Sōgetsu Art Center in Japan in 1962, the works were presented as written texts alone. The instructions, which the artist Toshi Ishiyangai transcribed in Japanese characters, consisted of a title heading followed by Haiku-like commands; examples include "*Painting for the Wind*. Make a hole, leave it in the wind" and "*Painting to Be Stepped On*. Leave a piece of canvas or a finished painting on the floor or in the street."

In 1964 Ono premiered *Cut Piece*, one of her most important works, at Yamaichi Concert Hall in

Kyoto. This performance was so psychologically and sexually charged that Gustav Metzger, via Al Hansen, requested her to present it in the Destruction in Arts Symposium held in London in September 1966. For this performance, Ono dressed in an elegant cocktail suit and invited the audience to cut away her clothing while she sat calmly in a state of contemplation on the stage. *Cut Piece* had lasting implications for a subsequent generation of performance artists, including Marina Abramovic, Ana Mendieta, Gina Pane, and Barbara Smith. It also anticipated the body-works of Vito Acconci and Chris Burden. Later in the 1960s, Ono created works such as *War Is Over* (1969), performed in collaboration with her husband John Lennon, that were stunning examples of an artist's ability to manipulate the press and to create a mass-media persona. What had begun with Pollock in *Life* in the 1950s was now becoming a strategy of worldwide significance.

Hi Red Center was a group of three Japanese artists associated with Fluxus — Genpei Akasegawa, Natsuyuki Nakanishi, and Jirō Takamatsu — formed in May 1963. The English name was derived from the first character of each artist's surname (Takamatsu: *high* pine; Akasegawa: *red* rapids; Nakanishi: *center* west). As Munroe has observed, "What connected these artists (who had been collaborating together for several months) was their conception of *objet* [a term that referred to assemblage-like objects] as the

57. Munroe, 218.

focus of 'events' that would go beyond the walls of the museum or gallery, as well as their informed leftist concern for the social inequities of modern Japan."[58] For an exhibition organized by the Tokyo Metropolitan Art Museum (the precursor of the Museum of Contemporary Art, Tokyo), Nakanishi covered his body with hundreds of metal clothespins, an act of self-mutilation that anticipated Acconci's, Burden's, Weibel's, and other 1970s performance artists' actions. This event also informed his own concurrent series of paintings in which he clipped clothespins to canvases attached to stretchers, about which Akasegawa remarked: "In the knowledge that this was not paint but simple, everyday objects, had we not discovered the minimum separation between painting and real life?"[59] For the same exhibition, Takamatsu contributed a string that originated in the busy Ueno train station, traveled through a vast park in the tradition of Gutai, and ended up in the museum. This seemingly low-keyed action became a subject of attention when an older woman stumbled on the string, fell down in the park, and reported the incident to the police, who found that the cause of the infraction was an event sponsored by a public institution, the museum.

However, the controversy inspired by this event paled in comparison to the scandal surrounding Akasegawa's November 1965 indictment for counterfeiting currency he had used in his work. In 1963 Akasegawa made copies of counterfeit 1000-yen notes, printed on only one side, that were being passed by a forger sought by the police. He used the counterfeit bills as wallpaper, as paper in which to wrap works of art, and as invitations to his one-person exhibition at Shinjuku Dai-Ichi Gallery. Akasegawa took the humor and irreverence of the commercial aspect of art distribution, which Oldenburg, Manzoni, and others had investigated, and used it as a rapier to taunt the municipal police, who appeared inept for their inability to capture the original forger. He was arrested as a counterfeiter when someone tried to pass one of his one-sided bills as legal tender. The trial, which was held in August 1966, became a highly publicized examination of per-

formance art. Defended by respected art critics and art historians on the grounds that his works were art, Akasegawa and his colleagues presented their controversial works to force the court to define what art was. These works included a Takamatsu string and a Hi Red Center *Shelter Plan* event in which reams of blueprints showing the artists naked were unfolded on the prosecutor's stand. This mockery of justice, occurring in a country whose judicial system had been remade by the United States, demonstrated the power of free speech and also gave performance art a political platform. It is difficult to imagine such an event occurring in the United States at that time; indeed, when the Chicago 7, who were aware of Happenings, used similar tactics in their trial, they were substantially restrained. And although Akasegawa ultimately lost, as Paik recounts in his 1994 essay "To Catch Up or Not to Catch Up with the West: Hijikata and Hi Red Center," the event "became a *cause célèbre*. People had used Grand Central Station, the armory, and airports for their Happening scenes and backdrops. But in the entire history of Happenings, I have never heard of any better scenery than this one — a real courtroom. I bet Ionesco would have been jealous of them."[60]

Through an interlocking network of friendships that included artists affiliated with *Nouveau Réalisme*, Happenings, Fluxus, and Destruction art, Wolf Vostell had the ability to influence a significant segment of the action community in the 1960s. He played an especially important role in forging connections among these tendencies through his journal *Dé-coll/age: Bulletin aktueller Ideen* (Dé-coll/age: Bulletin of Current Ideas), which he published from 1962 to 1967. In addition to publicizing the works and writings of artists with whom he felt an affinity, Vostell used the journal to promote his own work. The objects, installations, and Happenings that he had begun to produce in the late 1950s were all manifestations of a philosophy that he termed *dé-coll/age*. Derived from the French word *décollage*, which in the realm of art signifies the tearing of layers of glued papers from their support, Vostell became intrigued by the term after seeing it used in an article published

58. Ibid., 159.

59. Genpei Akasegawa, cited in ibid., 156.

60. Nam June Paik, "To Catch Up or Not to Catch Up with the West: Hijikata and Hi Red Center," in ibid., 81.

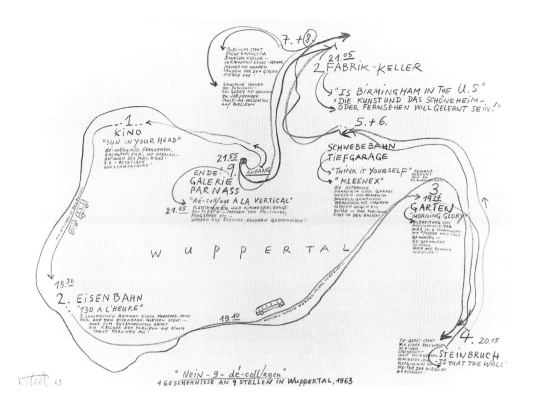

**Wolf Vostell**, *130 à l'heure*, *No. 3*, 1963. From the Happening, *Nein-9-dé-coll/agen*

in the 6 September 1954 issue of *Le Figaro* to describe the crash of an airplane. As Kristine Stiles has observed, "He appropriated the term to signify an aesthetic philosophy, applied also to the creation of live performances, by which the destructive, violent and erotic events of contemporary life were assembled and juxtaposed. Emphasizing the syllabic division, *dé-coll/age*, he underscored the dialectical meaning of the term applied to both the creative and destructive processes in natural and biological systems and in cultural and social structures."[61]

Vostell's ambitions were far more operatic than the more conceptually driven Fluxus artists. In fact, his romantic fascination with the power of technology and his conception of the modern city as a stage for performance forged an artistic vision that even exceeded Kaprow's during the same period. Yet, the experience of being a Jew who survived World War II endowed his work a sense of darkness that mediated his perception of machines such as weapons, automobiles, and television sets.

In 1958 Vostell conceived of a performance sculpture entitled *Das Theater ist auf der Strasse II* (The Theater Is in the Street II), which may be performed by anyone who follows the score. The sculpture is made by putting all the parts from an automobile accident onto the street or at a busy intersection and repeating this act "with accident after accident until traffic is impossible."[62] With this work, Vostell was attempting to create a sculpture based on the memory of tragedies that had occurred in a particular spot. Given the fact that he had witnessed the Holocaust, it could be interpreted as his monument to the lost souls of the war.

Vostell's actions became more complex with his presentation of *Nein-9-dé-coll/agen* at the Galerie Parnass in Wuppertal on 14 September 1963. Each of the nine parts of this Happening was, as with the German word *nein*, a negative provocation; participants were witnesses held captive in a bus transporting them to nine appointed places in the city. Between 6:00 p.m. and 10:00 p.m. they saw a film, a car wash, the cellar of a factory, and a locomotive engine crush an automobile at 130 kilometers per hour.

Though associated with Fluxus, Joseph Beuys engaged in actions that were closer to the complex range of sequential movements associated with Kaprow's and Vostell's Happenings than with the more modest actions of artists such as Brecht. While serving as a pilot for the Luftwaffe during World War II, Beuys was shot down over the Crimea in the winter of 1943 and rescued by native Tartar tribesmen. This experience provided him the elements of an artistic vocabulary that he would mine throughout his career. Although he spent the first twelve years of his career as an artist working making drawings, watercolors, oil paintings, and sculptures, he began to create performances in the early 1960s. Through the performances he was able to affect and influence a broad public to a degree that was never possible with his drawings. Beuys's hermetic artistic language, sophisticated manipulation of the media, and repositioning the figure of the artist from the aesthetic into the political arena profoundly altered the trajectory of art.

Beuys's first performance of *Eurasia: Siberische Symphonie* (Eurasia: Siberian Symphony) included many of the elements that he would use in subsequent actions, including the blackboard, the dead hare, and the piano.[63] The blackboard was a natural extension of the drawings he had made since the late 1940s; the hare had been a subject of these works since the 1950s; and the piano had been a staple of avant-garde performers from Cage, to Paik, Maciunas, and Ortiz. However, it was only with his first commercial exhibition, presented at Galerie Schmela in Dusseldorf in 1965, that Beuys began to develop a potent and manipulative relationship with the viewer — a dramatic change from most Fluxus stage performance. Beuys insisted that the gallery remain closed to the public, so that his performance was visible only through the doorway and street window. As Marcel Duchamp did with his last work, *Étant*

61. Kristine Stiles, "Décollage," in The Dictionary of Art, ed. Jane Turner, vol. 8 (New York: Grove, 1996), 608-609.

62. Wolf Vostell, "The Theater Is in the Street II" (1958), in dé-collage happenings, trans. Laura P. Williams (New York: Something Else Press, 1966), 11.

63. For complete documentation of Beuys's actions, see Uwe M. Schneede, Joseph Beuys: Die Aktionen: Kommentiertes Werkverzeichnis mit fotografischen Dokumentation (Ostfildern-Ruit bei Stuttgart: Verlag Gerd Hatje, 1994).

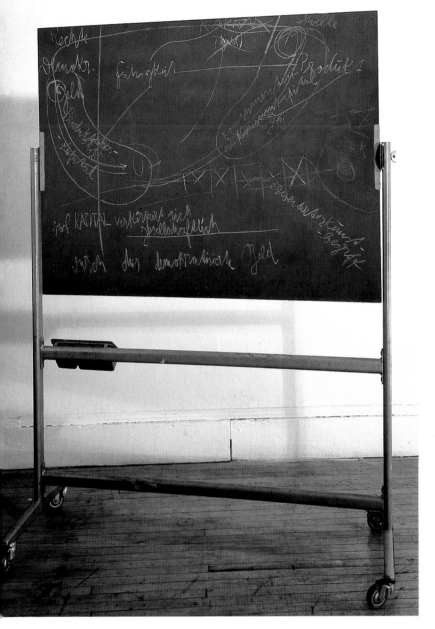

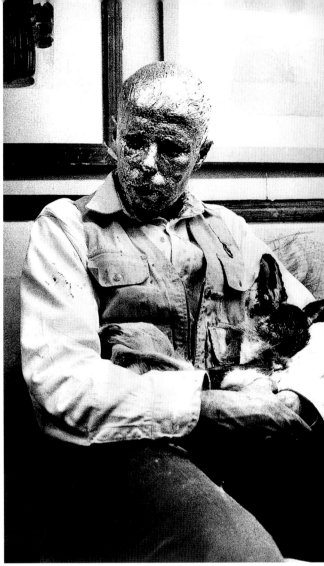

**Joseph Beuys**, *How to Explain Pictures to a Dead Hare*, 1965

**Joseph Beuys**, *Ausfegen*, 1972. Block Collection

**Joseph Beuys.** *Aus Berlin: Neues vom Kojoten.* 1979. Installation view at Ronald Feldman Fine Arts. Collection of Dia Center for the Arts, New York

Joseph Beuys, *I Like America and America Likes Me*, 1974. Block Collection

*donnés: 1. La chute d'eau, 2. Le gaz d'éclairage* (Given: 1. The Waterfall, 2. The Illuminating Gas, 1946–66), Beuys limited access to the work to ensure that it was a private experience. For disseminating his work to a larger public, Beuys relied on the mass media — particularly on the publication of photographs by Ute Klophaus, whose camera became the vehicle by which Beuys created and perpetuated the myths that enveloped his actions.

On 26 November 1965 Beuys performed *Wie man dem toten Hasen die Bilder erklärt* (How to Explain Pictures to a Dead Hare) at Galerie Schmela. For this important action, Beuys, his head covered with honey and gold leaf, mouthed silent words to a dead hare. Almost a year later, on 15 October 1966, he performed the thirty-fourth movement of *Eurasia: Siberian Symphony* at Galleri 101 in Copenhagen. For this ninety-minute action, Beuys got on his knees and pushed with his head two small crosses surmounted by stopwatches until he reached a blackboard on the other side of the room. On the blackboard he drew a cross, half of which he erased and then wrote the word *Eurasia* underneath it. As the Danish writer Troels Andersen remarked,

> The rest of the piece consisted of Beuys's slowly maneuvering, along a previously drawn line, a dead hare, whose legs and ears were extended by long, thin, black wooden sticks. When he held the hare on his shoulders, the sticks touched the ground. Beuys went from the wall to the board, where he laid the hare down. On the way back, three things happened: he scattered white powder between the legs of the hare, put a thermometer in its mouth, and blew through a tube. Then he turned to the blackboard with the half-cross on it and made the hare's ears quiver, while his own foot, to which an iron sole was tightly bound, hovered over another sole on the floor. From time to time he stamped on this sole.[64]

The relics that remained after the completion of the action have, over the ensuing decades, turned into a kind of shroud of Turin, in that they embody meanings that are functions of their mystical history. They include the blackboard, the hare, the sticks, and a felt-and-fat angle related to the degrees, as marked

on the blackboard, that lay between them. It was not until the end of the 1960s that Beuys began to remake objects associated with his performative activities into discrete sculptures that would stand on their own as representations of the actions for which they had been conceived. By this time, he had accumulated a large storehouse of objects, which he began to alter sculpturally by enclosing them in exhibit cases and introducing photographs, which allowed them to be displayed in museums and galleries and purchased by collectors. The transformation of the relic into sculpture was for Beuys a logical extension of the sculptural activities he had begun prior to his first performances. However, this decision ran counter to the anti-object mentality shared by many Fluxus artists. In fact, the generation of artists that emerged in the late 1960s and early 1970s was split between these two positions.

In 1974 René Block invited Beuys to present an action entitled *I Like America and America Likes Me* at his new gallery in New York. This action consisted of Beuys's quest to befriend a wild coyote named Little Joe that had been transported to the gallery. Upon his arrival at John F. Kennedy Airport on 21 May, Beuys was wrapped in felt and immediately driven by ambulance to the gallery, where the coyote was caged behind a wall made of wire mesh that divided the interior of the exhibition space. Beuys proceeded to enter this hay-strewn precinct. Dressed in his felt robe and holding a shepherd's staff, he arranged for fifty copies of the *Wall Street Journal*, a symbol of American capitalism, to be delivered to the gallery every day; he would arrange these newspapers in two columns of twenty-five. In addition, Beuys also made music with a triangle suspended from his neck. For the majority of the time, the coyote slept in the far corner, interacting only occasionally with Beuys and the newspapers, but eventually the two became accustomed to one another. The action ended on 25 May, when Beuys said farewell to the coyote and returned by ambulance to the airport. Although the action appeared to be about duration, at least in part, Beuys allowed himself the privilege of joining friends such as Paik and Block upstairs for din-

64. Troels Andersen, cited in Heiner Stachelhaus, Joseph Beuys, trans. David Britt (New York: Abbeville Press, 1991), 137.

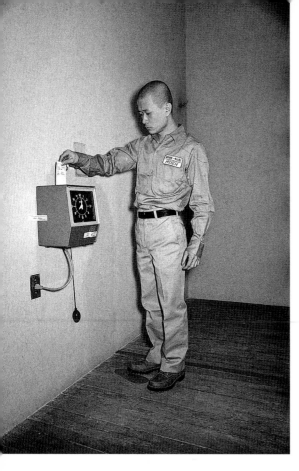

**Tehching Hsieh,** Punching the Time Clock on the Hour, One Year Performance, 11 April 1980 - 11 April 1981

ner when the gallery was closed. Yet, photographic documentation of the event reinforced the myth that the artist and coyote had interacted only with one other in the context of a caged performative environ-ment. Unlike artists such as Acconci, Burden, Tehching Hsieh, and others who emerged in the 1970s, Beuys thus embraced the symbolic traditions of his European heritage, instead of relying on the lit-eral, durational dimension of this performative work.

When Beuys remade the work five years later, he took elements he had saved, including copies of the *Wall Street Journal*, the shepherd's staff, and felt cloth, and made them into a new installation. Within this environment he created a pile of rubble that formed a substantial barrier between the viewer and the installation, which also contained a dusting of sul-fur on the floor and on all of the objects. The dramatic effect of this new installation relied on the complex symbolic meanings of the objects, rather than on the action in which they had originally been used.

In addition to his more dramatic actions, Beuys also presented an influential series of blackboard lec-tures in the 1960s and 1970s. These politically charged presentations were the antithesis of Mathieu's painting demonstrations with their dia-grammatic histories of battles, which evidenced his fascination with Europe's romantic age of chivalry. Although Beuys would diagrammatically draw, erase, and redraw throughout these presentations, their material supports were merely objects with no the-atrical connotations. Through these blackboard lectures Beuys transformed the role of the artist from that of entertainer to teacher, from clown to politician, from shaman to professor. As a result, artists of the next generation were accorded a new responsibility for defining the geopolitical culture in which they lived.

**Viennese Actionism** The *Wiener Aktionsgruppe* (Viennese Action Group), which included Günter Brus, Otto Muehl, Hermann Nitsch, and Rudolf Schwarzkogler, was officially formed in July 1965, although the participating artists had performed their works since 1962. The performances of the Viennese Actionists, which emerged from their work in the sta-tic mediums of painting, collage, assemblage, and installation, as well as from theater, were ritualistic actions accompanied by music in which the artists manipulated the carcasses of slaughtered animals. Christened *Abreaktionsspiele* (Abreaction Plays) by Nitsch, these performances manifested the Actionists' interest in a variety of cultural phenom-ena, including the cult of Dionysus; the rituals of the Catholic church; the psychoanalytic theories of Sigmund Freud, Karl Jung, and Wilhelm Reich; and the work of Austrian artists such as Egon Schiele and Oskar Kokoschka, as well as certain artists affiliated with Happenings and *Nouveau Réalisme*.

Although performance painting originated in the mid-1950s experiments of the Gutai group, it reached the provincial capital of Vienna in its most emphatically corporeal incarnation in Nitsch's work. By the early 1960s he had transformed what had begun as a third wave of abstraction from the New York School into one of the most gestural, body-ori-ented, sexually provocative, and psychologically inflammatory art forms ever developed. On the one hand, Nitsch's paintings, which manifested his con-tinuing adulation of Pollock and action painting, could be perceived as one of the last remnants of the New York School. However, as early as 1960, in works such as *Brot und Wein* (Bread and Wine), he was introducing themes generally alien to action painting, such as memory, history, and biography, into his artis-tic vocabulary. Through this more personalized language, his paintings came to express a certain darkness, just as works by artists as diverse as the Gutai artists, Grooms, and Vostell did. They also began to take on a more specific ritualized quality through their exchange with blood, which he would pour onto his canvases. In addition, they led directly to his performances, the first of which was presented on 19 December 1962 in Muehl's apartment, which reintroduced the ritualistic and religious sentiments that had characterized the weight of European his-

**Hermann Nitsch**, *Untitled*, 1961. Collection Julius Hummel, Vienna

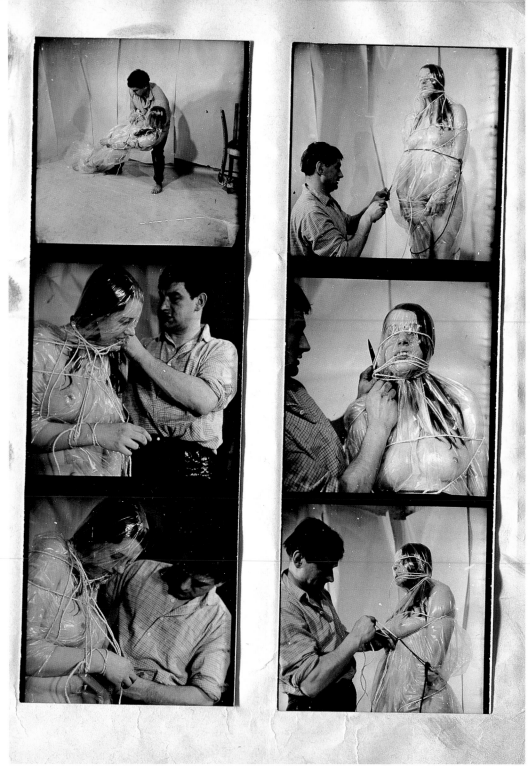

**Otto Muehl**, *Materialaktion*, 1965. Collection Julius Hummel, Vienna

**87**

Gustav Metzger, *South Bank Demo*, 1961/1998. Collection of the artist

**Robert Morris,** *Untitled (Standing Box)*, 1961. Solomon R. Guggenheim Museum, New York. From the Morris Archives

tory and psychology for centuries. Vienna's long traditions of psychological introspection, as well as its complicity in the destruction of World War II, made this last vestige of traditional figuration a ripe ground for performance-based painting, which would add complex layers of meaning to create a final flourish almost Baroque in its theatricality.

Like Nitsch, Muehl also wrestled with the stranglehold of *art informel*, also known as *tachisme*, by physically altering the relationship of the maker to the object. His accretions did not have the aesthetic quality of assemblage, but were objects encrusted with histories that had been left behind after the floodwaters had receded. In spite of the importance of these works, which eventually metamorphosed into his actions, it is the photographic and filmic documentation of the actions themselves that provides the clearest understanding of his work, characterized by its obsessions with the dual phenomena of sexuality and history. For example, works such as *Leda and the Swan* and *O Tannenbaum* are at once outrageous provocations against tradition, even while they are embedded within it.

Although not a member of the Viennese Action Group, Gustav Metzger played an important role in the promotion of their work. By 1966 Metzger had become well-known for his writings on the beauty and creativity of destruction, which appeared in his first manifesto of 4 November 1959. Metzger brought together the first international gathering of artists affiliated with Fluxus, Viennese Actionism, and other movements, including Nitsch, Muehl, and Jerzy Beres from Vienna; Hansen, Ono, and Ortiz from New York; and Barry Flanagan, Latham, and John Sharkey from London. Dressed in his signature gas mask, protective clothing, and heavy gloves, Metzger was known for actions in which he sprayed acid onto nylon, which created abstract patterns as the fabric dissolved — symbolic protests against the danger of weapons of mass destruction.

**1960s Performative Sculpture** Just as Cage's experimental music influenced the development of art in the 1950s, contemporary dance had a major, yet less recognized, effect on the reductive vocabulary of "performative sculpture" in the 1960s, as well as on aspects of Minimalist sculpture. Robert Morris, already well schooled as a third-generation Abstract Expressionist painter of the Bay Area mode, attended, with the dancer and choreographer Simone Forti, a number of Ann Halprin's dance workshops in San Francisco. The two formed their own dance and theater group in that city in 1957, and Forti's improvisational use of props and rule games to structure movement played a significant role in the development of the early performative sculptures that Morris created after he first moved to New York in 1960.[65]

During this period, Morris literalized in sculpture concepts being explored in the Living Theater, which emphasized the positioning of bodies in space, and in Forti's work with the Judson Dance Theater, with its focus on scale based on the human body. In fact, Morris's *Column*, *Passageway*, and *Untitled (Standing Box)* (all 1961) were prophetic of work that would be made by the artists who would directly translate avant-garde dance theories into sculptural body-oriented performance. With *Column*, Morris built his first sculptural object, which anticipated, in form and scale, his future Minimalist sculptures. Using a column based on the scale of his own body, Morris stood quietly erect inside the structure for three-and-one-half minutes and then tipped himself over.[66] The fact that he received a head injury during practice and subsequently chose to tip the column with strings rather than his body does not diminish the importance of this piece as a performative sculpture scaled to the body of the artist. Given the fact that there are easier ways to tip over a column than by jeopardizing one's own body, it is worth noting that Morris, even while inhabiting a cool, manufactured, Minimalist sculpture felt the need, at least initially, to participate in a repressed gestural action.

In Ono's 1961 Chamber Street Series, Morris created a viewer-activated performative environment

65. For more information on this subject, see Maurice Berger, Labyrinths: Robert Morris, Minimalism, and the 1960s (New York: Harper and Row, 1989), ch. 1.

66. Robert Morris: The Mind/Body Problem, exh. cat. (New York: Solomon R. Guggenheim Foundation, 1994), 90.

entitled *Passageway*. Just three years after the first Happenings — those participatory environments that incorporated a chaotic assemblage of fragments of daily life — Morris constructed a reductive environment with a choreographer's brutal simplicity. The plywood-lined corridor, which extended fifty feet, narrowed gradually to a point. The participant was completely controlled by this three-dimensional sculptural environment. In an ironic gesture, the artist reversed the action of breaking through and emergence that had characterized so much previous action-based work and created instead an aggressive compression that had containment as its ultimate aim.

In *Untitled (Standing Box)*, Morris created a rough pine coffin to fit his height and width exactly. As with *Column*, he "performed" the box by standing inside of it, a clear precedent for Bruce Nauman's 1966 sculpture, *Neon Templates of the Left Half of My Body Taken at Ten Inch Intervals*. Performative and autobiographical, Morris's box nevertheless eliminated any specific reference to the figure or narrative content: The body was represented through the geometry of the box; the figure was implied through its absence. Morris's sculptural, dance-inspired, proto-Minimalist object documented his role as both maker and participant. Sculpture, installation, and

performance (as well as its documentation through photography, film, and video) all were essential parts of Bruce Nauman's work from the time he graduated from art school in 1966. *Flour Arrangements* (1966) documented his month-long activity of arranging on the studio floor a pile of dust. This Man Ray-inspired gestural piece was related to Nauman's figurative performative sculpture, *Light Trap for Henry Moore, No. 1* (1967), which he recorded on film. In this work, Nauman parodies Henry Moore's figurative drawings of the early 1940s, not as static objects for contemplation but as traps that captured the movement of light. Making circular motions with a flashlight, Nauman formed figures in space whose traces were frozen in photographs. Even at this time he understood the deceptive nature of documentation. "I guess the film becomes a record of what went on," he recalled. "Maybe also because you tend to believe what is shown on a film is really true — you believe a film, or a photograph, more than a painting."[67]

In 1968 Nauman met the dancer and choreographer Meredith Monk. This encounter helped reinforce his feelings that movements, even those of an amateur, could be made into art. "The earliest performance things that were filmed were things like you sit in the studio and what do you do. Well, it turned out that I was pacing around the studio a lot. . . . That

67. Bruce Nauman, in Joe Raffaele and Elizabeth Baker, "The Way-Out West: Interviews with 4 San Francisco Artists," *Art News* 66, no. 4 (Summer 1967): 40, cited in Paul Schimmel, "Pay Attention," *Bruce Nauman*, ed. Joan Simon, exh.cat. (Minneapolis: Walker Art Center, 1994), 72.

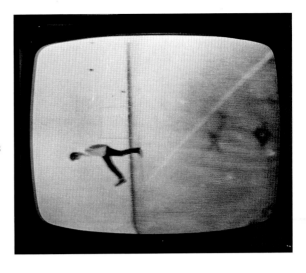

**Bruce Nauman**, *Slow Angle Walk (Beckett Walk)*, 1968

was an activity that I did so I filmed that, just this pacing. So I was doing really simple things like that. . . . I was familiar with some of the things that [Merce] Cunningham had done and some other dancers where you can take any simple movement and make it into a dance just by presenting it as a dance. . . But anyway, talking to Meredith helped, because she is a dancer and thought about things in that way."[68] For Nauman, the repetition of such simple actions had the potential to force the viewer into his loop. Eschewing narrative, he opted for a type of repetition that could ruthlessly wear down the viewer, for an engaging tension that would never be resolved.

While Nauman's early films and videotapes directed attention to ordinary or everyday occurrences, those made after 1967 took on the quality of extended tests, challenges, and discomforting experiments. For example, he set up difficult situations that made him angry, as in *Bouncing Two Balls between the Floor and Ceiling with Changing Rhythms* (1967–68). In this performance documented in film, he attempts to get a rhythm going by bouncing one ball off the floor and the other off the ceiling and then catching it and by bouncing another ball twice off the floor and once off the ceiling. However, he was unable to control the game.

With such works as *Performance Corridor* (1968-70), Nauman attempted to engage the viewer as a participant in the situations he created. As he once stated, "somebody else would have the same experience instead of just having to watch me have that experience."[69] *Performance Corridor* began as a prop for Nauman's videotape *Walk with Contrapposto* (1968), in which he records himself walking up and down a corridor, constructed of two 8 x 20–foot freestanding walls twenty inches apart, in a stylized manner for an hour. He reconstructed this corridor as *Performance Corridor* for the exhibition "Anti-Illusion: Procedures/Materials," presented at the Whitney Museum of American Art in New York from 19 May to 6 July 1969. He explained that "That

piece is important because it gave me the idea that you could make a participation piece without the participants being able to alter your work." He also observed that "a lot of strange things happened to anybody who walked into it."[70] Indeed, the critic Peter Schjeldahl described this work as "ruthless . . . somber . . . claustrophobic."[71] *Performance Corridor* inaugurated a series of works that exemplified Nauman's growing interest in corridors, passageways, and psychologically defined spaces. Moving decisively away from the freewheeling aspects of performative activities, Nauman created a "way of limiting the situation so that someone else can be a performer, but he can only do what I want him to do. I mistrust audience participation. That's why I try to make these works as limiting as possible."[72]

**1970s Performance** Vito Acconci abandoned his career as a poet to create a series of important performances before moving on to produce performative works in other mediums. Acconci created performances only from 1969 through 1974. Through these brilliantly simple and psychologically penetrating actions, he successfully and literally played himself in public to the point that by his presentation of *Command Performance* (1974), he insisted that the spectator take on the role of the artist. The body explorations of artists such as Burden, McCarthy, Marina Abramovic, Gina Pane, and others are inconceivable without the conceptual precedent that Acconci established and quickly left behind.

In Acconci's early task-oriented works, formal exercise quickly began to take on physically and psychologically assaultive qualities, both for him and for the audience. Employing the concept of mark that began with Fontana, Acconci in *Trademarks* (1970) bypassed the canvas and performed for the camera: "Biting myself: biting as much of my body as I can reach. Applying printers' ink to the bites; stamping bite prints on various surfaces."[73] Other short films

68. Bruce Nauman, in unpublished interview with Lorraine Sciarra, Pomona College, Claremont, California, January 1972, in Schimmel, "Pay Attention," 73.

69. Ibid., 78.

70. Nauman, ibid., 77.

71. Peter Schjeldahl, "New York Letter," Art International 13, no. 7 (September 1969): 71, cited in Neil Benezra, "Surveying Nauman" in Bruce Nauman, 26.

72. Bruce Nauman, in Willoughby Sharp, "Nauman Interview," Arts Magazine 44, no. 5 (March 1970): 26, cited in Schimmel, 77.

73. Vito Acconci, Avalanche, no. 6 (Fall 1972): 14-18. All descriptions of Acconci's work are from this source.

recorded other actions. In *Shadow Box* (1970) Acconci shadowboxed himself into exhaustion. In *Blindfolded Catching* (1970), he stood "blindfolded while rubber balls one at a time are repeatedly thrown at me." In *Hand and Mouth* (1970), he pushed "my hand into my mouth until I choke and am forced to release my hand; continuing the action for the duration of the film."

Acconci engaged in a virtual explosion of performances from 1970 to 1972. Constructed more like a notebook than a refined script, his quickly drawn and executed actions were created at a rapid and no doubt exhaustive pace. For example, for *Runoff New York* (July 1970), he ran in place for two hours until he developed a heavy sweat. Then, "Leaning back against the wall; moving around against the wall — the sweat reacts with the paint, the paint spots my body."[74] In a reversal of Klein's *anthropométries*, the body does not apply paint to a surface, but paint is transferred to the body.

By 1972 Acconci was already beginning what would become a lifelong interest in psychologically activated architectural spaces. In *Seed Bed* (1972) he had constructed a low wooden ramp that rose gently from the floor to the rear wall of the Sonnabend Gallery. Positioning himself beneath the floor, he masturbated and spoke to his "member" as the sounds were transmitted via loudspeaker into the gallery. Physically separating himself from the viewer, he began the process of reversing the viewer's role, incorporating the movements he or she made above him into his own orgiastic fantasies. This performance represented Acconci's first attempt to communicate with the viewer while physically apart from him or her. Because the viewer could not see Acconci, he or she had to confront him abstractly; however, this experience was also charged with intimacy, because of the nature of the monologues Acconci spoke while masturbating. Even though the act of masturbation set up the psychological intensity of the performance, he has stated that "the masturbation part came no more than a week before the piece began."[75]

The reversal of roles between artist and viewer evident in *Seed Bed* became complete in *Command Performance*, a performance incorporating video presented at 112 Greene Street in New York in January 1974. As Kate Linker has written, in this performance Acconci used the three columns "bisecting the gallery as 'exchange points' in a line of transmission. At the foot of one column Acconci placed a video monitor that faced a spotlit stool. . . . [A] video camera focused on the stool relayed the image to another monitor located at the third column in the line. At the base of this column Acconci positioned a rug for seating." She goes on to observe that the artist commanded the members of his audience to "'Come on, baby, move . . . move into the spotlight . . . that stool's all yours . . . take it baby . . . give it to them' . . . , ending with the self-realization of the auditor in the form of a superman ('You look so huge out there . . . bigger than life . . . / You'll be grand out there.')" In collusion with his audience, he confessed that his work has been "too private . . . I've been afraid to break out of myself . . . to throw myself into the world . . . you can show me how to be strong . . . big . . . public."

In this performance the viewer was repositioned to become the show and to exchange positions with Acconci, the artist. On the videotape Acconci changes gender, shifts from being commanded to being commander, and demands that the viewer, "Like a little dog . . . jump up, on the stool . . . Sit up, come on up to me . . . / Show them your ass . . . show *me* your ass . . . now you're doing what I always had to do . . . wiggle your prick around."[76] Thus, in this work Acconci set up a new structural environment, a combative situation in which he manipulated the viewer as a prop in his sadistic play, which other viewers, who participated voyeuristically, watched on a second video monitor. Throughout the tape, Acconci is present only as a talking image on the monitor facing the stool.

In 1968, one year before Acconci created his first performances and Nauman exhibited *Performance Corridor*, Mowry Baden made *I Walk*

74. *Ibid.*

75. *Vito Acconci, interviewed by Robin White, View 2, no. 5-6 (October-November 1979): 23.*

76. *Vito Acconci, in Kate Linker, Vito Acconci (New York: Rizzoli, 1994), 61-62.*

**Mowry Baden**, *Instrument*, 1969. Collection of the artist

**Mowry Baden**, *Seat Belt (With Block)*, 1969

Chris Burden, *Five Day Locker Piece*, University of California, Irvine, 26-30 April 1971

FIVE DAY LOCKER PIECE
University of California, Irvine: April 26-30, 1971

I was locked in locker number 5 for five consecutive days and did not leave the locker during this time. The locker measured two feet high, two feet wide, and three feet deep. I stopped eating several days prior to entry. The locker directly above me contained five gallons of bottled water; the locker below me contained an empty five gallon bottle.

**Chris Burden**, Relic from *Five Day Locker Piece*, 1971. Courtesy of Gagosian Gallery, New York

*the Line,* a sculpture that required viewers to walk a 20-foot passageway with a sculptural "line" between their legs. Baden's pieces forced viewers into awkward situations that expressed his interest in kinesthetics — physical perceptions and the changes that took place in neuromuscular memory as the body moved through the work. In *Seat Belts* (1969–71) Baden explored the difference between what it *felt* like to walk around a modified circle while tied with a strap from the waist to the floor and what it *looked* like it would feel like. He wanted to manipulate the "body prints" of viewers to alter their perceptions of balance, and creating a new "sensory imprint" was his sculptural aspiration. With *Instrument*, a 16-foot long aluminum and steel passageway with an undulating opening for the head, the viewer's participation was limited to the eyes and head. Passing through this visual corridor, a series of wavelike compressions and expansions penetrated the viewer's brain. Baden's experiments with sculptural-psychological, body-oriented works in the late 1960s and early 1970s would prove to be highly influential on artists such as Charles Ray and Chris Burden, both of whom were his students.

Unlike his teacher, who has worked in relative obscurity, Chris Burden received an extraordinary level of international attention early in his career. In 1971, while still a graduate student at the University of California, Irvine, Burden created a work that had an impact far beyond its modest origins. *Five Day Locker Piece,* which he executed for this graduate thesis exhibition in sculpture, consisted of being locked in a locker two feet high by two feet wide by three feet deep for five consecutive days. A bottle of water was placed in the locker above him, and an empty bottle in the locker below. This early work had many of the attributes that were to constitute Burden's work for the next several years. In subsequent activities, Burden would investigate in depth the implications of creating a situation in which the artist simultaneously endangered himself and involved the viewer as a witness to the seemingly life-threatening situation, thus implicating him or her as complicitous. The inextricable relationship between destruction and creation that had been important for Gutai, early Happenings, and *Nouveau Réalisme* was

**Chris Burden**, *Prelude to 220, or 110*, September 1976

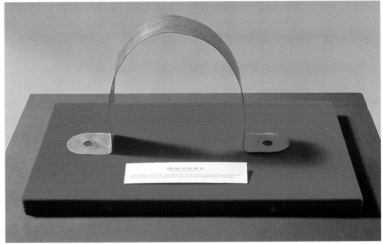

**Chris Burden**, Relic from *Prelude to 220, or 110*, September 1976. Courtesy Frayda and Ronald Feldman

**Chris Burden**, Relic from *Through the Night Softly*, 1973 Collection Wexner Center for the Arts, The Ohio State University; purchased in part with funds from the National Endowment for the Arts, 1979.09

**Chris Burden**, *Through the Night Softly*, Main Street, Los Angeles, 12 September 1973

**Chris Burden**, *Doorway to Heaven*, 15 November 1973

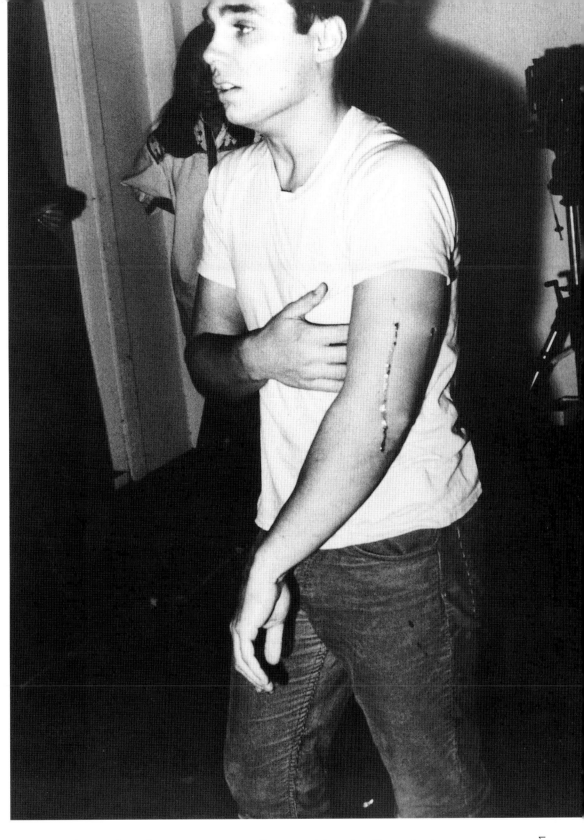

**Chris Burden**, *Shoot*, F Space, 19 November 1971

brought to its logical conclusion in the performances of artists such as Burden, who used his body, penetrated by push pins and bullets, as a receptacle for the assaultive actions of others.

With a visual simplicity stemming from his Minimalist background, Burden devised viscerally reductive actions characterized by a non-narrative, durational quality. These actions were further distinguished by their ability to be captured in a single photographic image and described in a brief paragraph. In addition, in many instances a residual object remained to remind the viewer that the action really did occur. This documentation was intended to preclude subsequent distortions by viewers or witnesses. For some artists, such as Abramovic, who also performed physically self-destructive actions during the early 1970s, the so-called "relics" of the actions that were commercial manifestations of performance were essentially pointless — a criticism also leveled at Beuys. In Burden's case, however, this criticism is unfounded; his performances were to a large degree centered on the object itself. Indeed, there would be no *Five Day Locker Piece* without the lock, no *Prelude to 220, or 110* (1976) without the copper bands, no *Through the Night Softly* (1973) without the glass chips, no *Doorway to Heaven* (1973) without the two wires. Burden, who had been an avid collector of miniature toys since childhood,

**Chris Burden**, *The Big Wheel*, 1979. The Museum of Contemporary Art, Los Angeles. Gift of Lannan Foundation

understood that objects could convince the viewer of the reality of the unbelievable. As Klein had done with *Leap into the Void*, he attempted to combat the skeptical by providing fragments of forensic evidence, three-dimensional truths supported by photographic documentation.

By performing actions witnessed by groups of individuals who could substantiate that they had actually occurred, Burden avoided the debate on truthfulness that dogged previous actions such as Klein's leap. Working in a quack scientific matter, he dreamed up psychologically charged experiments that in their simplicity were more suited for coverage in the mass media than the more extended works of other artists of his generation. His visibility in the media had an immediate impact, not just in the centers of the European and New York art world, but on the performance art of Eastern Europe, South America, and Japan as well. In their sensationalist quality these actions went beyond critics' and the general public's imagination of what seemed extreme. For example, over a period of five years,

Burden had himself shot, electrocuted, impaled, cut, drowned, incarcerated, and sequestered not to make a grand social, political, or religious statement or to reveal a deep psychological meaning, but just because he knew he could. These risky acts revealed much not only about Burden's psyche, but that of his viewers.

The sheer descriptive simplicity of Burden's events led many individuals to claim they had witnessed them. For example, several swear they remember seeing the artist crucified to the back of the Volkswagen Bug driven around Venice, California, in *Trans-Fixed* (1974). However, as Burden himself attests, in actuality only a handful of witnesses saw him for two minutes as the car was pushed and rolled, not driven, back into the garage. Burden conceived and designed his actions as succinct experiments through which he could test, define, and draw conclusions about their meaning as much for himself as for others. "How do you know what it feels like to be shot if you don't get shot?" he asked.[77] Or, as he also remarked, these experiments provided him with

77. *Chris Burden, in Paul Schimmel,* "Just the Facts," Chris Burden: A Twenty- Year Survey, exh. cat. *(Newport Beach: Newport Harbor Art Museum, 1988), 17.*

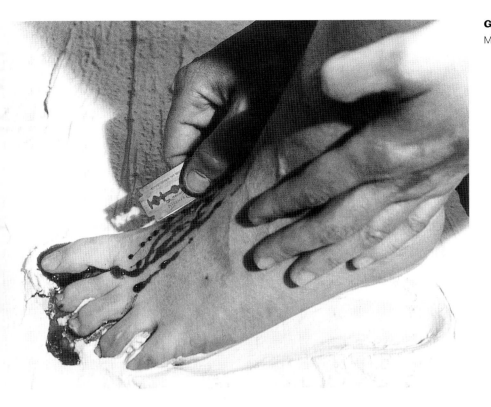

Gina Pane, *Le corps pressenti* (detail), 1975
Museum moderner Kunst Stiftung Ludwig, Wien

Gina Pane, *Le corps pressenti,* 1975
Museum moderner Kunst Stiftung Ludwig, Wien

"knowledge that other people don't have, some kind of wisdom" via renewed encounter with the facts.[78] Yet, beyond the factual evidence the artist has provided for posterity through photographs and objects, many who have learned about his performances have felt a need to elaborate on them. Similar misconceptions, like those surrounding Schwarzkogler and his self-castration events, became part of the mythology that surrounded the extreme, durational, self-destructive actions performed by many artists during the 1970s.

In Burden's masterpiece, *The Big Wheel* (1979), an 8-foot-diameter, 6,000-pound, cast iron flywheel is mounted vertically on a support structure. Behind the flywheel a stationary motorcycle is positioned in such a way that, when started up, its spinning rear wheel transfers its energy directly to the mass of the flywheel, which is able to store it. The motorcycle is then turned off and the massive flywheel keeps spinning. Four times a day, in public view, an operator repeats this process, imparting all the momentum normally used to propel him- or herself and the cycle forward into the cumbersomely elegant flywheel. Demonstrating a basic principle of physics, in its precise simplicity this work appears to pose a threat to everyone involved — the motorcycle operator, the viewer, and the institution that exhibits it; all are accomplices in a pseudoscientific engineering experiment. Like Burden's actions, it is hypnotically and terrifyingly beautiful. The artist has turned a scientific fact simple enough for a child to understand into a monumental sculpture that imparts a fearsome giggle in the viewer. Like other performance artists of his generation, including Acconci, Rebecca Horn, and Paul McCarthy, Burden shifted from performance to sculpture and installation while continuing to acknowledge the primacy of

the act — even though he eliminated the direct participation of the artist.

In 1971, about the same time that Burden created *Shoot*, Gina Pane created *Escalade non-anethesie*, a piece performed for a small group of friends at her studio and later in a public gallery. She climbed up a ladder structure that had small blades protruding where her bare feet would rest. In *Le corps pressenti* (1975), cuts made between her toes left permanent bloodstains on the plaster cast in which her feet rested as the incisions were made. Regarding these nonreligious sacraments, Pane explained, "my real problem was in constructing a language through this wound, which became a sign. Through this wound I communicate loss of energy. Physical suffering isn't a mere personal problem to me but a problem of language. The act of self-inflicting wounds on myself represented a temporal gesture, a psychovisual gesture which leaves traces."[79] In *Psyche* (1974) Pane kneeled in front of a mirror, methodically applied makeup to her face, and then cut small arch lines just below her eyebrow with a razor blade. By attacking her own body, she confronted her own vulnerability and that of women in general. One can see a similar belief underlying Orlan's extraordinary lifelong self-transformation, which began with *Le Baiser de l'Artiste* (The Kiss of the Artist) and continues to this day. Orlan's use of pain to break through the audience's anestheticization, like Burden's *Shoot*, creates

78. Ibid.,18.

79. Gina Pane, in Helena Kontová, "The Wound as a Sign: An Encounter with Gina Pane," Flash Art, nos. 92-93 (October-November 1979): 36.

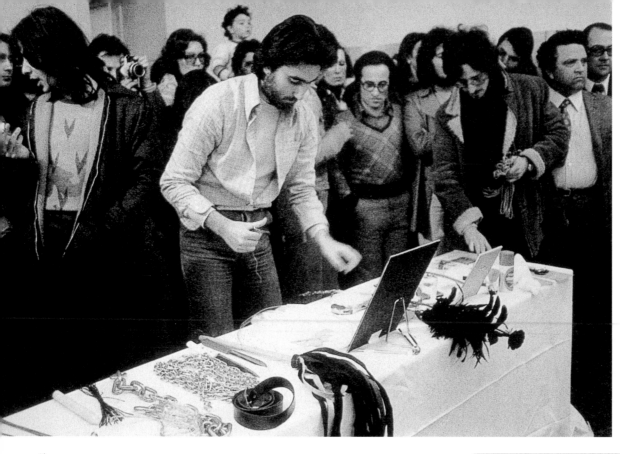

**Marina Abramović,** *Rhythm O*, 1974. Courtesy of the artist and Sean Kelly, New York

**Ulay/Abramović**, *Relation in Space*, Venice Biennale, 1976

a situation so extreme that even the most jaded viewer feels both empathy and complicity.

A few years after Burden's revolutionary *Shoot*, Marina Abramovic created a work that confronted her fears about her own body and at the same time demonstrated her seriousness toward her art: she placed that which was most visible, her body, into harm's way. In the public performance *Rhythm 0* (1974), Abramovic presented herself to an audience in Naples. She had placed various instruments of pleasure and pain on a table. The audience was told that for a period of six hours the artist would be passive and not exert her own will and that they were free to use the instruments during that time. She had committed to this ordeal for a predetermined length, a Cageian strategy adopted by many performance artists to give a nonlinear event a beginning and an end. What began rather modestly in the first three hours, with participants moving her around and touching her somewhat intimately, escalated into a dangerous and uncontrollable spectacle. All of Abramovic's clothes were cut from her body with razor blades; by the fourth hour, those same blades were used to create cuts in her skin from which blood could be sucked. It became evident to the audience that this woman would do nothing to protect herself and that she was likely to be assaulted and raped. A protective group began to develop, and when a loaded gun was thrust into Abramovic's hand and when her finger was placed on the trigger, a fight broke out between her protectors and the instigators, leaving her fully exposed to competing factions within the audience. [80]

Prior to becoming Abramovic's partner and collaborator in 1975, Ulay (Uwe F. Laysiepen), had also placed himself in emotionally and psychologically vulnerable positions in works that were more lifestyles than performances. His early works involved no public participants, but consisted of such activities as dressing as a female and entering the social milieu of transvestites and transsexuals continuously for two years or presenting himself as mentally impaired for one year, during which he sought out the company of persons with extreme physical abnormalities and modeled his own image on theirs. Although Ulay documented these activities, he has chosen to withhold the documentation from exhibition as an aspect of the activity. Unlike most artists who have created photographs to document their actions, Ulay morally questioned the commercial nature of such activities, as well as the status of the truth. [81]

Together, Abramovic and Ulay created a series of works that investigated gender, sexuality, and trust in a manner that would have been impossible as individuals. Their first performance, *Relation in Space* (1976), which they created for the Venice Biennale, involved a simple but increasingly risky action: "Two bodies repeatedly pass, touching each other. At higher speeds they collide. Time 58 minutes."

*Imponderabilia* (1977) involved the direct participation of the viewer in an intimate physical and psychological confrontation with the artists. "Naked, we are standing in the main entrance of the museum, facing each other. The public entering the museum have to pass sideways through the small space between us. Each person passing has to choose which one of us to face. Time 90 minutes." In the same year, they used a trusted Citröen SWAT-like police van, in which they had lived since they had first met and would continue to occupy throughout the 1970s, as an expression of a "relation in movement."

80. Thomas McEvilley, "Marina Abramovic/Ulay Ulay/Marina Abramovic," Artforum 13, no. 1 (September 1983): 52.

81. Ibid.

**101**

**Ulay/Abramović**, *Imponderabilia*,
Galleria Communale d'Arte Moderna, 1977

**Ulay/Abramović**, *Relation in Movement*, 10th Biennale of Paris, 1977

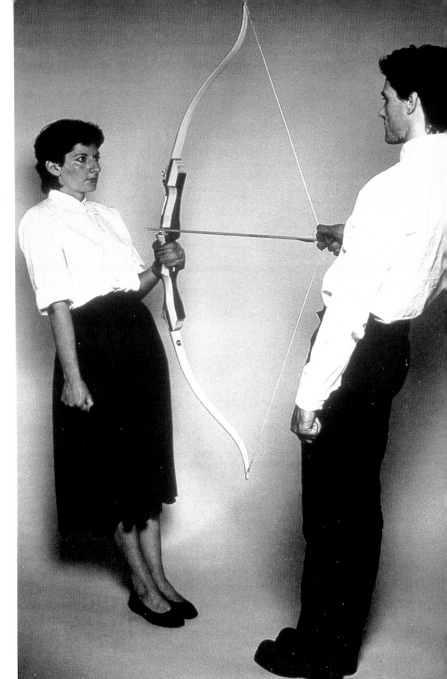

**Ulay/Abramović**, *Rest Energy*, 1980

Driving the van around the plaza of the Musée d'Art Moderne de la Ville de Paris, they left a mark in both the viewer's mind and on the plaza itself. Ulay stated, "I am driving the car for an indefinite time in a circle"; Abramovic, "I am sitting and moving for an indefinite time in a circle, announcing the number of circles by megaphone." They ultimately drove for sixteen hours, at which time oil began to leak, leaving an obvious circular pattern on the plaza's stone surface. The ring made by their van, with its precedents in the Rauschenberg–Cage automobile print and the tracks made by Kanayama's miniaturized remote-controlled cars, became for Abramovic and Ulay a public expression of their own life together as the subject of their art. In *Rest Energy* (1980), they demonstrated publicly their trust in each other: Abramovic held a bow, while Ulay notched the arrow in the string and aimed it at her heart.

Unlike the international recognition that Burden received while still in his twenties, Paul McCarthy worked for thirty years as a performance artist with a significant and loyal following in Los Angeles before he became widely acknowledged for

**103**

**Paul McCarthy**, performance mask from *Trunks*, 1973-83

**Paul McCarthy**, *Hot Dog*, 1974

**Paul McCarthy**, *PROPO*, performance prop from *Trunks*, 1973-83

**Paul McCarthy**, *Face Painting – Floor, White Line*, 1972

**Paul McCarthy,** *Sailor's Meat*, 1975

**Paul McCarthy**, *Assortment, Trunks*, 1973-83
Collection of Tom Patchett, Los Angeles

his complex kinetic narrative tableaux. While study-ing at the University of Utah in 1969, McCarthy executed several frighteningly dangerous perfor-mances that employed gravity as their literal and metaphorical vehicle. Pitching both himself — in *Too Steep, Too Fast*, performed in Marin County in 1969 — and a bowling ball — in *Mountain Bowling*, per-formed near Salt Lake City that same year — down slopes, he created missile-like trajectories that resulted in the obvious. No doubt these actions were part of the tradition of "performing" a line, as Paik did in *Zen for Head* in homage to La Monte Young's line composition, as well as in analogy with Manzoni, Rauschenberg–Cage, and Byars. In fact, as the critic Ralph Rugoff has observed, "In *Face Painting — Floor, White Line* (1972), [McCarthy] snaked across the floor of his studio, pushing a bucket of white paint with his head and torso to make a wide line across the room. Such pieces owe a debt to Klein's body prints. . . . But McCarthy's performances added raw slap-stick and an element of physical endurance that bears little resemblance to anything found in Klein's ironically packaged spectacles. Kazuo Shiraga's Gutai-associated works of the mid-1950s provide another partial precedent (McCarthy knew of this work through reading Kaprow's encyclopaedic *Assemblage, Environments, and Happenings*, 1966)."[82]

Between 1972 and 1974, McCarthy's formal, process-oriented work evolved into activities that were far more aggressive and sexually provocative. By 1974, he had achieved local renown for a series of brutally self-assaultive performances, including *Meatcake #1, #2* and *#3*, *Hot Dog*, and *Heinz Ketchup Sauce*, that raised questions of propriety among his audience. Ingesting raw meat, mayon-

82. Ralph Rugoff, "Mr. McCarthy's
Neighbourhood," in Paul McCarthy
(London: Phaidon, 1996), 38, 41.

**Rebecca Horn**, *Mechanical Body Fan*, 1972
Collection of the artist

**Rebecca Horn**, *Arm Extensions*, 1968

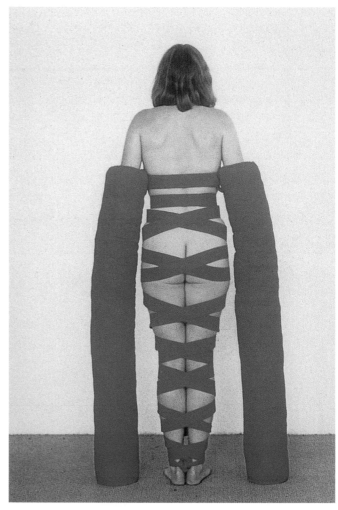

naise, ketchup, mustard, and other foodstuffs, as well as cold cream, McCarthy extended the ritualized and religious traditions of Muehl and the Viennese Actionists into a grotesque horror film that might be titled *American Popular Culture*. Out of packaged food products such as Hellman's Mayonnaise and Heinz Ketchup he created faux bodily fluids — semen ejaculations and blood hemorrhages — in addition to ingesting and regurgitating raw hamburger.

Rooted in the pervasive media-manipulated culture of Los Angeles, McCarthy explored in the 1970s and 1980s notions of artifice and spectacle through aberrant behavior that had no redeeming political, cultural, or psychological purpose. For his performances he would often create gender-bending characters that he would present via video — well in advance of the 1990s preoccupation with the grotesque and abject. From 1974 through 1983, and to a diminishing degree thereafter, he worked nude or partially nude with a series of props that included razors (with which he shaved until he bled), hot dog buns, hot dogs, and his genitals. As Barbara Smith has reported, one of McCarthy's performances involved "drinking catsup and stuffing his mouth with hotdogs, more and more until its seems inconceivable that anymore will fit. Binding his head with gauze and adding more hot dogs, he finally tapes his bulging mouth closed so that the protruding mass looks like a snout. I struggle inwardly to control the impulse to gag. He stands alone, struggling with himself, trying to prevent his own retching."[83]

Over the ensuing years McCarthy used dolls, wigs, underpants, Vaseline, rocks, GI Joe dolls, football helmets, fake breasts, and prosthetic male and female genitals, among other props, to create such performances as *Sailor's Meat, Grandpop, Pig Man* (1980), and *Popeye* (1983). After using these props again and again, he finally entombed them in a series of trunks stacked on top of one other in a post-Minimalist monument or above-ground burial. In this way McCarthy paid homage to his decade of

extremely repulsive performance. In a way, he needed to bury these objects of fascinating revulsion to make way for his new art based in the traditions of tableau.

Finally, even though McCarthy is foremost a performance artist who has more recently pursued the mediums of installation, tableaux, and sculpture, painting has always been an important subject of his work. At the beginning of McCarthy's career, the broad, gestural traces of his actions had painterly counterparts in his *Black Paintings* (1967–68). For these works, the artist used his hands to apply a flammable pigment to his body, which would then be covered with gasoline and burned. In the 1970s, McCarthy used his penis to make paintings in a deft parody of the macho posturing of Pollock and the action painters. And in his recent performance and videotape *Painter* (1995), in which a figure dressed in a smock and mask makes action paintings with an oversized brush and roller, he satirized Willem de Kooning.

Very different in character from the often brutal performances of Burden, Pane, Abramovic, Ulay, and McCarthy are the works of Rebecca Horn and Gordon Matta-Clark. In 1969, the same year in which Acconci made his first mature works as a visual artist, Horn was recovering from a critical bout with tuberculosis, an experience that changed her life. After a period of making large sculptures with polyester resin in the tradition of many process-oriented artists, Horn created a series of complex works that explored the delicate balance between life and death — a concern ignited by her confrontation with mortality.[84]

In her body sculptures of the late 1960s and early 1970s, Horn designed a series of devices that enhanced the organic activities that constitute life. Commencing with *Arm Extensions* (1968), she created "a personal art where the number of participants was limited, because intense interpersonal perception is only possible in a small circle of people";[85] the garment that constituted the work was constructed specifically for the body of the person who was to

83. Barbara Smith, LAICA Journal (January 1979): 46.

84. For complete documentation of Horn's work, see Rebecca Horn, exh. cat. (New York: Solomon R. Guggenheim Foundation, 1993). This catalogue includes two interviews with the artist by Stuart Morgan; essays by Germano Celant, Nancy Spector, Katharina Schmidt, and Giuliana Bruno; and a catalogue of works.

85. Rebecca Horn, in Rebecca Horn: Drawings/Objects/Video/Films, exh. cat. (Cologne: Kölnischer Kunstverein, 1977), 24.

**Gordon Matta-Clark.** *Photo-Fry,* 1969

wear it. In 1970 Horn transformed her respect for the biomechanical medical devices that had saved her life into a series of pseudomedical sculptures designed for physical and sensory awareness, including *Über-strömer* (Overflowing Blood Machine) and *Cornucopia, Seance for Two Breasts.* In the former, four horizontal belts hold eight tubes attached to a glass base on which a person stands. Blood pumped from the base pulses rhythmically through the exterior vascular system. The latter, which is most directly related to the illness that had so profoundly altered Horn's life, resembles a pair of black lungs connecting the mouth to the breast. This work expressed her desire to feel more intimately connected with herself.

In 1972 Horn continued her exploration of sensory awareness and movement in *Fingerhandschuhe* (Finger Gloves) — spiky finger extensions made of balsa wood covered with fabric that can be used to feel, touch, or grasp anything from an extended distance. In this work the "lever action of the lengthened fingers intensifies the various sense data of the hand; the manual activity is experienced in a new operational mode. I feel me touching. I see me grasping. I control the distance between me and the objects."[86] The same year Horn made *Bleistiftmaske* (Pencil Mask), a work that refers back to the mark-making so characteristic of the action painters and the Gutai artists. It consisted of a performance in which the artist wore a mask from which protruded rows of

sharpened pencils, arranged so that she could draw with her head. In *Aktion "Mechanischer Körperfächer"* (Mechanical Body Fan, 1972), Horn turned herself on an axis for a series of motions that were visually amplified through the semicircular fan that rested on her shoulders — an amplified version of Valie Export's geometrically structured photographs of street body works. In this series of performative sculptures that functioned as extensions of the artist's own body and were complete only when activated through their use, Horn extended the tradition begun by Tanaka and her *Electric Dress.*

From the time he graduated from Cornell University in 1969 through the early 1970s, Gordon Matta-Clark, although not as well known for his performance work as Horn, consistently created sculptural works that emerged from process-oriented activities. Although known more for his deconstructions of architectural structures, Matta-Clark's activity from 1969 to 1972 was dominated by performative work. For an exhibition in New York entitled "Documentations," organized by John Gibson, Matta-Clark created a work called *Photo-Fry* by frying photographs in an old-fashioned skillet filled with grease — an act as irreverent to photography as photography had been to painting. He exhibited the photographs, which were available for purchase and are still extant, along with the stove, pan, and gas tank.[87]

86. *Ibid.,* 41.

87. *Mary Jane Jacob,* Gordon Matta-Clark: A Retrospective, *exh. cat. (Chicago: Museum of Contemporary Art, 1985), 22.*

On 25 December of that year Matta-Clark organized an event entitled *Christmas Piece,* which was both a birthday party for his fellow Cornell University alumnus, Alan Saret, and an opening celebration of the 98 Greene Street Loft, an alternative space for poetry, music, performance, and art. About that time, he also photo-fried Christmas cards to send to his friends. As Mary Jane Jacob has written, "The performance installation consisted of a darkened room illuminated only by theatrical lights on three trees: a Christmas tree, a holly bush, and a flowering peach tree. One hundred chairs stood stacked against the back wall; as each guest entered and took a chair, the piece was diminished as the party grew."[88] The "undoing" of the chairs thus became the performance, with each guest becoming a performer as he or she took a seat.

In 1972 Matta-Clark created an important performative installation between 98 and 112 Greene Street entitled *Open House* (also called *Drag-On* and *Dumpster*). Using wood and found doors, Matta-Clark subdivided a large industrial refuse container lengthwise into thirds and then into multiple subdivided spaces with various openings. Sound from a tape made by Ted Greenwald resonated throughout the altered container, where a series of performances, including a dance by Tina Girouard, Suzanne Harris, and Barbara Dilley took place. Like *Christmas Piece, Open House* was a performance involving par-

ticipants who activated and altered the space as they moved through it.[89]

That same year Matta-Clark created *Hair,* a sculptural performance consisting of the cutting of his hair, which he had not shorn for a year. In a spoof of the systems and grids of Minimalist and Conceptual art, he made a schematic plan drawn like a phrenological map to divide his cranium into quadrants. In a private performance on New Year's Eve, he and Carol Goodden tagged, labeled, and plotted each clump of hair according to a corresponding numerical and alphabetical position on the grid. What remain today are the numbered and tagged clumps; the artist's plan to make a wig sculpture was never fulfilled.[90]

Finally, Matta-Clark's anarchistic deconstruction of buildings in works such as *Bronx Floors* (1972–73) and *Splitting* (1974) expressed his concerns about the way architecture controls and alters social interaction. Perceived today in formalist, post-Minimalist, and Conceptual terms, the highly provocative and dramatic actions necessary to create these works were guerrilla actions against vernacular architecture and what it stands for. These were not performances that could have been sanctioned by civil engineers or the police department; in fact, the authorities pursued Matta-Clark after he and a crew of friends spent the summer of 1975 cutting into Pier 52 on the Hudson River. The work, *Day's End,* resulted in a warrant issued for the artist's arrest and

88. *Ibid.,* 24.    89. *Ibid., 42–43.*    90. *Ibid.,* 48.

**Paul Cotton,** *The People's Prick*, February 1970

**Terry Fox**, *Cellar*, 1970

his eventual flight to Europe.

In the San Francisco Bay Area in the late 1960s and early 1970s, a remarkable generation of artists emerged, including Terry Fox, Paul Cotton, and Howard Fried. These performance artists had difficulty gaining recognition as visual artists who practiced a medium distinct from the region's long-standing tradition of poetry, dance, music, film, and theater. The legacies of the Beats in poetry, of Ann Halprin in dance, and of Steve Reich and Terry Reilly in music served as both justification for and a challenge to the highly specific performance-installation artists who were becoming active at the same time — and who have yet to be systematically and coherently chronicled.

While a graduate student in art at the University of California, Berkeley, Paul Cotton created a participatory performative environment in 1966 that explored the themes of framing and public interaction, which have held his interest throughout his career. *Random House Converter #6* consisted

of eight 8 x 5–foot canvases placed two feet apart, one behind the other. Each had a doorway in its center, and the doorways became successively smaller in each panel. A view through the openings suggested a corridor in perspective or a mirror reflected, and the repetition created a literal break in the picture plane. The work, though participatory, anticipates aspects of the "light and space" installations pioneered by various southern Californian artists, as well as certain qualities of James Turrell's environments. Cotton named the work after the Random House Publishing Company's logo — a peaked roof–shape similar to the configuration created by the guy wires that suspended the panels — because he found irony in the idea of a "random house." For an exhibition at Eugenia Butler Gallery in Los Angeles in 1969, Cotton constructed a booth with a divided partition that included a one-way mirror; in this mirror, the participant stared at his or her own face, which seemed to be attached to Cotton's white-gowned body.

Many of Cotton's works playfully engaged

**110**

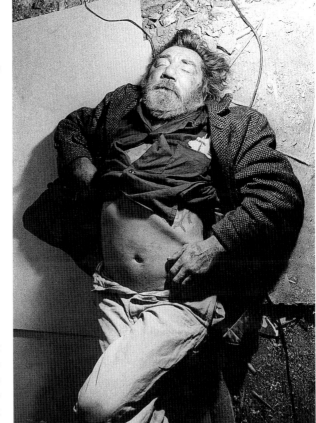

**Terry Fox**, *Cellar*, 1970

with current events. Three days after Neil Armstrong and his comrades had returned to earth from the first successful mission to the moon, Cotton performed a work entitled *The People's Prick*. In this work, he appeared in the People's Park March in Berkeley dressed as a giant penis. In this persona, his most renowned of the period, Cotton was a living embodiment of the spirit of the park and a symbol of the vitality of the neighborhood in which it was situated, which had been vitiated by the university. Placing a flag on the ground, he proclaimed the park the realm of I-Magi-Nation. His costume was buried there in a ceremony that recognized the end of an era.

In 1969 Terry Fox returned to San Francisco after having lived in Paris, where he had participated in the student riots of May 1968. This experience was to prove important to the activist performances that form a counterpart to the poetic, cerebral, and meditative aspects of his oeuvre. In contrast to Cotton, Fox did not make a dramatic move from more private to more public actions. In fact, in 1968, very early in his career, he began to create a series of public theater pieces in and around San Francisco. Once a month Fox would choose a specific time and site where people would be invited to watch and participate in an event that would disrupt the normal course of activities at that location. In *What Do Blind Men Dream?* (1969), for example, he asked a blind woman to leave her usual neighborhood and sing and play the accordion for an evening on a street corner he chose. To convince her to relocate to an unfamiliar context, Fox had to gain her trust. The persuasiveness he demonstrated played a significant role in the work that introduced him to the New York art world.

Arriving in the city in the summer of 1970, Fox stayed in the loft of his friend Robert Frank, the Swiss-American photographer who had published his famous book of photographs, *The Americans*, which included an introduction by Jack Kerouac, in 1959. The loft's location on the Bowery stimulated Fox's decision to create a work that reflected the gritty difference between San Francisco and New York. In *Cellar* (1970), a performance-installation presented at Reese Palley Gallery in July, he chose to reveal the

basement of the newly opened gallery, ignoring its beautiful white exhibition spaces. The resulting work became a living tableau, complete with a "bum" named Ronnie, who had been sleeping in the artist's doorway for three days. Fox persuaded Ronnie to inhabit the dark, rubbish-filled space as a participant in his social sculpture. As he remarked, "It was a piece that took in everything I felt about the place and that I was involved in from day to day. And the context, like the bums' sense of time. That was very clear to me, the Bowery bums' special relationship to time. . . . The Bowery bums are real New Yorkers."[91]

Upon entering this installation, the viewer was confronted with a dim, littered environment and the snoring sounds of Ronnie lying in the rubble, as well as the amplified sounds of the sewer that ran underneath the floor. In addition, Fox performed a series of actions in which he painted his face white with clown makeup, washed his hands with a bar of soap in a little pail of water, broke a window pane with a hunting knife (which he had borrowed from Frank), and spit soapy water out through the broken glass. To create a connection between himself, the windowpane, and the wall, he put a series of taped black X's on his face and on the wall; and he chalked white X's on his chest and on the black square that he had scraped into the white wall behind him.

That September Fox created a work entitled *Levitation* at the Richmond Art Center outside San Francisco, in which he lay on his back for six hours in a pile of dirt, experiencing a prolonged sense of being out of his body. "I drew a circle in the middle of the dirt with my own blood," he stated at the time. "Its diameter was my height. According to medieval notion, that creates a magic space. Then I lay on my back in the middle of the circle holding four clear poly-

91. Terry Fox, in Brenda Richardson,
Terry Fox, exh. cat. (Berkeley: University
Art Museum, 1973), n.p.

**111**

**Howard Fried**, *All My Dirty Blue Clothes*
(end disestablishment phase),
University Art Museum, Berkeley, 1970.
Courtesy of the artist
and Gallery Paule Anglim, San Francisco

**Howard Fried,** *All My Dirty Blue Clothes*, 1970. Courtesy of the artist and Gallery Paule Anglim, San Francisco

**Howard Fried.** *A Clock of Commercial Significance (from Synchromatic Baseball),* 1974-1978. Courtesy Gallery Paule Anglim, San Francisco

ethylene tubes filled with blood, urine, milk, and water. They represented the elemental fluids that I was expelling from my body. I lay there for six hours with the tubes in my hand trying to levitate. The doors were locked. Nobody saw me. I didn't move a muscle. I didn't close my eyes. I tried not to change my focal point."[92] After four hours Fox could not feel any part of his body and concluded that his legs and arms had probably fallen asleep. After six hours, viewers were allowed to enter into the room and see an imprint of his body in the earth. Fox considered this work his strongest sculpture because its terrifying quality deeply moved everyone who witnessed it.

The matrices of power and energy that had informed *Levitation* also influenced Fox's six-year investigation into the labyrinth laid into the floor of Chartres Cathedral — a common feature of many Gothic cathedrals; tracing one's way through the labyrinth symbolized the pilgrim's journey to knowledge of God. Fox was fascinated that this abstract form could exert such extreme physical control over the space in which it was situated. As he has stated, "I adopted the labyrinth of Chartres as my subject matter and as the structure of whatever I was doing. It was like somebody's life, autobiographical or biographical, for to go the twenty feet from the perimeter to the center, you had to walk 180 feet and cover every inch of the space."[93] Fox had been drawn to the labyrinths for personal reasons. In the late 1960s he had been diagnosed with Hodgkin's disease; following extensive surgery in the fall of 1971, he produced the first of several "hospital" pieces. When he was pronounced cured in 1972, he began his first investigations into the labyrinth, and throughout the 1970s he regarded the form as a metaphor for the cycle of health, sickness, and recovery. Like the process of following the pathways of a labyrinth, Fox's quest became obsessive. As he has stated,

"The years of working with it ended up in a very bad way for me — I became — I mean, it really was an obsession."[94]

Beginning in 1972 by making a plaster labyrinth, Fox explored the form in drawings, objects, sculptures, and musical elements. His labyrinth scored for cat purrs is an audiotape of the purring sounds of eleven different cats. At the beginning of the tape the sounds have a domestic quality, but they gradually change until the purrs merge to create the sound of a jungle cat, which, according to Fox, was heard at the center of the labyrinth. Unconventional sounds such as the sewer water and the snoring in *Cellar,* as well as those he produced by stroking a violin bow across his handmade musical instruments, produced an unorthodox music with a sacred and uplifting quality. This work strongly evokes the sensation of transcending the time-and-form-bound realities of material existence, a process Fox also achieved through the labyrinth, levitation, sleep, and the use of hallucinogenic drugs.

While Fox had discovered a public metaphor for his psyche in the labyrinth, Howard Fried, a close colleague also from the Bay Area, explored group dynamics and the psychology of social interaction. In *Synchromatic Baseball* (1971), Fried created a psychological and visual metaphor for opposing psychological types. He invited twenty people to participate in a night baseball game, which was to be played on a brightly lit, peaked roof with tomatoes instead of baseballs. The two teams were named Dommy (for dominants) and Indo (for indominant types). Members of the teams were not informed of the meaning of their team's name meant, nor of Fried's motives for choosing them. Fried himself, who had chosen the players based on their relationship with him, took the role of both coach and catcher. The Dommies functioned with efficiency and quickly cre-

92. Ibid.

93. Terry Fox, in Fred Martin, "Art and History," Artweek, 22 May 1976, 2.

94. Terry Fox, interview with Robin White, View 2, no. 3 (June 1979); 20.

**Tom Marioni**, First floor, Breens, The Saloon of the Museum of Conceptual Art, 75 Third Street, San Francisco, 1973

ated a hierarchy of power, while the Indos had neither leadership nor organization. The game came to an end when Fried fell through a skylight chasing a foul ball.

Two years earlier, in 1969, Fried had developed the hallmarks of his psychologically complex investigations into the pragmatic activities of daily life in *All My Dirty Blue Clothes*, which was originally conceived for the exhibition "Pollution," presented at the Oakland Art Museum in 1970. In this work, he proposed creating a chain structure along the perimeter of an exhibition space by tying together all of his dirty blue clothes. He described the installation in two detailed categories. "Accumulation" dealt with the period from 1957 in Cleveland, when he first acquired a long-sleeved polo shirt, to 1969 in Sacramento, when he acquired two pairs of pants. In "Establishment" he explained that he focused on clothes because they were the category of items in closest proximity to his life and on blue because it was the color he responded to most favorably. In addition, in "Notification" Fried made clear the changes he had made in the installation — specifically, the fact that he had to have surrogate clothing stand in for all but one of the originals. This work manifested Fried's interest in investigating, to an absurd degree, the common actions of daily life, thereby turning them into obsessively fastidious visual metaphors.

The artist most responsible for bringing together Cotton, Fox, and Fried, among others, was Tom Marioni. As curator of the Richmond Art Center from 1968 to 1971 and as founder of the Museum of Conceptual Art in San Francisco in 1970, Marioni played a crucial role in bringing wider recognition to the Bay Area's uniquely psychological, political, and conceptually oriented performative work. However,

he may be best known for *The Act of Drinking Beer with Friends is the Highest Form of Art* — an event Marioni organized for the evening of 26 October 1970 at the Oakland Art Museum. As Ann Goldstein has written, "On a Monday afternoon when the museum was closed to the public, he invited a small group of his friends to join him at the museum to drink beer. The activity of drinking beer and talking with friends comprised the work; the debris (empty beer cans, cigarette butts, melted ice, etc.) was exhibited for one month and constituted a record of the event. Since that original event and exhibition at the Oakland Art Museum, Marioni has recreated this work numerous times."[95]

By 1972 Marioni, who had studied violin as a youth, had developed a process by which sound could be used as a sculptural material. The rhythmic actions of drum-brushing on paper, for example, resulted in a drawing that was a record of the action. Invited in 1972 to participate in Richard de Marco's gallery in Edinburgh, where Beuys had performed the *Celtic Symphony*, Marioni recorded the length of his body moving from a crouch to a standing position in a series of pencil lines that traced the motion. This work is his largest drawing that documents a gestural performance. But Marioni's greatest legacy as an artist is perhaps his work as a curator. Although he does not consider his curatorial work as art, it is apparent from work for both the Richmond Art Center and the Museum of Conceptual Art that no one but an artist could have generated the types of projects that he did. The record of those activities may not be as traditional as the traces he left on pieces of paper, but they nonetheless have left an indelible mark on the history of Bay Area art during the 1970s.

Like many other artists in this exhibition, Mike

95. Ann Goldstein, "Tom Marioni," in Goldstein and Anne Rorimer, Reconsidering the Object of Art, 1965–1975, exh. cat. (Los Angeles: The Museum of Contemporary Art, 1995), 172.

**Tom Marioni**, *Drum Brush Drawing*, 1973
Courtesy of the artist, Gallery Paule Anglim, San Francisco,
and Margarete Roeder Gallery, New York

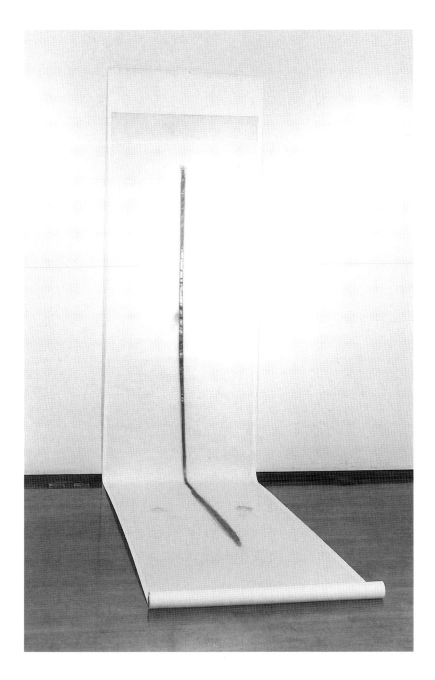

**Tom Marioni**, *Drawing a Line as far as I Can Reach*, 1972. Courtesy of the artist, Gallery Paule Anglim, San Francisco, and Margarete Roeder Gallery, New York

**Mike Kelley**, *Spirit View*, performance view, L.A.C.E. (with Don Krieger), playing back sounds (tube music) collected by the Spirit Collector, 1978

**Mike Kelley**, *Spirit Collector*, performance view, L.A.C.E., Los Angeles, 1978
Private Collection

Mike Kelley, *Indianana*, performance view (with Tony Oursler),
L.A.C.E., Los Angeles, 1978

Kelley created his first performative work while still a student — in his case at the California Institute of the Arts in Valencia. When completing his final term, Kelley made a series of demonstrational objects that he used in short pieces. These works dealt with the common theme of reversed or inverted perspective, both aurally and visually. *Perspectaphone* (1977–78) was performed at LACE in Los Angeles on 4 March 1978. As Timothy Martin has observed, "It's a measured but slightly Dr. Erwin Corey-ish lesson using two square megaphones, one hand-held, the other about eight feet long, to confuse the idea of voice projection with perspectival reduction. Shouting through the hand-held megaphone, Kelley demonstrates that it's 'loudest near the mouth,' and adds, 'you're not hearing it louder; I'm fooling you.' He traces the megaphone on a nearby chalkboard, turning it into a perspective diagram and adding big and little stick figures at the appropriate ends." Martin continues: "He then explains: 'the big person is near, has a big voice; little person is far, has a small voice.' The giant megaphone and a chair are brought out by an assistant (or 'stooge,' as Kelley calls them; this one's Donald Krieger), who takes the big end of the megaphone and sits down for a haranguing, dyslexic quiz demonstrating the logic of the Perspectaphone."[96]

At this time that Kelley was particularly interested in American history. He presented a performance entitled *The Monitor and the Merrimac* on 15 June 1979, in which he took the battle of the Civil War ironclads as a point of departure. As Martin remarks, "Flanked by two assistants, who use a drum and can to bang out the boom and clang of cannon balls on iron, Kelley stands behind a bucket, legs apart, wearing a pair of baggy lower pants legs made from garbage bags and attached to his belt by strings. The peculiar pant-dickeys, looking a little like sailors' bells and a lot like a flasher's accoutrement, get hoisted by its strings during the clamorous overture to reveal a cardboard *Merrimac* on one foot and a *Monitor* on the other. A discussion about spatial and temporal disorientation follows the observation that during the battle the *Monitor*'s speaking tube was inoperable and its turret window was barred with iron shutters. Blindfolded and brandishing a stick, Kelley mimics the 'wildly spinning turret' with 'no sense of direction' and

96. Timothy Martin, "Janitor in a Drum: Excerpts from a Performance History," in Elisabeth Sussman, Mike Kelley: Catholic Tastes, *exh. cat. (New York: Whitney Museum of American Art, 1993), 57, 59.*

**117**

reasons out its location: '*Monitor* is north, *Merrimac* is south. But two horizons are still left open. What is east and what is west?'"[97]

In *Indianana*, presented at LACE on 29 September 1978, Kelley used models of a spiral-shaped fort that protected the settlers in Indiana Territory, along with drawings of beehives to illustrate the communal nature and centralized controls often employed in frontier communities. With megaphones he described the social interactions of Native Americans and settlers. As in previous investigations into the disorientations of space, perspective, and sound Kelley investigated in *Indianana* the convoluted structure of social organizations. Like most of the artists in this exhibition, he used performance as a wellspring for ideas and associations that enriched his subsequent art. In addition, also like many of artists before him, he created performance for only a brief period.

For the vast majority of artists in this exhibition, the performative act was a wellspring of creative activity at the beginning of their careers. Liberating their thinking from the bonds of tradition, materialized in the object, the performative act offered artists the opportunity to investigate such compelling issues as destruction, mortality, and the tenuous boundaries of being in the world. It offered them the opportunity to unravel the systems and structures that provide a false sense of solidity in a world that is forever in flux. It offered them the opportunity to leap into the void — a singular act that embodied the optimism tempered by despair that is so characteristic of the period in which we live.

97. *Ibid.*, 61, 63.

**Kazuo Shiraga**, *Please Come In*, 1955

Shinichiro Osaki

# BODY AND PLACE:
## Action in Postwar Art in Japan

In recent years the contemporary art of non-European and non-American countries has been attracting attention. Many museums have organized exhibitions focusing on the art of Asia, Africa, and Latin America, while art journals routinely run features on the contemporary art of these regions. Of course, as Edward E. Said revealed in his *Orientalism*, for Europe and America the cultures of non-Euro-American countries have been a mere mirror confirming the orthodoxy and superiority of their own cultures; thus, some political elements are most certainly at work behind this phenomenon. Even the current exhibition, which surveys the aspects of action in postwar art on an international scale, cannot escape the effect of such politics.

The Japanese postwar art that derived from action deviated from most Modernist art in two important ways. First, obviously, was the shift in physical location, from Europe and America to the Far East, and the other was the deviation from the formalist orthodoxies of much art created after World War II.

The history of contemporary art in Japan is typified by these two factors. As some recent exhibitions have revealed, postwar Japanese art neither imitated the tendencies of European and American art nor followed their theories, but developed according to its own necessity.[1] It is interesting to note that the relationship between artist and action — central to the work created by numerous groups and artists in the 1950s and 1960s — has been a crucial concept in contemporary Japanese art. The long-assumed superiority and influence of postwar American art has been reassessed; to examine — with action as an axis — the possibility that postwar Japanese art concealed means articulating a fundamental criticism of modernist art as a whole.

From this point of view, postwar Japanese art should be considered in the context of two important movements that evolved in Osaka and Tokyo: the activities of the Gutai Art Association (*Gutai Bijutsu Kyokai*, hereinafter referred to as the Gutai) which was founded in Ashiya, near Osaka, in 1954, and the groups of artists who emerged from the Yomiuri Indépendant exhibitions held at the Tokyo Metropolitan Art Museum in the sixties. However similar these two groups were in terms of their use of action, there was almost no contact between the two and the circumstances that led them to action were completely different as well.[2] The meaning of the activities of these groups should be discussed from a contemporary perspective, based on fact. The activities of the Gutai and those associated with the Yomiuri Indépendant exhibitions often have been interpreted in connection with the Japanese traditions of Zen, Shintoism, and *Ukiyo-e*. However, rather than discuss the meaning and uniqueness of their activities in light of the past, they should be considered in the context of European and American art created at the same time.

The Japanese surrender in the Second World War had a great impact on the Japanese art circle. Jiro Yoshihara, who later became the leader of the Gutai group, reminisced about that time: "Although I was painting such works, I was thinking that something, a quite new, epoch-making idea which was not thought of before the war, must emerge in the art world as a mainstream, like Dada after the end of the First World War."[3] Only a few years after the end of World War II, the issues surrounding the artists' wartime responsibilities were vociferously questioned in Tokyo, where various art groups repeatedly merged

1. There are a number of recent publications that systematically addresses postwar art in Japan.

Dada in Japan: Japanische Avant-garde 1920/1970, Exh. cat. (Düsseldorf: Kunstmuseum Düsseldorf, 1984).

Reconstructions: Avant-Garde in Japan 1945-65, Exh. cat. (Oxford: The Museum of Modern Art, 1985).

Japon des Avant-Gardes 1910-1970, Exh. cat. (Paris: Centre Georges Pompidou, 1986).

Japanese Art after 1945: Scream Against the Sky (New York: Harry N. Abrams, 1994).

2. There was some contact between the two. For instance, the Gutai exhibited at the 7th Yomiuri Indépendant exhibition in 1955 in which all members of the Gutai who exhibited titled their works "The Gutai." In addition, when the artists who were associated with the Yomiuri Indépendants went to Kyushu at the invitation of the Kyushu-ha in 1962, Takumi Kazekura stopped in Osaka, visited the

Gutai Pinakotheca, and proposed to perform impromptu but was refused. This episode is recorded in the following publication, which suggests that for the young artists in the 1960s the Gutai was already an authority. "Special Issue, Takumi Kazekura," Kikan 12 (Kaicho-sha, 1981): 14.

3. Jiro Yoshihara, "Waga kokoro no jijo-den" (Autobiography of My Heart), Kobe Newspaper, 9 July 1967.

**Michio Yoshihara**, painting with a bicycle, 1956

and parted. The central artistic tendency at the time was social realism, which was strong in propaganda but lacked innovative, expressive ideas. In contrast, artists working in the Kansai region (which included the three major cities of Osaka, Kyoto, and Kobe) felt the impact of such a chaotic situation much less, thus offering a favorable environment to those of the Gutai group, led by Yoshihara, to realize "an epoch-making idea in the world of painting."

During this period various art movements and associations in Kansai were searching for a new mode of expression, crossing over different mediums. For example, the Genbi Contemporary Art Council (*Gendai Bijutsu Kondankai*) was founded in 1952: both experienced and young avant-garde artists in the Kansai region gathered to hold study sessions once a month, and organized a total of three exhibitions. The participating artists were amazingly diverse and included Yoshihara and Waichi Tsutaka, the notable abstract painters of the time in Kansai; young artists who later would be the central members of the Gutai group; Shiryu Morita, who influenced not only Japanese but also American painters; a group of radical calligraphers like Yuichi Inoue and Sogen Eguchi, who propelled an avant-garde movement in calligraphy along with Morita; and pioneering sculptors and architects. Besides these artists, other outstanding artists from a wide range of media — such as design, ceramics, and flower arrangement — gathered, argued, and exhibited together in the Genbi Exhibition. Morita and Inoue founded the *Bokujinkai*,

a group of avant-garde calligraphers, in 1952, and they published the journal *Bokubi*, with a readers' column called "alpha" that invited contributions of calligraphy that emphasized creativity over conventional calligraphic characteristics. Young artists who later would participate in the Gutai submitted entries to this juried column; Yoshihara and others selected the entries for publication. The exciting cultural environment in the Kansai region of the 1950s provided the groundwork for the unconventional and innovative ideas of the Gutai.

Jiro Yoshihara was born in 1905 into a prominent family with a cooking-oil business in Osaka. As one of the first generation of Japanese abstract painters, he had already assumed the role of leader in postwar art circles in Kansai. Around this time, Shōzō Shimamoto, Tsuruko Yamazaki, and other young artists gathered around Yoshihara, bringing their works and seeking his criticism of them, and gradually forming a group. These artists then began to recognize each other while participating in various exhibitions, such as the "Genbi Exhibition," the "Avant-Garde Exhibition by Young Artists" in 1954, and the "Ashiya City Exhibition," a radical exhibition open to the public and judged by Yoshihara: they formed the group that would be known as the Gutai. As no manifesto or exhibition marking the founding of the Gutai exists, there are various theories as to the exact time of its founding, but the artists chose the name Gutai Art Association (*Gutai Bijutsu Kyokai*) for the group and began to function as a group in the summer and winter of 1954. The first project they embarked upon was to publish a journal named after the group: *Gutai*, fourteen issues of which were published between 1955 and 1965 as the record of their activities and exhibitions. Captions and resumes were printed in English in the first three issues, which clearly indicated that the journals were meant to appeal to readers in foreign countries. This strategy was also used in Shiryu Morita's *Bokubi*, published with French text. It is very interesting to note that two journals published in the Kansai region at that time consciously sought communication with the radical minds of the world and were sent to artists and critics in other countries. While it is unclear exactly how they came to be in his possession, the second and third issues of *Gutai* were found in Jackson Pollock's

**Saburo Murakami**, *Work Painted by Throwing a Ball*, 1954. Private collection

studio after his death.[4] The second issue featured paintings utilizing chemical reactions and children's paintings, while the third featured the Gutai's first outdoor exhibition (which will be discussed later). Although the third issue also contained Kazuo Shiraga's radical aphorism on action, it only appeared in Japanese, so it is hard to imagine that it had a direct influence on Pollock. Nevertheless, because it was easy to understand the early activities of the Gutai through many plates and the English text and captions, the extent of this journal's influence should not be discounted.

The first issue of *Gutai*, published in January 1955, featured the works of eighteen founding members of the group but, surprisingly, most of them were moderate abstract paintings. However, many of these original members soon left the Gutai, for the teaching of Yoshihara, who urged his young artists to create paintings that no one else had done, was demanding; interestingly, artists who persisted in painting as their medium of expression dropped out of the group one after another.

As if to replace them, the four members of Group Zero (*Zerokai*) — Kazuo Shiraga, Saburo Murakami, Atsuko Tanaka, and Akira Kanayama — joined the Gutai. They had originally belonged to an academic art organization, but as each artist's radical tendencies intensified, they formed a separate group and called it Group Zero. It must be noted that these four individuals had already established their own unique artistic methods prior to joining the Gutai. They mounted an exhibition in the display windows of an Osaka department store in 1954; Shiraga's painting made with his feet, Murakami's work created by throwing a ball covered with paint at the canvas, Kanayama's painting in a far more simplified version of Mondrian's abstraction, and others were shown. They had already made contact with young artists of the Gutai, and they soon dissolved the Group Zero and joined the Gutai at the request of Yoshihara. With their involvement with the group, the Gutai's activity took more radical turns.

This radical tendency was shown in the "Experimental Outdoor Modern Art Exhibition to Challenge the Burning Midsummer Sun," held along the banks of the Ashiya River in July 1955. This epochal outdoor exhibition was sponsored by the local Ashiya City Art Association, where Yoshihara served as a representative; the members of the Gutai formed the nucleus of the exhibition, which presaged the coming of action and object which characterized the group. Kazuo Shiraga, wielding an axe, erected a cone of logs painted red; Saburo Murakami ran over a tarred roofing sheet thrown down, and tore it; Atsuko Tanaka stretched a pink sheet out over the ground; Sadamasa Motonaga, a new member joining

4. Francis V. O'Connor and Eugene Victor Thaw, eds., Jackson Pollock: A Catalogue Raisonne of Paintings, Drawings, and Other Works, vol. 4; 197 (New Haven, Conn.: Yale University Press, 1978).

**123**

the Gutai on this occasion, hung plastic bags of colored water among the pine trees; Tsuruko Yamazaki hung sheets of tin attached to one another; and Michio Yoshihara set out objects made from junk. This innovative exhibition, with its brightly colored works made of strong materials, defying the midsummer sun, was unparalleled at the time. Yozo Ukita's summary of the event, which appeared in the third issue of *Gutai* (published soon afterward), concluded: "At this outdoor exhibition we never tried to conquer nor confront nature. After all, it is heterogeneous. . . . We experimented as to how we can exist in the given pine forest, using all the knowledge we have about form, with enthusiasm, and our bodies."[5]

In October of the same year "The First Gutai Exhibition" was held at the Ohara Kaikan in Tokyo. The decision to mount their first exhibition in Tokyo, like the dissemination of their journal overseas, indicated the Gutai's determination to let the world know about their activities. What took place at that first exhibition was two actions: Saburo Murakami's *Paper Tearing* and Kazuo Shiraga's *Challenging Mud*, both of which have attained near-mythical status today. About a week before the exhibition, seven Gutai artists went to Tokyo to familiarize themselves with the location, work over their ideas, and prepare for the show. On the first day of the exhibition, Murakami thrust his body through packing paper, stretched over frames, and Shiraga, wearing only his shorts, struggled with a ton of clay that he had piled in the courtyard. What must be noted here is that the artists intended their actions to result in the creation of paintings. Murakami displayed his torn canvas in the hall, and Shiraga considered the clay shapes left by his struggle to be his works.[6] The exhibition, which became famous for these two actions, also included quite a few paintings by Jiro Yoshihara and other members. These paintings, which emphasized materiality, were discussed in terms of their similarity to the *art informel* that would develop in Europe later and, as this would suggest, the Gutai — led by painter Jiro Yoshihara — did not have Actions and

5. Yozo Ukita, "Manatsu no taiyo ni idomu yagai modan ato jikken ten" (Experimental Outdoor Modern Art Exhibition to Challenge the Burning Midsummer Sun), Gutai, no. 3 (October 20, 1955): 2.

6. Transcription of my interview with Kazuo Shiraga, July 10, 1985, in Document Gutai 1954-1972 (Ashiya: Ashiya City Museum of Art and History, 1993), 381.

Kazuo Shiraga (left), Hiroshi Yamazaki (front on the floor), Akira Kanayama (right), installation view of the First Gutai Exhibition, 1955

Kazuo Shiraga, *Challenging Mud*, 1955

Objects as a goal at the outset.

These two Actions later would be considered pioneers of Happenings by Allan Kaprow in his major text, *Assemblage, Environments and Happenings*[7]; however, Kaprow's book was published eleven years later (in 1966), and these two Actions preceded Kaprow's first Happening by two years. Many critics who visited the exhibition could find no words to describe the Actions, and it was as much as they could do to regard them as a repetition of Dada. A recollection by a critic clearly shows such bewilderment: "At that time we were bound by the conventional concept of form and we had no perception to accept these works. We were perplexed, as if we were confronting aliens from Mars."[8]

Although the exhibition was ignored by Tokyo's art establishment, *Life* expressed interest in the exhibition and sent their photographers to Japan; "One-Day Outdoor Exhibition" was mounted exclusively for them in some ruins on the banks of the Muko River and at the Yoshihara family's oil manufacturing plant in April 1956. Kazuo Shiraga made another version of his timber and axe piece, and Sadamasa Motonaga hung his colored-water objects. Unfortunately, the *Life* story never appeared but the photographs documenting the exhibition were kept in

the Gutai archive. "The Second Outdoor Exhibition" was held on the banks of the Ashiya River again in July of the same year. Works by Shimamoto and Murakami which enticed spectators to participate, grotesque objects by Shiraga, and conceptual pieces by Kanayama were displayed among the pine trees, while Atsuko Tanaka's huge figure decorated with light bulbs, *Stage Costume*, illuminated the site at night. The works had become larger than the ones shown at their previous outdoor exhibition; a typical example was a huge painting, ten meters by ten meters, by Shōzō Shimamoto, who spread a vinyl sheet between pine trees and shot paint at it with a toy cannon.

With this exhibition, it was clear that interest in painting using Action had intensified among the Gutai artists. Shimamoto recalls that Yoshihara considered action painting to be the way in which art would move beyond Mondrian, whose work was regarded as the acme of abstraction at the time. That is, Yoshihara saw the possibility of bringing the element of time into painting, something missing from Mondrian's; he discovered such a possibility in the calligraphy of a Zen priest, Nantembo, which he saw at a temple in Nishinomiya.[9] Shiryu Morita also became interested in Nantembo's calligraphy, which

7. Allan Kaprow, Assemblage, Environments and Happenings (New York: Harry N. Abrams, 1966).

8. Ichiro Haryu, "Sengo Bijutsu Seisuishi" (Up and Down of Postwar Art), Tokyo Shoseki (1979): 98.

9. Transcription of my interview with Shōzō Shimamoto, June 15, 1985, in Document Gutai 1954-72.

**Atsuko Tanaka**, *Electric Dress* and its drawings, 1956.

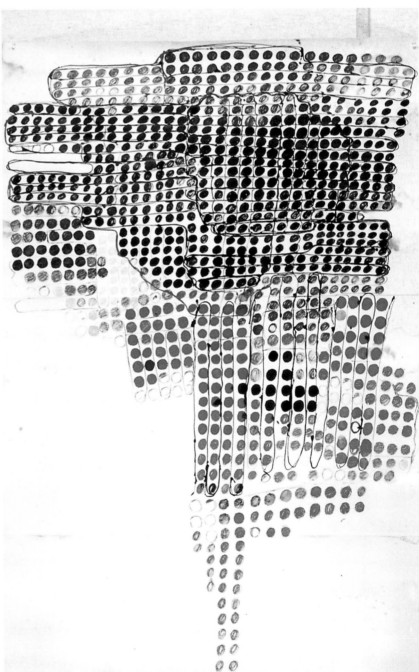

**Atsuko Tanaka**, Drawing for *Electric Dress*, 1956.
Hyogo Prefectural Museum of Modern Art, Kobe

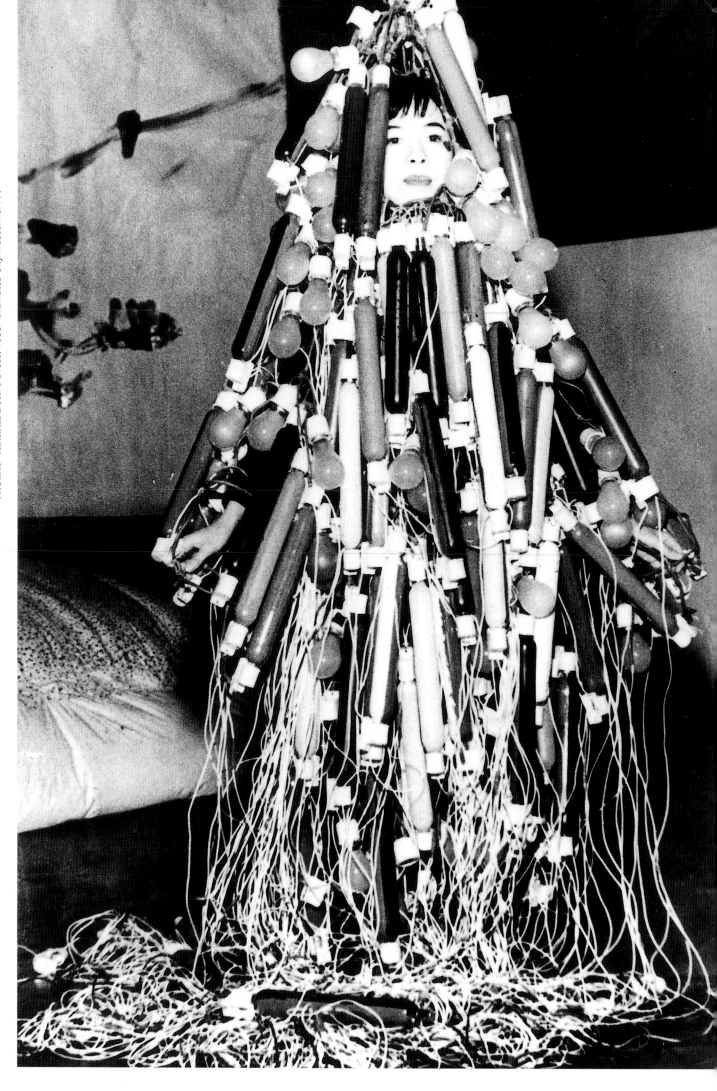

Atsuko Tanaka. *Electric Dress*, 1956. Takamatsu City Museum of Art

**Shōzō Shimamoto**, the artist making
a painting by throwing bottles of paint, 1956

**Kazuo Shiraga**, the artist painting with his feet, 1956

indicated that avant-garde calligraphy and abstract painting had something unexpected in common.[10] When Yoshihara later created paintings with a monochrome Zen-like circle, critical interpretations of this work strained to make comparisons between his art and the practice of Zen; in fact, all the Gutai artists were discussed in relation to that tradition. But the possibilities Yoshihara saw in calligraphy were in relation to form, not philosophy.

The seed of Action Painting that had germinated in the outdoor exhibitions fully bloomed at "The Second Gutai Exhibition" held once again at the Ohara Kaikan in Tokyo in October. The Actions by Shiraga and Murakami at "The First Gutai Exhibition" the previous year had left the relationship to painting still vague, but many of the Actions at the second exhibition made the relationship very clear: Actions led to the creation of painting. Suddenly, "painting as an arena" was referred to by Harold Rosenberg, "field painting" by Clement Greenberg.

Actions were performed for the press at a specified time, showing clearly the importance placed by the Gutai on the process of creation as well as the works themselves, but they were accused of simply seeking publicity. On the roof, Shimamoto created his work by throwing bottles of paint onto paper spread on the floor. Toshio Yoshida poured paint from a watering can high above the canvas. Murakami broke through many frames of Kraft paper, and Shiraga painted with his feet in paint spread over the surface of the paper. As documented by photographs taken at the time, Shiraga's huge work measured over two meters high and six meters long; except for Shimamoto's painting created by a paint-filled cannon at "The Second Outdoor Exhibition," paintings on such a large scale did not exist at the time.

As in the previous indoor exhibition, there were many objects and paintings on display, many of them reworkings or expansions of ideas first examined in the outdoor exhibitions. Atsuko Tanaka's *Electric Dress*, an elaborate costume made of numer-

10. The detailed reference to Nantembo and a record of the discussion about him between Shiryu Morita and Yoshihara were published in the following issue of Bokubi, edited by Morita. Special Issue, "Calligraphy of Nantembo," Bokubi, no. 14 (July 1952).

**Saburo Murakami**, *Many Screens of Paper*, 1956

Sadamasa Motonaga. *Water*, 1956

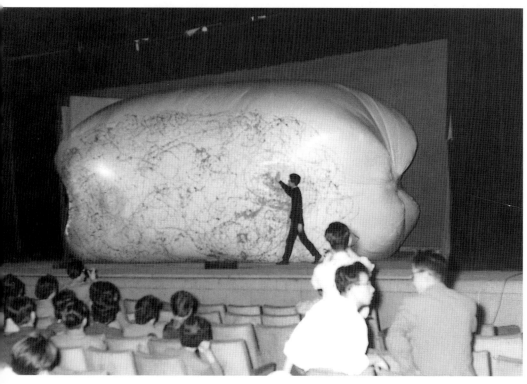

**Akira Kanayama**, performing *The Giant Balloon*, 1957

ous bulbs, filled the hall with garish light, as her *Stage Costume* had lit up the Ashiya River site. Kanayama and Motonaga created wonderful pieces using a balloon and tubes filled with colored water, similar to their work in previous outdoor exhibitions. The use of the elements — electricity, air, water — was also conceived at the outdoor exhibitions. Furthermore, Tsuruko Yamazaki's painting using tin and Yasuo Sumi's Action Painting made reference to their pieces created outside, revealing the significance of the experiments done in the outdoors in the early years of the Gutai.

In May of the following year (1957), the Gutai held their most radical exhibition yet: the "Gutai On-Stage Art Exhibition," in Osaka and Tokyo. The outdoor exhibitions played an important role in the conception of this event as well, as Yoshihara explained in *Gutai*: "It was an adventure to go out to a vast outdoor from a conventional idea of indoor space as the only venue to exhibit works, but such valuable experience gained through the challenging conditions seemed to have heightened the pioneering spirit of the artists. And since then, we began to think about the theatrical stage as the next project."[11] The "on-stage" exhibition consisted of two parts, with twelve scenes quite unlike an ordinary stage event. Besides using familiar objects such as an inflated balloon and an electric dress, the Actions — such as

*Sambaso-Ultra Modern* in which Shiraga, dressed in red, performed as a bogeyman, and *Destruction of Objects* by Shimamoto, in which he broke down objects and drawings by automatism — were performed without relevance to each other. Also shown were experimental works using images and sounds, which can be regarded as precursors of the intermedia art that would flourish in America in the 1960s.

It was also in 1957 that the Gutai was recognized internationally for the first time. Michel Tapié, the French critic who was the leader of an art movement, *art informel* or *un art autre*, became aware of the Gutai from their journals, given to him by the Japanese painter Hisao Domoto, who was studying in Paris. Tapié became deeply interested in the group's activities. As Gutai primarily featured the group's outdoor exhibitions and the Actions, it is hard to assume that Tapié was initially interested in the Gutai paintings. But when he arrived in Osaka in September 1957 with Georges Mathieu and saw paintings by Gutai members for the first time, he was "amazed at the high standard of their works."[12] He further stated: "I don't think I can find anywhere in the world today another group that encompasses such artists with powerful individuality in one area while keeping them as a group. I came to Japan with an idea to suggest something and realize it but I have found out that here it was already developed in per-

11. Jiro Yoshihara, "Butai wo shiyosuru Gutai bijutsu nitsuite" (On Gutai Bijutsu on Stage), Gutai, no. 7 (July 15, 1957): n.p.

12. Michel Tapié, "Dai ikkai nihon ryoko no seishin-teki kessai sho" (A Mental Account from the First Trip to Japan), Bijutsu Techo (October 1957): 101.

Georges Mathieu, public painting action, Japan, 1957

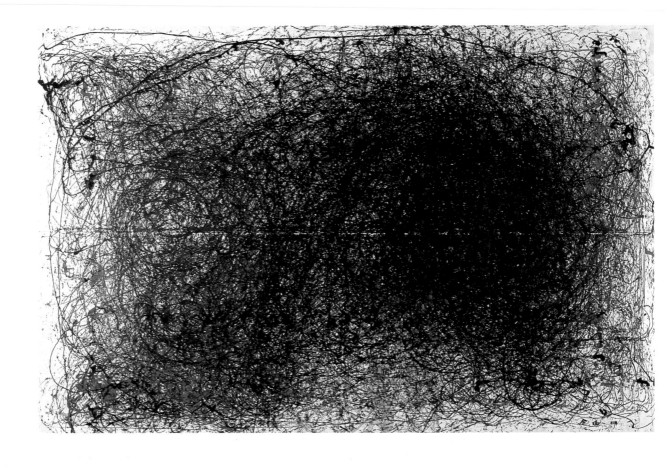

**Akira Kanayama**, *Work*, 1957. Hyogo Prefectural Museum of Modern Art, Kobe

**Shōzō Shimamoto**, *Work*, 1952. Hyogo Prefectural Museum of Modern Art, Kobe. Yamamura Collection

fection."[13]

It was probably Tapié's strategy to ally himself with the Gutai in order to emphasize the international extent of *art informel*, but for the Gutai members, who had been ignored and isolated in Japan, Tapié's support was a welcome encouragement. After that, the Gutai actively participated in international exhibitions organized by Tapié. When "International Art of a New Era: Informel and Gutai" (with paintings by Lucio Fontana, Antoni Tapies, Pollock, Franz Kline, and others) traveled to Japan in 1958, it was possible to compare the results of Gutai's Action Painting with works by these now internationally acclaimed artists. The Gutai also had an exhibition at the Martha Jackson Gallery in New York the same year, but the paintings were criticized as being secondhand versions of Abstract Expressionism.[14]

Contact with Tapié brought changes to the activities of the Gutai itself. Tapié was a collector and an art dealer as well as a critic, and he bought many Gutai works and sent them to Europe. It is important to reiterate that the Gutai had placed the creation of painting at the core of their activity from the beginning, and — although several Happenings were organized after Tapié's involvement — in the 1960s the Gutai gradually began to emphasize the Gutai Art Exhibitions rather than the outdoor and on-stage exhibitions. They concentrated on painting instead of Actions, complying with Tapié's priorities. The establishment of the Gutai Pinakotheca at Nakanoshima, Osaka, in 1962 provided a permanent place for the Gutai artists to show their works, and this also accelerated the domination of painting in their practice.

The Gutai ended their existence as a group in 1972 with the sudden death of their leader, Jiro Yoshihara. The first five years of the Gutai's existence, from 1954 to 1958, are the most important in terms of their influence on Action in Japan, but this does not mean that Action-oriented art waned, as epoch-making Happenings were performed one after

13. Tapié, "Gutai-ha raisan" (Homage to the Gutai), Gutai, no. 8 (September 29, 1957): n.p.

14. Dore Ashton, "Japan's Gutai Group," New York Times, 25 September 1958.

**Akira Kanayama**, *Work*, 1958. Museum of Contemporary Art, Tokyo. Gift of the artist

**Shōzō Shimamoto**, *Work (Sakuhin)*, 1961. Hyogo Prefectural Museum of Modern Art, Kobe

**Kazuo Shiraga**, *Work BB21*, 1956. Galerie Georg Nothelfer, Berlin

**Kazuo Shiraga**, *Work II*, 1958. Hyogo Prefectural Museum of Modern Art, Kobe

**Masanobu Yoshimura**, *Mr. Sadada's Drawing Room*, 1961

another in turbulent Tokyo in the 1960s. As the Gutai was guided by Yoshihara, who disliked to put narrative or social context into the works, the Gutai Actions were sometimes discussed in relation to Dada, but they never contained any social criticism or political implications: they were performed purely to make aesthetic statements. However, for those artists active in Tokyo in the 1960s, Action was not an aesthetic concern, but rather a medium of expression inextricably linked to society.

The "Japan Indépendant Exhibition" was a nonjuried exhibition, open to all artists who wished to participate; it was held annually from 1949 until 1963 at the Tokyo Metropolitan Art Museum, a total of fifteen times. In order to distinguish it from another exhibition with the same name organized by the Japan Art Society (*Nihon Bijutsu-kai*), it is usually referred to as the "Yomiuri Indépendant Exhibition" (*Yomiuri andepandan-ten*), after the name of its sponsor, the *Yomiuri* newspaper. This type of nonjuried show was quite rare in Japan at the time, but it can be seen as a glimpse of democracy brought about by Japan's defeat in the Second World War, which extended even to the Japanese art establishment. The first exhibition had more than one thousand entries, and many of Japan's prominent artists participated; there was even a message from Henri Matisse in the *Yomiuri* newspaper. At the third exhibition in 1951, in a special section introducing new works from abroad, two drip paintings by Jackson Pollock were hung, one of the earliest showings of his work in Japan. Upon seeing Pollock's paintings in Osaka, Jiro Yoshihara praised them highly at a time when the importance of Pollock's paintings was not yet fully recognized in Europe and America.[15] During the late 1950s, older, more well-known artists ceased to participate in the annual exhibition (as if a tide were ebbing as more space to exhibit was provided) and, instead, younger newcomers with their outrageous works dominated the scene. Beginning with the tenth show in 1958, a sense of chaotic euphoria had taken hold, and the most radical section of the exhibition became a show-

case for Japanese avant-garde art of the early sixties.

In 1960, a movement against the renewal of the Japan-U.S. Security Treaty (Anpo) was gaining overwhelming momentum, and over one-hundred thousand demonstrators filled the area around the Diet building in Tokyo day after day. Confrontation between the demonstrators and riot police culminated in tragedy on the evening of June 15 when a student demonstator, Michiko Kamba, was killed. Shusaku Arakawa, Ushio Shinohara, Masunobu Yoshimura, and other artists happened to be there at the Diet that night: the political and social upheaval of the time provides an insight into why these artists sought artistic expression and involvement with real life.

For those artists who sought contact with reality, the social realist style, which was prevalent at the time, seemed too indirect and tepid, so they began to incorporate actual objects into their paintings. Initially, the works resulting from such endeavors were likened to *art informel*, but the critic Shuzo Takiguchi made the following accurate observation: "They are not to be linked forcibly with the *informel* paintings, rather their pent-up desire for expression in search of direction is directly linked with action, *art informel* is only providing an opportunity."[16] As will be discussed later, the Yomiuri Indépendant artists did not need even the framework of painting itself; this differed from the Gutai, whose expression was eventually incorporated into paintings.

The Yomiuri Indépendant artists initially added mundane objects found in real life (such as scrubbing brushes and rubber tubes) to their paintings, but they became more radical and turned from painting to relief and *objet*. Their methods — utilizing everyday objects and destroying form — had much in common with the works of Allan Kaprow and Robert Rauschenberg, who tried to eliminate the distinction between everyday life and art. Especially notable is this artist group's use of assemblage: in Masunobu Yoshimura's *Mr. Sadada's Drawing Room* (1961), numerous empty liquor bottles were used to con-

15. Jiro Yoshihara, "Chusho kaiga no bi" (The Beauty of Abstract Paintings), Asahi Newspaper, 17 April 1951.

16. Shuzo Takiguchi, "Hyogen no kiki: dai 9 kai Yomiuri andepandan ten" (The Crisis of Expression: The 9th Yomiuri Indépendant Exhibition) (1957), reprinted in Ten (Points) (Tokyo: Misuzu Shobo, 1963), 299-300.

(right & left)
**Natsuyuki Nakanishi,** *Clothespins Assert Churning Action,*
1963

struct strange furniture; a 1962 work by Yutaka Matsuzawa was a fetish-like *objet* made by piling up discarded debris. These discrete objects gave way gradually to works that spread out into space. In the last years of the Yomiuri Indépendant exhibitions, such works as Natsuyuki Nakanishi's *Clothespins Assert Churning Action* (1963), a multitude of clothespins covering the entire wall, and Tetsumi Kudo's *Distribution Chart of Impotence and the Emergence of Protective Dome in Its Saturated Part* (1962), a room full of penis-like rolls dangling from the ceiling, were shown. This evolution in size and scope is consistent with artistic developments analyzed by Kaprow in his book, *Assemblage, Environments and Happenings*, and it was inevitable that these works would further evolve into Action.

The Yomiuri Indépendant exhibitions began presenting bizarre spectacles that incorporated action and obscenity, knives and noise, and fresh food into works which, of course, clashed with the institution of the museum and led to restrictions imposed by

the museum; the infamous 1962 "Standards for the Exhibits at the Tokyo Metropolitan Art Museum" prohibited the use of decomposed matter, knives, sand, etc., thus dictating the artists' choice of materials. The exhibition's organizer, the *Yomiuri* newspaper, forcibly ended the program in its fifteenth year, in 1963.

Many groups for whom Action and Happenings were their main mediums of expression coalesced around the Yomiuri Indépendant. The group *Kyushu-ha* (Kyushi School), formed in Fukuoka on the southernmost island of Kyushu in 1957, from the very beginning displayed their outrageous activities in pavement exhibitions. Members of the Kyushu School participated in the Yomiuri Indépendant exhibitions and from 1958 had shows at galleries in Ginza, Tokyo. In 1962 they organized a Happening, *Great Assembly of Heroes*, inviting Takehisa Kosugi, Takumi Kazekura, and other artists from Tokyo to the Momoji Beach in the suburb of Fukuoka. Their actions — setting fire to a huge object, crucifying a chicken, and digging a gigantic hole on the beach — were filled with a strong sense of ritual and destruction.[17]

Those artists who formed the nucleus of the Yomiuri Indépendant exhibitions, like Masunobu Yoshimura, Ushio Shinohara, Shusaku Arakawa, and Takumi Kazekura, formed the group Neo-Dadaism Organizers in April 1960 and held three exhibitions within the same year. At their first exhibition at the Ginza Gallery in April, they filled the gallery with debris, smashed a stove and a wash basin in the gallery, and went out onto the street in their bizarre costumes. As the demonstration against the renewal of the security treaty (Anpo) reached its peak and demonstrators and riot police fought day and night, the artists performed reckless Happenings; despite the fatality resulting from the clash on June 15 and despite violent opposition, the treaty was automatically ratified four days later.

In response to this political situation, the *Anpo Episode Event* was held at Yoshimura's studio the night before. Filled with hopeless frenzy, the half-naked artists drank heavily and destroyed nearby objects one after another; their actions were so outrageous and destructive that their works do not exist today except in photographs recording the events. On the occasion of their third exhibition at the Hibiya Gallery, the artists took to the streets. Yoshimura, who was bandaged like a mummy in leaflets announcing the exhibition, and Kinpei Masuzawa, whose back was bound by a string of light bulbs, paraded through the Ginza area, while in Hibiya Park, half-dressed Shinohara and others staged an Action where they savagely smashed steel plates. Perhaps lacking determination, the Neo-Dadaism Organizers was short-lived, and with this exhibition they ended their activity as a group. In 1961, Arakawa went to New York, and Tetsumi Kudo, active member of this group, went to Paris; other central figures, like Shinohara and Yoshimura, left for New York one after the other. These artists have since cultivated their own forms of expression in their own milieus.

The Zero Dimension (*Zerojigen*), founded by

17. See the following publication on the Kyushu-ha: Raiji Kuroda, "Isetsu: Bijutsu undou to shiteno Kyushu-ha" (A Different Perspective: Kyushu-ha as an Art Movement), in Group Kyushu-ha (Fukuoka: Fukuoka Art Museum, 1988).

**Tetsumi Kudo**, *Philosophy of Impotence*, 1962

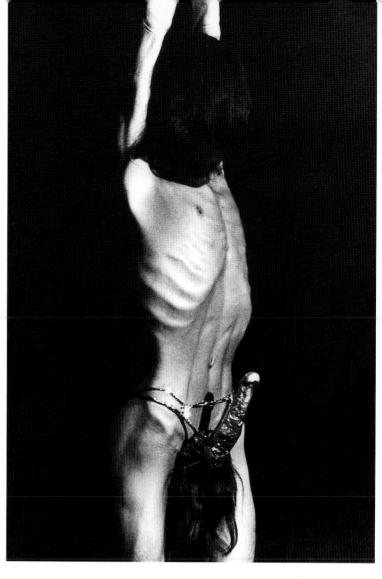

Yoshihiro Kato and active around Nagoya, exhibited at the last Yomiuri Indépendant in 1963; the members of the group performed a monotonous Happening in which they lay on cloth spread over the floor of the gallery space for nearly an entire day. They also regularly presented Happenings called *Ritual*, which took place on downtown streets. Their Happenings, often performed completely naked or sometimes in gas masks, often caused the police to intervene; eventually they focused their attention on the Japan World Exposition held in Osaka in 1970 when they did a series of "activities to crush the Expo." In addition, the Group Ongaku (Music), founded by Takehisa Kosugi, Yasunao Tone, and others became active around 1960 with a series of improvised concerts, but their Happenings at the Yomiuri Indépendant caused them to be ejected by the museum.

Although he had no direct contact with the Yomiuri Indépendant, during the same period Tatsumi Hijikata organized the *Ankoku Butoh-ha*, or the "Dance of Utter Darkness," which presented dark dance works, using native Japanese rituals and sexual metaphors. Natsuyuki Nakanishi and other artists affiliated with the Yomiuri Indépendant often helped out with stage sets, while the novelist Yukio Mishima wrote for the playbill: "The relationship between man and the object is full of tragic contradictions; the man's movements futilely lift himself in the air to reach the object or he moves completely controlled by the object." Hijikata performed at midnight doing a Happening stark naked at a Ginza intersection

around 1961. About the same time, Shuji Terayama suggested that there be stages on the street, and his plays involved the spectators. But it was the Hi Red Center that most strategically used street performance as a medium of expression.

The Hi Red Center, founded by Jiro Takamatsu, Genpei Akasegawa, and Natsuyuki Nakanishi in 1962, almost coincided with the cessation of the Yomiuri Indépendant exhibitions. These artists were already known for their series of action-inducing *objets*. Takamatsu's work of a string extending outside from the exhibition space, Nakanishi's assemblage of clothespins, and the wrapped works of Akasegawa (who was a member of the Neo-Dadaism Organizers), were exhibited at the Yomiuri Indépendant. Even before they began to start their activities as a group in earnest, Akasegawa, with Tatsumi Hijikata and Takumi Kazekura, staged an event in August 1962 in which they ate food continuously in front of spectators at a community center in Kunitachi, and in October of the same year Nakanishi and Takamatsu, carrying *objets* they had made, boarded the Yamanote Line in Tokyo and did Happenings on a train and the station platform.

The Hi Red Center is an English acronym for the first character of each artist's name: Takamatsu, Akasegawa, and Nakanishi; there were a few other members of the group, which emphasized its members' anonymity. They performed a Happening, *Miniature Restaurant*, in which they served toy plates filled with food to the visitors at the last Yomiuri

(center & below) **Jiro Takamatsu**, *The String of 1000 Meters*, 1963

**Hi Red Center**, *The 6th Mixer Plan*, 1963

**Hi Red Center**, *Movement to Promote the Cleanup of the Metropolitan Area (Be Clean!)*, 1964

Indépendant in 1963. They called these Actions that incorporated everyday life "agitation," and in May of the same year these three artists had a three-man show called "Mixer Plan" at the Shinjuku Daiichi Gallery and Naika Gallery in Tokyo. In January 1964 they rented a room at the Imperial Hotel and made life-sized blueprints of visitors; they constructed a personal shelter in *Shelter Plan*; and in June they presented *Grand Panorama*, in which they closed the gallery on the first day of the exhibition and opened it on the last day of the show. In *Dropping Event* in October they threw down baggage and bedsheets from the rooftop of a building. Six members, including Nakanishi, went out to Ginza, Tokyo, during the Tokyo Summer Olympic Games and wiped pavement and manhole covers with rags in *Movement to Promote the Cleanup of the Metropolitan Area (Be Clean!)*. This event, in which they cleaned up a streetcorner like deranged people, was, in the end, their last activity as a group (this event was later reenacted in New York by the Fluxus artists).[18]

The Hi Red Center Happenings were an art of pure and free action that did not materialize into form. Their group's provocative actions out on the streets were immediately filled with political implications in a time still troubled by antiwar demonstrations and student protests. They cleverly hid such implications and tried to imbue their actions with pure art, but as long as they questioned the boundary between life and art, a clash with the established system was inevitable. Genpei Akasegawa was indicted in 1966 on charges of counterfeiting currency and securities when a series of his works — exhibited at his one-

person show, the Yomiuri Indépendant, and "Mixer Plan" in 1963 — brought an accusation that he had counterfeited a thousand-yen note. Many artists and critics joined in as witnesses for the defense during the four-year judicial battle called the "One Thousand Yen Note Trial," notable in Japan as a rare case of art being arbitrated in court. The trial concluded in May 1970, and Akasegawa was found guilty. It is ironic that when almost no record of the art of Action in the sixties is extant today (except in photographs), the activity of the Hi Red Center was minutely recorded in public materials in the vast amount of evidence and testimony provided during the trial.

The Action formed the nucleus of postwar Japanese art, although some alienation occurred in subsequent art. For instance, while Pollock's gesture has been repeated and interpreted by numerous American artists who followed him, Action Painting by the Gutai was not referred to in any way by the artists who followed them, not even in a negative sense. The direct actions by the Hi Red Center did not give distinctive influence to the art of the next generation either, and they were discussed as events that were performed only once. I believe such alienation derived from the innate nature of the actions, and so it is important to consider the special qualities of the actions performed by Gutai and Yomiuri Indépendant artists, and the theoretical background.

Although Jiro Yoshihara, who was the leader of the Gutai, disliked creating works based upon theory, the Gutai was not a group without a theory. Shiraga and Shimamoto wrote radical theories on Action for Gutai, and Yoshihara himself contributed his famous *The Gutai Art Manifesto* to the December 1956 issue of the art magazine, *Geijutsu Shincho*. In the manifesto Yoshihara expressed the Gutai's theory in a most dignified manner:

> With our present awareness, the arts we have known up to now appear to us in general to be fakes fitted out with an affectation. . . . Gutai Art does not change the material. Gutai Art imparts life to the material. Gutai Art does not

18. This Happening was reenacted in June 1966 by George Maciunas and others at the Grand Army Plaza (58th and Fifth Avenues) in New York. Almost at the same time, the Shelter Plan was also reenacted with a new title, Hotel Event at the Waldorf Astoria Hotel. The photographs are published in: Thomas Kellein, FLUXUS (London: Thames and Hudson, 1995), 61-65.

**Akira Kanayama**, *Biological Balloon*, 1958

distort the material. In Gutai Art, the human spirit and the material shake hands while confronting each other. The material never compromises itself with the spirit. The spirit never dominates the material. When the material remains intact and exposes its characteristics, it starts telling a story, and even cries out. To make the fullest use of the material is to make use of the spirit. By enhancing the spirit, the material is brought to the height of the spirit.[19]

Easily understood in reference to the outdoor exhibitions, the "material" referred to here includes non-art mediums such as mud and water, vinyl and fabric. The use of such elementary materials may form a part of the Bataille-like "base materialism" that Rosalind E. Krauss and others take note of today,[20] and its relationship to *arte povera*, developed subsequently in Italy, should also be considered.[21]

The materials the artists chose to preserve their actions were not only conventional materials like paint and bronze, but also materials with a strong presence and hard-to-handle qualities, such as mud and timber, plaster and metal; the places where they wanted to imprint their actions were vast spaces (outdoors and stages), or in a huge painting that could be called a field. Their action was often physically violent: after finishing his Action *Paper Tearing*, Murakami was groggy from a concussion, and Shiraga's struggle with mud half-naked left his body bruised and cut.

It was Shiraga who put the meaning of such Action clearly into writing. Several of his contriubutions to Gutai complemented the theory of the material stated in *The Gutai Art Manifesto*. Shiraga stated: "My mind was filled with the thought of reducing art, which is an expression of man's spirit, to the condition of the body,"[22] and he called a such condi-

tion of the body "quality." "The quality of which I speak here is not the fragile one which we have called character thus far and which did not develop *a posteriori*, but the unified condition of the spirit and the body which is acquired through living and is founded on the body we are born with."[23] Shiraga recalls that what motivated him to create his work of red-painted logs scarred with an axe (shown at the outdoor exhibition), was the thought that he might attain something if he drove his body hard enough to make himself dizzy.[24]

The concept of reducing expression to the body and the material was shared, to a certain degree, among the radical-minded artists and critics of the time. For example, in the Manifesto, Yoshihara stated that he believed the paintings of Pollock and Georges Mathieu wrestled with materials. Written before the activity of Gutai, Jean Dubuffet's statement brings to mind a part of *The Gutai Art Manifesto*: "Art is born from the material and the tool. It must leave the trace of the tool and its struggle with the material. Man must speak. But so should the tool, and so should the material as well."[25] And Asgar Jorn — a central figure in the COBRA group, which developed a unique expressionist movement in Scandinavia — said as if in answer Shiraga's words: "One cannot express oneself in a purely psychic manner. Expression is a physical act which materializes thought. Therefore, psychic automatism is linked to physical automatism."[26]

As Jorn's words suggest, the Gutai's action can be regarded on the historical continuum as a radical form of automatism, and the Gutai artists were well aware of this point. Discussing Action Paintings by Shiraga and Shimamoto in the manifesto, Yoshihara noted: "When the quality of the individual was united with the chosen materials in the melting pot of automatism, we were overwhelmed by the

19. Jiro Yoshihara, "The Gutai Art Manifesto," Geijutsu Shincho, December 1956.

20. For more about the increasing interest in Bataille as his ideas relate to art, see the following exhibition catalogue, which included Shiraga's work: Yve-Alain Bois and Rosalind Krauss, L'informe mode d'emploi (Paris: Centre Georges Pompidou, 1996).

21. Barbara Bertozzi, "On the Origin of the New Avant-Gardes: The Japanese Association of Artists Gutai," in Gutai: Japanese Avant-Garde 1954-1965 (Darmstadt: Mathildenhohe Darmstadt, 1991).

22. Kazuo Shiraga, "Shishitsu ni tsuite" (On Quality), Gutai, no. 5 (October 1, 1956): n.p.

23. Ibid.

24. Transcription of my interview with Kazuo Shiraga, July 10, 1985, in Document Gutai 1954-1972, 380.

25. Jean Dubuffet, Prospectus aux Amateurs de Tout Genre (Paris: Edition Gallimard, 1946), 56.

26. Asgar Jorn, "Discours aux Pingouins," COBRA 1 (1949): 8.

**Kazuo Shiraga**, *Cho Gendai Sanbansou*, 1957

**Shōzō Shimamoto**, *Painting with Cannon*, 1956

shape of space still unknown to us, never seen or experienced before." Here was the revolution of pictorial space brought about by the innovation of automatism, with Shiraga's view on the "quality" of an individual as a premise. Automatism was advocated by the surrealists, who were interested in the associative characteristics of the images created by frottage and decalcomania. As Max Ernst, discussing the effect of frottage on his state of mind, explained:

> I put a few papers on the floor at random in order to enhance my ability to meditate and hallucinate. I traced over them with graphite and created a series of drawings. While I was looking at the dark parts or soft and shadowy parts of these drawings, I was surprised that my ability to visualize was suddenly enhanced, and various contradicting images, with a persistence and swiftness peculiar to the memory of an affair, overlapped each other and appeared in succession with hallucinations.[27]

In contrast, the automatism utilized by the Gutai placed importance on the temporal process of creation rather than on the created images. The traces of splashed paint and paint crushed by feet are, literally, the evidence of a violent struggle between the body and the material; they have nothing to do with hallucination or association. Automatism, thus far, has been divided into physical automatism and mechanical automatism. But the Gutai's automatism, which placed importance on the creative process, should be considered durational automatism to distinguish it from Ernst's associative automatism.[28] This very durational automatism is the

characteristic shared by Action Paintings of the time, and it is what most contributed to their qualitative difference. Pollock's paintings clearly have an awareness of durational automatism, but Georges Mathieu's works, which similarly used violent action in their creation, are not freed from the associative automatism of surrealism, in the end realizing the mystified images that Mathieu himself and Michel Tapié advocated. Although the Gutai shared affinities with *art informel*, the essence of their action is linked to the time process of painting a picture, that is, durational automatism. Yoshihara's interest in Nantembo's calligraphy can be considered in this regard, and both Shimamoto's paintings, created in an instant by exploding bottles of paint, and Motonaga's poured paintings in which images are formed over long hours, are concerned with the issue of the temporal process of creating a painting: they indicate a new phase of automatism.

An interest in the temporal and physical aspects of automatism was shared by many artists who used Action as their medium of expression: however, once it is taken to an extreme, the expression no longer needs to take the form of paintings or three-dimensional objects. The Gutai's Action was unique in this regard as well, for it must be remembered that despite their radical early action, the Gutai's Action was directed, in the end, toward painting. For instance, the two Actions staged at the "First Gutai Art Exhibition," *Challenging Mud* and *Paper Tearing*, were conceived as a way to create paintings. Shiraga said of his log piece that he sought to create an endless painting of white scars left by an axe on the inside of the red logs.[29] As for the works performed on stage, an extraordinary method of expression, some were conceived as live performances of painting by automatism and most had quite an effect on painting. As Murakami commented on the on-stage exhibition: "In the past, time itself has never been involved in the spatial aspect of painting. The desire for discovery among the Gutai

27. Max Ernst, Au-dela de la peinture (Paris: Cahiers d'Art, 1937).

28. I developed the idea of contrasting concepts of duration and association from the linguistic study of Ferdinand Saussure. He applies the words "syntag-

matique" for the former and "associatif" for the latter and considers them the two types of linguistic activity; similar views can be found in the following publications: Roman Jakobson, "Deux aspects du langage et deux types d'aphasie," in Essais de linguistique generale (Paris: Edition de

Minuit, 1963); and Roland Barthes, "L'imagination du signe," in Essais critiques (Paris: Edition du Seuil, 1964).

29. Transcription of my interview with Kazuo Shiraga, July 10, 1985 in Document Gutai 1954-1972, 380.

members demanded the use of both spatial and temporal elements in order to communicate our aesthetic inspiration completely. We discarded the frame, jumped out of the wall, moved from static time to live time, tried out a new painting."[30] Although the work was created in an extraordinary way, the Gutai's emphasis on the relationship of Action and painting was one of the essential qualities of the Gutai's art. In fact, it was quite rare for the Gutai's Actions to stand on their own in and of themselves.

As for objects, the Gutai members often reversed the process: the materials Tsuruko Yamazaki used for her works at the outdoor exhibition were incorporated into her paintings, and Atsuko Tanaka's magnificent object, an electric cloth, was transformed into a huge illuminated painting when it was dismantled and mounted onto the canvas, and it was transformed again with a series of circles and lines created by its wiring plan. While Yoshihara always supported artistic expressions by young artists which were hard to define, it is not surprising that he — who had belonged to traditional art groups and had established his career as a painter — saw painting as the final goal and considered other media to be preliminary processes. After 1958, when the Gutai artists realized the significance of their own paintings after their contact with Tapié, Yoshihara seemed to have urged them to create new painting by expanding upon their experiments with Action thus far. As a result, the Gutai paintings attracted international attention around 1960, but there was no critic at the time who could discuss these paintings.

For Allan Kaprow, Jackson Pollock's paintings created the possibility of dismantling the form of painting; he aspired to expand that possibility through the practice of Happenings.[31] Preceding Kaprow,

30. Saburo Murakami, "Gutai bijutsu nitsuite" (On Gutai, Art), Gutai, no. 7 (July 15, 1957): n.p.

31. Allan Kaprow, "The Legacy of Jackson Pollock," Art News 57, no. 6 (October 1958): 56.

32. Harold Rosenberg, "American Action Painters," Art News 51, no.8 (December 1952):56. The similarities between the writings of Shiraga and Rosenberg are pointed out in detail in the following text: Akira Tatehata,

"Seiseisuru taburo — Gutai bijutsu kyokai no 1950 nendai (Generating Painting: The Gutai in the 1950s)," in Action and Emotion — Paintings in the 1950s (Suita, Japan: The National Museum of Art, Osaka, 1985).

Harold Rosenberg introduced the concept of action painting, placing more importance on the process than the work, on action rather than painting.[32] On the other hand, the Gutai in the mid-1950s radicalized their Action to a degree unparalleled in the world and, at the same time, they continued to constantly reduce Action to painting. This was a fundamental difference between Gutai's Action and Happenings by Kaprow and others whose goal was to eliminate the boundary between life and art. As a result of their reduction of Action to form, the Gutai left many outstanding objects, which was exceptional for a group that worked in Action. This is in clear contrast not only to Happenings in Europe and America but also to Action by the groups that emerged from and were associated with the Yomiuri Indépendant exhibitions.

It becomes clear when examining the Action instigated in Tokyo in the 1960s that many were futile efforts, manifestations of aggressive and destructive impulses; as a result, it was rare for any works with form to be created. Georges Mathieu, who came to Japan with Michel Tapié in 1957, had a great influence on young artists as he demonstrated the process of creating his paintings in public, in Osaka and Tokyo. For instance, at his first one-person show in 1958, Ushio Shinohara, who was inspired by Mathieu's *Action Painting*, performed his own Action in which he wielded a brush and a knife on a canvas,

with a jazz band playing in the background, and left the canvas in shreds. Around 1960 Shinohara conceived the idea of boxing/painting by publicly punching with boxing gloves covered in *sumi*, creating in an instant a large pictorial surface. His Action, which can be interpreted as a parody of Mathieu and Pollock, differed decisively from their work as the painting itself was destroyed in the end.

During his visit to Japan, Tapié met not only the Gutai members but also other young artists in Tokyo. One of them was Tomio Miki, who, along with Shinohara, caught the attention of Tapié, and he often destroyed his works during the performance of his Action.[33] Shinohara wrote: "Our Action, which did not allow an incomplete fixed painting, was not related to the so-called Action Painting by Pollock. It surpassed Abstract Expressionism which gained tremendous but temporary popularity at publicly subscribed exhibitions and ran violently through Happenings which were metaphysical Action."[34]

We can see from the above comment that the Yomiuri Indépendant exhibitions artists did not intend to leave actual works, and the objects associated with these Actions bore the stamp of ruthless destruction. A sense of confrontation between the artist and the object that receives his action is quite easily associated with the Gutai as well as the Yomiuri Indépendant artists: a half-naked Yoshimura smash-

33. Ushio Shinohara, "Zenei no michi 5 (The Avant-Garde Road 5)," Bijutsu Techo (June 1966): 61.

34. Ibid.

**149**

ing a tin plate covered with sulfuric acid, Shiraga's Action of axing logs, or Shimamoto's automatism Action for the on-stage exhibition, certainly can be considered confrontational. However, while the Gutai artists tried to enhance the aesthetic quality of objects created by Action, younger Tokyo artists discarded what they created, without reluctance, once they had finished their Action; the waste materials piled up high beside Shinohara's atelier in those days amply illustrated this.

Except for a few works by Shusaku Arakawa, the works of Neo-Dadaism Organizers do not exist today.[35] There were some installations that were intended to be shown during the exhibition itself, but the materials used — glass fragments, scrubbing brushes, sand, sulfuric acid, bedding soiled by urine — were all waste items, and they defied adequate description. This clearly indicates that the artists were not interested in preserving their works. For this reason, it is fortunate to be able to confirm the existence of some works from photographs, but there were numerous works whose existence was recorded only in exhibition reviews and memoirs: the object was not the manifestation of aesthetic sensibility but only the record of an Action. The suggestion by Tapié that Shinohara should create his "Action Sculpture" — which was no better than waste materials — in bronze symbolizes the gap between the critics and artists at the time.[36] The artist Tetsumi Kudo stated at the time: "For me what matters most is not to create my works but how to live. The work happens to exist there as I excrete, eat meals or talk like I am doing now."[37] (These words remind one of the words of de Kooning, who regarded his works in the same light as his life[38]). Most of the objects shown at the Gutai's

early outdoor exhibitions no longer exist today because the places where they were displayed were quite extraordinary.[39]

Although young artists often ultimately destroyed their works, they did not show Action and objects at random. They presented their works effectively, based on a distinctive strategy. This is clear from the Neo-Dadaism Organizers' first exhibition, which was cancelled before its completion because it was too outrageous, and so made it difficult to find places to exhibit their works: the Yomiuri Indépendant exhibitions became their greatest objective because they guaranteed freedom of expression as well as many viewers. It was the raison d'être of an artist to be recognized there. Every year they exhibited their works, on which they had concentrated their energies, filling the place with a fantastic enthusiasm Shuzo Takiguchi called a "free spectacle." Without the Yomiuri Indépendant exhibitions, Japanese art in the 1960s could not have shown such intensity.

As is evident from their careful selection of where to show their works, the Action artists were very conscious of the importance of being seen and being photographed. As Raiji Kuroda points out, it was the time when television and weekly magazines — instant visual media — were developing rapidly, and the Neo-Dadaism Organizers were well aware of their influence.[40] Their outrageous Actions was a fascinating subject for the media, and they performed regularly at beaches and ateliers, complying with the schedules of weekly magazines and television programs.

Naturally the artists' "shocking" activities were often interpreted as simply being part of the lifestyle of the younger generation rather than art, which they

35. There have been no retrospective exhibitions of the Neo-Dadaism Organizers or the Yomiuri Indépendant exhibitions except one exhibition that introduced the works of the Neo-Dadaism Organizers in photographs, held at the Fukuoka Art Museum in 1993. The lack of exhibitions is mainly due to the fact that most of their works do not exist today; their disregard of the preservation of their works was shared by the Kyushu-ha. See Kuroda, "Isetsu: Bijutsu undou to shiteno Kyushu-ha."

36. Shinohara, "Zenei no michi 3," Bijutsu Techo (April 1966): 119.

37. Tetsumi Kudo, "Zadankai: wakai bokenha wa kataru" (Discussion by Young Adventurers), Bijutsu Techo (August 1961).

38. Willem de Kooning, "What Abstract Means to Me," Bulletin of the Museum of Modern Art 18 (1951), reprinted in David and Cecile Shapiro, eds., Abstract Expressionism: A Critical Record (Cambridge, U.K.: Cambridge University Press, 1990), 219-224.

39. The Ashiya City Museum of Art and History presented the Gutai's Outdoor Exhibition in July 1992, with twenty-three re-created works, along the banks of the Ashiya River; this was tried again at the 1993 Venice Biennale. Many objects relating to Action and on-stage exhibitions have been re-created and acquired by museums.

40. Raiji Kuroda, "Akarui satsurikusha sono shunkan gei no jutsu" (Cheerful Assassins: Their Instant Skill of Art), Neo-Dada Witnessed: Photo Documents (Fukuoka: Fukuoka Art Museum, 1993).

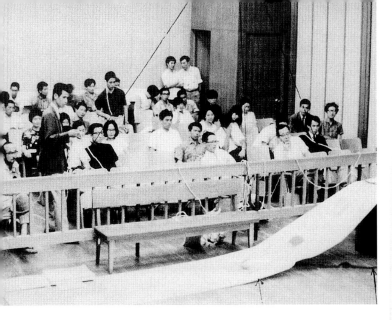

**Genpei Akasegawa**, *One Thousand Yen Note Trial*, 1967

willingly accepted. Akasegawa recalls: "Besides that, weekly magazines' feature sections swarmed to cover us in lowbrow interest and the Neo-Dadaists in art daringly complied with it. The star to be photographed was, of course, Ushio Shinohara in his Mohican hairstyle. Shinohara bragged that so many weekly magazines came to cover him this week, counting on his fingers. Because the media was vulgar, they dared us to use new materials."[41] "Because the Yomiuri Indépendant exhibition was sponsored by the *Yomiuri Shimbun*, the largest newspaper publisher in Japan, to be recognized at the exhibition and taken up in the press had great merit and gained the artists more publicity.

Furthermore, they actively sought contact with art critics, from the famed Shuzo Takiguchi to younger critics like Yoshiaki Tono and Yusuke Nakahara. Many critics visited artists' ateliers and exhibitions, sometimes arguing about the concept of "Anti-Art;" they also rose to the occasion and defended artists by appearing as special witnesses for the defense at the "One Thousand Yen Note Trial." It must be noted that, contrary to their anti-authority stance, the Neo-Dadaism Organizers were really an elite group of artists from the Yomiuri Indépendant exhibition who cultivated and deepened their relationship with the critics rather than the general public.[42]

In opposition to the aggressiveness, the disregard of the object in contrast to Action, and the cultivation of the media that characterized the Yomiuri Indépendant exhibitions, the Hi Red Center (which started their activity in earnest after the Yomiuri Indépendant was discontinued), approached Action from a different angle. The object did have an important meaning for them. The central members — Takamatsu, Akasegawa, and Nakanishi — exhibited strings, broken glass, and numerous clothespins at the Yomiuri Indépendant: the strings and clothespins were spread through the gallery space by the hands

of viewers, and broken glass made viewers feel the pain as if their skin was cut. All of the Action was meant to directly involve the viewers.

While the objects by Shinohara and others bore the marks of the artists' physical involvement, the works by the Hi Red Center artists remained anonymous and their relationship with the unspecified viewers became a theme instead. Prior to starting their activity in earnest, Akasegawa and other members performed a Happening in which they ate dinner on stage in front of a hungry audience, aiming to provoke the spectators; as to his relationship with the object, Akasegawa's comment that "in order to antagonize the other party, I become an object"[43] is suggestive. Nakanishi (and others), with their faces made-up, used objects attempting to provoke an involuntary audience of passengers on the Yamanote train line. To explain why he chose a train as a stage for a Happening, Nakanishi states: "A train is a very special place. When I thought about where people can get close together in Tokyo, it was in a train that I can be close to the maximum of unknown people on maximum times."[44]

While they worked under the name of Hi Red

41. Genpei Akasegawa, *Imaya akushon aru nomi! Yomiuri andepandan to iu gensho* (Now there is only action! The Yomiuri Indépendant Phenomenon) (Tokyo: Chikuma Shobo, 1985), 149.

42. Quote from Raiji Kuroda, ibid., 9. The Zero Dimension and the artists who were associated with the Yomiuri

Indépendant exhibitions also criticized the elitism of the Neo-Dadaism Organizers.

43. Genpei Akasegawa, "Zadankai: Chokusetsu kodoron no kizashi II" (Discussion: A symptom of Direct Action II), Keisho 8 (1962).

44. Natsuyuki Nakanishi, "Sen-en-satsu saiban ni okeru Nakanishi Natsuyuki shogenroku 1" (The Record of Verbal Evidence by Natsuyuki Nakanishi at the One-thousand-Yen Note Trial), Bijutsu Techo (October 1971): 96-97.

**151**

**Yayoi Kusama**, *Silver Coat*, c. 1962

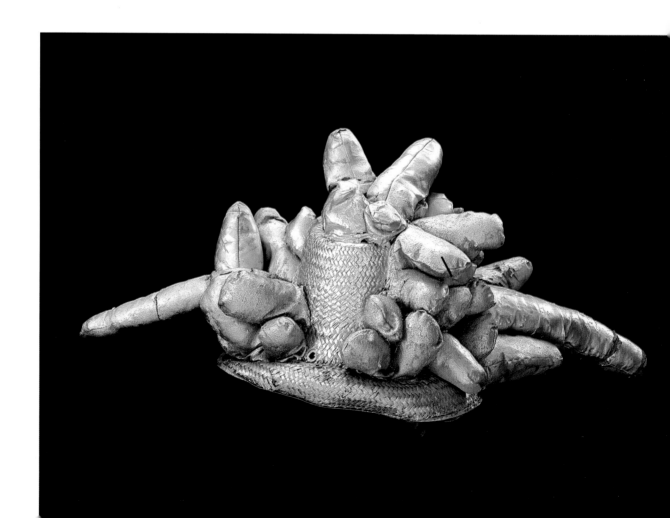

**Yayoi Kusama**, *Silver Hat*, c. 1966

Center, which made them appear to be associated with a group or an organization, they continued their activity but intentionally kept their own identities anonymous;[45] the members of the group were not specified at the time. Even an article on the Hi Red Center which appeared in *Bijutsu Techo* in 1971 listed a highly dubious "Encyclopedia Hi Red Centanica" as the source, with author unknown.[46] The Hi Red Center also made use of the media to approach a large number of unspecified people. While the members of Neo-Dadaism Organizers maintained close contact with the visual media, the Hi Red Center's relationship with the mass media was more complex. Maintaining their anonymity, they announced Happenings through invitations and "Hi Red Correspondences," or they issued warnings by leaf-lets.[47] Sometimes these correspondences, issued by an ambiguous organization but purporting to have been sent by public offices, literally agitated the city of Tokyo in the 1960s; therefore, their Happenings blurred the relationship between art and the institution by simulating a certain authority. This was a sharp criticism against Action associated with the Yomiuri Indépendant exhibitions, which was unable to convert political messages into any effective expression. For instance, at their last Happening, *Movement to Promote the Cleanup of the Metropolitan Area (Be Clean !)* (1964), in the meaningless act of mopping the streets of Ginza leaflets given out to passersby, listing the name of a real public organization as a supporter and making the nature of the Happening more ambiguous. Their idea to simulate an institution and forcefully create a relationship between art and society looked similar to the "counterfeit one thousand-yen note" Akasegawa made around the same time. From this point of view, the activity of the Hi Red Center resembles the "One Thousand Yen Note Trial" itself, an art on trial. It was inevitable that the activity of the Hi Red Center — Happenings created by anonymous artists — was brought to light through testimony at the trial.

Although there are large differences in the times, circumstances, and intentions of the Action performed by the Gutai and the artists associated with the Yomiuri Indépendant exhibitions, there are some important aspects they have in common. First, the body of the artist has an important meaning in both groups' Action. Of course, as Action is a form of expression with the body of the artist as a medium, it is inevitable that the body becomes obvious. But when we consider their activity with the entire postwar Japanese art scene in mind, this issue begins to have another meaning.

The very issue of the body has always constituted a central theme in contemporary Japanese art, beginning with the painting by On Kawara of a bloody and dismembered body strewn around a bathroom in the early 1950s. After that, Kazuo Shiraga struggled with mud, and the paintings by the Gutai artists were the manifestation of a certain physicality. In the 1960s, Ushio Shinohara and Tetsumi Kudo performed Action paintings repeatedly, and Takumi Kazekura and Nobuaki Kojima exhibited works that made use of their own bodies in the Yomiuri Indépendant exhibitions.

Once again it becomes necessary to consider the numerous objects they created as not only a record of the artists' action, but also metaphor for the body. Many objects suggested the body directly or indirectly: *Vaginal Sheet* by Genpei Akasegawa, made of slimy material, suggestive of a female sexual organ; *Sand Vessel* by Shusaku Arakawa, which used sponge and liquid, also suggestive of an organ; the penis-like rolls dangling from the ceiling by

45. *Akasegawa recalls that the combination of the social conditions, which led to the formation of many groups and sects (both in politics and art) and his personal distrust of originality, led him to organize the Hi Red Center. Interview with Genpei Akasegawa, September 17, 1996, Tokyo.*

46. *"Hi Red Center," from "Encyclopedia Hi Red Centanica,"* Bijutsu Techo *(October 1971): 70-71.*

47. *Before performing* Yamanote Line Event *and other Happenings, a prospectus with the date and place was mailed, not just to art critics but also to people who were selected at random from the telephone directory. Such activity can be compared with that of the mass media, which transmit information to a multitude of unspecified people. Telephone interview with Nakanishi Natsuyuki, July 31, 1997. On the activity of the Hi Red Center in general, see the following publication: Genpei Akasegawa, Tokyo mikisa keikaku: Hi Red Center chokutsu kodo no kiroku (Tokyo Mixer Plans: Documents of the Hi Red Center's Direct Actions) (Tokyo: Parco Co., 1984).*

**153**

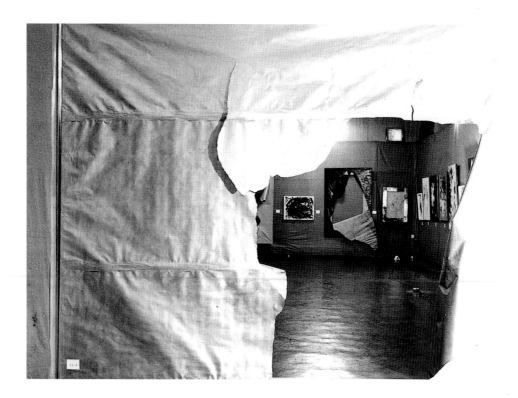

**Saburo Murakami**, *Entrance*, 1955. Collection of Makiko Murakami

Tetsumi Kudo; and a grotesque penis-like object by Yayoi Kusama, created while she lived in New York.

Why were such explicit expressions of the body repeated in the history of Japanese postwar art? By emphasizing physicality, the relationship to opticality can be contrasted. Contemporary art in the United States developed upon the principle of visual superiority, with the genealogy of optical art progressing from abstract expressionism to color field painting to formalism, accompanied by a powerful critical tradition that advocated it. In contrast, physical expression had an overwhelmingly superiority in Japan and the same optical-art genealogy almost did not exist, either in practice or criticism. This is why the Gutai paintings have long been ignored. For instance, everyone agrees today that Pollock and Shiraga are the most influential pracitioners of Action Painting, but once Pollock's paintings — created as a result of violent gesturing action — were placed on the wall, they were highly valued for their visual quality by Clement Greenberg and Michael Fried, becoming the prototype of formalist painting. In contrast, the tactile paintings of Shiraga, which similarly sealed the marks of the artist's body, were opaque and refused visual evaluation. The Japanese critics could not understand the unique quality of Shiraga's works, which could not be defined within the framework of formalism.

It has been only recently that the critical meanings of material (in form or time) suggested by Shiraga's paintings have been understood even in Europe and America. The Gutai were an extraordinary group that produced a large quantity of work by distilling their Action into paintings, and their paintings were latent with a possibility comparable to formalism; however, there was no "other criteria" anywhere able to recognize and evaluate them anywhere at that time. Furthermore, there was no critic

in Japan like Harold Rosenberg, who sought to examine the relationship between action and art, so the issue has never been seriously discussed; in the 1960s it was banished from museums and was critically assessed not in art discourse but court, in legal language.

Another characteristic shared by the Action artists in Japan was site-specificity. In the early days of Gutai during the 1950s, the choice of extraordinary places — a pine forest under the burning sun, or a stage — to exhibit their works facilitated the epoch-making expression of Action. In their words: "We experimented as to how we can exist in the given pine forest, using all the knowledge we have about form, with enthusiasm and our bodies."[48] Furthermore, the First Gutai Exhibition (where Murakami performed his *Paper Tearing*) was held at the Ohara Kaikan in Tokyo, a venue unknown to them. Upon examining the space, the artists chose Action as the appropriate medium of expression for that particular place. The artists chose varied and extreme places to exhibit their works, which were conceived in relation to each specific place. While Pollock considered his action to be a secret ritual performed alone in his atelier and revealed to only a limited number of photographers, the Gutai invited reporters to the site of their Second Gutai Exhibition and created their works in the open, in front of spectators, with the intention of creating paintings linked to the specific site.

The same awareness of place can be seen in the art of the 1960s. First, the Tokyo Metropolitan Art Museum was the special place for the Yomiuri Indépendant exhibitions. As mentioned earlier, it was difficult for those artists who exhibited and performed outrageous works to find places to exhibit, so it was inevitable that radical expressions would emerge in an exhibition without a jury. Those works that were exhibited stimulated other artists in turn, evoking

48. *Yozo Ukita, op. cit.*

Hi Red Center, *The Ochanomizu Drop (Dropping Event),* 1964

even more radical expressions. For instance, Akasegawa spoke about a technique to incorporate everyday materials into works, and these mundane objects were often seen in works in the Yomiuri Indépendant: "Sand which we mixed into paint, cautiously at first, filled the gallery as a technique, then, the next year, stones were mixed in the paint, surpassing sand. Then as if to compete, tin fragments and pieces of undershirt appeared and numerous nails were hammered onto canvas, starting a race to project the texture of the pictorial surface."[49]

The museum is a medium to radicalize expression as well as guarantee the relationship between exhibited objects or performed Action and art. Takamatsu's strings and Nakanishi's clothespins were considered not as the banal everyday objects they were but as works of art, and guerilla-like Happenings performed by the Hi Red Center were not considered as commercial operations but Actions as art; but it is not possible to talk about them without mentioning their relationship to place. Therefore, it was not the works that provided the place for the Yomiuri Indépendants, but the place that provided the works. In addition, there was the atelier of Masunobu Yoshimura — the so-called "Radical Artists's White House," designed by Arata Isozaki and a key place for artistic activity — where the second exhibition of the Neo-Dada Organizers was held. Speaking about the importance of this space where the members gathered every Saturday, Kuroda points out: "Yoshimura, the artist, and the space he owns alienated those young artists with enthusiasm and talent from their sense of daily life and functioned as a place to nurture and breed them as elite avant-garde artists."[50]

When the Yomiuri Indépendant exhibition was discontinued in 1963, the relationship with the place was severed and works were taken out onto the streets. The Hi Red Center, whose activity lost the shelter of the Yomiuri Indépendant exhibition, spread out centrifugally into the large metropolis of Tokyo: their first activity, *Yamanote Line Event,* was a Happening performed on a loop line in Tokyo, addressing the issues of metropolis, transportation, and commuting. They then performed various Happenings in other areas of Tokyo such as Shinbashi, Shinjuku, Ueno, and Ginza.

While the Neo-Dadaism Organizers went out into the streets in bizarre costumes, they acted as a kind of sideshow for the exhibition; in contrast, the Hi Red Center had a definite strategy in performing their Happenings in the streets. Their mopping of the streets in downtown Tokyo, and the Happenings performed at train stations where many people gathered, incorporated the place where they were performed as an element of their works. Nakanishi, one of the members, recalls that he was inspired to do a Happening by a certain place.[51] Each chapter of Akasegawa's detailed record of their activity, *Tokyo Mixer Plans,* bore Tokyo place-names and the title of the Happening performed there. The record of the activities of the Hi Red Center — published by Shigeko Kubota and Fluxus — was written on a map of Tokyo, which is suggestive of their ideas about urban theory.[52] Their Happenings were not simply induced by a place, but rather were more strategically chosen by incorporating the place as a constituting element of the Action. Furthermore, wasn't Hi Red Center, an anonymous organization itself, a place?

49. Genpei Akasegawa, "Jikaisuru kaiga no uchigawa" (The Inside of the Self-destructive Painting,) Art Vivant, no. 21 (1986): 92.

50. Raiji Kuroda, "Akarui satsurikusha sono shunkan gei no jutsu," 9.

51. Telephone interview with Natsuyuki Nakanishi, July 31, 1997.

52. Shigeko Kubota, ed., Hi Red Center, quoted in Akasegawa's Tokyo Mikisa keikaku: Hi Red Center chokutsu kodo no kiroku, double-spread title page.

**Masanobu Yoshimura** (right) **Kinpei Masuzawa** (left), untitled, 1960

This group was constituted only by the gathering of unspecified artists to perform Happenings. The Hi Red Center, the place, questioned the relationship between the individual and the group itself and prepared the way for the practice of art that was neither by an individual nor by a group.[53]

In postwar American art, the physicality contained in works was suppressed, and the relationship between the work and a particular place was severed. The tendencies of Happenings and body art, which emphasize body and action, or the site-specificity of much minimal art and earthworks, were a fundamental criticism of mainstream postwar art. From the Gutai to the Yomiuri Indépendants to Hi Red Center, these same two issues emerge, but in contrast to American art, physical and site-specific works were the mainstream postwar art in Japan, and they continue to be important aspects of contemporary Japanese art. From the activity of "Mono-ha" in the 1970s, and installation work of the 1980s, to the recent activity of Yasumasa Morimura, who slips his own body into the masterpieces of Western painting, the relationship between body and site continues to be examined.

Postwar art in Japan has often been considered regional or imitative. However, it is obvious that it has developed around the concrete issues of body and place, resulting in an art form entirely different from contemporary art in Europe and America. The physical and site-specific aspects are the exterior of the work, elements that cannot be analyzed by the traditional critical language of formalism. Indeed, the possibility which remains latent in postwar art in Japan can be found such aspects. What possibility does such art conceal? What assertive meaning does it have for the art of today, whose direction is hard to determine? It is not a simple comparison of West to East, modernism to postmodernism, but more analysis of the essential quality of postwar art in Japan is eagerly anticipated.

*(Translated by Tomoko Matsutani)*

53. *The Hi Red Center was intentionally vague about its members and the length of the group's existence. See "Hi Red Center" from "Encyclopedia Hi Red Centanica" in* Bijutsu Techo *(October 1971). It is noted in that publication that* after their Happening Movement to Promote the Cleanup of the Metropolitan Area, *the Hi Red Center was absorbed into a larger group called Hi Group.*

**Valie Export** and **Peter Weibel**, *Aus der mappe der Hundigkeit*, 1968

Hubert Klocker

## GESTURE AND THE OBJECT
### Liberation as Aktion:
#### A European Component
#### of Performative Art

We know that the performative work of art, be it Happening, performance art, body art, or *Aktion*, is an ephemeral and participatory event. As such, it is primarily a direct experience and loses its immediacy upon being realized. Its presence can then only be conveyed by the media, or by means of representational objects. This does not necessarily imply a dissolution of the art object. It indicates rather a new, expansive, and free conception of the artwork and art itself, for eventually in the performative work, even thought achieves plasticity. It then becomes a gesture that in the conceptual and performative work can not only stand by itself, but can also lead one to a reevaluation of the art objects. This then provides the languages of art new contextual possibilities and conceptual variations.

History, in particular the history of art, confronts us with the problem of recognizing past realities and of dealing with their individual and collective memory. Reflection on the past and bringing it back to mind is not static, but rather a constantly flowing interconnection of information, an unending process. The conditions of these interconnections are also determined by the subjective interests of the moment and their projection into the future, in the sense of expectations and visions. Perception of past reality is formed out of a sum of information — the result of an either direct or conventional flow of communication. Those who assure and convey this flow of information assume various forms. In the Age of Enlightenment and Modernism, their productivity was intensified by information machines. These apparatuses, from the smallest to the most massive concentrations of meanings belong, as profaned ritual sites, to the core of modern societies. They are organized in a spectrum that ranges from totality to collective participation, providing accordingly opportunities for extreme didacticism and influence, as well as for self-discovery and self-reflection. Their most advanced forms are called "library," "archive," "museum" — the new media and the data-highway being, after all, radically accelerated components of these institutions. Such mechanisms of communication and ritual spaces symbolize the external power of societies that produce and operate them and also become available to the other structures of power. In their complex forms of organization and identity, they

are themselves symbols in the flux of time. It must, however, be noted that their significance lies only in the aggregate of what they are meant to convey.

One of the most complex units of information is the work of art. It is the vehicle of the most individual, but possibly also the most collective meta-language, since it resorts not only to conventional forms of spoken or written language, but invents new systems of information in its own form in an individual, yet collectively learnable and comprehensible accumulation of meaning. The aesthetisized object is, so to say, a test case for society's willingness to communicate. As the creator of the object, the artist is the agitator who challenges the collective and forces it to uninterrupted communication with the aid of his coded message. This leads to movement and perception. The collective as well as the individual is called upon to guarantee this flow of communication on all levels.

The aesthetic object thus possesses an energy-laden, one could almost say a sense-endowing or even metaphysical, quality, which in its turn draws upon the flow of communication. This quality can be measured by the quantum of agitative abilities the object is equipped with. A successful agitation is dependent on the interaction arising from openness of communication and simultaneous enigma. The central component of this enigmatizing quality of art, namely the individual metaphor, functions as a source of energy. There is an interaction between its complexity and the duration of validity of the aesthetic object. Ideally, this source of energy would never extinguish and its potential to agitate would be endless.

The desire to possess such objects, the collection and exploitation of their sense-endowing qualities, becomes central to the conception of the information mechanisms and legitimizes, so to speak, their existence. Nevertheless, the idealistic process of collecting cannot be accepted unconditionally by the modern artist, whose process of autonomous creation results from his own self-conception. If the artist were to become a *collaborator* in this point, it would lead to a collective functionalization of art, which would lose the autonomy it had achieved. The flow of communication would freeze and be robbed of the agitative capabilities which form the nucleus of its being.

**159**

The artist of the modern period, especially of the avant-garde, is constantly caught in a critical, potentially deconstructive relationship with the persistent information mechanism and strives to escape the danger of stagnation between the object and its container. This pattern, in some ways, is comparable to Karl Popper's insistence on the "falsifiability" of legitimate theories. Just as a theory should not become immune to refutation, the object too should remain enigmatic and continue to possess its openness to interpretation.

This outline of some of the basic problems of modern and contemporary art indicates yet "another" dimension that the artist has assigned to the artwork. The focus then shifts from the self-contained and autonomous artwork towards an emphasis on process and motion in art, the inclusion of the environment as part of the artwork, and the emancipation of thought (which, although independent of the object, nevertheless reflects it) as form. Vilém Flusser defines the performative, multi-dimensional component as "enigma," a "puzzle that can be solved through decryption."[1] The introduction of the subjective "enigma" by means of the gestic element is thus to be viewed as art's reaction to the tightened grid of communication and information channels, into which it has been interwoven by the collective and thereby become objectified. Although art constantly runs the risk of being undermined by the tendencies to interpret, paraphrase, and be relegated to the museum, its enigmatic quality remains the immanent guarantor of the preservation of the artist's potential to liberate.

Flusser subsequently speaks of the necessity to formulate a "general theory of gestures" in an attempt to reveal the enigma of art. He describes art as causally inexplicable and sets it in contrast with semantic analysis. According to him, the advantage of this procedure lies in the property of art to unfold the phenomenon under inspection only in the course of analysis, since the various levels of "reading" bring different meanings to light. This gives rise to a multiplicative effect which enriches the phenomenon and which is in keeping with the agitative spirit of the

object under discussion. For after all, "it is not the objective of an analysis of the gesture of painting to do away with the problem of painting itself. It is, rather, far more the desire to delve deeper into the enigma of painting in order to experience it ever more richly."[2] The beginning point and origin of the desire for such a "Theory of Gestures" is the sense, addressed by Flusser and represented in art, of a revolutionary process in our reality. Flusser expresses the necessity to develop a new methodology to deal with the reality of the future by means of our present knowledge. This is particularly relevant in the wake of the mega-catastrophes of this century and the demographic and ecological problems,[3] which will probably dominate the future and are already recognizable. He has no reserves in this respect about referring to the theory of gestures as the "discipline of an emerging 'post-historical' future." It is, in both theoretical as well as practical terms, a possible "discipline of the so-called 'new human being'."[4] The drive of freedom inherent to the theory is also reflected in Flusser's definition model. For him the gesture or the gestural is "man's active presence in the world,"[5] an appeal for free, conscious and analytical action. In its optimistic striving, his model basically adheres to the dynamics of a spiritual search. Yet, this theory-model possesses an avant-garde passion, which makes it seem capable of conveying and revealing the positions and energies of the art of the second half of the century — particularly the dynamism that the emphasis on the processual and eventful infused it with since the 1950s.

The imperative of freedom and openness is central to Flusser's call for revolutionary activity. This not only defined the position of postwar American art, especially that of the New York School, but also substantially determined the position of European Modernism in its constant state of conflict with the unrestrained excesses of totalitarian, twentieth-century ideologies. On the geopolitical level, this process still continues due to the reunification of Europe and its reintegration with the East. It has by no means

1. Vilém Flusser, Gesten – Versuch einer Phänomenologie (Bensheim:Bollmann Bibliothek, 1993), 91.

2. Ibid., 91.

3. See Eric Hobsbawn, Age of Extremes (New York: Viking, 1994).

4. Flusser, Gesten – Versuch einer Phänomenologie, 236.

5. Ibid., 223-224.

ended and is ultimately merely a step in the striding globalization of today. Seen in a historical perspective, the first half of the twentieth century witnessed a restructuring of political and ideological powers and radical changes in the cultural paradigms of the Western world. This re-evaluation triggered the beginning of the end for the West's Eurocentricism, which has now been replaced by an inclination towards globalization and an increase in ideological free-spaces. The 1950s, at the same time, witnessed an expansive phase of American-culture art with international reverberations.

For the New York artists, freedom was synonymous with the liberation from a European spirit of totalitarian ideologies and the burden of European art history. Barnett Newman, the most outspoken demagogue of the Abstract Expressionists, called it "geometrization" in European art. In his "Statement," published in the catalogue of the demonstrative propaganda exhibition "The New American Painting," organized by The Museum of Modern Art, he drives straight to the very core of his theory.[6] In the very first sentence he calls "geometry" a "death image" which must be resisted without compromise. In the course of the text the "principles of geometry" are defined as principles of the art of World War I, which continue to tie it to the art of the nineteenth century. With this he addresses the fact that the most important — for him the most valid — avant-garde movements formulated and developed their concepts in the first two decades of our century. Newman, however, denies every connection between these concepts and his own art. He indeed demands the rejection of Pablo Picasso's Cubism and Piet Mondrian's Purism, since they can only "end up with the collage scheme of free-associated forms."[7] These too, like Joan Miró or Kasimir Malevich, are still "caught in the same geometric trap." According to him, there is no hope for freedom as long as these traditional concepts are not adamantly resisted and new possibilities discovered and evolved.

Newman's text and the degree of his criticism of two of the best-known contemporary European artists in the United States at the time, is an exemplary illustration of the position and self-confidence of the Abstract Expressionists and the artists of the New York School toward the end of the 1950s. These artists were initially confronted by the Surrealists who lived in exile in New York and dominated the current discussion. This preoccupation with the works of the Surrealists pervades the art of Arshile Gorky, Mark Rothko, and Jackson Pollock, to a lesser degree that of Clyfford Still and Newman. Yet Newman, though writing of the death of Surrealism in the spring of 1945, concedes to it a certain truthfulness and authentic quality when — in the face of the terrible photo-documentation of the atrocities in German concentration camps that had then reached America — he speaks of the prophetic dimensions of the shocking tableaux.[8] In his manifestative texts, however, Newman clearly marks the territory for a discussion that has influenced the intensive discourse and dialogue between American and European art and criticism until today. This was particularly true of the two decades following the war due to the new political relations between Europe and America. Beyond that he, like Clement Greenberg, was involved in the redefinition of Modernism. This new perspective, free of the European conception, was to give way to a freshly emerging American position. It thus ensured New York and American culture a dominant place in the field of art.[9]

In 1958 Dorothy Miller, an influential curator of New York's Museum of Modern Art, curated a traveling show for Europe entitled "The New American Painting," which opened at the Basel Kunsthalle. Its successful conclusion at the Tate Gallery in London was celebrated with a party in MOMA's sculpture garden. It became apparent to Alfred Barr, the members of the museum's International Committee, and the guests from the art scene, that the project had achieved its desired effect. The works of Pollock, Willem de Kooning, Sam Francis, Philip Guston, Franz Kline, Robert Motherwell, Newman, Rothko, and Still, among others, made clear that the New York artists had led painting from what had evolved in Paris to a

6. Barnett Newman, "Statements: From The New American Painting," Selected Writings and Interviews (Berkeley: University of California Press, 1990), 178.

7. Ibid., 179.

8. Ibid., "Surrealism and the War," 94.

9. See Serge Guilbaut, How New York Stole the Idea of Modern Art: Abstract Expressionism, Freedom and the Cold War (Chicago: University of Chicago Press, 1983).

wholly new dimension. The influence of the New York School on the local American scene, as well as on European art, reached its peak after the Basel show and its strong presence at Documenta II in 1959 in Kassel. Pollock and Newman in particular, each in his own way, had formulated the basics of the anti-centric and subtle "allover," that pointed beyond the confines of the canvas. They refused to give painting an illusionistic structure and above all expanded the format in a psychologically effective manner beyond the dimensions of the human body. Painting was thereby taken to the farthest point possible. This moment of culmination was reflected in Pollock's "drippings," which he worked on until 1950-51. It was apparent in his subsequent exhaustion and general lack of orientation, even in personal tragedy, which turned him into a legend. Pollock, however, did not possess the creative means to evolve the new possibilities that would transcend the culmination of painting that he himself had formulated. In the months preceding his fatal accident he was unable to paint, his gesture became petrified, and it was left to the following generation to work on new solutions and conclusions. In the final analysis, Pollock's greatest achievement was his refusal to corrupt the magical gesture of his "drippings" by becoming repetitive.

One of the first theoretical reflections by an artist on the path paved by Pollock was Allan Kaprow's documentary recapitulation in his essay, "The Legacy of Jackson Pollock," written two years after Pollock's death in 1958. Towards the end of the text, he used the terms "Happenings" or "Events" and envisioned them as a possible direction that future developments could take. The Abstract Expressionists, as a result of their self-confident reaction to the European positions before World War II, succeeded in producing models of valid parameters for a new avant-gardism. The radical reduction to the immediate subject in Surrealism led to a new transformative path which opened doors into yet uncharted territory. The suggestion of a realm beyond the confines of the canvas was typical for the gestural painting of the Abstract Expressionists, especially for the works of Pollock and Newman. This substantial gesture, which catapulted art into a new dimension, had great international impact and provoked extensive renewals in American art. It was this dynamic

that led Robert Rauschenberg and Jasper Johns to focus on the real object in painting, thereby linking the illusionistic level with immediate reality. Both raised the painted picture from a subjective expression of personal experience in gestural abstraction to a structural level. A dialogue between the surface of the painting and the object thus became possible. Subsequently in American art, however performative, the manifested object played a central role — be it objects from the immediate surroundings, as in the work of Rauschenberg or Kaprow, or artificial fetishes brought into a performative context, as in Claes Oldenburg's *Store*. It is thus the object that occupies the central place in American art of this period; the human being on the other hand freezes in a distanced stance as the white, life-sized figures of George Segal. The existential aspect of the physical, the human tragedy and comedy, are released to aloof observation through the filter of the media, as in the works of Andy Warhol and Bruce Nauman. It was now left to the European artists to use all the means at hand to tell about the drama of human existence, about the loss and recovery of the subject's conditions, as a part of their own terrible experience. It can undoubtedly be maintained that the American and subsequently European discussion was dominated after 1958-59 by object-oriented art. While Pop art and its use of the media gained success concurrently with the rapid expansion of possibilities in mass-media, the postmodern phase saw a demonstrative waning in the importance of the avant-garde. Almost parallel to this, a development in American art could be observed that rejected every sequentially narrative aspect of language. This became an even more legitimate heir to the legacy of Abstract Expressionism than Pop art, to which it was diametrically opposed. Pollock and Newman had reached a degree of gestural abstraction in their works that corresponded more closely with the intentions of the younger generation, whom Michael Fried had named "Literalists" in his essay "Art and Objecthood," than the canvases of Frank Stella, Kenneth Noland, and Morris Louis. The Color-field painters, in transfixing the moment of transformation from painting to object, picked out a decisive but limited process which in turn proved to be their own limitation: the literalists, at the same time, defined the artwork as all encompassing. It included the spatial, the performative and the concept-oriented, and was thus in the position to fully exploit the spectrum of all the new possibilities it made available. The various concepts in the works of Vito Acconci, Carl Andre, Chris Burden, Dan Flavin, Dan Graham, Michael Heizer, Donald Judd, Gordon Matta-Clark, Robert Morris, Nauman, Richard Serra, Robert Smithson, or Keith Sonnier are a direct consequence of the performative gesture in the works of Pollock and Newman. They represented an American genre which had a lasting effect on art in the second half of this century and which, together with the European movement that developed simultaneously to it, most deserves to be termed a *konkrete* art form. An art form which, by prolonging the gestural element of the avant-garde — updated by the Abstract Expressionists — into the present, once again questioned the classical aspect of art as illusion and representation. Fried is right in saying it is much "more than a mere episode in the history of taste."[10] He defines the essence of this new dimension in art not as a singular development, but rather as "the expression of a general and all-permeating state."[11] Although he categorizes it as a part of "the history — almost the natural history — of sensibility,"[12] he takes a critical stand against the development of what was correctly diagnosed by him as a revolutionary shift of paradigms in art. Flusser however, had he already thought in terms of his theory of gesture at the time, would probably have been delighted to see it confirmed. But theory always follows the idea.

The real power of the ideas formulated by the Abstract Expressionists challenged both American and European artists. In order to comprehend the position of European art, one has to place it in a transcontinental context. Also one has to be aware of the situation of the war-devastated avant-gardes from the early part of the century. Modernism and the avant-garde witnessed a terrible decline in those European societies which had previously bred totalitarianism and fascism in all its facets — such as the corruption of the educated classes, expulsion of the intelligentsia, anti-semitism, genocide, and the total subordination and subjugation of art by state tyranny. It took more than a decade in Germany, Austria, and Italy for artists to take up a new and challenging position and to establish a link with pre-war traditions. Russian art today is guided more by a persistent trend to exile than by the construction of a fundamental basis within the country itself. Austria, which lies at the epicenter of a newly forming Europe, between transcontinental, Atlantic contexts and a volatile East European situation, was fraught by catastrophic discontinuity in the first half of this century. A conception of art that operated more in retrospect and from the desire to retain traditional values emerged from the intellectual ruins. One clung to the past and longed for the fair, collective memory of a monarchically-centralized Hapsburg world. It was the task of postwar art to create a link back to the intellectual tradition at the turn of the century, when the energies released by the fragility of the Austro-Hungarian empire and the entire Europolitical structure had been transformed in Viennese modernism into trail-blazing achievements in art and science. Furthermore, the postwar generation had to find its own identity through an intensive international exchange of ideas. It was faced with the problem of finding answers to the recent aberrations of the National-Socialist phase and to the intellectual and cultural inclinations, rooted far in the previous century.

In contrast to the Austrian situation, where legends of victimization overshadowed the complicity of the country — suppressed until recent times — Germany went through a process of cathartic purging. The Nuremberg Trials, the restructuring of modern media, universities, public life, and cultural institutions — all contributed to a future-oriented change and fundamental modernization. One could, however, look back to a modern tradition just before the war that ranged from Munich, the Rhineland, Dessau, to Berlin, which lent contemporary art a new impetus in the 1950s. New collections, museums and the Documenta proved to be projects that assisted Germany in establishing its position in contemporary art today. The artists could look up to Josef Albers,

10. Michael Fried, "Kunst und Objekthaftigkeit," Minimal Art – eine kritische Retrospektive (Dresden/Basel: Fundus/Verlag der Kunst, 1995), 353.

11. Ibid., 353.

12. Ibid., 353.

Jean Arp, Max Beckmann, Max Ernst, George Grosz, Hans Hartung, Paul Klee, Kurt Schwitters, and Alfred Wols.

Especially in the works of Wols, a European position manifests itself in contrast to the gestural painting of the New York Expressionists. His art mirrors the individual and existential catastrophe with an immediacy without distance. Wols's gestural abstractions and keen, realistic photography date back to a time when *Tachism*, the *Informel*, and Abstract Expressionism were nowhere in sight. More than any other, Wols achieved a landmark state of dissolution in his paintings and anticipated a great deal of what followed in the 1950s and the 1960s. The stark realism of his photographs depicts a strong desire to comprehend reality in a concrete manner. The penetrating concentration on the canvas, the intensity with which the author delves into the picture, corresponds to Antonin Artaud's theoretical stance in literature. Both were outsiders during their lifetime and died under tragic circumstances. They are both embodiments of the terrible social conditions of the 1940s and the 1950s in Europe, occupying heroic positions in European art and remaining paradigmatic points of reference to this day. Artaud's and Wols's legendary positions, along with the works of Pollock, make a continuity of anthropomorphic themes possible; indeed, they seem even necessary. Along with these points of departure that found their justification in the historical events of the immediate past, the art of postwar Europe stood in direct contrast to the reactions by American literalists regarding the gestural in expressionism, since it primarily insisted on the subjective in its confrontation with reality.

Artaud's comprehensive theoretical-poetic writings and Wols's relatively small number of paintings and photographs reveal a desire to transcend the conception of work itself, to give a greater presence to the subject. Text and picture are infused with an immediate, indeed, a tactile presence of personality. Pollock's method of ritualized painting, in which the subject enters directly into the painting in a transcendental gesture, also holds for the work of Wols and for Artaud's writing, but with different aesthetic solutions and consequences. It is not just the emer-

gence, but the implosion of a state of personal exposure that finds its expression in the painting. Each, however, is an individual act of liberation. In his "The Theater and its Double," Artaud said, "If anything infernal, really abominable exists in our times, it is the artist's clinging to forms — rather than being like the condemned, those one immolates and who send signals from their funeral pyres."[13] Already in 1923, after Jacques Reviere's refusal to publish his poems in the *Nouvelle Revue Française*, Artaud had begun his criticism of the object as an act of freedom. He finds it increasingly difficult to produce for the "warehouse of literature." In "The Nerve Meter," Artaud declares on behalf of all art forms that the writing of literature amounts to the production of garbage. He insists on an irreconcilable unity of thought and action, of concept and gesture, as a strategy for liberation. Seen from this perspective, even his negation of the difference between art object and thought, between literature and truth, between object and empirical reality, become comprehensible. Breathlessly, he circumvents the gnostic concept of the melding of body and mind by defining spirit — thought itself — as the object, and thereby vows to abolish the authority of the object.

It is obvious that an isolated view of the traditions that European postwar art referred to is no longer possible without also considering the revolutionary developments in American art since 1945. The transatlantic balance of power has shifted too much as a result of the wars in Europe. For a valid and varied understanding of the developments in the second half of the century, it is important to determine the roots that are present as links to the past in the immediate European traditions. Particularly in reference to the performative gesture of art, a genealogy exists which has in the past been too partial to the American positions of the 1950s and their undeniable influence on European art. This genealogy is challenged by the positions of Artaud and Wols. Their works, along with those of the Dadaists, Marcel Duchamp, and Pollock, contain further historical references for a general interpretation of the history of certain performative positions in European art.

With the removal of the Soviet sphere of influ-

13. See Antonin Artaud, "Das Theater und die Kultur," in **The Theater and its** **Double** (Munich: Matthes und Seitz, 1996), 15.

ence against the backdrop of the fall of communism and the changing face of capitalism, a fundamental geopolitical restructuring and a shift in paradigms faces us today, which resembles one of these dualistic American-European postwar situations. We are only now in possession of the information that can give us some insight into the era following Josef Stalin's regime of bondage and suppression after the 1920s. The extent of the gradual changes, since the 1960s, in autonomous positions of Russian art — independent of state machinery — is becoming increasingly apparent. It is also becoming clearer that a comprehensive history or phenomenology of transcontinental relations between modernism and the avant-garde would be impossible and would be greatly wanting without the integration of post-Stalinist Russian art. The radical global and socio-political changes of the last few years have ultimately linked the positions of Russian art of the early part of this century — along with their ideological effects on the development of modernism — with the non-conformist art of the avant-garde of the past decades. The obscurity that they were steeped in for over thirty years was not merely the consequence of the conflict between totalitarianism and art. It was much more the tragic result of the idealistic pragmatism of the Stalinist era being transcended by the individual.[14] The Russian poet Joseph Brodsky coined a metaphor for the state as "a place instilling fear through its own devastation."

The artists who insisted on their autonomy were faced with this void, which has been a consistent motif in Russian art during the last forty years. The repressive influence of the Stalinist machinery led to extremely regressive forms of fanatically rapturous avowals to subjective traditionalism and of personal isolation in the 1950s and the 1960s, as in

14. Andre Erofev points out that Göring's art collection did include works of the impressionists. Stalin, on the other hand, forced all spheres of independent artistic activity — including the art made by children or folk-art — to fit the framework of his system.

the work of Dimitri Crasnopevchev. The 1970s, however, saw the emergence of the movement called "Moscow Romantic Conceptualism," a name coined by Boris Groys in the late 1970s. This circle mounted a subtle counterattack on the persistently suppressive machinery. The artists distanced themselves from all current norms, formulated their symbols and aestheticized the commonplace from this position of alienation. In the period after Leonid Brezhnev's death, this seemed to be a logical reaction to the interesting fact that one could now speak of alienation and a loss of meaning. As a consequence, ideology was aestheticized and brought into the context of the museum, which in turn determined the reality. *Perestroika* and *glasnost* brought radical changes in the life of the Soviet citizen, which affirmed, accelerated and finally stopped this movement. Russian art today is in a still more radically transitional phase. While the generation of Moscow Romantic Conceptualists was at least confronted with a partially functioning ideological machinery, whose pitiable condition filled them with courage, the present generation of artists is caught in a possibly even more frightening schism between exile and ideological void. Several Romantic Conceptualists like Ilya Kabakov and Eric Bulatov left Russia a long time ago to live in Europe or America, where their art has since been shown and interpreted in an international context. The present generation, however, sees itself as confronted by unpredictability. It no longer thematizes the collective and subjective states of a degenerating system from the superior position of the active opposition. Russian artists are now rather confronted with an actual loss of identity, which signifies a substantial qualitative difference in the social context after the breakdown of the system. The result is a controversial, spontaneous and authentic art with a strong performative element. Maybe the most radical exponent of contemporary Russian Actionism is Alexander Brener. He, in the name of the Russian citizen, describes the coordinate-system of his reality

**165**

HOMO SAPIENS
КЛАСС МЛЕКОПИТАЮЩИХ
GROUP OF MAMMALES
САМЕЦ И САМКА
MALE AND FEMALE

**Valery Gerlovin** and **Rimma Gerlovina**, *Zoo*, 1976

as "sex, violence and helplessness."[15] Brener was imprisoned for several months in Amsterdam at the beginning of 1997, after he sprayed an Andy Warhol-like dollar sign over a Malevich. Yet, before one denounces such an act, it would be good to know that Malevich himself, in a text about the museum, recommended the burning of all old art in order to enjoy the view of the ashes.[16] Groys points out that in the face of this statement, Malevich's *Black Square* (1923) can be interpreted as the result of the burning of all other paintings and as the "living origin of the world." This analogy of the void is also valid for the *White Square on White* (1918). The avant-garde gesture with which Malevich formulated the beginning as not a "fearful," but rather a "fruitful" void, is reflected in the neo-avant-garde of the Romantic Conceptualists as well as in Brener's work.

A photograph from 1976 shows a nude rear-view of Valery Gerlovin and Rimma Gerlovina. A placard saying "Homo Sapiens – Délai de Conservation 100 ans" hangs from their hips. The bare white, coordinate-less background of the photos make them seem to be metaphoric links between contemporary Russian art and the heroic avant-garde of Suprematism. The action *Zoo*, on the other hand, is an actionist gesture and represents the circumstances of the Moscow Romantic Conceptualists. Again in 1976, the group called Collective Action, founded by the philologist Andrej Monastyrskij, performed for the first time. His position is interdisciplinary and performatory from the very outset — his interest being poetry and minimal music. Not only did Monastyrskij soon take on the leadership of the group, but he went on to be an important theoretician of unofficial 1970s Muscovite culture. He started making objects around 1975, which were then employed in his actions. Collective Action Group performed about sixty times between 1976 and the end of the 1980s. The performances, due to the political situation of the times and analogous to the exhibitions of non-conformist art, were always held for an intimate circle. Apart from Monastyrskij, the artists Nikita Alekseev, Georgij Kizeval'ter, Nikola Panitkov, and Sergej Romaschko were also involved during the first few years. The same friends were invited to all the performances, these being mainly Joseph Bakstein, Bulatov, Kabakov, Dmitrij Prigov, and a few others. Three elements are essential to the structure of Monastyrskij's works — the landscape, the journey, and language in the form of commentary. The performances were preferably held in winter in a neighborhood of Moscow, where Monastyrskij also projected the Suprematist *White Square* and its productive void onto the landscape. The activities of the group members, observed and experienced by the friends who were present, could only take place after a journey or a walk, during which one left the urban context behind. With the aid of the white landscape and the semi-meditative journey out of the ideologized flow of language of the urban environment, the members of Collective Action Group formulated that free space which Groys had christened the "Zero

15. *The artist in a video interview with Josef Bakstein for the show "For a Better World — Aktionismus in Moskau," Secession, Vienna, 1997.*

16. *Kasimir Malevich, "On the Museum,"* in Essays on Art, 1915-1933 *(New York: G. Wittenborn, 1971), 68-69.*

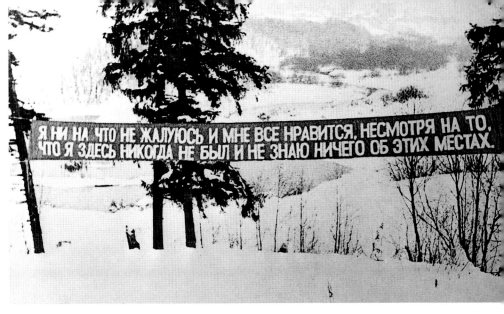

**Collective Action Group**,
*Slogan – Manifesto, 1976*

Solution" in one of his first texts on the Moscow scene. It was this free space that they subsequently filled with their specific language and activities. In the fifteen years of its existence, the Collective Action Group developed almost into a discursive sect, with Monastyrskij, who now barely leaves Moscow or even his apartment, taking the role of the shaman who designed the participatory performances. The continuity of his work and that of his group had the effect of inspiring many artists, writers, and critics to participate in it over the years. With this, it became a sort of bridge between the generations for the art world in Moscow.

In the 1970s and 1980s, it became increasingly possible for artists to move in a certain, if only small and permanently threatened, space. They met regularly in overflowing apartments, usually in the suburbs. The machinery lost its ability to control due to the anonymity this granted, while at the same time the artist forfeited his public presence. It was only in these little, tolerated niches that the non-conformist artist could survive. The lives of this small circle of friends turned into a series of domestic actions and rituals. The sacred objects of art nestled in the wretched lodgings, in the overflowing kitchens of the minuscule apartments on the outskirts of Moscow. The mundanity of life and the lack of context led to despair and to the questioning of the art object itself. The only interpretation of art and the museum then permitted was "archive" or "garbage dump of history." Archives and museums simply exhibit various "languages" as equals next to each other, turning them into mere instruments of the institution. They are thus deconstructed in their very essence, creating spaces devoid of sense and meaning and transforming them to the "garbage dumps" Groys refers to in his texts.[17]

The positions of Kabakov and Groys are reminiscent of Artaud. He, too, refused to supply the "warehouse of literature" with further "garbage" and saw his task as the concretization of thought itself through a direct — indeed, physically painful — expe-

rience of it. He called for the return to a concrete subjectivity, through the projection of thought on the body. Artaud's demand, arising from the pervasive crises in European societies, became a central theme of Actionism, whether it be the works of Collective Action Group in Moscow since 1975, or those of the *Wiener Aktionisten* and Joseph Beuys in Western Europe since 1960.

The present-day Actionism in Moscow can now refer to the performative developments of the Russian avant-garde of the revolution, to Happenings, Fluxus, *Wiener Aktionisten*, and performance art, as well as to the more recent history of Russian performative art, represented by artists such as the Gerlovins and the group around Monastyrskij. The gesture and the action were, after all, parts of the vocabulary of Russian Conceptualism from the very start. One should keep in mind the fact that several of these artists did not have a background in fine arts; they came from literature and linguistics. As such, they were possibly better equipped and had greater talent for dealing with a system that communicated its ideology through language and texts. In order to combat this potentially suppressive homogeneity of the system, it was of primary importance to analyze and deconstruct its language. To this purpose, the Romantic Conceptualists developed a method of alienation through the media, with the help of ironic and detached commentary, and the liberating gesture of the action.

While retaining the conditions that existed after the clash of modernism with totalitarian and homogeneous political ideologies, let us now move the time and location to forty years ago in central Europe. Vienna gradually emerges from the agonizing downfall of the Hapsburg empire, the trauma of Austro-Fascism during the period between the wars, the Anschluss, and the catastrophes of both wars. The basic achievements of modernism in Vienna — the early expressionism of Richard Gerstl, Gustav Klimt, Gustav Mahler, Egon Schiele, and Arnold Schoenberg; Sigmund Freud's theories of psycho-

17. See Boris Groys, "Sammeln und Gesammelt werden - die Rolle des Museums wenn der Nationalstaat zusammen bricht," *in* lettre international *(2, no. 33, 1996).*

**167**

analysis; the literature of Georg Trakl and Robert Musil; the new Vienna School of music of Alban Berg, Schönberg, and Anton Webern; the Vienna circle consisting of Rudolf Carnap, Ernst Mach, Fritz Mauthner, Moritz Schlick, and Ludwig Wittgenstein — are all gone, their representatives either in exile or dead. Brodsky's literary image of a "place instilling fear through its own devastation" aptly describes the extent of destruction. Even the most progressive thinkers of the time were afraid in their social and cultural isolation — as were also the many National Socialists, who had lost their identity and their moral and cultural integrity. In this context, it is quite apparent that even after 1945 Austria was, and to a certain extent still is, under the influence of Austro-Fascism and National Socialism.[18] The cultural climate in Austria was long determined by a basic anti-modern mood of retrospection. One can in no way speak of an open-minded, dynamic and progressive spirit, although contemporary historians like to speak of it as the "Zero Hour," suggestive of a new beginning. Only much later, in a gruelling, still on-going process did the country begin to deal with the collective burden of the past. Historians in Austria aptly define this rigid and stagnant aspect in the social development of the Second Republic as an "Historischer Block."[19] Only in the recent past does this inflexibility of the somewhat provincial obstinacy seem to be approaching an end. This is a consequence of a final inclination towards a united Europe, of the sudden emergence of a geopolitical situation resulting from the opening of Eastern Europe and of increased self-reflection regarding the disastrous role of the country at the time of Fascism and National Socialism.

If one wishes to understand the radicality or the degree with which the avant-garde desired to agitate in Austria, one must keep in mind that Austria's art was unable to develop a language equivalent to that of Europe's classical modernism. Barely had modern painting in Austria begun, than it came to a premature end with World War I. A loss of identity gave way to heroic individual positions reflected in

the literary works of the early Wittgenstein, of Elias Canetti, Franz Kafka, Karl Kraus, Musil, and Trakl. Art could not come up with any equivalent achievements after the death of Schiele, Gerstl's suicide, and Oskar Kokoschka's exile. Singular positions were formulated later during the 1950s in the Second Republic. Arnulf Rainer and Maria Lassnig, but first and foremost the *Wiener Gruppe* and later in the 1960s, the *Wiener Aktionisten*, found the thread back to modernist art and, through somewhat difficult processes, reestablished a link to the Austrian situation. These are the historical conditions that marked the *Wiener Gruppe* as the first real Austrian modernist movement. It owed its allegiance not to a visual tradition but rather to that of linguistics and literature. For Friedrich Achleitner, H.C. Artmann, Konrad Bayer, Gerhard Rühm, and Oswald Wiener, the points of reference were primarily the abovementioned literary achievements, especially the criticism of language practiced by Wittgenstein and the *Wiener Kreis*. Oswald Wiener was, in fact, the first to read Wittgenstein and Mauthner after the war. The history of the *Wiener Gruppe* is closely knit with the positions of these thinkers. Rühm, for example, assumed concrete structural-analytic positions in his early work.

The *Wiener Gruppe* was formed in Viennese clubs of the postwar art scene around 1952. The literary work of this group is uncompromising in its criticism of structure. For the first time in Austrian art emerged a position that interpreted literature and art as representatives of social and political realities, behavioral patterns, and attempts to intervene in their processes of communication. In the course of the following years, this trend intensified and led to the events of the *literarische cabarets* (literary cabarets) in 1958-59. In these, they criticized the literary text to such an extent that the conceptual vacuum thus created was filled by eventful scenes or, in the diction of the *Wiener Gruppe*, "incidents." Wiener reports a remark made by Konrad Bayer that, were they to carry on this way, one would "end up

18. See Peter Weibel, Die Wiener Gruppe — a moment of modernity *(Vienna and New York: Springer Verlag, 1997), 775.*

19. See Gerhard Botz/Albert Müller, *"Über Differenz/Identität in der Österre-* ichischen Gesellschafts- und Politikgeschichte seit 1945," in Identität: differenz — eine Topografie der Moderne *(Vienna, Cologne, Weimar:Böhlau Verlag, 1992), 525.*

**Valie Export**, *Tapp und Tastkino*, 1968

**Valie Export**, *Tapp und Tastkino*, 1968

with a mere display of objects."[20] Structures emerged in 1957 which then determined the position of the Aktionisten. The criticism of the representational in art imbued their own works with a performative character, with the purpose of gaining insights into reality. Just the way the *Wiener Gruppe* developed performative models around 1957, through the use and analytical deconstruction of language and its patterns, *Wiener Aktionismus* also turned the art object into a tool for the study of representation models, thereby gesturally charging it with significance. Oswald Wiener described this mechanism very precisely in the introduction to Hermann Nitsch's first book. He called it *Politik der Erfahrung* (Politics of Experience). In his analysis he refers to the common adversary, namely "culture and reality," as a pole of an unemancipated consciousness. The common goal is the creation of a "Sense," which in the words of Wiener, "does not [wait] to be

discovered," but rather "is produced." Furthermore, "Sense" — that is, "Meaning" — is a "dimension of communication."[21] Here, Wiener gives an introduction to the phenomenology of the gestural. He calls it the act of inducing sense, in the context of Flusser's theory of the gesture mentioned earlier. Central is an understanding of art, in which the active, "sense-endowing" gesture — one could also say *Aktion* — primarily assumes a causal significance. In the late 1950s, a position equivalent to the emerging international artistic paradigms becomes apparent through Wiener's works. In the shift of balance the static definition of the process of art, of the situation, the concept, the action, is replaced by the performative plasticity of thought.

Several factors appear to me to have been the major influences and points of reference for the *Wiener Aktionisten*. They include the expressionist tradition of Viennese modernism at the turn of the

20. See Oswald Wiener, "das 'literarische cabaret' der wiener gruppe," in Die Wiener Gruppe — a moment of moder-nity (Vienna and New York: Springer Verlag, 1997), 309.

21. Oswald Wiener, in the foreword to

Hermann Nitsch Orgien Mysterien Theater (Darmstadt: März, 1969), 21.

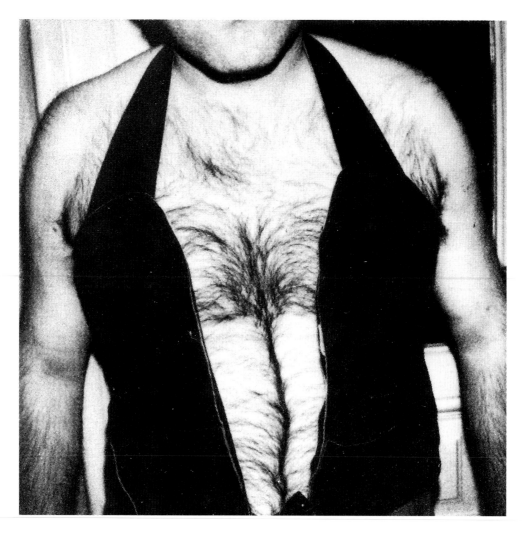

Peter **Weibel**, *Media Lung*, 1968

century; the confrontation with the radically transformed surrealism of the American Abstract
Expressionists and certain European positions; an
analytical and performative basis concentrated in the
works of the *Wiener Gruppe*; and the artists' desire
to cling to the analytic and narrative interpretation of
Modernism. The *Wiener Aktionisten* added to Oswald
Wiener's conceptual, structure-analytical, and linguistic positions, an adherence to the concrete object
and novel ways of interpreting it. In the "literalist"
positions of the American Minimalists, or of the
European *Nouveaux Realistes*, the painting or the
sculpture became the object and the space became
the subject matter. On the other hand, the *Wiener
Aktionisten* demanded the presence of the body, as
the object of the art of a "politics of experience." They
thereby stand not only within the context of the
European reaction to the American modernism of
Abstract Expressionism and its effects, but primarily,
along with Beuys, in that of a so far underexposed
European tradition of performative art. An art which
still echoes the shocks of the cultural and existential
catastrophes following the widespread destruction of
European societies between 1914 and 1945. Not until
the works of the *Aktionisten*, as for example in
Austrian postwar art, were steps taken to formulate
and comprehend the dissolution of social mores which
led to totalitarianism, National Socialism, Holocaust,
and genocide. Not even the *Wiener Gruppe* attacked

the taboos and repressions of the collective and its
systems as relentlessly as *Aktionismus* did in its act
of liberation during the sixties.

In the same way that the *Wiener Gruppe* cannot be perceived as a relatively homogeneous avant-
garde group for longer than a period of four years, the
*Wiener Aktionisten* too existed as a group for a short
period, without any long-term program. *Aktionismus*,
as an activist gesture pertaining to the body, can be
applied to a number of Austrian artists until the present, depending on how liberally one understands its
definition.[22]

As an example, the earliest works of Valie
Export and Peter Weibel refer to the *Aktionist* theme
of the body. Under the influence of Oswald Wiener
and Parisian Structuralism, they developed their initial conceptual positions. They expanded on these in
their work through an analytical use of the media in
1968-69. While the *Aktionisten* developed the *Aktion*
in a critical confrontation with gestural painting,
Export's and Weibel's performative positions refer to
a radical analysis of the communicative potential of
texts and technical media, like film and video. The
representational art object is of secondary importance in their early works. In its stead, as in the case
of Günter Brus or the early performative works of
Acconci or Burden, the body takes on the role of a
projection surface for the compulsion to communicate determined by the communication technologies

22. *Peter Weibel's and Valie Export's*
*book-collage* WIEN-Bildcompendium
Wiener Aktionismus und Film *presents*
*such an expanded interpretation of it.*

**Peter Weibel**, *Space of Language*, 1973

of the media. The metaphor becomes a demonstration. In the case of Export and Weibel, the deconstructive analysis of the media always points towards the body as a phenomenon of socialization. This eminently political act of liberation determines their early performative work and links it with the positions of Brus and Otto Muehl. The latter had undertaken a radicalization of their actions, from approximately 1966 onwards, by intensifying the role of the body as the theme and by investigating it through the analysis of its functions, with all the violations of taboos related to it. Works such as the joint performance *Aus der mappe der Hundigkeit* (From the Portfolio of Doggishness) in 1968, Export's *Tapp und Tastkino* (Grope and Touch Cinema) in 1968, or Weibel's *Space of Language* (1973) and *Media Lung* (1968), thematize the body as the vehicle of the code under analysis.

The work of Franz West also developed from a dialectical relationship of reaction and contradiction to the specific situation of Austrian postwar art,

which was undoubtedly dominated by the *Wiener Gruppe, Wiener Aktionismus*, and their environment. As a result of their participatory conception, the *Paßstück* (Adaptives), created in the mid-1970s, mean to provoke psycho-physical gesticulations and poses in the user. The *Paßstück* themselves are sculptural forms made of cheap materials such as found objects, papier-mâché and pieces of wire. Their language lies in a fantastical area between concrete legibility and amorphous abstraction. They gain their meaning not from their sculptural perfection, but rather from their animistic and actionist character. Gesticulation, the combination of the form with the body of its user, make the process visible. During this process, as West says, the *Paßstück* mutates to "a

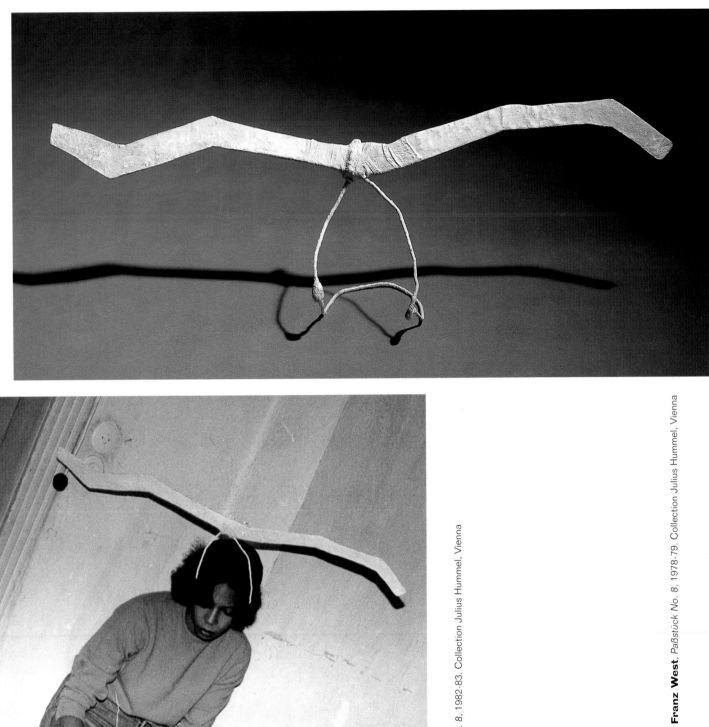

**Franz West**, Model with *Paßstück No. 8*, 1982-83. Collection Julius Hummel, Vienna

**Franz West**, *Paßstück No. 8*, 1978-79. Collection Julius Hummel, Vienna

**Alfons Schilling**, *Untitled (Rotation-painting)*, 1962

**Alfons Schilling**, *Untitled (Rotation-painting)*, 1962

depiction of neurosis,"[23] and its carrier to a potentially transparent and sensitized being. These earlier works, as well as those that follow, including the installations and spatial collages, show that his primary interest lies in the communicative process. In the open conception of West's work, the balance tips in favor of the many possibilities available to the recipient. The artists who, in *Wiener Aktionismus* and even in the work of Weibel and Export, placed themselves in an heroic avant-garde pose in the forefront, recede into the background in West's work. Only when the actor performs the communicative act of wandering about with the object does the thought manifest itself.

The basic character of Alfons Schilling's work emerged out of the confrontation between a younger generation of painters — still on the fertile soil of an expressive Austrian modernism — and the liberating international developments in the art of the 1950s. Schilling, who was born in Basel, came in contact with the gestural painting of the New York School around 1959 through the Documenta catalog and somewhat later at the Venice Bienale.[24] He subsequently became intensely involved in the position of Pollock and painted his radical, large-format abstractions in ecstatic procedures beyond the surface of the picture into space itself. The *Rotationsbilder* (Rotation-paintings) of 1962-63 and their later development into optical devices contributed significantly to the commentary on surmounting preconceptions, which also had an impact on Muehl, Nitsch, and Brus in their action paintings at the beginning of *Aktionismus*. The Rotation-paintings, where Schilling pours paint onto rapidly rotating round canvases, marked the beginning of this path of overcoming the gesture of painting. He left for New York after a short stay in Paris, where he began to experiment with the mechanism of the eye. With the aid of optical devices and so-called *Sehmaschinen* (seeing machines), he gained insight into the processes and various possibilities of seeing itself. His analytical involvement with

the concept that the conditions of seeing form the source of artistic creation, the radical manipulations of the functions of the eye, reveal him as having been in the vanguard of the art of the new media.

Those concepts that one associates with the term *Wiener Aktionismus* are, however, most concentrated in the works of Hermann Nitsch, Günter Brus, Otto Muehl, and Rudolf Schwarzkogler. At the very onset, it was essentially left to these artists to place the body in the center of their work, in the context of the general trend towards a *konkrete* conception of art. Having already done this in their own radical form since the early 1960s, they were in a position to formulate basic structures and themes of performative developments in art. In *Wiener Aktionismus*, the body becomes a concrete projection surface for what Wiener calls the "politics of experience." As such, it anticipates the positions of performance art as formulated in the 1970s. The extent of liberation that the actions tried to achieve idealized the cognitive capabilities of the empiric and is thereby entirely in the tradition of a specific Austrian school of analytical philosophy and science. It applies their *Ansatz* (stance), which is critical of the system, to art by way of object and material-oriented painting, which breaks into the realm of performative artwork. The *Wiener Aktionisten*, on the other hand, never totally abandoned the representative object. On the contrary, they were concerned with giving back to the art work, be it painting or object, the narrative potential of the text which had been lost to abstraction. They attempted this by means of the actionist — what Flusser called the "sense-endowing" — gesture in art. In short the basic consensus, which had already been proposed in a large segment of postwar Austrian art, defining the body and its empirical potential for cognition as a coordinate-system of art needing fundamental analysis, underwent several phases. Until today, this basic consensus forms a wide-reaching spectrum — the direct, dynamic effect of Schilling's Rotation-

23. See catalog to **Ausstellung in Kunstzentrum,** *no. 66 (München-Neuperlach, 1985)*, 5.

24. *Schilling met Günter Brus at the University of Applied Arts in Vienna, where he studied. In the early gestural* abstractions of both friends, an intense and critical preoccupation with Pollock's adamant concentration on the picture could be seen. They, in contrast to Pollock, emphasized an actionistic gesture of the body to the point of an ecstatic, even physical fusion of the artist with his painting. Schilling made a direct attack on the eye in his experiments with the fast rotating discs. The subject matter of Brus's work was his own body. He saw it as a concrete material and surface of his expression.

paintings on the eye; the recurrent theme of the body arising from abstraction in the early canvases and self-painting and self-mutilation *Aktionen* of Brus. It spans as well the synaesthetic analyses of Nitsch, Schwarzkogler, and Muehl, the agitative experiments of Wiener, the conceptual ideas of Weibel and Export, and finally, the participatory *Paßstück*, the *Möbel* (Furniture) and diacritical *Zitatinstallation* (Quotation Installations) of Franz West. The foundation was laid in the 1950s through such manifestative gestures as Arnulf Rainer's abuse of his audience, H.C. Artmann's surreal, romantic activities, and the *literarische kabarett* (literary cabarets) of the *Wiener Gruppe*.

In 1962 Nitsch worked on a comprehensive series of action paintings. The results were large-format paintings onto which he squeezed color from a sponge. The color flowed downwards, leaving a curtain of dripping tracks upon the white primer of the canvas. Or in an explosive gesture, he flung buckets of paint at canvases lying on the floor. This palpable dualism in action painting — consisting of contemplation and ecstasy — underlies the concept of

Nitsch's performative oeuvre; that is, the *Orgien-Mysterien-Theater* (Orgies-Mysteries-Theater). The complete concept of his six-day long *Aktionscollage* had been developing in stages from early literary concepts, and especially from the action paintings since 1960. At the end of 1962, Nitsch took the step from action painting to the *Aktion* itself in his first performative work. Wearing a long white shirt and tied to a crucifix, he had Otto Muehl splash him with blood. Experienced by the artist in a highly dramatic manner, this gesture of the synaesthetic union of painter and artwork, with a comprehensive (in the sense of its decipherability) symbolic content, stands at the forefront of *Wiener Aktionismus*. This gesture, judged by the basic structures, also marks the beginning of Muehl's and Brus's performances, which took place somewhat later. In Muehl's *Die Versumpfung einer Venus* (Degradation of a Venus) (1963) and Brus's *Ana* (1964) as well, the distance between the painting and its creator is eliminated in a dramatic gesture. Painting was thus replaced by the psycho-dramatically constructed performance, with its collagelike use of real, significance-laden materials and objects.

**176**

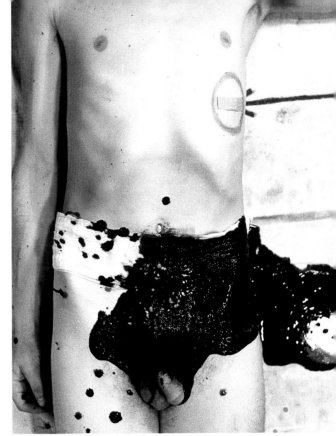

**Hermann Nitsch**, *12th Action*, 1965

**Hermann Nitsch**, *4th Action*, 1963

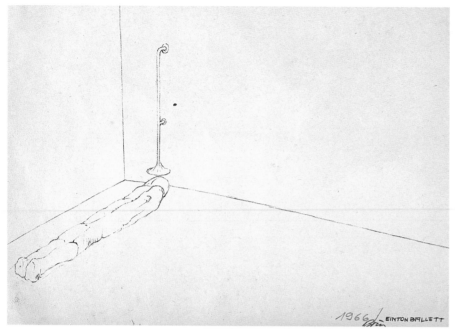

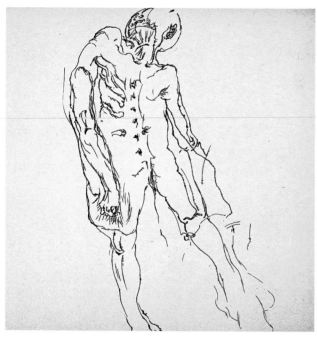

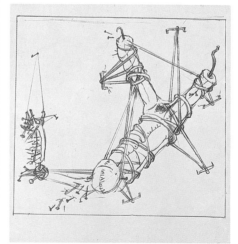

**Günter Brus**, *Untitled*, 1963. Private Collection

**Günter Brus**, *Ana*, 1964

**Günter Brus**, *No.2 Aktion*, 1964. Archiv Conz, Verona

Otto Muehl, *Materialaktion*, 1965. Courtesy Gallery Krinzinger, Vienna

**Otto Muehl**, *Aktionobject*, 1963-1964. Sammlung Friedrichshof, Zurndorf

**Otto Muehl** (with Günther Brus), *Aktion (Ten Rounds for Cassius Clay)*, 1966.
Archiv Conz, Verona

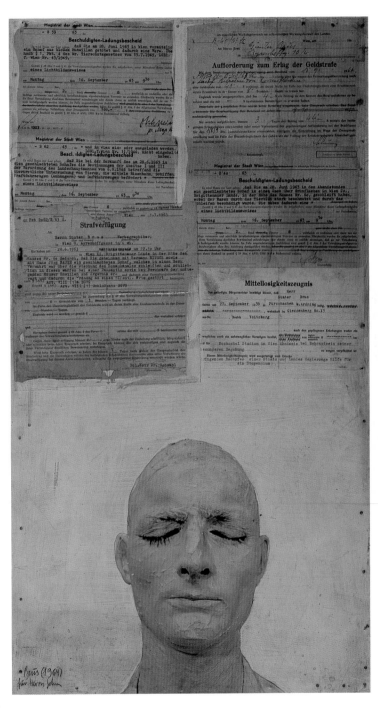

In 1966, the *Wiener Aktionisten* were invited by Gustav Metzger to the  Destruction in Art Symposium in London. This meeting marked the first direct contact with the international performative scene. Shortly after this encounter a cycle of *Aktionen* commenced. The means available to the body and material-actions of Brus and Muehl, which were developed in the preceding years, as well as the critique of language and of the established system by Wiener and Weibel, were combined, tried and tested in the socio-political context of the time. This led to serious conflicts with post-fascist Austrian society, with the result that the artists involved finally left the country. Günter Brus was sentenced to several months in prison and lived in Berlin until his pardon in 1976. In the *Aktion Zerreißprobe*, which was staged in Aktionsraum 1 in Munich in 1970, he concluded his investigative analyses of the body. He then withdrew to a self-constraining subjectivism of drawing and writing. Muehl, on the other hand, remained in Vienna, where he founded a commune to develop his material actions further into a group-therapeutical model of analysis. The AA-Kommune (*Aktionsanalytische Kommune*) was founded on the principles of free sexuality and collective property and had up to 300 members until its final breakup in the early 1990s.

Meanwhile, Nitsch's sacrificial gesture of 1962, which formed the nucleus of his model of the *Aktion*, had developed into a comprehensive, performative, and even dramaturgically constructed collage. All the performances that he has so far staged were a form of demonstration or rehearsal for his great *Orgien-Mysterien-Theater*, which has yet to be realized.

In 1969, Rudolf Schwarzkogler died as the result of a fall from his apartment window. In 1966 he had realized his last and possibly the most complete of his *Aktions*, and he left behind a dense and com-

**Günter Brus**, *Untitled*, 1965.
Scottish National Gallery of Modern Art

prehensive photographic oeuvre. In his view, the performative work could only be regarded as complete in the context of a dialectical approach to photography. On this point, he stands for an important aspect of *Wiener Aktionismus*. The photographs for *Aktionssitzungen* were made during an *Aktion* staged expressly for the photographer. The theme of the photograph and the performative art work, of the object and the gesture, reached its peak in Schwarzkogler's performative work. With the considerable distance of time one often forgets that the focal point in the work of Brus, Nitsch, and Schwarzkogler in the early 1960s was the dramatically eventful art work. This mechanism of reception can also be observed in the work of Beuys. One can

only see his work in this context once individual performances are brought to mind through installations such as the *Beuys-Block*, on display in Darmstadt. As in the case of Beuys, the performances of the Viennese artists, are also, each in its own way, accompanied by the aura of representational objects. A traditional view often tends to perceive these as independent and autonomous art works. It is, therefore, important to be aware of the fact that ultimately they always refer, either directly or by context, to the eventful gesture of the *Aktion*. The object is therefore the blueprint, icon, document, approach, analysis, clue, bookmark — the focal point and even shadow of the concrete art form of the *Aktionists*.

If, for example in the case of Beuys and also

Rudolf **Schwarzkogler**, *3rd Action*, 1965-66.
Collection Shashi Caudill and Alan Cravitz

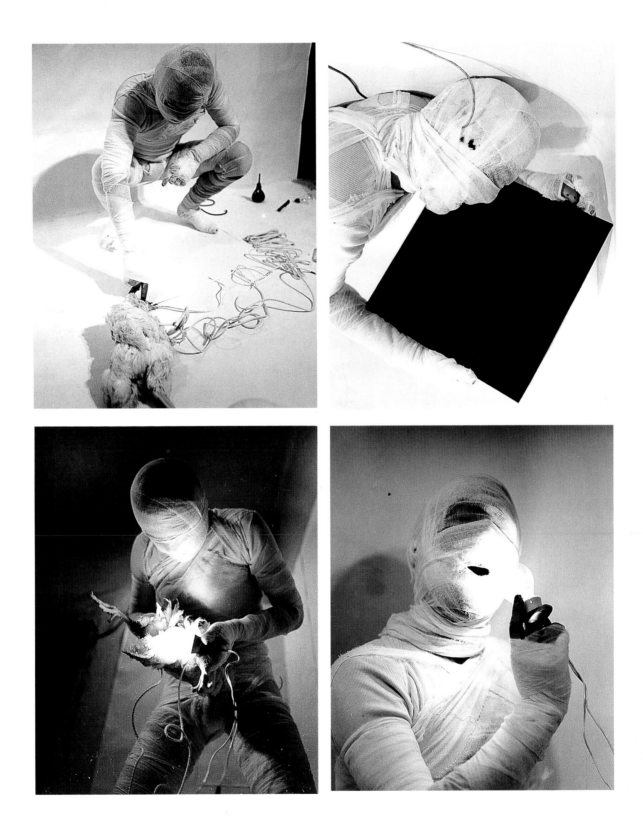

Rudolf Schwarzkogler, *Untitled (Sigmund Freud-Bild)*, 1965.
Museum moderner Kunst Stiftung Ludwig, Vienna

analogous to his roots in sculpture, the relationship between gesture and object — in the sense of stretching the concept of sculpture into spatial installations — is in the forefront, then photography assumes an important role for the *Wiener Aktionisten*. From 1963 onwards an important database of photographs emerged, which documented the *Aktionen*. This material, in particular, gives us some insight into the performative gesture of these artists. After all, only Nitsch still makes it possible to experience his concept of the *Orgien-Mysterien-Theater*. It is accessible either directly or through the installation of the relics, the remnants, of past performances. The *Asolo Raum* (1971) is the earliest and most representative example for this. The desire to capture the *Aktion* in the photograph spans from distanced documentation to the aesthetic photograph as artwork. We would today call the former a scientifically aloof analysis and the latter an aesthetic transformation of the object into a fetish. Each artist in his own way had a claim to both definitions. It would be a grave simplification to say that the frozen and over-composed snapshot was the domain of just Schwarzkogler and that Muehl's interest lay purely in the voyeuristic aspect of photography. It would be equally one-dimensional to criticize the photographic oeuvre as being the regression of the *Aktion* to the static picture. At the beginning, as well as towards the end of the 1960s, it was the documentary position and thus the eye of the photographer that dominated the photographic works of the *Wiener Aktionisten*. At about the same time between 1964 and 1966, photography entered an aesthetic and analytical phase, alongside the progressive use of a variety of material-languages in the *Aktionen*. The artists started intervening in the process once they had become aware of the qualities of the medium. The photograph allowed Schwarzkogler to concentrate on the performative gesture of the eventful

**Hermann Nitsch**, *4th Action*, 1963

(above & right) **Hermann Nitsch**, *Asolo Raum* (details), 1971. Archiv Conz, Verona

**Joseph Beuys**, teaching 1968

*Aktion* itself. This enabled him to free himself from "the constraints of the relics as the ultimate goal." His artist friends were of the same view and photos of this period are the ones mostly associated with *Wiener Aktionismus*. Schwarzkogler's "man with fish on his back," Brus's "face divided by a line," Muehl's "nude with an umbrella," and Nitsch's "torso with a wound in the side" all stem from this flood of pictures.

Apart from this, Muehl, Brus, and Schwarzkogler increasingly employed the photograph as the basis for their *Aktionen* and collages. The photographs of the *Aktionen* became raw material, making narrative expression in the picture possible again. The episodic revival of this (actually avant-garde) method made the picture, which had initially been rejected, again seem possible and meaningful before the phase of radicalization of the *Aktionen* from 1967 onwards. The artists, particularly

Brus and Muehl, assumed political positions through the collage. *Wiener Aktionismus* thus became synonymous with the criticism of the hegemonies of the state and church and their intrusions on individual freedom. In 1968 Brus announced an *Aktion* on a poster saying "Der Staatsbürger Günter Brus betrachtet seinen Körper" (The Citizen Günter Brus regards his body). Here, at the latest, art becomes a political gesture, its basis being the ritual of critical self-observation in the *Aktion* and its analytical reflection in photographic reproduction. An act like this qualifies photography as a medium of liberation and the *Wiener Aktionisten* most certainly made use of it as such.

There are several similarities between *Wiener Aktionism* and Joseph Beuys, stemming from the process and structure of the work. Although the Viennese artists (with the exception of Muehl) belong

**190**

to a younger generation, their work converges in the development of the performative dimension. The first public *Aktionen* of Beuys as well as Muehl and Nitsch were staged between 1962 and 1963. Beuys, Brus, Muehl, Nitsch, and Schwarzkogler saw nothing fundamentally in common with the American Happenings and Fluxus movements. On the contrary, they found their work to be in a purely European tradition, based on Surrealism and the assumption that an aesthetic expression of the subconscious is still possible.

Despite all the differences in content and form, structural similarities in the performative forms that emerged are conspicuous. The semi-dramaturgical and ritualistic structure of the performances points to the artists' interest in the narrative language of the object. Within the framework of the anthropocentric artwork, the artist assumes an extremely subjective position. Beuys, Nitsch, and Schwarzkogler employ the magical gesture by assuming the role of the shaman or the priest. Brus, on the other hand, uses the body as a projection surface for the subconscious collective potential. It then turns into an expression of the sacrificial act. They, as well as Monastyrskij's Collective Action Group, claim that art has a cathartic and healing function and that the artist is an antithetical, indeed, a tragic subject in the center of the art work itself. A socio-political element emerges as a direct consequence of this. It manifests itself in the work of Beuys through his politically-oriented projects and in his willingness to negotiate, as well as in his idea of the *Soziale Skulpture*. The *Wiener Aktionisten* have added to it an alternate model that is socio-politically more isolated and has therefore also faced corresponding resistance, be it the anarchistic-agitative performances of Brus, Muehl, Wiener, or Weibel, the ex-territorial ritual arena of the *Orgies-Mysteries-Theater* of Nitsch, or the utopic AA-Kommune of Muehl and his friends based on the *Aktionsanalyse* (which ultimately failed on account of its idealistic secludedness).

The isolation resulting from the nature of the projects shows the identity crisis of Austrian postwar society. The subject matter of Beuys's work, however, is the entire social and geopolitical position of German expansionism, although, it is important to emphasize, in a framework of liberation and reconciliation. One can safely say that the insistence on a synthesis of the basic principles of East and West by the German visionary was not, as some claim, a striving for a form of totalitarianism. The central idea behind his work was presumably much more a clarifying and productive process. In the face of the current political developments in Europe that this analysis refers to, his work gains in fascination precisely because of its critical stand from a dogmatically structuralist and Marxist angle.[25]

In 1967, along with the Danish Fluxus composer Henning Christiansen, Beuys was invited to the St. Stephen Gallery in Vienna to stage *Eurasienstab*. The focus of the *Aktion* was the gestural act. A solid and heavy copper staff, over three meters long and specially crafted, was installed in the space defined by Beuys's grease and felt corner. The *Eurasienstab* is now part of the comprehensive installation called the *Beuys-Block* in Darmstadt, Germany. By way of initiating Christiansen into the symbolism and procedure of his performance, Beuys made a series of sketches, which clarified the meaning of the staff, bent back on one end into a "U" form. This set of drawings, completed later, is of crucial importance for the comprehension and understanding of his work today. The process of unification, reconciliation, and resurrection — intrinsic to the Eurasia theme — is insinuated either by a sketchily drawn symbol called "new cross" or by a note saying "Element 3." Beuys sketched a map of Europe for Christiansen, where he drew a vertical line instead of the wall dividing not only Germany, but indeed the entire world. It had already appeared in his "Eurasia" performances and symbolized a radical division between the basic principles of East and West, far beyond the internal political problems of Germany. A line in the form of the *Eurasienstab* hooks the vertical dividing line and points eastward, beyond the confines of the sheet. Eurasia is the definition of the enormous land mass that stretches from Western Europe all the way to China, whose cultural and political histories have always been linked together. On the top left corner of

25. See discussion between Benjamin Buchloh, Catherine David, and Jean-François Chevrier, on "Josef Beuys und der Surrealismus," in "Politics-Poetics," in Documenta X, exh. cat. (Ostfildern: Cantz Verlag, 1997), 392-94.

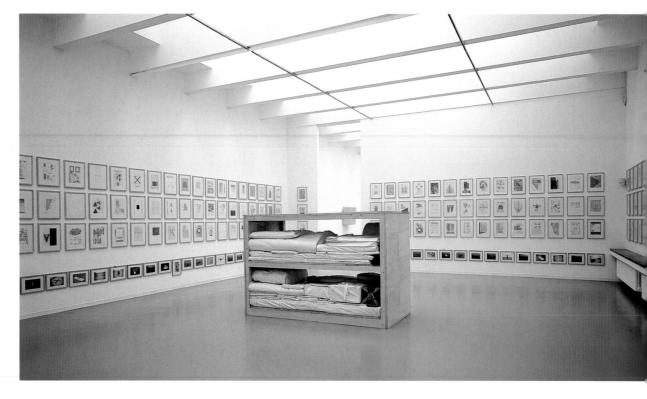

the sheet, Beuys sketched a new cross-form which stemmed from this thought and led to new ideas. With this symbol of conciliation he played directly on the historical conflict between the Eastern and Western church, which has determined the history of Europe. At the same time, he hoped to penetrate into the consciousness of the Christian *Westmenschen* with the line pointing far into the East and with the methods, perception, and dimension of a Far Eastern spirituality.

There are several reasons why the artist repeated the Eurasia idea precisely in his Vienna performance and created a sculpture in the form of his *Eurasienstab*. The geopolitical situation of the city, with an inclination to the East due to its imperial past and its role as cultural mediator on the fringes of the iron curtain between East and West — all these factors played a role in the piece. The idea of the unification of the ideas of the East and the West goes back primarily to Rudolf Steiner's anthroposophic teachings. This all-encompassing view of life, with which Beuys had come in contact as early as 1940, pervaded his entire oeuvre. It is fascinating to observe how this transcendence of boundaries, especially in the view of a divided Germany and its recent totalitarian past, its negative energies flowing into the East, became a visionary theme in the work of Beuys.

Eurasia can then be seen as the main theme that ran through all his work. It not only permeated the actions *Eurasia Sibirische Symphonie* (1963) and the Viennese and Antwerpian *Eurasienstab* (1967-

68), but also a third and decisive action which dates back to 1966 called *Manresa*. This remarkable act of liberation and reconciliation is conveyed directly through the performance and points at the most problematic political events in Germany's recent past, which had caused a deep impression on Beuys. His oeuvre is a clearly formulated model of the fundamental relationship between the gesture and the object, of the performative act and the art object. The first homogeneous show of his truly sculptural pieces called *Parallelprozess I* was held at Mönchengladbach in 1967. It was largely constituted of all the pieces and installations — divorced from any context of the actions — that he had used in his performances since 1963. This material is the focal point of the *Beuys-Block* at the Darmstadt Museum, which is permitted neither to change nor disassemble the work. It therefore is the most complete object representation of Beuys's "expanded definition of art." This step enabled the artist to stress the essence of his work. Today it can only be seen in showcases or as free spatial arrangements.

This step also represents a structural system of coordinates which led to an almost reflex action by a whole range of artists — from Anna and Bernhard Blume, Rebecca Horn, Jürgen Klauke, Klaus Rinke, to Franz Erhard Walther. The performative *Aktion* is central to the work of almost all these artists. They thematize the relation of the body — as subject matter or as an objective vehicle of meaning — to the individually experienced and created social reality.

**Franz Erhard Walther,** *Werksatz* (demonstration), 1967

The totality of this redemptive art work of Beuys is contrasted with the analytical-investigative conception of art. This brings art back from a magical dimension to that of an enlightening conception of artistic modesty. The work of the above-mentioned artists is no longer intrinsically concerned with an ideological definition of art. It is much more a partially de-ideologized, expanded concept of the work process itself. This a critical reflection on the homogeneity of the entire work of Joseph Beuys. To this idea, which has been criticized as too self-contained, an aspect of measurable or free-action is added by many in the successive generations of German artists, e.g. by his student Blinky Palermo or even Sigmar Polke.

In this context, Franz Erhard Walther's emancipative conception of art, in particular, is to be seen as an explicit antithesis. He contraposes the range of actions offered by the liberating participatory object to the iconographic language of art determined by the artist. He says, "I do not make things that one has to decode."[26] The artist as the subject distances himself from the work and performative art leaves the object behind it as a narrative vehicle of symbols. It is replaced by the concrete, reduced object, which operates as a purely functionalist instrument that determines and orders the border conditions of the action-space. In contrast to Beuys's magical conception of reality, Walther's participatory objects, which

always include the performative process, create a measurable and clear space. Only when the willing recipient walks around with the objects does the work become complete. With this, Walther transforms the viewer into a creator. He presupposes a growing awareness in the viewer, which through the process of handling the work, conveys an understanding of it. Through this experience, the work also gives him the feeling of completeness and self-containedness, of cognition and acceptance of himself.

Such a reduced and thereby concentrated immediacy of experience is also evident in the work of Jochen Gerz. The central theme in his works is also the attempt, through the process of creating awareness, to overcome that which separates representation and reality. In his work *Ausstellung von Jochen Gerz neben seiner fotographischen Reproduktion* (Exhibition of Jochen Gerz beside his photographic reproduction), produced in Basel in 1972, this process is set in motion through an analysis of the relationship between the artist and his potential audience. It became apparent that the majority of the passersby hurrying past were most interested in the photographs and avoided direct contact with the actor. The complicated relationship between illustration and reality, object and gesture, is revealed through this simple act, which is more the manifestation of a thought than a scientific investigation. A deep criticism of culture underlies Gerz's

26. See Bernd Growe, "Werk-Handlung," in Das Haus in dem ich wohne — Die Theorie zum Werkentwurf von Franz Erhard Walther (Klagenfurt: Ritter Verlag, 1990), 120.

**193**

**Jochen Gerz**, *Ausstellung von Jochen Gerz neben seiner fotographischen Reproduktion*
(Exhibition of Jochen Gerz beside his photographic reproduction), 1972

actionist demonstration. Art for him is a regressive substitute for life not lived, for the loss of authenticity. In the further development of the artist's work, this attitude is expressed on the one hand in textual criticism and analysis and on the other in works for retrieving experiences of nature.

The above-mentioned positions of the avant-garde of performative art in Germany, Austria, and the former U.S.S.R. are characterized by concepts of reconciliation and healing, and are independent of differences in content, form, and date of origin. They were developed in societies whose cultures gave rise to those totalitarian systems and personalities that put an end to the first half of this century with a long-lasting European epoch of disasters and calamities. The works of the artists link the partially shattered and authentic knowledge of experienced reality with future-oriented artistic visions. The revolutionary concepts of art and work had to arise from the tension between the individual needs of the artist to surmount the tragic, collectively suppressed reality and Theodor Adorno's criticism of art. This criticism was in the context of the genocide, in the civilized countries of Central and Eastern Europe, of those who were different. After all, Adorno had denied art that possibility which could produce reasonable perception through collective action in the following, deeply pessimistic sentence: "To write a poem after Auschwitz is barbaric. It even corrodes the perception of why it became impossible to write poetry today."[27] Especially those artists whose societies created the conditions that attracted such shattering criticism, had to deal with these grave considerations.

We see quite the contrary here. It is as though the struggle with the same past led to a critical experience of the present and a revolutionary insight into the future. A revolutionary vision underlies even the theory of gestures that Flusser wished to develop shortly before his fatal accident. He stressed the fact that it has become extremely difficult for us, due to the pervading feeling of obscurity and indistinctness, to either locate or to name this revolution objectively. However, the permanent desire for re-orientation that makes one capable of any action at all, led him to assume its existence. He felt the need, within these circumstances, to evolve new ideas and perspectives. The entire history of contemporary art and science and of Modernism thus becomes a laboratory for an integrative model. For Flusser, the gesture is a "phenomenon of our active presence in the world." Thus liberating, free, and creative action is a factor which is continuously developed in this laboratory. This idealistic emphasis on free, self-reflective action offers a parameter for the interpretation of the development of art in this century and beyond it, whose activist and anthropocentric aspect was formulated primarily in the post-fascist and post-communist societies. Indeed, in the twentieth century, there was a constant state of conflict between the rise of totalitarian political and technological systems of thought, with all their terrible and inconceivable consequences, and the demand for the freedom of thought. Modernism, with its avant-garde advances and the development of the gesture as a performative intervention in art, in the form of an autonomous construct, achieved a mechanism for permanent liberation and emancipation.

*(Translated by Nita Tandon)*

27. Theodor W. Adorno, **Gesammelte** Schriften, 10 (Frankfurt am Main: Suhrkamp Verlag, 1977), 30.

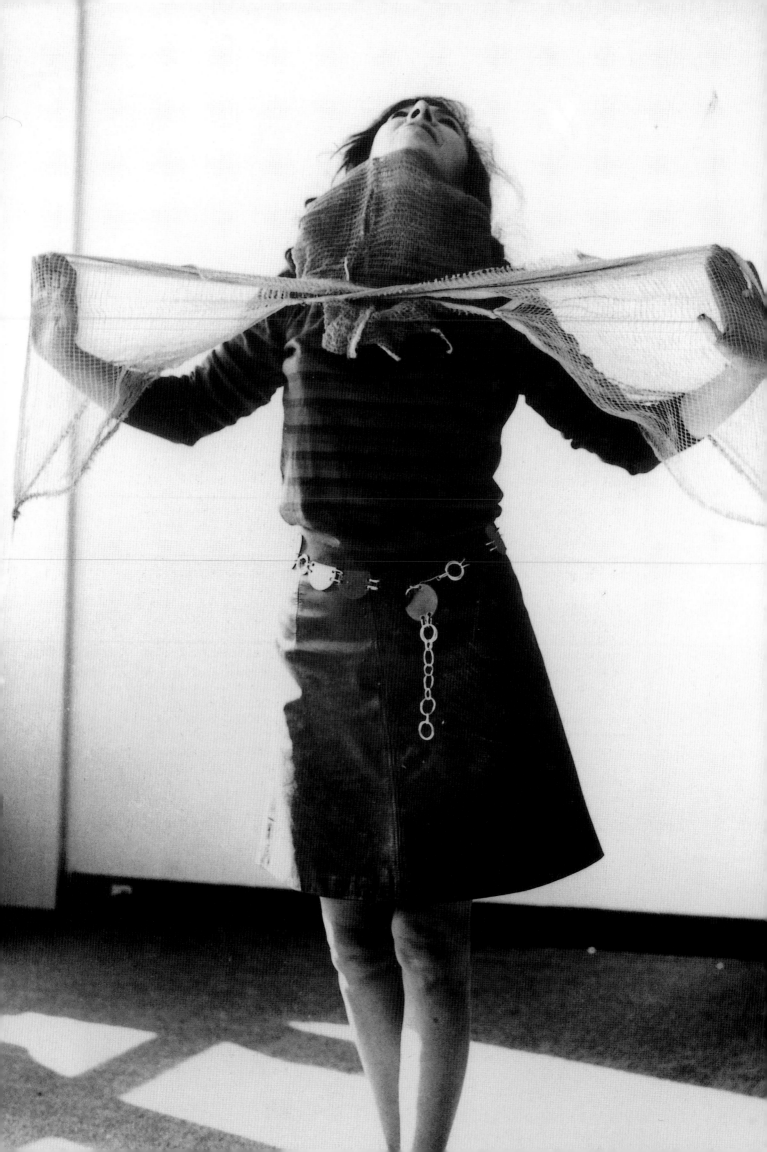

**Guy Brett**

## LIFE STRATEGIES:
## OVERVIEW AND SELECTION
### Buenos Aires / London / Rio de Janeiro / Santiago de Chile
### 1960 - 1980

To write about "live art," performance, action, participation, surely requires an attentiveness towards the complexity of life itself, its flux, its tendency to exceed systems and dogmas. In a paradoxical way, to write about this subject requires an admission of the partiality of one's viewpoint and knowledge, at the same time as an acceptance of the validity of one's subjective history and lived experience.

After all, who can be an expert in live art? Artists' events and performances have been so many, varied, and scattered that one person cannot know more than a fraction of the whole phenomenon. One happened to be at a certain place at a certain time; one saw a photo of one moment of a performance; one saw an image which suggested or encapsulated an imaginary event; one read the report of an eye-witness; one remembers a part of what one saw and forgets the rest, and so on. In other words, one surrenders to, or celebrates, the selectiveness of memory as part of the necessary workings of sense and inspiration. Likewise, an attentiveness to the analogy with life itself should propel the writer past the stage of treating "live art" as another packageable style, art form, or ism. Brave words! In writing this essay I've found a system of classification inevitably creeping in, and I became painfully aware how much of the artists' work was lost in fitting them into it. Even to invoke "life itself" is not to point to any agreed-upon thing or common ground, for didn't Paul Klee rightly say that in an artist's work "curiosities become realities, realities of art which help to lift life out of its mediocrity?"

Perhaps, nevertheless, we are referring to the same thing. In Klee's formulation, "mediocrity" becomes the key term. We are still speaking of something that constantly fights the tendency to reduce artistic insights to commodities, bureaucratic categories, and institutional formulae. If we use a broader, more suggestive notion than terms like "performance" or "happening" suggest, such as the "live element" in art, many doors begin to open. We begin to see a common project running through a significant cross-section of the art of the sixties and seventies, wherever it originated and whatever stylistic category it was eventually consigned to. The desire to reconnect art with life was inseparable from a challenge to all limiting and ossifying structures:

institutions founded upon hierarchical ordering of practices (painting and sculpture at the top); on national chauvinism or economic power; on product rather than process; on the "do not touch" principle of the separation of artist and spectator; on the commercial logic of the art market, etc. A clear interconnection becomes visible between the art/life experiments of artists in fields which later came to be called "kinetic," "process," "conceptual," "performance," "participatory," "environmental," "pop" art, and so on. Many of these connections lie dormant, though, because they have been suppressed by institutional histories, leading to many injustices. Assiduous research would reveal them again, a kind of research which would have to be as uninfluenced as possible by the fact that some artists' references may stretch over several shelves of art historical libraries, while others are barely mentioned. The accent should be on experimentation, on art as a method of investigating reality.

It would then be revealed that we have a cultural phenomenon whose spread is matched by its subtlety, which usually went against the grain, taking risks, confounding stereotypes, and often making use of the Zen-like practice of negation: not fabricating the habitual object, not looking in the expected places, indicating things which have always been there but have never been noticed. "Live art," typically, responds to the modern world by embracing its polarities: playing simultaneously with the mobility of the artist and the art work which has come with new transport and communications, and the uniqueness, localness, untranslatability, and ephemerality of an experience or event. This phenomenon crosses the heavily-defended territory of gallery and museum art at certain points only to reveal what lies beyond it: ephemeral structures, collective endeavours, unrealised or impossible projects, infinitely extendable proposals, reconstituted or "do-it-yourself" objects, and so on.

Since the early 1960s I have lived in London and written about its art. For almost as long I have had a great interest in work produced by artists in other parts of the world — all parts, but for the specific theme of this essay, the countries in southern Latin America. Is it possible to write about both Europe and Latin America in one text? Relations

**197**

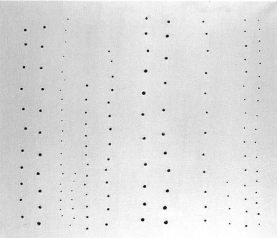

Lucio Fontana, *Concetto spaziale* (Spatial Concept) *C49-50 B 3*, 1949-50
Fondazione Lucio Fontana, Milan

between these two spheres have always intrigued me: on the one hand their interpenetration, manifested openly in the travels of certain artists and thinkers, footloose in one way or another; on the other hand, all that separates and divides them. "Truth to experience" would make a distinction between what is lived in the mind — ideas in the air at a given moment, and what is lived in the body: daily life in particular nations, cultures, political systems, neighbourhoods. And yet the two dimensions are continuously interacting. Frances Yates, in her study of Elizabethan drama, *Theatre of the World*, pointed to the significance of the name of Shakespeare's theatre, The Globe, as part of a great change of ideas then taking place: "Emerging from a Renaissance world of thought the English public theatres, such as The Globe, adapted to the English situation and expressed a Renaissance, rather than a medieval outlook on man and the universe."[1] I believe it is a similar combination of an "outlook on the universe" and a local situation — a kind of interflow or fusion of the ethereal/spiritual and the earthly/corporeal — which charges the most vital phenomena of contemporary art. But universal/local, mind/body, must be understood in a multiple, and not a single or absolute sense. All experience is contradictory (for example, my closeness to the work of certain Latin American artists is mitigated by my distance from their everyday conditions of life; my everyday familiarity with certain aspects of London is mitigated by my alienation from nationalist myths of "British art," and so on).

One global idea, shared sign, or material metaphor that emerged in the art of the sixties independently in different parts of the world, was the *permeable membrane*. In its simplest terms a translucent, elastic, relative division between opposites — for example between inside and outside — it perfectly expressed the 1960s liberationist drive to supersede ossified, dichotomous structures in art and life. It was a sign for a new relation with nature, the body and the psyche. It appears in many guises.

Thus, Lucio Fontana's cuts and punctures turned the canvas into a membrane and Gordon

Matta-Clark's cuts into buildings turned them into membranous structures. Extending Fontana's gesture, with or without conscious connection — it doesn't matter — Lea Lublin in Santiago, Chile, projected the images of famous paintings on translucent and cut screens for people to pass through (1971). Christo's *Oceanfront* (1974) involved a vast polythene sheet lying half submerged in water, half supported by rock and sand, on the margins between sea and land, retained by a large crowd of people around its edges acting like fisherfolk pulling in a gigantic net.[2] Similarly, but six years before and presumably unknown to Christo, Lygia Pape in Brazil had invited people to put their heads through a vast collective cotton sheet (*Divisor*, 1968). In Lygia Clark's sensorial clothing, using airbags, polythene sheets, stone weights and elastic bands, and Hélio Oiticica's *Parangolé Capes* and cellular penetrable structures, the membrane becomes a means of both accentuating and crossing the boundary between the inside and the outside of the body, the self and other person, the individual and collective life-space (how intriguing to compare, for example, Christo's *Oceanfront* with Lygia Clark's *Air & Stone* (1966), one on an environmental scale, the other a small, air-filled bag weighted with a pebble and squeezed between the hands).

Such ideas, arising globally with neither check nor hindrance, meet the constraints and possibilities of each particular milieu. The art I would like to write about here emerges out of two kinds of urban experience: that of Europe, specifically London, and that of Latin American cities, especially Rio de Janeiro, Buenos Aires and Santiago de Chile. To begin with I had gone right back to the basic points of difference between these two realities: cities of the new world against those of the old; cities of post-colonial economic dependency against the metropolises of empire and global capitalism; divided cities polarised between rich and poor against social-democratic consensus and consumerism. Such gulfs remain, but a more complex picture emerges if we cease to see the two realities as monolithic and impermeable. Pockets of the First World exist in the Third, and vice versa.

1. Frances Yates, Theatre of the World (London and New York: Routledge & Kegan Paul, 1987), xii.

2. This work was the subject of a fine book, Oceanfront, text by Sally Yard, photography by Gianfranco Gorgoni

(Princeton: Princeton University Press, 1975).

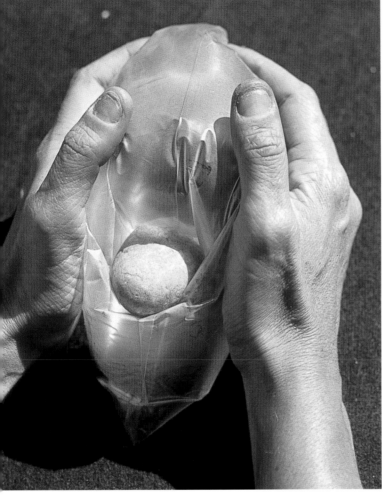

**Lygia Clark**, *Ar e pedra* (Air and Stone)
1966, a participatory proposition

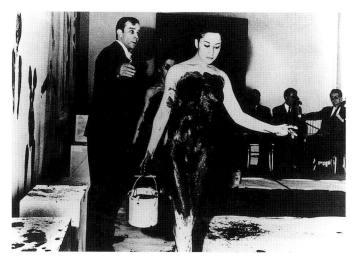

**Yves Klein**, *Anthropométries et Symphonie monoton,*
exhibition at the Galerie internationale d'art contemporain,
rue Saint-Honoré, Paris (9 March 1960)

Both are subject to the accelerating mix-up of cultures in the late twentieth century. Both are honeycombed with intricate paradoxes and contradictions. In Latin American cities, for example, socially divided in a way Europe has not known since the nineteenth century, the rich appear to appropriate culture, consigning the rest to a misery out of which, in actual fact, arise aspirations and improvisations which continually expose the official culture as a hollow sham. Conversely, a city like London, with all its ancient layers and preserved customs, is the scene of a modern revolution, turning it into probably the world's greatest cosmopolis, exposing all national-exclusive models of English culture as another hollow sham. It is precisely on this terrain of the new and changing, and the need to understand it and its liberating possibilities, rather than trying to fit it within the old conceptual frameworks of prejudice and injustice, that many artists have fought their battles.

Despite their social extremes, in other ways Latin American cities present themselves as homogeneous. Most people are insiders. London, on the other hand, has become increasingly heterogeneous. It was always a mess, higgledy-piggledy, cheek-by-jowl accretions, where the kind of master-plans familiar in Paris or Rome peter out, after a few streets, into a maze of byways and bylaws. Today the cacophony of voices, the multiplicity of cultural phenomena co-existing in the city has vastly grown; and regret at the unwillingness of institutions, including art institutions, to recognise this reality is mixed with relief at their inability to control or appropriate it. Most art institutions still work to outmoded nationalist priorities, stultified criteria as to what constitutes a "British" artist, rather than the more elastic notion, both spatially and temporally, of a "Britain-based" artist. A recent anthology exhibition, for example, devoted to the London art scene of the sixties, presented an almost entirely British, white phenomenon, whereas the vitality of the period was certainly due to its cosmopolitan and multiracial character.[3] London was a magnet promising a kind of freedom. A little research would show the presence of many young

artists from different parts of the world who had escaped from designated career, structured family, and formality. London became a mutual testing ground where different inherited forms of relative uptightness and freedom rubbed against one another and fused to create something new. In my view, such meetings have been synonymous with vitality in Britain. When they cease, the pull of the establishment takes over, the "live element" ossifies and artists retreat to the conservative monumental formalism they originally set out to challenge. By no means, however, is a love of experimentation incompatible with a sensibility to London's ancient layers.

To mention the two different contexts is immediately to follow with the names of artists who have moved in, out, and between them. The pattern has been more complex than a simple move from periphery to center, although this may be the dominant force. There were the Argentinians Lucio Fontana, whose extremely influential *White Manifesto* was written during a seven year stay in Buenos Aires during a life mainly spent in Italy; Alberto Greco, who stayed for periods in Paris and especially Spain; Lea Lublin, who moved permanently to Paris in 1964; and Leopoldo Maler, who spent much of the sixties and seventies in London and now lives in the Dominican Republic. The Brazilians included Lygia Clark, who worked in Paris between 1968 and 1975; Hélio Oiticica, who stayed in London in 1969-70 and later lived in New York before returning to Rio in 1978; Artur Barrio, born in Portugal, who emigrated to Brazil at the age of ten; and Mira Schendel, who arrived in Brazil as a young woman from Italy in 1949 (she had been born in Zurich). Two influential writers of the Chilean *Avanzada* movement in the 1970s, Nelly Richard and Ronald Kay, moved to Chile from France and Germany, respectively. Among the London artists, David Medalla came from the Philippines in 1960; Rasheed Araeen from Pakistan in 1964; Carlyle Reedy from the United States in 1964; Susan Hiller from the U.S. towards the end of the sixties; Paul Neagu from Romania in 1969. And those who didn't travel (much) were as susceptible as those who did to the exchange of ideas by which artists

3. David Mellor, The Sixties Art Scene
in London (London: Phaidon Press with
the Barbican Art Gallery, 1993).

**Alberto Greco**, *Vivo Dito*, 1964

constitute themselves as a kind of "research community" with a common language.

Looking back at the entire period this exhibition covers, one can perhaps divide it into three streams. They roughly follow one another chronologically, but not completely, with much interplay between them. The first considers actions which *explode the concepts of painting and sculpture*. The second, which I call *liberation strategies*, refers to a wide range of practices. The third is more closely associated with performance, focusing — but again in so many, often contradictory ways as to be an extremely complex phenomenon — on *the protagonist*. The categorisation is mainly one of mode, reflecting changing thinking on a basic problem common to all art: the relationship of subject and object, self and other, artist and audience.

**Exploding painting and sculpture** The 1950s and 1960s witnessed a great many proposals for the transformation of the traditional categories of painting and sculpture. Many embodied a typical paradox of twentieth-century art: anticipation of the future by means of reinvoking the ancient past, the beginnings, even, of art. The emancipatory charge contained in these proposals was essentially a renewal, a revitalisation. A strong element of showmanship was involved in Fontana slashing and puncturing the canvas, in Piero Manzoni signing living bodies, or Yves Klein in evening dress directing naked women to mark the canvas ("living brushes," he called them, just one of the arch references to visual art's traditional paraphernalia). The contradiction here is striking. In the very gesture of negating the art object and affirming life, these artists exaggerated the myth of the artist as master and unique author. Perhaps the exaggeration was itself ironic. In any case it set the scene for the radical changes in the concept of creativity and authorship represented by the participatory works of Lygia Clark and Hélio Oiticica in Brazil, and practices like those of David Medalla and Susan Hiller in Britain. These bodies of work are too complex and multivalent to be subsumed under any one label. At the same time, the more impersonal, "objective" processes of material transformation explored in kinetic art and other forms had closely allied aims of

reconnecting art with the processes and rhythms of nature. The two approaches sometimes coincided in the same work. For all their parody of the artist's gesture with the brush, Fontana's cut canvases were also "Spatial Concepts." They answered the need, in his own words, for "an art springing from materialism (not from ideas) which in a sense generates itself in accordance with natural forces."

Releasing ourselves from a strictly linear chronology, we could first consider strategies where the performative element immersed traditional, monumental conceptions of painting and sculpture in the flux of a living process. In Latin America these include the work of Alberto Greco, Victor Grippo, Lea Lublin, Leopoldo Maler, and Marta Minujin in Argentina; Artur Barrio, Lygia Clark, Antonio Manuel, Hélio Oiticica, Lygia Pape, and Regina Vater in Brazil. In Britain they include the work of Stuart Brisley, Paul Burwell, Susan Hiller, Anthony Howell, John Latham, Li Yuan-chia, David Medalla, Gustav Metzger, Paul Neagu, Carlyle Reedy, the early work of Bruce McLean, Gilbert & George, Barry Flanagan, Richard Long, etc. Out of some of these strategies arose the participatory practices between artist and spectator which shook established and institutional models of artistic activity in the sixties and seventies in a fundamental way that is still, I think, to be fully appreciated.

Alberto Greco's memory should be kept alive by some means or other. The objects he left behind cannot really do it, because he lived in his example: a perpetual rebel against all the formalising and institutionalising tendencies of art. He was born in Buenos Aires in 1931 and committed suicide in Barcelona at the age of thirty-four. Oscillating between Argentina, Paris, and Madrid, he was present at Yves Klein's events during a show called "Antagonisms 2: the Object," at the Musée des Arts Decoratifs in Paris in March 1962. He arrived wearing a sandwich-board, on which was written "Alberto Greco, oeuvre d'art hors catalogue." On the same occasion, in hommage-emulation of the French artist, Greco launched his *Vivo Dito*, his "adventure in reality." Going out into the street he would simply draw a chalk line around something or someone and sign it.

"Vivo" derived from *vivencia* (life-experience) and "Dito" from *dedo*, a finger, the action of pointing or signalling. "While live art seeks its object," he wrote, "once that object is found, it leaves it in its place; it does not transform it or carry it off to an art gallery."[4] Greco's life and its mementos, fired by a restless desire for communication, dramatise the most ancient dilemmas between reality and representation, between action and contemplation. "Why can we not look and live at once?" asked Jane Harrison poignantly in her book about the way in which ancient art originally separated itself from ritual.[5] But in a way we do, and the object sought is never neutral.

Susan Hiller's "Hand Paintings," made soon after the artist moved to England from the United States in 1969, have echoes of Klein, but perform a transformation of painting of a completely different kind. Participants were invited to make their hand prints on communal canvasses. An atmosphere was conjured up of "the earliest and most widespread (universal) form of art, the hand print as 'my' mark: archetypal, ceremonious, magical, basic." "The hand print," Hiller wrote, "is simultaneously a symbol and a representation, a trace and image."[6] The works were kept in this form until 1972 when the artist, on leaving her studio, ceremoniously burned some of the paintings. She collected the ashes in glass flasks, tagged with the names of the individual paintings. They were placed in a glass bowl like a still-life and collectively titled *Hand Grenades*. Ironies abound. The apparent death of the paintings — these traces of life — was not the actual death they might suffer if immured in museums, but really only their transformation into another state: ashes. And these "archived" dead things had the implied capacity (triggered by the title) to explode into new life. Hiller herself said, much later, that one of the ideas behind her work was her wish for "everything to be seen as having the same potential for insight," and that the glass grenades were "just as interesting to look at and experience as paintings."[7] Who can say we are not looking at paintings here? We may also, inadvertently, be looking at a cunning allegory for the dilemmas of the MOCA exhibition itself. Can the ashes of live art explode, by some process of poetic re-presentation, into new life?

The role of the living body in these transformations of painting also takes place for sculpture. The old conceptual category becomes a spring-board for launching a new and liberated perspective. Instances can be found in Takis's *Man in Space* (1960),[8] Klein's *Leap into the Void* (1960), Manzoni's *Magic Base and World Pedestal* (1961), Medalla's *Astro-acupucture Man* (1965),[9] Paul Neagu's *Anthropocosmos* (1969),[10] Lygia Clark's *Relational Objects* (from 1964), Oiticica's *Parangolé* (from 1965), and so on.

There was often a tender humor in the way the

4. Quoted in Jorge Glusberg, Art in Argentina (Milan: Giancarlo Politi Editore, 1986), 69.

5. Jane Harrison, Ancient Art and Ritual (London: Williams & Northgate, 1913), 133.

6. Susan Hiller, unpublished notes, reprinted with the artist's kind permission.

7. Stuart Morgan, "Beyond Control: An Interview with Susan Hiller," in Susan Hiller (Liverpool: Tate Gallery, 1996), 35.

8. At the Galerie Iris Clert in Paris, Takis floated a man in space using magnets. It was a few months before Yuri Gagarin became the first human to escape earth's gravitational pull. The man in Takis's event was the poet Sinclair Beiles. He recited from space his poem "I am a Sculpture."

9. "I dream of the day when I shall create sculptures that breathe, perspire, cough, laugh, yawn, smirk, wink, pant, dance, walk, crawl . . . and move among people as shadows move among people . . ." In David Medalla, Mmmmmmmm . . . Manifesto, 1965 [reprinted in Guy Brett, Exploding Galaxies (London: Kala Press, 1995), 61].

10. This concept described a series of honey-combed, cellular human figures, made soon after the artist moved to London from Rumania. One life-size sculpture was made of waffles and was communally eaten at a participatory event at the Sigi Krauss Gallery, London, in 1971.

**Bruce McLean**, *Pose Work for Plinths*, 1971
Tate Gallery, London

**Carlyle Reedy**, *Human Visual Sculpture in Contemplative Time*, 1972

living body emerged from protocols of the sculptural and the theatrical. Carlyle Reedy, for example, in her work of the seventies conducted a mischievous cross-play of genres in which sculptural and theatrical time clashed. This was seen in works such as *Human Visual Sculpture in Contemplative Time* (1972) at the Royal Court Theatre Upstairs, one of a small number of London venues prepared to show work that, whether riotously or meditatively, questioned some of the fundamental tenets of theatre. Reedy had worked for a long period prior to the performance with the four participants. She made body-bags for them, "the colours of crocus flowers in the spring." Slides taken of the performers in their bags, from above in an abandoned church, were then projected over their actual bodies during the performance, so they moved in response to the pool of colour and light forming their own image. The artist acted as pacer of changes by bell, rattle, gong, and the occasional verbal statement. Expectations of drama and of acting were denied in favour of what Reedy called "visual sculptural living time": a kind of slow emergence into presence, analogous to the growth of plants. Performers stirred within their bags and gradually shed them to take up positions in the theatre, guided by their intuition to achieve "an authentic deviceless being-in-performance."[11] Reedy has continued to work with great subtlety between verbal language (often using several languages), theatre and visual art.

Although their work was never compared at the time, it is possible to see today that Reedy's piece and those of Bruce McLean have something in common in trying to rescue a notion of the living from the stereotypical expectations and social conventions of established art forms. They proceed by opposite means. If Reedy sought a naked existential "being," McLean adopted all the mannerisms of the contemporary art world in his own person in order to ridicule them. *Pose Work for Plinths* (1971) jestingly returns the monumental rhetoric of sculpture to the living human being. The artist, dressed in flared trousers and sweater, balances heroically, leisurely or awkwardly on three white cubes. These may have been the work of a (very young) "son" mocking the "fathers," and it is perhaps characteristic of the British psyche that they were quite quickly absorbed into the milieu they criticised. But McLean had a serious purpose. His isolation of the "pose" as a key sign of the times was refined and extended in later works and took on a broader social relevance.

**Liberation strategies** Having suggested how the performative element transformed some ancient generic forms of visual art, we can go on to consider the broader liberationist tendencies of the 1960s. Although we may appear here to narrow a global phenomenon to the specific geographical scope of this essay, I believe that Latin America represents a vital kernel of these movements. In no way can it be considered merely a contributor, still less an "outpost." Certain values essential to the liberating implications of these movements vis-à-vis the widely-shared

11. Carlyle Reedy, "Human Visual Sculpture in Contemplative Time," unpublished notes. Reprinted with the artist's kind permission.

Lygia Clark, *Respire comigo* (Breathe With Me), 1966
Projeto Hélio Oiticica/Lygia Clark Estate, Rio de Janeiro

dilemmas of contemporary culture came to fruition there. This could be attributed to many causes. Perhaps it lies partly in the energising potential of the very contradictions which underlie it: the pursuit of an Edenic "dream of happiness" in the face of authoritarian repression; the belief in art as a force of cultural emancipation in the face of the precariousness of art's production, survival, and continuity; a vision of the body's sensuality and equilibrium in the face of starvation and abuse. Of course it lies in the vision and strength of character of certain individual artists, but one has the feeling that this very strength is partly inspired and buoyed up by the presence of a popular energy and creativeness to which the artists are in one way or another witnesses. I have always thought that art in Latin America, especially in Brazil during the 1960s, had certain points in common with that of the Soviet avant-garde in the early 1920s: formal innovations which led to a broad social vision, "experimental exercises in freedom" (Mario Pedrosa). If the dynamo of the Soviet vision was the machine and technology (tempered by Tatlin's later reconsiderations), in Brazil it was the body.[12] It was in reference to the body that traditional artistic structures were revolutionised: specifically the nature of the object and the relationship between artist, work and spectator. And it was because of Brazil's historical Afro-Euro-Amerindian "popular culture of the body" that experiments in Brazil took the participatory forms which so clearly distinguishes them.

The extraordinarily fertile work and concepts of Lygia Clark and Hélio Oiticica carry many implications for the future interrelationship of art and life. One might almost characterize the vitality of their work by the simplicity and economy of their propositions. Take Clark's *Air and Stone* (as a matter of fact one can actually take it. It is not an art object but a proposal: simply inflate an ordinary plastic bag, seal it, place the stone in one corner and squeeze the bag between your hands). The interplay of solid mass and empty space, of weight and lightness, sums up the whole of sculptural history, yet the object is analogous to a body, breathing between our hands and sustained by our gestures. "We are the mould: the breath inside the mould is yours: the meaning of our existence."[13]

Clark, Oiticica, and Lygia Pape emerged from the seminal Neo-concrete movement in Brazil (1959-1961). These artists assimilated European abstract and concrete art (especially the examples of Mondrian and Malevich) in the most creative and critical fashion. It has always seemed to me significant that the grounding in those rigorous forms — the sweeping away of representational illusionism, traditional symbolism and naturalistic colour — underlay their later experiments. The transformation of Concretism in Brazilian conditions is a fascinating phenomenon. In a daring but logical process, Lygia Clark revealed the "organic" in the schemata of geometric abstraction. She, like Oiticica and Pape, took the *tabula rasa* of abstraction as an invitation to plunge into it bodily. Having penetrated the idealist construct of the plane as a projection of our "poetics" outside ourselves, Clark announced its death and proceeded to rediscover this poetic inside ourselves, with the body as the motor. The external object became the means of a radical internalisation. Proceeding from metal-hinged sculpture to rubber möbius ribbons, to sensorial hoods, to clothing which put one's insides out to be handled in a metaphorical game, often shared with a group of others, she arrived at collective experiences which are hard to name. *Baba Antropofágica* (1973) is not a performance, since there is no spectator. "We arrived at what I call 'collective body,'" the artist wrote, "an exchange between people of their intimate psychology. This exchange is not a pleasant thing . . . and the word communication is too weak to express what happens in the group."[14]

By the mid-seventies Clark had a whole reper-

---

12. See, for example, the Neo-concrete Manifesto (1959), to which Lygia Clark, Hélio Oiticica, and Lygia Pape were among the signatories: "If we have to look for an equivalent to the work of art we will not find it in the machine, or even the object as such, but . . . in living organ-

isms." The manifesto is reprinted in English in Dawn Ades et al., Art in Latin America: The Modern Period (London: Yale University Press, 1989), 335.

13. Lygia Clark, quoted in Paulo Herkenhoff, "Having Europe for Lunch,"

Poliester (USA-Mexico), no. 8: 14.

14. Lygia Clark, quoted in Guy Brett, "Lygia Clark: The Borderline between Life and Art," Third Text (London), no. 1 (Autumn 1987): 87.

**Lygia Clark**, *Baba Antropofágica*, 1973, from the series Collective Body

**Hélio Oiticica**, Inauguration of *Parangolé*,
Museu de Arte Moderna, Rio de Janeiro, 1965

*Lygia Clark, The I and the You: Clothing-Body-Clothing, 1967*

cannot really be discussed in one field only. Only when both fields have changed and communicated much more will her work have its long-term effects. The implication of her innovations in the sixties and seventies context of "live art" is the transformation of the artist/spectator relationship. No longer "Me the artist, YOU the spectator," in Ricardo Basbaum's words, but "YOUwillbecoME."[15]

toire of what she now calls *Relational Objects*. So convinced had she become of the inter-connections between the "physical" and the "metaphorical" in a person's lived experience that she felt she had evolved a "language of the body." By means of the *Relational Objects*, an interaction was possible with experiences locked in the body's memory at a non-verbal, or pre-verbal, level. The therapeutic possibilities of this process interested Clark increasingly, and from 1976 to about 1982, in her Rio studio, she treated many individuals with psychological problems ranging from profound psychotic crises to minor neuroses, although she had no regular psychiatric qualifications. Clark kept detailed notes on each experience, and found her best results with her most seriously disturbed patients.

  The implications of Clark's work are profound and still to be widely understood. She entered an area *between* art and medicine, such that her discoveries

Oiticica began with an extremely keen sense of the liberty promised by innovations of earlier modern art. A diary entry, written when he was twenty-four, speaks of Mondrian's aim in art as being "neither the mural nor applied art, but something expressive, which would be like the 'beauty of life,' something he could not define, because it did not yet exist."[16] The clean beauty and pure colours of Oiticica's early paintings might have suggested that he would adopt a technicist, constructivist position in the contemporary modernising enthusiasm of Brazil. Instead he identified himself with the most marginal sections of the population: *favela*-dwellers, outlaws, vagrants. It was not in a modernist utopia, but in the "desperate search for happiness," the rebellious acts, the yearning and finesse of the *samba*, the improvisations of shanty builders, the earth, the abandoned objects of

15. Ricardo Basbaum, "Clark and Oiticica," in Blast 4: Bioinformatica (New York: X-Art Foundation), 1994.

16. "Hélio Oiticica," diary entry, 16 February 1961, in Hélio Oiticica (Rotterdam: Witte de With et al., 1992), 42.

**Hélio Oiticica** with *Parangolé P22 Cape 18, Nirvana*,
with Antonio Manuel, 1968.
Centro de Arte Hélio Oiticica, Rio de Janeiro

the wastelands of the city, that he found indications
of a new culture. Oiticica combined his sensuous
response to the environment with a highly imaginative system of conceptual orders, intended to identify
a creative nucleus, both aesthetic/structural and eth-
ical/social, at each level of experience, from the
object up to the entire environment. Two suggestive
concepts encompassed the whole: *Worldshelter*, the
notion of a habitable world, and *Crelazer* or
*Creleisure*, a neologism made of the Portugese *crer*
(to believe), *criar* (to create), *lazer* (leisure), and perhaps *creole*. *Creleisure* was a refutation of a whole
system of values lying behind colonialism and racism,
imagining a "world which creates itself through our
leisure, in and around it, not as an escape, but as the
apex of human desires."[17]

 *Parangolé* (1964) was perhaps Oiticica's
finest invention: a transformable art work incorporated into the body and the emanation of each unique
being. Each of his capes had a different structure and
character, usually inspired by a particular individual or

collaboratively made. When it is worn or danced in,
the participator veils and unveils its various layers.
*Incorporo a Revolta* (I embody revolt) was made with
Nildo, a samba dancer of the Mangueira *favela*. The
constructivist rationale still shows gently through a
layered structure which has been astutely analysed
by Rosangela da Costa Motta:

> There is a general feeling of weight, of something
> to be carried. However what is in contact with the
> body is soft. . . . The text "Incorporo a Revolta" is
> covered by a skin of straw mat which symbolises
> rest and laziness. This indolence covers the sack-
> ing which is related to hard work. However, revolt
> is lit up by the red cloth. On the other hand, the
> contact of this blazing revolt with the body is
> deadened by the filling of flax. . . . The participa-
> tor experiences this cape as if it was a toy that
> provokes strange feelings of conflicting weights.[18]

 Certain works of Lygia Pape also give the
sense (more powerfully than words) of the way struc-

17. *Ibid.*, 136.

18. Rosangela da Costa Motta, from a
PhD thesis on Hélio Oiticica and the city
of Rio de Janeiro, at the Architectural

Association, London, 1997, unpublished.
Quoted with the author's kind permission.

**Lygia Pape**, *Egg*, 1967

tures of abstraction and minimalism were opened to the body and immersed in the flux of life in Rio de Janeiro. In Pape's *Eggs*, (1967) the minimalist cubes were wooden structures stretched on one side with a plastic membrane, out of which the participants burst in an analogy of birth. In *Divisor* (1968) we immediately recognise the device of the grid and the all-over composition. The cloth is a vast plane of cotton which holds a large number of people together in a group while at the same time separating them by the regular arrangement of holes. Pape also experimented with further dividing the head from the body by allowing a freezing draught of air to blow over the upper part and warm air to circulate in the nether regions. However, as soon as the piece becomes collective, the divisive and isolating elements disappear in a tide of energy and interactions ("Energy spreads over the whole of this primordial plane of light," in Paul Herkenhoff's words[19]).[20]

Many strategies appeared among Brazilian artists for questioning art's separation of the visual from the other senses. In *Wheel of Delights* (1968), Pape arranged bowls of colour pigments in a circle with droppers, for a light-hearted game in which one's visual attraction to a beautiful colour was often contradicted by a vile taste on the tongue.

Lea Lublin constructed a number of vast participatory environments in Argentina and Chile. Each was in a sense a "world" to be explored by the visitor, sensory and metaphorical elements combined by the artist according to a systematic didactic sequence. *Fluvio Subtunal* (1969) covered 900 square metres. It was partly inspired by the building of an underwa-

18. Rosangela da Costa Motta, from a PhD thesis on Hélio Oiticica and the city of Rio de Janeiro, at the Architectural Association, London, 1997, unpublished. Quoted with the author's kind permission.

19. Paulo Herkenhoff, "Lygia Pape — Fragmentos," in Lygia Pape (São Paulo: Galeria Camargo Vilaça, 1995).

20. Other remarkable expressions of this immersion could be mentioned: Mauricio Cirne's photos of pages in Pape's Neoconcrete Book of Creation (1959),

inserted in the everyday cacophony of Rio's streets; Regina Vater's inscription of the word ART ephemerally in nature's ebb and flow (Veart, 1978); Leonora de Baro's poem-performance in which her tongue seduces the keys of a typewriter (1980); and so on.

(left & below) **Lygia Pape**, *Divisor*, 1968

**Lygia Pape**, *Wheel of Delights*, 1968/1998. Collection of the artist

ter tunnel between the cities of Rosario and Santa Fé, and questioned the relationship between nature and technology. Visitors passed through nine zones (the Fountain, zone of winds, technological zone, production zone, sensorial zone, discharge zone, tunnel, nature zone, and participation area). The core of the work was the long inflated plastic tunnel into which one was virtually sucked, traversing and being expelled in a clear analogy to bodily processes. *Terranauts* (1969) (built at the avant-garde Instituto de Tella in Buenos Aires) was a spiral labyrinth in form. Barefoot and equipped with a miner's helmet, the visitors made their way through, discovering by the light of their lamps some essentials of life (earth, water, sand, wood, seeds, onions, potatoes, etc), amid smells, tactile sensations, music, and illuminated messages. Among a pile of vegetables a sign read: "Art will be life." At the exit a "cabin for thought" was provided. Lublin has characterised these works as early stages in a life-long project to "put in question the cultural conditioning of vision and perception, of the seen, of the known."[21] They were experiments to test the possibility of a "multi-dimensional perception acting equally on our psychic, sensorial and intellectual experiences."[22] It sounds reasonable enough, yet the ramifications of challenging our "visual conditioning" soon extend up to the normative dictates of the State. While making these essentially playful proposals in the Argentina of the early 1970s, Lublin had to defend herself against interference and censorship. She sometimes made works which wittily

documented this very process (e.g., her photographic montage, *A Police Inspector's Reading of a Work by Lea Lublin*, 1972).

A violent police response to the apparently innocuous appeared illogical but perhaps bore witness to a deeper challenge by artists to the ruling values. A work like Victor Grippo's, despite his conscious philosophy of minimum disturbance, or "a minimal sensitization," became at a certain point a target in this sense. In 1972 police invaded a public exhibition site in the center of Buenos Aires and smashed *Traditional Rural Oven for Making Bread* which had been temporarily constructed there by Grippo, Jorge Gamarra, an artist, and A. Rossi, a rural worker. Bread was baked in the oven and handed out to passers-by in a dramatisation of the polarisation of the city and hinterland in Argentina.

In 1974, at the height of the state terror of death squads and disappearances, Leopoldo Maler's uncle, the well-known editor of Argentina's leading liberal newspaper, was abducted and subsequently murdered. Looking at his uncle's typewriter in his house, "the image of fire replacing the sheet of paper came suddenly to my mind."[23] Maler made the typewriter in flames as an object, entitled *Homage* (the flames were maintained by a gas supply emerging through the carriage), and exhibited it in London in 1974. Alternating between Buenos Aires and London during the sixties and much of the seventies, Maler was a flamboyant experimenter with new media. He used television in theatre pieces, choreographed a

21. Jérôme Sans, "The Screen to the Real: Interview with Lea Lublin," in Lea Lublin: Mémoire des lieux, mémoire du corps (Quimper: Le Quartier Centre d'Art Contemporain, 1995), 57.

22. Lea Lublin, "Procés à l'image - Eléments pour une réflexion active," in Lea Lublin: Présent suspendu (Paris: Hôtel des Arts, 1991), 106.

23. Leopoldo Maler, from a letter to the author, April 1997.

Leopoldo Maler, *Crane Ballet*, 1971

**Victor Grippo**, *Construction of a Traditional Rural Oven for Making Bread*, 1972

ballet for dancers suspended from a construction crane in London in 1971, and showed an early, and memorable, example of expanded cinema in Britain, the tableau *Silence* (1971), which incorporated a film projected on the board of a hospital bed, and a live "nurse." In 1976, Maler returned to the theme of death and transience, and the technology of gas-jets, for an exhibition at London's Whitechapel Gallery, "Mortal Issues." Fire and air he saw as the live performing elements, playing around transparent or fragmented effigies of the human figure. An iron figure haloed in fire completed the installation. Interestingly enough, the life/fire, creation/destruction metaphor can be traced extensively in recent Latin-American art (unmistakably announced by Hélio Oiticica's *Bolides* (Fire-Balls) of 1963).

Marta Minujin was a pioneer of Happenings on an international stage and an early collaborator with Wolf Vostell and Allan Kaprow. Yet her work is not nearly as well known as it should be. Among her projects have been "deconstructed monuments" of a scale and logistical panache that rivals Christo's, though their *raison d'être* was rather different. Alberto Greco said of Minujin that she was "revitalising the graveyard." Desires for a dynamic art, subversion of the patriarchal and pompous myths of the state, a tapping of popular energies and tastes, an invitation to the spectator's participation, all come together in a typical Latin-American fusion. After events and environments culminating in *Sensmindenvironment* (c. 1974) (one circular and six cubic rooms of self-reflection designed to awaken "the creative energy which everyone potentially possesses"), Minujin launched her *Popular Myths* series, her "ephemeral art." At the São Paulo Bienal in 1977 she exhibited a full-size version of the Buenos Aires Obelisk (Argentina's equivalent of the Washington Monument), lying on its side ("everything is so straight and rigid and perpendicular that I want to make it all lie down"[24]). Two years later she erected in Buenos Aires another version of the Obelisk in the midst of a crowded industrial fair. The towering structure was made of 30,000 *panatone*, or raisin-buns, eaten by everyone in Argentina at Christmas. At a signal, six fire engines arrived with their ladders extended, surrounded the obelisk and distributed the buns to the audience. "When you eat the myth, you de-sacralise the myth. You make the old myth fall to make room for the new myth," in the artist's words.[25] You also perpetuate certain old myths which themselves signify renewal, like the tradition of constructing carnival giants, symbols of the people's cares, which, after being paraded the streets, were often ceremoniously burnt, destroyed, or otherwise consumed.

24. Richard Squires, "Eat me, Read me, Burn me: The Ephemeral Art of Marta Minujin" (interview), Performance (London), no. 64 (Summer 1991): 20.

25. Ibid., 20.

**Marta Minujin**, *The Obelisk of Raisin Buns*, 1979

Marta Minujin, *Mattress House*, 1963

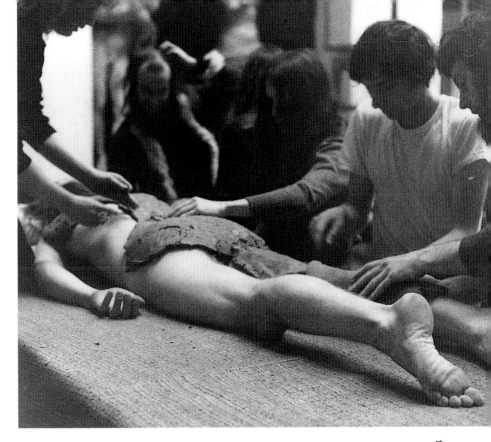

**David Medalla**, *Porcelain Wedding*,1974

A consideration of participatory and collective experiments which evolved in Britain during the same period (or slightly later) will show what they had in common with Argentinian and Brazilian work in bringing art out of institutional confines, but also some piquant differences.

David Medalla saw his participatory works as arising directly from his kinetic experiments of the sixties, for example his *Bubble Machines* (1964). The artist's relinquishing of control, the surrender to chance, and the allowance of natural forces to go beyond artistic choices excited him. If the metaphor for creation in the *Bubble Machines* was biological, there was no reason why this cellular structure of proliferation should not be translated to the social sphere: to people's energies and imaginations. Although he was already giving performances in the 1960s, Medalla felt the need also for an object or installation, potentially open to the passer-by and chance encounter, which could focus creative energies within contemplative time and space.

*A Stitch in Time* (1968), *Porcelain Wedding* (1974), and *Eskimo Carver* (1977) were the results. With the passage of time and hindsight, it is perhaps even easier to see the fluid and intricate metaphor of production which these experiments put in evidence.

In *Porcelain Wedding* a couple lay down naked and were encased in clay over their bodies by the other participants. The clay was decorated with linear designs and then cut into small squares to be baked and threaded together to form suits (similar to the jade burial suits recently unearthed in China).

As a prelude to the symbolic wedding visitors were invited to make small clay sculptures alluding to the seven days of creation: a form of "offering." *Porcelain Wedding* could also be seen as a fantastic parody of the life drawing class. The relationship between "artist" and "model" was revitalised by the hands-on collective game of molding the art material directly to the body, obliterating the element of cold detachment and surveillance, and at the same time becoming fused with the loving union of the couple in the marriage. The death suits were changed into vehicles of life. In *A Stitch in Time*, people were invited to sew anything they liked on long sheets of cotton. Installed differently each time, the work filled the room with a non-rigid, hanging, hammock-like structure, incorporating the sheets, the multitude of bobbins of coloured thread, and the needles. It was easy to enter ("people can walk in and out of my sit-

**213**

David Medalla, *A Stitch in Time*, 1968-72. Arts Council Collection, London

uations," the artist explained[26]), and the invitation to sew took away all preconceptions associated with high art, yet the ambience exerted subtle psychological pressures. To hurry by, or to offer your time, something of yourself, in an atmosphere of collective expectation? "Each one in his or her own time could be involved in a very simple activity. . . . and in the process of stitching, in the rhythm of the stitching, you'll find that the material will determine its half of the entire rhythm."[27] In place of an artist's traditional "achieved work," here was a growing kinetic model of a creative process in which artist and spectator, individual and collective, fabricator and material, reciprocally produced each other.

It is instructive, and perhaps liberating once again, to move the notion of a participatory and collective "live" work from corporeal frames of reference to an "out of the body" experience. To move, too, from an expressive mode of utterance to an analytical, investigatory one. We bear in mind of course the relativity and interdependency of all these terms: a conclusion perhaps intended by Susan Hiller's ironic, but admiring, application of the "objective" practices of measuring and mapping to the insubstantiality/subjectivity of dreams, in her *Dream Mapping* (1974). The project proceeded as follows. After a few practice weeks spent learning to notate their dreams, seven participants were invited by Hiller to sleep in a Hampshire field for three nights, a place noted for its large concentration of mushroom rings. Participants recorded and mapped their dreams each morning, and from their individual maps, composite maps were produced by superimposition. The piece raises intriguing questions about the influence of location on the highly specific life history reflected in each indi-

26. Steve Thorn, interview with David Medalla, quoted in Guy Brett, Exploding Galaxies (London: Kala Press, 1995), 98.

27. Ibid.

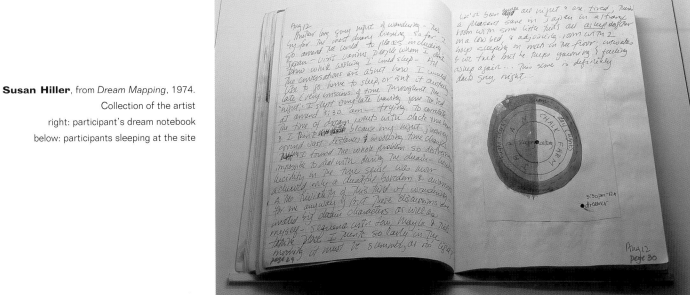

**Susan Hiller**, from *Dream Mapping*, 1974.
Collection of the artist
right: participant's dream notebook
below: participants sleeping at the site

**Susan Hiller**, *Street Ceremonies, 1973*

vidual's dream and his or her mode of "mapping" it, whether the circles of mushrooms gathered the participants in any form of collectivity, and so forth. But Hiller discounted the desire for "results." She stressed instead a process which would sensitise people to, and place into thought-provoking uncertainty, the boundary between individual and social, private and public. This fascinating experiment, and related investigations such as *Street Ceremonies* (1973), still radical in their implications today, were "deliberately non-theatrical. They are conducted among creative equals in the spirit of a collective endeavour, for which all participants are responsible," the artist wrote. "Individual experiences, reactions, and expressive acts function as aspects of a structure . . . designed to intensify a sense of shared subjectivity."[28]

**Protagonists** There is no twentieth-century art history which gives these participatory experiments their due.[29] They have not been included in the roll-call of recent art movements, and this must be because, although we know the art market can even-

tually make a saleable commodity out of almost anything, these works still disturb the prevailing conventions of art institutions. Oiticica likened his proposals to "mother-cells," plural and proliferating. Medalla described his as "endless" ("I could easily inundate, say, the Tate Gallery"[30]). Lygia Clark felt her experiments fundamentally changed the model of creation inherent in the division of artist and spectator, subject and object. It was this relationship which mattered, not whether the artist produced an object or a live event. For this reason, Clark distinguished her work from many forms of "body art" and performance, taking the radical position that these forms perpetuated the myth of the artist "to the extent to which the myth becomes the object of the spectacle."[31] Her work remained consistent with these principles. At the same time, however, participatory experiments had opened a field of unknown possibilities. They were lucid demonstrations of the fact that, as Hiller put it, "identity is shared, the self is multiple." "My 'self' is a locus for thoughts, feelings, sensations, but not an impermeable corporeal boundary. 'I AM NOT A CONTAINER.'"[32] There were many ways of manifesting and applying this expanded (or, if one wants to equalise the implications of duality, fragmented) view of the self, many ways, one might almost say, of transforming the ancient mode of the "self-portrait." A genre like "performance" therefore became a site for complex struggles between the presentation of a persona of the old monolithic type and a multiple self, a fluid identity, which is not constructed by annihilating its "other," but which can be many things at once.

Times change too, of course, sometimes subtly, sometimes grossly. Even the gross change is perhaps a violent form of conflicts which have continuously existed, and in relation to which the artist has always taken a position. The response of artists in Brazil to the trauma of military dictatorship (at its worst in the early seventies) would have to be read

28. Susan Hiller, quoted in Susan Hiller, op. cit., 50.

29. An exception is Frank Popper's Art–Action and Participation (New York: New York University Press, 1975), one of the conscienscious and generous books he produced on the art of the 1960s and 1970s.

30. Steve Thorn, interview with David Medalla, in Exploding Galaxies, 110.

31. Lygia Clark, "De la suppression de l'objet," Macula (Paris) no. 1 (1973): 118.

32. Susan Hiller, Sisters of Menon (London: Coracle Press, 1983).

**Artur Barrio**, *Situation T/T,* 1970

through the complex of liberating strategies which had been explored by the Brazilian avant-garde, an achievement whose effects were too powerful to be simply obliterated. The subtlety of artists' responses was a mark of these strategies' vitality and civilizational values.

Artur Barrio comes from a more expressionist direction than Clark, Oiticica, or Pape, without the element of constructivist ordering in his background. He found another route towards a similar (Brazilian? or perhaps more strictly Rio de Janeiro – *carioca*?) ethos, "tossing us into the . . . realm of the random, of chaos, into the uncontrollable flux of life."[33] Barrio expresses a characteristic position vis-à-vis reality and the spectator: "In my works things are not indicated (represented); they are lived. And it is necessary that one plunges into them. My work has its own life because it is all of us."[34] At the turn of the seventies Barrio organised in Rio and other cities a number of events involving *Trouxas Ensangüentadas* (Bloody Bundles), horribly suggestive objects which he left outside the museum (Museu de Arte Moderna, Rio, 1969) to be deposited in city streets or washed up along river banks. Cloth, bound with string, bulged with human detritus (blood, fingernails, hair, spit, urine, shit, bones), toilet paper, old newspapers, bandages, food scraps, ink, bits of film, etc. The photos of passers-by encountering these anonymous objects on the pavement, or witnessing their sinister defilement of nature, gives a powerful sense of remote authority perpetrating atrocities against the people. Yet Barrio also referred to the bundles more abstractly, as "inciting objects" and "cumulative centres of energy."[35] He insisted that his "rubbish" — strewn in provocative events usually broken up by the police — was as much a revitalising of art as a social protest.

In Cildo Meireles's *The Sermon on the Mount: Fiat Lux* (1973-79), actors dressed as presidential

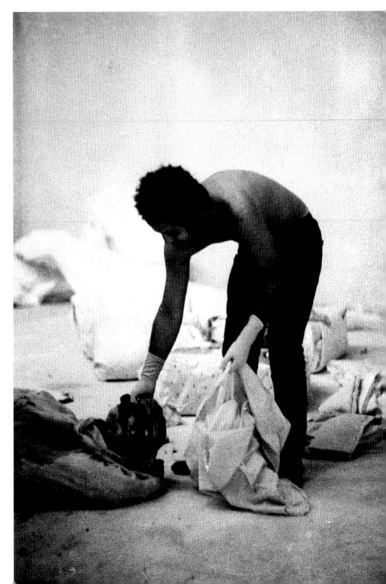

33. Marcio Doctors, "O Todo Nós/ The All of Us," in Situações: Artur Barrio: Registro (Rio de Janeiro: Centro Cultural Banco do Brasil, 1996), 6.

34. Artur Barrio, quoted in Doctors, ibid., 6.

35. Ibid., 16.

**Roberto Evangelista**, from *Mater Dolorosa, In Memoriam II*, 1979

**Cildo Meireles**, *The Sermon on the Mount: Fiat Lux*, 1973-79

bodyguards, or secret police, surround a large stack of packaged goods, such as one might find in a warehouse. These packages contain in fact 126,000 boxes of matches of a brand common in Brazil, *Fiat Lux* (Let there be light). Biblical allusions continue with the mirrors around the walls on which are printed Christ's beatitudes. On the floor the spectators', as well as the actors', feet rub against emery paper of the kind glued to the sides of match boxes. Despite its avoidance of any militant stance, its cunning deployment of the Duchampian ready-made, Meireles's work was shown publicly only with difficulty, being cancelled and withdrawn twice before being finally performed for twenty-four hours in 1979. In fact, in this work, I believe Meireles went beyond a denunciation of the political authorities to produce a brilliant allegory of art. It is as effective in its performative aspects (the oppressive presence of the heavies, precise down to the smallest detail), as in its use of the object. In the context of Christ's assurances to the humble and powerless that they will one day inherit the earth (which we peruse superimposed on our own self-image), is a huge nucleus of latent energy and light, nervously guarded by officials whose feet may set it off at any minute. The matches can be seen as both the popular energy repressed by the rich and powerful, and as the artist's work. Can either exist in Brazil and come to fruition? The "guarded" scenario asks guardedly the question which motivated so many in the avant-garde of the sixties. We would not expect an answer, unless it is at another level of the allegory. The cube may be suddenly transformed. As Ronaldo Brito wrote poetically in his study of Meireles: "the work is against solids, a physics of solids, a politics of solids. Against all that restrains energy, communication, the flux of transforming densities."[36]

The theme of immersion, which runs through so much of Brazilian art of this period, is strikingly present in Roberto Evangelista's work. Evangelista was born, educated, and lives and works in Manaus, on the Amazon, and like other artists scattered in different parts of Brazil, has been pre-occupied with environmental questions for much of his career. For him this has meant an intense involvement in the local: a specific place, history, people, and the problematic of how to "infect" the international avant-garde discourse with his knowledge of the long history of foreign despoliation in the Amazon.

In works like *Mater Dolorosa*, the waters of the Rio Negro have been both "support" and "medium:" a surface for the movement of commonplace local elements (such as the gourd and bamboo), and a metaphor for the reality in which one is immersed with fellow beings. The lyrical sequences in *Mater Dolorosa* suddenly come to an end in a disturbing, memorable image. Several people appear in the water in the semi-distance, their heads bobbing among the gourds, making up a group (the artist among them) from which desperate cries are issuing. It is like a cry of agony which can also be read as a shout of survival. In the same sense, Evangelista's metaphor of immersion can be read in two ways: as the drowning, the shipwreck of a land and culture (in a text written in 1970 Oiticica had described the whole of Brazil as a "drowning country"); and also as the artist's plunging with the body into the space of the work, and into the local environment and the people.

36. Ronaldo Brito, "Freqüência Imodulada," in Cildo Meireles (Rio de Janeiro: Funarte, 1981), 8.

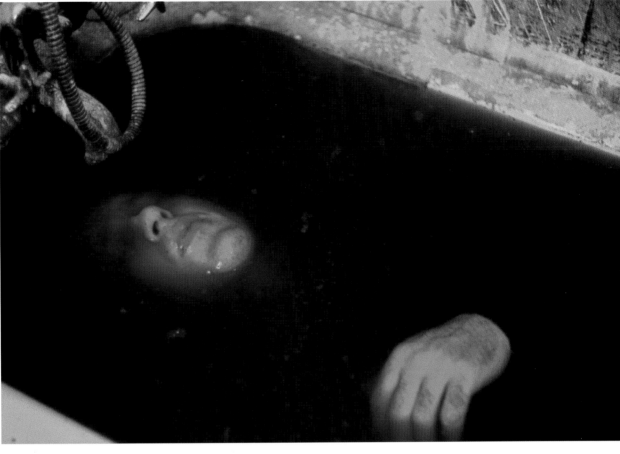

Stuart Brisley, *And for Today . . . Nothing*, 1972. Collection of the artist

In an intense series of performances between 1973 and 1980 — apparently the first to be done in Chile — Carlos Leppe provided a sort of experimental cell where the general physiognomy of the official order was challenged through the presentation of the body. Nelly Richard has spoken of "the intransigence of the military for whom the body is the first disciplinary mould of the normative identity,"[37] enforced by training and torture. In direct contrast, Leppe exhibited — not with bombast but in terms of vulnerability and struggle — the transvestite body, where the rigid determination of sexual roles is parodied. In Chile at this time the exposure of the body had a special intensity since, as Nelly Richard has observed, under the pervasive regime of censorship applied to the use of language in general, "any superfluous discourse or unspoken pressures, which undermine the syntax of the permitted, can only surface as bodily gestures."[38]

Interplay between presentation of the self as an artist (self-portrait) and self-representation as an ordinary person, "traversed by the social conflicts which make one conform to society,"[39] is not a new theme in art. However, performance art gave the whole process a new inflection by translating the artists from their customary discourse (painting, sculpture, etc.) to one where they were naked and unformed, on exhibition and in direct contact with the audience. Immediately tensions were created between "being oneself" and "acting a role," between material reality and symbol or metaphor. It seems, in retrospect, that this change signalled two great desires: the artist's desire to rescue the vitality of communication from an art system increasingly besotted with the commodity, and the "ordinary person's" desire to come to know himself or herself through their lived experience, particular history, identity, and subjectivity. It is as if artists presented this twofold desire in an embryonic and a testamentary form, facing the audience as if facing the world.

Concentration on the artist's individual person and subjectivity would seem to suggest an inescapably solo mode, yet the fruitful paradox was that the appearance of the visual artist in the role of "actor" was simultaneously a deconstruction, and an expansion, of the notion of the protagonist. The wave of performance art that swept Britain in the late seventies threw up a fascinating variety of protagonists. While in one sense the performers were "naked" before the audience, in another they came to represent the complex amalgam, the "infinity of traces" (Gramsci), which make up identity. Therefore there was no break, but a continuity, between the solo mode, duos, ensembles, and a range of devices including absent or surrogate performers, stand-ins,

37. Nelly Richard, "A Matter of Style," in Adam's Apple Chile – Transvestites (Paddington NSW: Australian Centre for Photography, 1989).

38. Nelly Richard, "Margins and Institutions," op. cit., 72.

39. Fernando Balcell's "Analysis" in Nelly Richard, "Margins and Institutions."

Gilbert & George, *Singing Sculpture*, 1970

Bruce McLean, *Nice Style Pose Band event, High Up on a Baroque Palazzo*, 1974

alter egos, and disguises, and inanimate objects which sometimes seemed more alive than the live performers.

In a highly impressionistic survey of this rich field, whose records are still scattered and often inaccessible, one could range from those performers whose work seems to stem from the "agony" contained in the word "protagonist," artists such as Stuart Brisley, Kerry Trengove, or Alastair MacLennan, who have grappled with dark and subterranean aspects of society through feats of endurance and stamina; to those who have adopted a cool and sartorially unblemished appearance such as Gilbert & George or Bruce McLean.

The impact of Gilbert & George's early performances as the Human Sculptures can only be understood in the context in which they first appeared. A typical scenario would be a Rolling Stones concert in a summery Hyde Park at the end of the sixties, where the long-haired, languid, liberated crowds looked up to see a buttoned-up male couple with faces painted metallic silver and gold, gingerly promenading and striking poses like a thirties fashion print. Their robotic choreography was the antithesis of everything hippie. It was mesmeric, funny, and perhaps ultimately frightening. Like their gallery presentations of the *Singing Sculpture* (1970), miming to a portable tape-recording of the Edwardian music-hall song, "Underneath the Arches," it appealed to a perennial fascination with automata, effigies and mannequins. It seemed an illustration of the liberty art offers for a play of opposites. When one style is becoming a cliché, its contrary produces an electrifying effect. Against a pursuit of the natural, the fluid, interactive and plural, was set the artificial, rigid, remote and single (despite Gilbert & George being a duo). McLean's Nice Style ("the world's first

pose band"), which followed from his early performances, was prescient in transposing a traditional British obsession with the visual and gestural signs of rank to a general condition of fakery, involving broad swathes of the bureaucracy, academia, and the consumer society.

In these examples, however, many elements are familiar and represent a transposition to the field of live art of a traditional model of the artist as demiurge or master. With the emergence of a large number of outstanding women artists in Britain in the 1970s, as well as others whose representation within British society had been denied or stereotyped, such as artists from countries of the Third World, these models changed.

A new perception of the relationship between the artist's dreams and the demands of everyday life were expressed in the invention of a new kind of protagonist. To examine the whole tradition of the artist as master was not to abandon it but to reconfigure it ironically as inseparable from its opposite: uncertainty, ambivalence, "our fruitful incoherence," as Susan Hiller once called it. The new protagonists constructed themselves in the process of dissolving many rigid dichotomies which had defined the old: between passive receptiveness and active enquiry, between power and powerlessness, between artist and audience, male and female, adult and child, stage and world. Thus we had Tina Keane's dialogue with her daughter Emily through a series of performances based on children's songs and games; Rose Finn-Kelcey's invention of the "absent" or "surrogate" performer; the elegant and unending ritual of witnessing in Hannah O'Shea's *Litany for Women Artists* (1976) or the hesitant and painful one in Sonia Knox's *Echoes of the North* (1979); Rasheed Araeen's experiments in how the artist/black person in Britain could produce a self-portrait, and so on.

The date chosen as the cut-off point for this exhibition, 1979, produced no interruption of this process in Britain. In fact performance was probably at its liveliest in the mid-eighties, with artists of older and younger generations appearing together in a number of memorable events. Only the barest indication here can trace the efflorescence of personae:

**Kerry Trengove** *An Eight-Day Passage*, 1977

Bow Gamelan's fire-raisers (Anne Bean, Paul Burwell, and Richard Wilson) re-orchestrating artistic visions of the river Thames; Nick Stewart's pilgrim; Nick Payne's incisive dandy; Mona Hatoum's powerful peformances interweaving oppression and resistance; Sylvia Ziranek's poseur, whose words and attributes both mockingly define and fantastically exceed her suburban persona; Rose English's move from solo performer to become the artist of magnificent live events, both entertaining and profound, where a host of theatrical languages and persons of great skill such as acrobats and conjurers combine with "ordinary people" within a charmed arena of philosophical and cosmological enquiry. Many of these artists first emerged in the seventies and came to maturity in the eighties. Artists who were already performing in the sixties, such as Carlyle Reedy and David Medalla, also produced brilliant new work in the eighties, unfortunately beyond the time-span of this essay.

Stuart Brisley's earliest performances departed from the body/sculpture borderline. He often used body casts, and the performers themselves resembled white effigies, disposed within a geometric framework. Although, as the critic Paul Overy has remarked, time replaced the space-frame as the favourite structuring device of Brisley's live works,[40] a kind of stasis persisted. The elapse of time in the performance intensified the impact of a single image. Brisley has disclaimed the role of the subjective in his actions: "The work is never seriously about one's own problems."[41] In the critic John Roberts's words,

> The world of dark things that Brisley's art inhabits is not the workings of the mind directed inwards but outwards to those "mechanics of power" — the family, the public institutions, the State — which regulate our lives in their myriad, ubiquitous ways.

By using his own body as a metaphoric or allegorical site, Roberts continues, "Brisley enacts and comments upon how the individual manoeuvres himself fitfully, haplessly, between authority and freedom."[42] The rationale is remarkably similar to that of Carlos Leppe in Chile, working some years later in conditions ostensibly very different. It may be that the sheer mess, stench and repellent aspects of many of Brisley's performances were expressions of his determination to overcome the slick and self-satisfied surface of modernising capitalist states that ride over decrepitude and deprivation — an exercise in which he sees the art world as implicated. At the 1977 Documenta, Brisley was offered an outdoor space next to the American artist Walter de Maria, who had been sponsored by an American millionaire to sink a thin brass rod one kilometre into the earth.

40. Paul Overy, introduction, in Stuart Brisley (London: Institute of Contemporary Arts, 1981), 8.

41. Stuart Brisley, quoted in John Roberts, "Stuart Brisley," ibid., 11.

42. John Roberts, "Stuart Brisley," ibid., 11.

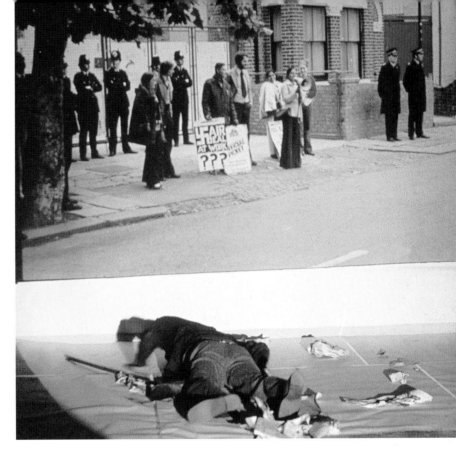

**Rasheed Araeen**, "*Paki Bastard*", 1979

Brisley removed himself to another part of Kassel, where, with the help of a collaborator, he laboriously dug his own hole by hand and lived at the bottom of it, amidst the mud and debris, alone for a period of two weeks (*Survival in Alien Circumstances*). More than a mere critique of the waste of money and manpower nearby, Brisley's action equated this expense with blandness, and seemed to suggest that his pit was where life-affirming energy could really be found.

In a romantically symbolic act, Kerry Trengove tunnelled his way out of a small sealed space in the foundations of the Acme Gallery in London (*An Eight-Day Passage*, 1977). It took him eight days to emerge into the daylight to a blaze of media attention. Again an artist eschewed the white-painted cleanliness of the art gallery for a subterranean cell whose rubble walls and constricted space, where the artist was seen moving about by the light of a miner's helmet or sleeping, were relayed to visitors in the gallery above by closed-circuit TV to produce the maximum contrast. In this unexpected and very literal struggle by the Artist, a figure conventionally seen as ethereal and fanciful, to escape from self-imposed limits of time and space, Trengove clearly intended to raise broader questions about stereotyped modes of behaviour, control and freedom in general, a theme he

often returned to before his premature death in 1991.

In the mid and late-seventies Rasheed Araeen became concerned with the problematic question of how to represent himself, how to make a self-portrait. He increasingly identified his life-situation in Britain with that of immigrant workers from Asia and Africa, exploited and denied a political and cultural voice. The freedom represented by his earlier abstract work came to seem to him to occupy a mythical space "inversely proportional to the real space at the bottom of the hierarchical pyramid."[43] "*Paki Bastard*" (1979) was Araeen's unique foray into live performance, a moving experience as much for the artist's dignified awkwardness before the audience as the social realities he was evoking. Identity as an artist, identity as a black person, identity as exploited worker were the three themes whose interrelationship was continually questioned in the piece. Again, Araeen's minimalist sixties *Structures* appear in the scenario, playing a role as part of the critical polemic, but also perhaps contradictorily as a talisman of artistic exploration, suggesting that the "identity" forced on him by circumstances only represents a part of his humanity.

Rose Finn-Kelcey's live works of the seventies and early eighties are a fascinating reflection on the notion of protagonist. All could be interpreted partly in terms of her search for an appropriate voice for her experience as a woman artist, one where "the doubts are given equal substance as the certainties in the realisation of the piece."[44] Ironic questioning of the myth of mastery led her to a succession of unique and poetic scenarios. In *One for Sorrow, Two for Joy* (1976), she spent two evenings in a gallery window with a live magpie. She made various approaches to the bird, with whose wayward reputation in folklore

43. Rasheed Araeen, "Paki Bastard," in Making Myself Visible (London: Kala Press, 1984), 114.

44. Catherine Elwes, "About Time," Primary Sources (London), (Christmas 1980).

she had long identified, offering it food and addressing it in its own language as arranged into seventeen cries and transcribed into French phonetics by an eighteenth-century scientist. Could she be flexible enough in this encounter to find her way back from the codified information to the bird's experience, thus linking it with her own? *Mind the Gap* (1980) was, famously, the performance in which the artist did not appear; or rather she appeared only after a woman's voice had apologised for her absence and read a selection of working notes towards the unfinished event. Having made her own ambivalence about performing the subject of the event, Finn-Kelcey introduced her notion of "surrogate performers" and "the vacated performance," a nice conceit capable of giving paradoxical insights into the phenomena of power.

If the reader is still with me after these hurried raids through so many artists' work, I would like to offer a few thoughts on the guiding theme the curator has used to bring this huge historical compendium together. "Out of Actions: Between Performance and the Object": significant procedures are encapsulated in these titular phrases. Besides the introduction of the notion of the object into a field which seems to represent its opposite, the performative, the insistent little pun implies that something vital may have died when the ephemeral event is over and only the material residue remains. By introducing the category of the object, which it basically exists for and is most comfortable with, while suggesting that this object is the dead result of something living, the museum or the institution subliminally suggests that this process always triumphs.

However, I would like to open the question up beyond such deterministic conclusions and reconsider the relationship between performance and the object. It is a complex one, shot through with all the paradoxes of life. It is as varied as all the procedures by which an object, a substance, a word, a gesture, may become efficacious or not. It does not reside in the object, finally, but in a relationship, in this case

(left and opposite) **Rose Finn-Kelcey**, *One for Sorrow, Two for Joy*, 1976

between artist, work, and spectator: a reality which most of the bodies of work above bear out.

For example, a sensitive eye-witness account of an ephemeral event may be a more precious residue than some other material object, although it cannot be fetishised. Its efficacy lies in its participatory aspect: its vision (a combination of seeing and imagination). Hélio Oiticica made his *Parangolé Capes* for active participation, to be worn, danced in, simultaneously a reverie for the wearer and a spectacle for others. They look forlorn displayed on hangers as art objects in a museum. Yet, applying his irony and "critical ambivalence," as he called it, Oiticica also made static objects which invite action only in imagination: for example in 1968 he made a grey basin filled almost to the top with water. Visible in cut-out letters at the bottom, through the water, were the words *MERGULHO DO CORPO* (plunging of the body) — a temptation to plunge and a kind of encapsulation of his art/life aesthetic. This was another way of suggesting that it was not the object which was important but the way it was "lived" by the spectator/participant.

MOCA has placed Jackson Pollock at the beginning of the show as an originary figure in fusing visual art and the performative. Oiticica referred to Pollock several times in his early writings, and it was primarily a transformation of the artist-work-spectator relationship which took Oiticica past the stage of Pollock's drip paintings. Noting that, in Pollock, "the picture virtually 'explodes' — transforms itself into the acting field of graphic movement,"[45] he went on to lift this "acting field" out of the graphic transcription of the artist's expressivity and to give it to the spectator, so to speak. His *Area Bolides* of 1967 —

low rectangular enclosures strewn with sand or straw — were designated voids where "the participator will 'act' upon those areas looking for 'internal meanings' within himself, rather than trying to apprehend external meanings or sensations."[46]

Lygia Clark's *Relational Objects* also proposed a relationship with the participator in which, in Lula Wanderley's words, "the object [is] lived in an 'imaginary inwardness of the body' where it finds signification."[47] Treading a parallel path, David Medalla in 1970 memorably recast the art object as a "thought." As a contribution to a survey of multiples — the supposed means of a democratisation of art in the sixties — Medalla proposed his *Ephemerals*: miniatures to be made by anyone out of anything to "illuminate for an instant a transitory experience."[48]

Such experiences lead to a fusion of the subject and object, of the subjective and objective, which, in a sense, we have always known. We know, for example, that Brancusi's sculptures look physically different in the photographs he took than they do in other people's; that different selections of the same artist's work vary wildly in efficacy; that an object apparently exhausted by consumption can be reconfigured. This is perhaps one of the great themes of Susan Hiller's work: a practice and a poetic of mediation. "A wish for everything to be seen as having the same potential for insight:" a way of working in the world by means of mapping, reselection, editing, changes of state, boxes within boxes.

It follows that, in the museum also, we are responsible not only for an act of preservation but also of re-creation.

45. Hélio Oiticica, diary entry, 16 February 1961, in Hélio Oiticica, op. cit., 43.

46. Hélio Oiticica, "Eden," ibid., 12.

47. Lula Wanderley, "The Memory of the Body," unpublished, 1993. Quoted with the author's kind permission.

48. David Medalla, statement, in 3 > ∞: new multiple art (London: Arts Council of Great Britain, 1970), 54.

**John Latham**, *Art and Culture*, 1966-69. The Museum of Modern Art, New York. Blanchette Rockefeller Fund

Kristine Stiles

# UNCORRUPTED JOY: INTERNATIONAL ART ACTIONS

It may be some time before the potential of material/transforming art,
and its implications for art and society have been worked out.
When carried into practice, it may be regarded as one of the most radical
steps in the twentieth century.
— Gustav Metzger, 1965[1]

**I. Art in Culture**  In late August, 1966, John Latham withdrew Clement Greenberg's collection of essays, *Art and Culture*, from the library of London's St. Martin's School of Art where he worked as a part-time art instructor. Together with one of his students, the now well-known British sculptor Barry Flanagan, Latham organized a party at his home, mysteriously entitled *Still and Chew*. When the guests arrived, Latham invited them to tear and chew up pages from Greenberg's widely influential book on the theory of art. "If necessary," the forty-five year old artist sardonically instructed, "spit out the product into a flask provided."[2] Those assembled complied, expectorating about a third of the volume in a heap of masticated pulp. Latham then immersed the wad in a solution containing thirty-percent sulfuric acid, left it until the solution converted to sugar, neutralized the remains with sodium bicarbonate and introduced a yeast — an "Alien Culture" — into the substance to create a "brew." Latham allowed his cultured brew to "bubble gently" for nearly a year until the end of May, 1967, when he received a postcard labeled: "Art and Culture wanted urgently by a student." Latham decanted the distilled mass into a suitable glass container, labeled the jar "Art and Culture," and returned it. "After the few minutes required to persuade the librarian that this was indeed the book which was asked for on the postcard," Latham left the object and returned home. The next morning he received a letter from the Director of St. Martin's who apologized for being "unable to invite [him] to do any more teaching." Latham's teaching career came to an abrupt end after his encounter with art and culture.

By manifesting the interdependence of the body and its object, in his conceptual and physical relationship to Greenberg's text, Latham produced a counter-illusionistic work of art, for which the object, *Art and Culture*, stands as commissure. Latham's object would have little meaning without the action. In fact, without his action there would be no "brew,"

no clash between art and culture. The materials that constitute *Still and Chew* now reside in a leather briefcase, in the collection of The Museum of Modern Art, New York. The case is filled with powders and liquids, letters, photostats, and the invitation the artist sent for the event. It also includes the written dismissal Latham received from St. Martin's School of Art, a copy of Greenberg's *Art and Culture*, and other memorabilia from the action. As objects their categorical status is quite mundane. It is their relationality to an artist's action that constitutes them as art. They are entrusted to share that act with us. Greenberg could only metaphorically re-present what Latham could metonymically make present by linking action to its object. These tropes comprise a central axis along which actions in art have shifted the conventional subject-object relations instantiated in traditional viewing conditions away from their sole dependence on re-presentation (metaphor) to connection (metonymy).[3] Latham's action rematerialized Greenberg's book in terms of the body, wryly suggesting that, as conceptual "food for thought," the text was mush, unpalatable for artists.

This very term — art and culture — exhibits the relationality of art to something else, just as such phrases as "art and politics," "art and technology," "art and life," disclose how art cannot be without an other to which it cleaves. To cleave to is not the same as to become one with. The unique aspect of action art is that, when the body is used in action, it exemplifies the means by which all art is relational with the world. Moreover, action in art draws viewers closer to the fact that it is the body itself that produces objects and that such an art is a unique vehicle enabling perception and contemplation of the truth that the "made object [is] a projection of the human body."[4] Action art makes palpable this projection between objects and subjects. By showing the myriad ways that action itself couples the conceptual to the physical, the emotional to the political, the psychological

1. Gustav Metzger, Auto-Destructive Art: Metzger at AA *(London: Creation/Destruction, 1965), 25.*

2. All descriptions here of Latham's event, Still and Chew, are taken from his own account of the project, August 1967, and printed in John Latham: least event, one second drawings, blind work, 24

second painting (London: Lisson Publications, l970), 8.

3. Much of this section on the function of metonymy in action art is taken from my unpublished dissertation, "The Destruction in Art Symposium (DIAS): The Radical Project of Event-Structured Live Art," 1987, University of California at Berkeley. See also my "Synopsis of

The Destruction in Art Symposium (DIAS) and Its Theoretical Significance," The Act (New York) 1 (Spring 1987): 22-31.

4. Elaine Scarry, The Body in Pain: The Making and Unmaking of the World (Oxford: Oxford University Press, 1985), 281.

to the social, the sexual to the cultural, and so on, action art makes evident the all-too-often-forgotten interdependence of human subjects — of people — one to another. The body is the medium of the Real, however multifarious that Real becomes and is manifest. By making this interconnection itself material, action art renders both the relationality of individuals within the frame of art and culture visible. In this way, action in art *acts* for all Art — for better or worse — to bring the relation between seeing and meaning, making and being, into view.

The essay that follows consists of an interrelated set of brief meditations, each of which explores only a fragment of the infinite number of correspondences that action art traverses. My essay, in this regard, is not an historical survey, and is not concerned with a particular chronology of events. Nonetheless, a chronology exists, however multiple its mappings may be. That chronology begins certainly somewhere in action painting and moves into Happenings that themselves reflect and overlap with the aftermath of World War II, the emergence of the *hibakusha* (bomb victims), the Beat generation, the Angry Young Men of England, the reconstruction of world economies and cultures, as well as violent conflicts, especially in Korea, Vietnam, and Algeria. During these volatile decades, the communication between artists creating Happenings around the world, and the loose affiliation of artists who comprised Fluxus, help to make it possible to understand that the individuals who made actions as art were equally employed in a project that recognized no national boundaries, *even as* the particular conflicts and contingencies that individual artist's work exhibited reflected the exigencies of national identity.

Unusual events often result in paradigmatic shifts that happen at critical conjunctions. I have long contended that the body as material in art after 1950 was deeply tied to the need to assert the primacy of human subjects over inanimate objects, and was a response to the threatened ontological condition of life itself in the aftermath of the Holocaust and the

advent of the atomic age. To write this is not to suggest that there were no precedents for such an art. There were many, and the body as visual medium existed in almost every European avant-garde movement before World War II. But the regular, systematic, and international use of the body over the past fifty years defined it as new medium and genre in the visual arts. An art of actions meant that art could be simultaneously representational *and* presentational, simultaneously claiming the primacy of the body as metaphorical content *and* as concrete presentational form. Such an art has made more concrete the metonymic relationship of exchange that exists between the viewer and the work of art. But it has further altered that relationship by presenting an acting subject in a real exchange with another acting subject: in short, action art presents two human beings who negotiate meaning with one another, however complicated that mode of communication might be.[5] Indeed, communication *between human beings* is the issue when actions become art. Action in the real social condition of everyday life is what lost Latham his teaching position. He proved how much is at stake when one weds action to art and culture.

I think that the proportional significance of the cultural to the political became especially vivid in the art actions generally associated with "The Sixties" primarily because of the hyper-awareness in the period that human action in the social realm impacts the political domain. For me, "The Sixties" begin in 1955 with Rosa Parks, the black seamstress from Montgomery, Alabama, who refused to give up her seat on a city bus to a white person (as she was legally required to do); and end some time between 1973 and 1975, when the U.S. withdrew troops from Vietnam, and the ignoble helicopter flights from the roof-top of the American embassy there forever etched on my mind.[6] Watergate, the demise of the New Left in the aftermath of May 1968 in Europe, and the violence of the Chinese Cultural Revolution destroyed any remaining shreds of confidence in the

5. Daniel Buren's "Sandwich Men," an action in which people carried placards consisting merely of alternating white and colored stripes around Paris in 1968, exhibited just how difficult communication over the slippery territory of signs

may be even when, and no doubt because, action is involved.

6. For a discussion of history written by decades, see Fredric Jameson, "Periodizing the 60s," in The 60s Without

Apology, ed. Sohnya Sayres, Anders Stephanson, Stanley Aronowitz, and Fredric Jameson (Minneapolis: University of Minnesota Press in cooperation with Social Text, 1984), 178-209.

**228**

beneficence of government, causing an inward turning away from the civic.

The extraordinary degree of interplay between action and politics which characterizes "The Sixties" is paralleled by the wide range of terms artists used then to describe their work: concrete art, Happenings, Fluxus, action, direct art, ceremonies, demonstrations, kinetic theater, arte povera, earth or ecological art, process art, interactive art, actual art, activities, guerrilla art, guerrilla theater, guerrilla art action, street theater, live art, event art, eventstructure, consciousness raising, survival research, and many more. This linguistic variety itself delineates the rich interface between the social and aesthetic content of art. Such a fertile etymology displays how vital and how committed artists were to laying bare the very real intersections already existing between aesthetics, activism, and culture; conjunctions that depended not only on the example provided by the Civil Rights movement, but the international experience of a divided planet in the Cold War, the emergence of post-colonialism, the space race, the beginning of the electronic revolution in communications (especially television and computers), the new global ecological awareness, the rise of the New Left and feminism followed by the activation of other special interest groups such as Gays and Lesbians, and the multiculturalism that began in the late 1970s.

Perhaps the homogeneity of the ubiquitous term Performance Art, which now generically designates, administers, and manages a wide range of cultural actions, and whose widespread appearance marks the end of the period under investigation by this exhibition, also indicates how conceptually removed culture has become from an awareness of its own conditions of, and potential for, action. Perhaps this homogenization process — manifest in a dissociation from actual involvement as one moves from being engaged to theorizing change — has subsumed action into theory, which itself may be overwhelmed by the task of balancing the two in praxis.

## II. Commissures: Art Actions as Objects

Jackson Pollock's No. 1 (1949) is an excellent place to begin. Although it was painted on the floor, as was Pollock's habit, No. 1 also hung on his studio wall during the summer and fall of 1950, a silent witness to Hans Namuth's camera. In a famous series of photo sessions, Namuth produced images that form the bridge from action-painting to the first events of action art.[7] No. 1 is one picture in a series of painting-actions, each considered singular and so titled, yet also connected and interconnected with others: No. 1 (1948), No. 1 (1949), One (1950), and Lavender Mist (No. 1) (1950). The continuities between Pollock's titles might be said to begin and end on a chain of resemblances. Pollock's painting then, is to the exhibition of objects of actions in the museum, what Latham's Art and Culture is to a text about the exhibited objects and actions: an integral link in a chain of meaning that begins in actions, moves through objects and texts into institutions and the lives of people interested in art, in a continuous series of linkages and reciprocities.

The central issue of this exhibition is the dimensionality between actions and objects, and all that it entails. Latham's Art and Culture demonstrates this relationship with humor and insight, engaging us at the level of the artistic act (whether textual or visual) and its reception in culture. Pollock also seemed to have grasped this essence in his eccentric numbering system. For one painting is also a part of an other, poised together in a titular matrix that identifies Pollock's actions as belonging to the task of someone making objects. There is a symmetry here between objects and human actions that is the critical aesthetic point to which action art has attended. But this symmetry passes over an interstice that is abstract. This description is difficult to grasp and needs a more concrete means for thinking about the space that sets up a congruence between the object and an action. If this space is objectified and its linkage labeled, it may become more substantial. I think that the term "commissure" may enable us to think about the space of connection in a

7. See the diagram of Pollock's studio in E.A. Carmean, Jr.'s essay, "L'art de Pollock en 1950," in Hans Namuth, L'Atelier de Jackson Pollock. Along with No. 1, 1949, the other works in the room included Autumn Rhythm, on which Pollock was working, No. 32 (1950), One, and, in an adjacent room, Lavender Mist (No. 1), (1950).

broader, more theoretical way that ultimately entails commitment, the value that I believe is preeminent in performance art.

Commissure is derived from the Latin terms *commissura*, meaning to join together, and *committere*, meaning to connect, entrust, or to give in trust (from which the English word "commit" is derived). Among its many meanings commissure also refers to the corporeal slit separating the two eye-lids and the lips. Thought of as commissures, the objects that come "out of actions" might gain the rich multiplicity and multiple articulation of that term. First of all, objects that come out of actions (action-objects) may signify in the same ways that conventional art objects (paintings, sculptures, assemblages, installations) communicate meaning, as discrete things made to be viewed formally. But what about the traces of use that many of these objects suggest, or the meaning connected to the actions from which they derive or in which such objects participated? In this sense action-objects become commissures, announcing their contingency to signifying acts. Understood as commissures, the objects that come out of actions can clarify how actions signify both as works of art themselves (*as objects*), and as modalities bonding viewers back to actions in a chain of interdependence. Thinking of the objects as connected, as commissures, one may grasp that *those actions constitute* artistic behaviors that are made to be viewed in the same way that we look at the object. As commissures, these objects must be understood as linked to behavior that itself is made for viewing. Thus in art actions, objects are entrusted, delegated to act as connections leading back to aesthetic concepts. The objects that come out of actions, seen as commissures, must be understood as signs of commitment to viewers that are given in a desire for communication about an artist's acts.

Removing art from purely formalist concerns and the commodification of objects, artists employing action sought to reengage both themselves and spectators in an active experience by reconnecting art (as behavior) to the behavior of viewers. Art actions and their related objects move through the body of the artist in his/her material circumstance to the viewer in the social world. Such action-objects are carriers of that information enlivened by action. They announce that it is never enough to simply look at the object of an action without entering into a committed relation, a situation in which the object draws viewers back to actions completing the cycle of relation between acting subjects, objects, and viewing subjects.

The commissural quality of action art invokes consideration of the phenomenal relations between intention and act, as well. As Ludwig Wittgenstein observed: "Let us not forget this. When 'I raise my arm,' my arm goes up. And the problem arises: what is leftover if I subtract the fact that my arm goes up from the fact that I raised my arm?"[8] In terms of Wittgenstein's example, the action of the artist may be understood to be the moment that provides visual access to "what is leftover when the fact that my arm goes up is subtracted from the fact that I raised my arm." Action art draws attention to the psycho-physical, cognitive-intuitional mechanism that produces the act and its object in all their dimensionality; and the object directs our attention to the interstice that is the space of this difference. While actions in art enable us to appreciate, even highly value, objects, there is something of much greater significance to be grasped about action art. Wittgenstein's example requires us to pay attention to that which is left over, after we subtract the fact that an art object occurs from the fact that an action produced that object, is the primary aim of action art.

M.M. Bakhtin sought to understand the "difference between what is *now* and what is *after-now*" and what manner of connection might bridge that difference. As Michael Holquist has written:

Bakhtin [sought] the sheer quality of happening in life before the magma of such experience cools, hardening into igneous theories, or accounts of what has happened. And just as lava differs from the rock it will become, so the two states of lived experience, on the one hand, and systems for registering such experience on the other, are fundamentally different from each other.[9]

8. Ludwig Wittgenstein, Philosophical Investigations, *trans. G.E.M. Anscombe (New York: Macmillian, 1953), sec. 621.*

9. Michael Holquist, "Foreword," to M.M. Bakhtin's Toward a Philosophy of the Act, *translated and notes by Vadim Liapunov,* and edited by Michael Holquist and Vadim Liapunov (Austin: University of Texas Press, 1993).

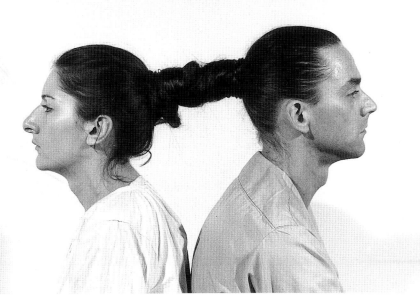

**Marina Abramović and Ulay**, *Relation in Time*, 1977

The objects that come "out of actions" are other than the action itself. But just as lava may differ from the rock it will become, so it is also the same as what it was. In this regard the objects used in, or which have become relics of an action, extend the implicit temporality experienced in the *now* beyond now to the *after now*.

In this manner, George Brecht's elegant and economical scores for events often employ action as a unit of measure connecting different physical states.

> *Three Aqueous Events (1961)*
> ice
> water
> steam

The performer of one of Brecht's "event scores" can enact the score in any way s/he chooses, or merely receive the message conceptually, or ignore it. Already in this range of choice, it is possible to see that the number of responses and the acts through which one might imagine how to realize ice, water, and steam — whether to demonstrate their properties, to use them, to exchange them, etc. — is infinite. In *Three Aqueous Events*, the action of the artist is employed to evince the result of divergence in acts that relate together the simultaneous existence of difference in one element.

What I am suggesting is that the objects which come out of actions describe how *what is now is also connected to what comes after now*, just as the future is comprised of everything contained in the past that the present manifests as the ongoing, yet simultaneous, transitory site between states. The unprecedented value of action art is to articulate this connectivity. But to suggest this does not mean that actions are robbed of their own artifactuality; it is, after all, the aesthetic dimension to which these objects point. This phenomenon has been disregarded regardless of how carefully the work of art has been interpreted — whether in terms of intentionality, iconography, iconology, or semiotics; or with regard to the work's social history and reception.

Action is a truth of art. The processes involved in the making of things have been neglected, except, of course, in the ways we have attended to questions of connoisseurship and the material construction of things (*how* an etching was made, or *how* the "lost wax technique" was achieved). This elision is all the more remarkable since Marxist art history has carefully considered labor both as it relates to the conditions in which art is produced as well as artistic representations of people at work. However significant these ways of looking and interpreting have been, the artifactuality of artistic action, that initiating modality from which the entire history of art and aesthetics unfolds, has been overlooked and has remained disregarded until artists focused attention on action.

Artists producing actions as art have taught that artifactuality is only an index of art, it is *not* art itself. In this regard, it is useful to remember that the Greek meanings of the term "aesthetics" include: "*aisthanesthai*, 'to perceive,' *aisthêsis*, 'perception,' and *aisthêtikos*, 'capable of perception.'"[10] Aesthetics was the "'science of sensory knowledge'," even though it "was soon restricted to the 'science of sensory beauty.'"[11] Perception itself is an act. It requires taking possession of something, obtaining and receiving something, and it is through this act of possession that a science of sensory knowledge is achieved. Action art assists perception in noticing the dynamic intersection between intentionality, actuality, and the complex social context of reception and interpretation within which art occurs. Action art augments perception and sensory knowledge, or, in Allan Kaprow's words:

> As art becomes less art, it takes on philosophy's early role as critique of life. Even if its beauty can be refuted, it remains astonishingly thoughtful. Precisely because art can be confused with life, it forces attention upon the aim of its ambiguities, to "reveal" experience.[12]

In actions and their objects, experience is laid open in relation. "Relation" is the theme of the remarkable series of actions Marina Abramovic and Ulay did during the period they lived and worked together.

10. See Michael Inwood, "Commentary," on Hegel's Introductory Lectures on Aesthetics (London: Penguin Books, 1993), 98.

11. Ibid.

12. Allan Kaprow, "Manifesto," in Manifestoes, a Great Bear Pamphlet (New York: Something Else Press, 1966), 13.

**Alison Knowles** (with Philip Corner and Bill Fontana),
*Gentle Surprises for the Ear*, 1975. Collection of the artist

**Dick Higgins**, *Symphony 607 — The Divers*, 1968. Block Collection

*Relation in Time*, an action that took place over seventeen hours in October 1977, at Studio G7 in Bologna, shows how deeply objects can represent otherwise unnoticed actions of subjects themselves. In *Relation in Time*, the couple sat back to back with their long hair tied together into a continuous bun, linking the backs of their heads together and holding them fast to each other. The sequence of photographs from this action shows how with weariness, eventual loss of concentration, and the weight of the body, the neatly roped hair gradually pulled and tugged until it began to show signs of strain — eventually slipping out of the knot that held them together. This ligature of hair is not an object that may be exhibited, bought, or sold, but it was, nonetheless, an artificial thing created as a point of juncture across which the artists visualized a quality of their exchange. In its eventual unraveling, the band of hair exhibited physical properties of force, movement, tension, the invisible dynamism and magnetism that drew the couple together and eventually set them apart.

Relation in one circumstance becomes something altogether different in another. In *Gentle Surprises for the Ear* (1975), Alison Knowles, with the composers Philip Corner and Bill Fontana, rescued and related to discarded objects found on the street. Growing out of Knowles's earlier soundworks, the three artists began to collect abandoned debris, things whose provenance, identity, and character were lost or broken. These small bits and pieces, fragments of discarded objects, could be held in the hand: a tiny metal spring with a loop at the end, a small glass cylinder, a ten-inch 45rpm record broken in half, part of a brush or comb, two stick pins with white balls at the end, a bent plastic straw, many unidentifiable objects, and so on. Such things, however devalued, became for Knowles, Corner, and Fontana sources for producing sound. After carrying out the business of collecting the objects, the trio affixed "tickets" with hand-written instructions on each one, explaining how to use them as musical instruments. This process was not undertaken all at once, but from time to time for several years. The

tagging system itself required an attentiveness to the object, and demanded close observation of its qualities and character in line with its potential for the production of sound. The instructions for carrying out the sound-task included: "twirl by ear;" "drop, roll;" "hold open to get whirring sound;" "holding to ear gently, surprise;" "crinkle;" "tinkle;" "twist;" "brush;" "scratch;" "insert and let rock back and forth like a teeter-totter;" "push in and out;" "rocking at its own rhythm." Such instructions elicited a sensual response and, themselves, invoked sensual associations.

Indeed, Knowles considered the objects the three friends recuperated "intimate because people aren't watching; they become your own discovery."[13] As Theodor Adorno observed:

Academic philosophy has assigned aesthetics a place in the division of philosophical labour. True aesthetics reacts to this debasement by demanding that phenomena be lifted out of their mere existence and made to reflect on themselves. Philosophy is reflection on what has become petrified in the sciences, not another science beside or beyond them. This means that aesthetics must try to articulate what its object in its immediacy is driving at.[14]

Similarly, by lifting objects out of their "mere existence," Knowles, Corner, and Fontana facilitated reflection on objects in their immediacy. Minute attention to the world may be traced back to at least Leonardo da Vinci's observations of images in the swirls of marble and grain of wood, up through Dada artists like Kurt Schwitters whose *merzbau* and *merzbild* were constructed from commercial debris found on the city streets, Duchamp's "readymades," the Surrealists' "found" and augmented objects, to

*13. Alison Knowles in conversation with the author, 1 August 1997, New York. All quotes from Knowles on* Gentle Surprises for the Ear *come from this discussion.*

*14. Theodor Adorno, "Additions, A-1," in Appendix I of* Aesthetic Theory, *translated by C. Lenhardt and edited by Gretel Adorno and Rolf Tiedemann (London and*

*New York: Routledge & Kegan Paul, 1972), 370.*

Cage's attention to common forms and ambient sound, and Rauschenberg's combines.

It has, of course, been difficult to see beyond the individual artist's body to the visual, auditory, and haptic concerns of all bodies for which artists' bodies signify in all their ontological, phenomenological, and epistemological complexity, in part because the presence of a body acting before other bodies is so powerful, and also because the presentational mode itself constitutes such a radical shift in the normative aesthetic context of traditional representational objects. The very idea of presenting the self (and the artist's ideas) instead of an objective substitute for that self (her or his ideas embodied in an object) was and remains challenging to traditional ideas of art. In Michael Fried's influential article, "Art and Objecthood" (1967), the art historian attacked all art that "includes the beholder . . . in a situation" as a denigration of art into "the condition of theater," and demanded nothing less than a "war" against it as an enemy of art, an "anti-art."[15] A passage in Fried's argument reveals his deep aversion to the actual body and his neo-Platonic insistence upon resemblance. Objects, he wrote, must merely re-present the "innumerable ways and moods [the body] makes meaning" rather than present that body as the concrete self-evidential material in which meaning constantly shifts. Acts and action-objects have a greater trust: as commissures they draw subjects closer to a confrontation with their primary conditions of interaction.

The concept of commissure is also a useful construct enabling reflection on the problem of the commodification of "Performance Art" as an object. Many artists who turned to action as an alternative to the production of objects (and many of the scholars who have written about action, myself included), did so with the aim that actions might escape commercialization and commodification. Kaprow summarized this aim in 1966 when he observed that "Painting had become symbol rather than power . . .

something which *stood for* experience rather than *acting directly upon it*."[16] He urged artists to make "new values" not objects. Six years later, Lucy Lippard expressed a similar hope — and its disillusion — in the "Preface" and "Postface" to her monumental catalogue of conceptual art actions and objects, *Six Years*. "Hopes that 'conceptual art' would be able to avoid the general commercialization, the destructively 'progressive' approach of modernism," she wrote, "were for the most part unfounded."[17]

Regardless of the voracious appetite of the culture, consciousness, and theory industries, the hope to create non-commodifiable art continues, as Peggy Phelan reiterated in 1993:

> Performance's only life is in the present. Performance cannot be saved, recorded, documented, or otherwise participate in the circulation of representations of representations: once it does so, it becomes something other than performance. To the degree that performance attempts to enter the economy of reproduction it betrays and lessens the promise of its own ontology. Performance's being . . . becomes itself through disappearance.[18]

Yes, and no. The temporal moment of the act disappears. But the objects that were used in, and are a part of, that action remain. So too does the documentation that is saved not only by the collector and the museum, but most significantly by the artists themselves. Even the artists who have most stridently avoided commodifaction of their events have saved photographic negatives, made catalogues, artists' books, and other kinds of relics that are *connected* to the work. If any single transition toward the commodification of actions has occurred it has been discursive and then associative, the absorption of "action" into the theatricalized, spectatorial condition of "Performance." But even given that significant shift in the discursive conditions of culture, which I will revisit below, "performance" does not "become"

15. Michael Fried, "Art and Objecthood," Artforum 5, no. 10 (June 1967); reprinted in Gregory Battcock, ed., Minimal Art: A Critical Anthology (New York: E.P. Dutton, 1968), 116-147.

16. Allan Kaprow, Assemblage, Environments, and Happenings (New York: Harry Abrams, 1966), 156.

17. Lucy Lippard, Six Years: The dematerialization of the art object from 1966 to 1972 (New York: Praeger

Publishers, 1972), 263.

18. See Peggy Phelan's immensely intelligent book, Unmarked: The Politics of Performance (London and New York: Routledge, 1993), 146.

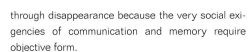

**Kazuo Shiraga,** *Challenging Mud*, 1955. The Ashiya City Museum of Art and History

through disappearance because the very social exigencies of communication and memory require objective form.

Objects are tools *of* life necessary *to* life in order *to do* and *to communicate*. Objects contain the traces of the history of action (life) from the past through the present and into the future. Objects are not commodities in and of themselves; rather, attitudes about and uses of objects make them so — or do not — in relation to the actions that bring them into being. Action in art would have us respond to objects of art as things made by a maker in action. For example, when one is presented with an object, such as a guillotine, then pain, suffering, torture, murder, capital punishment — all enacted by someone to someone else — come to mind. The object, guillotine, is a vivid example of an action-object relating thought back to human institutions and behaviors. But all objects function in this way, which is why we understand their meaning and use. What is missing from art objects, what artists engaged in action restore to them, is that relationality between making and doing and the artifactuality itself. What artists do is alter the meaning and use of objects through their actions in order to remake vision and, thereby, our action (and thought) in the world.

Action in art is pedagogical in the sense that it instructs visuality back to the primary conditions of making and viewing, and then out to the communicative experience between the making subject and the viewing subject. If we think of the objects that come out of actions as commissures, entrusted to *do* something (have agency by the mere fact that *they exist in relation*), then these objects retain the energy of that relatedness both to the originating action and in our reception — however objects may also be aestheticized and become coveted and fetishized. If we think of art actions as the events produced by one subjectivity aimed at communicating with another subjectivity, then acts in art may be understood as commissures as well, commitments by artists to interpersonal connection. *Action art and action objects teach us to remember the value of the individual subject who creates objects — both in the narrow sense of the artist as producer and in the*

*much larger sense of elevating human subjects over objects — as the highest value.*

**III. From Action to Performance** So far, I have emphasized the term "action" rather than the more generic term "performance" to maintain attention to the difference between action and objects, and to stress *process* at the foundation of what has become known as Performance Art. Moreover, the term "action" keeps the pressure on the political reference inherent in the term activism that was, and remains, so central to the use of the body as a medium. Action was a term that reflected a highly determined strategy for artistic intervention in public life. Action in art was imagined as a means to remedy the aestheticism that transformed art as an integral part of the production of meaning in culture into the empty category of "art for art's sake," a shift in the social role of art that robbed art of its cultural efficacy in favor of its surface appearance prized as a prestigious emblem of status and taste.

Such a powerful transition in the media and means of art occurred in an entirely altered planetary condition in the wake of the Holocaust and the advent of the nuclear age. Given these unprecedented conditions, the use of the body in action seemed not only necessary, but urgent. Ten years after the bombing of Hiroshima, in 1955 Kazuo Shiraga used his body in *Challenging Mud*. That same year, Saburo Murakami violently broke through a series of large paper screens by running with his whole body against the structures. Murakami's action was accomplished "with such a speed, in almost an instant, that the cameramen failed to catch the moment;" and, more importantly, the experience left the artist feeling that, "I became a new man."[19] The particular type of new man that Murakami had become most certainly had been affected by what Japanese poet Hara Tamiki described in "*This Is a* Human Being" (1950), a poem that uses italics to create multiple readings of the text: "This is a human being./ *Please note what* changes *have been affected* by the atomic bomb./ This body *is grotesquely* bloated,/ Male *and* female characteristics *are indistinguishable*./ Oh, that black,

19. Jiro Yoshihara, "On the First 'Gutaiten' (the First Exhibition of 'Gutai' Art Group)," Gutai 4 (1959): 2.

**235**

**Charlotte Moorman**, *Cello Bombs*, C. 1965/ 1990s. Sammlung Hoffmann

seared, smashed and/ Festering face, from whose swollen lips oozes a voice/ *"Help me"*/ In faint quiet words./ *This is a* human being./ *The* face *of a* human being."[20]

In 1952, Murakami and Shiraga created the *Zero-kai* (Group Zero), and two years later, both joined the Gutai Group under the leadership of Jiro Yoshihara. Yoshihara, a representative of the Ashiya City Art Association, was himself a resident of the city of Ashiya (near Osaka) where the war "had harmed half of Ashiya's residents and forty percent of their homes."[21] It was during this period that Yoshihara's work "went through a transitional period from a dark representational style . . . to a linear form of abstract expressionism."[22] And it was Yoshihara who proclaimed in the first Gutai Manifesto:

> Gutai art does not change the material but brings it to life. Gutai art does not falsify the material. In Gutai art the human spirit and the material reach out their hands to each other, even though they are otherwise opposed to each other. The material is not absorbed by the spirit. The spirit does not force the material into submission. . . . Keeping the life of the material alive also means bringing the spirit alive, and lifting up the spirit means leading the material up to the height of the spirit.[23]

Like the Gutai Group itself and its works, Yoshihara's emphasis on the relationship between concrete materiality and the spirit must, I believe, be considered at least in part in terms of what it meant to be a survivor living in post-Hiroshima/Nagasaki Japan. He was interested in "keeping the life of the material alive" in order to keep the "spirit alive."

Given this context, Yves Klein's experiences in Japan in 1952 may have been a significant factor — more than has been appreciated — in motivating his move from painting concrete, non-objective mono-chromes into the use of the human body as a "living brush" in 1959. This idea is supported by his power-ful essay "Truth Becomes Reality," a text that accounts for Klein's desire to "leave my mark on the world," and to associate the traces left by the bodies in his images to those "shadows of Hiroshima [which] in the desert of the atomic catastrophe . . . consti-tuted evidence, terrible evidence beyond any doubt, but still evidence of hope for the permanence (though immaterial) of the flesh."[24] The technological power of "rockets, Sputniks, and missiles," was not what Klein valued, but rather the "affective atmosphere of the flesh itself . . . [as a] powerful yet pacific force of . . . sensitivity." Klein published this essay in the third and last issue of the German publication, *ZERO*, in July 1961. In the original publication, he had the last page of his article burned off — dematerialized by fire.

For Shiraga, Murakami, and Klein, the very corporeality of the human body defeats technological and scientific determinism. Action is the core of performance from its earliest manifestations in action-painting to the Gutai and Happenings. In Carolee Schneemann's *Snows* (January 1967), the artist used montages of Vietnam atrocities along with colors and other kinds of representations from the media in order "to concretize and elucidate the geno-cidal compulsions of a vicious disjunctive technocracy gone berserk against an integral, essentially rural culture."[25] In this climate Jon Hendricks wrote his manifesto "Some Notes," December 11, 1967, decrying commercialism, the Vietnam war, and race riots; in this climate Hendricks, Raphael Ortiz, Al Hansen, Jean Toche, and Lil Picard wrote the "Judson Manifesto," stating that "the function of the artist is to subvert culture, since our culture is trivial;" in this climate Ortiz and Hendricks cancelled an exhibition — "DIAS USA" — at the Judson Church to protest the assassination of Dr. Martin Luther King Jr.; in this climate Toche and Hendricks lay down in the doorway of the Metropolitan Museum for an hour, protesting the museum's refusal to take a stand against the war

20. Quoted in John Whittier Treat, Writing Ground Zero: Japanese Literature and the Atomic Bomb (Chicago: University of Chicago Press, 1995), 168.

21. Atsuo Yamamoto, "Gutai 1954-1972, Introduction," in Gutai I.II.III. (Ashiya: Ashiya City Museum of Art and History, 1994): unpaginated.

22. Ibid.

23. Jiro Yoshihara, "Gutai Manifesto," Geijutsu Shincho 7, no.12 (December 1956).

24. Yves Klein, "Truth Becomes Reality," in Yves Klein 1928-1962: A Retrospective, exh. cat. (Houston: Institute for the Arts, Rice University, and New York: The Arts Publisher, 1982), 230-231.

25. From the program for Snows, reprinted in Carolee Schneemann, More Than Meat Joy: Complete Performance Works & Selected Writings, edited by Bruce McPherson (New Paltz: Documentext, 1979), 129.

**237**

Guerrilla Art Action Group. *Museum of Modern Art Action (Number 3)*, New York, 18 November 1969

in Vietnam; and in this climate Hendricks and Toche defined themselves, March 4, 1970, as the Guerrilla Art Action Group (GAAG), a collective organized around the concept and practice of non-violence for "symbolically dramatizing the danger of reality-violence, of oppression, and of repression," and for questioning and provoking "people into a confrontation with the existing crises."

For his part, political activist Abbie Hoffman had learned enough about actions from artists to stage events that disrupted the New York Stock Exchange, August 24, 1967. At that time he and a group of about twelve individuals (including Jerry Rubin) threw dollars at the traders from the overhanging balcony of the exchange floor; an action that stopped trading for a few seconds when the brokers lunged to grab the money in a classic image of greed in the heart of capitalism. Such media events culminated in the disruptions of the Democratic Convention in August 1968, and the subsequent trial of "The Chicago Seven." While such political happenings had been inspired by artistic Happenings, they also contributed to reshaping actions in art. Stunning proof of this interrelation is Terry Fox's *Defoliation Piece* (1970), the artist's self-proclaimed "first political work:"

> I wanted to destroy the flowers in a very calculated way. By burning a perfect rectangle right in the middle, it would look as though someone had destroyed them on purpose. The flowers were Chinese jasmine planted five years ago which were to bloom in two years. It was also a theatrical piece. Everyone likes to watch fires. It was making a beautiful roaring sound. But at a certain point people realized what was going on — the landscape was being violated; flowers were being burnt. Suddenly everyone was quiet. One woman cried for twenty minutes.[26]

In the heart of suburban Berkeley, *Defoliation*

*Piece* called direct attention to the "scorched earth" policy of the United States in Vietnam. Fox used a flamethrower of the type used in Vietnam to cremate the plants. His reminder of napalmed land and scorched bodies of Vietnamese flesh was a symbolic act re-presenting the ontological value of the life and land of the Vietnamese people in terms of the value of the Chinese jasmine. It was also a concrete act of destruction, metonymically contingent with the destruction of war.

Actions in art offered an alternative paradigm for artistic practice by presenting the human being as the materialization of the gap, the *contiguous* point between art and life. An emphasis on contiguity is *not* to say a merging of art and life, but to highlight the commissural commitment between them. When the term "performance art" gained currency in the burgeoning literature on action that appeared in the mid-1970s, many artists initially rejected it for the term's connotations and association with entertainment and traditional theater. This was especially the case in Europe.[27] Only with the advent of extensive textual narrative in performance did the once largely non-verbal physicality of body action become associated with the theatricality and spectacle implicit in the term "performance art." Vito Acconci is significant in this etymological history. He not only ushered in text-based action (in no small measure due to his practice as a poet) but he also stopped performing in 1973, only five years after he had begun to make actions. Acconci, by his own account, stopped performing when he realized that the reception of the artist as a theatrical spectacle interfered with his own visual and intellectual goals as an artist.[28]

In Acconci's notorious action, *Seed Bed* (1972), at the Sonnabend Gallery in New York, for example, the artist is said to have masturbated for some six hours a day, twice a week, while concealed under a low wooden ramp built into the gallery. What we

26. Terry Fox, quoted in Carl E. Loeffler and Darlene Tong, eds., Performance Anthology: Source Book of California Performance Art, rev. ed. (San Francisco: Last Gasp Press and Contemporary Arts Press, 1989), 17.

27. Stuart Brisley and Leslie Haslam argued that the term inadequately and inappropriately connoted theater, not

visual art. See Brisley and Haslam, "Anti-Performance Art," in Arte Inglese Oggi 1960-1970 (Milan: Palazzo Reale, 1976). See also Hugh Adams, "Editorial: Against a Definitive Statement on British Performance Art," in a special issue on "Performance Art," Studio International 192, no. 982 (July-August 1976): 3. For the etymology of "performance art," see Bruce Barber, "Indexing:

Conditionalism and Its Heretical Equivalents," in A.A. Bronson and Peggy Gale, eds., Performance By Artists (Toronto: Art Metrople, 1979), 183-204.

28. Panel discussion at the symposium, Performance Art in the 1960s, 1970s, and 1980s (Baltimore: Maryland Institute of the Arts, 1989).

**Vito Acconci**, *Seed Bed*, Sonnabend Gallery, New York, 15-29 January 1972. Courtesy of the artist and Barbara Gladstone Gallery, New York

actually know is that the artist responded verbally to visitors in the gallery, using them as catalysts, presumably to stimulate his own sensual experience, but their's as well. In mental images spurred by his narrative, Acconci conjured the conjoining of his own and the viewer's identity, commingling aesthetic production with metaphors of human reproduction, impeded by a narcissistic lack of connection. This (simulated?) auto-erotic action lacked the capacity for the mutual exchange of information prerequisite for meaningful relationships and the reproduction of life. Language was effective in perpetuating the "aesthetic distance" demanded by traditional conventions of art in the viewer/object dyad. But together with action, language functioned as commissure committing Acconci to interaction with the visitor and vice versa. Aggressive and violating, language transformed a desensualized emptiness into a sexualized threat in which visitors were forced to respond with agency and participate, if only to stop up their ears and leave. The assault by language in Acconci's work performed the spectacle his hidden body refused to make.

Throughout the 1980s and 1990s, language-based performance dominated in the United States and Europe. Such performances did conform more to the connotative and denotative meanings of theatricality implied by the term "performance art." Moreover, such a shift seems to have been not only reasonable, but necessary, given the general exhaus-

tion experienced internationally at the end of the 1970s. For the three decades that comprise this exhibition were inscribed by extraordinary poles of psychologically demanding experience. The devastation after World War II was subsumed by the remarkable economic recovery of Japan and Germany and the production of a lavish surplus of goods, both in terms of consumable commodities and the staggering development of advanced technologies. This situation only augmented existential anguish which quickened and deepened with the unprecedented threat of Cold War nuclear annihilation — what British Happening artist Jeff Nuttall identified in 1968 as the "Bomb Culture," the title and subject of his extraordinary book, charting the history of the "Ban-the-Bomb" movement in England in the late 1950s through the international, underground, counter-cultural revolution in art, poetry, and music, that used London as a cross-roads.[29]

At the same time, social movements from civil rights to feminism set the standard for the identity politics, multiculturalism, and post-colonialism that emerged full-blown in the 1970s to claim for itself a shifting historical paradigm and the emergence of "postmodernism." The *coup de grace* of this tumultuous period was the Vietnam War. Witnessed globally on television, this despicably immoral and bloody battle ended in a pyrrhic victory for a tiny Communist nation that had triumphed first over the

29. *Jeff Nuttall*, Bomb Culture *(New York: Dell Publishing, 1968).*

**John Duncan**, *Blind Date*, 1980

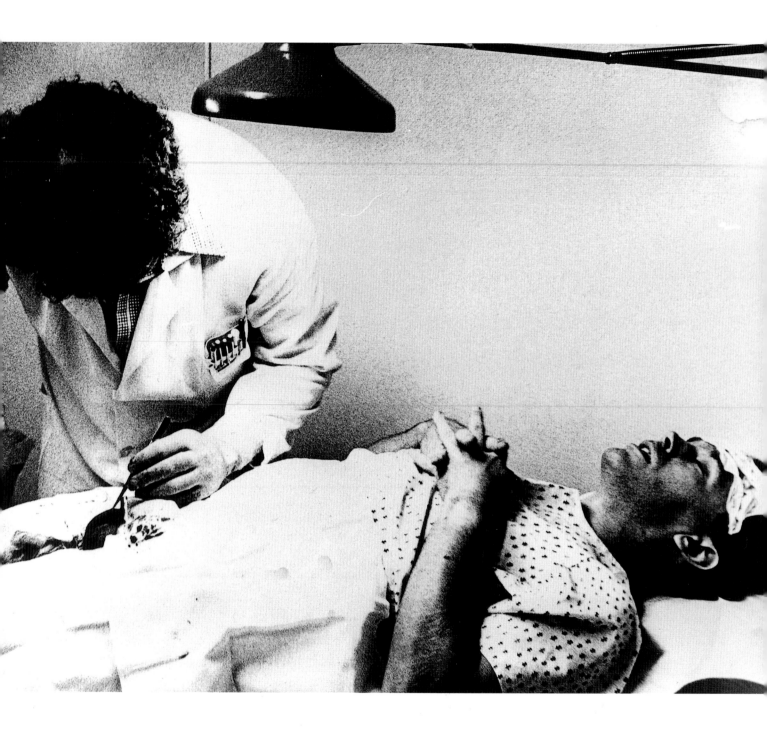

Communist nation that had triumphed first over the French, then over the Chinese and the Soviets, finally winning against the United States, wreaking humiliation and disillusionment on that putative super-power and self-proclaimed leader of world democracy. When the 1970s came to a close, it was not just the end of a decade, it was the ignoble conclusion of a traumatic era of struggle and decay. Its immaterial internal pain was perfectly and self-destructively embodied in the material external sign of safety pins stuck through the flesh of young punks. This picture of abjection and alienation was symmetrically balanced by an international disco scene, itself a mode of action epitomizing widespread dissociation from larger questions of survival that, paradoxically and inevitably, slipped through the denial into discourse in the Bee Gees' song, "Staying Alive."

As for "staying alive," there is no act as pitiable and tragic as the attempt to assert one's life (manifested in *eros*) against the actual experience of one's desperate numbness unto death (*thanatos*). Such is the image of pathos that the violent debasement of John Duncan's loathing in *Blind Date* (1980) recalls. In May, Duncan purchased a female corpse in Tijuana for the purpose of sex, and taped his sex act with it. After this experience of "indescribable intense self-disgust," he returned to have a vasectomy in order, he later wrote, "to make sure that the last potent seed I had was spent in a cadaver."[30] Photographs he had taken of this operation anticipate Orlan's equally self-destructive/self-reconstructive cosmetic surgery in the 1990s. Duncan had to wait six weeks for the vasectomy, the waiting period required then in California, and after the operation he scheduled a performance of *Blind Date* before a public to whom he recounted the experience, saying that he "wanted to show what can happen to men that are trained to ignore their emotions." Linda Burnham, the indefatigable and courageous editor of *High Performance* magazine (1976-1997), refused to publish an account of *Blind Date* because she found it "highly morally objectionable" and preferred to be "guilty of censorship" rather than to be "responsible for putting that material in front of any one, especially my kids."[31]

When she imagined that the incident was a "rape" of a body whose "spirit" may not have yet "gone from her body," Duncan responded that it was like "having sex with meat."[32]

However contemptable Duncan's desperate event, the artist presented his own excruciating lack, a psychic pain that is palpable. For such an act unfolds within the epistemological spaces insured by white male hegemony, the phallic rule which must guarantee its virility by any means. In *Blind Date*, this ideal is carried to the extreme as caricature. But what it unmasked was the reality of impotence, suffering derived from the fact that while the artist embodied the representation of white maleness with all its accreted power, he psychologically cohabitated the disempowered space of the lifeless woman whom he violated, fucking *himself* to death: "I risked the ability to accept myself. I risked the ability to have sex . . . and the ability to love."[33]

The extreme self-loathing in Duncan's action may be traced, I think, to experiences the artist recounted anonymously in an installation five months later, entitled *If Only We Could Tell You* (1980), in which a text describing the verbal abuse of a child includes such statements as: "We hate you little boy," "We always knew you'd be half-human baggage." "You're a blight on our lives," "Why don't you do everyone a favor and kill yourself," and "DIE.DIE.DIE.DIE.DIE.DIE.DIE." Every example of violence or destruction in art, especially when it is related directly to the artist's body, contains a lingering trauma still present from the past. An absent presence animates the unorganized psychic experiences of the artist either unconsciously or consciously and drives the production of the work. Such art is an overture, a sign that visually signifies the invisible, the process of destruction itself operating within the psyche of the artist. Duncan's art represents trauma, makes it visible. In this way, art actions and performances offer access to the inexpressible interiority of individual suffering in a way that few other representations can provide. I interpret *Blind Date* as a warning signal of intense distress. *Blind Date*, however reprehensible, is about many

30. Louis MacAdams, "Sex with the Dead," Wet 30 (March-April 1981): 60.

31. Ibid.

32. Ibid., 61.

33. Ibid.

Paul McCarthy, *Sailor's Meat*, 1975

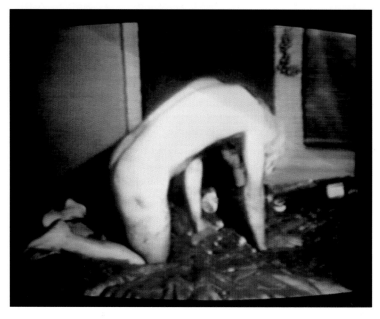

bodies and minds, for which Duncan's acts require attention, empathy, and care. It was in this spirit that artists at the end of the 1970s entered areas of the dissociated cultural unconscious with the aim of unpacking its consequences personally and socially but not always with the ability to reorganize, reconnect, and redirect the knowledge gained in such acts to recovery in everyday life.

The kind of pain expressed in Duncan's work could also be seen in his friend and mentor Paul McCarthy's sculptural translation of internal pain into visual communication. In such deeply disturbing performances as *Meatcake* (1974), and *Sailor's Meat* (1975), McCarthy created visual models through which highly volatile and excessively self-abnegating internal images were communicated in a set of invented corporeal actions that signify the operations of the numbed, and often amnesiac, mind of the trauma "survivor." The performative language of trauma — what I consider a sculptural language — includes visualizing dissociation through spatial and temporal drift. For example, it might be expressed in numbed and repetitive moving in and out of spaces, around and around tables, and/or other physical and speech acts as in the work of McCarthy. It could be exemplified in the self-denigrating and self-destructive imagery often present in women's actions. Risk-taking, excessive expressions of anger, self-victimization, self-revictimization, and victimization of others, are all constant visualizations of tropes of pain and suffering, as could be whimpering, sobbing, and other sounds of distress or irrational eruptions of erratic laughing, and so on.[34] McCarthy has said, for example, that he might, "spin for an hour and something would begin to happen." Building momentum through repetition, the action permits the artist to arrive at a particular state of consciousness that brings that internal experience into physical expression even though it may be bereft of speech.

Trauma may also be expressed in violence, as in McCarthy's *Whipping a Wall with Paint* (1974), in which the artist unleashed an internal force (rage ?, power as yet undefined?, sorrow?, pain?) against a huge store-front window and throughout the space on the walls, pillars, and floor that he beat (whipped) with a paint-soaked blanket, slamming the paint against the window for thirty to forty minutes. This act is loaded with explosive potential, a violence infinitely more troubling than the metaphors for bodily fluids he makes with such visceral, yet kitschy, materials as catsup and mayonnaise. Nonetheless, such materials also possess dissociative qualities; for McCarthy uses condiments that have a distant relationship to the "real" food they are meant to enhance, but the absence of which they symbolically represent. The construction of violence in McCarthy's work raises the specter of the memory of an actual experience unrecoverable to language but present in powerful, disturbing, and touching actions — touching because the work is about profound corruption.

McCarthy's and Duncan's actions recall the Viennese Action artists — Günter Brus, Otto Muehl, Hermann Nitsch, and Rudolf Schwarzkogler. But one of the lesser-known landmark actions to which McCarthy and Duncan are also indebted is *Self-Destruction* (1966), a performance realized by Raphael Montañez Ortiz at the Mercury Theater in London. Prior to the action, Ortiz selectively cut the middle-class business man's suit he was wearing so that it would easily tear away from his body. He then entered the space already set with milk bottles, a large rubber duck toy, a diaper, and a large talcum powder canister. Entering from the back of the stage, Ortiz cried softly: "Mother, mother, I am home; Ralphie is here; your son is here." When his mother did not appear, the artist began calling for her in angry tones that gave way to screaming. Finally Ortiz explained:

I sat down and I guzzled the milk and I can hardly breathe. I grab another bottle. I guzzle it and pour it all over me: there is Mommy's presence right there in all the milk. I get real hysterical again and I throw up. I reject Mommy. I throw up, first spontaneously, then deliberately sticking

34. See for example Robert Jay Lifton's "From Hiroshima to the Nazi Doctors: The Evolution of Psychoformative Approaches to Understanding Traumatic Stress Syndromes," in International Handbook of Traumatic Stress Syndromes, eds. John P. Wilson and Beverley Raphael (New York and London: Plenum Press, 1993), 11-13. Such repetition as the obsessive-compulsive writing of numbers or letters — as, for example, in the case of the German conceptual artist Hannah Darboven — is also a sign of trauma.

35. Kristine Stiles in converation with Paul McCarthy, in Paul McCarthy (London: Phaidon Press, 1996), 6-29.

my finger down my throat, vomiting up about two pints of milk. I then slap the puddle of vomit angrily over and over calling, "Mommy, Mommy." Accepting the puddle of milk as symbolic of Mommy, I calm down. I crawl off. "Mommy, ma, ma . . . "[36]

Four years after Ortiz's *Self-Destruction* action in London, Arthur Janov, a psychologist and psychiatric social worker, published his book *The Primal Scream*. He opened his introduction with an account given him by a patient, "Danny," who had witnessed Ortiz's *Self-Destruction* and demanded Janov's help in reenacting critical early experiences of his life in the manner Ortiz had demonstrated in his action. Janov explained Ortiz's action "changed the course of my professional life."[37] In developing his theory of the primal scream Janov — like Ortiz before him — drew on Otto Rank's notion of the birth trauma (*The Trauma of Birth*, 1929) and Jacob Moreno's work on psychodrama (*Who Shall Survive*, 1953). Primal scream therapy was popularized, ironically not by Ortiz, but by Yoko Ono and John Lennon, who underwent work with Janov after his book appeared. Primal scream therapy was also important to Otto Muehl.

Ortiz had arrived at the idea of destruction as a creative psychological and physical process in the late 1950s through montage in filmmaking. Between 1960 and 1967, he destroyed objects of furniture (mattresses and arm chairs) fixing the remains as sculptural objects to create his *Archaeological Finds* (1961-67). In 1962, he wrote the first of several manifestos on the use of destruction in art: "Destructivism: A Manifesto." Between 1965 and 1970 he carried out numerous "Destruction Ritual Realizations," the most famous of which were his ritualized piano destructions. In the early 1970s, he returned to psychology and aspects of the human potential movement, studying Tantrism, bio-energetics and macrobiotics, psychic healing, and also undergoing rebirthing at the Rocky Mountain Healing Arts Institute. By 1979 he was fully engaged in developing a process for "inner visioning" that led to his "Physio-Psycho-Alchemy," a theory of psycholog-

ical and physical aesthetic action for which he earned a doctorate in 1982 from Columbia Teachers College.

Ortiz, like McCarthy and Duncan after him, invented visual and physical discourses on everything that remains hidden from conscious verbalization. The languages these artists have created constitute corporeal languages of abuse that discredit abuses to the body that have been sublimated in the unconscious. Their actions speak a rhetoric of abuse that is created in order *to show* their discreditation of all those beings and values which have been abused, for which there is no longer discourse, they act *through* that corruption. The action becomes a negation of all the things that the action itself exhibits and deplores. In this sense, a double negation goes on where something is recuperated. And it is this restorative element that permits us to continue to look at their work.

However liberating this work may have been for the individual artists and for many who viewed it, such work was also intolerable, exhausting, too theatrical and dramatic. Michael Peppe, an artist himself working in performance, described this emotional saturation as "boring" in a 1982 essay entitled "Why Performance Art Is So Boring." This insightful and funny essay registered a need to release from the strain of such psychologically demanding work. In a parody of action art, Peppe imagined the following stereotypical early 1980s club-scene performance:

You walk into the "space." A girl with spiky hair is playing electric guitar with a nail file. A fellow with pale skin and one earring is shaving his head. A tape of the Mutants is playing, overdubbed with the girl's voice enumerating the contents of her bathroom shelf. The backdrop is painted deliberately to look childish. On it are projected slides of suburbia. The fellow begins

36. *Ortiz quotes, unless otherwise cited, come from discussions with the artist since 1982. See also my* Rafael Montañez Ortiz: Years of the Warrior

1960, Years of the Psyche 1988 *(New York: El Museo del Barrio, 1988).*

37. *See Arthur Janov's* The Primal

Scream: Primal Therapy, the Cure for Neurosis *(New York: Praeger Publishers, 1970), 9-11.*

talking about how his parents forced him to be Macho. The girl begins smashing on the guitar with the file.[38]

Peppe located the problem in the late 1970s and early 1980s "Me Generation" which followed the "*sauvage* license and *engagé* politics of the Assassination Era [when] art-as-refuge replaced art-as-revolution with minimalist boredom . . . something to be endured . . . a phone call during dinner from a dull uncle."[39] Peppe named Laurie Anderson as queen of "A.P.E.M.E. (Art Performance Equals Minimalism as Entertainment)," noting sarcastically that although she had "brilliantly pointed out, 'Let X = X.' — it didn't matter since such cultural pablum as Werner Erhart, or Guru Maharaji Ji, or the Electric Light Orchestra" all might have said the same thing.[40]

Peppe reacted to the dramatic shift — in every sense of the word "dramatic" — that occured at the end of the 1970s when performance became entertainment, moving away from the intense physicality and task-oriented work that Willoughby Sharp defined in his important essay "Body Works," published in the inaugural issue of *Avalanche*, the important artist's journal edited by Sharp and filmmaker Liza Bear that specialized in covering international body art, concepts, installations, process, and other experimental practices between 1970 and 1976.[41] Peppe singled out Anderson, and rightly so, as the most visible of performance artists who had made this shift broadly accessible, and whose own theatricality endorsed an exploration of the body in ways that did not necessarily carry the weight of sacrifice previously associated with Body Art.[42] In this regard, Anderson is an important transitional figure, creating constructive movement out of the 1960s through the 1970s and into the 1980s.

Many artists, especially women involved with feminist narrative-performance — Joan Jonas, Yvonne Rainer, Rachel Rosenthal, Martha Rosler, Faith Wilding, Martha Wilson, Mary Beth Edelson — had throughout the 1970s integrated text and

body, as had such artists as Vito Acconci, Dennis Oppenheim, David Antin, Bruce McLean, Gilbert & George, and so on. But as Peppe had caricaturized the period, many of the works overflowed with ideological, idiosyncratic, compulsive, or private experiences. Anderson, by contrast, moderated between the private self and the public arena, performing text-based theatricalized works in accordance with the spectacularized spaces of public life. In addition, as Valie Export has pointed out, Anderson armed the body with the prosthesis of technology, prosthetics which "cannot be separated from the cultural process, from civilizatory development" itself.[43] Moreover, Anderson's story-telling anticipated what the French theorist Michel de Certeau would later identify as the fusion of theory and practice in "narrativization" as the central "oppositional practice in everyday life."[44]

Anderson's first actions, done in the early 1970s, were related to body art. In 1972, for example, she created public sleeping pieces called *The Dream Before*. In these, she fell asleep in public places, and later recorded her dreams, the narratives of which (taking her cues from Acconci, she has explained) became the material for story-telling. During this same period, she began to create unique musical objects like *Self-Playing Violin* (1974), a violin that contained a tape of the instrument being played which could be activated by itself, or could be played in a "duet" when Anderson, playing the same violin, played along. *Duets on Ice* (1974-75) is one of the earliest of her works to combine all the elements that would eventually identify her unique style: electronic technology, physical action, and story-telling in a matrix of multi-media electronic music and narrative. In this work, she had pre-recorded "mostly cowboy songs" on ninety-minute cassettes for the action, and would play along wearing ice skates embedded in ice as a timing mechanism. When the ice melted and she lost her balance, the concert was over:

In between songs I talked about the parallels

38. Michael Peppe, "Why Performance Art Is So Boring," High Performance 5, no. 1 (Spring-Summer 1982): 3-12.

39. Ibid., 4-5.

40. Ibid., 7.

41. Willoughby Sharp, "Body Works,"

Avalanche 1 (Fall 1970): 14-17.

42. For an excellent article that considers the subject of "sacrifice," see Jindrich Chapupecky, "Art and Sacrifice," Flash Art, nos. 80-81 (February-April, 1978): 33-35.

43. Valie Export, "The Real and Its Double: The Body," Discourse: Theoretical Studies in Media and Culture 11, no. 1 (Fall-Winter 1988-89): 5.

44. See de Certeau's "On the Oppositional Practices of Everyday Life," Social Text 1, no. 3 (Fall 1980): 3-43.

**245**

between ice skating and violin playing: blades over a surface, balance, simultaneity, the constant state of imbalance followed by balance followed by imbalance, like walking, like music, like everything.[45]

With her remarkable timing and sense of humor, Anderson could entertain in a way few action artists could. Freeing the imagination from its inhibitions, humor betrays and undermines power.

A tale Anderson told about *Duets on Ice* perfectly conveys her acute sensitivity to the way nuanced speech abruptly transforms the average into the uncanny, suddenly disrupting normativity. While performing the piece in Genoa, Italy, Anderson told her stories, in what she described as her "awkward Italian," to the people watching her on the street. "I am playing these songs," she told them, "in memory of my grandmother because the day she died I went out on a frozen lake and saw a lot of ducks whose feet had frozen into the new layer of ice."[46] After the artist had offered this poignant, but really banal picture (correlating her grandmother's death with the death of nature [winter] and frozen ducks), Anderson rescued her own conventional tale by later elaborating: "One [Italian] man who heard me tell this story was explaining to newcomers, 'She's playing these songs because once she and her grandmother were frozen together into a lake.'"

This modification of the original story becomes not only self-deprecating, but augments the original tale: frozen in the lake together, it is now possible to understand how parts of Anderson — like the duck's feet frozen into the ice in the earlier version of the tale — died with her grandmother. Standing with her feet embedded in ice, Anderson is the frozen duck, and the duet becomes a lament and a dirge for the grandmother. But all of this is set in a scene as absurd as the set of a dream: a young woman, who looks like a girl, plays cowboy songs on a self-playing violin, with her feet in ice-skates embedded in blocks of melting ice, in a city far away from the site of her story, telling her audience about the formal similarity between the skills of playing a violin and ice skating,

speaking a language she barely knows, which the listeners barely understand. Just this kind of conflation of the real-absurd was needed in the aftermath of the 1970s, just when the Cold War heated up for the last time under Ronald Reagan.

Just when J.L. Austin's *How To Do Things with Words* (1962) was reprinted in 1975 by Harvard University Press, the term "performance art" gained ascendency — as a speech act.[47] Austin differentiated between "constative" utterances (describing things) and "performative" utterances (utterances that do something) — in other words, *utterances that act*! Just when, in the early 1980s, scholars in the burgeoning field of "cultural studies" who had followed structuralism through semiotics into poststructuralism (from the 1950s through the 1970s), and who were powerfully influenced by French cultural theory (Foucault, Barthes, Lyotard, de Certeau, Baudrillard, Bourdieu, and Derrida), suddenly became interested in Performance Art.

**IV. Assimilations and Supressions** In retrospect, that "action" became a modality of aesthetic production seems a reasonable response to the 1949-1979 period. The concept of action remained so great at the end of the 1970s and with the rise of "performativity," that "the gesture" itself became a trope, distilled in Brian O'Doherty's well known 1981 article, "The Gallery as a Gesture," in which the exhibition space itself is figured as an embodied site:

> The gallery's implicit content can be forced to declare itself through gestures that use it whole. That content leads in two directions. It comments on the "art" within to which it is contextual. And it comments on the wider context — street, city, money, business — that contains it.[48]

A comparison between O'Doherty's description of the gallery space and Kaprow's 1958 description of the evolution from action painting to Happenings, some twenty-three years earlier, is instructive for just how deeply the theory of Happenings, actions, body

45. *Laurie Anderson,* Stories from the Nerve Bible: A Retrospective 1972-1992 *(New York: HarperPerennial, 1994), 40.*

46. *Ibid., 44.*

47. *J.L. Austin,* How to Do Things with Words *(Cambridge: Harvard University Press, 1962).*

48. *Brian O'Doherty, "The Gallery as a Gesture," Artforum 20, no. 4 (December 1981): 27.*

art, and performance had penetrated general cultural discourses and institutions by the early 1980s:

> This is what happened: The pieces of paper curled up off the canvas, were removed from the surface to exist on their own, became more solid as they grew into other materials and reaching out further into the room, finally filled it entirely. Suddenly, there were jungles, crowded streets, littered alleys, dream spaces of sci-fi, rooms of madness and junk-filled attics of the mind. People are moving colored shapes — sound — odors.[49] — Allan Kaprow, 1958

> From the '20s to the '70s . . . the pedestal melted away leaving the spectator waist deep in wall-to-wall space. As the frame dropped off space slides across the wall, creating turbulence in the corners. Collage flopped out of the picture and settled on the floor as easily as a bag lady. The new god, extensive homogenous space, flowed easily into every part of the gallery. All impediments except "art" were removed.
> — Brian O'Doherty, 1981

Even while action art continues to remain peripheral to mainstream art, art history, and exhibitions, the concepts explored in its practices were, nonetheless, being assimilated into them as well as other fields. In 1983, in a widely discussed and important essay, "Art in the Dark," Thomas McEvilley already observed that "the conceptual and performance genres changed the rules of art till it became virtually unrecognizable to those who had thought that it was theirs," and furthermore threatened his readers that "it will not go away [because] the strange record is there."[50] But even McEvilley's eloquent demonstration and theory of performance practice did not prevent this history from creeping back into the dark recesses of aesthetic consciousness. The assimilation of notions of action and process, from the field that has come to be known as Performance Art, within various humanist disciplines — especially cultural studies — has never been made explicit, even though its conceptual structures routinely turn up in their discourses.[51] This is not, of course, to suggest that art is the only tradition for such thought, but it is the most public, visible expression of a corpus of ideas made explicit in body actions.

A recent example within art history itself may make this point vivid. Art historian David Summers begins an account of the Western tradition of representation from Plato to the present with a definition of *repraesentatio* as "a construction around the verb 'to be'"; and he links *repraesentatio* to "*praesens* . . . a participial form of *praeesse*, 'to be before' (both in the sense of spatial location and precedence)."[52] At the close of his discussion, Summers proposes a "shift" in art historical focus and interpretation away from representation and related tropes of "'realism' and 'worldview' and 'ideology' to constructions of common human corporeality and of personal, social, and political spaces, both our own and those alternative to our own."[53] But while he suggests such a shift, neither Summers nor any of the other twenty-one eminent scholars who contributed to *Critical Terms for Art History*, a book that is superb in every other aspect, discuss performance or mention any artists associated with the body as an aesthetic medium except Yvonne Rainer, who is described as a "feminist [film] director."[54] As a result of this exclusion, radical transitions from conventional representations of art brought about by the embodied presentations enacted by artists remain unacknowledged for their contributions to contemporary art and critical theory. Such an exclusion is all the more distressing since the volume contains an entire section on "Social Relations," where one might most expect to find a discussion of artists' actions. Especially in the chapters on "Ritual" and "Gender," there is a curious absence of feminist performance and discourses

49. Allan Kaprow, Assemblage, Environment, Happenings, 165.

50. Thomas McEvilley, "Art in the Dark," Artforum 21, no. 10 (June 1983): 62.

51. A book, simply entitled Performances, by Greg Dening, Professor Emeritus of History at the University of Melbourne, is devoted to a theory of history-writing as Derridian "ambivalence" under the trope of "performance." See Greg Dening, Performances (Chicago: University of Chicago Press, 1996), xiii.

52. David Summers, "Representation," in Robert S. Nelson and Richard Shiff, eds., Critical Terms for Art History (Chicago and London: University of Chicago Press, 1996), 6.

53. Ibid., 16.

54. Margaret Olin, "Gaze," in Critical Terms for Art History, 216.

**Giuseppe Pinot Gallizio** *Industrial Painting*, Alba, 1958
Galleria Martano, Torino

**Giuseppe Pinot Gallizio** and his son surrounded by
the *Industrial Painting*, Alba, 1958

which, it could be argued, have made their greatest contributions to the histories of art in the arena of women's art actions, a field in which women have also not only made some of the most intense and sustained work since the 1960s, but a field that — after 1970 — might justifiably be said to have been defined primarily by women.

What these examples suggest is how instantiated in art history the discourses of action art are while its actual practices are often invisible to the canon. A 1994 "round-table" discussion conducted by the editors of *October* on the subject of "The Reception of the Sixties" is the most vivid example of this neglect. Not until mid-way through their extensive conversation did any mention of performance come up at all, and then only in the context of what was described as the "tableau-like, or pictorial space [of] Carolee Schneeman [sic] or of Valie Export."[55] To his credit, Benjamin H. D. Buchloh confessed his ignorance of such art, but his honest admission was flatly rejected by Rosalind Krauss, who argued that it is "richer" to develop an "elaborated model . . . and then we can go back to the body as something that's suppressed not just by the aesthetic paradigm but by that of a paradigm of 'administration.'"[56] Finally, Annette Michelson commented that "historians and theorists of the visual arts" are at "fault" for ignoring performance, a neglect that the "field of 'visual culture' may remedy."[57] Her unchallenged comment suggests that the general suppression of the vast amount of writing by both artists and art historians on performance would be banished to obscurity by refusing to acknowledge its very existence. But as Guy Debord, the principal theorist of the Situationist International (SI), wrote: "All usurpers have shared this aim: to make us forget that *they have only just arrived*."[58]

55. *Slivia Kolbowski, in "The Reception of the Sixties," October 69 (Summer 1994): 10.*

56. *Rosalind Krauss, ibid., 19.*

57. *Annette Michelson, ibid, 20.*

58. *Guy Debord,* Comments on the Society of the Spectacle, *trans. Malcolm Imrie (London: Verso, 1990), 16. Originally published in Paris by Gérard Lebovici, 1988.*

**Giuseppe Pinot Gallizio**, *Industrial Painting*, 1958. Galleria Martano, Torino

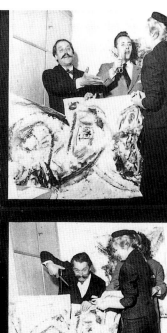

Giuseppe Pinot Gallizio, auction sale of pieces of the *Industrial Painting*, Galerie Van de Loo, Munich, April 1959

Although *October* published excellent articles in 1994 on the SI, they are a newcomer to the field. The SI formed in 1957 and included Debord, Michèle Bernstein, Attila Kotanyi, Raoul Vaneigem, and others. Their method included "experiments in behavior" aimed at altering conduct through the creation of "situations" leading to the construction of what they imagined might be authentic collective environments and personal experiences. The SI published their theoretical texts, the primary vehicles of their practice, in the *Internationale Situationnist* (1958-1969), and these form the conceptual basis for a practical realization of *situationnisme* — the instigation of circumstances through which political and social conditions might be effectively altered — something they rarely actually did, even if there is no question but that the SI offered a sustained, compelling, and inspiring critique of captialism, imperialism, colonialism, the political division and control of urban space, and the general poverty of intellectual life.

One of the artists associated with the Situationists, who created interactive environments and who was eventually excommunicated from the group, was Giuseppe Pinot Gallizio, whose studio in Alba, Italy, served as the site for the Experimental Laboratory of the International Movement for an Imaginist Bauhaus (MIBI), a group comprised of Asger Jorn, Enrico Baj, Ettore Sottsass, Simondo, and himself. They called themselves "free experimental artists" as opposed to "industrial designers," and formed the MIBI "in opposition to Max Bill's work and theories at the Hochschule für Gestaltung in Ulm, Germany."[59] A collaboration in 1956 between Guy Debord's Lettrist International and the MIBI resulted in an agreement that the two groups would join in a program of unitary urbanism (*urbanisme unitaire*), "the theory of the combined use of arts and techniques for the integral construction of a milieu in dynamic relation with experiments in behavior," that later characterized Situationist ideology.[60] The Situationist International was born of this association in 1957. In his own work, Pinot Gallizio aimed at creating playful environments that emphasized luxury, free time, "brightly painted freeways, massive archi-

59. Mirella Bandini, "an enormous and unknown chemical reaction: the EXPERI-MENTAL LABORATORY in ALBA," in on the Passage of a few people through a rather brief moment in time: The Situationist International 1957-1972 (Cambridge: MIT Press, 1989), 68. See also, Bandini's L'estetico il politico: Da Cobra all'Internazionale situazionista, 1948-1957 (Rome: Oficina Edizioni, 1977).

60. Iwona Blazwick in consultation with Mark Francis, Peter Wollen and Malcolm Imrie, eds., An endless adventure . . . an endless passion . . . an endless banquet: A Situationist Scrapbook (London and New York: Verso, 1989): 22.

tectural and urbanistic constructions, fantastic palaces of synesthesia, the products of 'industrial poetry' and sites of 'magical-creative-collective' festivity."[61] In his exhibition, "Cavern of anti-matter," at the Galerie René Drouin, in Paris, in May 1959, he draped the gallery walls, ceiling, and floor entirely with a continuous roll of paintings, and with "mirrors and lights to create the effect of a labyrinth, filled with violent colors, perfumes, and music, producing a drama that would transform visitors into actors."[62] He sold work at the show by the meter, merely cutting off lengths of the painted roll in a parody of automation.[63]

However important the SI were, they constituted only *one* circle in a broad field of artists and intellectuals proferring contentious forms of cultural engagement characteristic of action art during that period. Moreover, it is a measure of their programmatic theory and Marxist orthodoxy that the SI were championed with relative ease and speed by academic discourses and absorbed into art world legends, the thought of which was deplorable to them. Debord's alcoholism and suicide in late 1994 was tragic even as a voluntary philosophical act.

Jean-Jacques Lebel is an artist who could not be tamed by "elaborate models," and rejected dogma in any form. Similarly, he refused to specialize in any one of his diverse talents as a poet, painter, theorist, organizer, and political activist.[64] A year before the Situationist International was formed, Lebel engaged directly in actual political struggle as a draft resister against the Algerian war in 1956, at the age of twenty. At that time, he fled to Italy and began to publish a poetry-protest magazine called *Front Unique* (1956-60).

Lebel's first happening, *The Anti-Procès* (July 8, 1960), was the culminating event in a series of manifestations he and the poet Alain Jouffroy orga-

nized as "collective opposition" to the Algerian War between 1960 and 1961. *The Anti-Procès* took place in Paris, Milan, and Venice and included the collective production of a painting, *Le Grand Tableau Antifasciste Collectif* which he realized with Enrico Baj, Roberto Crippa, Gianni Dovam, Errò (then named Ferrò), and Antonio Recalcati. The painting represented a collective outcry of revolt against colonialism, torture, Napalm, and racism. Pasted to the painting is philosopher Maurice Blanchot's "Manifesto of the 121: Declaration of the Right of Insubordination in the Algeria War," a manifesto signed by Lebel and 121 other French intellectuals including Jean-Paul Sartre, Simone de Beauvoir, Françoise Sagan, and André Breton. The signatories to this tract were considered "traitors" to France. When the group attempted to exhibit *Le Grand Tableau* in 1961 at the *Anti-Procèss III* in Milan, Lebel was arrested and, in his words, "the painting was torn off the wall and kidnapped by the police."[65]

On the seventh anniversary of the Algerian war, November 1,1961, Lebel left France and traveled to the United States. There he participated in Oldenburg's "Ray Gun Theater," gave a poetry reading at the Living Theater (organized by Carolee Schneemann), in the Hall of Issues exhibited a large bomb-shaped metal construction collaged with male and girlie clippings that he said was the "phallic symbol of today," and publicly debated the Algerian revolution in a New York synagogue before returning to France.[66]

Back in Paris, he created a scandal when he organized *Pour Conjurer l'Esprit de Catastrophe*, November 27, 1962 at Galerie Raymond Cordier, during which Tetsumi Kudo performed *Philosophy of Impotence*.[67] The happening was again performed in 1963 at the Boulogne Movie Studios in a "differ-

61. Peter Wollen, "Bitter Victory: The Art and Politics of the Situationist International," in on the Passage of a few people through a rather brief moment in time, 50.

62. Ibid.

63. Mark Francis, "It's All Over: The Material (and Anti-Material) Evidence," in on the Passage of a few people through a rather brief moment in time, 22.

64. In fact Lebel met Debord, five years his senior, when he was 16 in 1952.

65. Unless otherwise noted, all quotes by Lebel come from an interview with the author 27 October 1980, Paris, and subsequent discussions.

66. In 1969 Lebel published an extended interview with the Living Theater, the first publication on the revolutionary work of Judith Malina and Julien Beck in Europe. See Lebel's Entretiens avec 'Le Living

Theatre' (Paris: Editions Pierre Belfond, 1969).

67. Jouffrey, Ferrò (a.k.a. Gudmundur Ferrò, a.k.a. Errò), Jacques Gabriel, Philippe Hiquily, Robert Malaval, Norman Rubington, and Gian-Franco Baruchello all exhibited paintings and sculptures or participated.

**Jean-Jacques Lebel**, *Les manuscrits de Pascal*,
from *To Conjure the Spirit of Catastrophe*, 1962

**Jean-Jacques Lebel**, *New York/New Guinea*,
from *To Conjure the Spirit of Catastrophe*, 1962

**251**

**Jean-Jacques Lebel**, *Christine Keeler Tabloid*,
from *To Conjure the Spirit of Catastrophe*, 1962

ent, extended, and developed" form.[68] Sexual abandon distinguished this and all of Lebel's happenings. The Situationists denounced such happenings in 1963 for including "drugs, alcohol, and eroticism, poetry, painting, dance, and jazz," claiming that they resembled "the ordinary surprise party or the classic orgy," and were assembled like "hash" by "throwing together all the old artistic leftovers."[69] This kind of response was typical of the way in which the Situationists dismissed the construction of any competing "situations."

Lebel inherited Surrealism directly from André Breton, who played a pivotal role in his adolescence. Son of Robert Lebel, the first biographer of Marcel Duchamp, Jean-Jacques Lebel grew up in the milieu of Dada and Surrealist artists.[70] Family friends included Breton, Man Ray, Duchamp, Benjamin Péret, Meret Oppenheim, and Victor Brauner.[71] In 1947, at the age

of eleven, Lebel became involved with street gangs stealing cars. He ended up in a reform school at age twelve. There he was frequently "beaten, . . . saw kids my own age jump out of windows and commit suicide, . . . and learned total desperation." Among his few possessions was Breton's *Arcane 17* and Lebel wrote to the poet about his situation. Breton answered Lebel's letter, telling the boy, "Don't despair." When Lebel escaped from the reform school, he went straight to Breton. The poet became a mentor, but not one Lebel viewed uncritically. He was "a fantastic expresser of life in privacy," Lebel recalled, "but when he got into a group situation, he became like Mussolini." A decade later Breton, in 1959, "expelled" Lebel from Surrealism for being "undisciplined, in permanent revolt, and for direct action." Lebel felt "liberated" yet remained on close terms with Breton.

It is not surprising that Breton disapproved of

68. Production of a film, poorly executed by Titanus (MGM), was released under the title "Il Malamondo." Participants included Jouffrey, François Dufrène, Lilian Lijn, Ferrò, Johanna Lawrenson, and others. Lawrenson and Lebel became involved in Europe, in 1958. They lived together in Paris and New York until 1962. Johanna participated in two of Lebel's happenings. He called her the "chimera à la Gustave Moreau." They also participated together in Oldenburg's happening in New York, and returned to Paris where she worked as model. She would eventually meet Abbie Hoffman in

1974, and later marry him. In his biography of Hoffman, Jonah Raskin explained that Lawrenson "had been raised in a highly intellectual and very political family. . . Her father, Jack Lawrenson, had been a Communist and a leading trade union organizer in the thirties and forties, and she identified with the workers of the world. Her mother, Helen . . . wrote for Esquire and Vanity Fair." See Jonah Raskin, For the Hell of It, xxv.

69. "The Avant-Garde of Presence," Internationale Situationniste, no. 8 (January 1963): 109, reprinted in Ken

Knabb, ed., Situationist International Anthology (Berkeley: Bureau of Public Secrets, 1981), 109.

70. See Robert Lebel, Marcel Duchamp, with chapters by Marcel Duchamp, André Breton & H. P. Roché, translated by George Heard Hamilton (New York: Grove Press, 1959).

71. Lebel called this the "Situationist's. . . violent and, I thought, absurd attack on Breton and Péret (who were my friends) [that] kept me at a distance" from the Situationists.

**Carolee Schneemann**, in her studio, New York, 1963

the blatant sexuality of Lebel's happenings. Sexuality as a synthetic principle pervades Lebel's art, but not the sublimated sexuality of Breton, the desublimated eroticism associated with Bataille, Wilhelm Reich, and Herbert Marcuse. The imaginary, for Lebel, was based on redefinitions of the erotic and its relation to freedom of will, a prerequisite for human freedom. In this regard, it must be remembered that Lebel is a poet-painter. The free-wheeling "sexual revolution" epitomizing Lebel's happenings and attributed to the 1960s was laid out in the 1950s milieu of the Beat poets, and draws heavily on Henry Miller, Surrealism, jazz, unconstrained behavior, ecstatic, mystical, romantic, mind-altering release in drugs and alcohol, eroticism, and the savage transformation of personal life against, and interlaced with, commitment to social change of urban life, all of which Lebel wrote about in his book, *Anthologie de la poésie de la Beat Generation* (1966).

All of these aspects of Lebel's intellectual formation were evident in the "Festivals of Free Expression" he organized between 1964-1967. More than any other environment for art actions, Lebel's activities were international, joining together a cross-section of Fluxus and *Nouveau Réaliste* artists who had created happenings with Beat poets and Concrete poets, playwrights, jazz musicians, movie stars, intellectuals, and Dada and Surrealist artists such as Man Ray and Duchamp. In the first Festival, Carolee Schneemann performed *Meat Joy*, an action that was described by the Parisian press as an "orgy." During the second Festival of Free Expression (at the American Center in Paris), Lebel organized the sacrificial destruction of an automobile. As the car was being beaten with axes and hammers, a motorcycle slowly roared through the crowd carrying a naked woman up and onto the stage. The hall became a

frenzied scene of lights, sounds, and motion. Spaghetti was systematically applied to one woman's body and then hurled through the crowd, while Lawrence Ferlinghetti read a poem about revolt.

From a late-1990s perspective, the men and women who invented some of the aesthetic modes aimed at "liberation" were incapable of recognizing the potential misogyny inherent in their practices. But the historical context is critical. In *Le Happening*, published in 1966, Lebel laid out his thinking further. He quoted Herbert Marcuse from *Eros and Civilization*: "psychological problems become political problems," and Bataille from *Eros and the Fascination with Death*: "Eroticism is born of the forbidden, and lives from the forbidden." He rejected Merleau-Ponty's observation that "hallucinatory phenomena are not part of the world nor accessible" as a "condemn[ation] of art and its languages."[72] In contrast, Lebel claimed: "Happenings are not content to interpret life, they participate in the unfolding of life." All transumutation begins in violation and subversion, he argued, and recalled how Kandinsky had arrived at abstraction through the experience of viewing a painting by Monet turned upside down, and how Marx had reversed Hegel. Most importantly, he stated: "every happening possessed a network of significations that are derived from the precise social and psychological context in which they occur," and for this reason, "there can be no [general] theory of happenings." "After action painting," he continued, "there could be nothing but ACTION. . . . We have a sensation of apocalypse in us, . . . an insurmountable disgust for a 'happy civilization' and its Hiroshima." For Lebel, the Happening constituted a "psycho-social environment", was a "psycho-physical experience", could be augmented by hallucinogenic drugs like 'L.S.D.', "*must transform voyeurs into*

72. *Jean-Jacques Lebel*, Le happening
*(Paris: Edition Denoël, 1966), 22.*
*My translation.*

**253**

**Lynda Benglis**, advertisement in *Artforum*, November 1974

**Barbara T. Smith**, *Feed Me*, 1973. Collection of the artist

**254**

*seers*" (IL FAUT ÊTRE VOYANT, PAS VOYEUR); and, finally: "*The most urgent question of contemporary art has become the renovation and intensification of perception*".

Regardless of whether one appreciates or condemns such images and actions, they (he) did push the boundaries of stifling, hypocritical, conventional morality and somatic phobias (fear of the body that occasions its suppressions) out into the open for public airing. The discourses in which such actions participated belonged to a wide range of liberationist positions especially explored by the New Left that, paradoxically, led to, and were a part of, the explosion of feminism in the late 1960s. But neither Lebel, the women who performed in such events as Yves Klein 's "living brushes," for example, nor the culture at large could pose the same kinds of questions that were possible a decade later. By 1974, Lynda Benglis was prepared to respond with critical distance, irony, humor, and parody to a photograph of Robert Morris on a poster advertising his April exhibition at the Castelli-Sonnabend Gallery in New York in which the artist appeared nude from the waist up wearing a metal dog collar, chains hanging from his neck, and a metal helmet which turned the image of Morris into a huge greased phallus with a helmet head. As Mira Schor has pointed out, such a picture only worked by erasing the actual image of Morris' own penis by cropping the picture just above the waist.[73] Benglis answered this image with a series of pin-up type photographs in *Artforum*, culminating in the November issue where she appeared naked with her own body greased, wearing sunglasses, and sporting a huge phallus between her legs. Visually ridiculing his

pathetic patriarchal posturing, Benglis demonstrated just how powerful and self-confident feminist discourse had become. Clearly the world had changed radically between 1960 and 1974.

Barbara T. Smith's *Feed Me* (1973) marks a moment in the shift from Lebel's erotic objectification of women to feminism, and helps to illustrate one of the ways in which the sexual revolution carried over into the 1970s. *Feed Me*, an intensely intimate piece, was staged in the center of a highly masculinized event — "Sound Sculpture As" — organized by Tom Marioni at his San Francisco Museum of Conceptual Art. Marioni's *Pissing* piece (enacted by Allan Fish, the fabricated persona he invented to enable him to function both as an artist and curator) was typical of the kinds of sound pieces created by the male artists on this evening. Fish's (a.k.a. Marioni's) action included drinking beer all night and, when he needed to relieve himself, going up a ladder and pissing into a metal tub where "the sound pitch went down as the water level went up."[74] Mel Henderson "paced up and down the large loft with a .30 caliber rifle [and] took aim and fired a single shot at a film image of a tiger being projected on a paper-covered saw horse."[75] In contrast, Smith had constructed a private space in which she remained nude throughout the night inviting visitor-participants, one at a time, to enter and interact with her. Her private boudoir-like space was fitted with a mattress, incense, flowers, body oils, wine, perfume, shawls, and music, tea, books, marijuana, a heater to warm the area, and participants were invited to "feed" her and themselves in an exchange of "conversation and affection." When asked how she felt about creating an image of a

73. Mira Schor, "Representations of the Penis," M/E/A/N/I/N/G 4 (November 1988).

74. Tom Marioni, quoted in Performance Anthology, 12. Lebel explained that: "There were also pissing scenes in '120 minutes'. . . . Billy Copley pissed up on a ladder into a tube (a reference to a Huichol Indian habit of collecting the piss of the person who has eaten peyote because piss retains the psychotrope alkaloid and, when drunk, the others can get ritually high too for free. This is because peyote was too expensive for these Indians, thus it enabled all to participate in the ritual with only one pey-

ote bud). Also in the same Happening, Marianne, a naked lady, pissed on the audience from the theatre balcony before descending on a rope and doing other things. All this was years before Karen Finley, Cicciolina or Annie Sprinkle (and I really admire these ladies as performers, pissers and artists) even though today, all this pissing sounds a little childish. But in 1966, I can assure you it was dynamite and just about the wildest body language you could dream of doing. Today, according to articles in the Italian press, the prostitution industry openly advertises pissing in commercial sexual transactions. Perhaps because the worldwide

AIDS epidemic has forced "new" or different forms of sex into the open. Perhaps because all human actions or desires are prone to winding up as supermarket commodities swallowed up and imitated by fashion victims. If art is a social "laboratory," which I hope it is, artists do not exert control over the use to which their work is put. In May 1968, my feeling was that the "social laboratory" of art had very positive results. That's not always the case, is it?" Lebel letter to the author, 23 October 1997.

75. Barbara T. Smith, "Birthdaze," High Performance 4, no. 3 (Fall 1981): 19-24.

woman as a "courtesan and [an] odalisque," Smith responded that such images of women are part of "real life" and part of "fantasy." In this and subsequent works, Smith, like Orlan in France, attempted to negotiate between the cultural image of woman as "virgin and whore," between patriarchal and feminist discourses, and between her own utilization of performance as a "vehicle for personal transformation" and a mode of "expanded consciousness in the world."[75]

When the body is used as a psychological and political weapon as Lebel employed it in his Happenings, when the condition of art as a commodity and its rapacious promotion is exposed as $hit (Lebel's term), the only way to defeat such art actions (and bodies) is to ignore them: suppress the body *and* the discourses that deal with it until they can be administered back into the system of exchange which they deny.

## V. We, Multiples

For a long time I have hesitated to write a book on woman. The subject is irritating, especially to women; and it is not new.
— Simone de Beauvoir, 1953[76]

CONVERSATION PIECE
Bandage any part of your body.
If people ask about it, make a story and tell.
If people do not ask about it, draw their attention to it and tell.
If people forget about it, remind them of it and keep telling.
Do not talk about anything else.
— Yoko Ono, 1962[77]

In 1970, Valie Export posed nude for a photograph in which her upper thigh appears tattooed with the representation of a garter that holds up the edge of an imaginary stocking. A semiotics of gender

enslavement, Export's *Body-sign action* is a corporeal signifier of "repressed sexuality . . . belonging to a class that demands conditioned behaviour," and it served her as a reminder to "keep alive" what she described as "the problem of self-determination and/or other-determination of femininity."[78] But while the image of the tattoo is compelling, what is even more commanding is the closeness the photograph permits to the delicate triangle that is Valie Export's public area. There, it is possible to see her labia lightly covered in pubic hair, looking vulnerable and innocent, beside the aggressive tattoo. One photograph depicts much that is women's pain, pleasure, and multiple identity: our sex, our socialization, and our representation. I stated above that feminist performances "have made their greatest contributions to the histories of art in the arena of women's art actions." For these reasons, I situate a specific discussion of women's art actions here, in the center of this essay, even while I long for the time when a "special" section on *any* particular group will no longer be necessary.

Even the most cursory view of women's performances over the last forty years presents a collective picture of that explosive energy erupting from within culture, a rage acted out in multiple ways and often as multiplicity itself. Adrian Piper's work is a case in point. Like many feminists' performances, Piper's work comes out of her own life experience and is intended as political analysis, a social critique grounded in personal biography that reflects the 1970s feminist slogan "the personal is the political." As an African-American woman living under racism and sexism, Piper's work refused that cultural erasure.

The daughter of light-skinned parents of African descent, Piper grew up in Harlem, and was educated in mostly white, economically advantaged schools. She lived in two worlds. Responding to these conditions, Piper began her *Catalysis* series in 1970. Aggressively confrontational in character, Piper would appear on the streets of New York in some highly obnoxious manner. For example, she once "soaked

76. Simone de Beauvoir, "Introduction," in The Second Sex (New York: Alfred A. Knopf, 1953), reprinted in Linda Nicholson, ed., The Second Wave: A Reader in Feminist Theory (New York and London: Routledge, 1997), 11.

77. Yoko Ono, Grapefruit (New York: Simon and Schuster, 1970), 11. Grapefruit was originally published in a limited edition of 500 copies by the Wunternaum Press in Tokyo in 1964.

78. Valie Export, Valie Export (Vienna: Austria Biennale di Venezia and Galerie in der Staatsoper, 1980), 46.

**Adrian Piper,** *Catalysis IV,* street performance, New York, 1970

Linda Montano (with Tom Marioni), *Handcuff: Linda Montano and Tom Marioni*, 1973

some clothing in a smelly broth of vinegar, milk, cod liver oil and eggs for a week and then, wearing this malodorous costume, she rode the subway and browsed in a bookstore."[79] Later she would appear as the *Mythic Being*, an "angry, cigar-smoking, third-world man wearing sunglasses and a mustache."

Piper's extraordinarily creative and constructive strategies and tactics combat pyschic turmoil, to survive whole, analytic, and productive in a social situation in which her identity remained under constant and continuous assault. Piper herself has reported that her interest in the performative aspect of "the object (herself) — subject (audience) dichotomy began to dissolve with the dialogues she had with a psychiatrist in early 1972."[80] An essay by the artist from 1985 — "Two Conceptions of the Self" — suggests that the artist's self-analysis extended to an analysis of the deep divisions in philosophy itself regarding the character and development of the self, split between "the Kantian notion [favored by Piper] that what ultimately motivates the self is 'the disposition to render all our experiences, including our experiences of our own conscious behavior, rationally intelligible,' [and] the Humean idea that the self is motivated primarily by desires, which rationality, in a subordinate capacity, serves to fulfill."[81]

The artist who most consistently sustained a constantly evolving invention of personae is Linda Montano. Perhaps Montano's personae began, as she suggests, in "The Chicken Show," the artist's M.F.A. exhibition (May 20, 1969), in which she exhibited chickens on the roof of the art department and throughout the city of Madison, Wisconsin. After this she created herself as *Chicken Woman* (1970). Her first performance, *Lying: Dead Chicken, Live Angel* (1971), eventually evolved into numerous personifi-

cations of herself as a composite being: *Home Nurse*, (1973), a *Bell-Ringer for the Salvation Army*, (December, 1974), her sister in *Talking about Sex while Under Hypnosis* (1975), *The Screaming Nun* (1975), *Guru* (March 22, 1975), and *Dr. Jane Gooding and Sister Rose Augustine (1975)*. (It is important to note here that Montano's several personae as a nun are some kind of aesthetic reincarnation of her former life as a nun. She entered Maryknoll Sisters Missionary in 1960 at the age of 18, and left two years later weighing eighty-two pounds and diagnosed with anorexia nervosa.) As another form of creating composite personae, the artist also permitted herself to be bound to male artists: Tom Marioni in *Handcuff: Linda Montano and Tom Marioni* (1973) — a three-day action in which the two artists were handcuffed together; and Tehching Hsieh in *One Year Art/Life Performance*, a year-long action that included being tied together by an eight-foot rope from 1983 to 1984.

Like Montano, Lynn Hershman has sustained the representation of split subjectivity in multiples that continue — as do Montano's — into the present. "Roberta" began in an advertisement for a roommate that Hershman placed in a San Francisco newspaper. When people responded, she extended her fabricated reality to encompass them.[82] "Roberta" had a driver's license, checking accounts, and credit cards. She went to Weight Watchers, EST, saw a psychiatrist, had her own speech patterns, handwriting, apartment, clothing, gestures, and moods. The public, friends, and other artists assumed that Hershman was, indeed, "Roberta," even though Hershman denied it, insisting that Roberta was "her own woman" with separate defined needs, ambitions, and instincts. "Roberta" was Hershman's "underside . . .

79. Ken Johnson, "Being and Politics," Art in America 78, no. 9 (September 1990): 156-57.

80. Rosemary Mayer, "Performance & Experience," Arts Magazine 47, no. 3 (December-January 1973): 35.

81. Ken Johnson, "Being and Politics," Art in America 78, no. 9 (September 1990): 156-57.

82. The origins of "Roberta Breitmore" are difficult to pin down. In a 1977 article Hershman cited 1975 as the beginning of

this performance. [See Lynn Hershman, "Lynn Hershman," Data 27 (July-September 1977): 4.] In 1992, she dated Roberta as "1971-78." [See Lynn Hershman, "Simulations and Performances: Roberta Breitmore," in Lynn Hershman (Montbéliard and Belfort, France: Chimaera, 1992), 64.] But in 1995, she stated that her installation, "The Dante Hotel," was the work of art that "led to a ten-year project entitled 'Roberta Breitmore.'" [See Lynn Hershman Leeson, "Reflections and Preliminary Notes," Paranoid Mirror

(Seattle: Seattle Art Museum, 1995), 13.] I personally experienced and lived through the period in which Roberta Breitmore was active; and I was not only the first "Roberta" multiple, but was present at "Roberta's" exorcism in 1978. In the 1995 essay, Hershman writes that the beginnings of Roberta were "private." It is, indeed, very likely that "Roberta Breitmore" began in a private experience. Therefore, as a public performance, "Roberta" probably dates from 1975 to 1978. But the riddle is not so simply solved.

**Robert Rauschenberg** firing at *tirs* (shooting paintings) with a .22 rifle, near Stockholm, 23 May 1961

**Niki de Saint Phalle** with a .22 rifle creating a shooting painting, Impasse Ronsin, Paris, 15 June 1961

a dark, shadowy cadaver that we try with pathetic illusion to camouflage."[83] "Roberta" was a material manifestation of the psychological interface between a whole and fragmented psyche. Simultaneously real and a fabrication, she personified the space of passage between states of being-knowing and dissociation: space that is the territory of art where visuality and subjectivity overlap in the artifact of action.[84]

In 1980, Hershman again duplicated herself by separating her artistic development between "B. C. (*Before Computers*) and A. D. (*After Digital*)."[85] During the A. D. period, Hershman has produced numerous new multiples in video, laser disc, and virtual reality. In *Electronic Diary* (1985-89), she whispered — "Don't talk about it," reminding viewers, turned witnesses, of the family secrets surrounding her own multiple experiences with incest which she cites as the origins of her autobiographical series. In this video series, the Jewish artist undergoes an auto-analysis of her own eating disorders, originating in violations she equated with Hitler, the vampire, and Holocaust survivors. As recently as 1996, Hershman wrote:

The work in which I am presently engaged is the creation of a fictional persona, designed as an updated "Roberta," who is navigating through the Internet. Surveillance, capture and tracking

are the DNA of her inherently digital anatomy. They form the underpinning of her portrait.[86]

Unlike *Roberta,* however, who was exorcised in an alchemical death of air, fire, mirrors, and smoke in the Palazzo dei Diamonte in Ferrara, Italy (1978), Hershman's 1990s "portrait" seeks to "erase" the separation between "death that separates one reality from the surface reality lived."[87]

While often sublimated and dissociated into alternate personae, the rage and psychic turmoil I have been describing was directly expressed by Niki de Saint Phalle in her *Tir à Volonté* (Fire at Will) paintings, a series of constructions onto whose surface the artist attached bags of liquid pigment that burst when she (or others) fired a .22 caliber rifle at her work. She first publicly presented these "shoot paintings" on June 30, 1961, at Pierre Restany's Galerie J. in Paris. De Saint Phalle herself wrote:

I shot because it was fun and made me feel great. I shot because I was fascinated watching the painting bleed and die. I shot for that moment of magic. It was a moment of scorpionic truth. White purity. Sacrifice. Ready. Aim. Fire. Red, yellow, blue — the painting is crying the painting is dead. I have killed the painting. It is reborn. War with no victims.[88]

All of these works convey the wisdom and invention of a narrative of woman's survival, as do the

83. Lynn Hershman Leeson, "Reflections and Preliminary Notes," Paranoid Mirror, 13. It is worth remarking that in sometimes using her husband's name, Hershman continues to appear multiple since "Leeson" is not a name that she consistently uses.

84. For a longer discussion of Roberta's multiplicity, see my "1.1.78 - 2.2.78: Roberta Breitmore," in Roberta Breitmore Is Not Lynn Hershman (San Francisco: De Young Memorial Museum, 1978), 5-14. In this article, I attempted to mirror

Hershman/Breitmore's "schizophrenia" by alternating between two very different discursive voices. Twenty years later, my text itself has become a study of fragmentation. Moreover, as the first "multiple" of Roberta, a role I enacted in 1977 in San Francisco when I went with Hershman as Roberta to gallery openings, her condition of fragmentation was palpable.

85. Lynn Hershman, "The Floating Museum," Data 27 (July-September 1977): 11.

86. Lynn Hershman Leeson, "Romancing the Anti-Body: Lust and Longing in (Cyber)space," in Lynn Hershman: Captured Bodies of Resistance (Warsaw: Centre for Contemporary Art, Ujazkowski Castle, 1996), 25.

87. Ibid., 26.

88. Niki de Saint Phalle, quoted in Carla Schulz-Hoffmann, Niki de Saint Phalle (Bonn: Prestel-Verlag, 1987), 53.

following: Yayoi Kusama's obsessive environments and clothing of the 1960s that become a claustrophobic space, a horror-vacuii, of phallic forms, dominating and reducing the vaginal image to a dot repeated over its surfaces like decorative fluff; Martha Rosler's *Vital Statistics of a Citizen, Simply Obtained* (1973), a performance that acknowledged the many ways in which women are dehumanized into statistical categories, our bodies disciplined and controlled; Mary Beth Edelson's *Proposals for: Memorials to the 9,000,000 Women Burned as Witches in the Christian Era* (1977), a group ritual organized to remember and mourn the women who — because of their knowledge, independence, intuitions, information, social and (unauthorized and uncontrolled) sexual practices, love, care for and compatibility with animals (cats in particular) — were tortured, tried, and murdered; Judy Chicago, Suzanne Lacy, Sandra Orgel, and Aviva Rahmani's *Ablutions* (1972), a work based on the oral histories of women rape and incest survivors, collected by Chicago and Lacy in 1971; Leslie Labowitz and Suzanne Lacy's *In Mourning and in Rage* (1977), a public media action realized in Los Angeles that marshaled the entire city to an awareness of violence against women; Mierle Laderman Ukeles's manifesto, "Maintenance Art" (1969), that expressed her attention to the time spent by women in domestic, service-related labor and that led to actions such as *Touch Sanitation* (1978-80), in which the artist attempted to greet and shake hands with New York's 8,500 sanitation workers.

Sometimes the sheer weight of the continuous experience of oppression drives one to self-destruction and self-mutilation in a desperate attack on the self as somehow inadequate, in a dangerous effort to cut the dissociative numbing that separates feeling from the persistence of psychic pain that becomes physical. Gina Pane climbed the spiked stairs of a ladder in *Escalade non anésthesiée* (Non-anesthetized Climb, 1971), in order to "protest against a world where everything is anesthetized."[89] Art historian Kathy O'Dell has pointed out that Pane's "self-attacking . . . self-negating, and self-mutilatory [performances] highlighted the vulnerability that can be entailed in conforming to conditions of masquerade [and that rendered] Pane's denial of pleasure . . . explicit."[90] These performances also represent a desperate attempt to feel something, *anything*, but the suffering self, the internal physical and psychic pain that is so intense that it must be shut out, dissociated, or deferred, only to be cut through to be re-experienced. Writing on masochism, the performance artist Rachel Rosenthal, whose work has deeply explored the territory of psychic suffering, explained that:

> Some of us seek pain. Not as an end in itself, but as a technique, a trigger, a channel. As a path. Pain may be a path to orgasm, to the dissolution of ego, to growth, understanding, spiritual enlightenment, moral well-being, and the feeling of being somewhat special and superior in the culture.[91]

In the late 1960s and throughout the 1970s, some men responded to the sexual revolution and feminism by fashioning an androgynous look typified by rock stars and hippies. Such films as *Performance* (1968), featuring Mick Jagger, promoted gender ambiguity and an attitude about identity and sexuality as performative; while works like Lou Reed's 1973 album *Transformer* (a record produced by David Bowie) contained the song "Walk on the Wild Side," a favorite amongst drag queens. Performance artists who explored this territory included Urs Lüthi, Katharina Sieverding, Günter Brus, Michel Journiac, Gilbert & George, Vito Acconci, Lucas Samaras, Paul McCarthy, Luigi Ontani, and many others, like Jürgen Klauke.

In the early 1970s, Klauke often collaborated with Ulay (a.k.a. Uwe Laysiepen, who later collaborated with Marina Abramovic). They created gender-ambiguous and transsexual images of himself in

89. Gina Pane, quoted in Ezio Quarantelli, "Travels with St. Francis," Contemporanea 1, no. 4 (November/December 1988): 46.

90. Kathy O'Dell, "The Performance Artist as Masochistic Woman," Arts Magazine 62, no. 10 (June 1988): 96-97.

91. Rachel Rosenthal, "Stelarc, Performance and Masochism," Obsolete Body/Suspensions/Stelarc, compiled and edited by James D. Paffrath with Stelarc (Davis, California: JP Publications, 1984), 69-70. Rachel Rosenthal studied dance and theater in France before coming to the United States where she created "Instant Theatre," was involved in the Women's Art Movement in Los Angeles, and created and taught Performance Art.

**Jürgen Klauke,** *The Harder They Come II*, 1978. Courtesy Galerie Bugdahn and Kaimer, Düsseldorf

sado-masochistic like rituals, with accessories and appendages that mimicked both male and female genitalia. Klauke especially investigated unconventional representations of sexuality and identity in "coolly straightforward" self-portrayals in sequential photographs suggestive of the performative context of the photographic display as well as of "facile notions concerning photography's ability to capture both the 'truth' and a fixed identity."[92] Indeed, one of the most striking qualities of Klauke's "image" was exactly his cool, unreachable demeanor, a manner of self-presentation that was augmented by his physical appearance: tall, slender, handsome, with shoulder-length hair and a provocative way of dressing in tight pants, open shirt, and lots of long gold chains around his neck. He created an aura of untouchability augmented by clothing that was exactly the element of identity that made his performance, *The Harder They Come*, which I attended at the Student Cultural Center in Belgrade, 1978, so poignant.

Dressed all in white with his tight pants tucked into elegant cowboy boots, and his silk shirt open nearly to the waist revealing the gold chains and amulets on his chest, and using the codes of representation that connoted a rock star, Klauke entered the room. In the center of the space a labyrinth of large concrete masonry blocks were tied together with strings in concentric circles. Klauke walked in to the music of Jimmy Cliff's famous reggae song "The Harder They Come, The Harder They Fall" which had been recorded on a continuous tape loop. The room itself was semi-circular with windows facing the busy, noisy street; it was dusk and slightly dark except for lights that shone into the space irregularly from passing cars on the Belgrade street. This urbane, complicated, extremely aloof, distant, and apparently self-contained man began to find his way around and through the concentric circles of blocks which had been carefully tied together in such a way as to permit access to the next inner circle only in specific places. If the artist was not careful, he tripped over the string. Klauke continued to circle, dancing with an increasing vigor to the music. The more he danced,

92. J. Fiona Ragheb, "Artists' Biographies," *in* Rrose is a Rrose is a Rrose, 210.

the harder it became to navigate the strings, the more his fancy boots caught in the labyrinth, until they were hopelessly entangled in the strings and the weight and pull of the concrete masonry bricks brought him crashing to the floor. *The Harder They Come* was a simple piece. But it was very compelling to watch this guarded, artificial, self-conscious, sexually ambivalent white man create an obstacle course augmented by radical black oppositional music that inevitably obviated, hindered, invalidated, and ultimately annulled everything his carefully constructed self-presentation was manufactured to convey.

Clearly Klauke had taken his cues from feminist performance, as did Sherman Fleming, who in 1976 also created an alternate persona, RodForce, in order to move "forward through this morass of repressed power-seeing bodies as the all-powerful Black Male, active in a city of Monuments essentialized in the Washington Monument: unyielding and invulnerable!"[93] In RodForce, Fleming condensed the representation of black males in popular media into one massive phallic personification of force: the "commanding intellectualism of Malcolm X, the spiritualism of Martin Luther King, the emotive eroticism of James Brown, and the physical endurability of the mythic John Henry." Fleming realized that such an image was a farce and that the media myth makers

for the consumers of culture could, in the blink of an eye, by the same mechanisms that created his heroes reduce them into "negative and mythic constructions: a violent lunatic, a womanizer, a fanatic partisan, and a plagiarizer."[94]

In *Something Akin to Living* (1979), the audience faced a spot light aimed at two Doric columns between which Fleming, as RodForce, a tall, slender African-American man, nude except for an array of feathers woven around his dreadlocks and a silver-lamé thong gathered around his genitals, entered and positioned himself between the columns.[95] His assistant, Haig Paul, measured and cut pieces of lumber to fit at various angles between the columns and Fleming's body. Standing immobile during an action that lasted thirty-five minutes, RodForce strained to support the weight of this cumbersome and irrational architecture. Adjusting himself like a static juggler, RodForce kept up the unwieldy and increasingly weighty timbered structure around him until, straining and exhausted, he could no longer sustain the imprisoning edifice and simply walked off, letting the entire weight fall around him.

This action pointed to how abstract power systems, symbolically represented by architectural monuments, arbitrarily and artificially order and regiment life to fit into schematized systems that neither

93. Sherman I. Fleming, Jr., "Living in a City of Monuments, Or Why I No Longer Walk with an Erection," Washington Review (Washington, D.C.) 17, no. 5 (February-March 1991), 5.

94. Ibid., 6.

95. The performance took place at Wayne Higgs' studio gallery space at 930 F Street in Washington, D.C., the office

building that soon thereafter housed the "9:30 Club," a punk-music and performance space.

support nor sustain the individual necessity of human beings who themselves, ironically and pathetically, continue to support and sustain such systems. Through the parody of the sexualized persona, RodForce emphasized not only *how* the body is the material that bears the weight of such symbolic edifices, but *how* it was in the labor of the black male body that part of the edifice that is the United States was constructed, a body that was then mythically eroticised as a means to control and suppress it.

Suppression and segregation were the primary experiences of Sherman Fleming's life, experiences that he detailed in an essay in 1990, "Nigger as Anti-Body." He grew up "obsessed" with the word "nigger," which he looked up in Webster's Dictionary at the age of nine in 1962, only to discover that "it seemed that I had already known it then, all my life."[96] "Starting in the fourth grade," he wrote, "I would welcome each school year by looking for Nigger in the dictionary."[97] As one of fourteen students out of 750 who were the first generation forced by busing to desegregate his junior high school, and later as the first generation to desegregate Virginia Commonwealth University, Fleming understood the implications of the term only too well.

Fleming's attention to the "fitness" of the body as a mythical indicator of its sexual prowess also anticipated and parodied the fitness craze of the 1980s that regulated the "healthy body" as a commercial commodity similar to what the "black male" himself became in the 1980s and early 1990s. Richard Powell has written that Fleming's work "merged the spectacle of a perceived racial difference with notions of desire, contagion, concealment, and emancipation, all within his theoretical construct of physical (as well as psychological) endurance."[98] Eleven years later, in 1987, he gave up performing under the pseudonym.[99] A cross between "Superman and a Clown," RodForce eventually became a "prison

of expectations — both of my own and those of my audience." As Fleming wryly pointed out, "RodForce could not keep it up." After abandoning this persona, he experienced a "freedom that permits me to no longer walk with an erection."[100]

The radical questioning of gender roles that began in the late 1960s has continued through several successive developments of feminism. Initially, the Women's Liberation Movement faced the task of "getting others in the New Left (women as well as men) to recognize women's oppression," its presence across history, and its fundamental importance "as a principle of social organization."[101] Because Women's Liberation was aligned with the New Left, it also reflected the impact of Marxism on critical thought, which meant that women needed to account for oppression by writing *across and through* the discourses of Marxism, and by including considerations of reproduction and the labor involved in the care of human beings in more generalized theories of production and work. By the end of the 1960s and early 1970s, some feminists understood that by emphasizing the similarities between the sexes, they might advance women's issues, while other feminists — associated with radical feminism, or "gynocentric" feminism, emphasized differences between the sexes.[102] Within these two tendencies of the early 1970s, other divisions emerged. Black feminists argued that the very term "Black feminist" classified African-American women regardless of their experiences as the same, and pointed out that a Black feminist might equally be Frederick Douglass or William E.B. DuBois as a woman.

Reductive labels were assigned to these complex and heterogeneous debates: the term "essentialist" came to stand for first generation feminists (often associated with gynocentric feminism), while "constructivist," or "post-structuralist," feminism represented the second generation (heavily

---

96. Sherman Fleming, "Nigger as Anti-Body," WhiteWalls 25 (Spring 1990): 54, a special issue on "Art and Healing," edited by the author.

97. Ibid., 56.

98. Richard J. Powell, Black Art and Culture in the Twentieth Century (London: Thames and Hudson, 1997), 198.

99. In 1986, Fleming invited me to collaborate on performances with him. I agreed only if he abandoned the name RodForce, which had nothing to do with the collaborations we then performed from late 1986 until the end of 1992.

100. "Living in a City of Monuments," 7.

101. Linda Nicholson, The Second Wave, 1-2.

102. See Iris Young, "Humanism, Gynocentrism and Feminist Politics," in Hypatia: A Journal of Feminist Philosophy 3, a special issue of Women's Studies International Forum 8, no. 3 (1985): 173-183.

**Valie Export**, *Tapp und Tastkino*, 1968

influenced by the psychoanalytic views of Jacques Lacan and the deconstruction of Jacques Derrida). Lacan and Derrida offered a critique of the notion of "autonomous, preconstituted conceptions of the subject and theories of language that construed meaning in representational or essentialist terms," as expressions of "phallocentric" and "logocentric" logic.

Mira Schor, along with feminist artists Cheri Gaulke and Suzanne Lacy, and art historians such as Moira Roth and Lucy Lippard, especially active during the early phases of feminism, have all documented the origins of feminist performance during this period. Roth identified the conjunction of feminist performance with feminist street theater, such as the "disruption of the Miss America Pageant in Atlantic City in 1968," and "the raw eggs and sanitary napkins littering pristine museum spaces protesting the low percentage of women in the Whitney Museum's Biennial in New York," in 1970.[103] She identified the beginning of performance in America on the East Coast as integrally connected with Happenings, experimental dance and music, and with minimal and Conceptual art. She noted that performance on the West Coast emerged from equally varied sources, reflecting the "improvisatory theater" of Rachel Rosenthal, the experimental music and dance events associated with Ann Halprin and Pauline Oliveros, the process, ecological, and minimalist oriented works of Barbara Smith and Bonnie Sherk, as well as the Feminist Art Program in Fresno led by Judy Chicago. Most chronologies in the United States begin with the "Consciousness Raising" (CR), that took place in many centers including the Fresno Feminist Art Program (begun by Judy Chicago); the Feminist Art Program at Cal Arts in 1971 (under Chicago and Miriam Shapiro); the month-long series of activities sponsored by Womanhouse — an "environmental artwork collaboratively created by women in the Cal Arts Program in Los Angeles," in 1972; and the Woman's Building which opened in 1973.[104]

In Europe, Valie Export's guerilla performances were among the first feminist actions. In 1968, she collaborated with Peter Weibel on such actions as *Tapp und Tastkino* (Touch and Taste Film). Export appeared on the street with a miniature theater-stage set constructed around her bare, but hidden, breasts. Using a bull-horn, Weibel invited the public to step up, reach through the stage curtains, and touch her breasts. Export's 1968 statement about this performance demonstrates how avant-garde consciousness often leads social consciousness:

> In that I, in the language of film, allowed my "body screen," my chest, to be touched by everybody, I broke through the confines of socially legitimate social communication. My chest was withdrawn from "the society of spectacle," which had drawn the woman into "objectification" with it. Moreover, the breast is no longer the property of one single man; rather, the woman attempts through the free availability of her body to determine her identity independently: the first step from object to subject.[105]

In 1969, dressed in a black shirt and pants with the crotch cut away and a machine gun slung over her shoulder for a performance, entitled *Genital Panic*, Export entered a theater in Munich that was screening pornographic films. Addressing the audience that had come to watch genitals on the screen, she announced that "real" genitalia were available and they could do whatever they wished. She remembered:

> I moved down each row slowly, facing people. I did not move in an erotic way. I walked down each row, the gun I carried pointed at the heads of the people in the row behind. I was afraid and had no idea what the people would do. As I moved from row to row, each row of people silently got up and left the theatre. Out of film context, it was a totally different way for them to connect with the particular erotic symbol.[106]

Also in 1969, COUM Transmissions was founded by Peter Christopherson, Cosey Fanni Tutti

103. Moira Roth, The Amazing Decade: Women and Performance Art in America 1970-1980 (Los Angeles: Astro Arts, 1983), 16.

104. Cheri Gaulke, "Performance Art of the Woman's Building," High Performance 3, nos. 3-4 (Fall/Winter 1980): 156-163.

105. Export, quoted in Peter Nesweda, "In Her Own Image: Valie Export, Artist and Feminist," Arts Magazine 65, no. 9 (May 1991): 71.

106. Valie Export, in an interview with Ruth Askey, High Performance 13 (Spring 1981): 80, quoted in Barry Kapk, "Body as Sign: Performance and Film Works of Valie Export," High Performance 45 (Spring 1989): 35.

**Valie Export,** *Genital Panic,* 1969

**Valie Export,** *Vagire,* from *Körper-Konfigurationen,* 1972

# PRICK TEASE TORMENTOR
## AND KEITH THE RANDY TYCOON

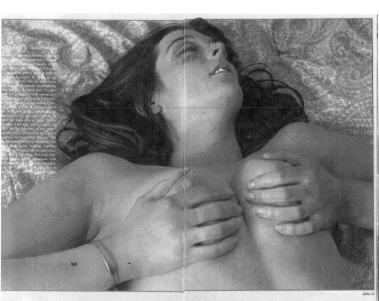

**album**
your private collection

JOANNA   JANE   COSEY

### Porno panto

### Private view

### X-certificate

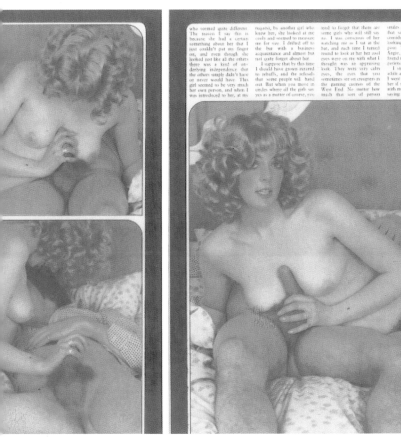
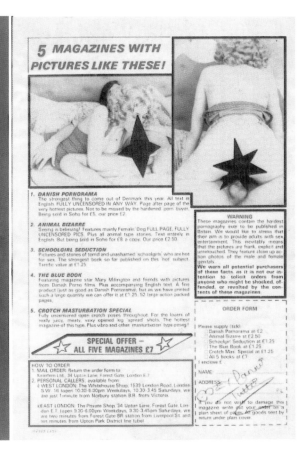

**COUM Transmissions (Cosey Fanni Tutti)**, *Exhibit No. 10 (Park Lane No. 15)(Sex Magazine Art Action Performance)*,
from "Prostitution" Exhibition, Institute of Contemporary Arts, London, October 1976. Collection of Cosey Fanni Tutti

**COUM Transmissions (Cosey Fanni Tutti)**, *Exhibit No. 29 (Alpha No. 5) (Sex Magazine Art Action Performance)*,
from "Prostitution" Exhibition, Institute of Contemporary Arts, London, October 1976. Collection of Cosey Fanni Tutti

and Genesis P-Orridge in London. On October 16, 1976, at the London Institute of Contemporary Arts, they opened "Prostitution," an exhibition inspired by Cosey's work in the sex industry and publication of sex magazines in which she herself appeared. By 1976 she had already worked for two years posing as a "glamour/porno model" for some forty pornography magazines, a deliberate performative strategy from which pictures were used for "Prostitution," COUM's "sexhibition." Cosey was particularly interested in the ways in which British laws classified prostitution as an "act," and pointed out that "soliciting or loitering in public is not an offence if done by any person [except] a female common prostitute," and cited a 1959 law, the Street Offences Act, as directed primarily against female prostitutes.[107] Cosey understood her work in sex magazines and films to be an infiltration of the mass consciousness through its own structures, a clinical analysis of the commercialization and commodification of sex:

> My projects are presented unaltered in a very clinical way, as any other COUM project would be. The only difference is that my projects involve the very emotional ritual of making love. To make an action I must feel that the action is me and no one else, no influences, just purely me. This is where the photos and films coum in. I am laying myself open, fully to myself, and through my action to other people also. . . . Here you will see COUM only as you want to see us. The world dictates what it deems to be reality, thereby annihilating reality and we, COUM, cease to exist.[108]

Predictably the media and the public made a furor over "Prostitution." "If this is art — what will happen next" the London *Evening News* screeched Monday, October 25, 1976. As it nearly always does, the media reflected only a shallow view of the role of

107. Cosey Fanni Tutti, "Prostitution: Sex magazine action performance," Curious 46, Exhibit No. 36, 1976. She details extensively what "Act" means in the legal sense of arrest in the article.

108. Statement in I.C.A. Bulletin (October/December 1976).

**269**

art and artists, and failed to address the problems COUM had raised regarding prostitution, the sex industry, porno-film business, or any of the other issues facing sex-workers and culture in general.

Prior to this exhibition the group had performed actions in streets, galleries, and festivals, but often in a context outside of what had become standard "alternative spaces" for exhibiting Performance Art. Cosey Fanni Tutti adapted her name as a pun on the title of Mozart's famous *opera buffa*, *Così Fan Tutte* (1790), the eighteenth-century Naples setting of which finds two young officers, Ferrando and Guglielmo, boasting to their friend Don Alfonso of the fidelity of their fiancées, Dorabella and Fiordiligi. Don Alfonso makes a bet that both sisters will take new lovers, given the opportunity, and the three devise a plan to fool the women by disguising themselves as Albanians. After initially rejecting their advances, Dorabella and Fiordiligi succumb to the two exotic men and agree to wed the Albanians. They are once again tricked by the men into a false wedding, and finally shamed for their inconstancy. All ends well, of course, because Ferrando and Guglielmo forgive them, and Don Alfonso, having won his bet, states: "Così fan tutte" (Girls are all like that). Double standards and duplicity: is it any wonder that women's identities multiply?

One year before the formation of COUM, Carolee Schneemann performed "Naked Action Lecture," at the London Institute of Contemporary Arts, June 27, 1968. Unambiguously and explicitly feminist, she dressed and undressed during an action that entailed such questions as:

Can an art istorian be a naked woman?

Does a woman have intellectual authority?

Can she have public authority while naked and speaking?

Was the content of the lecture less appreciable when she was naked?

What multiple levels of uneasiness, pleasure, curiosity, erotic fascination, acceptance or rejection were activated in an audience?[109]

Schneemann had read Simone de Beauvoir's *Second Sex* in the 1950s, and she was aware already then, not only in her personal relationships (especially with her husband, the composer James Tenney, and their friend Stan Brakhage) but professionally, that she continually had to fight for recognition and equality. At the same time, the works of Reich and Artaud had equally influenced her, and Schneemann participated in her generation's celebration of sensuality. She and Tenney appeared in Brakhage's *Loving* and in her own *Meat Joy* (1964), which the artist described as a "propulsion . . . toward the ecstatic — shifting and turning between tenderness, wildness, precision, abandon: qualities which could at any moment be sensual, comic, joyous, repellent, [and] an erotic rite: excessive, indulgent, a celebration of [male and female] flesh as material."[110] So too is her erotic film *Fuses* (1964-65), a heterosexual celebration of sexuality. But these works, which heralded sexual freedom for women, were also self-conscious actions that insisted on the centrality of a woman producing her own image. In 1974, in a text prophetically titled "Istory of a Girl Pornographer," that anticipated COUM's "Prostitution," Schneemann wrote: "I WAS PERMITTED TO BE AN IMAGE/BUT NOT AN IMAGEMAKER CREATING HER OWN SELF-IMAGE."[111]

The struggle to produce an image of oneself — to have, in Virginia Woolf's terms, "a room of one's own" — was explored by Ulrike Rosenbach again and again, but never as eloquently, in my view, as in *Don't Believe I'm an Amazon* (1975). Rosenbach confronted stereotypical representations of women: the pure Mother/Madonna with the war-like, masculine (read: lesbian) Amazon. The artist shot arrows at a target covered with a black and white photographic reproduction of Stephan Lochner's famous *Madonna and Child*. Meanwhile, a video camera, placed behind the target and shooting through a square hole cut in the center, filmed Rosenbach's actions. In a subsequent video of the performance "the image of Rosenbach shooting arrows is superimposed on the image of the Madonna."[112]

In 1971, at the same moment when Linda

109. All quotes from Naked Action Lecture *may be found in* More Than Meat Joy, *180-81*

110. Ibid., 63.

111. Schneemann, "Istory of a Girl Pornographer," in More Than Meat Joy, 194.

112. Claudia Lupri, "Essay: Transformations," in Ulrike Rosenbach: Video, Performance, Installation 1972-1989 (Toronto: Art Gallery of York University, 1989), 15.

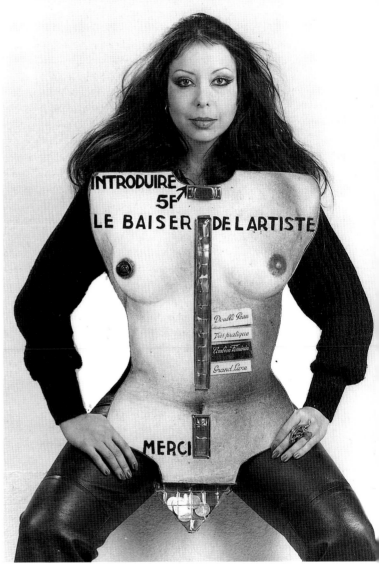

**Orlan**, *Baiser de l'Artiste*, 1976-77. Collection of the artist

**271**

**Gustav Metzger**, *South Bank Demo*, London, 1961

Montano was presenting herself as a nun-like "Living Angel," Orlan baptised herself St. Orlan and began draping her body in various elaborate baroque cloakings and posing in *tableaux vivants*. In fact, the name "Orlan" itself is a fictive identity which, apparently, the artist assumed as a teenager. In 1990, Orlan began *The Reincarnation of St. Orlan*, undergoing the first of a series of cosmetic surgery operations — performances to transform herself into a composite of the male-defined notion of idealized female beauty based on a careful selection of five famous Renaissance and Baroque images: the nose of *Diana* (an unattributed School of Fontainebleau sculpture); the mouth of Boucher's *Europa*; the forehead of Da Vinci's *Mona Lisa*; the chin of Botticelli's *Venus*, and the eyes of Gérôme's *Psyche*.

Elaine Scarry has argued that, "the only state that is as anomalous as pain is the imagination," and that, "while pain is a state remarkable for being wholly without objects, the imagination is remarkable for being the only state that is wholly its objects."[113] Invented and real wounds — bandaged (as in Ono's *Conversation Piece*) or bleeding, as in Gina Pane's many masochistic actions — articulate real psychophysical pain. These actions narrate and visualize suffering. They describe the unspeakable conditions that can be woman's interior life. Voicing these psychic-shattering lesions is central to finding a voice through, and by which, to repossess and recover a sense of the concreteness of personal experience and the integrity of self. Even more urgent is the need to communicate the interior reality to someone else — to materialize it. Pain and trauma need someone to bear witness to the contents of that identity-splitting experience of women's violation and destruction by patriarchy. The bodies of women in such performances offer evidence for beholders to witness. Feminist performance artists have created bodily enactment of the multiple contradictions of the pressures and pains of being a woman under patriarchy, thereby creating a visual language that can be seen and heard and perpetuated in the political movement that is feminism.[114]

**VI. DIAS** Gustav Metzger authored the first of five manifestos laying out the basis for "Auto-Destructive Art" in 1959.[115] Written contemporaneously with the first Happenings, Metzger systematically formulated a theory and a practice concerned with destruction as a social and aesthetic phenomenon:

*Auto-Destructive Art*

Auto-destructive art is primarily a form of public art for industrial societies.

Self-destructive painting, sculpture and construction is a total unity of idea, site, form, color, method and timing of the disintegrative process.

Auto-destructive art can be created with natural forces, traditional art techniques and technological techniques.

The amplified sound of the auto-destructive process can be an element of the total conception.

The artist may collaborate with scientists, engineers.

Self-destructive art can be machine produced and factory assembled.

Auto-destructive paintings, sculptures and constructions have a lifetime varying from a few moments to twenty years. When the disintegrative process is complete the work is to be removed from the site and scrapped.

Realized as public monuments on civic sites, "Auto-Destructive Art" would contain sophisticated technological and electronic internal devices causing them to implode and self-destruct. Site-sensitive and site-specific, requiring collaboration between scientists and artists, these sculptures were to visualize aspects of decay and disaster related to the culture of crisis within which they were imagined. The very concept of "Auto-Destructive Art" condensed a vast experiential and technological territory of destruction (and its concomitant survivalist ethos) into a manageable representation. Most importantly, Auto-Destructive Art would disappear.

Metzger formulated his theory precisely twenty years after he was sent to England at the age of twelve in 1939, following his family's arrest by the

113. Scarry, The Body in Pain, 162.

114. Hélène Cixous, Inside, trans. C. Barko (New York: Schocken, 1986), 97.

115. See Metzger's manifestos, reprinted in Kristine Stiles and Peter Selz, eds., Theories and Documents of Contemporary Art (Berkeley: University of California Press, 1996), 401-404.

Gestapo in Nuremberg. Twenty seconds, then, is a temporal analog for the time it took to destroy his personal world by killing his family; twenty years, the time of gestation in his own auto-transformation. Temporality in destruction art is the index of duration that confronts consciousness with the cycle of construction and destruction manifest in cultural artifacts and technological objects as well as in nature. This temporality reinscribes the psyche of the social body with a memory of the finite which must function as an affective agent in the reaggregation of consciousness around the concept of survival itself.

A vivid example of Metzger's practice was his *South Bank Demonstration* of July 3, 1961. Wearing a gas mask as a protective device, Metzger sprayed hydrochloric acid on three nylon tarpaulins — white, black, and red, a reference to Kasimir Malevich and Russian Suprematism — stretched over a series of three frames seven-feet high, twelve and one-half feet long, and six-feet deep. The nylon dissolved within fifteen seconds after contact with the acid. Metzger had positioned himself against a complex of urban office buildings and a crowd of men, many in business attire.

However fascinating and original Metzger's *South Bank Demonstration* may have been, his concept of Auto-Destructive Art was overshadowed by the spectacle created by Jean Tinguely's *Homage to New York*, which disassembled itself by accidentally bursting into flames on March 17, 1960, just three months after Metzger's first manifesto. Always ready for an extravaganza, New York itself exploded with attention to Tinguely. The work, at The Museum of Modern Art, was promoted by the powerful MoMA

curator of painting and sculpture, Peter Selz. An official press release was issued by MoMA that forewarned the audience: "Space is limited and we are naturally eager to be able to accomodate the press and the invited audience so that both can see the spectacle."[116] Alfred H. Barr, Jr. (then the museum's Director), compared Tinguely's vision to no less than Jules Verne, Leonardo da Vinci, Rube Goldberg, Piranesi, Alexander Calder, Man Ray, Francis Picabia, and, of course, Marcel Duchamp. Given the public relations blitz, it is not surprising that Tinguely's fame was immediate and his art historical place secured. The work itself was magical and dangerous, bringing in the full force of the New York fire department to extinguish its flames.

Metzger's most impressive work, however, was his realization of the Destruction in Art Symposium (DIAS) throughout the month of September in London, in 1966.[117] This multi-national, multi-disciplinary, international event attracted nearly one-hundred artists and poets (most of whom were the pioneers of Happenings and Concrete Poetry) from fifteen countries in Eastern and Western Europe, the United States, South America, and Japan. The diverse collection of artists and poets who participated either directly or indirectly in DIAS were unified in their response to the theme of destruction in art. Yet they never comprised a movement nor produced a manifesto or publication as a group. They never established a meeting place to discuss and share ideas, nor did they exhibit as a group again after DIAS.[118] Apart from the month of events, DIAS represented a special moment in which a small body of international artists shared a discriminating atti-

116. The Museum of Modern Art, New York, press release issued 8 March 1960, Library, Museum of Modern Art, Jean Tinguely artist file.

117. For a complete reconstruction not only of DIAS but Metzger's biographical development as an artist and the theoretical and practical development of the use of destruction in art in the late 1950s and throughout the 1960s, see my unpublished doctoral dissertation, op. cit, fn #3, and numerous other publications of mine on the subject cited throughout this essay. Unauthorized and uncited aspects of my dissertation also appear in Justin Hoffmann's Destruktionskunst:

Der Mythos der Zerstörung in der Kunst der frühen sechziger Jahre (Munich: Verlag Silke Schreiber, 1995), and in Gustav Metzger: "damaged nature, auto-destructive art", essay by Andrew Wilson (London: Coracle and Lanmet, 1996).

118. During DIAS a number of discussions took place about staging further DIAS events in New York City and in Tokyo. When Ortiz returned to New York, he began to organize "DIAS: NYC" with Jon Hendricks. This event was eventually canceled by Ortiz and Hendricks after the murder of Martin Luther King, but a DIAS preview took place in 1968 featuring works by Hermann Nitsch, Charlotte

Moorman, Bici Hendricks, Ortiz, and others. Ortiz was also an advisor for the exhibition "Destruction Art," organized by Elaine Varian at Finch College Museum in New York, 1968. In addition, Jon Hendricks and Ortiz collaborated in "12 Evenings of Maniputions" at the Judson Church, New York, 1967, an event in which destructive processes were included in many actions such as Nam June Paik's "Cutting My Arm," in which the artist cut long X-shaped or cross-shaped marks into his arms with a razor blade. See photographs in John G. Hanhardt's Nam June Paik (New York: Whitney Museum of American Art in association with W.W. Norton, 1982), 40.

**Wolf Vostell**. *130 à l'heure, No.1. from Nein-9-dé-coll/agen, 1963*

tude about the use of destruction as an element in the creation of art, as a conceptual frame, as an attitude to the world, and as a way of relating subject matter in art to events and conditions in society. Among those who formed the resonant core of artists associated with the counter-cultural underground in the mid-1960s were Brus, Henri Chopin, Ivor Davies, Hansen, Kurt Kren, Latham, Lebel, Anna Lockwood, Muehl, Nitsch, the Dutch Provos, Ono, Ortiz, Vostell, and Weibel. Among those who sent works to DIAS, but were unable to attend, were Enrico Baj, Milan Knížák, Ad Reinhardt, Dieter Roth, and many others including a group of Argentinian poets and painters (Jorge Lopez Anaya, Jorge Roiger, Silvia Torras, and Luis Alberto Wells) who had been assembled by the Argentinian painter Kenneth Kemble to exhibit under the title "Arte Destructivo" in the Galeria Lirolay in Buenos Aires, in 1961. Kemble sent documentation to the DIAS organizers of the group's activities, photographs of altered and destroyed objects that they had exhibited as sculpture, and sound-tapes of their destruction music and poetry. Shortly after this exhibition the group dissolved, and not until DIAS did the material resurface. Finally, two American psychiatrists participated in DIAS: Ehrling Eng, an American

working with Vietnam veterans, and Joseph Berke, an American collaborating with R.D. Laing at Kingsley Hall, the radical center in London's East End for anti-psychiatry where Berke worked with the famous patient, Mary Barnes.[119]

A list of those who participated in the organizing committee of DIAS, alone, suggests how this event marked a significant moment in the history of international exchange amongst artists and poets associated with the Left counter-culture concerned with destruction in art and society at this time. The Irish poet John Sharkey helped Metzger assemble the participants and organize the events. The poet Bob Cobbing, then manager of Better Books, a London book shop that functioned in the mid-1960s as a gathering place for poetry readings and performances of the international literary and artistic underground, participated in the organizing committee along with the Benedictine monk Dom Sylvester Houedard, also a concrete poet. Roy Ascott, a British artist, theorist, and educator interested in cybernetics, participated along with Mario Amaya, then editor of the new art journal, *Art and Artists*.

As the first person to make Happenings in Germany, and an artist whose symbolism and repre-

119. Berke went to Kingsley Hall in 1965 and lived there through most of 1966. There he worked with Mary Barnes, a nurse in her forties who had been diagnosed as a severe schizophrenic and whom Laing and Berke brought through what they described as an "emotional death and rebirth experience" as a radical means to heal her. Once at Kingsley Hall, she was encouraged to "regress" to re-experience the trauma of birth as a means through which to reconstruct her present life-experience. On Berke, see "Anti-Psychiatry.'" See also Berke's Butterfly Man *and* Counter Culture. *See also Barnes and Berke,* Mary Barnes: Two Accounts of a Journey Through Madness *(New York: Harcourt Brace Jovanovich, 1972).*

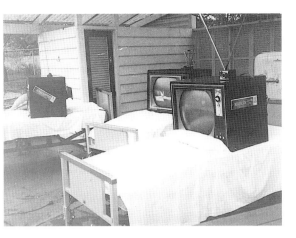

**Wolf Vostell**, *TV-Hospital Beds/From "You"*, Great Neck, New York, 1964.
Collection of the artist

sentations were based on destruction and violence in the media and society, Wolf Vostell's name on the organizing committee lent it a certain authority with the culture of Happenings, Fluxus, and action art in Germany. Vostell was also the publisher of *dé-coll/age: Bulletin Aktuellen Ideen* (1962-1969), a comprehensive periodical of original artists' writings theorizing the wide range of international activities in Happenings, Fluxus, action, and pop art taking place at the time. Vostell concentrated on the conjunction of destruction, violence, and sexuality, especially as represented in the media.[120]

In 1959, Vostell began to transfer photographs culled from popular magazines onto canvas and paper (a process developed independently by Rauschenberg in 1958); and, also in 1959, in *TV dé-coll/age for Millions*, he used actual television sets in the installation, the first time this medium was used in art. He acknowledged television as the disseminator of the "two great twentieth-century themes: destruction and sex." Vostell arrived at his concept of *dé-coll/age* in Paris, in 1954, when he noticed the term used in the newspaper *Le Figaro* to describe the simultaneous take off and crash of an airliner.

Dividing the word into syllables to emphasize both the difference and continuity of creative and destructive processes ("coll" for collage, or construction, and "dé" for disassembly or deconstruction), Vostell employed the term as a synthesizing principle for the destructive/creative dialectic of Western epistemology, and as the defining theoretical principle of his art. In 1958, he created *Theater on the Street*, his first large-scale *dé-coll/age* Happening. Functioning in the social arena like "weapons to politicize art," *Nein-9-dé-coll/agen* received widespread media attention in 1963.[121] In this work, the artist hired a locomotive to run into and destroy a Mercedes Benz parked across the railroad tracks. Both a dramatic spectacle and a critique of German commodity culture, Vostell's willful destruction of a prized object of German craftsmanship also summoned memories of German trains that carried humans to destruction only eighteen years earlier. As much as he was central to the development of happenings, Vostell was also a founder of Fluxus in Europe, introducing artists such as Nam June Paik (who had come to study avant-garde music in Germany at the time) and Joseph Beuys (then teaching at the Düsseldorf Kunst

120. See the special issue on DIAS in dé-col/lage: Bulletin Aktuellen Ideen 6 (July 1967). The ZERO group (Otto Piene, Heinz Mack and, in 1961, Günter Uecker) had begun to produce public spectacles focusing on the intersection between art and technology, and using projections, smoke, fire, reflections, shadows, vibrations, and other phenom-

ena of light and motion.

121. Dé-coll/age also emerged in the work of Raymond Hains, who began to collect torn posters (affiches lacérée) from billboard hoardings in Paris in 1949. Hains and Jacques de Villèglé, François Dufrêne, and Mimmo Rotello exhibited the torn posters as public relics

recontextualized as art. Reframed in the conditions of display, affiches lacérée visualized the interconnected processes and links between destruction and creation, construction and deconstruction, and the objects and institutions of the fine art and the artifacts of popular culture.

**Wolf Vostell,** *You*, Great Neck, New York, 1964.

Yoko Ono, *Cut Piece*, Carnegie Recital Hall, New York, 1965

Akademie) to George Maciunas, the artist who in September, 1962, launched the first of a European tour of Fluxus festivals in Wiesbaden. In 1964, in the United States Vostell participated in the Yam Festival organized by George Brecht and Robert Watts, producing *You*, a disturbing Happening that in its conjured war-like and barbed-wire-wrapped televisions reflected on the Vietnam war. Joseph Beuys has often been credited as the artist who made discussion of World War II possible in Germany. But it was Vostell who first paved the way to the discussion and cultural confrontation with the Nazi era in his happenings and installations of the late 1950s and early 1960s. These were undeniably symbolic of war, critical of commodity culture, and visually reminiscent of destructive processes of life.

Yoko Ono's presence at DIAS was key for Metzger not only because she was a woman (he tried to involve as many women as possible, including Schneemann, who, lacking the funds and the ability to raise them, could not attend) but because of the way in which Ono's work related destruction to interpersonal, often intimate, human relations. This element was particularly thought-provoking in *Cut Piece*, one of many actions she did at DIAS. Ono had first done the performance in 1964, in Japan, and again at Carnegie Hall, in New York, in 1965. Ono sat motionless on the stage after inviting the audience to come up and cut away her clothing, covering her breasts at the moment of unbosoming. *Cut Piece* entailed a disrobing, a denouement of the reciprocity between exhibitionism and scopic desires, between victim and assailant, between sadist and masochist; and, as a heterosexual herself, Ono unveiled the gendered relationship of male and female subjects as objects for each other.[122] *Cut Piece* also recalled the psychological impact of being an object for others that Ono later expressed in a "Statement" made in 1971: "People went on cutting the parts they do not like of me finally there was only the stone remained of me that was in me but they were still not satisfied and wanted to know what it's like in the stone."[123]

*Cut Piece* also went beyond the social, political, and gender issues to aesthetic concerns. For *Cut Piece* deconstructed the subject/object relationship that resides behind the edifice of art — the often presumed opaque neutrality of the ubiquitous art object and distant, removed art observer. In *Cut Piece* Ono demonstrated the accountability that the viewer has to the condition, reception, and preservation of objects of art by addressing the ways in which viewing without responsibility cuts into and destroys the object of its perception.

Such works may be said to typify her feelings of marginalization in the New York art world during the 1960s. "[I was] not well accepted even in the avant-garde," she explained, "because the New York avant-garde was into cool art, not hot [and] what I do was too emotional; in a way they thought it was too animalistic."[124] In the post-Abstract-Expressionist school of Beatnik cool that hardened in New York into the ice of minimalism and the restraint of Fluxus, Ono's work — like that of many of the artists associated with happenings and DIAS — was felt to be too much. Indeed Ono, Schneemann, and Shigeko Kubota, all women whose work dealt with visceral expression of sexuality and emotion, felt ignored within their own milieu.

122. For a longer discussion on the problem of relationality not only in her work but in her coupling with Lennon, see my "Unbosoming Lennon: The Politics of Yoko Ono's Experience," Art Criticism 7, no. 2 (Spring 1993): 21-54, reprinted by the University of Havana, Cuba, 1994.

123. See Ono's "Statement" in the Village Voice (7 October 1971): 20.

124. Yoko Ono, in Melody Sumner, Kathleen Burch, and Michael Sumner, eds., The guests go in to supper: John Cage, Robert Ashley, Yoko Ono, Laurie Anderson, Charles Amirkhanian, Michael Peppe, K. Archley (Oakland and San Francisco: Burning Books, 1986), 174.

**278**

**Shigeko Kubota**. *Vagina Painting*, Perpetual Fluxus Festival, New York, 4 July 1965

Kubota, for example, remembered that her friends and colleagues in Fluxus hated her performance *Vagina Painting* (July 4, 1965), performed exactly one year after she arrived in New York.[125] Kubota placed paper on the floor and, squatting over it, began to paint with a brush that she had earlier fastened to her underpants. Moving over the paper, she dipped the brush in red paint to produce an eloquent gestural image that redefined Action Painting according to the codes of female anatomy, exaggerated female sexual attributes and bodily functions, and was funny! The direct reference to menstrual cycles seems to compare the procreation/creation continuum lodged in the interiority of woman with the temporal cycles of change and growth she experienced in her own art and life after moving from Japan to the United States. Her artistic progeny may be accessed in the action-text of metaphorical blood through which she objectified the immaterial creative biological center of woman and in the concrete image it manifested of her artistic powers. "To have material form," Elaine Scarry has written, "is to have self-substantiating form."[126] Although she may not have intended the work to suggest a rejection of woman as the female muse, Kubota's *Vagina Painting* did just that.[127] In this action, she recovered woman as the source of her own artistic inspiration, as the gender able to produce both actual life and representational form.[128] Kubota's event also posits female bodies as the nexus of art and of life, their material synthesis. While Kubota did not participate in DIAS, it was this kind of action by a woman that Metzger

125. *Kubota in a telephone conversation with the author, 12 June 1991; and Yoko Ono, in ibid.*

126. *Elaine Scarry,* The Body in Pain, *117. Kubota has continued her gendered and sexual discourse in her subsequent video installation work. In* Video Poem *(1968-1976), Kubota encased a nineteen-inch monitor with a single-channel, color-synthesized tape of self-portrait in a nylon bag with zippered openings to create a sculptural form resembling the vaginal cavity. A poem accompanying this work and reflecting* Vagina Painting *appears as* Video Poem *(1968-1969) in "Duchampiana,"* Tracks: A Journal of Artists' Writings *3, no. 3 (Fall 1977): 63; and in Mary Jane Jacob, ed.,* Shigeko

Kubota: Video Sculpture *(New York: American Museum of the Moving Image, 1991): 18.*

127. *Historically consigned to the passive position of the mythic "muse," the female in Western culture has served as the creative inspiration for man, stimulating his imagination and redirecting his sexual drive into productive channels that provided his salvation in the creation of music, poetry, and visual art. The male Surrealists' obsession with the muse is legendary. Writing about the ways in which women artists of the Surrealist movement were utilized "to make the whole psychosexual field of human experience available to the [male] artist," Whitney Chadwick has observed that*

"the muse, an eternalized source of creative energy and a personification of the female Other, is a peculiarly male invention." *Whitney Chadwick,* Women Artists and the Surrealist Movement *(Boston: A New York Graphic Society Book and Little, Brown, 1985), 66.*

128. *In her* Interior Scroll *(1975), Carolee Schneemann made concrete the metaphorical connection between procreation and creation suggested in Kubota's* Vagina Painting. *See Schneemann,* More Than Meat Joy: Complete Performance Works and Selected Writings, *ed. Bruce McPherson (New Paltz, New York: Documentext, 1979), 234-239.*

**279**

**Mark Boyle and Joan Hills**, *Son et Lumière: Bodily Fluids and Functions*, 1966

had tried to incorporate in DIAS.

Two more artists to participate in DIAS were the couple Mark Boyle and Joan Hills. They had become interested in destruction when they left a slide too long in a projector and it accidentally burned. Fascinated with the potential of the unique image, they introduced destructive elements into their work in *Suddenly Last Supper* (1963), an event that took place in their London flat. Guests were invited to a party, and at some point led into a room in absolute darkness. Hill projected a film of random images onto mannequins painted white, while Boyle projected slides — which he simultaneously burned with acid or flame — onto a white paper surface serving as a screen. At a certain point an assistant painted the white screen black. Then the assistant tore down the black paper, revealing a second white screen onto which Boyle then projected an image of Botticelli's *The Birth of Venus*. The screen was then cut down and the image projected on the nude figure of a woman standing behind the screen in exactly the same pose as Botticelli's Venus. But it was only when Boyle burned the slide of *The Birth of Venus* that the nude woman could be seen. Her body was then painted black (destroyed as a screen) while Boyle continued to show slides on a third screen behind her. When the last screen was destroyed, a group of actors dressed in white began to pantomime against a black wall while more film was projected onto them. During their pantomime, Boyle and Hills moved their family and belongings out of the flat, from which they had been evicted. When the event was over, the audience discovered that the layers of black and white creation/destruction transformations which had occurred in the illusory performance had taken place in actuality in the emptied flat.[129]

Developing their projection technique, for DIAS, Boyle and Hills realized a section of their series, *Son et Lumière*, for three aspects of nature: one for the elements — Earth, Air, Fire, and Water — one for Insects, Reptiles, and Water creatures, and one for Bodily Fluids and Functions. The work was simply called *Presentation*, and involved the projec-

tion of microscopic life. But something went wrong and the audience was confronted with the actual death and destruction of some of the insects:

At a certain moment, wasps were projected onto a huge screen, which gave them a length of six to seven feet. These wasps had been placed in a specially constructed container in which they were protected from the heat of the projector lamp by a water-cooling system. This system suddenly developed a leak, and water slowly entered the chamber holding the wasps. As the water-level rose, the wasps attempting to reach the air and stay alive began to fight fiercely with each other. Their mortal struggles and the entire process of drowning could be seen in enormously enlarged detail on the screen. It was a terrible spectacle. Many people left in dismay, others begged that the projector be turned off.[130]

Perhaps even more compelling than the DIAS performance was the *Son et Lumière* they did for Bodily Fluids and Functions, in Liverpool, in 1966, and again at the Roundhouse in London. It included an electrifying performance that Boyle recounted:

In the sperm sequence a couple wired up to ECG (electro-cardiogram) and EEG (electroencephalogram) celebrated intercourse [hidden behind a screen], while the oscilloscopes of the ECG and EEG were televised on closed circuit television and projected with an Eidofor TV projector on to a large screen behind the couple. Thus, their heartbeats and brain waves were instantly revealed. . . . Everyone that was there seemed to find the experience very moving. The dirt and the mystique, the secretness and the sacredness were washed away. For me, provided the participants are free, all sexual manifestations are marvelous and from that moment on I knew that it doesn't matter whether people are guilty, lascivious, pure, perverse, or promiscuous, the mechanism that drives them is unbelievably complex and totally fascinating.[131]

By 1967, the couple had perfected their projection techniques and would produce extraordinary

129. I do not know whether or not Ulrike Rosenbach was familiar with Boyle and Hill's Suddenly Last Supper, when she did her own strikingly similar perfor-

mance, Reflections on the Birth of Venus, in 1976.

130. J.L. Locher, Mark Boyle's Journey to the Surface of the Earth (Stuttgart and

London: Edition Hansjörg Mayer, 1978), 68.

131. Ibid., 72-73.

**280**

**Mark Boyle and Joan Hills**, *Suddenly Last Supper*, 1963

light shows for rock and roll groups such as the Soft Machine (with Jimi Hendrix), Pink Floyd, Cream, and the Animals.[132]

DIAS ended in litigation when Metzger and Sharkey were brought to trial 19 July 1967, for having presented Hermann Nitsch's 21st action of the "Orgies Mysteries Theatre" on 16 September 1966. They were found guilty of "unlawfully causing to be shown a lewd and an indecent exhibition." This guilty verdict is the sign of the State's own guilt as an accomplice in constructing and then protecting the very systems, institutions, and epistemologies that utilize and manufacture destruction as a central organizing and controlling principle of power. The artists were merely used as scapegoats, allowing the State to repress its own guilt. But the artists' putative "guilt" must be read as the single most important evidence of the ability of DIAS to reveal the fundamental hypocrisy of a system that "talks" about reform, but does not "act" and, moreover, punishes those who do.

**VII. Activities** Allan Kaprow remembered the sense of high publicity surrounding DIAS, including the anticipation of massive press coverage, but by 1966 he had moved toward private, self-reflective actions avoiding media exploitation. He declined to participate because he judged the focus on destruction at DIAS as "too narrow."[133] In fact, by the time Kaprow had established guidelines for Happenings in his landmark book *Assemblage, Environments and Happenings* (1966), he had already abandoned them himself for simpler actions he would later call "Activities".

Kaprow had already become discouraged by the lack of committed response to his Happening, *Push and Pull: A Furniture Comedy for Hans Hofmann*, in 1963. This elaborate work was a tribute to, and jousted with, the German artist's pedagogy regarding the "push-pull" dynamics of the picture

plane. It included such inventive and playful activities as a "Persian rug" made of food. Participants were invited to "eat your way through the designs, right across the room, making new ones behind you as you went along."[134] But when the participants failed to engage in the event in a sufficiently interactive way Kaprow responded: "From reports, I gather that this arrangement has not worked out optimally. In an exhibition atmosphere people are not geared to enter into the process of art. Hence, this kind of work is much better off away from the habits and rituals of conventional culture."[135]

The origins of the ideas for Activities date from about 1968-69, especially to his *Days Off Calendar* (1969), a nine-month visual calendar project that chronicled and photographically documented his own activities for the year. Activities themselves consist of private actions undertaken by consenting participants who agreed to realize a scored event. The contents changed with each action but all addressed problems of perception and the observation of the performance of particular aspects of everyday life. The differences between Kaprow's Happenings, interactive environments and Activities are worth noting. The Happenings included multiple, complex, physically demanding, and energized, sometimes baroque events that required participation. They could even become extravagant structures that eventually were associated with what Kaprow called "high jinks," qualities in which he quickly lost interest.[136] In an interactive environment, such as *Yard* (1961), participants were immersed in a built space to be negotiated physically and experientially. In such an environment, one could decide to actually engage in an activity or a task, or simply look around and leave. Happenings and environments were mostly (although not exclusively) public.[137]

There are many individual elements in both Kaprow's Happenings and environments that anticipated the Activities. But the Activities are very different especially in terms of how they require indi-

132. See "When the Dust Settles: Mark Boyle Interviewed by Mark Bloch," High Performance 4, no. 3 (Fall 1981): 73-74.

133. Allan Kaprow, unpublished interview with the author, 27 March 1981.

134. Allan Kaprow, "Just Doing," Tulane Drama Review (Fall 1977):314.

135. Ibid., 316.

136. Allan Kaprow, in conversation with the author, 23 October 1997. All other quotes from Kaprow unless otherwise

cited are from this conversation.

137. See Michael Kirby's detailed discussion of the structures of Happenings in two important books: Happenings (New York: E.P. Dutton, 1965); and The Art of Time (New York: E.P. Dutton, 1969).

viduals to take responsibility for engaging in committed agreements to act together. Their interpersonal contract reiterated on an intimate aesthetic level the concept of the social contract on a public political plane. Those who took the responsibility to act were obliged to examine the nature of their acts while being occupied as subjects doing something. At the same time, they became subjects observing themselves as objects doing something. The agreement itself functioned as a commissure relating everyday activity to aesthetic activity.[138] Most of the Activities required close attention to phenomenological conditions of the body either alone or in a social exchange.

Because of the capacity of mind both to participate in, and also view, its actions, Kaprow's Activities constantly visualize the reciprocity of cultural values between the work and its reception, as well as the complex interactions between biography and socio-historical context. For example, in *Sweet Wall*, an activity undertaken in Berlin, November 1970, Kaprow created a meta-discourse on political space (the activity involved building a wall of bricks with mortar comprised of bread and jam), a meditation on Passover (the exodus and the liberation of the Israelites) that recalled his Jewish origins, and an infinite number of other associations that might be made between the labor, the object, the artist, and the site.

Kaprow's Activities can be associated with Pinchas Cohen Gan's *activities*, undertaken in Israel during some of the same period. These two artists share not only a point of linguistic contact, but aesthetic and social content as well. In the spring of 1973, Cohen Gan chiseled through layers of paint and plaster to sculpt *Place*, a cut-away image of an upright figure in the wall of the Yodfat Gallery in Tel Aviv. He then placed pegs inside the figure, inviting visitors to assume the position of the figural representation on the wall. A Moroccan born, Israeli artist, Cohen Gan stated his intention "to represent physical and social place [as] a symbolic imposition of presence in matter."[139] *Place* was one of his first *activities*, a group of works carried out between 1972

and 1974, in which the artist made his life into a formula, creating aesthetic forms that figured the viewer as actively engaged in the social, political, and cultural environment.

Cohen Gan's *Action in the Jericho Refugee Camp* (February 10, 1974) grew out of his feelings about the Yom Kippur War. In this activity in the north-eastern sector of the ancient city of Jericho, Cohen Gan constructed a temporary tent shelter in the refugee camp, and gave a lecture on the subject of the conditions for peace in Israel "in the year 2000." The questions raised in his lecture were, for the artist, both spiritual and physical because, as he later noted: "The legal attitude towards establishing who is a refugee and/or the United Nations definition of a refugee, make no difference to the refugee's actual existence and feelings about the territories where he was or has passed."[140] "A refugee is a man who cannot return to his birthplace," Cohen Gan declared. This work can be seen as a personal meditation on what it means to be "in a continual state of being a refugee," a condition that the artist knows from his own personal experience.

In Kaprow's and Cohen Gan's activities one discovers an actual event that has occurred. Something concrete has happened. Someone, as Kaprow repeatedly points out, "just does something." Now, the fact that someone does something — that *someone can do something* — that something happens rather than nothing — is more than notable. It sets action artists apart. They operate as commissures entrusted with the idea of communicating the value and image of *anyone doing something*. This is why performance artists are considered so dangerous. They propose that something can be done, and then they make it happen. People who make things happen present potential problems to normative behavior and values. Doing is what action art is. Activities are object-lessons in "doing."

Making something happen is the intentional, causal essence of an empowered political act. In making something happen, one survives. But beyond

138. On the subject of the "social contract" and participatory interactivity, see my project "Lettres/Livres," 1982 (which were strongly influenced by Kaprow's work), in Questions 1977-1982 (San Francisco: KronOscope Press, 1982), 78-

85. For a theorization of the relation between performance art and the social contract, see Kathy O'Dell's forthcoming Contract with the Skin: Masochism, Performance Art, and the 1970s (Minneapolis: University of Minnesota

Press, 1998).

139. Yona Fischer, Pinchas Cohen Gan, activities (Jerusalem: Israel Museum, 1974).

140. Ibid., 36.

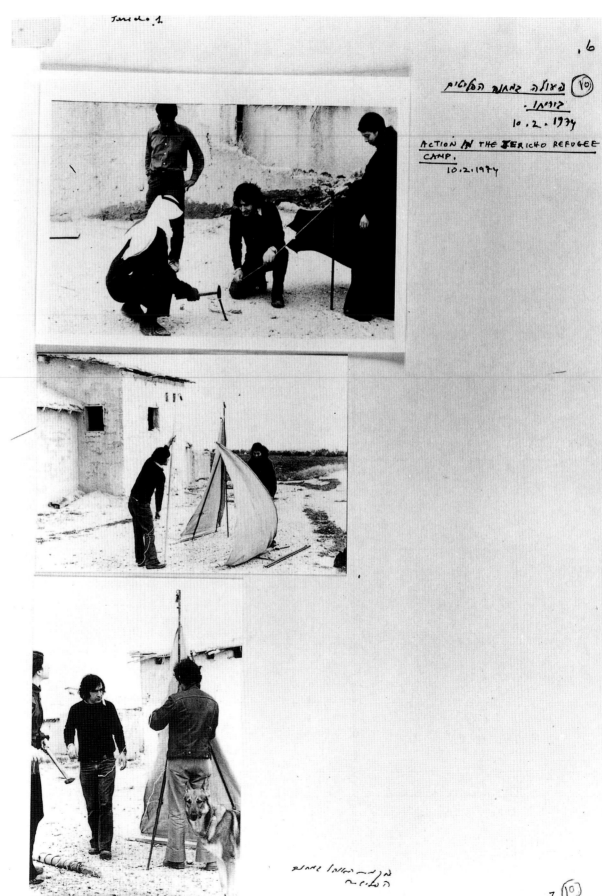

Jericho 2

צילום ואתור וכתובות ציונו
10.2.1974

mere survival, belief may emerge from making things happen rather than nothing without which it is practically impossible to live. This is not the belief so frequently associated with faith or organized religion, or even with notions of God. It is belief in, and for, itself. For to survive and live well, individuals act with belief and with a sense of responsibility toward others with whom one commits to acting together.

## VIII. Painting-Photography-Performance

Any discussion of action art and its objects must consider the central role of photography in the dissemination of images that led to the artifactuality of actions. Most famous amongst them are the photographs taken in the summer and early fall of 1950 by Hans Namuth in Pollock's studio. During this period, Namuth made over 500 photographs, a black and white movie, and a color movie (with Paul Falkenberg), all of Pollock at work. These photographs and films are pivotal to reckoning Pollock as a mythical figure. His legendary status was achieved, in no small measure, by the ways in which Namuth's published photographs were often cropped to make it appear as if Pollock was closer to the viewer and more engulfed in the painting itself. A problem with one of Namuth's cameras blurred some of the pictures, a serendipitous accident that, as the photographer eventually recognized, contributed to enhancing the perception of motion in the still image.

This "special effect of blurred focus," Griselda Pollock and Fred Orton have observed, "became [a] component of the codes which constituted Namuth's representation of Pollock."[141] Orton and Pollock remind us that photographic "truth" is suspect, and "mediates historical actuality" by producing meanings that are "contingent on the spectator's interests."[142] Indeed, the unfocused photographic image did establish the visual impression of Pollock *in* his work that could be intuited by artists who were looking for a way to continue in Pollock's direction while, at the same time, go beyond him and away from the highly individualized signature works characteristic of Abstract Expressionism in general. This

multiple directionality is apparent in Kaprow's leap of imagination that conceived a trajectory reaching back to Cubist collage and up through action painting (and Namuth's photographs) to Happenings. As Kaprow wrote:

> The pieces of paper curled up off the canvas, were removed from the surface to exist in their own, became more solid as they grew into other materials and reaching out into the room they filled it entirely. Suddenly, there were jungles, crowded streets, littered alleys, dream spaces of science fiction, rooms of madness, and junk-filled attics of the mind.[143]

Namuth's photographs inhabited the social and cultural context of the discussions surrounding Pollock from the moment they were published in late 1950. Moreover, Namuth's images contributed to a representation of Pollock as the heroic artist, a larger than life presence that, Amelia Jones has pointed out, is consistent with the modernist trope of creativity associated with masculinity and divinity:

> The male artist is paradigmatic of the ideologically centred subject of modernism, acting as paternal origin for subsequent lineages of artistic production, a genius whose fully intentional creative acts are invested with transcendental value by art history. . . . The artist has come to epitomize . . . the construction of the masculine self as a coherent individual at the expense of female subjectivity, which is thus rendered impossible to conceive. . . . The artist might [even] be said to replace God.[144]

Writing particularly about Klein, Morris, Acconci, and Burden, Jones observed that the exaggerated display of masculinity that is characteristic of much male performance is, paradoxically, *not* a sign of the same kind of inherited patriarchal authority, but rather instantiates a masculinity that is negotiated. By "displaying and performing their own bodies," she states, "these 'body artists' shift to varying degrees away from the transcendental and singularly masculine conception of artistic authority put in place within modernism."[145]

However ambiguous and "negotiated" gender

141. Fred Orton and Griselda Pollock, "Jackson Pollock, Painting, and the Myth of Photography," Art History 6, no. 1 (March 1983): 117.

142. Ibid., 118-119.

143. Allan Kaprow, Assemblage, Environments, and Happenings, 165.

144. Amelia Jones, "Dis/playing the Phallus: Male Artists Perform Their Masculinities," Art History 17, no. 4 (December 1994): 547.

145. Ibid.

may become when the body is used as the material for art, Mira Schor has argued that the "patrilineage" of art history itself is still based on male forebears, even when women artists . . . are involved."[146] This claim is certainly true in terms of the pivotal role photography played in the evolution of action painting into Happenings, and, later, body art and performance. The Namuth photographs are a case in point, and they fit into the series of articles, begun in 1949 in *Art News*, that featured an artist — almost exclusively male — "painting a picture." Even when women came to be pictured to "paint a picture," their paternity had already been secured. Schor writes: "Works by women whose paternity can be established and whose work can safely be assimilated into art discourse are privileged, and every effort is made to assure this patrilineage."[147]

Realizing the importance of Namuth's photographs, Georges Mathieu was the first artist to stage live action paintings as the subject of photography, and as a performance before a viewing public. On January 19, 1952, he had his picture taken in his own studio while painting *Hommage au Maréchal de Turenne*, a canvas that he consigned to his "Zen" period, and one loosely in the style of the German gestural painter Hans Hartung, whom he admired. The conceptualization of *painting a picture for the camera* clearly emerged from Mathieu's deep admiration for Pollock, whom he considered the greatest living painter, and was keen to emulate. As Pollock's progeny — or to be more exact — the son of Namuth's photographs' of Pollock, Mathieu realized the powerful potential connection between painting, photography, performance, and the public. *As a commissure, the photograph carried the content of painting and the process of performance to the public*. Mathieu was the first to make this connection.

There was, however, a stark and bizarre difference between the dramatic images of Pollock hovering or leaping in a blurring splash over a paint strewn "field," and the pictures of a half-naked, bare-chested Mathieu with a loin-cloth-like material wrapped around his waist and barely reaching his knees, in his shoes and socks, painting a picture hung on the wall, not placed on the floor. When Mathieu first saw these photographs of himself in 1952, he must have realized just how strange they looked, because, two years later, on April 25, 1954, when Robert Descharnes filmed him at the Paris Salon de Mai painting *Battle of the Bouvines* (a thirteenth-century French battle in which one of his forebearers had taken part), Mathieu dressed in a striking costume reincarnating medieval military gear: black silk pants and jacket, a white helmet and greaves fastened to his shins with white cross-straps. Although Mathieu now painted a masculine militarized theme, the photographs still failed to picture him as the quintessential patriarch. Rather, he appears fascinatingly androgenous.

In the *Battle of the Bouvines*, for exactly the duration of the legendary battle, Mathieu physically enacted the historical drama in paint. "Speed, intuition, excitement," were his driving "methods." His action suggested analogies between artistic innovation, historical battle, and the relationship between political and aesthetical transformation. But most importantly the photographs depict a man fully in control of his medium and able to execute Harold Rosenberg's theory that the canvas had become an "arena" for an event, an "encounter" between artist and material if not history and its battles.[148]

A year later, in February, 1955, when *Art News* featured "Mathieu Paints a Picture," the article produced a slew of sarcastic and denigrating letters from its readers in the United States:

In these days when avant-garde painting is so open to the charges of quackery and fraud, it was a special treat to read, in the article on Mathieu, the intimate and exacting portrayal of so intricate a creative process. What a brilliant concept — to regurgitate an entire battle in paint. But one wonders — was it paint? Did not some of those horses (so prone to conventional emergencies) stand around too long?[149]

Damaging as it may have been, comparing the paint on the surface of Mathieu's canvas with horse feces, it was not as insulting as the comments of the highly respected, Abstract-Expressionist painter,

146. Mira Schor, "Patrilineage," Art Journal 50, no. 2 (Summer 1991): 58.

147. Ibid.

148. Harold Rosenberg, "The Action Painters," Art News 51, no. 8 (December 1952): 22-23, 48-50.

149. This and all subsequent citations of "Editor's letters," may be found in Art News (March 1955.

**287**

Clyfford Still:

> Is the *Art News* really so desperate that it has to devote its pages to the cynicism and lies of its Mathieu feature, or has it just become its way of life to grope in sewers of journalism for its ethics and performers? I blush with the embarrassment all artists must feel when viewing this sordid parody — especially for those sincere men who in the late 1940s went from here and the West Coast to Paris and exposed their work to this parasitical and antic "tramp." To the *Art News* the back of my hand.

Renowned for his argumentative, caustic, and even bitter temperment, Still's letter fits into a pattern of his behavior. To be sure, Mathieu's photograph in *Art News* (depicting the elegant French aristocrat in his silk smoking jacket, poised at his writing table adjacent to his famous and enormous painting, *Battle of the Bouvines*) was *anything but* the mythic image of the angst-ridden, whiskey-drinking, troubled American cowboy turned heroic artist.

Throughout the late 1950s, *Time* magazine featured articles on Mathieu that ambiguously celebrated and denigrated the artist. For example: "He drives a Rolls-Royce;" "has learned Salvador Dali's stunt of playing the capped and haughty aristocrat;" "is quite capable of making long trips through the most beautiful countryside without even seeing a thing."[150] This last comment, a direct quote from Michel Tapié's 1953 article on "Mathieu Paints a Picture," is, not surprisingly, taken completely out of context. Tapié had attempted to establish Mathieu's enormous powers of concentration and research before making a painting! *Time* went on to suppose, however, that Mathieu, "paints as he drives — as much to be seen as to see;" and it concluded insultingly that his work was as much about "equivocation" as "reverberation" (March 7, 1955).

More damaging in the minds of Americans than his personal wealth (accustomed as they were to understanding Abstract Expressionism as a private, existential struggle to achieve a sublime image) was the fact that Mathieu reputedly "whipped out small paintings in as little as ten minutes, and even

his huge pictures require no more than a couple of hours to paint" (April 5, 1954). If comparing his pigments to toothpaste and tar was not insulting enough, *Time* compared him to a fast-changing "art fashion."

Mathieu's reception in other countries was substantially different. When in August, 1957, he traveled to Japan with Tapié, they were warmly received by the Gutai as colleagues in exploring a new aesthetic direction. In Tokyo alone, Mathieu painted twenty-one canvases in three days including a fresco fifteen-yards long before fascinated crowds.[151] *Time* reported extensively on this trip and gave a long, vivid description of his action that conveys something of the atmosphere of the moment:

> Visibly shaking with nervousness and anticipation, Mathieu paced barefooted [in a kimono] beside a huge, 25-ft. by 7 ft. canvas stretched on the garage floor, glowering as his assistants laid out boxes of paint tubes, a big sake bottle filled with turpentine, bundles of brushes, and a dozen brass mixing bowls. Of a sudden, in a burst of movement, Mathieu was at work. Tearing paper cartons with his teeth to gain time, he began squeezing blobs and curlicues of violet paint straight from the tubes, and then squirted whole tubes of black pigment. He gripped four tubes in either hand, emptied them in one mighty salvo, next grabbed the sake bottle of turpentine and up-ended it over the canvas, then dropped to his knees, began fiercely swabbing the surface with a towel, finally swarmed directly onto the canvas itself. With the canvas well primed, Mathieu paused to swig down a frothing glass of Japanese beer while assistants propped the work up against the easel. Then glaring like a buccaneer about to board ship, he kicked at the debris of brushes, tubes, and bottles, plunged one brush into a bowl of white paint, grasped a second brush in his teeth and rushed at the canvas. A white cross with red outline appeared on one side, a yellow squiggle on the other. He returned to the beer and charged again. Aiming a five-foot brush

150. The notion that Mathieu could drive without "seeing a thing" comes from an article on Mathieu written by Michel Tapié, "Mathieu Paints a Picture," Art News 53, no. 10 (February 1953): 50, 51, 74-75.

151. See Jirō Yoshihara, "On 'The International Art of A New Era,' dedicated to 'Osaka International Festival'", Gutai 9 (1958): 7.

**Georges Mathieu**, public painting action, 1957

like a lance, he carved broad, pink lines running the length of the twenty-five foot canvas. From then on, the battle raged with such fury that Mathieu was soaked in paint, turpentine, and sweat. Soon the Japanese, usually polite before foreigners, were roaring with laughter, shouting delightedly after each stroke.

"It's the new Ford!" cracked one. "It's not a who-dunit, but a hedunit," cried another, in good doughboy English. Mathieu was too engrossed to hear. He banged the canvas with a towel soaked in yellow paint, kneaded flake-white pigment into snowballs, and pitched them at the dripping oil, slapped on more paint with rapier-quick strokes, seized handfuls of paint tubes and leaped up and down the length of the battlefield. At the peak of his fury, he was ejecting tubes over his shoulder with the cyclic action of a machine gun, until he finally slowed down, devoted the last twenty minutes to adding only a touch of paint here and there.

Total elapsed time: 110 minutes. Title: The Battle of Hakata (A.D. 1281 — when the Japanese defeated Kublai Khan).[152]

Mathieu's reception in Europe was mixed. He was acknowledged by Yves Klein as a mentor and fellow monarchist. Indeed Klein's notorious photographic *Leap into the Void* (1960), which purports to document a single, spontaneous, risky leap into space, demonstrates his debt to Mathieu in terms of staging his art for photography. But Klein's debt to his mentor is also conceptual and intellectual. Klein's attention to risk, spontaneity, speed, and improvisation, carried out in his living brushes and other works, echoes Mathieu's thinking. Mathieu was also recognized by the Viennese action artists, who acknowledged his performance in Vienna April 2, 1959, at the Theater am Fleischmarkt, as significant in their move into action.[153]

Why is it that Mathieu's contribution to the history of art (and particularly the history of

Performance) was not recognized in its time? Why have his theoretical writings been all but forgotten? I think that the negative critical reception of Mathieu's work in the United States points to the long-standing suspicion of public display especially as photographically captured in popular magazines like *Time*. It did not help in the puritanical climate of the United States that he was rich, eccentric, aristocratic, and flaunted it. In Europe some artists associated with the political Left dismissed Mathieu for his monarchism. This might be understandable if Yves Klein's monarchism had interferred with the reception of his work by the avant-garde. All of this animosity was cleverly camouflaged in criticisms of Mathieu's work as facile, lacking in seriousness, decorative, and just plain bad, subjective aesthetic judgments merely posing as objective ones.

Mathieu was stunned and deeply hurt by this nearly universal negative reception in the United States of his work and person. He had, after all, been one of the first European artists to champion American Abstract Expressionist painting in many statements, exhibitions, and essays. Mathieu always understood himself to be a lyrical, abstract action-painter. As late as 1994, he still denied that his work had anything to do with performance.[154] In his own words, his public actions were efforts "to make the public participate in the creation [of a painting] itself," whereas the goal of Happenings "seemed to be the destruction of every trace of an artistic event," this, despite the fact that he "painted in public before almost all the countries of the world."[155] Most certainly Mathieu is not "one of the pioneers of Happenings"[156]: if anything, he is a forerunner of action art.

152. *Time*, September 1957. The work was reputedly sold for "3,000,000 yen, or $8,333 at the time."

153. See Robert Fleck, Avantgarde in Wien: Die Geschichte der Galerie Nächst St. Stephan 1954-1982, Kunst und Kunstbetrieb in Osterreich, Band I: Die Chronik (Vienna: Galerie Nächst St. Stephan, 1982), 186-96.

154. Mathieu, in conversation with the author, Paris, October 1994.

155. Unpublished letter from Georges Mathieu to Jean de Loisy, 27 January 1994, upon being invited to participate in the exhibition "Hors Limites," an exhibition on the history of performance art at the Centre Georges Pompidou, 1994.

156. See Wollen's statement in an unpublished letter from Judith Hanson (Project Director for Anthony McCall Associates) to Mathieu, 14 October 1994.

Returning to the patrimonial lineage of Namuth's photographs of Pollock's painting process and its germination of an entirely different dimension in Mathieu's work, it could be said that by theatricalizing the stock macho artist who "paints a picture," photographs representing Mathieu as an effete, French, aristocratic dandy destabilized the received conventions of the male artist as paradigmatic of the ideologically centered subject of modernism. At least one could argue that Mathieu diminished that patriarchal image of man at the center of art, even if he had not fully deconstructed it.

The evolution of action-painting into action — through the transit of the photograph — pinpoints a means and a medium (photography) by which the hegemony of the stable aesthetic medium of painting shifted to the unstable medium of the body. But, paradoxically, as the vehicle for the presentation of ephemeral actions, it was also the technological apparatus of reproduction that displaced painted representations of figurative subject-matter with photographic ones, stabilizing action in a conventional form. This duality of the photographic object has not been examined in the rush to claim photography as "the transgressive medium par excellence."[157] Photography was not "transgressive." It was, however, the best means by which to convey the representational and figurative content of the presentational medium of action. Photographs materialized (as image) the contiguity between action and its object. In this way the body in action — augmented by the camera's ability to show a fraction of a second of that moment of being-in-the-world — could briefly visualize the contingency and interdependence of one human subject (the artist) identified with another human subject (the viewer). This is what Roland Barthes identified as the "punctum," the charged aspect of a picture.[158] Moreover,

the photograph was cheap, available, and could be manipulated. In a succession of images, one could select the "best" representation, and could manipulate the way the action was read. The image could be cropped and, in many ways, it could fool the viewer.

One of the most notorious myths of performance art and the evidentiary capacity of the photograph is the story that Viennese artist Rudolf Schwarzkogler cut off his penis in a performance and died from the action, a story still recounted today.[159] This fiction was circulated by Robert Hughes in 1972, in *Time* magazine:

Schwarzkogler seems to have deduced that what really counts is not the application of paint, but the removal of surplus flesh. So he proceeded, inch by inch, to amputate his own penis, while a photographer recorded the act as an art event. In 1972, the resulting prints were reverently exhibited in that biennial motor show of Western art, Documenta V at Kassel. Successive acts of self-amputation finally did Schwarzkogler in.[160]

The confusion of the fictional with the documentary haunts not only Schwarzkogler's work, but performance art in general. And the Schwarzkogler myth is summoned by anyone aiming to compromise, trivialize, sensationalize, or simply discredit artists using the body as material for art.

The facts are that Schwarzkogler matured as an artist in the circle of Viennese artists that included Hermann Nitsch, Günter Brus, and Otto Muehl, began to participate actively in action-happenings in October, 1964, and served as the model in several of Nitsch's actions. After this period, Schwarzkogler began to create his own action images. In the summer and fall of 1965, Schwarzkogler directed five discrete photographic works, entitled *Aktion mit einem menschlichen Körper* (Action with a Male Body).[161] These works, which differed markedly from

157. Nancy Spector, "Performing the Body in the 1970s," in Rrose is a Rrose is a Rrose: Gender Performance in Photography, 159.

158. Roland Barthes, Camera Lucida (New York: Hill & Wang, 1981).

159. For more on Schwarzkogler, see my "Notes on Rudolf Schwarzkogler's Images of Healing," WhiteWalls: A Magazine of Writings by Artists 25 (Spring 1990): 13-26. Reprinted

in Rudolf Schwarzkogler (Vancouver: University of British Columbia, 1993): 29-39.

160. Robert Hughes, "The Decline and Fall of the Avant Garde," Time (18 December 1972): 111.

161. Sources differ on the number of photographic tableaux Schwarzkogler did before his own last live actions. The pamphlet issued by the Galerie Nächst St. Stephan in 1970, and the catalogue

entry for Documenta V, 1972, both list one Happening (Hochzeit), five Actions with a Male Body in the summer and fall of 1965, and one last action with his own body in 1966. Two recent books, Von der Aktionsmalerei zum Aktionismus, Wein, 1960-1965, and Wiener Aktionismus, 1960-1970, describe Schwarzkogler's last action as #6. The discrepancy resides, I think, in whether the authors consider Schwarzkogler's Hochzeit an action or not.

Rudolf **Schwarzkogler**, *Hochzeit*, 1965. Archiv Conz, Verona

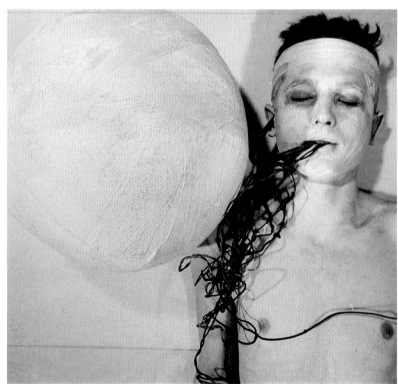

**Rudolf Schwarzkogler**, *3rd Action*, 1965-66.
Private Collection

the gestural, live body-actions and happenings created by his friends, have been described since by Nitsch as "Apollonian," and thus distinguished from the more "Dionysian" actions of the others.[162] Using his friend Heinz Cibulka as his model (the same artist that Nitsch also often employed) Schwarzkogler conceived and orchestrated a series of still tableaux which were then photographed by Ludwig Hoffenreich, a photographer who had worked with Nitsch since the early 1960s.[163] Together in private studio sessions, Schwarzkogler created the *mise en scène*, Cibulka provided the physical body-object for the construction of the image, and Hoffenreich took the pictures. These private studio pieces did not include a developmental action through time, as in a happening, and were not performances, but were strictly arranged by Schwarzkogler as discrete, simulated events.

Seeming to be photographic documents, these seductive images actually presented only an artificial construction, a series of fictional events, symbolic not only in form but in content. Apparently signs signifying the real, these photographs are signifiers of the imaginary. Finally, Schwarzkogler did not die in a body action, nor do the photographs of staged, fictional castration even depict him.[164]

By the end of 1968, Schwarzkogler hardly communicated with anyone at all. His withdrawn condition alarmed his partner Edith Adam, as well as Nitsch and Nitsch's wife Eva, a psychologist who suggested individual treatment by a well-known Munich psychotherapist.[165] This plan was never carried through. By 1969, Schwarzkogler had begun to experiment with various physical health regimes which he hoped both to cleanse and purify his own body and mind. At the time of his death, he had arrived at a prolonged state of extreme agitation. His diet was often restricted to a self-imposed regime of milk and bread.[166] During this period, Edith Adam remembered that Schwarzkogler experienced severe hallucinations which led him at times to cower in his room, imagining himself surrounded by snakes.[167]

Schwarzkogler also became increasingly obsessed with Yves Klein's photomontage, *Leap Into the Void*. On the day of his death, he had been experiencing a period of severe hallucinations and was sitting in the window of their apartment while Adam worked in another room. She conjectures that he either fell (owing to his altered mental state), jumped (a suicide resulting from depression), or actually attempted to fly (like Klein) from their second story apartment window. Whatever the truth may be,

162. Hermann Nitsch, Rudolf Schwarzkogler, in Schwarzkogler 1940-1969 (Vienna: Galerie Nächst St. Stephan, 1970).

163. By Nitsch's 12th Action, 6 September 1965, he too employed Cibulka as the principle model in his work.

164. Aside from Schwarzkogler's first event, Hochzeit, of 5 February 1965, an action that included Schwarzkogler, Cibulka and Anni Brus, photographed by Michael Epp, and his last action, performed alone in 1966, Schwarzkogler is never the figure in his images.

165. Wiener Aktionismus, 380-81.

166. Dr. Franz Xavier Mayr, Die Darmtragheit: Stuhlverstopfung (Wien: Verlag Neues Leben, 1953): 273.

167. Edith Adam in conversation with the author, April 1978, Vienna.

Carolee Schneemann, *Eye Body*, 1963.
Collection of the artist

**Carolee Schneemann**, *Interior Scroll*, 1975.
Collection of Peter and Eileen Norton, Santa Monica

Schwarzkogler plunged to his death on June 20th, 1969, perhaps with a photograph in mind.

Six years before Schwarzkogler's tragic death and three years before he began to work with a photographer to realize his images, Carolee Schneemann performed *Eye Body*. This, her first body action, was made in private for the expressed purpose of producing photographs, taken by her friend, the Icelandic artist Errò. The photographs of *Eye Body* are still generally accepted as among the first visual images that constitute the lexicon of an explicitly feminist avant-garde vocabulary. Not until the publication of Schneemann's book, *More Than Meat Joy* (1979), in which the artist historicized and theorized her own work, did *Eye Body* begin to receive widespread attention. But then it was in an entirely different cultural climate, both for the reception of feminist performance work and in terms of the increasingly different discourse brought to bear on it by post-structuralist theory, heavily laden with psychoanalytic and cultural theories of "transgression" and "resistance."

Schneemann is partially responsible for encouraging associations between her early work and the "transgressive" art of the 1980s. Moreover, the photographs from *Interior Scroll* (1975), in which the artist is shown pulling a text from her vagina, enabled her to be appropriated into the context of the "bad girl" of the 1990s. But when Schneemann turns up in those contexts, they threaten to undermine the very values she has so courageously fought to achieve.[168]

168. For a powerful critique of the very notion of "bad girls" see Laura Cottingham, How Many "Bad" Feminists Does It Take to Change a Light Bulb? (New York: After words, 1994). Cottingham described the "historicized usage of 'Bad Girl' [as] distinctly derogatory [functioning] to regulate the behavior of women toward self-sacrifice, sexual repression, and assimilation into the heterosexual contract of marriage and family, toward the very 'Good Girl' model" against which the shows were a reaction; and she correctly added that "an appropriation of the good/bad model, from any woman's perspective, even if consciously attempted as subversive, is still nothing more than a parroting of a male supremacist construct. Such rhetoric, she concluded, "relies on a false, pseudo-Hegelian premise that thesis ('good girl') and anti-thesis ('bad girl') will provide synthesis (emancipation) — ignoring how obviously this dialectic willingly writes the terms of women's emancipation according to patriarchy itself. She also pointed out the shallowness of Marcia Tucker's definition of the "bad girl," as "honest, outrageous, contentious, wanton, self-indulgent, and even vulgar;" and Cottingham noted: "Much of the rhetoric associated with these exhibitions reeks of such unexamined self-hatred and self-contempt."

**Hannah Wilke**, S.O.S. *Starification Object Series, An Adult Game of Mastication, Box*, 1974.
Courtesy of the Estate of Hannah Wilke and Ronald Feldman Fine Arts, New York

For example, Rebecca Schneider writes: Within twenty-five years of "Eye/Body" [sic], explicit body work would include such feminist artists as Orlan, who, in the 1990s, takes her own "flesh as material" as she undergoes a series of plastic surgery operations to rearrange her bodily "parts" to conform, with ironic mimicry, to women depicted in canonical art.[169]

However excellent in theory, on this point Schneider misreads Schneemann, whose exploration of "flesh as material" in *Eye Body* was very different than the ways in which Schneider theorizes its relation to Orlan's use of "flesh as material." What Schneemann acturally wrote must be examined more closely:

In 1962 I began a loft environment built of large panels interlocked by rhythmic color units, broken mirrors and glass, lights, moving umbrellas and motorized parts. I worked with my whole body — the scale of the panels incorporating my own physical scale. I then decided *I wanted my actual body to be combined with the work as an integral material* — a further dimension of the construction . . . (my emphasis).[170]

Schneemann wanted "to do a series of physical transformations" of her body *in* her "constructions and wall environment," as a means for making her body into "visual territory, [exploring] the image values of flesh as material."[171] This environment eventually became *Eye Body*, comprised of several constructions: *Four Fur Cutting Boards* (1962), *Ice Box* (1962), *Window to Brakhage* (1962), *Fur Wheel* (1962), and *Gift Science* (1963).

As a painter, it was *the image values* of flesh as material that concerned the ways in which Schneemann positioned her body in her work, understood her body to "remain erotic, sexual, desired, desiring but [also] votive," and conceived of herself as an "extension" of her "painting-constructions [and] myself — the artist . . . a primal, archaic force which could unify energies discovered as visual information [by] my creative female will." Schneemann's language has always been grounded in the visual

problems — "image values" — of painting, and the sculptural "rhymic interlocking" of her body with her assemblage-constructions. The source of Schneemann's work — then as now — is painting. She has always described herself as a painter, and her theoretical orientation has always been toward the fractured visual fields of Cezanne in whose work she saw the breakdown of perspectival orientation which occasioned a radical shift in the visual relation to the picture plane, a shift that also drew the body of the artist into the work.

*Eye Body*, performed in late 1963, and *Meat Joy* (1964) belong to a history of assemblage, environments, and Happenings of the early 1960s, not feminist performance of the mid-to late 1970s (when she did *Interior Scroll*), or of the 1990s when "bad girls" like Annie Sprinkle or Karen Finley appeared, even if their work grew out of interpretations of her performance. To put her into these contexts is to imagine that her path-breaking work has also been celebrated, supported by dealers (such as that of Wilke and Orlan), or any of the other financial and personal rewards that other women's work now achieves. It has not.

Schneemann still has little institutional support in the art world despite the fact that she has been the model for the practices of so many other men and women for three decades. Most importantly, her work was never about violence to the body, but about, in her own words, "erotic, sexual, desired, desiring" bodies, and about flesh as "joy" — all qualities vividly conveyed in *Eye Body* as her own body diagonally intersects the picture-surface, extending metaphorically from painterly space into the lived space in which she created her actions.

Schneemann created acts of primary observation. She reconstructed the ways in which we see and interpret the world. *Observation that reconstructs interpretation is radical and original.* And it is the radicality of her vision, her originality that is worth defending. For Schneemann's art has been full of the joy and celebration of female bodies in and for themselves.

169. Rebecca Schneider, The Explicit Body in Performance *(London and New York: Routledge, 1997), 331-32.*

170. Carolee Schneemann, More Than Meat Joy, 52.

171. Ibid.

**Milan Knížák**, street performance, Prague, 1964

### IX. Balancing Between a Dusthole and Eternity

Milan Knížák painted *Preacher of an X Time* in 1958. It was a gestural painting peopled by elongated figures. In a photograph of the now destroyed painting, Knížák stands before his larger than life-size image wearing a beret and the alienated, suspicious expression of a James Dean.[172] On the face of the photograph is written: "My first dreams about a new society. I was eighteen." During this period and much later, Knížák was "kicked out" of the university and the art academy where he planned "a wild celebration on the first of May and the school was upside down and they kicked me out: it was 1959." A year later, the artist was drafted and spent two years and four months in the army, during which time he was always in jail for refusing to follow orders.

After being discharged from the army, the artist began to paint in a raw style similar to the painters of the "realism of emotions," and to make assemblages of a crude and rough character. At that time, he also began to put objects directly on the streets. By 1962-63, the AKTUAL Community began to take shape in Prague. The community of artists consisted of Sonja Svecová, Jan Trtilek, the brothers Jan and Vit Mach, and Zdenka Zizkova. Between 1964 and 1966, Knížák created his first "ceremonies" and "demonstrations." Robert Wittmann joined during this period and remembered the group as "a living embodiment of the problems of society, problems that had so far been violently forced out of sight...."[173] A typical AKTUAL event created by Knížák was *How to Make Clothing Actual* (1965):

> A sleeve is ripped off the coat./ The collar is painted a clashing color./ On the bottom (hemline) of the coat, a thirty-centimeter long fringe is attached. Its ends may be braided./ The coat is cut apart along its entire length./ We wear each half separately./ A square twenty by twenty centimeters is cut out on the bodice of an overcoat, the wide side is parallel to the shoulders. The same on the jacket, shirt./ Undershirt. Easter decals are printed on the skin./ Clothes which are taken off are rolled into a bundle and carried on one's/ back like a knapsack, etc., etc.

By 1965, Knížák was shooting at books to make *Killed Books*, encasing books in cement to make *Documentary Books*, and making *Destroyed Music* from records he scratched, drew on, broke, and reassembled. He was also in constant contact with Fluxus, the PROVOS, Vostell, DIAS, and many other artists in Europe and the US. He communicated with these artists principally through his *samizdat* publications, handmade books containing written, typed, painted, drawn, and mimeographed manifestos, drawings, poems, and theoretical writings on art, mathematics, destruction, and many other topics. Knížák initially thought of the events he made with the AKTUAL group as "ceremonies" and "demonstrations." But by the end of 1965, he began to refuse to use any names to describe his work at all because he felt they were too artificial and he wanted to dissolve his art "into the stream of everyday life":

> I smuggled [art] into their lives. . . . I wanted people to live richly every millimeter of their everyday life. . . . Look, I was very influenced by

172. Milan Knížák in conversation with the author 23-24 May 1995, Prague. All quotes from Knížák, unless otherwise cited, come from this interview.

173. Robert Wittmann, quoted in *Milan Knížák Actions (Prague)*, n.p.

**Milan Knížák**, *Dress Jewelry*, 1969. Collection Feelisch, Remscheid

**Milan Knížák**, *Actualized Coat*, 1965-70. Collection of the artist

**Milan Knížák**, *My Destiny*, 1969. Collection Feelisch, Remscheid

**Milan Knížák**, *Dress with Iron Cuffs, Pockets, Collar*, Model 1970

the Communist ideal. We lived in it. Even if I was never a Commie, never. But I was very much influenced by the idea that life is important, that we have to make life very rich, we have to live really and deeply. We have to trust in justice. They said these things but they never did it. We were taught at school about fantastic stuff and there was a great contrast between this and the reality. They were totally different. I always thought about revolutions, changes in life, change in the life. That is at the base of my being. I was taught about it. I was taught that revolutions brought something new and important. I didn't want to make social revolution, I wanted to make revolution in everyday life.

Knížák came to the U.S. and created *Lying Ceremony* in 1968. Increasingly interned for his work, Knížák did not even participate in the realization of his *The March* (1973), because he was in jail. In late 1974 and early 1975, Knížák spent four more months in prison, and they "wanted to kick me out of the

174. The exhibition was a group show including Jiri Kolár, Bela Kolarova, and Jan Ságl.

country; so I married." The artist had no employment or way to make money in a country where it was forbidden not to have a job. His wife supported him, as did the German collector Ruepp, who often sent him two hundred marks a month, which the police sometimes returned saying that they could not locate the artist, or, as he recalled, "some other blah blah blah: but that was the life." Eventually, he stopped making events. "I found the space of the mind (because I was studying mathematics), a real space, like the other spaces, and maybe even a little bit more free. It was the only free space I could use under the Communists in the 1970s." Much in the tradition of George Brecht's *Event Scores* of the late 1950s and early 1960s, he wrote:

ACTIONS THAT CANNOT HAPPEN.
ACTIONS THAT CANNOT EVEN BE
THOUGHT ABOUT.
ACTIONS THAT ARE NOT ACTIONS (1978).

Zorka Ságlová exhibited her first and last public installation-event, *Hay–Straw*, at the Václav Spála Gallery, in Prague, in August 1969.[174] As part of a group exhibition entitled "Something Somewhere," she

**Zorka Ságlová**, *Hay-Straw*, August 1969.

installed yellow bales of straw and green bales of dried alfalfa in one room, and in another she "tossed about" hay that she and friends had dried and tied together into bales. Rock music was played throughout the space on pre-recorded tapes. Visitors to her exhibition, Ságlová explained, "spontaneously" interacted with the natural and dyed materials, creating "new compositions of the hay and straw each day [while] a large number of grasshoppers chirped on the walls."[175] Milena Lamarová, a Prague critic, described this exhibition as "one of the most important events in the art world of the 1960s," and Jiri Padrta explained why:

> The title itself — "Something Somewhere" — is an exhibition of something possible at any time and at any place, it was not given beforehand, nor previously selected, prepared and closed. The absence of depiction, the indifference of all those present to each *a priori* artistic form and, finally, perhaps the most marked feature, namely the submission of the reality of things into the completely raw factual concept of the location. Reality is neither reproduced in this concept nor evoked through art, but it is simply seen, exposed, treated outside of its original environment and taken into a new context to be transposed to a vision, feeling, hearing framework, and to the manipulation which can change the static fact of its existence via the physical action.[176]

However important to those who experienced her work in 1969, the exhibition cost Ságlová two decades of her artistic life. After this exhibition, she was banned from exhibiting for nineteen years.

Perhaps now it is possible to understand what it meant when in an action on December 20, 1974, Jan Mlcoch simply took off his clothes, and, in the presence of a few friends, washed his whole body; or in another action, on August 5, 1974, let himself be suspended by his hands and feet on a nylon rope in a large attic, blindfolded by a black scarf and his ears plugged with wax. Perhaps an action by Petr Stembera realized at the Galerie Repassage in Warsaw on September 5, 1977, enables visualization of what it was like to live

175. Zorka Ságlová, quoted in Zorka Ságlová — 1965-1995 (Prague: Galerie vytvarného uméni v Litomerichich), unpaginated. All quotes unless otherwise cited are from this catalogue.

176. Ibid.

**Jan Mlcoch**, *The Emigrant's Suitcase: Across the Sea*, Gallery Remont, Warsaw, 5 May 1976. Collection of the artist

**Jan Mlcoch**, *The Classic Escape*, Hradec Kr·lávé, 26 November 1977. Collection of the artist

Petr Stembera, *The Way*, 1977

as if a one were a lighted fuse:

> Stembera drew himself along the floor, flat on
> his stomach, hands tied behind him, over two
> lines of black and white powder, one for each
> leg. He was striving to reach the end of these
> lines, but as he moved, an assistant poured acid
> onto strings trailing behind his bare feet. The
> acid burned away the strings so that gradually,
> like a lit fuse, the splashes of acid came closer
> to his bare, upturned feet. Would he be able to
> reach the end of the lines of powder before the
> acid burned away the strings that touched his
> feet? The same year, 1978, he balanced his chin
> on a thin sheet of glass and pushed it forward
> along the floor.[177]

Until Mlcoch witnessed Stembera's actions, he had made no art. "In the early Seventies, after the Soviet occupation, we felt we were 'falling through time,' and I wanted to create some firm points for myself in the shapeless present we were experiencing," Mlcoch said.[178] Stembera and Mlcoch emphasized "physical presence" and "self-knowledge" as the decisive elements in their work. They made art that responded with personal necessity to their urgent situation.

Stembera had begun painting in 1966 in a style influenced by the Spanish painter Tapiès, but a visit to Paris during the Prague Spring altered his direction. For two years, the artist worked with his own blood "trying to decide what to do," and practiced yoga and various ascetic regimes. This physical regimentation might be understood as a kind of personal resistance training. "It's important to be prepared," he told me, "for this physical psychological aggression: prepared with meditation and yoga."

Stembera's first "body action," in 1971, was a simple trip to the countryside where the artist collected "many heavy stones" and transported them

back to the city. By 1974, his actions had become increasingly ritualistic. In *Narcissus, #1*, for example, performed in December 1974, Stembera stood gazing at his portrait placed on an improvised "altar" lit with candles. Then blood was drawn from his vein with a hypodermic syringe by Mlcoch. Stembera mixed the blood with his own urine, hair and nail clippings, and drank the mixture in front of his altar. Such an action recalls shamanistic and voodoo practices for accumulating power, protecting against evil spirits, and generally guarding the soul. In *Grafting*, performed in April of the following year, Stembera attempted to graft a plant to his body (using the normal gardening method that included poisonous materials for grafting), explaining that he wanted, "to make contact with the plant, to put it in my body, to be together with it as long as possible." The desperation that was clearly communicated in these actions was not intentional, Stembera believed: "It is a question of the position of one man who was nobody (myself), and another situation for a man who might be known; it was political for that one person who is known, but not for me."

That Stembera's actions may not have been "political" in a public sense is understandable because they had been stimulated, in part, by Eastern philosophy and existentialism (especially the work of Gabriel Marcel) which he said was "fashionable" at that time. The artist also read literature on Zen, information theory by Marshall McLuhan, and remembered that:

> The essence of these ideas was the discovery of
> one's own body, of physical experience and physical being in the world. But I should stress that
> all of these studies were not done in depth. I was
> concerned with defining my own experience,
> not with the assimilation of some systems. The
> actual form of my performances evolved under
> the direct influence of Western art. In those days
> I was in relatively close contact with Terry Fox,
> Tom Marioni, Chris Burden and others, and I had
> a pretty good idea of what was going on in
> the world. But I was repelled by the "Viennese
> school" and its perverse "end of the century"
> atmosphere. (Freud could only exist there).[179]

177. Roland Miller, "The Curtain Rises,"
Variant 12 (199 ): 20-21.

178. Jan Mlcoch, quoted in Vytvarne
Umeni: The Magazine for Contemporary
Art 3/91 (1991): 77.

179. Stembera, in conversation
with Ludvik Hlavacek, "vzpominka na
akeni umeni 70. let," in ibid., 66.

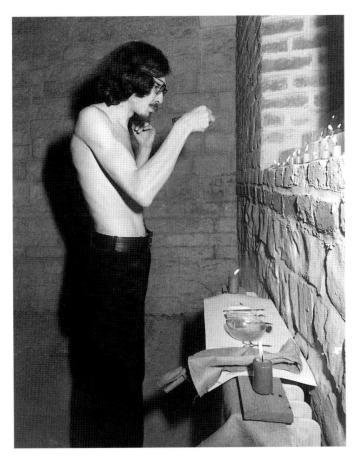

**Petr Stembera**, *Narcissus #1*, 1974

**Petr Stembera**, *Grafting*, 1975

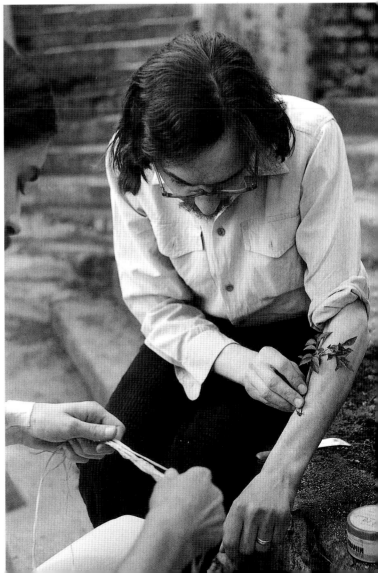

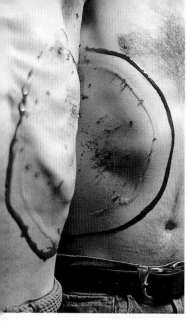

**Petr Stembera**, *Joining with Tom Marioni*, 1975

In April, 1975, Tom Marioni traveled to Prague as part of the research for the very important special issue of *Vision* magazine on Eastern European experimental art. While he was there, Marioni and Stembera created *Joining*, an action in which the two artists joined their bodies with circles of condensed milk and cocoa to which they applied hungry ants, the circular pattern signifying their brotherhood within the conflict of East and West.

Is it any wonder in Eastern Europe of the 1970s that Yugoslavian artist Raša Todosijević would perform *Was Ist Kunst?* repeatedly between 1976 and 1978? Standing with his back to the audience before a microphone into which, in various tones and intonations, he whispered, shouted, ranted, screamed, pleaded, begged, simply asked the same question over and over again — "What is Art?" — while facing a hand-written backdrop on which the same words were boldly written, and against which a silent woman (Marinela Kozelj) sat impassively facing the audience and a man stood with a black cloth over his head and shoulders tied with a rope around his neck. The action lasted some twenty-five minutes until Todosijević was exhausted and his deep, husky, powerful voice could barely be heard. It was excruciating to watch, to hear, to witness. For the question inextricably connected to the artist's own cultural conditions, wherein the unremitting challenge to any attempt to visualize authentically the actual experiences of contemporary life was suppressed, but also to know as an artist how irrepressible art is whether within the voracious consumption of capitalism or the compulsive repression of communism. While the staged interrogation placed the validity of art itself in question, the mute response but constant presence of the witness (Kozelj) and the tortured man only served to confirm art's resistance, and by extension, humanity's ability to oppose, confront, and persist through the absolutely uncontrollable imaginative powers that no discipline so powerfully cultivates as art.

In *Drinking of Water* (April 28, 1974), the artist, bare-chested, repeatedly drank water from a fish tank from which the fish had been emptied out on the floor before the audience. Trying to "harmonize the rhythm of the fish breathing," the artist drank twenty-six glasses of water at the same time as breathing, eventually vomiting out the intolerable quantities of water he had forced himself to consume in imitation of the environment of a creature that he was not.[180] Such an action also recalls Marina Abramović's *Rhythm O* (1974), in which the artist laid threatening objects out on a table and announced: "There are some objects on the table you may use on me. I am an object."

These and a series of other actions Abramovic, Stembera, Mlcoch, Todosijević, and many other Eastern European artists created have been described as "masochistic." While certainly expressing the inversion of external suffering back on the self, they were accomplished neither for the sake of personalized erotic pleasure or desire, but as vital culturally shared communications between the artists and tiny groups of individuals partaking in the context and experiences metaphorically enacted and metonymically shared. Metonymy conveys some incorporeal or intangible state in terms of the corporeal or tangible, requiring connection along the axis of combination, enabling one to perceive the contiguity of relations between two things. When such a connection includes human relations, it may have the effect of reducing human actions "to a less complex and usually more concrete realm of being."[181] These qualities are of particular relevance to the function and structure of the altered communicative means of live, performed art. For by literally acting in the space between a human viewing subject and the conventional art object — as the mediator between the two — the artists who produced action-paintings and later actions, exhibited the intersection where subjects meet object, where the artifactuality of the object is born in an event, and where the artist becomes both a subject who produces an object, and the object itself. Such art exhibits how the metonymic process precedes the signifying capabilities of metaphor (objectified in representational objects). The very artifactuality of the artist and the event,

180. Raša Todosijević, in *Vision*, op. cit., 31.

181. See Robert J. Matthews and Wilfried Ver Eecke, "Metaphoric-Metonymic Polarities: A Structural Analysis," Linguisitics: An International Review 67 (March 1971): 49. Quoted in my unpublished dissertation, "The Destruction in Art Symposium (DIAS)," 1987, op. cit.

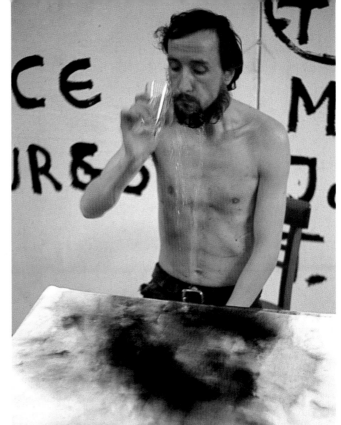

**Raša Todosijević**, *Drinking of Water — Inversions, Imitations and Contrasts*, 1974.

**Raša Todosijević**, and Marinella Kozelj, *Drinking of Water — Inversions, Imitations and Contrasts*, 1974.

then, holds the potential to link the alienated Hegelian subject to his/her object through the transit of the body, shifting visual art's traditional and exclusive dependence on the communicative mechanisms of metaphorical objects to metonymical actions. Indeed, some philosophers of language have even suggested that the metonymic process precedes the signifying capabilities of metaphor.

Artists in the Eastern Bloc had varying degrees of contact with other countries. Aside from perhaps the Albanians, however, the Romanians were the most isolated. Action in Romania in the 1970s occurred primarily in the context of environmental installations and photography, since it was nearly impossible for the artists to gather and perform together. In the mid-1970s, Ion Grigorescu organized several exhibitions at the Friderich Schiller House in Bucharest focused on the use of photography in which the camera, as he explained, "treat[s] tools just as persons."[182] Refering to his own work, Grigorescu described his "Autophotographies" as emerging out of "a few happenings" that he considered related to his own "personality" in a context of "individual voyeurism."[183]

One of these "Autophotographies" resulted in his series entitled, *Pole Vault — River Traisteni* (1976). The photographs, taken by Andrei Gheorghiu, document the artist in various actions by the river. Grigorescu is seen sitting on a huge tree stump, screaming into the air, pole-vaulting into space, and then appearing with his neck ringed in a metal crown. In another self-portrait the artist appears with an elongated neck over which is superimposed the image of the Egyptian King Tut's renowned coffin. Other photographs from the period show Grigorescu performing body-actions in his own living quarters. *The Tongue* (1976), shows only the artist's mouth, gaping wide open, in what appears to be a scream. Just the exhibition of such an image would have brought questions by authorities as to Grigorescu's motives for "screaming," hence Grigorescu's subtle attention to the body part (the tongue and its inability to speak) rather than the political context within which such speech was repressed. An untitled series

182. Ion Grigorescu, "Short presentation of Romanian photography,"*Oosteuropese Conceptuele Fotografie (Eindhoven:* *Technische Hogeschool, 1977),* 8.

183. *Ibid.*

**Ion Grigorescu**, *Male/Female*, 1976

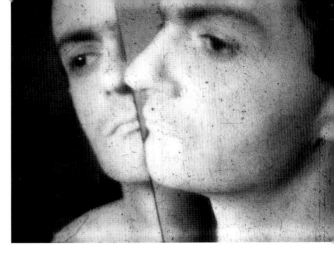

**Ion Grigorescu**, *Boxing*, 1977

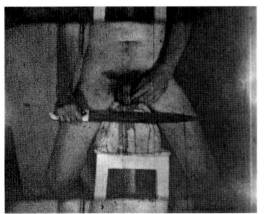

depicts the artist nude in frantic action confined to the tiny space of his room. In this group of images, Grigorescu left the shutter open as long as he could while quickly moving in front of the lens.

In all of these photographs, the artist appears multiplied again and again. They represent not only auto-portraits of the artist, but they picture the dissociated psychic condition in which so many Romanians existed as their ruptured national identity was reinforced in, and echoed by, the shattering of personal identity. Katherine Verdery, an American anthropologist specializing in Romanian culture, recognized a "social schizophrenia" among Romanians which she described as an ability to experience a "real meaningful and coherent self *only* in relation to the enemy party."[184] In addition, she argued that while coercion was the most obvious process by

which Romanians were traumatized into obedience, a double bind existed (comprised of intense nationalism coupled with economic shortage) that left the people incapacitated to perceive themselves as anything other than "absolutely dependent upon a government which they could not criticize without being labeled unpatriotic."[185] This paradoxical predicament reinforced what Verdery described as the "symbolic-ideological" discourse in Romania, a discourse that utilizes "the Nation . . . as a master *symbol*," and that pervades Romanian art, wherein the body and its actions are identified as both self and enemy.[186]

In short, Romanians felt conflicted, paradoxical, doubled, and contaminated. This doubling and splitting appears throughout the photographs and films Grigorescu made of himself. In *Male/Female*

184. Katherine Verdery, "Nationalism and the 'Transition' in Romania," a lecture given at Duke University, 23 February 1993. This use of the term "schizophrenia" is different from the popularization of that notion as a theorization of postmodernity in the work of Gilles Deleuze and Felix Guattari. On the contrary, it is used in

the psychoanalytic sense of severely disturbed cognitive and emotional responses that are physiologically, psychologically, and/or socially grounded. This distinction is the basis for my theorization of Romania itself as a "culture of trauma." See my "Shaved Heads and Marked Bodies: Representations from Cultures of Trauma," in Strategie II:

Peuples Mediterraneens (Paris) 64-65 (July-December 1993), 95-117.

185. Katherine Verdery, National Ideology Under Socialism: Identity and Cultural Politics in Ceausecu's Romania (Berkeley: University of California Press), 101.

186. Ibid., 122.

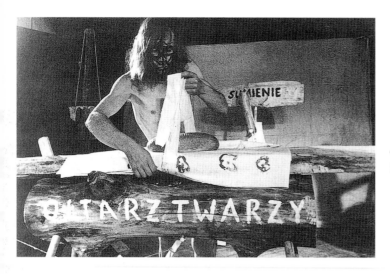

**Jerzy Beres**, *Altar of Face (Oltarz Twarzy)*, 1974.
Muzeum Narodowe, Wroclaw, Poland

(1976) he appears as two genders. In *Boxing* (1977) the artist boxes with himself. In *Âme-am* (1977) he grapples with his soul. In *Dialogue with Nicolae Ceausescu* (1978), a six-minute black and white film, the artist assumes the role of both the dictator and himself in a dialogue. Grigorescu's representation and presentation of himself — as self-recriminating, filled with guilt, anger, futility, and a fractured sense of social experience — also reflects what Alexandra Cornilescu, a linguist from Bucharest University, explained was a Romanian survival technique: the ability to "hedge, to cultivate and live multiple lives, to say one thing and to mean something else, to speak in layered codes impenetrable to informers (often even confusing to friends), to use one's eyes and gestures as if they were words."[187] Or, as the Romanian-American poet Andrei Codrescu wrote: "I lie in order to hide the truth from morons."[188]

The influence of Tadeusz Kantor on avant-garde art throughout Eastern Europe cannot be underestimated. Born in 1915 and trained as a painter, Kantor survived the war in Kraków, staging plays at a time when all artistic life under German prohibition was prevented upon penalty of death. Immediately following the war, he was one of the organizers of the First Exhibition of Modern Art in Kraków in 1948. These activities must be contextualized within the massive destruction that occurred throughout Poland. Six million Poles had died. Every major city except Kraków was bombed to rubble. There was massive illiteracy, and the "rich diversity of the country [had] vanished: [most of] the Jews were dead, the Germans expelled, the Ukrainians and Belorussians swallowed by the Soviet Union."[189] And Poland remained under Stalinism until 1956.

Kantor established his experimental theater, Cricot 2, at Galeria Krzysztofory (one of two avant-garde galleries in Poland) in 1955. Cricot 2 represented a "theatre of concrete reality, not scenic illusion," and expressed Kantor's interest in the real-

ity of destroyed, degraded, and rejected materials that fascinated so many artists in the immediate post-war years. That same year he visited Paris, discovering Wols, Mathieu, and Pollock, and, in 1957, he began to paint in an *informel* style, and to use the French word *emballer* (to pack, to wrap up) for his practice of wrapping people and objects as packages in the productions of Cricot 2 (a practice that perhaps influenced the Bulgarian artist, Christo). In 1963, he organized the "Anti-Exhibit" in Kraków, and wrote "The Zero Theater," a manifesto asserting the important relation between art and reality. Kantor visited the United States in 1965, where he met Allan Kaprow and thereafter began to think of his own process of "depicting reality via reality," as a Happening. He organized eight Happenings between 1965 and 1969.[190] In *Panoramic Sea Happening* (1967), the artist started rumors to emphasize the mysterious contents of a large trunk whose contents were never shown to the audience and which was thrown into the sea before they could be discovered.[191]

Galeria Foksal played a critical role in the history of Happenings and actions in Poland, presenting not only Kantor's work but that of Zbigniew Gostomski, Zygmunt Krauze, Maria Stangret (who married Kantor), Edward Krasinski, Jerzy Beres, and others. In Beres's event, *Prophesy I*, 1968, the artist presented his views on the act of creation and its prerequisites: "independence — work — action — discovery." In this action, Beres appeared nude and carved a sculpture (using an ax and a saw) from the trunk of a tree brought to the gallery. At the end of his performance, the artist tied himself to his sculpture, making him inseparable from his work. Beres had used organic materials in his work since the 1950s, and had made wooden sculptures placed in urban settings in the early 1960s. His earliest actions in the late 1960s often included dialogue with the spectator. In the 1970s, they assumed more mystical

187. Alexandra Cornilescu, "Transitional Patterns: Symptoms of the Erosion of Fear in Romanian Political Discourse," unpublished talk at the Modern Language Association Annual Meeting, New York, 1992. All further quotes by Cornilescu come from this article.

188. Andrei Codrescu, Monsieur Teste in America and Other Instances of Realism (Minneapolis: Coffee House Press, 1987), 14.

189. Tina Rosenberg, The Haunted Land: Facing Europe's Ghosts after Communism (New York: Vintage Books, 1995), 145.

190. Michal Kobialka, "The Quest for the Self/Other: A Critical Study of Tadeusz Kantor's Theatre," in Michal Kobialka, ed., A Journey Through Other Spaces: Essays and Manifestos, 1944-1990, Tadeusz Kantor (Berkeley: University of California Press, 1993), 293.

191. Tadeusz Kantor, from the script of the Panoramic Sea Happening, 1967 in Documentation (September 1971), broadside from the Galeria Foksal.

**Tadeusz Kantor**, *Panoramic Sea Happening*, 1967

and ritualistic qualities, with references to transubstantiation, altars, and transfiguration — such as changing the consumptive function of bread into an aesthetic one by covering sides of bread with paint (*The Beautiful Altar*). In 1981, the artist pushed a heavy wooden cart through the market square in Kraków, then lit five bonfires signifying Hope, Freedom, Dignity, Love, and Truth. This action reflects the central role that the Catholic Church has played in creating modes of resistance in Poland (as it did in Romania and elsewhere throughout the Eastern Bloc), as well as the speech that Pope John Paul II (the former Polish Cardinal Stefan Wyszynski) delivered October 16, 1978, in the Kraków cathedral, in which he advised: "The future of Poland will depend on how many people are mature enough to be nonconformists."[192]

The extraordinary intelligence, beauty, complexity, élan, and tragedy expressed in Eastern European action art remains a rich source for research. The absence of general recognition of these artists' work, even now when they are supposedly free to participate in the world beyond the Iron Curtain, makes it extremely difficult emotionally for many to continue. This situation is exacerbated by an even more ironical paradox: whereas *before* 1989 it was difficult to work *inside* one's country, *after* 1989 it has become difficult to work *outside* of one's country, because interest in Eastern European art is, by and large, marginal and passing. Given this reality, perhaps it is wise to remember Rasheed Araeen's 1978 warning:

> The usage of the term international. . . does not imply the participation of all people, or the cross-fertilization between the different cultures of the world, but merely the evolution of art styles in the West and their imposition on the rest of the world. It is in the global context of domination that we see the actual role of international art. . . . Although the present-day cultural domination in the Third World is part, and an instrument, of neo-colonialism, the concept of Western domination predates the emergence of multinationals. In fact it developed right from the beginning of the modern Western era, paradoxically as part of its humanistic concept of the world.[193]

**X. Cosmologies** Cosmology is a branch of systematic philosophy that deals with the character of the universe as a cosmos by combining metaphysics and scientific knowledge, and is particularly concerned with the processes of nature and the relation of its parts. Cosmogonic speculations consider the problem of creation and origins, or the coming into

192. Rosenberg, The Haunted Land, 160.

193. *Rasheed Araeen paper at "Session 3: The Multinational Style," for special issue on "The State of British Art," by* Studio International 193, no. 987 (1978): 103.

**Al Hansen**, *Hansen Breaks into the Unknown*, 1966

being of the world. From its roots in the Greek terms *kosm* or *kosmo*, such interrelated concepts evolved as "cosmopolitan," meaning knowledge and appreciation of many parts of the world, and as opposed to the provincial, local, or limited; "cosmopolite," one who is at home in every country and a citizen of the world; and "cosmorama," an exhibition of views of various parts of the world made to appear realistic by mirrors, lenses, and illumination.

Action art is a cosmopolitan art, made by cosmopolites creating cosmoramic views of their cultural, social, political environment in all of its infinite dimensions on the surface of their bodies. Those corporeal spaces reflect back fragments, flickers of illumination about the condition of Being in a period of the world that is coming to a close as fast as it is opening new possibilities. Through the lenses of their minds, these artists have fashioned a picture displayed as so many somatic crystalline representations in ephemeral events that visualize how humanity goes about its life.

A close look at the work of artists in this exhibition will reveal how each anticipated, contributed to, and participated in the global order that has not only recently been made visible and manifest in the electronic communications revolution, but which emerged as a discourse regarding cosmopolitanism at the turn of the last century, if not long before. By discussing the many ways in which artists' actions have altered everyday life for the past fifty years I have tried throughout this essay to locate their accomplishments at the intersection of the aesthetic and social worlds. They have permanently changed the ways in which art, visuality, and interaction amongst us all must be thought and rethought ever after. And it is my view that they have been operating as aesthetic cosmonauts exploring modes of being and living and doing and thinking that will become models for radically changing futures augmented by bio-, endo-, and nano-technologies, cybernated bodies, artificial forms of life and intelligence, and virtual realities and worlds.

There is no doubt but that in a period of television, film, advertising and now digital imagery, altering

and controlling meaning in the visible world is an infinitely more complex task than it was in the shattered shadows of World War II. Across the time/space of this exhibition, these artists have participated in the divide of a world poised on the trigger of annihilation only to live to see one small wall break open, on November 9, 1989; to watch Nelson Mandela walk free after twenty-seven years in a racist prison to become the President of a new South Africa; to witness the announcement of the cloning of animals; and the strategic and psychological defeat of the greatest human chess master by a computer program. In a world of such worlds, the speculative explorations that these artists have shared in their body's actions have offered gifts for remaking and rethinking experience that are incomparable resources for a constructive, more humane future faced with changes that will make everything I have described above appear naive and crude. Below I highlight a few unusual aesthetic cosmologies suggestive of alternative ways to relate parts of the processes of nature — from actual biological systems to societal relations — to a larger whole.

**Brief Life on a Third Rail** "Pole-vaulting around" — a self-description of his manner of living — Al Hansen was a particularly rich source of energy in the international art community, and he became a conduit of information connecting artists involved in Happenings, Fluxus, and later performance in Europe and the United States.[194] Hansen also described himself as a "'natural,' and a bit of a primitive." Much of his life, Hansen lived from hand-to-mouth as a kind of street artist, traveled a great deal, and was always on, around, and making "the scene," whether in the United States or Europe. "I was always involved in just communication, just moving it around and whatnot, making things happen," he said. And he did.[195]

Hansen was electric. He brimmed with energy that he turned into information, calling his "living happening space," the Third Rail Gallery of Current Art. Sometimes written "3rd Rail Gallery," the name referred to the dangerous third metal rail of a train track through which high voltage current flows to the

194. All quotes from Hansen come from his unpublished letters to the author between 1979 and 1980 unless otherwise cited.

195. Al Hansen interview with Jan Van Raay, "Interview," 7 August 1979, Artzien (Amsterdam) 1, no. 9 (September 1979): n.p.

**Al Hansen**, *Hansen Does the New Year's Boogie with a Dancer*, 1966

**Al Hansen**, *Al Does a Newspaper Snow Job, from McLuhan Megillah*, Time Space Theatre, 12 February 1966

**Al Hansen**, *Hansen Weaves Valentine's Day Love Web with Dancer and Grail*, from *McLuhan Megillah* at the Time Space Theatre, 18 February 1966

**Al Hansen**, *Al Does a Newspaper Snow Job, from McLuhan Megillah,*
Time Space Theatre, 12 February 1966

motors of electric locomotives. Hansen began calling his "living quarters" by this name when he was doing "machine art." Commenting on Hansen's view of his living-exhibition space as a "third rail," Allan Kaprow stated:

> We saw it as a kind of danger metaphor where electrocution was possible at any moment; if he calls his own home a third rail, he might see the rest of his life with all its changes of forces as a dangerous world. He had to keep moving for all those reasons.[196]

It was Kaprow, moreover, who most clearly distinguished a difference between Hansen and many artists involved with Happenings: "Al was impulsive. Happenings were poetic. Al was openly adventuresome. Happenings were quietly exploratory. Al was a dare-devil who made people admire him but fear him. He picked up on the fear-attraction."[197] Although Hansen was included in both the environment and events of Fluxus, his highly visceral work and overt references to sex and violence did not comfortably fit that context. In Fluxus, sexuality was more sublimated than the overtly hedonistic performance practices of Happenings and Pop Art that coexisted, overlapped, and sometimes interlocked with it in the 1960s.

In a certain sense then, Hansen existed betwixt and between artists involved with Happenings, Fluxus, Pop Art, and later Performance and rock music. A perpetual outsider, his personality constituted the difference that mattered in terms of commercial and personal success. While other artists concentrated on building reputations, Hansen free-wheeled it: "I like to freak it and party, and I like to just disappear out of the scene regularly too. Drop back in after a year or two and challenge all the quick draw cats and chicks who've been building up a rep."

Hansen never served the commercial art community. He neither produced a marketable body of work (however inventive and delightful his collages

are), an obedient Happening (by his own admission, his events were so unpredictable as to be actually physically injurious on some occasions),[198] nor did he create a marketable persona as a performance artist (although he was more commercially successful in this endeavor). Hansen's Happenings had a raw character. He used refuse that was "detritus that couldn't be retrieved," Schneemann observed, "unlike Oldenburg's magical, embedded objects of degraded materials where something remained after an event." "The end of a Hansen Happening," she laughed, "looked like the toilet in the restaurant had flooded."[199]

*What the art industry could never fathom was Hansen's ability to be what a Happening was theorized to be.* Hansen understood the multifarious world of qualities and experiences and propagated them in a prodigious array by making marvelous objects and events. *But he also recovered life as a work of art.* Art history based on artist's biographies has been held in contempt for over a decade, threatened with being not sufficiently "theoretical," and coupled with the critique of art historical conventions connected to the critique of originality and artistic aura.[200] But examination of an artist's life, especially when that life is lived as it was by Al Hansen, sheds more light on the institutional practices, cultural situations, and political interactions in the avant-garde than if that biography were denied. For the critical point that Hansen's life/art raised about Happenings was: Could they be about *that* much life? To what degree were Happenings and Fluxus capable of accommodating the extremes to which he was capable of living and working? Would these artists ride the third rail? And if not, how did they go about excluding that part of life from the shape of events?

Hansen made it difficult both to accept or reject him, and he created circumstances filled with tension, contradictions, and all the actual dialectical conditions that life situations entail. Hansen's life and

196. Allan Kaprow, in conversation with the author, 12 November 1996, State College, Pennsylvania.

197. Ibid.

198. Hansen's description of his "Hall Street Happening" reads as if the experience was pure bedlam. See A Primer of

Happenings and Time/Space Art (New York: Something Else Press, 1965), 11-20.

199. Schneemann, in conversation with the author, 4 August 1997.

200. For the critique of originality, see Rosalind E. Krauss, "The Originality of the Avant-Garde," October 18 (Fall 1981), reprinted in Krauss's The

Originality of the Avant-Garde and Other Modernist Myths (Cambridge: MIT Press, 1985). For the effect of aura, see Walter Benjamin, "Work of Art in the Age of Mechanical Reproduction," in Illuminations, ed. Hannah Arendt and trans. Harry Zohn (New York: Harcourt, Brace, 1968).

**315**

**Joshua Neustein** (with G. Marx and G. Battle), *Jerusalem River Project:*
*Sound of Flowing River in the Dry Wadi of Abu Tor,* 1970

Joshua Neustein, *The Sound of Pine Cones Opening in the Sun*, Tel Aviv, November 1973

his life's work *itself* were comprised of an assemblage of simultaneous, unrepeatable, unpredictable, and unrelated occurrences and actions that defeated attempts at producing meaning, while at the same time embodying a remarkable coherency and unity. Hansen believed that "Art always wins!" He led his life in the manner John Cage taught, where conscious-ness is not a thing but a process; where art must entail the random, indeterminate, and chance aspects of nature and culture; where behavioral processes continually inform a work of art; where "the real world . . . becomes . . . not an object [but] a process."[201] And, in theory at least, such a life sounds ideal. But in practice it is quite another thing, as witnessed by the paradox that Cage himself regarded Hansen with distant caution.[202] As his childhood friend the cele-brated columnist Jimmy Breslin remembered in his remarkable obituary of the artist, Hansen was some-one "they tried to hold onto . . . like everybody else," but who, nevertheless, "tried everyday to put some-thing bright and different into the lives of people trying desperately to live like each other." And then, like a cosmonaut, "he stepped into the sky."[203]

**Powdered Light and the Sound of Water**
Contrasting natural and cultural systems, Joshua Neustein created several action-installations that addressed points of conflict between geo-political formations and State-supervised institutionalization of space and human exigencies. Prompted by the fact that ancient maps, biblical stories, and Israeli folklore mentioned a river near Jerusalem, a memory on which Israeli and Palestinian writers and painters had long meditated, the following year Neustein created a "fantasy river" that, in his words, "should-be-and-is-not." *Jerusalem River Project: Sound of Flowing River in the Dry Wadi of Abu Tor* (1970), responded to the real and unconscious need for "a wet element in the landscape of Jerusalem." The activity began when Neustein, working with Gerry Marx and Georgette Battle, traveled throughout Israel to tape-record the sounds of water flowing from all of the country's natural water sources. Then Neustein searched for a source for an electrical outlet in the dry mountain valley outside of Jerusalem so that the sounds they had recorded could be played over the land. Neustein found the convent of St. Claire Monastery and approached the nuns, explaining that he needed electricity for an art work. The women refused to let him use their convent as a source for art, but when he further explained that the piece was about water flowing over the dry valley, they responded enthusiastically and immediately cooperated.

The artists then laid electrical cord over the hillside to which, at various points, they attached sty-rofoam cups to function as loud-speakers. The electrical wires followed the bed of the valley and ended at the Valley of Kidron. The piece was two kilo-meters in length, and its width extended as far as the sound emitted from the Styrofoam cups could be heard. After installing the piece, Neustein and his col-laborators returned home planning the next day to return to begin playing the piece. That night he was violently awakened by the Israeli police who had been called to investigate the wire strewn all over the val-ley outside of Jerusalem. Only three years after the Six Day War, inexplicable objects — especially elec-trical wire in the hills outside of Jerusalem — seemed intentionally provocative. The authorities had been alerted to the potential threat of explosives. In their frantic search for bombs, the police had crushed the installation, which had to be reconstructed. While the poetry of a river of sound was ostensibly the theme of *Jerusalem River Project* the artists unintentionally evoked political tensions between Israel and its neighbors over vital resources. These latter meanings accrued to the work from the lived context of the installation.

The theme of war and its relation to somatic circumstance appears in many guises in Neustein's work. In *The Sound of Pine Cones Opening in the Sun* (1973), Neustein commemorated the Yom Kippur War in Israel that broke out on the holy Day of

201. John Cage and Daniel Charles, For the Birds: John Cage in Conversation with Daniel Charles (Boston and London: Marion Boyars, 1981), 80.

202. "Cage always had strong reservations about Al. He was senstive to the physical energy and movement in him. But in those days silence in which nothing happened was golden," Kaprow explained in a conversation with me, 12 November 1996, at State College, Pennsylvania.

203. Jimmy Breslin, "The Happening of a Lifetime", A2.

**Joshua Neustein**, *Territorial Imperative, 1976-78*

Atonement. This piece evolved from his actions and thoughts immediately prior to departing for military duty. During those hours, Neustein gathered up from his backyard what he referred to as the "fall" — a term that conflated the season of the year with the fallen soldiers of war. The collection of materials — pine needles, cones, and branches — was done with the proviso that after the war he would separate the materials and exhibit them. The war as an intervening element was crucial to the conception and exhibition of the piece. When he returned to civilian life in December 1973, he installed the work, including the tape-recorded sound of pine cones ejecting their seeds as they opened. This poetic natural sound, like the sound of the "fantasy river" in *Jerusalem River Project*, provoked a memory of nature in transition as much as it signified the destructive sound of culture, the distant sound of gun-fire and the fall of bodies over territories mapped by authority.

Deemphasizing his intentionality in order to highlight viewers' perceptions, Neustein systematically avoided drawing parallels between his works and his life. Without denying the inevitability of self-expression, he stressed place, reception, and context. Neustein's facility for hiding the body — even while simultaneously presenting and using his

body — is clarified when one learns that until he was six-years-old, the artist and his family were displaced Jews, wandering Europe during the aftermath of World War II:

> Living in basements as a child with my parents, . . . it was dark, safe and confined. The light was laden with danger and still one looked to it as essential to survival, like a breath of air. I remember . . . subterranean light was another light, a powdered haze that blurred more than defined.[204]

A Polish, Jewish, American who spends part of his life living and working in Israel, Neustein's ethnic identity and his art bespeaks, and has mapped, a diasporic consciousness made visual in art and expressive of a state of mind and body in which most of the world now lives. "Neustein's art is deterritorial, political, and collective (it has an 'active solidarity in spite of skepticism' with [art history])."[205]

In 1976, Neustein began a series of actions — *Territorial Imperative* — that demarcated points of violent international boundary dispute. He first visited the Golan Heights, Israeli/Syrian border (1976), then Belfast, Northern Ireland (1977), Kassel, East/West border (1977), and Krusa, German/Danish border (1978) with a male dog that urinated on the land at each site. Neustein photographed the animal in its

204. Joshua Neustein, in conversation with D. Schultz (1992), as quoted in Neustein, Tzaig and Grossman in the National Library Archives (Vienna:

Venice Biennale and The Israeli Pavilion, 1995), 28.

205. Jeannette Ingberman, "The Road

Not Taken . . . ", in Joshua Neustein (New York: Exit Art, 1987), 5.

**Bonnie Sherk** (with Howard Levine), *Portable Parks II*, June 1970

**Bonnie Sherk**, *Public Lunch*, Lion House, San Francisco Zoo, February 1971

act and created a series of posters with its image and the words "Territorial Imperative" stamped on the poster. Neustein then created a map of the area which showed the territory marked by the dog next to the political territory marked by nations. Neustein juxtaposed the instinctual habit of male animals to make territories with the distinctive odor of their bodily excretions, with the extension of these primal acts into command and control over territory through powerful technological means.

**Crossroads**[206]  Crossroads Community, better known as "The Farm," was a functioning farm and art space in San Francisco from 1974 until 1980. Founded and directed by Bonnie Sherk, its President, The Farm was a "multicultural art and life center" located at 144 Potrero Avenue adjacent to the main freeway interchange leading up to San Francisco and across into its southernmost districts, Potrero Hill, Bernal Heights, and the Mission. Sherk described her project in 1977 as a vehicle for connecting "physical and conceptual fragments," a place of unity despite age, race, class, cultural background, and, finally, species. The Farm presented a "strong, visual contrast to the technological monolith of the freeway" graphically framing life. In its programs, The Farm created a dialogue with governmental systems and Sherk was successful in "persuading the city of San

Francisco to acquire the acres of open space, land bordered by the Farm buildings and a public elementary school, leasing a strip of land immediately next to the freeway from the state for 4H gardens, and gaining access to city land directly in the middle of the freeway complex for park and garden purposes."[207] Describing herself as an environmental performance sculptor whose work includes the development of public and sometimes participatory site-specific works, Sherk integrated her actions and programs into a whole experience.

Before creating "The Farm", Sherk collaborated with Howard Levine on creating situations in which she intervened in the urban landscape. In *Portable Parks* (1970), they installed living environments (containing such things as sod, palm trees, and cattle) on various concrete sites in San Francisco. *Public Lunch* took place in the San Francisco Zoo. In February, 1971, she sat eating her lunch (catered by a well-known San Francisco restaurant) in the feeding cage, an action for which she had prepared by familiarizing the animals in the next cage with her presence. This was a "key piece that triggered her further explorations into ecology . . . investigating the natural relationships between plants and animals." Sherk explained that *Public Lunch* actually came out of an experience she had in New York in 1970 when she was awarded "Woman of the Year" by

206. Linda Burnham, "Between the Diaspora and the Crinoline: Bonnie Sherk Interviewed by Linda Burnham,"   High Performance 15 (1981): 49-50. All quotes unless otherwise cited come from this remarkable and inspiring interview.   207. Bonnie Sherk, "Bonnie Sherk," Data 27 (July-September 1977): 67.

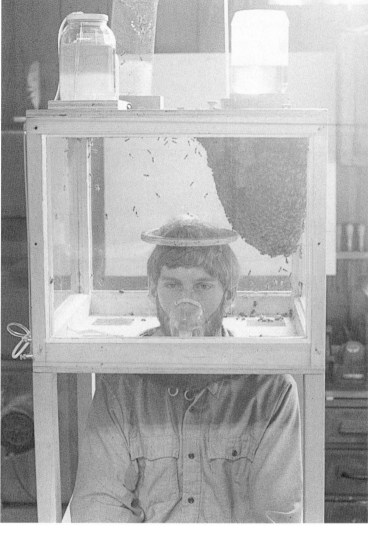

*Mademoiselle* magazine and, while living at the Waldorf-Astoria, realized how much "waste and ceremony" she experienced. After *Public Lunch*, she began working regularly with animals, merging her interests in performance, ecology, and installation.

Perhaps the best way to think about Bonnie Sherk's work is in cosmogonic terms. She has considered not only the problem of origins, or the coming into being of worlds, but she has created worlds for the needs of others. In a manner that recalls Harvard psychologist and feminist Carol Gilligan's famous research on the ways in which women's care-taking ethics are formed on a basis of emphatic extension to and with others, Sherk has continually performed a nurturing role.

**Everyone of the sun's rays** *carries with it bees. Then everything starts buzzing and one's head is a hive, the hive of the sounds of the sun.*
— Gaston Bachelard, *The Poetics of Space*

Mark Thompson began his *Live-In Hive* project in 1976. He imagined the hive as a shared living situation centered around, and inspired by, Gaston Bachelard's poetic connection between the energy of the sun, space, life as expressed in the action of bees, and the phenomenological conditions of human experience. Thompson constructed a glass-walled beehive that would permit him to live with his head inside the hive for twenty-one continuous days. This structure enabled the honeybees to have free access to the outside and to move around in the hive, drawing out wax combs, and carrying on their normal hive activities in relation to the artist's head. Through the three week period that Thompson envisioned living in the hive, he planned to have an automated, single-frame motion picture camera record the changing visual space around his head as the honeybees filled the hive with comb. At one point he also considered redesigning the hive for a more suitable living environment in which his body would float in a saline solution with waste discharged through a filtration system, while his head would have been centered in a sixteen-foot long, fifteen-inch square, corridor with the bees having free access to the outside through a wire mesh tube. He imagined that his diet would consist of water and liquid protein food. Along with the visual materials, the artist planned a sound recording

of his impressions and dreams during the three-week period. At the end of the period, the artist planned to make a sixteen-millimeter sound film determined by his experience of time during the twenty-one day period.

The *Live-In Hive* was a visionary project, partially realized at various points since its inception, when Thompson immersed his head in the hive for short periods of time. The very idea of immersion was also the subject of his film *Immersion*, shot between 1977 and 1978 with the artist Reese Williams. This work, still unfinished, expressed the artist's concept of the nature of sculptural space, and its relation to his work with the bees. In *Immersion*, Thompson was concerned with visualizing (in an extended, filmic exploration) the nature of physical and psychological space both in terms of the conditions of matter, and as matter/space/time generated by thousands of flying honeybees. The concluding segment of the film records the actual immersion of Thompson's head into this particle space with the swarm of honeybees slowly covering him. In order to induce the honeybees to swarm about his head, he placed the queen in a small cage carefully pinned to his hair. The bees swarmed to protect the queen creating long, heavy masses of rapidly moving insects clinging to each other that eventually covered his head and shoulders as if in chainmail.

In order to capture his vision of particle space, Thomspon was careful to use a shooting speed related to the changing intensity of the honeybee flight activity. The film begins with empty, blue sky, shot at twenty-four frames per second, and gradually changes to two frames per second as the flight activity intensified. Finally he slowed the camera speed to 150 frames per second, as the bees clustered and formed chains around his head. At the moment his head was fully covered, the filming speed returned to twenty-four frames per second, a normal viewing frame.

I cannot emphasize enough how Thompson's own living and working environment was/is intrinsic to the *Live-In Hive* itself. For the artist never conceived of his work in any of the categories that have subsequently been ascribed to the broad intersection of experimental practices (conceptual /installation/ body/ecological, etc.) at the end of the 1960s out of which his own art emerged. The *Live-In Hive* was

**Gideon Gechtman**, *Shaved Nude*, 1974. Collection of the artist

never intended as a public performance, or "body art," but rather was part of his research and ongoing relationship with honeybees. For Thompson is a beekeeper, caring for his bees year round, harvesting their honey and comb, and making special labels for the jars of honey he gives to friends or sells. In order to get a sense of Thompson's experience, try to imagine the *Live-In Hive* as part of a lived environment with all of the sensual qualities that filled that space: the humming sounds of the bees; the golden semi-transparent color of the honey, the pollen, the combs, and the bees themselves; the fragrant scent that filled the old warehouse with its soft filtered light; the constant movement of the honeybees inside and out-of-doors where they constantly traveled through mesh tunnels where one might observe their constant labor, and the warmth they seem to generate. It was a space of great comfort, quiet, and safety where one felt in harmony not only with nature but with the industry just outside the door. For in 1976, when Thompson gave the *Live-In Hive* its first trial, it was in his studio and living space in Howard Terminal — a railroad and shipping area on the Oakland docks. Envisioning such a place, with the artist in his daily routine living with the bees in a completely symbiotic way, one may better approach the vital relationship between Thompson's life and the species he studies.

**Between the Real and Somewhere Else**
Gideon Gechtman had open heart surgery to replace a heart-valve in April 1973. After his recovery, the Alexandrian born, Israeli artist carried out a documentation of his operation, which he exhibited in 1974. During the exhibition, the artist staged the shaving of his body in the gallery at the same time that he amplified the sound of his heart beating with the artificial valve. The exhibition included photographs of the artist before and after the shaving, a series of boxes each containing shaved hair from head, underarm, public hair, and so forth, jars with the medications he took for his illness and operation, containers of his urine under which he displayed charts showing the quantities and varieties of foods he had ingested during the day, chest x-rays, photographs of his chest scar, photographs of the attending physicians, and other relics related to the operation. In 1979, Gechtman created his *Shaving Hair* action, a performance in which he cut his hair publicly and made a brush from it.[208] Earlier, he had made brushes from his wife and son's hair: direct and poignant references to the Holocaust permeate Gechtman's work, family history, and memory.

Even before his operation, Gechtman proposed a series of "conceptual" works in November 1971. In *Mausoleum for Ten Anonymous People*, the artist imagined selecting ten anonymous people and relating to each as if s/he were a "famous military commander or emperor, down to the smallest details — including objects connected with their lives — and placing these in the framework of the familiar tradition of immortalization." Then in January 1972, Gechtman exhibited himself as "a living portrait." With his head shaved, he sat before a series of life-size rubber casts of his head, that had been cast from a model, painted red and positioned before the rows of death-mask-like sculptures. Immediately following his exhibition, "Exposures," the artist published obituary notices announcing his death in local newspapers. Gechtman later reprinted and posted the same obituary notice on colored paper, on large plywood advertising signs, in fluorescent light (flashing in blue to the rhythm of his heartbeats), and embroi-

208. In my essay, "Shaved Heads and Marked Bodies," op. cit., I comment extensively on the practice of shaving heads as an image of subordination, humiliation, and trauma. See also the biblical traditions in Isaiah 3:16-26, for example, or Deuteronomy 21:10-14.

**322**

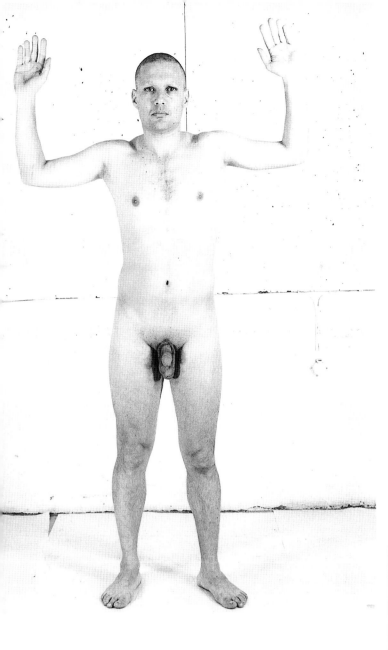

**Gideon Gechtman**, *Brushes*, 1974-79

Stelarc, *Street Suspension*, Mo David Gallery, New York, 21 July 1984

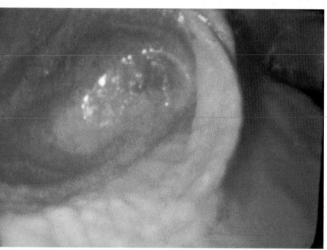

dered on a satin *parocheth* (the cloth curtain over the "ark" where Torah scrolls are kept in synagogue). Unraveling the relations between the real, the documentary, the ficitive, and the artificial, Gechtman explores the infinite ways in which life and death are simulated in the various institutions and practices of knowledge and being, simulations that create a mausoleum of life itself. Finally, "Exposures" and *Mausoleum* offer a profound consideration of the place of death in Jewish history, and the replacement of death in postmodern society. Gechtman's art is cosmoramic, exhibiting and illuminating the real by reproducing it somewhere else.

In this regard, Stelarc's art is equally cosmographic. In 1972, Stelarc (b. Stelios Arcadiou) made color videos of the inside of his stomach, bowels, and lungs. To make such images, he swallowed a telemetering capsule containing a camera. The procedure required an injection to prevent the stomach from rejecting the foreign object and then the spraying of

his throat with local anesthetic to numb the feeling. Stelarc's first successful stretched skin suspension took place in Tokyo in 1976. In Stelarc's suspensions, the artist had large fish- or meat-hooks inserted into his skin, supported by cables and pulleys by which his body was hoisted and suspended in space. Such rudimentary experiments represented the first steps in his aim to design a post-biological human body and further his research on artificial intelligence and robotics. Identifying the complex skeletal, muscular, and circulatory structures of human anatomy as incompatible with the information and technological environment created by humans — especially as demands to travel in outer space increase — Stelarc argued that electronic technology had rendered "The Body" intellectually and physically obsolete. When accused of "masochism," the artist responded: "This talk or emphasis on masochism in the context of what I'm doing is utterly, totally wrong. My events are involved with transcending normal human parame-

**324**

**Stelarc**, *Event for Lateral Suspension*, Tamura Gallery, Tokyo, 12 March 1978

Paul Neagu, *Ramp-Hyphen*, 5-10 December 1976

ters, including pain — to manifest an all-important concept."[209] Personally, I understand Stelarc's work to be a visionary corpus of research about the body on the body, even while the visualization of that research may be utterly disturbing to some to view, conjuring associations with masochism as a familiar narrative to explain the unknown or unimaginable. Moreover, his work is vulnerable to promotion and representation by those who do find pleasure in, or are fascinated by, masochism, in which case his own intentionality is only a part of the interpretive process.

Stelarc's suspensions were primarily research on the skin as a complex plastic membrane able to support and contain "The Body" in the computerized environments of the future. Other research the artist undertook included the amplification of his body sounds during suspensions as a means of gathering biofeedback (externalizing the internal structure of the body), and development of a prosthetic "third arm," a computerized robotic device controlled by bio-sensors. Stelarc understood these experiments to be prototypes for more invasive technology that would permit "The Body" to be implanted with electronic devices. In this regard, he envisioned the bionic artist of the future as an architect of internal body spaces and an evolutionary guide.

**Going Tornado**  Beginning at the age of about sixteen in 1954, Paul Neagu began to evolve a cosmological theory of aesthetics in drawings, assemblages, sculptures, writing, and, eventually performance. Organized around a trinity of forms, symbols, attributes, and behaviors, he divided his system of human evolution into three cycles, each with its own particular characteristics, beginning with

basic nature and progressing through levels of higher consciousness. These concepts originally appeared in the form of a humanoid figure, "Anthropocosmos," that transformed into the artist himself in actions, and were resolved in *Hyphen* — the form of connection between two principles or states, that dynamic commissure creating linkage and relationship.

In 1976, in an installation and performance, *Ramp-Hyphen*, Neagu summarized the three cycles. He performed an action in the midst of an installation of drawings and a large *Hyphen*, placed in the middle of the Serpentine Gallery in London. Neagu undertook the action with a female partner, Perry Robinson, who with her eyes blindfolded and standing against the gallery wall, marked the wall where she "felt" Neagu had landed after the artist ran and jumped, landing with his feet as high as possible on the wall (ramp). Each time Neagu jumped, Robinson felt the vibration of his impact and intuited its place, then marked it "blindly" on the wall. Neagu, in turn, marked each of his jumps on the inside of the *Hyphen* structure. When Neagu became too exhausted to execute the jump, Robinson began the performance, making the jumping and marking a reciprocal act. This was Neagu's last performance:

> I had come to believe that the essence of true performance could not be confined within the boundaries of "theatrical" arrangements, with audience and performers as separate categories, helplessly wishing for a common platform of understanding. With the same need for depth communication, the performer that I was and his gesture had to be felt from inside, so I discovered that this idea of the static and staring spectator gives a one-track communication much too shallow for my ardent ambitions. Thus

209. James D. Paffrath with Stelarc, *Obsolete Body/Suspensions/Stelarc* (Davis, California: JP Publication, 1983), 8.

210. Paul Neagu, "Gradually Going Ahead," Artscribe 16 (1979): 50, quoted in Overy, op. cit.

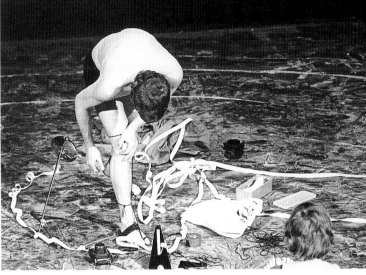

Paul Neagu, *Going Tornado*, Traverse Theatre, Edinburgh, February 1975

Paul Neagu, *Gradually Going Tornado*, Arnolfini Gallery, Bristol, March 1976

I decided to keep such impulses to myself and show to the public only a formalised record.[210]

That "formalised record" of Neagu's cosmology is the *Hyphen*. But before he stopped performing, Neagu had realized a number of performances based on his metaphysical system. They included *Blind Bite* (performed with variations in 1971, 1972 and 1975), *Horizontal Rain* (1973), *Going Tornado* (1975), and *Gradually Going Tornado* (1976). In each of these actions, Neagu conceived a total environmental relationship between physical and psychical existence.

*Hyphen* is the physical metaphor for all these transformative powers, and it bears the entire symbolic weight of Neagu's alternative epistemological, ontological, metaphysical, and aesthetic system. But *Hyphen* was also the result of a long process of art-making. The first form in which it appeared was a sculpture he titled *The Subject Generator* (1975). It consisted of a rectangular table-like surface (made of glass one-centimeter thick) supported by three wooden legs, two short and one extended from the middle out into space. Together the rectangular top, the triangular shape formed by the legs, and the fact that if the sculpture was rotated in space the long element would draw a circle meant that the triangle, rectangle, and element for spiralling were contained within one form. Moreover, on the glass surface of the table top, Neagu placed a magnifying glass, mirror, spotlight, snake, wooden board, gesso on canvas, a metal lamp, and a transformer. A 1974 pencil drawing of the object labeled, "The Subject," clearly offers evidence of the fact that the object is an anthropomorphic representation of the artist himself and the objects placed on its surface represent not only the "new subjects" but the elements of energy it "generates."

This drawing gives insight into the meaning of his work. By literally drawing a parallel between himself as artist and "The Subject," he suggests that the powers of generating art are likewise transfered to "The Subject." The agglomeration of standard art-making materials on its surface and the basic geometric shapes of its support structure are, then,

the materials for the generation of art. "The Subject" is a meta-art artwork: a work that embodies all the possibilities and preconditions for art.

In *Going Tornado*, the artist became a whirling dervish spinning like a gyroscope. Attached to his spining body, he fastened cultural baggage (his rolled up clothing) which he used as a kind of 'ballast' to enable him to spin faster. As he wrote, "The quasi-estatic character of a 'tornado' as culminative within the cycle is its expurgative and absorptive flow, that is to say it is an extravagant and wasteful disentanglement transcending everything which enters its whirls."[211] For the artist, *Gradually Going Tornado* signified "respect for physical life and spirit," at the same time as an appreciation of the "'supra-humane' dimensions . . . blend[ing] together EVOLUTION as forcible extraction, and REVOLUTION as sudden violent change of feeling."[212]

The *Hyphen* represents the condensation and displacement in sculptural form of Neagu's elaborate and complex system of energy, consciousness, and evolution. It began with organic life and moved through social life to quantum forces that metaphorically represented speeds that expand consciousness into a higher realm. Neagu has worked with a commitment to the belief that human existence on earth has a definite purpose to evolve, and that his role as an artist is to create forms in all media from drawing to action whereby in "reshaping a more suitable vehicle/body", society might arrive at a more constructive and "better understanding of the complex characteristics of the transformation of energy" through art.[213]

211. Paul Neagu, in Gradually Going Tornado! Paul Neagu and his Generative Art Group (Sunderland, England: Sunderland Arts Centre, 1975), 24.

212. Ibid., 27.

213. Ibid., 24.

**Paul Neagu**, *Gradually Going Tornado*, Arnolfini Gallery, Bristol, March 1976

**XI. Uncorrupted Joy** But what about uncorrupted joy? It is mine: pure and unalterable, inspired by the artists who have employed their bodies to redefine vision and to demonstrate how vital art is to the qualitative substance and conditions of every aspect of life. "I love what I'm . . . " Jim Dine wrote in his Happening, *The Smiling Workman* (1960), just before drinking the can of paint with which he was writing, and then crashing through the paper on which he wrote these words. Dine's language and acts depict a belief in the self as a subject — "I love what I am." — but they also portray an intimate understanding of the relationship between subjectivity and the objects that enable and constitute the subject.

Throughout this essay, I have described many instances of "anger" about the human condition presented and represented on the body and its objects. This fury is a condition of the post-Holocaust, post-atomic bomb, post-biological, post-modern world that carries with it not only the old sexism and racism and classism and ethnic divisions of the past, but the new "post" human condition. Action art is an aesthetic practice that specifically presents the most threatening and delighting conditions of human experience. I have described actions and action-objects as commissures, written about the artifactuality of objects, and proposed that action may become an object — all in an effort to persuade consideration of the idea that underlying the deep poetry and poignancy of action art is the recondite issue of relationality between subjects and objects, but more importantly between we human subjects ourselves. Action art is so difficult because it announces that intersubjectivity — that *Hyphen* — an interstice that these artists have identified and asked us to engage, drawing us into a dialogue that may threaten, repulse, dismay, or seduce; even as they educate and illuminate.

In this sense, artists who produce actions are, as Mark Boyle described them in August, 1967, "antennae of this multicellular organism humanity."

And he claimed that such persons were "not so much artists as feelers, not so much transmitters as receivers." By emphasizing the act of reception — *not* in the viewer, as is conventionally assumed, but in the artist, Boyle enunciated a major reversal in the subject/object relation inscribed in traditional art. I have theorized this new relation as an augmentation of the metaphorical capacities of conventional static forms of art with the communicative function of metonymy, wherein artists, as "receivers," visualize worlds of experience experienced, showing themselves as connected to what society itself transmits. Such artists "expand our ability to absorb" the world in new and different ways, as Boyle put it. As they do so, artists who make actions increasingly make themselves "unnecessary." Unnecessary, that is, Boyle concludes:

UNTIL IF WE'VE CAPACITY WE BECOME ONLY SENSITIVE BEINGS TOTALLY PERMANENTLY OPEN TO EVERYTHING WITHOUT THE FILTERING OF PSYCHOLOGICAL SHOCK BARRIERS OR THE DISTORTIONS OF INTELLIGENCE OR DRUGS DISCOVERING JUST HOW MUCH REALITY HUMAN KIND CAN BEAR.[214]

The question remains: How much reality can we bear? Whatever one's response, the artists who have made action art received, transmitted, and made visual more reality than we knew before their actions, creating new worlds, new cosmologies of human experience.

214. Mark Boyle, Journey to the Surface of the Earth: Mark Boyle's Atlas and Manual (Cologne, London, Reykjavik: Edition Hansjörg Mayer, 1970), unpaginated.

* I want to thank Paul Schimmel and Russell Ferguson for recognizing and believing in my work. Thanks also to Diane Aldrich, Kim Cooper, and Linda Genereux for all their assistance, and Mark D. Hasencamp who supported much of this research during another period of my life. Most of all I want to acknowledge my husband Edward Allen Shanken who repeatedly read, discussed, and edited this manuscript while also cooking, cleaning, and caring for me and our home during its seemingly endless gestation. For his loyal support, only love returned is adequate. This essay is excerpted from a much longer manuscript to be published as a book by the University of California Press.

**1943** "Jackson Pollock: Paintings and Drawings" (first solo exhibition). Art of This Century, N.Y.  9-27 November.

**1946** Jackson Pollock's first "allover" poured paintings. Late 1946-1947.

**1947** Yves Klein, first work on *Symphonie Monoton-Silence*, which will be completed in 1949.

**1949** Robert Rauschenberg makes a work with the imprints of students' feet as they walk through a doorway. The Art Students League, N.Y. Late summ

**1950** Hans Namuth films Jackson Pollock painting. September-October.

Shōzō Shimamoto begins *Hole* series. Japan.

**1955** Members of Zero Society join Gutai group collectively, at 7th Yomiuri Indépendant.Tokyo. Spring.

"Experimental Outdoor Exhibition of Modern Art to Challenge the Mid-summer Sun". Ashiya, Japan.

First exhibition of the Gutai Art Association. July.

First publication of *Gutai* journal, which will be produced through 1965. February.

Gutai group first shows work, signed collectively, at 7th Yomiuri Indépendant. Tokyo. Spring.

"Experimental Outdoor Exhibition of Modern Art to Challenge the Mid-summer Sun". Ashiya, Japan.

First exhibition of the Gutai Art Association. July.

First publication of *Gutai* journal, which will be produced through 1965.

**1956** "One Day Only Outdoor Exhibition (The Ruins)". Mukogawa River, Amagasaki, Japan. Gutai group event for *Life* magazine. 9 April.

Georges Mathieu paints *Hommage aux Poètes du Monde Entier*. Before an audience, on stage at Théâtre Sarah Bernhardt, Paris. 28 May.

Georges Mathieu paints *La Bataille de Hastings*. Prince's Gate Mews, London. Sponsored by Institute of Contemporary Arts. 23 June.

Festival d'art d'avant-garde. In Le Corbusier's Unité d'Habitation, Marseilles. Organized by Jacques Poliéri and Michel Ragon. Participants include Yves Klein and Jean Tinguely. August.

**1951** "Abstraction in Photography". The Museum of Modern Art, N.Y. Exhibition organized by Edward Steichen.

Robert Rauschenberg's and Susan Weill's *Blueprint: Photogram for Mural Decoration* (now titled *Female Figure*, ca. 1950) exhibited. 2 May – 4 July.

Hans Namuth's Pollock film debuts. The Museum of Modern Art, N.Y. 14 June.

**1952** John Cage organizes untitled event, later known as *Theater Piece No. 1*. Dining Hall, Black Mountain College, near Asheville, N.C. Participants include Merce Cunningham, Charles Olson, Robert Rauschenberg (whose white paintings are hung from the rafters), M.C. Richards, and David Tudor. Summer.

John Cage, *4'33"*. Woodstock, N.Y. Debut, performed by David Tudor. Late summer.

"A Retrospective Show of the Paintings of Jackson Pollock" (first retrospective exhibition). Bennington College, Bennington, Vermont, and touring to Lawrence Art Museum, Williams College, Williamstown, Mass. 17-30 November.

Formation of Zero Society (*Zero-kai*) by Akira Kanayama, Saburō Murakami, Kazuo Shiraga, and Atsuko Tanaka. Osaka, Japan.

**1953** Robert Rauschenberg and John Cage, *Automobile Tire Print*. Fulton Street, N.Y. Fall.

**1954** Georges Mathieu paints *La Bataille de Bouvines* (The Battle of the Bouvines) for the Salon of May. Château de la Muette, France. Filmed by Robert Descharnes. 25 April.

Georges Mathieu paints *Les Capétiens Partout*. Saint-Germain-en-Laye, France. 10 October.

Gutai Art Association formed in Ashiya, Kansai, Japan by Jirō Yoshihara. December.

Jackson Pollock dies in car accident, in which his passenger Edith Metzger is also killed. East Hampton, N.Y. 11 August.

Jirō Yoshihara writes *Gutai Manifesto*. October.

"2nd Gutai Art Exhibition". Ohara Kaikan Hall, Tokyo. Events include: Saburō Murakami, *At One Moment Opening Six Holes*; Shōzō Shimamoto, bottle throwing painting action; Kazuo Shiraga, *Challenging Mud* and foot painting demonstration; and Atsuko Tanaka wearing her *Electric Dress*. October.

**1957** Yves Klein, *Aerostatic Sculpture* (1,001 blue balloons released at exhibition opening) and performance of the *Symphonie Monoton*. Galerie Iris Clert, Paris. 10 May.

"Gutai Art on the Stage". Sankei Kaikan Hall, Osaka, Japan. May.

Yves Klein, *One Minute Fire Painting*. Galerie Colette Allendy, Paris. 14 May.

"Gutai Art on the Stage". Sankei Kaikan Hall, Tokyo. July.

Georges Mathieu paints twenty-one canvases in three days, including *La Bataille de Gowa* and *La Bataille d'Hakata* (Galerie Shirokiya, Tokyo), and *L'Hommage au Général Hideyoshi* (public performance, Osaka). Japan. September.

The Gutai group's first stage performance is discussed in Sunday art section, *The New York Times*. 8 September.

Hermann Nitsch begins developing idea of the Orgien Mysterien Theater, a six-day multi-media festival.

Yayoi Kusama moves to New York.

**1958** Allan Kaprow, *Untitled* (environment with sound and light). Hansa Gallery, N.Y. 11 – 29 March.

"Patriotism and the American Home," panel discussion moderated by Frederick Kiesler. Eighth Street Club, N.Y. Panelists include Allan Kaprow and Robert Rauschenberg. 17 March.

Allan Kaprow, *Untitled* (Happening). Douglass College, Rutgers University, New Brunswick, N.J. 15 April.

Yves Klein, "Le vide" (exhibition). Galerie Iris Clert, Paris. 28 April.

*Twenty-five Year Retrospective Concert of the Music of John Cage*. Town Hall, N.Y. Organized by Emile de Antonio, Jasper Johns, and Robert Rauschenberg. Music selected by David Tudor, conducted by Merce Cunningham. Exhibition of Cage scores held concurrently at Stable Gallery, N.Y. 15 May.

Yves Klein, *The Anthropometries of the Blue Period*. Robert Godet's apartment, Paris. Spring.

Georges Mathieu paints *La Bataille de Brunkeberg* before an audience. Musée Hallwylska, Stockholm. 23 July.

Red Grooms, *A Play Called Fire* (Happening). Sun Gallery, Provincetown, Mass. August-September.

Yves Klein in collaboration with Jean Tinguely, "Vitesse pure et stabilité monochrome" (exhibition). Galerie Iris Clert, Paris. November.

Allan Kaprow, *Untitled* (environment with sound, light and odors). Hansa Gallery, N.Y. 25 November-13 December.

Jean-Jacques Lebel, *Movie* (Happening). Ibiza. Date unknown.

**1959** Georges Mathieu paints *Hommage au Connétable de Bourbon*.

Fleischmarkt Theater, Vienna. With live musical accompaniment by Pierre Henry. 2 April.

Jean-Jacques Lebel, *Conception surréaliste du monde* (conference demonstration). Centre française d'études et d'information, Milan. 28 April.

Allan Kaprow, *Intermission Piece* (sound happening). Reuben Gallery, N.Y. 11 June.

Wolf Vostell, *Fernseh-de-coll/age für millionen*. Cologne. August–September.

Red Grooms, *The Walking Man* (Happening). Sun Gallery, Provincetown, Mass. September.

"8th Gutai Art Exhibition". Kyoto Municipal Museum of Art, Japan. September.

Allan Kaprow, *18 Happenings in 6 Parts*. Reuben Gallery, N.Y. Participants include: Sam Francis, Red Grooms, Dick Higgins, Jasper Johns, Robert Rauschenberg, Lucas Samaras, George Segal, and Robert Whitman, among others. 4 and 6-10 October.

George Brecht, *Towards Events — An Arrangement* (assemblage objects with instructions for performances). Reuben Gallery, N.Y. 16 October–5 November.

Gustav Metzger publishes his first manifesto, *Auto-Destructive Art*. 4 November.

Nam June Paik, *Hommage à John Cage: Music for Tape Recorder and Piano*. Galerie 22, Düsseldorf. 13 November.

Red Grooms, *The Burning Building* (Happening). Delancey Street Museum, 148 Delancey Street, N.Y. 4-11 December.

Georges Mathieu paints *Macumba* (before an audience, Museu de Arte, Rio de Janeiro), *Le Massacre de la Saint-Barthélemy* (with live musical accompaniment, television studio, Paris), and *Hommage au Général San Martin* (before an audience, Buenos Aires). Dates unknown.

Hermann Nitsch begins writing his unfinished *a lust play*, the stage directions of which call for a butchered bull to be hung on the stage.

**1960** Reuben Gallery, N.Y. Allan Kaprow, *Four Evenings* (Happenings); Red Grooms, *The Magic Train Ride* (changed from *Fireman's Dream*); Allan Kaprow, *The Big Laugh* (changed from *January Happening*); and Robert Whitman, *Small Cannon*. 8-11 January.

"Ray-Gun" (two-artist exhibition: Jim Dine, *The House*; Claes Oldenburg, *The Street*). Judson Gallery, Judson Memorial Church, N.Y. 30 January-17 March.

Jean-Jacques Lebel, *Poésie Directe et Jazz*. Galerie 55, Paris. With Gregory Corso and Max Harstein. 20 February.

*Ray Gun Spex*. Judson Gallery, N.Y. Happenings include: Jim Dine, *The Smiling Workman* (performed in the environment of *The House*); Al Hansen, *Projections*; Dick Higgins, *Edifices, Cabarets & Einschlusz*; Allan Kaprow, *Coca-Cola, Shirley Cannonball?*; Claes Oldenburg, *Snapshots from the City* (performed in the environment of *The Street*); and Robert Whitman, *Duet for a Small Smell*. 29 February–2 March.

Yves Klein, *Anthropométries de l'Époque Bleue* (performance). Galérie internationale d'art contemporain, Paris. 9 March.

Gustav Metzger publishes second manifesto, *Manifesto Auto-Destructive Art*. 10 March.

*A Concert of New Music*, program arranged by Nicola Cernovich and James Waring. The Living Theatre, N.Y. Works by George Brecht, John Cage, Al Hansen, Ray Johnson, Allan Kaprow, and Robert Rauschenberg, among others. 14 March.

Jean Tinguely, *Homage to New York*. Sculpture garden, The Museum of Modern Art, N.Y. Tinguely's kinetic sculpture accompanied by Robert Rauschenberg's *Money Thrower for Tinguely's H.T.N.Y.* 17 March.

Dick Higgins, *Saint Joan at Beaurevoir*. The Players Theater, N.Y. 21 March.

*Anti-Procès* (collage happening-theater-music). Galerie des Quatre Saisons, Paris. Organized by Jean-Jacques Lebel. 29 April-9 May.

**1960** (cont'd) *A Program of Happenings? Events! & Situations?*, directed by Al Hansen. Memorial Hall, Pratt Institute, N.Y. Music and performances by George Brecht, Al Hansen, Allan Kaprow, and Jackson Mac Low, among others. 2 May.

Claes Oldenburg, *The Street* (revised version of installation at Judson Gallery). Reuben Gallery, N.Y. 16-19 May.

Gustav Metzger develops technique for painting on nylon with acid. London. June.

"New Media — New Forms in Painting and Sculpture". Martha Jackson Gallery, N.Y. Group exhibition, seventy-one artists including: George Brecht, Jim Dine, Red Grooms, Allan Kaprow, Claes Oldenburg, Robert Rauschenberg, and Robert Whitman. Catalogue. 6-24 June.

Piero Manzoni unrolls his *Line 18 Metres Long*. In Nicolaj Plads, Copenhagen. 10 June.

An Evening of Sound Theatre — Happenings. Reuben Gallery, N.Y. Events include: George Brecht, *Gossoon* (a chamber event); Jim Dine, *The Vaudeville Show* (happening); Allan Kaprow, *Intermission Piece* (Happening); Richard Maxfield, *Electronic Music*; and Robert Whitman, *E.G.* (an opera). 11 June.

*Anti-Procès 2*. Galleria il Canale, Venice. Organized by Jean-Jacques Lebel, Alain Jouffroy and S. Rusconi. 18 June.

Gustav Metzger's first lecture/demonstration, *Auto-Destructive Art*. Temple Gallery, London. 22 June.

Piero Manzoni executes *Line 7,200 Metres Long*. Herning Avis Printing House, Herning, Denmark. 4 July.

Jean-Jacques Lebel, *L'Enterrement de la chose de Tinguely* (Happening). Palazzo Contarini-Corfou, Venice. 14 July.

Piero Manzoni, "Consumazione dell'arte dinamica del pubblico, divorare l'arte" (exhibition-event). Galleria Azimut, Milan. 21 July.

Wolf Vostell, *Plakat Phasen* (dé-coll/age action). Plaza de Cataluña, Barcelona. August.

*New Music* (concert). The Living Theatre, N.Y. Works by Al Hansen, Dick Higgins, Ray Johnson, Larry Poons, Jackson Mac Low, among others. Sponsored by New York Audiovisual Group. 1 August.

**1961** Jim Dine, *Rainbow Thoughts* (environment). Judson Gallery, Judson Memorial Church, N.Y. January.

Series of concerts organized by La Monte Young at Yoko Ono's loft, 112 Chambers Street, N.Y. Performances, dance and music by Jackson Mac Low, Robert Morris, and La Monte Young, among others. January-June.

Piero Manzoni, *Living Work of Art* and *Living Sculptures*. Studio Filmgiornale Sedi, Milan. Filmed by Gianpaolo Macentelli. 13 January.

Niki de Saint Phalle stages the first of more than a dozen shooting actions which will be held through 1962. In a vacant lot behind the artist's studio, 11 Impasse Ronsin, Paris. Spectators include Pierre Restany, Daniel Spoerri, and Jean Tinguely. 12 February.

Claes Oldenburg, *Circus (Ironworks/Fotodeath)* (two-part Happening, including *Pickpocket* slide presentation during intermission). Reuben Gallery, N.Y. 21-26 February.

Niki de Saint Phalle, second shooting action. Impasse Ronsin, Paris. 26 February.

Series of *Literary Evenings and Musica Antiqua et Nova Concerts: Festival of Electronic Music and Concert of New Sounds and Noises*. AG Gallery, N.Y. Sponsored by *Bread &* literary magazine and AG Gallery. Works by John Cage, Dick Higgins, Jackson Mac Low, Robert Morris, Yvonne Rainer, among others. March-July.

Georges Mathieu paints *Le Grand Dauphin*. Action is then broadcast on French television. 15 August.

Robert Filliou, *L'Imortelle mort du monde* (auto-theater). Paris. September.

Günter Brus clears his studio at Ayrenhoffgasse 10, Vienna, puts primed packing paper on all surfaces, and begins painting in three dimensions. Autumn.

"New Media — New Forms in Painting and Sculpture, Version II". Martha Jackson Gallery, N.Y. Group exhibition, seventy-two artists including: George Brecht, Jim Dine, Red Grooms, Allan Kaprow, Claes Oldenburg, Robert Rauschenberg, Robert Whitman. 28 September-22 October.

Gustav Metzger gives a lecture/demonstration at Heretics Society, Trinity College, Cambridge. Organized by Ian Sommerville and attended by William Burroughs and Brion Gysin. October.

Gustav Metzger shows his acid painting to Lucio Fontana at Temple Gallery, London. October.

Nam June Paik, *Étude for Pianoforte*. Atalier Mary Bauermeister, Cologne. 6 October.

Festival d'avant-garde, Palais des Expositions, Pavillon américain, Porte de Versailles, Paris. During "Nouveaux Realistes" group exhibition, Yves Klein creates *Anthropometry of the New Realists* with the imprints of Arman, Hains, Raysse, Restant, and Tinguely. Also, Daniel Spoerri's first *Tableaux-piège* (snare pictures) exhibited. 18 November-15 December.

Jim Dine, *Car Crash* (Happening). Reuben Gallery, N.Y. 1–6 November.

Hermann Nitsch, exhibition with Fritz Kindl. Loyalty-club, Vienna. Nitsch shows his Rinnbilder paintings and *Kleiner Existenzalter*. 3 November-early December.

Hermann Nitsch, *1st Painting Action*. Nitsch's studio in the Technical Museum, Vienna. 18 November.

Yves Klein, *Le Journal d'un seul jour, Dimanche* (four-page newspaper, featuring photograph of Klein leaping into the void, and signifying the artist's appropriation of all human activities on the planet that day). 27 November.

Robert Whitman, *The American Moon* (theater piece). Reuben Gallery, N.Y. 29 November–7 December.

Allan Kaprow, *An Apple Shrine* (environment). Judson Gallery, Judson Memorial Church, N.Y. 30 November-24 December.

*Christmas Varieties*. Happenings include: Jim Dine, *Shining Bed*; Simone Morris [Forti], *See Saw* and *Rollers*; and Claes Oldenburg, *Blackouts*: (in four parts; "Chimneyfires," "Erasers," "The Vitamin Man," and "Butter and Jam"). Reuben Gallery, N.Y. 16-20 December.

Robert Filliou with Peter Cohen, *Performance Piece for a Lonely Person in a Public Place*. Performed several times in Paris, circa 1960.

Al Hansen, *Hi-Ho Bibbe* (Happening). Pratt Institute, N.Y. Date unknown.

Georges Mathieu paints *L'Entrée de Louis XIII et de la Reine Anne D'Autriche dans Paris le 14 Mai 1616 À leur retour de Bordeaux* before an audience. Château de Courances, France. Date unknown.

Hermann Nitsch writes his *1st Abreaction Play*. Two more such plays follow in 1961 and 1962.

Niki de Saint Phalle makes her first "target" pictures. Paris.

**1962** (cont'd) "Art in Motion". Stedelijk Museum, Amsterdam; Moderna Museet, Stockholm. Exhibition
includes Allan Kaprow's *Stockroom* (environment consisting of instructions only). March-
September.

Otto Muehl rents cellar studio at No. 1 Perinetgasse, Vienna. This will be the site of many of the most
important Aktionist performances. March.

Hermann Nitsch, *2nd Painting Action*. Nitsch's studio in the Technical Museum, Vienna. 10 March.

Niki de Saint Phalle, shooting action. As part of "Bewogen Beweging" exhibition. Stedelijk Museum,
Amsterdam. 12 March.

Allan Kaprow, *A Spring Happening*. Reuben Gallery, N.Y. 22-27 March.

"Geist und Form". Union building of the Catholic students, No. 8 Eberndorferstr., Vienna. Participants
include Günter Brus, Hermann Nitsch, and Alfons Schilling, among others. April.

Robert Whitman, *Mouth* (theatre piece). Reuben Gallery, N.Y. 18-23 April.

Piero Manzoni, *Living Sculpture* (exhibition/performance). Galleria La 334 Tartaruga, Rome. 22 April.

Hermann Nitsch, *3rd Painting Action*. Nitsch's studio in the Technical Museum, Vienna. 25 April.

Piero Manzoni, *Living Works of Art* (numerous authentication actions). Milan. 30 April-6 May.

Otto Muehl alters his paintings by slitting canvases, smashing frames, and integrating objects.
Creates room-sized installation of tied-and-nailed-together pictures, *The Overcoming of the Easel
Picture by the Representation of its Destruction Process*. May.

Allan Kaprow, *Chapel* (environment) and *The Night* (or *A Happening for Ann Arbor*). Open House
61 festival, University of Michigan, Ann Arbor. 12-13 May.

Ben Patterson, *Situationen für 3 Klaviere, duo für Stimme und Streicher, Komposition für Papier,
Dé-Coll/Ages solo für Wolf Vostell*. Cologne. 14 May.

Günter Brus and Alfons Schilling joint exhibition. Galerie Junge Generation,
Vienna. 23 May-10 June.

Niki de Saint Phalle, tir shooting event. Staket sandpit, near Wik on
Värmdö, Sweden. As part of touring exhibition "Bewogen Beweging",
retitled "Rörelse i konsten", Moderna Museet, Stockholm.
Participants include Robert Rauschenberg. 23 May.

Yoko Ono, *A Grapefruit in the World of Park, A Piece for Strawberries and Violin*, and *AOS — to
David Tudor*. Carnegie Recital Hall, N.Y. Concert with sound and movement by George Brecht,
Philip Corner, Jackson Mac Low, Yvonne Rainer, and La Monte Young, among others. 24 November.

Claes Oldenburg, *The Store*, revised version of installation of reliefs shown at Martha Jackson
Gallery in May. Ray-Gun Mfg. Co., 107 East Second Street, N.Y., in cooperation with Green
Gallery, N.Y. 1 December-January 1962.

Alfons Schilling moves to Paris. Buys electric motor and begins constructing rotating two-meter disks
for painting. December 1961-January 1962.

"The Hall of Issues I" (exhibitions and actions for everyone). Hall of Issues, N.Y. Artists include
Allan Kaprow. 3 December-March 1962.

"Environments, Situations, Spaces". Martha Jackson Gallery and David Anderson Gallery, N.Y.
Group exhibition, including: George Brecht, *Iced Dice* (event); Jim Dine, *Spring Cabinet* (environment);
    Walter Gaudnek, *Unlimited Dimensions* (event); Allan Kaprow, *Yard* (environment); Claes
    Oldenburg, *The Store* (environment); and Robert Whitman, *Untitled* (environment). Catalogue.
    25 May-23 June.
*Homage to David Tudor*. Théâtre de l'Ambassade des États-Unis, Paris. Organized by Darthea
    Speyer. Simultaneous performance events by Robert Rauschenberg, Niki de Saint Phalle
    (assisted by a marksman), Jean Tinguely, David Tudor, and featuring static contributions from
    Jasper Johns. 20 June.
Niki de Saint Phalle, shooting action. Impasse Ronsin, Paris. 26 June.
"Feu à volonté". Niki de Saint Phalle exhibition with audience-participation shooting actions.
    Galerie J, Paris. Organized by Pierre Restany. 28 June (opening), 30 June-12 July.
Robert Filliou, *Poi-Poi* (environment/play). Galerie Køpcke, Copenhagen. June-September.

           Gustav Metzger demonstrates Auto-Destructive Art on the South Bank, London. His third
               manifesto, *Auto-Destructive Art, Machine Art, Auto Creative Art*, dated 23 June, is given out to
               spectators. 3 July.
           "Who Is Who". Vienna Secession. Anonymously-hung exhibition, organized by Hans Staudacher.
               Participants include Günter Brus, Otto Muehl, and Alfons Schilling. 11-23 July.
           Hermann Nitsch, *4th Painting Action*. Nitsch's studio, No. 7 Mitterhofergasse, Vienna. 12 July.
           Niki de Saint Phalle, shooting action. At Abbaye Roseland, for opening of Festival of Nouveaux
               Réalistes, Galerie Muratore, Nice. Organized by Pierre Restany. 13 July.
           Niki de Saint Phalle and Jean Tinguely construct life-sized paper and plaster bull which explodes
               during fireworks display honoring Salvador Dalí. Arena, Figueras, Spain. August.
           Wolf Vostell, *Cityrama 1*. Galerie Schwarz Mailand. 15 September.
           Nam June Paik, *Simple* (presented as part of *Action Music* program). Liljevalchs Konsthall,
               Stockholm. 18 September.
           Daniel Spoerri, *L'épicerie* (installation). Galerie Addi Køpcke, Copenhagen. 28 September-
                     28 October.
                    *9 Evenings: Theatre & Engineering*. 25th Street Armory, N.Y. Presented by The Foundation for
                       Contemporary Performance Arts Inc., in cooperation with Experiments in Art and Technology, Inc.
                       Includes works by John Cage, Yvonne Rainer, Robert Rauschenberg, David Tudor, and Robert
                       Whitman, among others. 13-23 October.
                  Piero Manzoni, "Artist's Shit, Living Works of Art" (exhibition). Galerie Køpcke, Copenhagen. 18
                     October.
                  Karlheinz Stockhausen, *Originale*, featuring Nam June Paik. Theater am Dom, Cologne. 26 October.
                  Piero Manzoni, *Living Work of Art* (action). Angli Shirt Factory, Herning, Denmark. November.
                  Otto Muehl shows junk sculptures for first time as part of group exhibition at Galerie Junge
                     Generation, Vienna. 20 November-10 December.

**1962** (cont'd) "4 Kreuzwegstationen und Theoretische Manifestation. Die Kunst als Religionsgleiche Mystiche Auseinandersetzung mit der Existenz". Hermann Nitsch exhibition. Galerie Fuchs, Vienna. 4-20 December.

Robert Whitman, *Ball* (theater piece). Green Gallery, N.Y. 29-30 December and 2-6 January 1962.

Dick Higgins, *Danger Music*. Judson Church, N.Y.

*Anti-Procès 3*. Galleria Brera, Milan. Organized by Jean-Jacques Lebel and Alain Jouffroy.

Date unknown.

George Brecht, *Dithyramb* (music and objects). Henry Street Playhouse, N.Y. Presented by James Waring and Dance Company. 5 January.

Hermann Nitsch, *5th painting action*. Studio, Brunnerstr. 132, Vienna. 15 January.

Marriage of Yves Klein and Rotraut Uecker, Church of Saint-Nicolas-des-Champs, Paris. Performance of second, definitive version of monotone symphony. 21 January.

Jean-Jacques Lebel, *Poésie Directe*. Living Theater, N.Y. 22 January.

Hermann Nitsch, *6th painting action*. Studio, Brunnerstr. 132, Vienna. 5 February.

Yves Klein, immaterial transfer ceremony exchanging gold for a zone of immaterial pictorial sensitivity. Pont au Double, Paris. 10 February.

Claes Oldenburg, *Ray Gun Theater* (Happenings): *Store Days I* (23-24 February); *Store Days II* (2-3 March); *Nekropolis I* (9-10 March); *Nekropolis II* (16-17 March); *Injun (N.Y.C.) I* (20-21 April); *Injun (N.Y.C.) II* (27-28 April); *Voyages I* (4-5 May); *Voyages II* (11-12 May); *World's Fair I* (18-19 May); and *World's Fair II* (25-26 May). Ray Gun Mfg. Co., 107 East Second Street, N.Y. February-May.

Niki de Saint Phalle stages three tir performances with the help of Robert Rauschenberg and Jean Tinguely. Virginia Dwan's beach home, Malibu and in parking lot of Renaissance Club, Sunset Blvd., Los Angeles. 4 and 7 March, and early April.

"6th Contemporary Art Exhibition". Kyung Bok Palace, Seoul, Korea. Participants include Otto Muehl and Hermann Nitsch. 10 April-7 May.

Allan Kaprow, *Mirrors* (Happening, not performed). May.

Robert Rauschenberg, Jean Tinguely, and Niki de Saint Phalle collaborate with Kenneth Koch on his *The Construction of Boston* (play). Maidman Playhouse, N.Y. Saint Phalle contributes her only shooting sculpture created on stage, *Vénus de Milo*. May

Yves Klein dies of a heart attack. Paris. 6 June.

"Die Bloodorgel (The Blood Organ)". Group exhibition/action by Adolf Frohner, Otto Muehl, and Hermann Nitsch. Perinetgasse 1, Vienna. Artists are walled into cellar on 1 June in order to create installation. Open to public 4-8 June.

George Brecht, *Nectarine* (event). 80 Jefferson Street, N.Y. 12 June.

*Neo-Dada in der Musik* program. Kammerspiele, Düsseldorf. Organized by Nam June Paik. Paik performs *One for Violin Solo* and *Sonata quasi una fantasia*. Other performers: George Maciunas, Ben Patterson, Tomas Schmit, Wolf Vostell. 16 June.

Gustav Metzger, *Auto-Destructive Art, Auto-Creative Art: The Struggle for the Machine Arts of the Future* (lecture/demonstration) at Ealing School of Art, London. Pete Townsend, later guitarist/principle songwriter with The Who, attends. 22 June.

Yves Klein sees the film *Mondo Cane*, which includes 1961 footage of a restaged *Anthropométries*
de l'Époque Bleue*, and later that evening suffers a heart attack. Cannes Film Festival. March.

Jean Tinguely with Niki de Saint Phalle, *Study for the End of the World Number 2* (Happening).
Nevada desert. Filmed by NBC-TV for *David Brinkley's Journal*. March.

American Theater for Poets, Inc., Poets Festival. Maidman Playhouse, N.Y. Contributions include
music by Joseph Byrd, Philip Corner, Richard Maxfield, and La Monte Young; dances by Fred
Herko, Yvonne Rainer (5 March), Trisha Brown and Fred Herko, Aileen Passloff, Yvonne Rainer,
and James Waring (13 March); Happenings by Allan Kaprow, *A Service for the Dead, I*, and
Robert Whitman, *Movies with Sound, Movements, Song, play* (22 March); films by Stan
VanDerBeek and Nicola Cernovich. March.

Robert Filliou, *No-Play in Front of No-Audience*. Paris. Spring.

Alfons Schilling's brother Niklaus films *Cosmos Action Painting — Desperate Motion*. Paris. Spring.

"1961". Dallas Museum for Contemporary Arts. Group exhibition, including: Jim Dine, Claes
Oldenburg, and Robert Rauschenberg; Oldenburg presented a partial re-creation of *The Store*.
Catalogue. 3 April-13 May.

Claes Oldenburg, *Injun* (second version) (Happening, presented in conjunction with the exhibition
"1961"). Dallas Museum for Contemporary Arts. 6-7 April.

Wolf Vostell, *PC Petit Ceinture (Cityrama 2)* (bus Happening). Twenty boulevards in Paris. 3 July.

Alfons Schilling builds circular wooden disk on which to paint. Vienna. July.

Hi Red Center, *Dinner Party on the Anniversary of Non V-Day*. Citizens Hall, Tokyo. 15 August.

Ergo Suits Festival (Happenings and performance pieces): Allan Kaprow, *Sweeping*, Woodstock, N.Y.
(19 August); Al Hansen, *Car Bibbe*, East Hampton, N.Y.; Allan Kaprow, *A Service for the Dead,
II*, on the beach, Bridgehampton, N.Y. (25 August); Alison Knowles, *Light House*, East Hampton,
N.Y.; Walter De Maria, *Boxes + Balls, The Ball Game*, East Hampton, N.Y.; and La Monte Young,
*Sopranino*, East Hampton, N.Y.; among others. 18-25 August.

Robert Rauschenberg, Niki de Saint Phalle, Daniel Spoerri, and Jean Tinguely, among others. *Dylaby*
(*Dynamisch Labyrint*, environment). Stedelijk Museum, Amsterdam. September.

*Fluxus Internationale Festspiele Neuester Musik*. Hörsaal des Städtischen Museums, Wiesbaden.
Participants include Robert Filliou, Dick Higgins, Alison Knowles, George Maciunas, Nam June
Paik (*Zen for Head*), Wolf Vostell, and Emmett Williams, among others. 1-23 September.

**1962** (cont'd)Allan Kaprow, *Words* (environment). Smolin Gallery, N.Y. 11-12 September.

Hi Red Center event. Natsuyuki Nakanishi gives *Lecture on Art*, illustrated with pipe smoke. Opening day of Jiritu-Gattuko, Tokyo. 15 September.

Claes Oldenburg, *Sports* (happening; presented during his one-artist show). Green Gallery, N.Y. 5 October.

Niki de Saint Phalle, exhibition with *Homage to Le Facteur Cheval*, a participatory shooting installation. Alexander Iolas Gallery, N.Y. 15 October-3 November.

Hi Red Center event. On Yamanote Line, Tokyo. 18 October.

*Festival of Misfits* organized by Daniel Spoerri and Robert Filliou at Victor Musgrave's Gallery One, London. Gustav Metzger's proposed contribution is rejected by the organizers. Participants include Ben Patterson, Daniel Spoerri, Ben Vautier, and Emmett Williams, among others. 23 October-8 November.

During *Misfits* event at Institute of Contemporary Arts, London, Gustav Metzger distributes his fourth manifesto, *Manifesto World*, dated 7 October 1962. 24 October.

Allan Kaprow, *Words* (environment, second presentation). State University of New York at Stony Brook. 31 October-3 November.

Jean-Jacques Lebel, *Pour conjurer l'esprit de Catastrophe* (Happening). Studios de Cinéma, Boulogne. October.

Allan Kaprow, *Chicken* (Happening). YMHA, Philadelphia. 7 November.

Dick Higgins, *The Broadway Opera*. Cologne. 11 November.

Allan Kaprow, *Mushroom* (Happening). Lehmann mushroom caves, St. Paul; commissioned by Walker Art Center, Minneapolis. 17 November.

**1963** Ben Watts, *Yam Lecture* (lecture with events for five performers); co-organized by Watts and George Brecht. New York. 21 January.

Hi Red Center. Genpei Akasegawa exhibition invitations printed as counterfeit one-thousand-Yen notes. Stinjiku Daiichi Gallery, Tokyo. February.

*Festum Fluxorum Fluxus (Musik, Antimusik, Das Instrumentale Theater)*. Staatliche Kunstakademie, Düsseldorf. Performers include Joseph Beuys, George Brecht, Al Hansen, Dick Higgins, George Maciunas, Jackson Mac Low, Nam June Paik, Ben Patterson, Tomas Schmit, Daniel Spoerri, Wolf Vostell, Emmett Williams, and La Monte Young. 2 February-3 March.

Claes Oldenburg, *Gayety* (Happening). Lexington Hall, University of Chicago. 8-10 February.

Gustav Metzger gives lecture/demonstration with slide projections where nylon on a slide frame is disintegrated with acid. Bartlett Society, School of Architecture, University of London. February.

Dick Higgins and Alison Knowles, *Fluxus* (Happenings, danger music). Alle Teatern, Stockholm. 1 March.

Hi Red Center Group, *Yomiuri Andi-Pandan Show*. Ueno Museum, Tokyo. Participants include Genpei Akasegawa, Natsuyuki Nakanishi, and Jirō Takamatsu, among others. 1 March.

Hi-Red-Center, *Waseda University Event*. Tokyo. 22 November.

Allan Kaprow, *The Courtyard* (Happening). Mills Hotel, N.Y.; sponsored by Smolin Gallery, N.Y.
23-25 November.

*Festum Fluxorum*. Nikolaikirke, Copenhagen. Performers include Robert Filliou, Dick Higgins,
Alison Knowles, Jackson Mac Low, George Maciunas, Nam June Paik, Wolf Vostell, and Emmett
Williams. 23-28 November.

Jean-Jacques Lebel, *Pour conjurer l'esprit de Catastrophe* (Happening) and Tetsumi Kudo,
*Philosophy of Impotence* (Happening). Galerie Raymond Cordier, Paris. 27 November.

*Festum Fluxorum*. At American Students Center and at Artists Center, Paris. Performers include
Robert Filliou, Dick Higgins, Alison Knowles, George Maciunas, Tomas Schmit, Daniel Spoerri,
and Wolf Vostell, Emmett Williams. 3-8 December.

> Hermann Nitsch, *1st action* (with Otto Muehl). At Muehl's studio apartment, Augartenstr., Vienna.
> Crucifixion action with Nitsch as passive actor. 19 December.
>
> Robert Filliou, *Galerie Legitime* (street performance, Paris) and *13 Ways to Use Emmett Williams'*
> *Skull* (street performance with Emmett Williams, Paris, Frankfurt, and London). Dates unknown.
>
> Al Hansen, *Hall Street Happenings*. Third Rail Gallery of Current Art, Brooklyn. Date unknown.
>
> Tetsumi Kudo moves to Paris. Presents *Instant Sperm* (Happening, piece) there. Date unknown.
>
> Raphael Montanez Ortiz (then Ralph Ortiz) writes *Destructivism: a Manifesto*.
>
> Rudolf Schwarzkogler makes paintings and sculptures derived from Yves Klein's theories on the use
> of the color blue.

Robert Whitman, *Flower* (theater piece). 9 Great Jones Street, N.Y. Throughout March.

Daniel Spoerri, *Restaurant de la Galerie J* (working restaurant). Galerie J, Paris. 2-13 March.

Hermann Nitsch, *Aktion*. Galerie Josef Dvorak, Vienna. 8 March. Daniel Spoerri, remnants of
*Restaurant de la Galerie J* placed on view. Galerie J, Paris. 14 March.

> Nam June Paik, "Exposition of Music — Electronic Television" (exhibition). Galerie Parnass,
> Wuppertal, Germany. During show, performs *Listening to Music Through the Mouth*. 11 March
> (opening). Twelve-year-old ballerina murdered at Vienna Opera House. Among suspects arrested
> in subsequent days are gallerist Josef Dvorak, Otto Muehl, and Hermann Nitsch. 12 March.

> > Hermann Nitsch exhibition. Inaugural show at Galerie Josef Dvorak, Vienna. Nitsch paints directly
> > on jute-covered walls with blood, red paint, and colored water. At opening, Nitsch's *2nd action*.
> > Also, Otto Muehl makes a junk sculpture from materials left over from conversion of
> > basement. 16 March (opening).

> > > Georges Mathieu paints Victoire de Denain. Musée d'art moderne de la
> > > ville de Paris. 26 March.

**1963** (cont'd) Fluxus Concert (all kinds of stage pieces). Studentekroa, Oslo. Participants include Dick Higgins, Alison Knowles, Ben Patterson, and Emmett Williams, among others. 28 March.

Günter Brus receives 5,000 schilling grant from Institut zur Förderung der Künste to make series of large pictures. Stretched molino into labyrinths in Josef Dvorak's empty gallery, on which he paints *Painting in a Labyrinth-like Space*. Spring.

Rudolf Schwarzkogler, 2nd action, 3rd action and 4th action. Heinz Cibulka's apartment, Kaiserstr. 16, Vienna. Cibulka passive actor. Spring.

New York Audiovisual Group event, *Happenings — Events — Advanced Musics*. Old Gymnasium, Douglas College, New Brunswick, N.J. Organized by Al Hansen. Participants include George Brecht, Hansen, Dick Higgins, Ray Johnson, Alison Knowles, Ben Patterson, Emmett Williams, and La Monte Young, among others. 6 April.

Allan Kaprow, *Push and Pull: A Furniture Comedy for Hans Hofmann* (environment). As part of "Hans Hofmann and his Students," a circulating exhibition organized by Museum of Modern Art, N.Y. First at the Santini brothers warehouse, N.Y., then various stagings through April 1965. 17 April.

Robert Filliou, *Kabou'inema* (action poetry). Paris. 18 May.

Robert Whitman, *Hole* (theatrical piece). 9 Great Jones Street, N.Y. 27 May-1 June.

Kiki Kogelnik, an Austrian living in New York, visits Muehl and tells him he has been making "happenings." Muehl and Nitsch adopt the term. June.

*Programme des Manifestations*. Galerie Raymond Cordier, Paris. Participants include Robert Filliou and Emmett Williams, *Comptoir*; Jean-Jacques Lebel, *Tableaux-Happenings*; and Marta Minujin (with Lebel), *Le Coq*. 5 June.

*Pocket Follies*, benefit for the Foundation for Contemporary Performance Arts, Pocket Theater, N.Y. Organized by James Waring. Performers include George Brecht, Ray Johnson, Yvonne Rainer, and Robert Rauschenberg (*Prestidigitator Extraordinary*), among others. 10 June.

Harold Liversidge directs a fifteen-minute film, *Auto-Destructive Art — The Activities of G. Metzger*, South Bank, London. Summer.

Al Hansen, *Silver City for Andy Warhol*. Third Rail Gallery, N.Y. 22 June.

Nam June Paik, *Piano for All Senses*. Amstel 47, Amsterdam. Performed by Tomas Schmit, among others. 22 June.

Carolee Schneemann, *Chrome Lodeon* (4th concretion). Judson Memorial Church, N.Y. 24 June.

Claes Oldenburg, *Stars: A Farce for Objects* (Happening); presented as part of the Pop Art Festival
organized in conjunction with the exhibition "The Popular Image". Washington Gallery of Modern
Art, Washington, D.C. 24-25 April.

*George Brecht*, (object-events). 80 Jefferson Street, N.Y. April.

Niki de Saint Phalle, shooting action with *King Kong* sculpture. Los Angeles. Organized by Virginia
Dwan. May.

Yam Festival. Smolin Gallery, N.Y., George Segal's Farm, New Brunswick, N.J., and Hardware Poet's
Playhouse, N.Y. Happenings, performances, dance, music, events organized by George Brecht
and Ben Watts. Contributors include Brecht, John Cage, Lucinda Childs, Philip Corner,
Red Grooms, Al Hansen, Dick Higgins (*Lots of Trouble* at Segal's Farm, 19 May), Ray Johnson,
Allan Kaprow (*Tree*, Happening, 19 May), Alison Knowles (*Yam Hat Sale*, group show at Smolin
Gallery, 9 May), George Maciunas, Jackson Mac Low, Robert Morris, Wolf Vostell (*Television
Decollage* at Segal's Farm, 19 May; *Television Decollage*, action environment at Smolin Gallery,
22 May; *Morning Glory* de/collage happening at Third Rail Gallery, N.Y., 25 May), and La Monte
Young, among others. 1-31 May.

Hermann Nitsch shows action paintings. Vienna Secession exhibition, Graz. 4 May (opening).

Hi Red Center, *The Third Mixer Plan Show*. Shinjiku Daiichi Gallery, Tokyo. 7 May.

*Pelican*, choreographed by Robert Rauschenberg, Concert of Dance 5, performed by Judson Dance
Theater. Pop Festival, Washington, D.C. 9 May.

Hi Red Center, *Promotional Event*. Shinbashi Station Square, Tokyo. 10 May.

Otto Muehl and Hermann Nitsch, *Fest des psycho-physischen Naturalismus*. Outside and in
Perinetgasse 1, Vienna. Planned events include Nitsch's *3rd action*, after which police stop
event. Günter Brus snatches a sack containing a lamb carcass and throws it into Danube canal.
Murder alarm sounded, and Kari Bauer, Brus, and Nitsch spend three days in prison.
Subsequently, Muehl and Nitsch are sentenced to 14 days for causing a public nuisance and
disturbing the peace. 28 June.

Daniel Spoerri (assisted by Emmett Williams), *Lecture on what should
be said at the moment, but what may not occur to me* (improvisation).
Monastery, Klosterneuburg, Vienna. 5 July.

Allan Kaprow, *Bon Marché* (Happening). Bon Marché Department Store,
Théâtre Recamier and Théâtre des Nations, Paris. Participants include
Jean-Jacques Lebel. 11-13 July.

George Maciunas organizes *Fluxus Festival of Total Art* (one concert, seven street events). Hotel
Scribe and in the streets, Nice. Participants include George Brecht, Dick Higgins, Maciunas,
Nam June Paik, Ben Patterson, Daniel Spoerri, Ben Vautier, and La Monte Young.
25 July-3 August.

Al Hansen, *Parisol 4 Marisol* (Happening). Gramercy Arts Theater. 8 August.

Hi-Red-Center, *Ror Rogy*. Roof of Bijitu-Shuttupan Co., Tokyo.
15 August.

1st Festival of the Avant Garde. Judson Memorial Church, N.Y. Music
and performances organized by Charlotte Moorman. 20 August-4
September.

**1963** (cont'd) Robert Whitman, *Water* (theater piece-happening). Multicar garage in an alley behind 521
N. La Cienega, L.A. 3-4 September.

Allan Kaprow, *Out* and *Sea* (Happenings); *Sea* was not performed due to its cancellation by
Chairman Kenneth Tynan Courtyard of Mc Ewan Hall, International Drama Conference, Edinburgh
Festival. 7 September.

Wolf Vostell, *Nein-9-dé-Coll/Agen* (Happening). Wuppertal, Germany.
14 September.

Biennale de Paris — Arts du Langage. Participants include: Robert Filliou; Jean-Jacques Lebel,
*Incidents* (poésie-direct and Happening, with Tetsumi Kudo and others), Musée d'art moderne,
8 October; Tetsumi Kudo, *Harakiri of Humanism, Bottled Humanism* (Happening-piece), Musée d'art
moderne, 8 October; *Fluxus — Poesie et Cetera*, pieces by George Brecht, Al Hansen, Dick Higgins,
Alison Knowles, Jackson Mac Low, George Maciunas, Ben Patterson, Emmett Williams, and La
Monte Young, among others, Musée d'art moderne, 10 October. 1-30 October.

Allan Kaprow, *Fight (part I, version I)* (Happening, not performed). Smolin Gallery, N.Y. October.

Otto Muehl, *Versumpfung eines weiblichen Körpers — Versumpfung einer Venus (Degredation of
a Female Body — Degredation of a Venus)* (material action). Muehl's studio apartment, Obere
Augartenstr., Vienna. October.

Hi Red Center. *NHK Television Show*, pieces by Jirō Takamatsu (*Smoking Box*) and
Natsuyuki Nakanishi (*Foaming Fountain*), among others. Japan. 3 November.

Hermann Nitsch, *4th action* (with Otto Muehl). Nitsch's studio, private performance for camera.
21 November.

Claes Oldenburg, *Autobodys* (Happening). Parking lot, American Institute of Aeronautics and
Astronautics, Los Angeles. 9-10 December.

Al Hansen, *Oogadooga* (Happening). Judson Gallery, N.Y. 12 December.

*Happenings, Events, and Advanced Musics*, organized by Al Hansen.
Douglass College, Rutgers University, New Brunswick, N.J.
Performers include George Brecht (*Three Aqueous Events*)

Milan Knížák and Group (Vit Mach, Sona Svecova, Jan Trtilek,
Zdena Zizkoka), *Seances* (three performances, environment, non-
instrumental music, lectures, etc.). Novy Svet, Prague. Dates
unknown.

Milan Knížák, *Demonstrations of Objects* (short exhibition
on the street). Novy Svet, Prague, and Garten in Marienbad (bei der
Wohnung). Dates unknown.

Milan Knížák, *Short Carting Exhibition*. Prague.

Marta Minujin, *La destruccin*. Impasse Ronssin, Paris. Date unknown.

**1964** "Four Environments By Four New Realists". Sidney Janis Gallery, N.Y. Artists: Jim Dine, Claes
Oldenburg, James Rosenquist, George Segal. 3 January-1 February.

Hi Red Center, *Police Event*. Genpei Akasegawa interrogated by Tokyo Metropolitan Police
regarding his production of counterfeit one-thousand-yen notes. 8 January.

Wolf Vostell, *Sun in Your Head*. Leidse Plein Theater, Amsterdam. 11 January.

Allan Kaprow, *Eat* (environment). In caves of old Ebling Brewery, Bronx, N.Y., sponsored by Smolin
Gallery. 18-19, 25-26 January.

Robert Rauschenberg, *Shot Put* (performance). Concert for New Paltz, State University of New York,
New Paltz. 30 January.

Hi Red Center, *Human Box Event*. Imperial Hotel, Room 340, Tokyo. January.

Al Hansen, *Monica Har Monica*. New York University, Spring Festival. 11 February.

Allan Kaprow, *Birds* (Happening). Southern Illinois University Campus, Carbondale. 16 February.

Otto Muehl, *Klarsichtpackung — Versumpfung in einer Truhe — Panierung eines weiblichen
Gesässes — Wälzen im Schlamm (Transparent Packing — Degredation in a Trunk — Bread-
crumbing of a Backside)* (material action). Muehl's studio, Obere Augartenstr., Vienna.
26 February.

Robert Rauschenberg, *Shot Put* (performance). Once Festival, University of Michigan, Ann Arbor.
Also performs Steve Paxton's *Proxy* (1962). 27 February.

Hermann Nitsch, *5th action*, and Otto Muehl, *Kreuzigung eines männlichen Körpers*
(material action). Muehl's studio, Obere Augartenstr., Vienna. 3 March.

Allan Kaprow, *Orange* (Happening). Unused citrus warehouse, Coral Gables, Florida. Sponsored by
Miami Arts Council. 7 March.

Allan Kaprow, *Paper* (Happening). Parking lot, University of California, Berkeley. 23-24 March.

George Brecht and others, *Events and Entertainments*. Pocket Theater, N.Y. 23 March-27 April.

Ben Vautier, *Quelque Chose* (fluxus and *theatre d'art total*). Nice. 27 March.

Presentation of Nam June Paik and La Monte Young composition. Sogetsukaikan Hall, Tokyo.
29 March.

*12 Fluxus Concerts*. Fluxhall, 359 Canal Street, N.Y. Works by George Brecht, Robert Filliou,
Dick Higgins, Allan Kaprow, Alison Knowles, Shigeko Kubota, George Maciunas, Jackson
Mac Low, Robert Morris, Nam June Paik, Ben Vautier, Emmett Williams, and La Monte Young,
among others. March-May.

Dick Higgins, *Lecture Series* (eight lectures). New York. 2 April.

**1964** (cont'd) Robert Filliou, *Soumission au Possible — Berger Revant Qu'il Etat Roi* (action poetry — chance play). Café-Théâtre de la Vieille Grille, Paris. 6 April.

Otto Muehl, *Verschnürung eines weiblichen Körpers (*Tying up of a female body*)* (material action). Obere Augartenstr., Vienna. 10 April.

George Maciunas performs Nam June Paik's *One for Violin Solo* at a Fluxus concert. New York. 11 April.

Otto Muehl, first public performance of a material action. Vienna. Planned, but banned by police; Muehl fined 1,000 schillings. 14 April.

Allan Kaprow and Wolf Vostell, *The Art of the Happening* (lecture). Cricket Theatre, N.Y. Following lecture, audience is bussed to Long Island to participate in Vostell's *You*. 19 April.

Wolf Vostell, *You* ("décollage" Happening) during which occurs Ben Vautier's *Menote (La Clef est à Nice)*. Robert Delford Brown and Rhett Delford Brown property, Great Neck, N.Y. 19 April.

Otto Muehl, *Chattanooga* (material action). Chattanooga, Vienna. 21 April.

Hermann Nitsch's announced action for the Chattanooga is not carried out. 21 April.

Al Hansen, *Red Dog for Freddi Herko, Piano for Lil Picard, Oogadooga* (Happenings). Third Rail Gallery, N.Y. 25 April.

Robert Rauschenberg and Alex Hay, *Dredge* (improvisation). Judson Memorial Church, N.Y. As part of *Concert of Dance 14:*

*Improvisations by the Dance Theater*, Judson Dance Theater. 27 April.

Otto Muehl, *Nabelschnur — Darstellung einer Geburt (Umbilical cord)* and *Stilleben — Aktion mit einem weiblichen Kopf und einem Rinderkopf (*Still life with a female and a cow's head*)* (material actions). Muehl's studio, Obere Augartenstr., Vienna. May.

Allan Kaprow, *Household* (Happening). In town dump outside Ithaca, N.Y., sponsored by Cornell University. 3 May.

Festival de la Libre Expression (alternately Workshop of Free Expression). American Center, Paris. Organized by Jean-Jacques Lebel. Participants include: George Brecht (*Exit*, 30 May); Tetsumi Kudo (*Bottled Humanis*, Happening, 26 May); Lebel (*Déchirex*, Happening, 26 May); Carolee Schneemann (*Meat Joy*, visual drama, 29 May); and Ben Vautier (*Re-Fluxus Event*, Théâtre total/Happening, 28 May). 25-30 May.

*A Collage Happening*. Denison Hall, London. Generated by Jean-Jacques Lebel and organized by Michael White. Participants include Mark Boyle (*Bags*), Lebel (*Pour Conjurer L'Esprit de Catastrophe*) and Carolee Schneemann (*Meat Joy*), among others. 8-9 June.

Otto Muehl, *Stilleben — Aktion mit einem weiblichen, einem männlichen Kopf und einem Rinderkopf (*Still Life with a Female, a Male and Cow's Head*)* (material action). Hüttenstr. 104, Düsseldorf, sponsored by Galerie Haro Lauhaus. 11 June.

Hi Red Center, *The Great Panorama Show*. Naiqua Gallery, Japan. 12 June.

Gustav Metzger's fifth manifesto, *On Random Activity in Material/ Transforming Works of Art* and reprints of the first three manifestos published in the journal *Signals*. Summer.

Hermann Nitsch, *6th action*. Galerie Junge Generation, Vienna. Action performed at opening of his exhibition, which is closed by Mayor Franz Jonas after two days. 23 June.

Wolf Vostell and F. Mon, *Bloomsday 1964*. Galerie Loehr, Frankfurt. 26 June.

*Fluxus Symphony Orchestra in Fluxus Concert*. Carnegie Recital Hall, N.Y. Works by George Brecht, Dick Higgins, Yoko Ono, Nam June Paik, Emmett Williams, La Monte Young, among others. 27 June.

Hermann Nitsch, scheduled lecture forbidden. Galerie Junge Generation, Vienna. 30 June.

Otto Muehl repeats his 11 June action as *Still Life with a Female, a Male and Cow's Head*.
Perinetgasse 1, Vienna. 2 July.
Otto Muehl, *Mama und Papa* (filmed material action with Kurt Kren). Perinetgasse 1, Vienna.
4 and August.
Otto Muehl, *Leda und der Swan* (filmed material action with Kurt Kren). Perinetgasse 1, Vienna.
20 August.
*Maj Udstillingen* (Happenings, action-music). Billed Huggersalen Charlottenborg, Copenhagen.
Participants include Joseph Beuys (*Piece No. 1*, 30 August), George Brecht, Dick Higgins,
Tomas Schmit, Wolf Vostell (*Bustop*, 30 August), Emmett Williams, among others. 29 August-
11 September.
2nd Annual New York Avant Garde Festival. Judson Memorial Church, N.Y. Organized by Charlotte
Moorman and N. Seaman. Performance of Karlheinz Stockhausen's *Originale*, starring Robert
Delford Brown and directed by Allan Kaprow. Nam June Paik performs *Robot Opera* with
Charlotte Moorman and *Robot K-456*. 30 August (opening).
2nd Annual New York Avant Garde Festival. Street performance with Nam June Paik's *Robot K-456*. 31 August.
2nd Annual New York Avant Garde Festival. Nam June Paik performs *Simple* as part of Karlheinz
Stockhausen's *Originale*. 8 September.
Flux Fest. Washington Square Gallery, N.Y. Works by AY-O, Joe Jones, and George Maciunas,
among others. 8 September-3 November.
Robert Rauschenberg, *Shot Put* and *Elgin Tie* (performances, the latter with sound by David
Tudor). Moderna Museet, Stockholm. As part of *Five New York Evenings*. 13 September.

**1964** (cont'd) Milan Knížák (Aktual), *Demonstration of All Senses* (demonstration). Prague. Fall.

Nam June Paik and Charlotte Moorman, performance. Philadelphia College of Art. At the invitation of Dieter Rot. October.

Günter Brus. At Muehl's urging, carries out his first action, *Ana*, in Muehl's studio apartment in Obere Augartenstr., Vienna. Filmed by Kurt Kren. October-November.

Otto Muehl (with Rudolf Schwarzkogler), *Balloon concert* (musical action). Perinetgasse 1, Vienna. 9 October.

Hi Red Center, *Roof Event*. Roof of Ikenobo Building, Tokyo. 10 October.

Al Hansen, *Octopus* (Happening). Third Rail Gallery, N.Y. 16 October.

Hi-Red Center, *Be Clean!* (event). Nakimi Street, Ginza, Tokyo. 16 October.

Robert Delford Brown and Rhett Delford Brown, *The Meat Show*. Washington Meat Market, N.Y. 19 October.

Otto Muehl, *Cosinus alpha* and *Still life with penis* (material actions). Perinetgasse 1, Vienna. Filmed by Kurt Kren. November.

**1965** Günter Brus, *Silber (Silver)*, *Self-painting II*, *Self-mutilation* (with Anni Brus). Perinetgasse 1, Vienna. Filmed and photographed. January.

Allan Kaprow, *Raining* (Happening for O. and B. Klüver). Thus far unperformed. January.

Nam June Paik, *Electronic TV, Color TV Experiments, 3 Robots, 2 Zen Boxes + 1 Zen Can*. New School, N.Y. Charlotte Moorman performs Paik's *Cello Sonata No. 1 for Adults Only*. 8 January.

Hermann Nitsch, *7th Aktion (für Dr. Tunner)*. Nitsch's studio and apartment, Vienna. Financed by Dr. Wolfgang Tunner. 9 January.

Hermann Nitsch (action). Nitsch's studio and apartment, Vienna. Action and feast of fifteen hours' duration, assisted by Rudolf Schwarzkogler. 16 January.

Hermann Nitsch, *8th action*. Nitsch's apartment, Jedlersdorferstr. 171, Vienna. Rudolf Schwarzkogler is passive actor. 22 January.

Tetsumi Kudo, *Quiet Event (Action Lentes)* (event with electric apparatus). Galerie J, Paris. February.

Otto Muehl, *Silberarsch (Silver Ass)* and *Aktion mit einem toten Hasen* (material action). Vienna. February.

Allan Kaprow, *Soap* (Happening). Sarasota and Florida State University, Tallahassee. 3-4 February.

Rudolf Schwarzkogler, *Aktion — Hochzeit (Wedding)*. Heinz Cibulka's apartment, Kaiserstr. 16, Vienna. Anni Brus and Cibulka as actors. 6 February.

Al Hansen, *The Gunboat Panay*. Third Rail Gallery, N.Y. 15 February.

Café à Go-Go, N.Y. *Monday Night Letter* event series, arranged by George Brecht and Ben Watts.
    Participants include: Ay-O (21 December, *Rainbow-Happening No. 4*, rainbow dinner); Brecht
    (23 November, *Life of Geo. Washington*; 14 December with Watts, *Yam Lecture*); Robert Filliou
    (25 January 1965, *Ample Food for Stupid Thought — Yes*, action poetry); Al Hansen (2
    November, untitled happening; 28 December with New York Audiovisual Group, *Garbo-X mas-
    Bibbe*, happening;4 January 1965 untitled happening); Dick Higgins (2 November, *Danger Music
    No. 17*; 7 December, *An Evening of Opera [Hrusalk] the Pre-Christmas Rush*, three events);
    Alison Knowles (9 November, *Assorted Night Riders*; 19 July 1965 with Eric Andersen and A.
    Fine, *The Silent Circus*); Charlotte Moorman (8 November 1965, happening); Nam June Paik
    (4 October 1965, *Electronic Video Recorder*, trial for main November show at Gallery Bonnino);
    and Emmett Williams (25 January 1965, *The Work of Emmett Williams [Yes It Was Still There
    An Opera]*, performers include Brecht, Ben Patterson, Alison Knowles, Watts, Dick Higgins,
    Robert Filliou, among others). Large group event 4 October 1965 *World Theatre* (experimental
    music dance theater): participants include Christo, Al Hansen, Dick Higgins, Alison Knowles,
    Charlotte Moorman, Yoko Ono, Nam June Paik, Dieter Rot, Wolf Vostell, and Andy Warhol,
    among others. November 1964-November 1965.
Wolf Vostell, *In Ulm, Um Ulm und Um Ulm Herum. Ulm*, Germany. 7 November.
                    *Recitals d'Avantguardia*, participants include George Brecht, John Cage, and Dick Higgins. Galleria
                        Blu, Milan. 16 November.
                    Carolee Schneemann, *Meat Joy* (kinetic theater). Judson Memorial Church, N.Y. 16-18 November.
                    Zaj Group, *Traslado a Pie de Tres Objetos...* (action music). Performers include Ramón Barce,
                        Juan Hidalgo, and Walter Marchetti. Madrid. 19 November.
                    Robert Rauschenberg, *Shot Put* and *Tango* (performances). Sogetsu Art Center, Tokyo. 20 November.
                    Zaj Group, *Concierto de Teatro Musical*. Performers include Ramón Barce, Juan Hidalgo, and
                        Walter Marchetti. Avenida de Seneca, Madrid. 21 November.
                                    *Flux-Festival*. Kunstcentrum 'T Venster, Rotterdam. Performers include Robert Filliou, Arthur
                                        Køpcke, Ben Vautier, and Emmett Williams, among others. 23 November.
                                    Ben Vautier, "Nine Directions in Art" (exhibition). Galerie Amstel, Amsterdam. 25 November-
                                        12 December.
                                    Robert Rauschenberg, *Twenty Questions to Bob Rauschenberg* (event during which the combine
                                        *Gold Standard* is made in collaboration with Deborah Hay, Alex Hay and Steve Paxton, in
                                        response to questions from critic Yoshiaki Tono). Sogetsu Art Center, Tokyo. Filmed for
                                        Japanese television. 28 November.
                                    Günter Brus, *Selbstbemalung I (Self-painting I)*. John Sailer's studio, Opernring 21, Vienna.
                                        December.
                                    Otto Muehl, *O Tannenbaum* (material action). Hochschule für bildende Künst, Braunschweig. Filmed
                                        by Kurt Kren. 16 December.
                                                    Joseph Beuys, *Der Chef — The Chief*. Galerie Block, Berlin. 1 December.
                                                    Wolf Vostell, *T.V. — Happening — Weisser Als Weiss*. Landesstudio
                                                        Nordrhein, Dusseldorf. 11 December.
                                                    Mark Boyle and Joan Hills. *Suddenly Last Supper* and *The Street*
                                                        (events).
                                                        South Kensington, London. Dates unknown.
                                                    Yoko Ono, *Cut Piece*. Yamaichi Concert Hall, Kyoto, Japan.
                                                        Aktual (Milan Knížák), *An Individual Demonstration*. Streets of
                                                        Prague. Dates unknown.
                                                    Aktual, Milan Knížák, *Demonstration One* (home piece-score) and S.
                                                        Svecova, *Demonstration Two* (action). In a tram in Prague. Dates
                                                        unknown.
                                                    Group Aktual, *Manifestation of Aktual Art* (environment), three pieces
                                                        (concert). Streets of Prague. Dates unknown.
                                                    Marta Minujin, *La Feria de las Ferias*. Galería Lirolay, Buenos Aires,
                                                        Argentina. Date unknown.

Dick Higgins, *The Tart*, *Solo for Florence and Orchestra*, and *Celestials [for Bengt af Klintberg]*, directed by Gloria Graves. Sunnyside Garden Ballroom and Wrestling Arena, N.Y. 17 April.

Otto Muehl, *Bodybuilding* (material action). Perinetgasse 1, Vienna. Filmed by Ernst Schmidt. May.

First New York Theater Rally: Dance Concert III. Most events at former CBS studio, Broadway and 81st Street, N.Y. Organized by Steve Paxton and Alan Solomon. Participants include: Jim Dine, *Natural History (The Dreams)*; Robert Morris and Carolee Schneemann (*Site* by Robert Morris, 5-7 May); Claes Oldenburg (*Washes* [Happening] at swimming pool of Al Roons' Health Club, 253 W. 73rd St., 22-23 May); *Piece for Telephone* (first version), 24-26 May); Robert Rauschenberg (*Spring Training*, 11-13 May; *Pelican*, 24-26 May); and Robert Whitman (*The Night Time Sky*, 14-16 May; 24-26 May; *Shower*, 24-26 May). 1-26 May.

Otto Muehl, *Rumpsti-Pumpsti* (material action). Vienna. 8 May.

2. Festival de la Libre Expression (alternately Workshop of Free Expression). American Center, Paris. Organized by Jean-Jacques Lebel. Participants include Robert Filliou (20 May), Emmett Williams (20 May), Nam June Paik and Charlotte Moorman (21 May, concert), and Ben Vautier (22 May, *Public et Solo Happening*). 17-25 May.

Otto Muehl, *Turnstunde in Lebensmitteln (Gymnastics class in food)* (material action). Perinetgasse 1, Vienna. 24 June.

Hermann Nitsch, *10th action*. Nitsch's studio, Brünnerstr. 132, Vienna. Rudolf Schwarzkogler is passive actor. 24 June.

Otto Muehl, *Penisaktion* (material action). Perinetgasse 1, Vienna. Summer.

Yoko Ono, *Bag Piece*. Filmmakers' Cinematheque, N.Y. 27 June.

Hermann Nitsch, *11th action*. Nitsch's studio, Brünnerstr. 132, Vienna. Rudolf Schwarzkogler is passive actor. 30 June.

Günter Brus, *Lockjaw* and *Transfusion*. Perinetgasse 1, Vienna. Actions filmed by Otto Muehl. Mid-late 1965.

Günter Brus, *Vienna Walk*. From Heldenplatz to Braeunerstr., Vienna. Action culminating in police sending him home in taxicab. 5 July.

Günter Brus, "Painting — Self-painting — Self-mutilation" (Malerei — Selbstbemalung — Selbstverstümmelung) (exhibition). Galerie Junge Generation, Vienna. Self-painting action performed at opening. 6-25 July.

Marta Minujin, *Suceso Plástico*. Estadio Peñarol, Montevideo, Uruguay, 25 July.

Allan Kaprow, *Calling* (Happening). New York. 21 August.

Allan Kaprow, *Calling* (Happening). Privately presented in George Segal's farm/woods, New Brunswick, N.J. 22 August.

Nam June Paik and Charlotte Moorman concert. Philadelphia College of Art. Performances of
    works by George Brecht, John Cage, Nam June Paik, and Karlheinz Stockhausen, among others.
    26 February.
Robert Filliou, *Streetfighting Singing Sade (whispered art history)* (action-poetry). East End Theater,
    N.Y. 3 March.
Jean-Jacques Lebel, *Mode d'emploi du pseudo-Kini: Play-Tex* (Happening). Restaurant la Tour
    d'Argent, Paris. 11 March.
            Robert Filliou and thirteen others, *Key Event*. East End Theater and Penn Station, N.Y. 13 March.
            Otto Muehl, *Bimmel Bammel (Tinkle Tinkle)* (material action). Perinetgasse 1, Vienna. Filmed
                by Ernst Schmidt. 13 March.
            Yoko Ono, *New Works*. Carnegie Recital Hall, N.Y. 21 March.
                        Otto Muehl begins serving fourteen days in prison for his role in the *Fest
                        des psycho-physischen Naturalismus*. 27 March.
                        Wolf Vostell, *Phaenomene* (Happening). Autofriedhof automobile
                        graveyard, Sacksendamm, Berlin. Sponsored by Galerie René Block.
                        Hermann Nitsch assists. 27 March.
                                    New York Audiovisual Group, *Happenings* (Third Rail program of
                                        time/space arts) and Al Hansen, *Happenings at the Bridge*. The
                                        Bridge, The Bridge Theater, N.Y. 5 April.
                                    Kurt Kren's films of Brus' and Muehl's actions are shown at the
                                        Museum of the Twentieth Century, Vienna. 14 April.

The Bridge, The Bridge Theater, N.Y. New York Audiovisual Group,
    *Happenings* (Third Rail program of time/space arts) and Al Hansen,
    *Happenings at the Bridge*. 5 April. Zaj Group (Marchetti and Hidalgo),
    *hmc2 1965-y despues, en bandeja (2 etce'teras)*. Galeria Edurne, Madrid. 18 May.
Aktual (Milan Knížák, S. Knížák, Jan Trtilek, Vit Mach), *2. Manifestation of Aktual Art (AA)*,
    manifestation. Prague. 21 May.
            Tomas Schmit, *Ohne Titel (Komposition für Ein und Zwanzig uhr Drei)*. Galerie René Block, Berlin.
                28 May.
            Hermann Nitsch, *9th action*. Nitsch's studio, Brünnerstr. 132, Vienna, and in fields at Stammersdorf.
                Ten-hour action. Günter Brus is among passive actors. 2 June.
                        Claes Oldenburg, *Birth of the Flag* (film performance). Cottage of R. Wurlitzer, Brookside, N.Y.
                        4-7 June.
                        *24 Stunden*, group performance by Joseph Beuys, Charlotte Moorman, Nam June Paik, Tomas
                        Schmit, and Wolf Vostell, among others. Galerie Parnass, Wuppertal. 5-6 June.
                                    Nam June Paik, *Robot Opera*. Kurfürstendamm, Gedaechtniskirche,
                                        and Galerie René Block, Berlin. 14 June.
                                    *Fluxus Konzert (Siebente Soiree)*. Galerie René Block, Berlin. Works
                                        and performances by John Cage, Dick Higgins, Jackson Mac Low,
                                        Yoko Ono, Nam June Paik, Dieter Rot, Wolf Vostell, and Emmett
                                        Williams, among others. 14 June.

Third Annual New York Avant Garde Festival. Judson Hall, N.Y.
    Organized by Charlotte Moorman. Performers include John Cage (*Theater Piece*), Al Hansen
    (time-space drama), Dick Higgins (choreographic theater), Allan Kaprow (participation
    Happening), Nam June Paik (action music), Paik and Moorman (*Variations on a Theme by Saint-
    Saëns*). 25 August-11 September.
            Otto Muehl, Gehirnoperation (*Brain operation*) (material action). Perinetgasse 1, Vienna. 29 August.
            Otto Muehl, *Astronaut* (material action). Perinetgasse 1, Vienna. 30 August.

**1965** (cont'd) *First World Congress: Happenings*. Saint Mary's of the Harbor, N.Y. Presented by Al Hansen and Octopus Allstars. Works by George Brecht, Robert Filliou, Hansen (*Parisol 4 Marisol*), Dick Higgins, Ray Johnson, Alison Knowles, Jackson Mac Low, Yoko Ono, Nam June Paik, Ben Patterson, Wolf Vostell, Tomas Schmit, and La Monte Young. 30 August-1 September.

*Perpetual Fluxfest*. New Cinematheque, N.Y. Participants include Jackson Mac Low (12 September), Yoko Ono (3 October), Hi Red Center Group (10 October), Shigeko Kubota (*Vagina Painting*, 31 October), Ben Patterson (5 December). 5 September-12 December.

Hermann Nitsch, *12th action*. Heinz Cibulka's apartment, Kaiserstr. 16, Vienna. Cibulka is passive actor. Photographed by Franziska Cibulka. 6 September.

Gustav Metzger presents light projection *Notes on the Chemical Revolution in Art*. ICA, organized by Mark Boyle. This is the first large-scale light show presented in London. 7 September.

Allan Kaprow, *Push and Pull (second version)* (Happening). Judson Hall, N.Y. Sponsored by Third Annual New York Festival of the Avant-Garde. 7 September.

Yoko Ono, *Morning Piece (1964) to George Maciunas*. On the roof of 87 Christopher St., N.Y. 12 September.

Hermann Nitsch, *13th action*. Strebersdorf and Stammersdorf. Nitsch and Cibulka passive actors. 16 September.

Robert Rauschenberg, *Spring Training* (performance). Maynard Street Parking Structure, University of Michigan, Ann Arbor. As part of Once Again Festival. 18 September.

Robert Rauschenberg performs in John Cage's *Talk 1*. University of Michigan, Ann Arbor. As part of Once Again Festival. 19 September.

Rudolf Schwarzkogler, *5th action*. Hermann Nitsch's studio, Brünnerstr. 132, Vienna. Schwarzkogler and Nitsch actors. Fall.

Jean-Jacques Lebel, *Welsh Automotive Salad with Yoghurt* (Happening). Reardon Smith Hall, Cardiff, Wales. Presented during Poetry Conference, Cardiff Arts Festival. 24 September.

Wolf Vostell, *Wenn Sie Mich Fragen* (Happening). Rowohlt Verlagshaus, Reinbek/Hamburg. 24 September.

Daniel Spoerri, *Restaurant de la City Galerie* (working restaurant). City Galerie, Pelikanstrasse, 38, Zürich. 25 September.

Hermann Nitsch, *14th action*. Heinz Cibulka's apartment, Kaiserstr. 16, Vienna. Cibulka is passive actor. Photographed by Franziska Cibulka. 29 September.

Nam June Paik and Charlotte Moorman perform John Cage's *26'1.1499""* for a String Player. Café à Go-Go, N.Y. 4 October.

Hermann Nitsch, *15th action*. Heinz Cibulka's apartment, Kaiserstr. 16, Vienna. Cibulka is passive actor. Photographed by Franziska Cibulka. 10 October.

Nam June Paik, *New Cinema Festival I*. Filmmakers' Cinematheque, N.Y. Performers include Paik (*Zen for Film*) and Charlotte Moorman. 2 November.

**1966** Otto Muehl, *Das Ohr, Waschschüssel, Hinrichtung* (material action). Perinetgasse 1, Vienna. January.

Aktual (Jan Mach, Milan Knížák), *Fly* (event). Apartment house no. 26, Vaclavkova Street, Prague, involving post office, workers, police, and Aktual. January-December.

First meeting between artists and engineers for *9 Evenings: Theatre and Engineering* festival. New York. 14 January.

Al Hansen, *A Mc Luhan Megillah* (Happening). Al Hansen's Studio, 119 Avenue D, N.Y. 28 January.

Marta Minujin, *El Batacazo*. Bianchini Gallery, N.Y. February.

Otto Muehl, *Nahrungsmitteltest* (material action). Perinetgasse 1, Vienna. February.

Milan Knížák, *Have a Cat*, instructions for inhabitants of apartment house no. 8, Komenskemo, Marienbad. 25 February.

Robert Rauschenberg, with Alex Hay, Deborah Hay, and Steve Paxton, *Map Room [I]* (performance).
    Goddard College, Plainfield, Vermont. 4 November.
*Something Else — A Concert of New Music + Events*. ICA, London. P. Green, Dick Higgins,
    Alison Knowles, and Gustav Metzger perform Dick Higgins' *Sound of the Animals Dying 13 to 1*,
    George Brecht's *Shake* and *Sit-Stand-Walk*, and Alison Knowles' *Shoes of Your Choice*,
    *Interruption Music*, and *A Collage of Events*. 5 November.
Milan Knížák (Aktual), *Soldier's Game* (game). Prague. 7 November.
Wolf Vostell, *100 Ereignisse-100 Minuten-100 Stellen*. Galerie René Block, Berlin. 10 November.
Joseph Beuys, *Action "How to Explain Paintings to a Dead Hare."* Schmela Gallery, Düsseldorf.
    26 November.
Zaj Group, Zaj Festival Zaj 1. Colegio Mayor, Universidad de Madrid. 27 November-15 December.
            Otto Muehl, *Kopf* (Head) (material action). Perinetgasse 1, Vienna. December.
            The Expanded Cinema Festival, Filmmakers' Cinematheque, N.Y. Organized by Jonas Mekas and others. Events include
                Claes Oldenburg, *Moveyhouse*; Robert Whitman, *Prune Flat*; and Robert Rauschenberg, *Map Room II*. 1-18 December.
            The International Steamed Spring Vegetable Pie. University of California, Los Angeles. Fluxus festival sponsored by New
                Music Workshop and Graduate Students' Association. 2 December.
            Robert Rauschenberg, impromptu tire-painting performance at funeral of Frederick Kiesler. New York. 27 December.
            Mark Boyle and Joan Hills, *O what a lovely Whore* (event). ICA, London. Date unknown.
            Mark Boyle and Joan Hills, Random street studies, Shepherds Bush, London, Series (behavior events).
            Robert Delford Brown and Rhett Delford Brown, *Cow Lane Weekend* (two-day event, Great Neck, Long Island, N.Y.),
                *Out of Order, Please use the Toilet Down the Hall Across the Lobby* (event, Bel Air Sands Hotel, L.A.). Dates unknown.
            Milan Knížák (Aktual), *Why Just So* (lecture demonstration). Bank of Moldau. Date unknown.
            Marta Minujin, *El Batacazo*. Instituto Torcuato Di Tella, Buenos Aires, Argentina. Date unknown.

**1966** (cont'd) In a broadsheet, Gustav Metzger publishes first announcement of the *Destruction in Art Symposium (D.I.A.S.)*. London. March.

Otto Muehl, *St. Ana* (material action). Perinetgasse 1, Vienna. March.

Milan Knížák, *Do You Know How to Play Marbles* (four pieces), wall newspaper. Prague. 6-31 March

Nam June Paik and Charlotte Moorman perform *Avant Garde Music Pieces* by George Brecht, John Cage, Dick Higgins, Jackson Mac Low, Paik, Dieter Rot, Wolf Vostell, and Emmett Williams, among others. Times Auditorium, Philadelphia College of Art. 13 March.

Yayoi Kusama, *Kusama's Peep Show: Endless Love Show* (mirrored sound and light environment). Castellane Gallery, 764 Madison Avenue, N.Y. 15 March (opening).

Carolee Schneemann, *Water Light Water Needle* (kinetic theater). St. Mark's Church in the Bowery, N.Y. 17-20 March.

Günter Brus, Kurt Kren, Otto Muehl, Hermann Nitsch, and Peter Weibel are invited to participate in Destruction in Art Symposium, London. For this purpose, they establish the Institut für Direkte Kunst. Spring.

Zaj Group, *Concierto Zaj*. Aula Magna, Facultad de Derecho, Universidad Madrid. 26 March.

Milan Knížák, *Get Wet By Rain (1. manifesto '66 in Aktual newspaper, 2. a walk game)*, wall newspaper. Prague. April.

Hi Red Center, *Be Clean!* (event, performed by members of Fluxus). Grand Army Plaza, N.Y. 11 June.

Hermann Nitsch, 4. *Abrreaktionsspiel*. Galerie Josef Dvorak, Vienna. 16 June.

Nam June Paik and Charlotte Moorman perform John Cage's *26'1.1499"" for a String Player* as part of *Gondola Happening*, Ponte Rialto, Venice. 18 June.

Günter Brus and Otto Muehl, *Totalaktion 2* (Brus' *Action no. 14*), filmed by Peter Weibel. Galerie Dvorak, Vienna. 24 June.

Günter Brus and Otto Muehl, *Vietnamparty* (Brus' *Action no. 15*). Institut für Direkte Kunst, Perinetgasse 1, Vienna. Filmed by Peter Weibel; photographed by L. Hoffenreich. 4 July.

Milan Knížák, *Vacation Activity*. Prague. July.

Allan Kaprow in collaboration with Charles Frazier, *Gas* (Happening). Hamptons, Long Island, N.Y. Sponsored by Dwan Gallery, N.Y., and WCBS-TV. 6-8 August.

Robert Whitman, *Two Holes of Water No. 1*. North West Woods, East Hampton, Long Island. 26-27 August.

Gustav Metzger and John Sharkey present *DIAS 1966 (Destruction in Arts Symposium)*. Individual performances listed on dates of occurrence, below. London. 31 August-30 September.

DIAS. Morning press conference followed by Ralph Ortiz, *Chair Destruction*. St. Bride Institute, London. 31 August.

DIAS. Mark Boyle, *Presentation*. Jeannetta Cochrane Theatre, London. 1 September.

DIAS. Günter Brus, Otto Muehl, and Hermann Nitsch. Press conference about DIAS and Brus, *Aktion in einem Kreis (Action in a Circle, 16th action)*. Institut für Direkte Kunst, Perinetgasse 1, Vienna. 2 September.

Otto Muehl, *Stilleben mit Finger* (Still Life with Finger) (material action). Perinetgasse 1, Vienna. 2 September.

DIAS. Ernst Flesichmann, Gustav Metzger, and Ralph Ortiz, *DIAS at Speakers' Corner*. Hyde Park, London. 3 September.

DIAS. *An Evening with Ralph Ortiz*. Better Books, London. 5 September.

DIAS. Jean Toche (GAAG), *Typewriter Destruction*. Better Books, London. 6 September.

3. Festival de la Libre Expression (alternately Workshop of Free
   Expression). Théâtre de la Chimère, Paris. Organized by Jean-Jacques
   Lebel. Events include Robert Filliou, *New-York imprévu* (Happening, 26
   April); Tetsumi Kudo, *Your portrait* (Happening) and *Sneeze of Guinea
   Pigs* (experiment, both 26 April); Ben Vautier, *La Table* and *Paris by
   Night* (théatre total, 25 April), and *120 minutes dédiées au Divin
   Marquis* (collaborative happening by Lebel and others staged on 4
   and 27 April). Formation of the International Committee for DIAS,
   Gustav Metzger Hon. Secretary. Series of press conferences. London.
   April-May.

*Advanced Art, Akce, Novy Realismus, Happenings, Event* presented by
   Eric Andersen, Arthur Køpcke and Tomas Schmit. Statni
                Divadelni Studio, Reduta, Prague. 5 April.
        Nam June Paik presents *Toward A More Sensible Boredom*. Filmmakers' Cinematheque, N.Y.
           Performers include Charlotte Moorman, Paik, Wolf Vostell, and Emmett Williams. Works by
           George Brecht, John Cage, Dick Higgins, Jackson Mac Low, Paik, Dieter Rot, and Emmett
           Williams, among others. 21 April.
        NOW Festival. National Arena, Washington, D.C. Sponsored by Private Arts Foundation. Events
           include Robert Rauschenberg's *Pelican* and *Linoleum*, Robert Whitman's *Prune Flat* and *Untitled
           Pieces*, and an appearance by the Velvet Underground, Andy Warhol and cast. 26 April.
                    Wolf Vostell, *Dogs and Chinese Not Allowed* (Happenings). New York subway stations, Wantagh,
                       Long Island, and Something Else Gallery. 16-20 May.
                    Zaj Group, *Festival Zaj 2*. Madrid. 21 May.
                       Milan Knížák, *Give a Paper Rose (1. a club founded, 2. a speech to the long hair people)*
                       (wall newspaper). Streets and restaurants, Prague. May.
                            Yayoi Kusama, *Narcissus Garden* (outdoor mirrored-sphere
                               environment). Italian Pavilion, 33rd Venice Biennale. June.
                            Allan Kaprow. *Self-Service* (Happening). Boston, New York, and Los
                               Angeles. Co-sponsored by Institute of Contemporary Arts, Boston,
                               Harry N. Abrams, Inc., N.Y., and the Pasadena Art Museum. June-
                               September.
                            Günter Brus and Otto Muehl, *Ornament ist ein Verbrechen (Ornament
                               is Crime)* (Brus's *Action no. 13*, first total action). Adolf Loos Villa,
                               Vienna. 2 June.

DIAS. Al Hansen performs *Coin Piece* in Biff Stevens's *Pneumatic Environment*, London. 17 September.
　　Discussion on DIAS, chaired by John J. Sharkey. Participants include Ivor Davies, Al Hansen,
　　Gustav Metzger, Ralph Ortiz, and Jasia Reichardt. ICA, London. 20 September.
DIAS. Ralph Ortiz, *Self-Destruction*. Mercury Theatre, London. 22 September.
DIAS. Evening events include Al Hansen, a happening with children. London Free School Playground.
　　23 September.
DIAS. John Latham, *Film*. Mercury Theatre, London. 23 September.
　　　　　　Wolf Vostell, *Seh Buch* (de-coll/age Happening). Studentenhaus, Frankfurt.
　　　　　　　23 September.
　　　　　　*Juxtapositionen*. Galerie Aachen. Performers include Juan Hidalgo, Dick
　　　　　　　Higgins, Alison Knowles, and Wolf Vostell. 25 September.
　　　　　　DIAS. *Evening with Yoko Ono*, assisted by Anthony Cox. Africa Centre,
　　　　　　　　　London. 28 September.
　　　　　　　　DIAS. *Evening with Yoko Ono*, assisted by Anthony Cox. Works include
　　　　　　　　　*Line Piece*, *Bag Piece*, *Cut Piece*, *Strip-Tease for Three*, *Wall Piece*,
　　　　　　　　　and *Dawn Piece*. Africa Centre, London. 29 September.
　　　　　　　　DIAS. *Final Event*, including Mark Boyle (projections), John Latham (*Film*), Yoko Ono
　　　　　　　　　(*Disappearing Piece*), and Ralph Ortiz (event-film). Mercury Theatre, London. 30 September.
　　　　　　　　　　　Nam June Paik and Charlotte Moorman perform works by Joseph
　　　　　　　　　　　　Beuys, George Brecht, John Cage, Dick Higgins, Alison Knowles,
　　　　　　　　　　　　Yoko Ono, Paik, and Dieter Rot. Gallerie 101, Copenhagen. 30
　　　　　　　　　　　　September.
　　　　　　　　　　　Claes Oldenburg, *Massage* (performance, presented in conjunction with
　　　　　　　　　　　　the exhibition "Claes Oldenburg: Skulpturer och Teckningar").
　　　　　　　　　　　　Moderna Museet, Stockholm. 3-4, 6-7 October.

**1966** (cont'd) *4th Annual New York Avant Garde Festival*, organized by Charlotte Moorman. Central Park
on the Mall, N.Y. Participants and works include George Brecht (*Symphony #4*), John Cage
(*Variations III*),Al Hansen (*3 Events*), Dick Higgins (*Danger Music No. 2, Dick and his Little
Wagon*, performed by Emmett Williams and his Japanese tools, Alison Knowles and her all girl
team, and Jerry Agel and his slide projector), Allan Kaprow (*Towers*, a Happening for children),
Alison Knowles (*Shoes of Your Choice*), Shigeko Kubota (*Peeping into the Balla*), Charlotte
Moorman (performing Joseph Beuys' *Cello Sonata*), Yoko Ono (*Sunrise Event, Cut Piece*), Nam
June Paik (*Zen Smiles*), Ben Patterson (*It's Vital, Night Kite*), Dieter Rot (*Manifesto*), Tomas
Schmit (...), Carolee Schneemann (*Something*); Wolf Vostell (*From Morning Glory*), Emmett
Williams (*Duet, Counting Song no. II*) and La Monte Young (*Composition 1960 #13* sung by
Dick Higgins). 9 September.
DIAS. Destruction in Art Symposium. Africa Centre, London. Presenters include Günter Brus, Al
Hansen, Juan Hidalgo, Jean-Jacques Lebel, John Latham, Gustav Metzger, Otto Muehl, Hermann
Nitsch, Ralph Ortiz, Wolf Vostell, Peter Weibel, and Yoko Ono. 9-11 September.
DIAS. Günter Brus, *Head Destruction (17th action)* and Otto Muehl *Translation for Two Voices*.
Africa Centre, London. 10 September.
DIAS. Afternoon events include: Al Hansen, *Event with Motor-Cycle*; John Latham, *Skoob with
Powder*; and Jean-Jacques Lebel, *Distorted Postcards* (Happening). London Free School Playground.
12 September.
DIAS. Günter Brus and Otto Muehl, *Breath Exercises* (action music, Brus' *18th action*); Al Hansen,
*Paper Happening*; Yoko Ono, *Whisper Piece*; and Ralph Ortiz, *Paper Bag Event*. Conway Hall,
Red Lions Street, London. 12 September.
London Free School Playground, DIAS. Afternoon events include John Latham, *Flying Skoob*, and
Yoko Ono, *Shadow Piece*. 13 September.
DIAS. Günter Brus and Otto Muehl present Direct Art, *Ten Rounds for Cassius Clay* (Brus' *19th
action*). St. Bride Institute, London. 13 September.
DIAS. Wolf Vostell, *Rebellion Plus Minus De-Composition* (happening-action lecture). Performers
include Günter Brus, Al Hansen, Juan Hidalgo, Kurt Kren, Gustav Metzger, Otto Muehl,
Hermann Nitsch, Robin Page, John Sharkey, and Vostell. ICA, London. 14 September.
DIAS. Juan Hidalgo and Zaj Group present and perform *Afternoon
Concert*. Africa Centre, London. 15 September.
DIAS. *Simultaneous Action* by the Vienna Group with Al Hansen:
Günter Brus (*Self-Destruction, 20th action*); Al Hansen (*Event*);
Otto Muehl (*Lecture Demonstration*); Hermann Nitsch (film
projections); and Peter Weibel (action-lecture *Proposals on Non-
Affirmative Art*). Africa Centre, London. 15 September.
DIAS. Hermann Nitsch OM Theatre action, 5. *Abreaktionsspiel*. St.
Bride Institute, London. 16 September.

Performances by Eric Andersen, Dick Higgins, Alison Knowles, and Arthur Køpcke. Akademiet-
Charlottenborg, Copenhagen. 7-10 October.
Hi Red Center, The One-Thousand-Yen Note Trial begins. Tokyo District Court. 8 October.
9 Evenings: Theatre + Engineering. 25th Street Armory, N.Y. Presented by the Foundation for
Contemporary Performance and Experiments in Art and Technology, Inc. Works presented by
John Cage, Lucinda Childs, Öyvind Fahlström, Alex Hay, Steve Paxton, Yvonne Rainer, Robert
Rauschenberg, David Tudor, and Robert Whitman. Filmed by Alfons Schilling. 14-23 October.
Koncert Fluxus, by Dick Higgins, Milan Knížák, Alison Knowles, and Ben Vautier. Various sites
including Klub Umelcu, Prague. 13-17 October.
Joseph Beuys, *Action "Eurasia"* and *"34th Movement of the Siberian Symphony"*. Gallery 101,
Gruppe Handwagen 13, Copenhagen. 4-15 October.
Allan Kaprow (New York), Marta Minujin (Buenos Aires), and Wolf
Vostell (Cologne), Three country Happening, *Simultaneidad en
Simultaneidad*. 24 October.

**1966** (cont'd) Otto Muehl, *Aktionskoncert für Al Hansen*, performed by Günter Brus, Kurt Kren, Hermann Nitsch, Rudolf Schwarzkogler, and Peter Weibel, among others. Galerie Nächst St. Stephen, Vienna. 29 October.

Joseph Beuys, *Action "Eurasia"* and *"32nd Movement of the Siberian Symphony 1963"*. Galerie René Block, Berlin. 31 October.

Otto Muehl, *Funebre* (material action). Perinetgasse 1, Vienna. November-December.

Allan Kaprow, *Untitled* (environment). Westchester Art Society, White Plains, N.Y. 11-23 November.

Alison Knowles and Dick Higgins, *Events and New Music*. El Salon de Actos de la Escuela Tecnica Superior de Arquitectura, Madrid. 12 November.

Jean-Jacques Lebel, *Happening dans la rue* (conference-demonstration). Festival SIGMA, Bordeaux. 19 November.

Zaj Group, *Festival Zaj 3*. Several sites, Madrid. 7-8 December.

*Happening for Sightseeing Bus Trip in Tokyo*, presented by Ay-O. Pieces by Robert Filliou, Al Hansen, Dick Higgins, Allan Kaprow, Alison Knowles, Ben Patterson, Tomas Schmit, Daniel Spoerri, and Wolf Vostell. Tokyo. 18 December.

Mark Boyle and Joan Hills, *Dig* (event). Shepherds Bush, London. Date unknown.

Mark Boyle and Joan Hills form the Sensual Laboratory. Light shows *Son et Lumière for Insects, Reptiles and Water, and Son et Lumière: Bodily Fluids and Functions*, at Cochrane Theatre, London. Dates unknown.

Robert Delford Brown and Rhett Delford Brown, *Orgasm Event* (performance, Hotel Belle Rive, Juan les Pins), *Vous êtes invitez pour un cocktail* (event, bridal suite, Negresco Hotel, Nice), and *Free Striptease with Drum and Bugle Corps Accompaniment* (two-week event, London). Dates unknown.

Jean-Jacques Lebel, *Tant va la cruche à l'eau qu'à la fin elle s'enlace* (Happening with Barnadette Lafont, Taylor Mead and the Living Theater). Festival de Cassis, Port de Cassis, France. Date unknown.

Rudolf Schwarzkogler, *6th action* (final action). Vienna.

Paul McCarthy, *Saw* (performance). Little Theater, University of Utah, Salt Lake City. April.

*Zock-Exercises*, by Otto Muehl, Peter Weibel, and Oswald Wiener. Galerie Nächst St. Stephen, Vienna. 17 April.

*Zock Festival*, participants include Otto Muehl, Hermann Nitsch, and Peter Weibel. Restaurant "Grünes Tor," Vienna. 21 April.

Ben Vautier presents Fluxus concert, *Les Mots et les Choses*. Galleria il Punto, Turin. 26-28 April.

Marta Minujin, *Circuit*. Sir George Williams University, Montreal. 28 April.

*Manifestazione Internationale*, by Juan Hidalgo, George Maciunas, W. Marchetti, and Ben Vautier. Dioniso Teatro, Rome. 1 May.

Allan Kaprow, *Interruption* (Happening). State University of New York at Stony Brook. 10-11 May.

Wolf Vostell, *Miss Vietnam* (Happening). Various sites, Cologne. 27 May.

Otto Muehl, *Aktion für das Österreichische Fernsehen* (material action). Perinetgasse 1, Vienna. June.

Yayoi Kusama, *Self-Obliteration by Kusama : An Audio-Visual-Light Performance*. Black Gate Theatre, N.Y. 16-18 June.

**1967** Carolee Schneemann, *Snows* (kinetic theater). Martinique Theater, N.Y. 21 January-5 February.

Tadeusz Kantor, *Lettre*. Galeria Foksal, Warsaw. 27 January.

Allan Kaprow, *Flick* (Happening). New York. Sponsored by Angry Vets Against War in VietNam. 1 February.

Nam June Paik, *Opéra Sextronique*, performed by Takehisa Kosugi, Charlotte Moorman, Paik, and Jud Yalkut. Filmmakers' Cinematheque, N.Y. Moorman performs the first two of four acts of Paik's *Opera Sextronique*, and is then arrested, along with Paik. For appearing topless, Moorman is convicted of indecent exposure and receives a suspended sentence. 9 February.

Jean-Jacques Lebel, *Happening et Fluxus, une conférence-démonstration*, and pieces by George Brecht, Alison Knowles, Nam June Paik, Tomas Schmit, and La Monte Young, among others. Ampithéâtre AC, Faculté des Lettres de Nanterre. 10 February.

Robert Rauschenberg, *Outskirts* (performance). Loeb Student Center, New York University. Event coordinated by Irving Sandler. 7 March.

Jean-Jacques Lebel, *Venceremos* (conférence-démonstration and street happening). Instituto Torcuato Di Tella, Buenos Aires. April.

Joseph Beuys, *Action "Eurasienstab" 82 min. fluxorum organum*. St. Stephan Gallery, Vienna. 2 July.

Yayoi Kusama, *Body Festivals*. In Tompkins Square Park and Washington Square Park, N.Y. Throughout Summer.

Yayoi Kusama, *Self-Obliteration by Kusama: An Audio-Visual-Light Performance* and *Horse Play*. Woodstock, N.Y. July.

Beginning of four-day trial of DIAS functionaries at the Old Bailey, London, for the presentation of an indecent exhibition, Hermann Nitsch's event. Metzger fined 100 pounds and John Sharkey conditionally discharged. 19 July.

4. Festival de la Libre Expression (alternately Workshop of Free Expression). La Cour Interieure du Papa Gayo à Saint Tropez, France. Presented by Jean-Jacques Lebel. Events include Pablo Picasso's *Le désir attrapé par la queue* (mise-en-scène by Lebel and featuring The Soft Machine, Taylor Mead, and Ultra Violet), Lebel's *Sunlove* (happening with The Soft Machine), and *Mon Cul sur la commode* (happening with Taylor Mead, Ben Vautier, Ultra Violet, among others, 24 July). 12 July-28 August.

**1967** (cont'd) Tadeusz Kantor, *Happening Panoramique*. 23 August.

Yippie group members drop dollar bills from the visitor's gallery to the trading floor of the New York Stock Exchange. 24 August.

Robert Whitman, *Prune, Flat, A New Piece* (skirt). Southhampton College Theater. 27 August-1 September.

Günter Brus, *Action with Diana* and *Transvestitenaktion (Transvestite Action, action no. 25)*. Brus home, Adalbert-Stifter-Str., Vienna. September.

Yayoi Kusama's performances include one at Chrysler Art Museum in Provincetown, thirty-two performances of "Kusama Tea dancers" (Electric Circus, N.Y.), and a body-painting party (Cheetah Club, N.Y.). Fall.

Günter Brus, *20. September (action no. 24)*. Brus home, Adalbert-Stifter-Str., Vienna. 27 September.

5th Annual New York Avant Garde Festival. J.F. Kennedy Ferry Boat, Whitehall Terminal, Staten Island Ferry, N.Y. Organized by Charlotte Moorman. Participants include Joseph Beuys (*Piano Piece*), George Brecht (*Drip Music*), John Cage's (*Variations III*), Al Hansen (*Baker's Dozen*), Hi Red Center Group (*Cleaning Event*), Dick Higgins (*Symphony*), Allan Kaprow (*Noise [for ferryboat]*), Jean-Jacques Lebel (*Wise & Lebel Interview*), Charlotte Moorman (Nam June Paik's *Amelia Earhart in Memorium*), Yoko Ono (*Water Piece*), Ralph Ortiz (*Melting Pot*), Nam June Paik (*Electronic Television, Video Tape Study, Check or Money Order*), Ben Patterson (*Untitled*), Tomas Schmit (*Third Class Reader*, poetry), Carolee Schneemann (*Nightcrawlers II*), Jean Toche (*Mattress*), Wolf Vostell (*From Kleenex*), Emmett Williams (*Cellar Song for 5 Boys*, poetry), and La Monte Young (*Composition 1960 #15*), among others. 29-30 September.

*12 Evenings of Manipulations*. Judson Gallery, N.Y. Destructionist art show with performances by Al Hansen, Allan Kaprow, Charlotte Moorman, Yoko Ono, Ralph Ortiz, Nam June Paik, Tomas Schmit, Carolee Schneemann, and Jean Toche, among others. October.

Allan Kaprow, *Fluids* (final large-scale Happening). Los Angeles area and Pasadena Art Museum. 10-12 October.

Dick Higgins and Alison Knowles, *What Did You Bring*. Museum of Contemporary Art, Chicago. Higgins presents *Graphis 132* and *Danger Music no. 17*; Knowles presents *String Piece, Bean Roll Reading, Blue Ram, Proposition, Newspaper Music*, and *News of the Day*. 23 October.

Yayoi Kusama, *Love Room* (installation). Galerij Orez, The Hague. While in Holland, stages several polka-dotting actions. 3 November (opening).

*Direct Art Festival*, presented by Otto Muehl and Günter Brus, among others. Porrhaus, Institute für Direkte Kunst, Vienna. 9 November.

**1968** Otto Muehl, *Amore, Aktion mit einem Masochisten* and *Satisfaction* (with Brus and Rudolf Schwarzkogler). Vienna. Early 1968.

Günter Brus, *Fountain* (28th action, with Otto Muehl and Kurt Kren). Brus home, Adalbert-Stifter-Str., Vienna. January.

Carolee Schneemann, *Illinois Central* (kinetic theater). Museum of Contemporary Art, Chicago. 26-28 January.

Günter Brus, *Satisfaction — Günter Brus bittet um Ruhe, alles Gute zum Muttertag wünscht Otto Muehl (Satisfaction — Günther Brus Requests Silence, Kind Regards for Mother's Day from Otto Muehl, 29th action*, with Otto Muehl and Rudolf Schwarzkogler). Early 1968.

Günter Brus, *Der helle Wahnsinn-Die Architektur des hellen Wahnsinns (The Total Madness — The Architecture of the Total Madness, 30th action)*. Reiffmuseum, Aachen. 6 February.

Allan Kaprow, *Runner* (Happening). Suburbs of St. Louis and Washington University. 9-11 February.

Allan Kaprow, *Transfer* (a Happening for Christo). Wesleyan University, Middletown, CT. 18 February.

Günter Brus, *Direkte Kunst (Direct Art , 32nd action)*. Kunstakademie, Düsseldorf. February.

Hermann Nitsch, *25th* and *26th Aktions*, or *Orgien Mysteries Theater*. Filmmakers' Cinematheque, N.Y. 2-16 March.

Robert Rauschenberg, *Urban Round* (performance). School of Visual Arts, N.Y. For Fall Gallery
Concerts. 10 and 19 November.

George Maciunas and Fluxus Group, *A Paper Event by the Fluxmasters of the Rear-Garde*. Time
Life Building and Museum of Contemporary Crafts of the American Craftsmens Council, N.Y.
Maciunas performs *In Memorium to A. Olivetti for Paper Orchestra*, Flux-Group presents *Kill
Paper Not People*. 15 November.

Allan Kaprow, *Moving* (a happening for Milan Knížák). Museum of Contemporary Art, Chicago. 29
November.

Günter Brus, *Mit Schwung ins Neue Jahr (With Verve into the New Year, action no. 27*, with Otto
Muehl and Rudolf Schwarzkogler). Brus home, Adalbert-Stifter-Str., Vienna. 31 December.

Mark Boyle and Joan Hills. Produce light shows for UFO Club, London. Begin collaboration with
rock group Soft Machine. Jean-Jacques Lebel, *Hommage à Lautréamont* (Happening).
Montevidéo, Uruguay. Date unknown.

Jean-Jacques Lebel, *L'élection de Miss Festival* (Happening erotico-politique with Yoko Ono).
Festival de Film Expérimental de Knokke-le-Zoute, Belgium. Date unknown.

Raphael Montañez Ortiz performs *Henny Penny Piano Destruction Concert with Paper Bag
Destruction*. The artist's studio, N.Y.

Reese Palley Gallery opens in San Francisco, under direction of Carol
Lindsley. Until its closure in 1972, the gallery will host performances
and exhibitions by Terry Fox, Howard Fried, Paul Kos, Bruce
Nauman, and Dennis Oppenheim, among others.

Allan Kaprow, *Travelog* (a Happening without an audience). Fairleigh Dickinson University, Madison, N.J.
20 July.

Yayoi Kusama, *The Anatomic Explosion* (third in happening series). At statue of Alice in Wonderland,
Central Park, assisted by James Golata and Gordon Brown. New York. August.

Yayoi Kusama, *Body Painting* (Happening). Avanti Galleries, N.Y. August.

Yippie group activities, including nomination of the pig Pigasus as the Youth International Party's
presidential candidate. During 1968 Democratic National Convention, Chicago. 20-29 August.

Otto Muehl, *Piss Action*. Munich. September.

Yayoi Kusama, *The Anatomic Explosion* (fourth in Happening series). United Nations, N.Y. 8
September.

*6th Annual New York Avant Garde Festival* (a parade). Down Central Park West, from 95th to
67th Streets, N.Y. Organized by Charlotte Moorman. 14 September.

    Otto Muehl, *Aktion* (nightclub, Annagasse, Vienna); *Aktion* for film *Reise nach Kythara* (Muehl home,
      Praterstr., Vienna); and *Libi* (Muehl home, Praterstr., Vienna). Fall.

    Yayoi Kusama, "weekly flesh-in." Nirvana Headshop (a "psychedelicatessen"), Union Turnpike, Queens.
      22 September.

    Emmett Williams, *The Boy and the Bird*. Central Park Poetry Events, N.Y. 28 September.

    Yayoi Kusama, *Naked Demonstration/Anatomic Explosion* (Happening). Wall Street, N.Y.
      Scheduled for 13 October.

    Joseph Beuys, *Simultan-Eisenkiste, Halbiertes Kreuz*. Art Intermedia, Aktionsraum Cologne.
      14 October.

    Adrian Piper, *Meat into Meat* (loft performance). New York. October.

    Günter Brus, *Kunststücke (Art Pieces)* (action). Muehl home, Praterstr., Vienna. November.

    Günter Brus, *Strangulation* (action with Anni Brus). Brus home, Adalbert-Stifter-Str., Vienna.
      November.

    Yayoi Kusama, protest action with nude body painting of performers in Nixon, Humphrey and
      Wallace masks. Board of Elections, Varick St., N.Y. 3 November.

        Yayoi Kusama, nudist protest action. Reade Street and Broadway, N.Y. 11 November.

        Yayoi Kusama, protest happening. Canarsie subway line on the BMT at 14th Street, N.Y.
          17 November.

        Yayoi Kusama, *Homosexual Wedding* of Falcon McKendall and John deVries. Couple dressed in
          Kusama-designed "orgy" wedding gown for two wearers. 31-33 Walker and Church Streets,
          N.Y. 25 November.

        Yayoi Kusama, two naked Happenings. New York's Fillmore East Theatre. Other performers include
          Fleetwood Mac, Country Joe and the Fish, and Joshua Light Show. 6-7 December.

          Dick Higgins, *The Thousand Symphonies* (1967). Hickman Auditorium, The Gun Show, Art
          Department, Douglass College, Rutgers University, New Brunswick, N.J. 9 December.

        Otto Muehl, *Aktion für WDR*. Muehl home, Praterstr., Vienna. 16 December.

            Milan Knížák, *Lying Ceremony*. Douglass College, Rutgers University,
              New Brunswick, N.J. 17 December.

            Mark Boyle and Joan Hills. As Sensual Laboratory, tour United States
              producing Light-Environments for concerts by Jimi Hendrix and Soft
              Machine.

            Mark Boyle and Joan Hills, *Bodily Fluids and Functions* (event).
              Roundhouse, London.

            Robert Delford Brown and Rhett Delford Brown, *Demolition Party* (with
              classical Chinese orchestra, announcing beginning of construction
              on Great Building Crack-Up, N.Y.). Dates unknown.

            Tadeusz Kantor, *La leçon d'anatomie d'après Rembrandt* (Happening).
              Nuremberg, Germany.

**1968** (cont'd) Allan Kaprow, *Hello* (Happening [for the medium itself]), sponsored by WGBH-TV. Four sites,
Boston. 13 March.

DIAS USA 1968 (Destruction in Art Symposium). Judson Gallery, N.Y.. Organized by Jon Hendricks.
Performers: Al Hansen (*Sadomaso*), Bici Hendricks (*Ice Breaking*), Charlotte Moorman
(*Destruction*), Hermann Nitsch (*27th Aktion*, or *Carcus [sic] Mutilation*), Ralphael Montañez Ortiz (*The Death
of White Henny and Black Penny*), Nam June Paik (*Self Mutilation*), and Lil Picard (*Soft Burnings
Feathers and Coal*). 22 March.

Jean-Jacques Lebel, *Golden Duck Soup* (Happening). Festival Internationale del Teatro Universitario,
Teatro Regio, Parma. 23 March.

Allan Kaprow, *Record II* (a Happening for Roger Shattuck). University of Texas, Austin. 27 March.

Hermann Nitsch, *28th Aktion*, or *Introduction to the O.M. Theater*. Great Hall (Faculty Lounge),
University of Cincinnati, Spring Arts Festival '68. 4-6 April.

Wolf Vostell, *Hommage a Dürer* (technical Happening). Institute für Moderne Kunst, Nuremberg.
4 April-12 May.

Scheduled 1968 International Symposium of Destruction in Art at Judson Gallery is cancelled by
organizers "in deference to the memory and the spirit of the beautiful soul Dr. Martin Luther
King, Jr." 19 April.

Allan Kaprow, *Arrivals* (Happening). On the airfield, Nassau Community College, N.Y. 22 April.

Allan Kaprow, *Population* (Happening). For each of four square plots around countryside, Colby
Junior College. 30 April.

Paul McCarthy, *Leap* (performance), University of Utah, Salt Lake City, and *Too Steep, Too Fast*
(performance), Marin County, Calif. May.

Marta Minujin, *Minucode*. Center for Interamerican Relations, N.Y. May.

Robert Filliou, The Poetic Science (action-poetry). Moderna Museet, Stockholm. 10 May.

The Destruction Art Group 1968 Presents. Judson Gallery, N.Y. Performances by Al Hansen,
Bici Hendricks, Kurt Kren, Charlotte Moorman, Ralphael Montñez Ortiz, Nam June Paik,
Lil Picard, and Jean Toche, among others. 10-18 May.

Allan Kaprow, *Overtime* (Happening for Walter de Maria). University of California, San Diego.
14 May.

Fluxus West San Diego and Ken Friedman present Ben Vautier, *Vautier Day*. Santa Cruz, San
Francisco, Berkeley, and San Jose. 15 May.

Günter Brus, *Der Staatsbuerger Brus betrachtet seinen Körper* (action). Hip-Hop, Judenplatz,
Vienna. 17 May.

Jean-Jacques Lebel, *Théâtre de guérilla dans la rue* (street plays and actions with students of
Vincennes University), Paris. May and through 1969.

Günter Brus, Otto Muehl, Peter Weibel, and Oswald Wiener present
*Kunst und Revolution*. Vienna University. Sponsored by the Socialist
Austrian Student Association. For degrading state symbols, Brus,
Muehl, and Wiener arrested and sentenced to six months'
detention. 7 June.

Nam June Paik and Charlotte Moorman, *Mixed Media Opera*. Town
Hall, N.Y. Pieces by Paik and others, including John Cage's
*26'1.1499"" for a String Player*. 10 June.

Daniel Spoerri, *Restaurant Spoerri* (working restaurant). Burgplatz 19,
Düsseldorf. 17 June (opening).

Yayoi Kusama, *The Anatomic Explosion* (first and second in happening
series). First in front of statue of George Washington opposite New
York Stock Exchange, Wall Street; second in front of Statue of
Liberty. New York. July.

**363**

**1969** His legal appeals rejected, Günter Brus flees to Berlin. Early 1969.

Otto Muehl, *Apollo 10*. Muehl home, Praterstr., Vienna. Early 1969.

Allan Kaprow, *Six Ordinary Happenings (Charity, Pose, Fine, Shape, Giveaway, Purpose)*. Berkeley, 7 March-23 May.

Wolf Vostell, *Brotver Messung* (instant Happening). Opernhaus, Cologne. 15 March.

Yayoi Kusama, *Preview Bust-Out*. Bethesda Pond Boating Lake Fountain, Central Park, N.Y. 16 March.

Hermann Nitsch, *30th Aktion*. Forum of Galerie Van de Loo, Munich. 18 March.

Otto Muehl, *Pissaktion*. Hamburger Filschau. March.

Yippie group organizers, including Abbie Hoffman and Jerry Rubin, indicted by Federal Grand Jury for crossing state lines to incite riot and to resist and obstruct the police. March.

Yayoi Kusama, *Bust-Out*. Sheep's Meadow, Central Park, N.Y. 6 April.

Al Hansen, *The Hamlet of Gertrude Stein*. Studio of Gilles Larrain, 66 Grand St., N.Y. 25-27 April.

Yayoi Kusama opens fashion boutique at 404 Sixth Avenue, N.Y. 28 April.

Wolf Vostell, *Rasten + Tanken* (de-coll/age happening). Munich-Sauerlach-Autobahn, Galerie Van de Loo. 8 May.

Allan Kaprow, *Course* (Happening). On the Iowa River, University of Iowa. 9 May.

Nam June Paik and Charlotte Moorman premiere *TV Bra for Living Sculpture*. Howard Wise Gallery, N.Y. 17 May.

Wolf Vostell, *100 Mal Hoeren und Spielen*. WDR Cologne. 19 May.

Ben Vautier, *Non-Art, Verite Art, Anti-Art-Festival*. Nice, France. 1 June.

Robert Filliou and George Brecht, *The Eternal Network*. Staedt. Museum, Moenchengladbach. 18 June.

Rudolf Schwarzkogler dies after falling from window of his apartment. Vienna. 20 June.

Gordon Matta-Clark, *Photo-Fry* (performance remnant/installation) in "Documentation" exhibition. John Gibson Gallery. Summer.

Otto Muehl, *Champagne Rider's Club* (film by Kurt Kren, encompassing the actions *Aktion im Freudenauer Wasser — Geschlechtsverkehrsaktion unter Wasser [Action in Freudenauer Water — Sexual Intercourse Action Under Water]*, *Masochistische Reiteraktion im Schlamm [Masochistic Rider Action in Mud]*, and *Penis-und Vaginaaktion*). Vienna. Summer.

Robert Filliou, *Leeds* (a card game). Leeds College of Art, England. 26 June.

**1970** "The Pollution Show". The Oakland Museum. Artists include Tom Marioni. Howard Fried's contribution, *All My Dirty Blue Clothes*, is rejected. Catalogue. 10 January-15 February.

Wolf Vostell, *Thermoelektrischer Kaugummi* (happening room). Kunsthalle, Cologne. 14 February-18 May.

Terry Fox, *Wall Push* (performance). Museum of Conceptual Art, San Francisco. February.

Hermann Nitsch, 7. *Abreaktionsspiel*, and Günter Brus, *Psychodramolett* (action no. 41, supplement to Nitsch's action). Aktionsraum, Munich. Recorded by West German Radio/Television. Late February.

Günter Brus, a small action (action no. 42), and Otto Muehl, *Aktion*, presented as part of *Oh Gott, da sind sie* (Oh God, Here They Are) event. Club Bastion, Kirchheim-Teck, Germany. March.

Yayoi Kusama censored in her attempt to remove her clothing on television during *Narawa Morning Show*. Japan. 12 March.

Yayoi Kusama, topless Happening. Iwaibashi Park, Tsukiji, Tokyo. Kusama and three female Japanese participants arrested. 13 March.

Yayoi Kusama, *Grand Orgy to Awaken the Dead at MOMA (Otherwise Known as The Museum of Modern Art) — Featuring Their Usual Display of Nudes*. The Museum of Modern Art, N.Y. The artist and eight nude models removed from the premises after twenty minutes. 24 August.

Paul McCarthy, *Mountain Bowling* (performance). Salt Lake City, Utah. September.

*7th Festival of Avant Garde*. Wards Island, Mill Rock Island, in the East River at 102 Street, N.Y. Organized by Charlotte Moorman. 28 September-4 October.

Otto Muehl, *Scheisskerl = Shit Head* (filmed action). Private home, Frankfurt. October.

Otto Muehl, *Der Tod der Sharon Tate (The Death of Sharon Tate)* (action and installation). Galeria Milano, Milan. 9 October.

Howard Fried, *All My Dirty Blue Clothes* (first installation). In a classroom, University of California Davis. 6 November.

Gordon Matta-Clark, *Christmas Piece* (performance). Opening night, Holly Solomon's 98 Greene Street Loft, N.Y. 25 December.

Mark Boyle and Joan Hills, *Body Work* and *Taste and Smell* events. ICA, London.

Günter Brus, *Blumenstück (Flower Piece, action no. 36*, at Villa Raspe), *Impudence in Grunewald* (with Otmar Bauer), *Körperanalyse I (Body Analysis I)*, and *Körperanalyse II (Body Analysis II)*, *Intelligenztest (Intelligence Test)*. Berlin. Dates unknown.

Nam June Paik and Charlotte Moorman, *TV Bra*. Corcoran Gallery of Art, Washington D.C.

Barbara Smith, *Ritual Meal*. Home of Stanley and Elyse Grinstein, L.A.

Otto Muehl, poem recitation and a pig's butchering at the "Festival of the Pious Songs, Gluttony and the Battle Interlude in Vietnam" results in 17,000 citizens of Braunschweig signing petitions of protest. Late 1969.

Marta Minujin, *La Imagen Eléctrica*. Instituto Torcuato Di Tella, Buenos Aires, Argentina. Date unknown.

Terry Fox, exhibition with performances. Reese Palley Gallery, San Francisco. Performances include
Corner Push, Asbestos Tracking, and Opening My Hand as Slowly as Possible. 19 May-
13 June.

Adrian Piper, Streetworks (performance). New York. May.

Günter Brus, Zerreissprobe (Breaking Test) (action no. 43). Aktionsraum, Munich. Brus' final
action. 19 June.

Bonnie Sherk and Howard Levine install Portable Parks 1-3. Three locations, San Francisco.
25-28 June.

Allan Kaprow, Level (for Vaughan Kaprow, activity [Happening]). Aspen, Colo., Arts Council of the
Aspen University for Humanistic Studies. 6 August.

Terry Fox, Blowing Smoke. Museum of Conceptual Art, San Francisco. August.

Otto Muehl, Aktion. Galerie Ostheimer, Frankfurt. 20 August.

Terry Fox, Levitation (performance). Richmond Art Center, Calif. Curated by Tom Marioni.
17-21 September.

Joseph Beuys, Action "Celtic (Kinloch rannoch), Scottish Symphony". Edinburgh College of Art,
Scotland. 26-30 August.

Bonnie Sherk, Snowjob (installation). San Francisco. 15 October.

"The Act of Drinking Beer with Friends Is the Highest Form of Art".
Exhibition by Allan Fish (Tom Marioni), with private performance,
26 October. The Oakland Museum. Catalogue. 27 October-
8 November.

**1971** During Terry Fox's solo exhibition, Fox invites Vito Acconci and Dennis Oppenheim to participate in Environmental
Surfaces: Three Simultaneous Situational Enclosures, a performance event in which each staged a performance. Reese Palley
Gallery, New York. 16 January.

Bonnie Sherk, Public Lunch (performance). In a tiger's cage at San Francisco Zoo's Lion House. February.

"Fish, Fox, Kos". De Saisset Art Gallery and Museum, University of Santa Clara. Exhibition with performances (Fish's Chain
Reaction, Fox's Pisces, and Kos's rEVOLUTION). Catalogue. 2-28 February.

Otto Muehl, Aktion. Private home, Liège, Belgium. 27 February.

Terry Fox privately recreates Thomas Schmit's piece Zyklus. Museum of Conceptual Art, San
Francisco. March.

Broadcast of MOCA-FM, sixty one-minute audio pieces. Artists include: Allan Fish (Tom Marioni),
Terry Fox, Howard Fried. KPFA-FM radio, San Francisco. Re-broadcast 21 August 1978.
1 March.

**1970** (cont'd) "The Eighties". University Art Museum, Berkeley. Organized by Susan Rannells and Brenda
Richardson. Artists include Terry Fox and Howard Fried. Catalogue. March-April.

Otto Muehl, *The Wanton Woden* (film encompassing the actions *Manotest*; *Morschl*; *Psychotic Party*; *Aktion Investmentfond*
*[Investment Fund]*; *Manopsychotic Ballet*; *Oh, Sensibility*; *SS and Jewish Star*; and *Der geile Wotan [The Wanton*
*Woden]*). Spring-Summer.

Paul McCarthy, *Spinning* (studio performance, videotape). Los Angeles. April.

Yoko Ono and John Lennon, *Fluxfest Presentation of John + Yoko*. 80 Wooster Street, N.Y. 11 April-
14 May.

*Fluxus — Fluxtour*, with Ben Vautier (audience piece), and visits with Jonas Mekas, La Monte Young,
James Stewart and Lauren Bacall (the latter two at theaters where they were performing).
Various sites, N.Y. 30 April-8 May.

Terry Fox, *A Sketch for Impacted Lead* and *Liquid Smoke*. Museum of Conceptual Art,
San Francisco. April.

Adrian Piper, *Untitled Catalysis* (performance). Max's Kansas City, N.Y. April.

*Sound Sculpture As*, one-night sound event. Museum of Conceptual Art, San Francisco.
Participants include Allan Fish [Tom Marioni] and Terry Fox, among others. 30 April.

Terry Fox, *My Hand is a Fine Porcelain* and *Hand Slide*. Museum of Conceptual Art, San Francisco.
May.

Bonnie Sherk, *Sitting Still I* (performance). Army Street Circle, San Francisco. October.

Bonnie Sherk, *Sitting Still II* (performance). In cage at San Francisco Zoo and various sidewalk sites
in the city. November.

Otto Muehl realizes two actions (*Manopsychotik 1* and *Manopsychotik 2*, both 8 November, the
latter with Charlotte Moorman) as his contribution to the "Happening und Fluxus" exhibition,
Kunsthalle Cologne. Returns to Vienna to find his studio in the Perinetgasse has been cleared
by the Viennese Health Department, and much work from 1961-1964 taken to the dump.
November.

Paul Cotton gives unscheduled performance in guise of The Astral-Naught Rabb-Eye, the first
appearance of this character. At opening of the new University Art Museum, Berkeley.
8 November.

Otto Muehl, *Aktion*. For Wet Dream Festival, Nederlands Filmmakers Coop, Amsterdam. Event
disrupted by Heathcote Williams. 26 November.

Otto Muehl, *Aktion mit Hammel*. Bremen, Germany. 13 December.

Otto Muehl, *Aktion*. Aktionsgalerie R. Jaeggli. 16 December.

Terry Fox, *Defoliation Piece* (performance). University Art Museum, Berkeley.

Alison Knowles moves to California to teach at Cal Arts, staying through 1972. Builds the House of
Dust, where many performances were staged.

Terry Fox, *Isolation Unit*. Extended play disc, recording of *Action* by Fox and Joseph Beuys, made
at the Kunstakademie, Düsseldorf. November 1970.

Niki de Saint Phalle, altar shooting action at opening of tenth-anniversary festival celebrating the
Nouveaux Réalistes. Milan.

**1971** (cont'd)"Body Movements". La Jolla Museum of Contemporary Art. Artists include Mowry
Baden, Chris Burden, and Bruce Nauman. April.

Adrian Piper, *Streetworks II* (performances). New York. April.

*A Collaboration Between Allan Fish and Tom Marioni*, identity-transfer video work marking the end
of Marioni's use of the Fish name. Berkeley Gallery, San Francisco. 13 April.

Chris Burden, *Five Day Locker Piece* (performance). University of California, Irvine. 26-30 April.

Chris Burden, *Bicycle Piece* (performance). University of California, Irvine. 6-20 May.

Otto Muehl, *Aktion*. Leasingstudio für Photo und Film, Zürich. 14 May.

Adrian Piper, *Food for the Spirit* (private loft performance). New York. June-July.

As his contribution to group show "6 x 6 x 6", Tom Marioni stages a
dinner, then leaves remnants on view. Civic Arts Gallery, Walnut
Creek, California. June.

Gordon Matta-Clark, *Untitled Performance*. For Projects series,
organized by Willoughby Sharp. Suspension action at Pier 18,
photographs exhibited at The Museum of Modern Art, N.Y. July
(exhibition).

Tom Marioni, *Allan Fish Drinks a Case of Beer*. Reese Palley Gallery,
San Francisco. 10 August.

**1972** Gordon Matta-Clark and Caroline Yorke Goodden, *Hair* (private performance). New York. 1 January.

*Notes and Scores for Sounds*, organized by Tom Marioni. Mills College Art Gallery, Oakland. Artists
include Vito Acconci, Terry Fox, Howard Fried, Nam June Paik, Barbara Smith, and John White.
9-30 January; broadcast on KPFA-FM 26 January.

Second showing of Terry Fox *Hospital*. Reese Palley Gallery, N.Y. January.

Chris Burden, *TV Hijack* (performance). During interview by Phyllis Lutjeans, Channel 3 Cablevision,
Irvine, C.A. 9 February.

"The Source Show", by Bonnie Sherk. San Francisco Art Institute. Featuring installation with animals,
*The Universe May Not be as it Appears*, with contributions from Terry Fox, among others.
10 February-11 March.

Chris Burden, *Bed Piece* (performance). Market Street Art Program, Venice, Calif. 18 February-
10 March.

Paul McCarthy, *Too Steep, Too Fast* (performance). Hollywood Hills, Calif. March.

Tom Marioni's exhibits *My First Car*, spending his budget on a Fiat, which he exhibits. De Saisset
Gallery, University of Santa Clara. Scheduled to run from 3-30 March, but closed after three
days by the university president.

Linda Montano performs *Chicken Dance: The Streets of San Francisco*. Various outdoor locations,
San Francisco. 3, 6, and 9 March.

Howard Fried exhibits videos *Sea Sell Sea Sick at Saw/Sea Sea Soar* and *Fuck You Purdue*, and
the set for *Seaquick*, which was performed and videotaped on the final day of the show. Reese
Palley Gallery, San Francisco. 11 March-8 April.

"San Francisco Performance". Newport Harbor Art Museum. Organized
by Tom Marioni. Artists include Terry Fox, Howard Fried, and Bonnie
Sherk. Catalogue. 12 March-16 April.

Chris Burden, *Match Piece* (performance). Pomona College,
Claremont, Calif. 20 March.

Paul McCarthy, *T.V.* (performance). Art Department, University of
Southern California, Los Angeles. April.

Easter celebration by Paul Cotton and seven performers in
Astral-Naught costumes. Live Oak Park, Berkeley. 2 April.

Tom Marioni, *The Creation* (live-in installation). Reese Palley Gallery,
San Francisco. 16 April-13 May.

*Six Comedy Sonatas*. Museum of Conceptual Art, San Francisco. Performance program featuring
   *Pie in the O Zone* and *Youth in Asia* by Terry Fox and Howard Fried, and *Pig Sonata* by Bonnie
   Sherk. 17 August.
Howard Fried, *Synchromatic Baseball*. Roof of 16 Rose Street studios, San Francisco. The game is
   briefly halted when Fried falls through a skylight, and resumes when he returns from the emergency
   room. August-September.
Chris Burden, *Shout Piece* (performance). F Space, Santa Ana, California. 21 August.
Chris Burden, *Prelude to 220, or 110* (performance). F Space, Santa Ana, California. 10-12 September.
Chris Burden, *I Become a Secret Hippy* (performance). Museum of Conceptual Art, San Francisco.
   3 October.
Chris Burden, *220* (performance). F Space, Santa Ana, California. 9 October.
   Terry Fox, *Hospital* (installation). Reese Palley Gallery, San Francisco. 23 October-6 November.
   Terry Fox, *Clutch* (studio performance). 16 Rose Street, San Francisco. November.
   Chris Burden, *You'll Never See My Face in Kansas City* (performance). Morgan Gallery, Kansas
      City, Missouri. 6 November.
   Chris Burden, *Shoot* (performance). F Space, Santa Ana, California. 19 November.
   Howard Fried stages *40 Winks*, which becomes a mass walking event ending in Hayward, California,
      at 2:00 A.M. Sponsored by University Art Museum, Berkeley. 10 December.
   Chris Burden, *Disappearing* (performance). 22-24 December.
                  Mark Boyle and Joan Hills, *Requiem for an Unknown Citizen* (event). Rotterdam, Netherlands.
                  Gordon Matta-Clark creates performance piece involving performers hiding beneath piles of
                     leaves, then running away. 112 Green Street, N.Y.
                  Gordon Matta-Clark, Tina Giraourd, Carol Goodden, Suzanne Harris, and Rachel Lew open Food
                     Restaurant in SoHo, N.Y.
                  Paul McCarthy, *Ma Bell* (studio performance and videotape). Los Angeles.
                  Otto Muehl begins to focus his energy on development of his commune, which will later settle
                     at an abandoned farm, the Friedrichshof, in Burgenland. Late 1971.

**369**

**1973** Museum of Conceptual Art, San Francisco, moves to 75 Third Street. Beginning of unscheduled events and free beer on Wednesday afternoons. 3 January.

Chris Burden, *747* (performance). Near Los Angeles International Airport. 5 January.

"The Four: Judy Chicago, Lynda Benglis, Miriam Schapiro, Bonnie Sherk". De Saisset Gallery, University of Santa Clara. Includes Sherk's live-in environment, *Living in the Forest: Demonstrations of Atkin Logic, Balance, Compromise, Devotion, etc.* 9 January-25 February.

Linda Montano, *Odd Jobs*, in which the artist sent cards announcing her availability for various casual employments. San Francisco. 15 January.

Paul McCarthy, *Gray Shirt*, *Couch*, *Stomach of the Squirrel*, and *Dress* (performance-videotapes). Los Angeles. February.

Womanspace, Los Angeles. Inaugural performance works by Aviva Rahmani, Vicki Hall, and Barbara Smith. 2-3 February.

Museum of Conceptual Art, San Francisco. Performances by Chris Burden (*Fire Roll*), Howard Fried (*Interaction*, performance for video), and Paul Cotton with Diana Coleman (*Home-Age to N.O. Brown*). 28 February.

Tom Marioni and his musical MOCA Ensemble present *Sculpture in 3/4 Time*. San Francisco Museum of Modern Art. 20 March.

Linda Montano, *Home Endurance*, in which the artist stays home for one week, documenting all thoughts and actions. San Francisco. 26 March-2 April.

Chris Burden, *Icarus* (studio performance). Venice, Calif. 13 April.

*All Night Sculptures*. Museum of Conceptual Art, San Francisco. Sunset to sunrise event, curated by Tom Marioni and featuring the participation of Terry Fox (*Cell*), Bonnie Sherk (*Adaqtation and Imbulgence*), and Barbara Smith (*Feed Me*), among others. 20-21 April.

Chris Burden, *Movie on the Way Down* (performance). Oberlin College gymnasium, Ohio. 1 May.

*Performance Festival 1973*, San Francisco Art Institute. Participants include Linda Montano (*The Story of My Life*) and Bonnie Sherk (*Adaqtation and Imbulgence: Sifting and Shifting, part 3d*). 7-8 May.

Chris Burden, *B.C. Mexico* (performance). Sea of Cortez beach, San Felipe, Mexico; then at Newspace, Newport Beach. 25 May-10 June.

Bonnie Sherk, living-art project as Saturday evening short order cook (for 6 months), then as waitress. Andy's Donuts, Castro and Market Streets, San Francisco. June 1973-May 1974.

Gordon Matta-Clark, *Graffiti Truck*. Mercer Street, between Third and Bleeker, N.Y. Alternative to Greenwich Village art fair. 8-9 and 15-16 June.

Marta Minujin, *Kidnappenning*. Museum of Modern Art, N.Y. 24-26 August.

"Terry Fox". University Art Museum, Berkeley. Exhibition with performances and catalogue. 5 September-21 October.

Chris Burden, *Through the Night Softly* (performance). Main Street, Los Angeles. 12 September.

**1971** (cont'd) Adrian Piper, *Two Untitled Streetworks*. Rochester, N.Y. April.

Gordon Matta-Clark, *Open House* (installation with dance performance by Barbara Dilley,
Tina Girouard, Suzanne Harris, and others). Between 112 and 98 Greene Street, N.Y. May.

Chris Burden, *Jaizu* (performance). F Space, Santa Ana, Calif. 10-11 June.

"Documenta 5". Kassel, Germany. Performances by Paul Cotton (*Triumph and Redemption of the
Prince of Peace; Astral-Naughty Rabb-Eyes* with Diana Coleman), Terry Fox (*Action for a Tower
Room*), and Howard Fried (*Indian War Dance* and *Indian Rope Trick*). Catalogue.
30 June-8 October.

Terry Fox, *Counter for Dorothy* (studio performance). 16 Rose Street, San Francisco. July.

Marta Minujin, *Interpenning*. Sculpture Garden, The Museum of Modern Art, N.Y. August.

Reese Palley Gallery, San Francisco, ceases its contemporary exhibition program. 17 August.

Gordon Matta-Clark (performing as George Smudge, with Juan Downey, Ted Greenwald, and
Ginger J. Walker), *Fresh Air Cart*. Wall Street, N.Y. 9 September.

Lynn Hershman with Eleanor Coppola, room installation. Dante Hotel, San Francisco.
October-July 1973.

Linda Montano performs *Don't Be Chicken Last Rites While Lying in My Own Shell*, a.k.a. *Dead
Chicken, Live Angel*, as part of *Women's Works: A Festival of Bay Area Women in the Arts*.
University Art Museum, Berkeley. 5-8 October.

Chris Burden, *Dos Equis* (event). Laguna Canyon Road, Laguna Beach, Calif. 16 October.

Joan Jonas, *Organic Honey's Visual Telepathy*. San Francisco Art Institute. 27 October.

For the month, Bonnie Sherk opens her studio to visitors, exhibiting the environment *Animal and
Vegetable Art*. 40 Gough Street, San Francisco. October.

Chris Burden performs *Deadman*, then is arrested for creating a false emergency. The case is
dismissed after three days of jury deliberation. On La Cienega Boulevard, outside Riko Mizuno
Gallery, Los Angeles. 12 November.

Vito Acconci, *Seed Bed* (performance installation). Sonnabend Gallery, N.Y.

Artists from Feminist Art Program at California Institute of the Arts create *Womanhouse*.
Los Angeles.

*Ablutions* collaboration performed by Judy Chicago, Suzanne Lacy, Sandra Orgel, and Aviva
Rahmani. Venice, Calif.

Laurie Anderson, *Automotive* (first performance). Vermont.

Eleanor Antin begins public performances in characters of a King, a Ballerina, a Black Movie Star,
and a Nurse. Solana Beach, Calif.

Tom Marioni, *Using My Body to Control Feedback*. Whitechapel Gallery, London.

Paul McCarthy, *Face Painting: Wall* and *Face Painting: Floor* (studio performances). Los Angeles.

Bonnie Sherk presents three-part theater situation, *Public Play, Act IV*. San Francisco Art Festival.
19-23 September.

Adrian Piper, *Untitled Streetwork* (performance). Rhode Island School of Design, Providence. October.

Adrian Piper, *Being Mythic on the Street* (performance) for "Adrian Piper: The Mythic Being" in *Other
Than Art's Sake*, a film by Peter Kennedy. October.

Linda Montano is handcuffed to Tom Marioni. Museum of Conceptual Art, San Francisco.
2-5 November.

Chris Burden, *Doorway to Heaven* (performance). Venice, Calif. 15 November.

The Woman's Building founded in Los Angeles. First performances are by Eleanor Antin,
Nancy Buchanan, Pauline Oliveros, and Barbara Smith.

Marina Abramović, *Rhythm 10/Part One* (performance). Richard Demarco Gallery, Edinburgh.

**1974** Chris Burden, *Back to You* (performance). 112 Greene Street, N.Y. 16 January.

Gordon Matta-Clark, *Splitting: Four Corners*. 322 Humphrey Street, Englewood, N.J. March-June, demolished August.

Chris Burden, *Trans-fixed* (performance). In a garage on Speedway Avenue, Venice, Calif. 23 April.

Chris Burden, *Velvet Water* (performance). School of the Art Institute, Chicago. 7 May.

Joseph Beuys, *I Like America and America Likes Me* (performance installation). René Block Gallery, N.Y. 23-25 May.

Chris Burden and Charles Hill perform *Kunst Kick* at the opening of the Art Fair. Basel, Switzerland. 19 June.

First issue of *Visions*, edited by Tom Marioni, published by Kathan Brown. Oakland, Calif. September.

Chris Burden, *Sculpture in Three Parts* (performance). Hansen-Fuller Gallery, San Francisco. 10-21 September.

Marta Minujin, *Imago Flowing*. Central Park, N.Y. 24 September.

*South of the Slot* performance series. 63 Bluxome Street, San Francisco. Performers include Terry Fox (*Halation*), Linda Montano (*Death and Birth: A Crib Event*), Tom Marioni (*Drum Brush Lecture*). Catalogue. October-November.

**1975** Chris Burden, *White Light/White Heat* (performance). Ronald Feldman Gallery, N.Y. 8 February-1 March.

Lynn Hershman, *Lady Luck: A Double Portrait of Las Vegas, The Personification of a Myth* (performance). Circus Circus Casino, Las Vegas. 2 March.

Chris Burden, *Doomed* (performance). Museum of Contemporary Art, Chicago. 11 April.

Chris Burden, *La Chiaraficazione* (performance). Galleria Alessandra Castelli, Milan. 5 May.

Chris Burden, *Oracle* (performance). Schema Gallery, Florence. 14 May.

Daniel Spoerri, *Restaurant de Coin du Restaurant Spoerri* (working restaurant). Galleria Multhipla, Milan. 19 May-5 June.

College Art Association conference, Washington, D.C. "Performance and the Arts" session, coordinated by Allan Kaprow, panel participants include Vito Acconci, Joan Jonas, Kaprow, and Yvonne Rainer. Summer.

Carolee Schneemann, *Interior Scroll* (performance). For the *Woman Here and Now* series. East Hampton, Long Island. August.

Marta Minujin, *La Academia del Fracaso*. CAYC, Buenos Aires, Argentina. 19 September.

"Tom Marioni: Thinking Out Loud". Galeria Foksal PSP, Warsaw. Catalogue. October.

Chris Burden conceives, designs and constructs *B-Car*. Los Angeles. 24 August-16 October.

Chris Burden re-assembles *B-Car* in four-day performance. De Appel Gallery, Amsterdam. 18-21 October.

Chris Burden, *Yankee Ingenuity* (performance with *B-Car*). Stadler Gallery, Paris. 23 October.

Chris Burden, *Working Artist* (performance). University Gallery, University of Maryland, Baltimore. 22-24 November.

Adrian Piper, *Some Reflective Surfaces* (performance). The Fine Arts Building, N.Y. December.

Chris Burden, *The Rise and Fall of Western Industrialism as Seen Through the Automobile* (performance-lecture). Hallwalls, Buffalo, N.Y. 5 December.

Marina Abramović, *The Lips of Thomas* (performance). Galerie Krinzinger, Innsbruck, Austria.

Marina Abramović, *Hot/Cold* (performance). Fruitmarket Gallery, Edinburgh.

Paul McCarthy, *Experimental Dancer-Rumpus Room* (performance, videotape). USC Medical Center, Los Angeles.

Paul McCarthy, *Sailor's Meat* and *Tubbing* (performance, videotapes). Pasadena.

Adrian Piper, *The Mythic Being* (performances). Cambridge, Mass. 1975-76.

Chris Burden, *Oh, Dracula* (performance). Utah Museum of Art, Salt Lake City. 7 October.

Chris Burden, *Dreamy Nights* (performance). Poolerie Gallery, Graz, Austria. 15 October.

Lynn Hershman, *Forming A Sculpture/Drama in Manhattan*. Chelsea Hotel, Plaza Hotel, Central
YWCA, N.Y. 21 October-14 December.

"University of California Irvine 1965-1975". La Jolla Museum of Contemporary Art. Artists include
Eleanor Antin (from *Carving: A Traditional Sculpture*), Chris Burden (*Photographic Book*), Bruce
Nauman (*Untitled Metal Sculpture*), and Barbara Smith (*The Art/Life Question*). Catalogue.
November-December.

"Barbara Smith". San Diego Art Gallery, University of California, La Jolla. Catalogue. 7 November-
4 December.

Chris Burden, *The Visitation* (performance). Hamilton College, Hamilton, N.Y. 9 November.

Chris Burden, *The Confession* (performance). Contemporary Arts Center, Cincinnati.
12 December.

Allan Kaprow joins the faculty of the University of California, San Diego.

Marina Abramović, *Rhythm 2* (Gallery of Contemporary Art, Zagreb, Yugoslavia); *Rhythm 4*
(Diagramma Gallery, Milan); and *Rhythm 0* (Galeria Studio Mora, Naples). Performances, dates
unknown.

Paul McCarthy, *Heinz Ketchup, Sauce* (performance, videotape). USC Medical Center,
Los Angeles.

Paul McCarthy, *Hot Dog*. Performance, videotape. Odd Fellows Temple, Pasadena.

Paul McCarthy. *Meat Cake #1*. Performance. Odd Fellows Temple, Pasadena.

Paul McCarthy. *Meat Cake #2*. Performance, videotape. Odd Fellows Temple, Pasadena.

Paul McCarthy. *Meat Cake #3*. Performance, videotape. Newspace Gallery, Los Angeles.

Marta Minujin and J. Cairol, *Four Presents*. Stefanotti Gallery, N.Y. Date unknown.

Bonnie Sherk forms The Farm (Crossroads Community) in San Francisco.

Transparent Teachers Ink., Paul Cotton, Medium. *33 Footnotes by Osmosis* (or *33 Foot-Notes by
Oz Moses*). Performance event staged at University Art Museum, Berkeley, during "Books by
Artists" exhibition.

**1976** Chris Burden, *Natural Habitat* (performance). Portland Center for the Visual Arts, Portland, Ore. 8-15 January.

Adrian Piper. *Some Reflective Surfaces* (performance). The Whitney Museum, N.Y. February.

Carolee Schneemann, *Up To and Including Her Limits* (performance-installation). The Kitchen, N.Y. 13-14 February.

Chris Burden, *Do You Believe in Television?* (performance). Alberta College of Art Gallery, Calgary, Canada. 26 February.

Terry Fox, *Timbre* (performance). Mount Tamalpais Ampitheatre, Marin County. 13 March.

Chris Burden, *Shadow* (performance). Ohio State University, Columbus. 26 April.

Paul Cotton, *The Second Norman Invasion*. Normon O. Brown's classroom, Cowell College, University of California at Santa Cruz. 18 May.

Marina Abramović and Ulay, *Relation in Space* (performance). Biennale di Venezia, Giudecca, Venice. July.

Chris Burden, *Garcon!* (performance). Hansen-Fuller Gallery, San Francisco. 3-7 August.

Chris Burden, *Death Valley Run* (performance). Death Valley, Calif. 14 October.

Chris Burden, *Studio Tour* (performance). Venice, Calif. 26 November.

Marina Abramović and Ulay, *Talking about similarity* (performance). Singel 64, Amsterdam. 30 November.

Gordon Matta-Clark, *Window Blow-Out*. Institute for Architecture and Urban Resources, N.Y. Censored window-shooting action for exhibition "Idea as Model". December.

Marina Abramović, *Freeing the Body* (performance). Künstlerhaus Bethanien, Berlin.

Paul McCarthy, *Class Fool* (performance, videotape). University of California at San Diego.

Paul McCarthy, *Political Disturbance* (performance). During American Theater Association Convention, Biltmore Hotel, Los Angeles.

Paul McCarthy, *Paid Stranger* (performance). Broadcast on Close Radio, KPFK-FM, co-produced with John Duncan. Los Angeles.

**1978** Marina Abramović and Ulay, *AAA-AAA* (performance). RTB, Liège, Belgium. February.

Kim Jones, *Telephone Pole* (performance). Los Angeles. 6 February.

Publication of debut issue of *High Performance*, edited by Linda Frye Burnham. Los Angeles. February.

Adrian Piper, *Collegium Academicum Freischrei* (performance). Haupstrasse, Heidelberg, West Germany. February.

Marina Abramović and Ulay, *Light/Dark* and *AAA-AAA* (performances). Amsterdam. March.

"Connecting Myths". Pasadena. Coordinated by Cheri Gaulke and John Duncan. Works include Duncan's *Every Woman*, Gaulke's *She is Risen Indeed*, and Leslie Labowitz's *Reenactments*. 23-26 March.

Marina Abramović and Ulay, *Incision* (performance). Galerie H-Humanic, Graz, Austria. April.

Marina Abramović and Ulay, *Kaiserschnitt* (performance). Internationales Performance Festival, Wiener Reitinstitut, Vienna. April.

"Lynn Hershman Is Not Roberta Breitmore, Roberta Breitmore Is Not Lynn Hershman". M.H. De Young Memorial Museum, San Francisco. Catalogue. 1 April-14 May.

Marina Abramović and Ulay, *Charged space* (performance). European performance series, One, Brooklyn Museum, N.Y. May.

LACE (Los Angeles Contemporary Exhibition) Gallery opens with a performance of a lamb dinner by Barbara T. Smith and Suzanne Lacy. The debut exhibition of women's work, sponsored by Double X, features Leslie Labowitz, Lacy, and Smith, among others. 9 July.

Chris Burden, *The Citadel* (performance/installation). Private studio, Los Angeles. 8-12 August.

Marina Abramović and Ulay, *Workrelation* (performance). Extract two, Arnhem Festival, Theater aan de Rijn, Arnhem. September.

Marina Abramović and Ulay, *Workrelation* (performance). Palazzo dei Diamanti, Ferrara. October.

**1977** Marina Abramović and Ulay, *Interruption in space* (performance). Kunstakademie/Klasse Rinke, Düsseldorf. January.

Eleanor Antin, *The Angel of Mercy* (performance). M.L. D'Arc Gallery, N.Y. January.

Barbara Smith, *Ordinary Life* (part one, performance). Venice, Calif. 22 January.

Barbara Smith, *Ordinary Life* (part two, performance). As part of *Performance Exchange* series, co-sponsored by 80 Langton Street, San Francisco, and LAICA. 12 March.

Marina Abramović and Ulay, *Breathing in – Breathing out* (1st part) (performance). Studenski Kulturni Centar, Belgrade. April.

Suzanne Lacy, *Three Weeks in May* ("a political art performance"). City Hall and other sites, Los Angeles. 7-24 May.

Marina Abramović and Ulay, *Imponderabilia* (Galleria Communale d'Arte Moderna, Bologna) and *Expansion in Space* (Documenta 6, Kassel). Performances. June.

Gordon Matta-Clark, *Jacob's Ladder*. Leipzigerstrasse and Melsungerstrasse, Kassel, West Germany. Project for Documenta 6. June.

Gordon Matta-Clark, *Descending Steps for Batan* (performance/installation). Yvon Lambert Gallery, Paris. June.

Paul McCarthy, *Grand Pop* (performance). USC Medical Center, Los Angeles. 23 July.

Marina Abramović and Ulay, *Relation in Movement* (performance). 10th Biennale de Paris, Musée d'art moderne de la ville de Paris. September.

Adrian Piper, *Danke(sehr)schon* (performance). Kurfurstendamm, West Berlin, West Germany. September.

Chris Burden, "Full Financial Disclosure" (exhibition). Baum-Silverman Gallery, Los Angeles. 20 September-8 October.

Marta Minujin, *Repollos*. Museo de Arte Contemporáneo, Sao Paolo, Brazil. 29 September.

Marina Abramović and Ulay, *Relation in Time* (Studio G7, Bologna) and *Light/Dark* (Internationaler Kunstmarkt, Cologne, Performance Programm, Messegelände, Cologne). Performances. October.

Eleanor Antin, *The Nurse and the Hijackers* (exhibition/video performance). Ronald Feldman Gallery, N.Y. 1-29 October.

Marina Abramović and Ulay, *Breathing out-Breathing in* (2nd part) (performance). Stedelijk Museum, Amsterdam. 30 November.

Marina Abramović and Ulay, *Balance proof* (performance). Musée d'art et d'histoire, Geneva. December.

**1979** Eleanor Antin, *Before the Revolution* (ballet-performance). Ronald Feldman Gallery, N.Y. 17 February-
  17 March.

Eleanor Antin, *Before the Revolution* (ballet-performance). The Kitchen Center for Video, Dance
  and Music, N.Y. 23-24 February.

Marina Abramovic and Ulay, *Installation "One"* (performance). De Appel, Amsterdam. March.

Chris Burden, *Send Me Your Money* (performance). Broadcast live on KPFK-FM radio, Los Angeles.
  21 March.

Chris Burden, *Honest Labor* (performance). Vancouver, B.C., Canada. 26-30 March.

Marina Abramović and Ulay, *The Brink* (performance). European Dialogue, 3rd Biennial of Sydney,
  Art Gallery of New South Wales, Sydney, Australia. April.

Marina Abramović and Ulay, *Go — Stop — Back... 1.2.3...* (performance). National Gallery of
  Victoria, Melbourne, Australia. May.

Tom Marioni recreates the Museum of Conceptual Art as an installation, including refrigerator, beer,
  and shelves for empty bottles. San Francisco Museum of Modern Art. May-June.

*Sound* (exhibition/event). Terry Fox, Mike Kelley, and Tom Marioni perform. Los Angeles Institute
  of Contemporary Art. 20 July.

Chris Burden, *Atomic Alphabet* (performance). San Francisco Art Institute. 17 November.

Marina Abramović and Ulay, *Communist Body — Capitalist Body* (performance). Zoutkeetsgracht
  116/118, Amsterdam. 30 November.

Chris Burden, *Pearl Harbor* (performance). National Guard Armory, Santa Barbara, Calif. 8
  December.

Mike Kelley, *The Monitor and the Merrimac*, *The Big Tent*, and *My Space* as part of *The
  Poltergeist: A Work Between David Askevold and Mike Kelley*. Foundation for Art Resources,
  Los Angeles.

Marta Minujin, *El Obelisco de Pan Dulce*. Il Feria de las Naciones, Buenos Aires, Argentina.
  Date unknown.

**1978** (cont'd) Chris Burden, *In Venice Money Grows on Trees*. Venice, Calif. 6 October.

Marina Abramović and Ulay, *Workrelation* (performance). Badischer Kunstverein, Karlsruhe. November.

Marina Abramović and Ulay, *Three* (performance). Harlekin Art, Wiesbaden. November.

Chris Burden, *Coals to Newcastle* (performance). Calexico, Calif. 17 December.

Chris Burden curates *Polar Crossing*, an exhibition of the work of Richard Kriesche, Gina Pane, and Petr Stembera. Los Angeles Institute of Contemporary Art.

Mike Kelley, *Actions Accompanied by Words* (performance). Exploratorium, California State University, Los Angeles.

Mike Kelley, *Indianana* (performance). LACE, Los Angeles.

*Mike Kelley in Performance*. La Jolla Museum of Contemporary Art. Performances include *My Space*, *Two Pieces of Tube Music*, *A Big Question (A Chocolate Kiss)*, *A Race Memory Story*, and *A Healthful Activity*.

Mike Kelley, *An Evening of Performance, Audio Tape and Film*. LACE, Los Angeles.

Paul McCarthy, *Contemporary Cure All* (performance, videotape). Los Angeles.

## WORKS IN THE EXHIBITION

The artists in this exhibition are represented by objects, photodocumentation, and videos. This is a selected checklist, listing only the primary representations for each artist. This checklist represents the exhibition at The Mueum of Contemporary Art, Los Angeles, and may change as the exhibition travels to other venues.

**Marina Abramović**
*Rhythm 0*, 1974
Objects and wooden table
Table: 31 1/2 x 21 5/8 x 118 1/8 in.
(80 x 55 x 300 cm.)
Collection of the artist

**Ulay/Marina Abramović**
*Relation in Movement*, 1977
1972 Citroën HY van
90 1/2 x 78 3/4 x 177 1/8 in. (230 x 200 x 450 cm.)
Collection of the artists

*Rest Energy*, 1980
Bow
27 1/2 x 7 7/8 x 6 in. (70 x 20 x 15 cm.)
Collection of the artists

**Vito Acconci**
*Service Area*, June-September 1970
Photodocumentation of activity at the "Information" exhibition at The Museum of Modern Art, New York (four black-and-white photographs)
11 x 14 in. each (27.9 x 35.6 cm.)
Courtesy of the artist and Barbara Gladstone Gallery, New York

*Untitled (Project for Pier 17)*, March-April 1971
Photodocumentation of activity at Pier 17, New York (black-and-white photograph)
11 x 14 in. (27.9 x 35.6 cm.)
Courtesy of the artist and Barbara Gladstone Gallery, New York

*Seed Bed*, 1972
Photodocumentation of activity at the Sonnabend Gallery, New York (two black-and-white photographs)
11 x 14 in. each (27.9 x 35.6 cm.)
Courtesy of the artist and Barbara Gladstone Gallery, New York

*Drawing for "Command Performance,"* 1974
Felt-tip pen on paper
8 1/2 x 11 in. (21.6 x 27.9 cm.)
Courtesy of the artist and Barbara Gladstone Gallery, New York

*Command Performance*, 1974
Mixed media video installation adapted to fit space requirements
Dimensions variable
San Francisco Museum of Modern Art, Accessions Committee Fund: Gift of Mrs. Robert MacDonnell, Byron R. Meyer, Modern Art Council, Norman C. Stone; and the National Endowment for the Arts

**Genpei Akasegawa**
*One Thousand Yen Note Trial Catalogue of Seized Works (Sen-en satsu saiban ōshuhin mokuroku)*, 1967
Poster
30 x 24 in. (76.2 x 61 cm.)
Nagoya City Museum

**Laurie Anderson**
*Duets on Ice*, 1974-75
Photodocumentation of performance (three color photographs)
11 x 14 in. each (27.9 x 35.6 cm.)
Collection of the artist

**Eleanor Antin**
*Jeanie, from "California Lives,"* 1969
TV tray, melamine plastic cup and saucer, pink hair curler, king size filter tip cigarette, matchbook from Jake's seafood restaurant
Approx. 24 x 20 x 14 in. (61 x 50.8 x 35.6 cm.)
Courtesy Ronald Feldman Fine Arts, New York

*Merrit, from "California Lives,"* 1969
Gasoline can with spout, bush hat, metal comb, and peace decal
Approx. 25 x 18 x 15 in. (63.5 x 45.7 x 38.1 cm.)
Courtesy Ronald Feldman Fine Arts, New York

*The Murfins, from "California Lives,"* 1969
Ladder, trowel, faux bricks, cement, and Fresca soda can
Approx. 96 x 84 x 48 in. (243.8 x 213.4 x 121.9 cm.)
Courtesy Ronald Feldman Fine Arts, New York

**Rasheed Araeen**
*"Paki Bastard" (Portrait of the Artist as a Black Person)*, 1979
Six texts and photodocumentation of performance (six color photographs)
14 x 17 in. each (35.6 x 43.2 cm.)
Collection of the artist

**Mowry Baden**
*Instrument*, 1969
Aluminum and steel
Approx. 96 x 84 x 48 in. (243.8 x 213.4 x 121.9 cm.)
Collection of the artist

**Artur Barrio**
*Situaçao T/T*, 1970
Text and photodocumentation of performance (one color and two black-and-white photographs)
14 x 17 in. each (35.6 x 43.2 cm.)
Courtesy of the artist and Galeria Cohn Edelstein, Rio de Janiero
Photographs by Cesar Carneiro

**Joseph Beuys**
*Ausfegen*, 1972 (Vitrine, 1985)
Sand, stones, paper, garbage, broom with red bristles, and plastic bag with printed appeal by Beuys
78 3/4 x 78 3/4 x 25 5/8 in. (200 x 200 x 65 cm.)
Block Collection

*Untitled (Technology, Analysis, Death)*, 1974
Chalk on blackboard
36 x 48 in. (91.4 x 121.9 cm.)
The Carol and Arthur Goldberg Collection

*Ecology and Socialism (Okologie und Sozialismus)*, 1980
Chalk on green chalkboard
Chalkboard: 39 x 51 in. (99.1 x 129.5 cm.);
with stand: 75 x 60 x 18 in. (190.5 x 152.4 x 45.7 cm.)
Courtesy Ronald Feldman Fine Arts, New York

**Mark Boyle and Joan Hills**
*Suddenly Last Supper*, 1963
Photodocumentation of performance (six black-and-white photographs)
9 1/2 x 7 1/8 in. each (24 x 18 cm.)
Collection of the artists

*Son et Lumière: Bodily Fluids and Functions*, 1966
Photodocumentation of performance (four color photographs)
12 1/4 x 12 1/4 in. each (31 x 31 cm.)
Collection of the artists

**George Brecht**
*Chair Event*, 1960
Painted wood chair, painted cane, and an orange
35 1/8 x 19 x 38 in. (88 x 48 x 95 cm.)
Collection Onnasch

*Coat Rack (Clothes Tree)*, 1962-63
Mixed media
76 x 27 1/2 x 27 1/2 in. (193 x 70 x 70 cm.)
Collection Onnasch

*Table with Rainbowleg*, 1962-63
Mixed media
24 1/2 x 17 3/4 x 16 in. (62.4 x 45.1 x 40.6 cm.)
Collection Onnasch

**Stuart Brisley**
*And for Today... Nothing*, 1972
Text and photodocumentation of performance (two color photographs)
11 x 14 in. each (27.9 x 35.6 cm.)
Collection of the artist

*Moments of Decision/Indecision, Warsaw*, 1975
Photograph on paper
21 1/2 x 16 3/4 in. (54.6 x 42.4 cm.)
Tate Gallery, London

**Robert Delford Brown
and Rhett Delford Brown**
*The Meat Show*, October 23, 1964
Installation with cloth and blood, box, taxidermied pig, pig's head, two sheep, and two cowskulls
Box: 16 x 21 x 12 in. (40.6 x 53.3 x 30.5 cm.); pig:
70 x 12 x 28 in. (177.8 x 30.5 x 71.1 cm.); pig's head: 11 x 11 x 14 in. (27.9 x 27.9 x 35.6 cm.); sheep:
42 x 12 x 22 in. each (106.7 x 30.5 x 5.9 cm.); cowskulls:
16 x 12 x 12 in. each (40.6 x 30.5 x 30.5 cm.)
Collection Robert Delford Brown

**Günter Brus**
*Untitled*, 1963
Emulsion paint on canvas
57 1/2 x 183 1/2 in. (198 x 467 cm.)
Private Collection

*Selbstbemalung*, 1964 (printed 1972)
Photodocumentation of performance (eight black-and-white photographs)
9 1/6 x 7 1/6 in. each (24 x 18 cm.)
Archiv Conz, Verona

*Untitled*, 1964
Collage, photographs, documents, and paint
29 1/8 x 16 1/8 in. (74 x 41 cm.)
Archiv Sohm, Staatsgalerie, Stuttgart

*Nine Drawings*, 1965
Pencil and ballpoint pen on paper
11 5/8 x 8 1/4 in. each (29.5 x 21 cm. each)
Sammlung Friedrichshof, Zurndorf

*Selbstbemalung 2*, 1965
(printed 1973)
Photodocumentation of performance
(eight black-and-white photographs)
9 1/6 x 7 1/6 in. each (24 x 18 cm.)
Archiv Conz, Verona

*Five Aktionsskizzen*, 1966-67
Pencil and ballpoint pen on paper
11 5/8 x 8 1/4 in. each (29.5 x 21 cm.)
Sammlung Friedrichshof, Zurndorf

*Der Helle Wahnsinn-Die Architektur des
Hellen Wahnsinns*, 1968 (printed 1972)
Photodocumentation of performance
(twenty-five black-and-white photographs)
9 1/2 x 7 1/8 in. each (24 x 18 cm.)
Archiv Conz, Verona

### Chris Burden
*Relic from "Five Day Locker Piece,"* April 1971
Lock
Case: 5 3/4 x 7 3/4 x 9 3/4 in.
(14.6 x 19.7 x 24.8 cm.)
Courtesy Gagosian Gallery, New York

*Relic from "Deadman,"* 1972
Plastic tarp
Case: 14 1/2 x 19 1/2 x 9 3/4 in.
(36.8 x 49.5 x 24.8 cm.)
Collection of the artist

*Relic from "Movie on the Way Down,"* May 1973
Kodak Instamatic movie camera
Case: 5 7/8 x 10 1/4 x 8 1/4 in. (14.9 x 26 x 21 cm.)
Courtesy Gagosian Gallery, New York

*Relic from "Through the Night Softly,"*
September 1973
Broken glass chips
Case: 5 3/4 x 8 3/4 x 8 1/4 in.
(14.6 x 22.2 x 21 cm.)
Collection Wexner Center for the Arts, The Ohio State
University; purchased in part with funds from the
National Endowment for the Arts, 1979.09

*Relic from "Dreamy Nights,"* October 1974
Corked bottle and spiritus
Case: 10 x 8 1/4 x 8 1/4 in. (25.4 x 21 x 21 cm.)
Collection Jasper Johns

*Relic from "Prelude to 220, or 110,"* September 1976
Copper neckband
Case: 11 x 15 x 8 1/2 in. (27.9 x 38.1 x 21 cm.)
Courtesy Frayda and Ronald Feldman

*The Big Wheel*, 1979
Three-ton, eight-foot diameter, cast-iron flywheel, pow-
ered by a motorcycle
9 ft. 4 in. x 14 ft. 7 in. x 11 ft. 11 in.
(2.8 x 4.44 x 3.63 m.)
The Museum of Contemporary Art, Los Angeles
Gift of Lannan Foundation

### James Lee Byars
*Untitled Object*, 1962-64
Crayon on Japanese handmade white flax paper, hinged
and folded
12 in. x 210 ft. 9 in. (30.3 cm. x 64.2 m.) (unfolded)
The Museum of Modern Art, New York
Gift of the artist

### John Cage
*Water Music*, 1952
India ink on paper
Overall: 60 5/8 x 39 7/16 x 1 3/4 in.
(154 x 100.3 x 4.4 cm.)
Whitney Museum of American Art, New York
Purchase, with funds from an anonymous donor

### Marc Camille Chaimowicz
*Arena: Art and Design, BBC-TV*, 1976
16mm film, black-and-white, 28 min.
Courtesy BBC-TV, London

### Lygia Clark
*Caminhando*, c. 1965/1998
Paper mobius strip
Dimensions variable
Projeto Hélio Oiticica/Lygia Clark Estate,
Rio de Janeiro

*Agua e conchas*, 1966/1998
Plastic bag, rubber strings, shells, and water
Dimensions variable
Projeto Hélio Oiticica/Lygia Clark Estate,
Rio de Janeiro

*Ar e pedra*, 1966/1998
Plastic bag and pebble
Dimensions variable
Projeto Hélio Oiticica/Lygia Clark Estate,
Rio de Janeiro

*Respire comigo*, 1966/1998
Rubber tubing
Approximately 15 3/4 in. (40 cm.)
Projeto Hélio Oiticica/Lygia Clark Estate,
Rio de Janeiro

*Máscaras sensorias: 1. Máscara cereja, 2. Máscara
branca, 3. Máscara de cor verde, 4. Máscara
cor-de-abobora, 5. Máscara azul, 6. Máscara preta,
7. Máscara vermelha*, 1967/1998
Seven cloth hoods with ear, eye, and nose
pieces of various materials
Dimensions variable
Projeto Hélio Oiticica/Lygia Clark Estate,
Rio de Janeiro

*Luvas sensoriais*, 1968/1998
Gloves (two pairs of chamois leather and
two pairs of rubber), balls of various materials
Leather gloves: 17 x 6 3/4 in. (43 x 17 cm.) and
11 x 7 in. (28 x 28 cm.), rubber gloves: 13 3/4 x 7 in.
(35 x 18 cm.) and 10 1/4 x 5 1/8 in. (26 x 13 cm.);
balls: various sizes
Projeto Hélio Oiticica/Lygia Clark Estate,
Rio de Janeiro

*Máscara abismo*, 1968/1998
Cotton net, pebbles, and plastic air bag
Dimensions variable
Projeto Hélio Oiticica/Lygia Clark Estate,
Rio de Janeiro

*Straightjacket*, 1968/1998
Rubberbands
Dimensions variable
Projeto Hélio Oiticica/Lygia Clark Estate,
Rio de Janeiro

### Lygia Clark and Hélio Oiticica
*Dialogue of Hands*, c. 1966/1998
Elastic mobius strip
3 x 8 in. (7.6 x 20.3 cm.)
Projeto Hélio Oiticica/Lygia Clark Estate,
Rio de Janeiro

### Pinchas Cohen Gan
*Action in the Jericho Refugee Camp*, 1974
Photodocumentation of performance
(two black-and-white photographs)
14 x 17 in. each (35.6 x 43.2 cm.)
Collection of the artist

### Collective Action Group
*Slogan-Manifesto*, 1976/1998
Cotton banner and acrylic paint
39 1/4 x 39 ft. 4 in. (1 x 10 m.)
Collection Andrej Monastyrskij

### Houston Conwill
*JuJu Bag*, 1977
Objects used in performance: fabric, herbs,
and other materials
24 x 60 in. (61 x 152.4 cm.);
with fringe: 26 x 77 in. (66 x 195.6 cm.)
"To My Grandfathers and Grandmothers";
from collection of W. L. Conwill and F.V. Harrison

### Paul Cotton
*Random House Converter #6*, 1966/1998
Eight freestanding acrylic on canvas paintings
Overall: 7 ft. 8 in. x 5 ft. x 17 ft. (2.3 x 1.5 x 5.2 m.)
Collection of the artist

*Betrayal of the Prince of Peace*, May 1971
Rubber stamped newsprint
17 x 11 in. (43.2 x 27.9 cm.)
Collection of the artist

### COUM Transmissions
### (Cosey Fanni Tutti)
*Exhibit No. 10 (Park Lane No. 15)* from
"Prostitution" Exhibition, Institute of
Contemporary Arts, London, October, 1976
Magazine
33 x 12 in. (83.8 x 30.5 cm.)
Collection Cosey Fanni Tutti

*Exhibit No. 29 (Alpha No. 5)* from "Prostitution"
Exhibition, Institute of Contemporary Art,
London, October, 1976
Magazine
33 x 12 in. (83.8 x 30.5 cm.)
Collection Cosey Fanni Tutti

### Guy de Cointet
*Halved Painting*, 1976
Acrylic on canvas
80 1/4 x 56 1/2 x 2 in. (203.8 x 143.5 x 5.1 cm.)
The Museum of Contemporary Art, Los Angeles
Gift of Paula and Brian D. Dailey

### Jim Dine
*Crash Drawing with White Cross #1*, 1959
Ink and gouache on paper
25 1/2 x 19 1/2 in. (64.8 x 49.5 cm.)
Collection of the artist

*Crash Drawing with White Cross #2*, 1959
Ink and gouache on paper
25 1/2 x 19 1/2 in. (64.8 x 49.5 cm.)
Collection of the artist

**Jim Dine** (continued)
*Untitled (Car Crash)*, 1959
Pastel on paper
24 x 18 in. (61 x 45.7 cm.)
Collection of the artist

*Untitled (Car Crash)*, 1959
Pastel on paper
24 x 18 in. (61 x 45.7 cm.)
Collection of the artist

*Household Piece*, 1959
Wood, canvas, cloth, iron springs, oil and
bronze paint, sheet copper, brown paper bag,
mattress stuffing, and plastic
54 1/4 x 44 1/4 x 9 1/4 in. (137.7 x 112.4 x 23.5 cm.)
The Museum of Modern Art, New York
Gift of John W. Weber

**John Duncan**
*Blind Date*, 1980
Text and photodocumentation of performance
(black-and-white photograph)
Text: 11 1/2 x 8 1/4 in. (29.2 x 21 cm.); photograph: 14
x 17 in. (35.6 x 43.2 cm.)
Collection of the artist

**Felipe Ehrenberg**
*A Date with Fate at the Tate*, 1970
Photodocumentation of performance
(two black-and-white photographs)
11 x 14 in. each (27.9 x 35.6 cm.)
Collection of the artist

*The Tube-O-Nauts*, 1970
Photodocumentation of performance
(two black-and-white photographs)
11 x 14 in. each (27.9 x 35.6 cm.)
Collection of the artist

**Roberto Evangelista**
*Mater Dolorosa: In Memoriam II*, 1979
Photodocumentation of performance
(three color photographs)
11 x 14 in. each (35.6 x 43.2 cm.)
Collection of the artist

**Valie Export**
*Aus der mappe der Hundigkeit*, 1968
Photodocumentation of performance
(black-and-white photograph)
11 x 14 in. (27.9 x 35.6 cm.)
Collection of the artist
Photograph by Josef Tandl

*Tapp und Tastkino*, 1968/1998
Wood, cloth, and styrofoam
9 7/8 x 19 3/4 x 19 3/4 in. (25 x 50 x 50 cm.)
Collection of the artist

*Genital Panic*, 1969
Two black-and-white offset prints
39 1/4 x 27 1/2 in. each (100 x 70 cm.)
Collection of the artist

*Körper-Konfigurationen: Abfüngung (1972),
Starre Identität (1972), Vagire (1972), Abrundung I
(1976), Der mensch als ornament (1976)*
Photodocumentation of performance
(five black-and-white photographs)
11 x 14 in. each (27.9 x 35.6 cm.)
Collection of the artist

**Robert Filliou**
*Automatic Poetry Machine*, 1962/1998
Two bicycle wheels and text
10 ft. x 15 ft. x 6 in. (3 m. x 4.6 m. x 15.2 cm.)
Courtesy Galerie Philip Nelson, Paris and Filliou Estate

**Rose Finn-Kelcey**
*Magpies Box from "One for Sorrow, Two for Joy"*
(made by H. Walton), 1976
Mixed media
14 1/2 x 19 3/4 x 7 1/2 in. (36.8 x 50 1/8 x 19.1 cm.)
Collection of the artist

**Sherman Fleming**
*Something Akin to Living*, 1979
Photodocumentation of performance
(black-and-white photograph)
14 x 17 in. (35.6 x 43.2 cm.)
Collection of the artist
Photograph by J. Wayne Higgs

**Lucio Fontana**
*Concetto spaziale* (C. 49 B 2), 1949
White paper mounted on canvas
39 3/8 x 39 3/8 in. (100 x 100 cm.)
Fondazione Lucio Fontana, Milan

*Concetto spaziale* (C. 49-50 B 3), 1949-50
Silver oil painting on canvas
23 5/8 x 29 1/2 in. (60 x 75 cm.)
Fondazione Lucio Fontana, Milan

*Concetto spaziale* (C. 50 B 4), 1950
Oil on canvas
33 1/2 x 25 5/8 in. (85 x 65 cm.)
Fondazione Lucio Fontana, Milan

*Concetto spaziale* (C. 50 B 9), 1950
White iron
29 5/16 x 25 3/16 in. (74.5 x 64 cm.)
Fondazione Lucio Fontana, Milan

**Terry Fox**
*Asbestos Tracking*, 1970
Photodocumentation of installation at Reese Palley
Gallery, San Francisco (black-and-white photograph)
11 x 14 in. (27.9 x 35.6 cm.)
Courtesy Gallery Paule Anglim, San Francisco
Photograph by Barry Klinger

*Cellar*, 1970
Photodocumentation of installation at Reese
Palley Gallery, New York
(three black-and-white photographs)
11 x 14 in. each (27.9 x 35.6 cm.)
Courtesy Gallery Paule Anglim, San Francisco
Photographs by Gianfranco Gorgoni

*Works from The Labyrinth: In the Box: Mason Jar with
Holes Containing the Triptych*, c. 1971-1978
Glass jar, metal lid, acetate, ink, and scotch tape
9 1/2 x 6 3/8 in. (24.1 x 16.2 cm.)
University of California, Berkeley Art Museum,
purchased with the aid of funds provided by the
National Endowment of the Arts and the
University Art Museum Council

*Works from The Labyrinth: In the Box: Metal Stamp
of the Labyrinth*, c. 1971-1978
Metal stamp, nail, plywood board, and paint
3 1/4 x 3 1/4 x 7/8 in. (8.3 x 8.3 x 2.2 cm.)
University of California, Berkeley Art Museum,
purchased with the aid of funds provided by the
National Endowment of the Arts and the
University Art Museum Council

*Works from The Labyrinth: In the Box: Photo of Stools*,
c. 1971-1978
Black-and-white photograph
10 x 8 in. (25.4 x 20.3 cm.)
University of California, Berkeley Art Museum,
purchased with the aid of funds provided by the
National Endowment of the Arts and the
University Art Museum Council

*Works from The Labyrinth: In the Box: Plaster
Labyrinth*, c. 1971-1978
Plaster cast
7/8 x 7 1/2 in. (2.2 x 19.1 cm.)
University of California, Berkeley Art Museum,
purchased with the aid of funds provided by the
National Endowment of the Arts and the
University Art Museum Council

*Works from The Labyrinth: In the Box: Scroll
Drawing of the 34 Turns*, c. 1971-1978
Pencil on paper
2 1/4 x 79 in. (5.7 x 200.7 cm.)
University of California, Berkeley Art Museum,
purchased with the aid of funds provided by the
National Endowment of the Arts and the
University Art Museum Council

*Works from The Labryinth: In the Box: Site Pendulum*,
c. 1971-1978
Lead ball, piano wire, and drinking glass
Lead ball: 2 1/4 in. dia. (5.7 cm.); wire: 14 ft.
(4.3 m.); glass: 6 1/4 x 5 in. dia. (15.9 x 12.7 cm.)
University of California, Berkeley Art Museum,
purchased with the aid of funds provided by the
National Endowment of the Arts and the
University Art Museum Council

*Works from The Labyrinth: In the Box: 3 Large
Drawings of the Triptych of Crosses*, c. 1971-1978
Pencil on paper
22 x 24 in. each (55.9 x 61 cm.)
University of California, Berkeley Art Museum,
purchased with the aid of funds provided by the
National Endowment of the Arts and the
University Art Museum Council

*Works from The Labyrinth: In the Box: Wooden Box
with Two Stacks of Glass Drawings*, c. 1971-1978
Wooden box, paint, glass slides, glass plates, and ink
Box closed: 1 1/4 x 12 x 10 3/4 in. (3.2 x 30.5 x 27.3
cm.); Box open for exhibition: 12 x 12 x 10 3/4 in. (30.5
x 30.5 x 27.3 cm.)
University of California, Berkeley Art Museum,
purchased with the aid of funds provided by the
National Endowment of the Arts and the
University Art Museum Council

*Works from The Labyrinth: Maltese Cross from the
Labyrinth of Chartres*, 1975
Metal hoop, nylon fishline, paint, and string
Hoop: 15 1/4 in. dia. (38.8 cm.)
Courtesy Frayda and Ronald Feldman

**Howard Fried**
*All My Dirty Blue Clothes*, 1970/1998
Clothes of various fabrics, metal and canvas laundry
cart, jointed wooden pool cues, paint, paint roller, roller
tray and skid, stencils, chalk, text
Dimensions variable, approx. 85 ft. (26 m.)
Courtesy of the artist and Gallery Paule Anglim,
San Francisco

*Prototype for A Clock of Commercial Significance
(from "Synchromatic Baseball," 1971)*, 1974-1978
Lacquered wooden frame, glass, black-and-white
photographs, metal clock hands, plastic clock
movement
58 1/2 x 58 1/2 x 3 in. (148.6 x 148.6 x 7.6 cm.)
Courtesy of the artist and Gallery Paule Anglim,
San Francisco

**Gideon Gechtman**
*Shaved Nude*, 1974
Black-and-white photograph
11 x 14 in. (27.9 x 35.6 cm.)
Collection of the artist

*Brushes*, 1974-1979
Wood and human hair
47 1/4 x 23 5/8 x 47 1/4 in. (120 x 60 x 120 cm.)
Collection of the artist

*Obituary Notice of the Artist*, 1975
Printed document
10 1/2 x 13 5/8 in. (26.7 x 34.6 cm.)
Collection of the artist

**Jochen Gerz**
*Exhibition of Jochen Gerz Beside
His Photographic Reproduction*, 1972
Photodocumentation of performance
(black-and-white photograph)
20 1/2 x 23 5/8 in. (52 x 60 cm.)
Courtesy of the artist and Gallery Paule Anglim,
San Francisco
Photograph by Galeria Stampa, Basel

*The Portrait*, 1972
Mixed media on paper
29 x 43 in. (73.7 x 109.2 cm.)
Courtesy Galerie Chantal Crousel, Paris
Photograph by Atelier Gerz

*To Write with My Hand*, 1972-73
Photodocumentation of performance
(six black-and-white photographs)
15 3/4 x 10 5/8 in. each (40 x 27 cm.)
Courtesy of the artist and Gallery Paule Anglim,
San Francisco
Photographs by Esther Shalev-Gerz

**Gilbert & George**
*Postal Sculpture*, 1969
Printed paper in envelope with wax seal
7 7/8 x 6 3/4 in. (20 x 17 cm.)
Courtesy Anthony d'Offay Gallery, London

*The Meal, A Living Sculpture*, 1969
Paper menu and ticket
4 1/5 x 3 1/5 in. (11.5 x 8.9 cm.)
Courtesy Anthony d'Offay Gallery, London

*George the Cunt and Gilbert the Shit*, 1970
Magazine sculpture
15 x 12 1/5 in. (38 x 31.8 cm.)
Courtesy Anthony d'Offay Gallery, London

*Smashed*, 1972
Ten black-and-white photographs
Overall: 75 x 52 in. (190.5 x 132.1 cm.)
Courtesy Sonnabend Gallery, New York

*Raining Gin*, 1973
Forty-four black-and-white photographs
Overall: 78 x 45 in. (198.1 x 114.3 cm.)
Courtesy Sonnabend Gallery, New York

*The Singing Sculpture* (a film by Philip Haas), 1991
Film transfer to video, 20 min.
Courtesy Sonnabend Sundell/Methodact Ltd.

**Alberto Greco**
*Vivo Dito*, 1964
Photodocumentation of performance
(four black-and-white photographs)
11 x 14 in. each (27.9 x 35.6 cm.)
Courtesy Greco Estate

**Ion Grigorescu**
*Action C (Caca)*, 1973-1974
Photodocumentation of performance
(four black-and-white photographs)
3 x 5 in. each (7.6 x 12.7 cm.), framed together
Private Collection

*Pole Vault - River Traisteni*, 1976
Photodocumentation of performance
(three hand-colored black-and-white photographs
and one black-and-white photograph)
Three photographs: 9 3/8 x 11 5/8 in. each
(23.8 x 29.5 cm);
one photograph: 14 x 17 in. (35.6 x 43.2 cm.)
Private Collection

**Victor Grippo**
*Construction of a Traditional Rural Oven for Making
Bread*, 1972
Photodocumentation of event
(three black-and-white photographs)
11 x 14 in. each (27.9 x 35.6 cm.)
Collection of the artist
Photographs by Mercedes Casanegra

**Red Grooms**
*Painting from "A Play Called Fire,"* 1958
Oil and enamel on canvas
53 1/2 x 91 in. (135.9 x 231.1 cm.)
Greenville County Museum of Art, Museum
purchase with funds from the Arthur and Holly Magill
Purchase Fund

**Guerrilla Art Action Group**
*Museum of Modern Art Action (Number 3)*, 1969
Two texts and photodocumentation of action
(three black-and-white photographs)
Texts: 11 x 14 in. each (27.9 x 35.6 cm); photographs:
14 x 17 in. each (35.6 x 43.2 cm.)
Collection Jon and Joanne Hendricks
Photographs by Ka Kwong Hui

*"People's Flag Show" (Number 12)*, 1970
Two texts
11 x 14 in. each (27.9 x 35.6 cm.)
Collection Jon and Joanne Hendricks

*The People's Flag*, 1970
Flag
Approx. 32 1/2 x 35 3/4 in. (82.6 x 90.8 cm.)
Collection of Eléonore Hendricks

**David Hammons**
*Untitled*, 1974
Mixed media on paper
28 x 22 in. (71.1 x 55.9 cm.)
Private Collection

*Untitled*, c. 1975
Mixed media on paper
29 x 23 in. (73.7 x 58.4 cm.)
Private Collection

**Al Hansen**
*Al Does a Newspaper Snow Job*, 1966
Photodocumentation of performance
(black-and-white photograph)
14 x 17 in. (35.6 x 43.2 cm.)
Collection Ronald Maker

*Hansen Breaks into the Unknown*, 1966
Photodocumentation of performance
(color photograph)
14 x 17 in. (35.6 x 43.2 cm.)
Collection Ronald Maker

*Hansen Does the New Year's Boogie
with a Dancer*, 1966
Photodocumentation of performance
(color photograph)
14 x 17 in. (35.6 x 43.2 cm.)
Collection Ronald Maker

*Hansen Weaves Valentine's Day Love Web
with Dancer and Grail*, 1966
Photodocumentation of performance
(black-and-white photograph)
14 x 17 in. (35.6 x 43.2 cm.)
Collection Ronald Maker

**Maren Hassinger**
*High Noon*, 1976
Photodocumentation of performance
(two black-and-white photographs)
11 x 14 in. each (27.9 x 35.6 cm.)
Collection of the artist
Photograph by Adam Avila

**Lynn Hershman**
*Roberta's Driver's License*, 1976
California driver's license
4 x 5 in. (10.2 x 12.7 cm.)
Courtesy Hess Collection, Napa and Berne

*Roberta's Check Book*, c. 1970s
Checkbook
3 x 6 x 1/4 in. (7.6 x 15.2 x .6 cm.)
Courtesy Hess Collection, Napa and Berne

*Roberta's Dress (Rust and White Polyester
with Polka-Dot Skirt)*, c. 1970s
Polyester
36 x 22 x 3 in. (91.4 x 55.9 x 7.6 cm.)
Courtesy Hess Collection, Napa and Berne

*Roberta's "Elura" Ash Blonde Frosted Wig*, c. 1970s
100% Mod acrylic fiber
12 x 7 x 6 in. (30.5 x 17.8 x 15.2 cm.)
Courtesy of Hess Collection, Napa and Berne

*Roberta's Jacket to Dress (Rust and White
Polyester)*, c. 1970s
Suede
30 x 25 x 3 in. (77.2 x 63.5 x 7.6 cm.)
Courtesy Hess Collection, Napa and Berne

*Roberta's Lost Button*, c. 1970s
Found object
10 x 8 x 3 in. (25.4 x 20.3 x 7.6 cm.)
Courtesy Hess Collection, Napa and Berne

*Three Roberta Breitmore Multiples*, c. 1970s
Photodocumentation (black-and-white and
color photographs)
30 x 40 in. each (76.2 x 101.6 cm.)
Courtesy Hess Collection, Napa and Berne

**Dick Higgins**
*Symphony 607-The Divers*, 1968
Five pages of music paper with bullet holes
and color spray
22 5/8 x 17 1/2 in. each (57.5 x 44.5 cm.)
Block Collection

**Tatsumi Hijikata**
*Tatsumi Hijikata and the Japanese-Revolt
of the Flesh*, 1968
Photodocumentation of performance
(three black-and-white photographs)
11 x 14 in. each (27.9 x 35.6 cm.)
Collection Tatsumi Hijikata Memorial Archives/
Theater Asbestos

**Susan Hiller**
*Hand Grenades*, 1969-72
Ashes of *Hand Paintings*, a series of twelve
collaborative group paintings, 1969; burnt and
presented in twelve glass jars with rubber stoppers and
tags, in Pyrex bowl, 1972; shelf added later
Overall: 4 3/8 x 7 1/8 x 7 1/8 in. (11 x 18 x 18 cm.)
Collection of the artist

*Dream Mapping*, 1974
Seven dream notebooks with drawings and texts
Notebooks: 9 x 7 in. each (23 x 18 cm.) (closed)
Collection of the artist

**Hi Red Center**
*Movement to Promote the Cleanup
of the Metropolitan Area (Be Clean!)*, October 16, 1964
Photodocumentation of event held in Ginza, Tokyo
(black-and-white photograph)
11 x 14 in. (27.9 x 35.6 cm.)
Nagoya City Museum

*The Ochanomizu Drop (Dropping Event)*, 1964
Photodocumentation of event held at Ikenobo
Kaikan Hall, Tokyo (black-and-white photograph)
11 x 14 in. (27.9 x 35.6 cm.)
Nagoya City Museum

**Rebecca Horn**
*Fingerhandschuhe*, 1972
Fabric and balsa wood
27 9/16 in. long (70 cm.)
Private Collection

*Mechanical Body Fan*, 1972
Fabric and metal
118 in. (300 cm.) (open)
Collection of the artist

*Paradieswitwe*, 1975
Black feathers and metal
78 3/4 x 31 1/2 in. (200 x 80 cm.)
Kunstmuseum Bonn

**Tehching Hsieh**
*Tehching Hsieh Punching the Timeclock on the Hour,
One Year Performance*, April 11, 1980-April 11, 1981
Photodocumentation of performance
(black-and-white photograph)
11 x 14 in. (27.9 x 35.6 cm.)
Collection of the artist
Photograph by Michael Shen

**Joan Jonas** (assisted by Linda Patton)
*Organic Honey's Visual Telepathy*, 1972/1994
Video: Black-and-white sound, 23 min.
Collection of the artist

**Kim Jones**
*Dog/Rat*, c. 1972, with later additions
Acrylic paint and ink on foam rubber, latex, nylon, wood,
and wire
42 x 17 x 6 1/2 in. (196.7 x 43.2 x 16.5 cm.)
Collection of the artist

**Michel Journiac**
*La messe pour un corps*, 1969-71
Installation with video, two wood "prie-dieu,"
three altoglas blood-plaquettes, mixed media and
collage on wood table-altar painting, and recipe
for human blood pudding
Dimensions variable
Collection Jacques Miège

**Akira Kanayama**
*Work*, 1957
Mixed media on vinyl
71 x 109 3/8 in. (180.3 x 277.8 cm.)
Hyogo Prefectural Museum of Modern Art, Kobe

*Work*, 1958
Synthetic polymer paint on canvas
70 3/4 x 102 1/4 in. (179.7 x 259.7 cm.)
Museum of Contemporary Art, Tokyo;
Gift of the artist

**Tadeusz Kantor**
*Panoramic Sea Happening*, 1967
Photodocumentation of performance
(black-and-white photograph)
18 x 24 in. (45.7 x 61 cm.)
Collection of the artist
Photograph by Eustachy Kossakowski

**Allan Kaprow**
*Hysteria*, 1956
Collage
72 x 67 in. (183 x 170 cm.)
Private Collection

*Rearrangeable Panels*, 1957-59
Mixed media assemblage
Overall: 95 11/16 x 59 1/16 x 55 1/8 in.
(243 x 150 x 140 cm.)
Mr. and Mrs. Rammant, Belgium

*18 Happenings in 6 Parts*, 1959
Photodocumentation of performance
(two black-and-white photographs)
11 x 14 in. each (27.9 x 35.6 cm.)
Collection of the artist

*Yard*, 1961/1998
Used automobile tires and other media
Dimensions variable
Collection Feelisch, Remscheid

**Mike Kelley**
*The Base Man*, 1970
Plastic megaphone, maraca, flashlights,
cardboard tubes, and paper
41 x 58 x 58 in. (104.1 x 147.3 x 147.3 cm.)
Collection of the artist

*Tube Music: The Flying Flower*, 1977-78
Cardboard tube, rubber whoopee cushion, painted
tin foil, rubber bands, and wood block
Dimensions variable
Collection of the artist

*Two Machines for the Intellect*, 1977-78
Two shoeboxes, tinfoil, optical lens, two electric
lightbulbs, and flashers
Boxes: 4 1/2 x 12 1/2 x 6 1/2 in. each
(11.4 x 31.8 x 16.5 cm.)
Collection of the artist

*Indianana*, 1978
Three black-and-white "leitmotif" photographs
23 5/8 x 27 in. (60 x 68.6 cm.)
Collection of the artist

*Indianana*, 1978
Main prop: wood, metal, caulk, and rubber
beehive airpump
12 in. high and approx. 48 in. dia. (30.5 x 121.9 cm.)
Collection of the artist

*Spirit Collector*, 1978
Painted wood with metal, masonite, batting,
and tape recorder
12 x 31 1/2 x 11 1/2 in. (30.5 x 80 x 29.2 cm.)
Private Collection

*Unstoppable Force vs. Immovable Object*, 1979
Cardboard tube and two whoopee cushions
Dimensions variable
Collection of the artist

*Wind and Crickets*, c. late 1970s
Cardboard tube, tinfoil, pushpin, and rubber band
Dimensions variable
Collection of the artist

**Jürgen Klauke**
*The Harder They Come (I and II)*, 1978
Photodocumentation of perfomance
(four black-and-white photographs)
9 x 12 in. (22.8 x 30.5 cm.)
Courtesy Galerie Bugdahn and Kaimer, Düsseldorf

**Yves Klein**
*Monochrome* (1KB Godet), 1957
Acrylic on paper mounted on canvas
59 x 77.9 in. (149.9 x 198.1 cm.)
Yves Klein Archives

*The Living Paintbrushes*, 1958
Photodocumentation of performance
(two black-and-white photographs)
14 x 17 in. each (35.6 x 43.2 cm.)
Yves Klein Archives

*L'Etoile* (ANT 73), 1960
Dry pigment and synthetic resin on canvas
53 1/2 x 39 3/8 in. (135.9 x 100 cm.)
Yves Klein Archives

*Leap into the Void*, 1960
Photodocumentation of action (black-and-white
photograph)
11 x 14 in. each (27.9 x 35.6 cm.)
Yves Klein Archives
Photograph by Harry Shunk

*Untitled Anthropometry* (ANT 106), 1960
Dry pigment on canvas
78 3/4 x 196 7/8 in. (200 x 500 cm.)
Yves Klein Archives

**Milan Knížák**
*Preacher of an X Time*, 1958
Photodocumentation of object
(black-and-white photograph)
11 7/8 x 8 1/4 in. (31 x 21 cm.)
Collection of the artist

*Demonstration of One*, 1964
Photodocumentation of performance
(five black-and-white photographs)
11 x 14 in. each (27.9 x 35.6 cm.)
Collection of the artist

*Everyday Suit of Milan Knížák*, 1964
Photograph pasted on cardboard
78 3/4 x 24 1/2 in. (200 x 62 cm.)
Collection of the artist

*Actualized Shirt*, 1965
Cut and burned textile
27 1/2 x 23 5/8 x 2 3/8 in. (70 x 60 x 6 cm.)
Collection of the artist

*Burned Shirt*, 1965
Textile
29 1/2 x 21 5/8 x 4 3/4 in. (75 x 55 x 12 cm.)
Collection of the artist

*Double-faced Jacket*, 1965
Textiles
33 1/2 x 25 5/8 x 4 in. (85 x 65 x 10 cm.)
Collection of the artist

*Actualized Coat*, 1965-70
Cut and resewn textile
43 3/8 x 17 3/4 x 4 in. (110 x 45 x 10 cm.)
Collection of the artist

*Make a Big Paper Glider*, 1965/1998
Paper
Dimensions variable
Collection of the artist

*Untitled*, 1968
Red paint on thin white cloth glued to a black board
21 1/4 x 15 3/4 in. (54 x 40 cm.)
Collection Hans Rueep

*Dress Jewelry*, 1969
Colored shirt with screw, matches, chewing gum,
scissors, and other materials
22 1/2 x 22 x 2 in. (57 x 56 x 5 cm.)
Collection Feelisch, Remscheid

*My Destiny*, 1969
White shirt with little Czechoslovakian flags
embroidered, patch burned off
29 1/2 x 20 1/2 x 2 in. (75 x 52 x 5 cm.)
Collection Feelisch, Remscheid

*Clothes Painted on a Body*, c. 1960s
Four ink on paper drawings
11 7/8 x 8 1/4 in. each (30 x 21 cm.)
Collection of the artist

*Untitled*, c. 1965-66
Military fatigue material and orange banner
Bag: 13 x 10 1/2 in. (33 x 26.7 cm.); banner:
2 3/4 x 11 in. (7 x 27.9 cm.)
Private Collection

**Alison Knowles** (with Philip Corner and Bill
Fontana)
*Gentle Surprises for the Ear*, 1975/1997
Installation with sound events, two wooden
platforms, and plexiglas sheet
Overall: 24 x 96 x 48 in. (61 x 243.8 x 122 cm.)
Collection of the artist

**Komar & Melamid**
*The Excavation on Crete*, 1978
Bone, horn, teeth, wire, and newspaper
with collage
The Solomon R. Guggenheim Museum, New York;
Gift, Professor and Mrs. Alexander Melamid,
New York

**Jannis Kounellis**
*Untitled*, 1960
Oil on cardboard
56 5/16 x 118 1/8 in. (143 x 300 cm.)
The Reiner Speck Collection, Cologne

*Untitled*, 1970/1998
Woman wrapped in a wool blanket on a steel base with
a propane gas torch tied to her foot
Base: 11 13/16 x 25 5/8 x 63 in.
(30 x 65.1 x 160 cm.)
Courtesy Christian Stein Gallery, Milan

*Untitled (Da inventare sul posto)*, 1972
Oil on canvas
97 1/4 x 118 in. (247 x 300 cm.)
The Reiner Speck Collection, Cologne

**Shigeko Kubota**
*Vagina Painting*, 1965
Photodocumentation of performance
(two black-and-white photographs)
8 x 10 in. each (20.3 x 25.4 cm.)
Courtesy Gilbert and Lila Silverman Fluxus
Collection Foundation
Photographs by George Maciunas

**Tetsumi Kudo**
*Philosophy of Impotence*, 1962
Photodocumentation of performance
(black-and-white photograph)
11 x 14 in. (27.9 x 35.6 cm.)
Courtesy Artist's Rights Society, New York

*Votre Portrait*, 1963
Wood, plastic, and polyester
78 3/4 x 19 11/16 x 19 11/16 in. (200 x 50 x 50 cm.)
Takamatsu City Museum of Art

**Yayoi Kusama**
*Avantgarde Fashion A*, c. 1960s/1998
Red net painting on white cotton
32 5/8 x 43 1/4 in. (83 x 110 cm.)
Collection of the artist

*Avantgarde Fashion B*, c. 1960s/1998
Yellow net painting on dark brown chemical velvet
35 1/2 x 43 1/4 in. (90 x 110 cm.)
Collection of the artist

*Avantgarde Fashion C*, c. 1960s/1998
Black chemical fiber
34 5/8 x 39 3/8 in. (88 x 100 cm.)
Collection of the artist

*Avantgarde Fashion D*, c. 1960s/1998
Colored dots on black polyester
39 3/8 x 35 1/2 in. (100 x 90 cm.)
Collection of the artist

*Hat*, c. 1962
Mixed media
13 x 30 x 18 in. (33 x 76.2 x 15.2 cm.)
Provenance Richard Castellane, Esq. (courtesy
D'Amelio Terras Gallery, New York)

*Silver Coat*, c. 1962
Mixed media
52 x 35 x 6 in. (132.1 x 88.9 x 15.2 cm.)
Provenance Richard Castellane, Esq. (courtesy
D'Amelio Terras Gallery, New York)

*Blue Tunic*, c. late 1960s
Mixed media
28 x 44 in. (71.1 x 111.8 cm.)
Courtesy Robert Miller Gallery, New York

*Brown Tunic*, c. late 1960s
Mixed media
30 x 60 in. (76.2 x 152.4 cm.)
Courtesy Robert Miller Gallery, New York

*Skirt*, c. late 1960s
Mixed media
19 x 22 in. (48.3 x 55.9 cm.)
Courtesy Robert Miller Gallery, New York

*Tie*, c. late 1960s
Mixed media
58 x 4 1/4 in. (147.3 x 10.2 x .6 cm.)
Courtesy Robert Miller Gallery, New York

*Untitled (Tunic)*, c. late 1960s
Oil on cloth
29 x 20 x 1/4 in. (73.7 x 50.7 x 6 cm.)
Collection of the Donald Judd Estate

**Leslie Labowitz and Suzanne Lacy**
*In Mourning and in Rage*, December 1977
Notebook of newspaper clippings and photodocumenta-
tion of performance (four color photographs)
Photographs: 11 x 14 in. each (27.9 x 35.6 cm.)
Collection Suzanne Lacy
Photographs by Maria Karras

**John Latham**
*Shaun II*, 1958
Assemblage on canvas
99 1/2 x 46 x 12  in. (252.7 x 116.8 x 30.5 cm.)
Arts Council Collection, Hayward Gallery, London

*Shem*, 1958
Hessian-covered door with books, scrap metals,
various paints, plasters, and cements
8 ft. 4 1/2 in. x 46 in. x 12 1/2 in.
(255.2 x 116.8 x 31.7 cm.)
The Museum of Modern Art, New York,
Philip Johnson Fund

*Soft Skoob*, 1964
Books, canvas, spray paint, and table
25 x 132 x 50 cm.
Courtesy Lisson Gallery, London

*Skoob Tower Ceremony*, 1964/1998
Ashes from burned  books and pedestal
Dimensions variable
Courtesy Lisson Gallery, London

*Art and Culture*, 1966-69
Book, labeled vials filled with powders and liquids,
letters, photostats, and other materials in a leather case
3 1/8 x 11 1/8 x 10 in. (7.9 x 28.2 x 25.3 cm.)
The Museum of Modern Art, New York, Blanchette
Rockefeller Fund

**Jean-Jacques Lebel**
*Pour Conjurer l'Esprit de Catastrophe #1 and 2*, 1962
Four "tableau-happenings" panels of collage
and paint on plywood
78 3/4 x 39 3/8 in. each (200 x 100 cm.)
Private Collection

**Lea Lublin**
*Fluvio Subtunal*, 1969
Photodocumentation of environment
(five color photographs)
11 x 14 in. each (27.9 x 35.6 cm.)
Collection of the artist

**George Maciunas**
*Instruction Drawing for "One Year"*, 1972
Ink on index card
3 x 5 in. (7.6 x 12.7 cm.)
Courtesy Gilbert and Lila Silverman
Fluxus Collection Foundation

*One Year*, 1972
Grocery packaging mounted on wood
82 11/16 x 137 13/16 x 4 3/4 in.
(210 x 350 x 12 cm. )
Block Collection

**Leopoldo Maler**
*Crane Ballet*, 1971
Photodocumentation of performance at Camden Music
Festival (two black-and-white photographs)
11 x 14 in. each (27.9 x 35.6 cm.)
Collection of the artist
Photographs by J. S. Lewinsky

**Piero Manzoni**
*Fiato d'artista*, 1960
Rubber and wood
7 1/16 x 7 1/16 in. (18 x 18 cm.)
Collection of Sante Falconér

*Fiato d'artista*, 1960
Rubber and wood
7 1/16 x 7 1/16 x 3/4 in. (18 x 18 cm.)
Collection of Alberto Bassi

*Corpo d'aria*, 1959-60
Rubber, metal and wood
1 7/8 x 16 3/4 x 4 7/8 in. (4.8 x 42.5 x 12.3 cm.)
Archivio Opera Piero Manzoni

*Corpo d'aria*, 1961
Wooden box with label, balloon, and metal stand
2 x 16 3/4 x 4 15/16 in. (5 x 42.5 x 12.5 cm.)
Block Collection

*Carte d'Authenticité*, 1961
Two unused blocks, ink on paper
1/8 x 2 3/4 x 6 3/4 in. (.32 x 7 x 17.1 cm.)
Archivio Opera Piero Manzoni

*Counterfoil of Carte d'Authenticité*, 1961
Ink on paper
1/8 x 2 3/4 x 2 3/4 in. (.32 x 7 x 7 cm.)
Archivio Opera Piero Manzoni

*Egg with Thumbprint, No. 13*, 1960
Egg, ink, and wood
2 1/4 x 3 1/4 x 3 1/8 in. (5.6 x 8.2 x 8 cm.)
Arturo Schwarz Collection, Milan

*Line 19.11 Meters*, 1959
Ink and paper on cardboard
Plexiglas box: 11 1/4 x 4 3/4 x 4 3/4 in.
(28.7 x 12 x 12 cm.)
Archivio Opera Piero Manzoni

*Line of 10.06 Meters*, 1959
Ink on paper and cardboard
Approx. 23 5/8 x 19 5/8 in. (50 x 60 cm.)
Arturo Schwarz Collection, Milan

*Line of Infinite Length*, 1959
Ink on parchment
2 1/16 x 8 3/8 in. (5.2 x 21.3 cm.)
Block Collection

*Line of Infinite Length*, 1960
Wood and paper
6 x 1 7/8 in. (15 x 4.8 cm.)
Archivio Opera Piero Manzoni

*Line of Infinite Length*, 1960
Wood and paper
6 x 1 7/8 in. (15 x 4.7 cm.)
Collection of Vanni Scheiwiller, Milan

*Thumbprint*, 1960
Ink on paper
4 x 3 in. (10 x 7.5 cm.)
Arturo Schwarz Collection, Milan

*Line 1000 Meters Long*, 1961
Chrome-plated metal drum containing a roll of paper
with an ink line drawn along its 1000-meter length
20 1/4 in. high x 15 3/8 in. dia. (51.2 x 38.8 cm.)
The Museum of Modern Art, New York
Gift of Fratelli Fabbri Editori and Purchase

*Base Magica*, 1961
Wood
31 1/2 x 31 1/2 x 23 1/2 in. (80 x 80 x 60 cm.)
Archivio Opera Piero Manzoni

*Merda d'artista, No. 55 and No. 80*, 1961
Metal and paper
1 7/8 x 2 1/2 in. dia. (4.8 x 6.4 cm.)
Archivio Opera Piero Manzoni

*Merda d'artista*, 1961
Can with printed label
2 in. high x 2 9/16 in. dia. (5 x 6.5 cm.)
Block Collection

**Tom Marioni**
*Drawing A Line As Far As I Can Reach
(Edinburgh Drawing)*, 1972
Pencil on paper
9 ft. 3 in. x 42 in. x 7 ft. 8 in. (2.8 m. x 106.7 cm. x 2.3 m.)
Courtesy of the artist and Gallery Paule Anglim,
San Francisco, and Margarete Roeder Gallery,
New York

*Drum-brush Drawing #1*, 1973
Steel on white paper
22 1/2 x 28 1/2 in. (57.2 x 72.4 cm.)
Courtesy of the artist, Gallery Paule Anglim,
San Francisco, and Margarete Roeder Gallery,
New York

*Drum-brush Drawing #2*, 1973
Steel on yellow paper
20 x 28 in. (50.8 x 71.1 cm.)
Courtesy Tom Marioni, Gallery Paule Anglim,
San Francisco, and Margarete Roeder Gallery,
New York

*Drum-brush Drawing #3*, 1973
Steel on sandpaper
22 x 28 in. (55.9 x 71.1 cm.)
Courtesy of the artist, Gallery Paule Anglim,
San Francisco, and Margarete Roeder Gallery,
New York

**Cusi Masuda**
*Self Digestion*, 1975
Photodocumentation of performance
(five black-and-white photographs)
8 x 10 in. each (20.3 x 24.2 cm.)
Collection of the artist

**Georges Mathieu**
*Hommage au Connetable de Bourbon*, 1959
Oil on canvas
98 7/16 x 236 3/16 in. (250.2 x 600 cm.)
Collection of the artist

**Gordon Matta-Clark**
*Fried Photograph*, 1969
Gold leaf photograph in box
1 x 5 x 3 3/4 in. (2.5 x 12.5 x 9.5 cm.)
Courtesy Lance Fung Gallery, New York,
and the Estate of Gordon Matta-Clark

*Photo-Fry*, 1969
Brochure with two black-and-white photographs
mounted on paper, with ink
13 1/2 x 9 1/8 in. (34.3 x 23.2 cm.) (closed)
Courtesy Gilbert and Lila Silverman Collection, Detroit

*Hair*, 1972
Five black-and-white photographs, four pencil
on paper drawings, and thirteen envelopes of hair
Photographs: 10 x 8 in. each (25.4 x 20.3 cm.);
drawings: 14 x 11 in. each (35.6 x 27.9 cm.)
Courtesy Lance Fung Gallery, New York, and
the Estate of Gordon Matta-Clark

**Paul McCarthy**
*Face Painting – Floor, White Line*, 1972
Photodocumentation of performance
(two black-and-white photographs)
20 x 16 in. each (50.8 x 40.6 cm.)
Collection of the artist

*Assortment, Trunks*, 1973-83
Suitcases and trunks containing objects from
performance work, 1973-83
Dimensions variable
Collection Tom Patchett, Los Angeles

*Meatcake*, 1974
Eight pages of scripts used in performance
Approx. 9 1/2 x 11 in. each (24.1 x 27.9 cm.)
Collection of the artist

**Bruce McLean**
*High Up on a Baroque Palazzo*, 1974
Photodocumentation of Nice Style Pose Band event
(black-and-white photograph)
20 3/8 x 20 in. (51.8 x 50.8 cm.)
Courtesy Anthony d'Offay Gallery, London

**David Medalla**
*A Stitch in Time*, 1968-72
Mixed media installation
Dimensions variable
Arts Council Collection, London

**Cildo Meireles**
*The Sermon on the Mount: Fiat Lux*, 1973-79
Photodocumentation of performance
(black-and-white photograph)
11 x 14 in. (27.9 x 35.6 cm.)
Collection of the artist

**Ana Mendieta**
*Burial of the Ñañigo*, 1976
Candles, slide projector, and projected slide image
79 x 39 x 10 in. (200.7 x 99.1 x 25.4 cm.)
Courtesy of the Estate of Ana Mendieta
and Galerie Lelong, New York

**Gustav Metzger**
*South Bank Demo*, 1961/1998
Metal, nylon, and acid
Approx. 5 x 8 ft. (1.52 x 2.44 m.)
Collection of the artist

*Daily Express*, 1962/1998
Newspaper
Collection of the artist

*Autodestructive Manifesto*, n.d.
Printed document
8 1/4 x 10 1/2 in. (21 x 27 cm.)
Collection Ben Vautier

**Marta Minujin**
*Mattress-House: La Pieza del Amor (1962),
Casa de Colchones (1963), Revuelsque (1964)*
Photodocumentation of installation
(color photograph)
30 x 40 in. (76.2 x 101.6 cm.)
Collection of the artist

*The Obelisk of Raisin Buns*, 1979
Photodocumentation of object (one color photograph
and two black-and-white photographs))
11 x 14 in. each (27.9 x 35.6 cm.)
Collection of the artist

**Jan Mlčoch**
*The Emigrant's Suitcase: Across the Sea*, 1976
Photodocumentation of object at Gallery Remont,
Warsaw, Poland (black-and-white photograph)
11 x 14 in. (27.9 x 35.6 cm.)
Collection of the artist

*No Return (The Terezin Concentration Camp –
A Prison Cell)*, 1976
Photodocumentation of performance
(black-and-white photograph)
11 x 14 in. (27.9 x 35.6 cm.)
Collection of the artist

*The Classic Escape*, 1977
Photodocumentation of performance
(black-and-white photograph)
11 x 14 in. (27.9 x 35.6 cm.)
Collection of the artist

**Linda Montano** (with Tom Marioni)
*Handcuff: Linda Montano and Tom Marioni*, 1973
Photodocumentation of performance
(black-and-white photograph)
11 x 14 in. (27.9 x 35.6 cm.)
Collection of the artist

**Charlotte Moorman**
*Cello Bombs*, c. 1965/1990s
Painted metal
47 in. high (119.4 cm.)
Sammlung Hoffmann

**Robert Morris**
*Untitled (Standing Box)*, 1961
Oak
75 x 24 1/2 x 11 in. (190.5 x 62.2 x 27.9 cm.)
Solomon R. Guggenheim Museum, New York,
Extended Loan of the Artist

**Otto Muehl**
*Materialbild (with sardine tin)*, 1961-62
Mixed media on hardboard
44 1/2 x 41 5/16 x 3 1/8 in. (113 x 105 x 8 cm.)
Sammlung Friedrichshof, Zurndorf

*Untitled*, 1963
Mixed media on hardboard
52 x 28 3/8 x 6 5/16 in. (132 x 72 x 16 cm.)
Sammlung Friedrichshof, Zurndorf

*Untitled*, 1963
Sand, plaster, stockings and emulsion on sackcloth
29 15/16 x 27 9/16 in. (76 x 70 cm.)
Sammlung Friedrichshof, Zurndorf

*Aktionobject*, 1963-64
Mixed media
98 7/16 x 98 7/16 in. (220 x 260 cm.)
Sammlung Friedrichshof, Zurndorf

*Collage*, 1964
Photographs and drawings on hardboard
19 5/8 x 25 5/8 in. (50 x 65 cm.)
Museum moderner Kunst Stiftung Ludwig, Vienna

*Materialaktion*, 1965
Photodocumentation of performance
13 3/4 x 7 7/8 in. (35 x 20 cm.)
Collection Julius Hummel, Vienna

*Materialaktion*, 1965
Photodocumentation of performance
9 x 13 3/4 in. (25 x 35 cm.)
Sammlung Friedrichshof, Zurndorf

*Materialaktion*, 1965
Photodocumentation of performance
13 3/4 x 7 7/8 in. (35 x 20 cm.)
Courtesy Galerie Krinzinger, Vienna

*Untitled*, n.d.
Photodocumentation of performance
(twenty-two Cibachrome photographs)
11 3/4 x 11 3/4 in. each (30 x 30 cm.)
Sammlung Friedrichshof, Zurndorf

**Saburō Murakami**
*Entrance*, 1955/1998
Paper and wood
Dimensions variable
Collection Makiko Murakami

*Work: Box (Sakuhin: Hako)*, 1956/1981
Wooden box with ticking clock
31 1/2 x 31 1/2 x 31 1/2 in. (80 x 80 x 80 cm.)
Museum of Contemporary Art, Tokyo

*Work: (Sakuhin)*, 1957
(also *Peeling Off Painting*)
Mixed media on board
36 5/8 x 72 5/8 in. (93 x 184.5 cm.)
The Ashiya City Museum of Art & History

**Natsuyuki Nakanishi**
*Clothespins Assert Churning Action*, 1963/1993
Underwear and tin clothespins attached to
five panels of partly burned canvas
Three panels: 46 x 35 3/4 x 5 in. (116.8 x 90.8 x 12.7
cm.); one panel: 13 x 15 x 5 in. (33 x 38.1 x 12.7 cm.);
one panel: 46 x 35 3/4 x 10 in. (116.8 x 90.8 x 25.4 cm.)
Collection of the artist

**Bruce Nauman**
*Performance Corridor*, 1968-70
Wallboard and wood
Approx. 96 x 240 x 20 in. (243.8 x 609.6 x 50.8 cm.)
Solomon R. Guggenheim Museum, New York:
Purchased with funds contributed by
the Louis and Bessie Adler Foundation, Inc.,
Seymour M. Klein, President

**Paul Neagu**
*Hyphen (The Subject Generator)*, 1975
Ash wood, bolts, and strings
39 1/2 x 40 x 83 in. (100.3 x 101.6 x 210.8 cm.)
Collection of the artist

*Codex for Hyphen*, 1976
Drawing
30 1/2 x 22 in. (77.5 x 55.9 cm.)
Collection of the artist

**Senga Nengudi**
*Respondez-vous s'il vous plaît—Studio performance,
Los Angeles*, 1976
Photodocumentation of performance
(black-and-white photograph)
11 x 14 in. (27.9 x 35.6 cm.)
Courtesy Thomas Erben Gallery, New York
Photograph by Adam Avila

*Freeway Fets* and *Ceremony for Freeway Fets*, 1978
Photodocumentation of performance
(color photograph)
11 x 14 in. (27.9 x 35.6 cm.)
Courtesy Thomas Erben Gallery, New York

*Masked Taping*, c. 1978-79
Photodocumentation of performance
(black-and-white photograph)
11 x 14 in. (27.9 x 35.6 cm.)
Courtesy Thomas Erben Gallery, New York
Photograph by Adam Avila

**Joshua Neustein** (with G. Marx and G. Battle)
*Jerusalem River Project: Sound of Flowing River
in the Dry Wadi of Abu Tor*, 1970
Photodocumentation of installation
(three black-and-white photographs)
11 x 14 in. each (27.9 x 35.6 cm.)
Collection of the artist

**Hermann Nitsch**
*Brot und Wein*, 1961
Tempera and emulsion paint on plaster,
mounted on synthetic support
59 x 59 in. (150 x 150 cm.)
Collection Julius Hummel, Vienna

*Rinnbild*, 1963
Blood and color on canvas
78 3/4 x 118 1/8 in. (190 x 340 cm.)
Sammlung Friedrichshof, Zurndorf

*4th Action*, 1963 (printed 1972)
Photodocumentation of performance
(eight color photographs)
23 5/8 x 19 3/4 in. each (60 x 50 cm.)
Collection of the artist

*Score to the 8th Action*, 1965
Ball-point pen in sketchbook
8 1/4 x 5 7/8 in. (21 x 14.8 cm.)
Archiv Sohm, Staatsgalerie, Stuttgart

**Hermann Nitsch** (continued)
*Asolo Raum*, 1971
Installation with objects, relics, and photographs
Room: 23 x 23 ft. (7 x 7 m.)
Archiv Conz, Verona


**Hélio Oiticica**
*Parangolé P5 (Cape 4), "Homenagem a Lygia Clark,"*
1964-65/1998
Acrylic on canvas with plastic, nylon, mesh, and burlap
55 1/8 x 23 5/8 x 4 3/4 in. (140 x 60 x 12 cm.)
Projeto Hélio Oiticica, Rio de Janeiro

*Parangolé P4 (Cape 1)*, 1964/1998
Acrylic on canvas with rope, plastic, and nylon mesh
55 1/8 x 19 5/8 x 3 7/8 in. (140 x 50 x 10 cm.)
Projeto Hélio Oiticica, Rio de Janeiro

*Parangolé P16 (Cape 12),"Of Adversity we Live,"* 1967
Acrylic on canvas with plastic, newspaper,
burlap, and pigment
55 1/8 x 23 5/8 x 4 3/4 in. (140 x 60 x 12 cm.)
Projeto Hélio Oiticica, Rio de Janeiro

*Parangolé P17 (Cape 13), "Estou Possuido,"*
1967/1997
Fabric, acrylic on nylon mesh, and straw
43 1/4 x 15 3/4 x 3 7/8 in. (120 x 40 x 10 cm.)
Projeto Hélio Oiticica, Rio de Janeiro


**Hélio Oiticica** (with Antonio Manuel)
*Parangolé P22 (Cape 18), "Nirvana,"* 1968/1998
Acrylic on fabric
51 1/8 x 23 5/8 x 3 7/8 in. (130 x 60 x 10 cm.)
Projeto Hélio Oiticica, Rio de Janeiro


**Claes Oldenburg**
*Business Cards from "The Store,"* 1961
Letterpress in one color on colored, metallicized
"fish scale" paper
Three at 2 x 3 1/2 in. each (5.1 x 8.9 cm.)
Collection Claes Oldenburg and Coosje van Bruggen

*Ledger from "The Store,"* 1961
Bound journal book with ink and pencil on paper
Closed: 7 7/8 x 5 1/4 in. (20 x 13.3 cm.)
Collection Claes Oldenburg and Coosje van Bruggen

*Poster from "The Store,"* 1961
Letterpress in two colors on cardboard
28 1/4 x 22 1/8 in. (71.8 x 56.2 cm.)
Collection Claes Oldenburg and Coosje van Bruggen
Published by the artist in cooperation
with The Green Gallery, New York

*Blue and Pink Panties*, 1961
Plaster soaked muslin
62 1/4 x 34 3/4 x 6 in. (158.1 x 88.3 x 15.2 cm.)
The Museum of Contemporary Art, Los Angeles,
The Panza Collection

*Bride Mannikin*, 1961
Plaster soaked muslin
61 x 37 1/2 x 36 3/4 in. (155 x 95.3 x 93.3 cm.)
The Museum of Contemporary Art, Los Angeles,
The Panza Collection

*Chocolates in Box (Fragment)*, 1961
Plaster soaked muslin
44 x 32 x 6 in. (111.8 x 81.3 x 15.2 cm.)
The Museum of Contemporary Art, Los Angeles,
The Panza Collection

*Cigarettes in Pack Fragment*, 1961
Plaster soaked muslin
32 3/4 x 30 3/4 x 6 3/4 in. (83.2 x 78.1 x 17.1 cm.)
The Museum of Contemporary Art, Los Angeles,
The Panza Collection

*Green Stockings*, 1961
Plaster soaked muslin
43 1/4 x 18 in. (109.8 x 45.7 cm.)
The Museum of Contemporary Art, Los Angeles,
The Panza Collection

*Man's Shoe*, 1961
Plaster soaked muslin
32 1/2 x 43 1/4 in. (82.6 x 109.0 cm.)
The Museum of Contemporary Art, Los Angeles,
The Panza Collection

*Mu Mu*, 1961
Plaster soaked muslin
63 1/4 x 41 1/4 x 4 in. (160.7 x 104.8 x 10.2 cm.)
The Museum of Contemporary Art, Los Angeles,
The Panza Collection

*Pepsi-Cola Sign*, 1961
Plaster soaked muslin
58 1/4 x 46 1/2 x 7 1/2 in. (148 x 118.1 x 19.1 cm.)
The Museum of Contemporary Art, Los Angeles,
The Panza Collection

*Store Cross*, 1961
Plaster soaked muslin
53 3/4 x 40 1/2 x 6 in. (136.5 x 102.9 x 15.2 cm.)
The Museum of Contemporary Art, Los Angeles,
The Panza Collection

*Blue Pants on a Chair*, 1962
Plaster soaked muslin
37 x 17 x 26 3/4 in. (94 x 43.2 x 67.9 cm.)
The Museum of Contemporary Art, Los Angeles,
The Panza Collection

*Breakfast Table*, 1962
Plaster soaked muslin
34 1/2 x 35 1/2 x 34 1/2 in. (87.6 x 90.2 x 87.6 cm.)
The Museum of Contemporary Art, Los Angeles,
The Panza Collection

*Hamburger*, 1962
Plaster soaked muslin
7 x 9 x 9 in. (17.8 x 22.9 x 22.9 cm.)
The Museum of Contemporary Art, Los Angeles,
The Panza Collection

*Pie A La Mode*, 1962
Plaster soaked muslin
20 x 13 x 19 in. (50.8 x 33 x 48.3 cm.)
The Museum of Contemporary Art, Los Angeles,
The Panza Collection

*Umbrella and Newspaper*, 1962
Plaster soaked muslin
38 1/2 x 19 1/2 x 6 in. (97.8 x 49.5 x 15.2 cm.)
The Museum of Contemporary Art, Los Angeles,
The Panza Collection

*White Gym Shoes*, 1962
Plaster soaked muslin
24 x 24 x 10 in. (61 x 61 x 25.4 cm.)
The Museum of Contemporary Art, Los Angeles,
The Panza Collection

*White Shirt on a Chair*, 1962
Plaster soaked muslin
39 3/4 x 30 x 25 in. (101 x 76.2 x 63.5 cm.)
The Museum of Contemporary Art, Los Angeles,
The Panza Collection

*Announcement from "Autobodys,"* 1963
Offset lithograph in one color on paper
11 x 8 1/2 in. (28 x 21.6 cm.)
Collection Claes Oldenburg and Coosje van Bruggen

*Poster from "Autobodys,"* 1963
Letterpress in one color over stock offset lithograph
"rainbow roll" in two colors on cardboard
22 x 14 in. (55.9 x 35.5 cm.)
Collection Claes Oldenburg and Coosje van Bruggen

*Program from "Autobodys,"* 1963
Offset lithograph in one color on paper
11 x 8 1/2 in. (28 x 21.6 cm.)
Collection Claes Oldenburg and Coosje van Bruggen

*Script for "Autobodys,"* 1963
Sixteen pages typescript on paper
11 x 8 1/2 in. each (28 x 21.6 cm.)
Collection Claes Oldenburg and Coosje van Bruggen


**Yoko Ono**
*Painting for the Wind*, 1961/1993
Sumi ink on stretched sunbleached linen, rope,
cloth, seeds, and bamboo screen
36 x 36 x 36 in. (91.5 x 91.5 x 91.5 cm.)
Collection of Ivam Centre Julio Gonzalez, Valencia, Spain

*Painting to be Stepped On*, 1960/1997
Figured tamo with a particular masame
14 1/2 x 10 5/8 x 1 1/4 in. (37 x 27 x 3 cm.)
Collection of the artist

*Painting to Hammer a Nail*, 1961/1998
Painted wood panel with 42 inch chain attached with
an eye screw; and a container with 1 1/2-2 inch
small finishing nails
Panel: 9 x 12 x 1 1/2 in. (22.9 x 30.5 x 3.8 cm.)
Collection of the artist


**Yoko Ono** (with John Lennon)
*Bed In (Bed Peace)*, 1969
Photodocumentation of event
(black-and-white photograph)
30 x 40 in. (76.2 x 101.6 cm.)
Courtesy Corbis-Bettmann


**Raphael Montañez Ortiz**
*Piano Destruction Concert*, 1966/1998
Destroyed piano
Variable dimensions
Courtesy of the artist


**Lorenzo Pace**
*Mummification Series*, 1978
Photodocumentation of performance
(black-and-white photograph)
11 x 14 in. (27.9 x 35.6 cm.)
Collection of the artist


**Nam June Paik**
*Integral Piano*, 1958-63
Upright piano with additions and alterations
53 1/2 x 55 x 25 1/2 in. (136 x 140 x 65 cm.)
Museum moderner Kunst Stiftung Ludwig, Wien

*Zen for Head*, 1962
Ink and tomato on paper and ink and tomato on tie
Paper: 63 x 5 1/2 in. (160 x 14 cm.); tie: 50 3/8 x 2 1/8
in. (128 x 5.5 cm.)
Museum Wiesbaden

*Piano K*, 1962-63
Piano with keyboard glued together
Approx. 51 3/16 x 55 1/8 x 25 5/8 in.
(130 x 140 x 65 cm.)
Block Collection

*Prepared Piano*, 1962-63
Piano prepared with various intrusions and objects
Approx. 51 3/16 x 55 1/8 x 25 5/8 in.
(130 x 140 x 65 cm.)
Block Collection

## Gina Pane

*Le corps pressenti*, 1975
Ink on paper drawing, color photographs, one
black-and-white photograph, one plaster cast
Various dimensions
Museum moderner Kunst Stiftung Ludwig, Vienna

*Le corps pressenti*, 1975
Five preparatory drawings
11 7/8 x 15 3/4 in. each (30 x 40 cm.)
Collection Anne Marchand

## Lygia Pape

*Wheel of Delights*, 1968/1998
Bowls filled with colored, flavored liquid;
and eyedroppers
29 1/2 x 29 1/2 x 15 3/4 in. (75 x 75 x 40 cm.)
Collection of the artist

## Giuseppe Pinot Gallizio

*Industrial Painting*, 1958
Mixed media on canvas
31 1/2 in. x 242 ft. 9 in. (80 cm. x 74 m.)
Galleria Martano, Torino

## Adrian Piper

*Catalysis III*, 1970
Photodocumentation of performance
(two black-and-white photographs)
20 x 24 in. each (50.8 x 61 cm.)
Collection of the artist

*Catalysis IV*, 1970
Photodocumentation of performance
(five black-and-white photographs)
20 x 24 in. each (50.8 x 61 cm.)
Collection of the artist

*Food for the Spirit*, 1970
Notebook and photodocumentation of performance
(fourteen black-and-white photographs)
Notebook: 14 1/2 x 15 in. (36.8 x 38.1 cm.)
Courtesy Thomas Erben

*Untitled Performance for Max's Kansas City*, 1970
Photodocumentation of performance
(two black-and-white photographs)
20 x 24 in. each (50.8 x 61 cm.)
Collection of the artist
Photographs by Rosemary Mayer

## Michelangelo Pistoletto

*Globe*, 1966-68
Pressed newspapers in iron cage
Iron cage: 70 3/4 in. dia. (180 cm.);
newspapers: 39 3/8 in. dia. (100 cm.)
Collection Lia Rumma

## Jackson Pollock

*No. 1*, 1949
Enamel and aluminum paint on canvas
63 x 102 in. (160 x 259.1 cm.)
The Museum of Contemporary Art, Los Angeles
The Rita and Taft Schreiber Collection
Given in loving memory of her husband, Taft Schreiber,
by Rita Schreiber

## William Pope L.

*Crawl Piece*, 1978
Photodocumentation of performance
(color photograph)
11 x 14 in. (27.9 x 35.6 cm.)
Collection of the artist
Photograph by Jim Pruznick

*Roach Motel Black*, 1978
Photodocumentation of performance
(two color photographs)
11 x 14 in. each (27.9 x 35.6 cm.)
Collection of the artist
Photographs by Jim Pruznick

*Thunderbird Immolation*, 1978
Photodocumentation of performance
(color photograph)
11 x 14 in. (27.9 x 35.6 cm.)
Collection of the artist
Photograph by Jim Pruznick

## Robert Rauschenberg

*Automobile Tire Print* (with John Cage), 1953
Ink on paper mounted on fabric (monoprint)
Extended: 16 1/2 x 264 1/2 in. (41.9 x 671.8 cm.)
Collection of the artist

*Trophy III (For Jean Tinguely)*, 1961
Combine painting
96 x 65 3/4 in. (243.8 x 167 cm.)
The Museum of Contemporary Art, Los Angeles,
The Panza Collection

*Second Time Painting*, c. 1961
Oil and assemblage on canvas
65 3/4 x 42 in. (167 x 106.7 cm.)
Rose Art Museum, Brandeis University, Waltham,
Massachusetts; Gevirtz-Mnuchin Purchase Fund, 1962

## Carlyle Reedy

*Living Human Sculpture*, c. 1972
Photodocumentation of performance
(forty-eight color slides)
Collection of the artist

## Klaus Rinke

*Zeitpunktueller Standortwechsel Kassel Documenta*,
1972
Photodocumentation of performance at Documenta,
Kassel, Germany
(black-and-white photograph)
95 1/4 x 49 1/2 in. (242 x 126 cm.)
Collection Barry Friedman, New York;
Courtesy of Galerie Rudolf Kicken, Cologne

## Ulrike Rosenbach

*Don't Believe I'm an Amazon*, 1975
Video: black-and-white
Collection of the artist

## Dieter Roth

*The Olivetti-Yamaha-Grundig-Combo*, 1965/1983
Mixed media
Overall: 78 3/4 x 67 x 47 1/4 in. (200 x 170 x 120 cm.)
Collection Onnasch

## Zorka Ságlová

*Hay-Straw*, 1969
Photodocumentation of performance
(ten black-and-white photographs)
10 x 10 in. each (25.4 x 25.4 cm.)
Collection of the artist

## Niki de Saint Phalle

*Tir de Robert Rauschenberg*, June 20, 1961
Wood, miscellaneous objects, and paint
74 x 21 11/16 x 14 3/16 in. (188 x 55 x 36 cm.)
Collection of the artist

*Tir de l'Ambassade Americaine*, June 20, 1961
Wood, miscellaneous objects, plaster of Paris,
and color
96 7/16 x 26 x 8 11/16 in. (245 x 66 x 22 cm.)
Collection of the artist

## Alfons Schilling

*Untitled (Rotation-painting)*, 1962
Emulsion paint on spinning canvas, box of
electronic control systems, and metal
construction for mechanical rotation of painting
84 1/2 in. dia. (214 cm.)
Collection of the artist

## Tomas Schmit

*Cycle for Water Buckets (or Bottles)*, 1963
Photodocumentation of performance
(black-and-white photograph)
11 x 14 in. (27.9 x 35.6 cm.)
Courtesy Dorine van der Klei

## Carolee Schneemann

*Eye Body*, 1963
Photodocumentation of installation
(twenty-seven black-and-white photographs)
11 x 14 in. each (27.9 x 35.6 cm.)
Collection of the artist

*Eye Body/Four Fur Cutting Boards Installation*, 1963
Mixed media installation
Dimensions variable
Collection of the artist

*Meat Joy*, 1964
Photodocumentation of performance (six photographs)
11 x 14 in. each (27.9 x 35.6 cm.)
Collection of the artist

*Interior Scroll*, 1975
Box with paper scroll
50 x 30 x 10 in. (127 x 76.2 x 25.4 cm.)
Collection Peter and Eileen Norton, Santa Monica

## Rudolf Schwarzkogler

*Untitled (Sigmund Freud-Bild)*, 1965
Mixed media on wood
42 1/8 x 20 7/8 in. (107 x 53 cm.)
Museum moderner Kunst Stiftung Ludwig, Vienna

*Hochzeit*, 1965 (printed 1972)
Photodocumentation of performance
(thirty-seven color photographs)
11 5/8 x 9 3/8 in. each (29.6 x 23.7 cm.)
Archiv Conz, Verona

**Rudolf Schwarzkogler** (continued)
*3rd Action*, 1965-66
Photodocumentation of performance
(four black-and-white photographs)
Approx. 7 7/8 x 5 7/8 in. (20 x 15 cm.)
Private Collection

*3rd Action*, 1965-66
Photodocumentation of performance
(two black-and-white photographs)
Approx. 7 7/8 x 5 7/8 in. (20 x 15 cm.)
Collection Shashi Caudill and Alan Cravitz

*6th Action*, 1966
Photodocumentation of performance
(fourteen black-and-white photographs)
15 3/8 x 15 3/8 in. (39 x 39 cm.)
Museum moderner Kunst Stiftung Ludwig, Vienna

*Drawing 4* (Cat. 103), 1965-66
Ink on paper
8 1/4 x 5 3/4 in. (21 x 14.5 cm.)
Museum moderner Kunst Stiftung Ludwig, Vienna

*Drawing 15* (Cat. 102), 1965-66
Felt pen on paper
11 3/4 x 8 1/4 in. (29.7 x 21 cm.)
Museum moderner Kunst Stiftung Ludwig, Vienna

*Drawing 16* (Cat. 205), 1968
Felt pen and pencil on paper
11 3/4 x 8 1/4 in. (29.7 x 21 cm.)
Museum moderner Kunst Stiftung Ludwig, Vienna

*Drawing 17* (Cat. 201), 1968
Felt pen on paper
11 3/4 x 8 1/4 in. (29.7 x 21 cm.)
Museum moderner Kunst Stiftung Ludwig, Vienna

*Drawing 18* (Cat. 191), 1968
Felt pen on paper
11 3/4 x 8 1/4 in. (29.7 x 21 cm.)
Museum moderner Kunst Stiftung Ludwig, Vienna

*Drawing 20* (Cat. 204), 1968
Felt pen on paper
11 3/4 x 8 1/4 in. (29.7 x 21 cm.)
Museum moderner Kunst Stiftung Ludwig, Vienna

*Drawing 22* (Cat. 194), 1968
Felt pen on paper
11 3/4 x 8 1/4 in. (29.7 x 21 cm.)
Museum moderner Kunst Stiftung Ludwig, Vienna

**Bonnie Sherk**
*Original proposal for "Portable Parks I-III,"* 1970
Six sheets of green construction paper
with typed text and collage
8 1/2 x 11 in. (21.6 x 27.9 cm.)
Collection of the artist

*Public Lunch*, 1971
Photodocumentation of performance at
the Lion House of the San Francisco Zoo
(black-and-white photograph)
11 x 14 in. (27.9 x 35.6 cm.)
Collection of the artist
Photograph by Vicente Saval

**Shōzō Shimamoto**
*Work*, 1952
Paint and newspaper
63 3/4 x 51 9/16 in. (162 x 131 cm.)
Hyogo Prefectural Museum of Modern Art, Kobe,
Yamamura Collection

*Work (Sakuhin)*, 1961
Mixed media
101 1/4 x 76 3/4 in. (257.1 x 194.9 cm.)
Hyogo Prefectural Museum of Modern Art, Kobe

*Work (Holes)*, c. 1950
Paint and pencil on newspaper
76 3/4 x 51 3/4 in. (194.9 x 131.4 cm.)
Museum of Contemporary Art, Tokyo

**Ushio Shinohara**
*Boxing Painting Action*, c. 1960-62
Photodocumentation of performance
(black-and-white photograph)
11 x 14 in. (27.9 x 35.6 cm.)
Collection of the artist

**Kazuo Shiraga**
*Work I*, September 1954
Oil on paper
44 x 30 1/2 in. (112 x 77.5 cm.)
Hyogo Prefectural Museum of Modern Art, Kobe

*Challenging Mud*, 1955
Photodocumentation of performance
(black-and-white photograph)
8 x 8 in. (20.3 x 20.3 cm.)
The Ashiya City Museum of Art and History

*Work BB21*, 1956
Oil, paper, and canvas
72 x 95 5/8 in. (183 x 243 cm.)
Galerie Georg Nothelfer, Berlin

*Sambaso Ultra Modern*, 1957/85
Mixed media
86 5/8 x 196 7/8 x 59 in. (220 x 500 x 150 cm.)
Hyogo Prefectural Museum of Modern Art, Kobe,
Yamamura Collection

*Work II*, 1958
Oil on paper
72 x 95 5/8 in. (183 x 243 cm.)
Hyogo Prefectural Museum of Modern Art, Kobe

*Kotei*, 1963
Oil on canvas
107 1/2 x 83 11/16 in. (273 x 212.5 cm.)
Hyogo Prefectural Museum of Modern Art, Kobe,
Yamamura Collection

**Barbara T. Smith**
*Ritual Meal*, 1968
Photodocumentation of performance
(black-and-white photograph)
11 x 14 in. (27.9 x 35.6 cm.)
Collection of the artist

*Feed Me*, 1973
Photodocumentation of performance
(black-and-white photograph)
11 x 14 in. (27.9 x 35.6 cm.)
Collection of the artist

**Daniel Spoerri**
*Le lieu de repos de la famille Delbeck*, 1960
Mixed media tableau
22 7/16 x 21 11/16 x 7 7/8 in. (73 x 73 x 19.5 cm.)
Collection Daniel Varenne, Geneva

*Le coin du restaurant Spoerri*, c. 1968
Mixed media
106 1/4 x 118 x 45 1/2 in. (270 x 300 x 150 cm.)
Vostell Museum, Malpartida de Caceres, Spain

**Petr Štembera**
*Narcissus #1*, 1974
Photodocumentation of performance
(three black-and-white photographs)
9 1/4 x 7 1/8 in. each (23.5 x 18 cm.)
Collection of the artist

*Grafting*, 1975
Photodocumentation of performance
(two black-and-white photographs)
9 1/4 x 7 1/8 in. each (23.5 x 18 cm.)
Collection of the artist

*Joining with Tom Marioni*, 1975
Photodocumentation of performance
(black-and-white photograph)
9 1/4 x 7 1/8 in. (23.5 x 18 cm.)
Collection of the artist

*The Way*, 1977
Photodocumentation of performance
(three black-and-white photographs)
9 1/4 x 7 1/8 in. each (23.5 x 18 cm.)
Collection of the artist

**Wolfgang Stoerchle**
*Jumping off Ladder through Layers*, 1970
Photodocumentation of performance
(black-and-white photograph)
11 x 14 in. (27.9 x 35.6 cm.)
Private Collection

**Jirō Takamatsu**
*The String in the Bottle*, 1963/1998
String and bottle
Dimensions variable
Courtesy of the artist and Akira Ikeda Gallery, Tokyo

*The String of 1000-Meters*, 1963/1998
String
39,370 in. long (1,000 m.)
Courtesy of the artist and Akira Ikeda Gallery, Tokyo

**Atsuko Tanaka**
*Drawing for "Electric Dress,"* 1956
Crayon on paper
43 5/16 x 30 5/16 in. (110 x 77 cm.)
Collection of the artist

*Drawings for "Electric Dress,"* 1956
Fifteen crayon on paper drawings
43 5/16 x 30 5/16 in. each (110 x 77 cm.)
Hyogo Prefectural Museum of Modern Art, Kobe

*Electric Dress*, 1956/1985
Painted light bulbs, electric cords, and timer
65 x 31 1/2 x 31 1/2 in. (165 x 80 x 80 cm.)
Takamatsu City Museum of Art

**Mark Thompson**
*Live-In Hive*, 1976
Wood, glass, netting, wooden chair, wire tubing,
and glass bottles
Box: 62 x 22 x 26 in. (157.5 x 55.9 x 66 cm.);
total height with wire-mesh tube: 108 in. (274.3 cm.)
Collection of the artist

**Jean Tinguely**
*Méta-matic No. 6*, 1959
Iron, wooden wheels, and electric engine
18 5/8 x 27 1/2 x 11 7/8 in. (50 x 70 x 30 cm.)
Private Collection

*Méta-matic No. 12 (Le grand Charles)*, 1959
Mixed media, mild steel, wood, and electrical devices
85 x 57 x 24 in. (215.9 x 144.8 x 61 cm.)
Collection Phyllis Lambert, Montréal

*Baluba*, 1962
Mixed media
Collection Niki de Saint Phalle

*Baluba*, 1964
Motorized assemblage: feather dusters, elastic
cords, electric motor, plastic toy, metal balls and parts,
rubber ball, tape, and cord on linoleum mounted
on wood
15 3/8 x 25 5/8 x 14 15/1 in. (39 x 65 x 38 cm.)
The Menil Collection, Houston; Gift of Jean Tinguely

**Raša Todosijević**
*Drinking of Water—Inversions, Imitations,
and Contrasts*, 1974
Photodocumentation of performance
(black-and-white photograph)
11 x 14 in. (27.9 x 35.6 cm.)
Collection of the artist

**Kerry Trengove**
*An Eight-Day Passage*, 1977
Photodocumentation of performance
(two black-and-white photographs)
11 x 14 in. each (27.9 x 35.6 cm.)
Courtesy Alison Radovanović and the Estate
of Kerry Trengove

**Ulay**
*Correspondence to the Situation—There is
a Criminal Touch to Art*, 1976
Photodocumentation of performance
(six black-and-white photographs)
16 x 20 in. each (40.6 x 50.8 cm.)
Collection of the artist

**Ben Vautier**
*Human Sculpture Certificate*, 1959
Handwritten certificate
7 x 7 in. (18 x 18 cm.)
Collection of the artist

*Death*, 1960
Text and photodocumentation
8 1/4 x 11 3/4 in. (21 x 29.7 cm.)
Collection of the artist

*Death. Ben Signs Death*, 1960
Two texts and photodocumentation
13 3/4 x 11 in. (35 x 28 cm.)
Collection of the artist

*Death - Signery*, 1960
Newspaper clipping
8 1/4 x 11 3/4 in. (21 x 30 cm.)
Collection of the artist

*Ben's Window*, 1962/1992-93
Mixed media
125 1/2 x 178 1/2 x 108 in. (318.8 x 453.4 x 274.3 cm.)
Walker Art Center, Minneapolis

*Death of Yves Klein*, 1962
Handwritten manuscript
10 1/4 x 8 1/4 in. (26 x 21 cm.)
Collection of the artist

*Gallery One*, 1962
Photodocumentation
7 1/2 x 11 7/8 in. (19 x 30 cm.)
Collection of the artist

*Human Sculpture Certificate*, 1961
Photodocumentation
12 1/4 x 15 in. (31 x 38 cm.)
Collection of the artist

*Human Sculpture Certificate Aguigue*, 1962
Two handwritten certificates
11 3/4 x 8 5/8 in. each (30 x 22 cm.)
Collection of the artist

*Human Sculpture Certificate for Alice*, 1962
Original unique photocopy
9 x 12 1/4 in. (23 x 31 cm.)
Collection of the artist

*Human Sculpture Certificate for Françoise Allongue*,
1962
Handwritten certificate
11 3/8 x 12 1/2 in. (29 x 32 cm.)
Collection of the artist

*Human Sculpture Certificate for Hochman*, 1962
Handwritten certificate
9 1/2 x 12 1/2 in. (24 x 32 cm.)
Collection of the artist

*Human Sculpture Certificate for Melidonian*, 1962
Photograph and text
8 1/4 x 11 3/4 in. each (21 x 30 cm.)
Collection of the artist

*Human Sculpture Certificate for Melidonian*, 1962
Two handwritten certificates
8 1/4 x 11 3/4 in. each (21 x 30 cm.)
Collection of the artist

*Human Sculpture Certificate Melidonian*, 1962
Photodocumentation
12 1/4 x 15 in. (31 x 38 cm.)
Collection of the artist

*Part of All*, 1962
Photodocumentation of performance
(four black-and-white photographs)
9 x 12 in. each (22.9 x 30.5 cm.)
Collection of the artist

*Vomit*, 1962
Text and photodocumentation of performance
(black-and-white photograph)
9 x 11 3/4 in. (23 x 30 cm.)
Collection of the artist

*Ben Vautier Signing Certificates, Nice*, 1963
Photodocumentation of event (photograph)
8 x 10 in. (20.3 x 25.4 cm.)
Courtesy Gilbert and Lila Silverman Fluxus Collection
Foundation

*Death by Ben*, 1963
Handwritten text
8 1/4 x 11 3/4 in. (21 x 30 cm.)
Collection of the artist

**Wolf Vostell**
*Drawing from "Nein-9-dé-coll/agen"*, 1963
Drawing, collage, and erasing on cardboard
27 1/2 x 39 3/8 in. (70 x 100 cm.)
Collection of the artist

*130 à l'heure from "Nein-9-dé-coll/agen"*, 1963/1998
Crashed Mercedes automobile
Dimensions variable
Collection of the artist

**Franz Erhard Walther**
*1. Werksatz in Storage*, 1963-69
Canvas, foam rubber, wood, plastic, nettle cloth,
cord, velvet and leather
Fifty-eight pieces on pile, dimensions variable
Courtesy John Weber Gallery, New York

*Drawings from "1. Werksatz in Storage,"* 1963-69
Fifteen mixed media drawings
Various dimensions
Courtesy John Weber Gallery, New York

**Peter Weibel**
*Media Lung*, 1968
Deer skin and miniature technical equipment
23 5/8 x 31 1/2 in. (60 x 80 cm.)
Neue Galerie am Landesmuseum Joanneum

*Scar Poems, Object*, 1970
Animal skin
7 1/8 x 9 1/2 in. (18 x 24 cm.)
Collection of the artist

*Space of Language*, 1973
Photodocumentation of performance
(black-and-white photograph)
11 x 14 in. (27.9 x 35.6 cm.)
Collection of the artist

**Franz West**
*Arbeitstudie im Aktionismusgeschmack*, 1974-77
Pencil, colored pencil, and adhesive tape on paper
8 1/4 x 11 3/4 in. (21 x 29.7 cm.)
Courtesy David Zwirner Gallery, New York

*Werkblatt im Aktionismusgeschmack*, 1974-77
Pencil, colored pencil, and ticket on paper
8 1/4 x 11 3/4 in. (21 x 29.7 cm.)
Courtesy David Zwirner Gallery, New York

*Drawing for Paßstück No. 2*, 1974/77
Pencil and colored pencil on paper
8 1/4 x 6 in. (21 x 15 cm.)
Collection Julius Hummel, Vienna

*Paßstück*, 1978-79
Plaster, emulsion paint, and wire
23 5/8 x 25 1/2 x 19 3/4 in. (60 x 65 x 50 cm.)
Collection Julius Hummel, Vienna

*Paßstück No.4*, 1978-79
Plaster, emulsion paint, and wire
14 1/8 x 13 3/4 x 11 3/4 in. (36 x 35 x 30 cm.)
Collection Julius Hummel, Vienna

*Paßstück No.5*, 1978-79
Plaster, emulsion paint, and wire
8 3/4 x 19 1/4 x 11 3/4 in. (22 x 49 x 30 cm.)
Collection Julius Hummel, Vienna

*Paßstück No. 8*, 1978-79
Plaster, emulsion paint, and wire
12 1/2 x 33 x 11 7/8 in. (32 x 84 x 30 cm.)
Collection Julius Hummel, Vienna

**Franz West** (continued)
*Paßstück No. 10*, 1978-79
Plaster, emulsion paint, and wire
26 3/4 x 26 3/4 x 8 1/4 in. (68 x 68 x 21 cm.)
Collection Julius Hummel, Vienna

*Model with Paßstück No. 8*, 1982-83
Photodocumentation of object in use
(color photograph)
9 1/2 x 7 in. (24 x 18 cm.)
Collection Julius Hummel, Vienna
Photograph by H. Hasieber

*Franz West with Paßstück No. 10*, 1982-83
Photodocumentation of object in use
(color photograph)
9 1/2 x 7 in. (24 x 18 cm.)
Collection Julius Hummel, Vienna
Photograph by H. Hasieber

*Participatory Combination with recent Paßstück*,
c. 1970/1998
Plaster objects
Dimensions variable
Courtesy David Zwirner Gallery, New York

**Hannah Wilke**
*S.O.S. Starification Object Series. An Adult Game
of Mastication, Box*, 1974
Game with photographs, sculptures, box, playing cards,
and instructions for play
Box: 12 x 8 1/2 x 2 in. (30.5 x 21.59 x 5 cm.)
Courtesy the Estate of Hannah Wilke
and Ronald Feldman Fine Arts, New York

**Emmett Williams**
*Alphabet Symphony*, 1963
Photodocumentation of performance
(twenty-six black-and-white photographs)
Archiv Sohm, Staatsgalerie, Stuttgart
Photographs by Barney Kirchoff

*An Opera*, c. 1957
Printed text
13 3/4 x 4 1/8 in. (34.9 x 2.9 cm.)
Collection of the artist

**Zaj**
*J'ai aimerais jouer avec un piano qui aurait
une grande queue*, 1976
Video: black-and-white
Courtesy RTVE and Museo Nacional Centro de Arte
Reina Sofia, Madrid

# GENERAL BIBLIOGRAPHY

## Books and Catalogues

*About time: Video, Performance and Installation by 21 Women Artists*. Exh. cat. London: Institute of Contemporary Arts, 1980.

*Action/Performance and the Photograph*. Exh. cat. Los Angeles: Turner/Krull Galleries, 1993.

*ADA: Aktionen der Avantgarde, Berlin, 1973*. Exh. cat. Berlin: Neuer Berliner Kunstverein in association with DAAD and the Berliner Festspielen, 1973.

Akasegawa, Genpei. *Imaya akushon aru nomi "Yomiuri andepandan" tu iu gensho* (Action Only, Now! The Phenomenon Called the "Yomiuri Independent"). Tokyo: Chikuma Shobo, 1985.

Akasegawa, Genpei. *Tokyo mikisa keikaku: Hai reddo senta chokusetsu kodo no kiroku* (Tokyo Mixer Plans: Documents of Hi Red Center's Direct Actions). Tokyo: PARCO Co., 1984.

*Aktionen, Vernissagen, Personen: die Rheinische Kunstszene der 50er und 60er. Eine Fotodokumentation von Manfred Leve*. Exh. cat. Nuremberg: Institut für Moderne Kunst in association with Cologne: Rheinland-Verlag, 1982.

Armstrong, Elizabeth, and Joan Rothfuss, eds. *In the Spirit of Fluxus*. Exh. cat. Minneapolis: Walker Art Center, 1993.

Armstrong, Richard, and Richard Marshall, eds. *The New Sculpture 1965-1975: Between Geometry and Gesture*. Exh. cat. New York: The Whitney Museum of American Art, 1990.

*L'art au corps: le corps exposé de Man Ray à nos jours*. Exh. cat. Marseille: MAC, galeries contemporaines des Musée de Marseille, 1996.

*The Art of Performance*. Exh. cat. Venice: Palazzo Grassi, 1979.

*Arte Italiana 1960-1982*. Exh. cat. London: Arts Council of Great Britian in association with Milan: Gruppo Editoriale Electa, 1982.

Ashiya City Museum of Art and History, eds. *Gutai shiryo-shu/Document Gutai 1954-1972*. Exh. cat. Ashiya, Japan: Ashiya City Culture Foundation, 1993.

Aue, Walter, ed. *Projekte, Conzepte & Actionen*. Cologne: Dumont Schauberg, 1971.

Auslander, Philip. *Presence and Resistance: Postmodernism and Cultural Politics in Contemporary American Performance*. Ann Arbor: University of Michigan Press, 1992.

*Avanguardia transavanguardia 68-77*. Exh. cat. Milan: Gruppo Editorale Electa in association with Mura Aureliane da Porta Metronia a Porta Latina, 1982.

Battcock, Gregory. *The New Art*. New York: E.P. Dutton and Co., 1966.

Battcock, Gregory, and Robert Nickas, eds. *The Art of Performance: A Critical Anthology*. New York: E.P. Dutton and Co., 1984.

Becker, Jürgen, and Wolf Vostell. *Happenings, Fluxus, Pop Art, Nouveau Réalisme*. Hamburg: Rowohlt, 1965.

Beeren, Wim, et al., eds. *Actie, werkelijkheid en fictie in de kunst van de jaren '60 in Nederland* (Action, Reality and Fiction in the Art of the 1960s in The Netherlands). Exh. cat. Rotterdam: Museum Boymans-van Beuningen and The Hague: Staatsuitgeverij, 1979.

Benamou, Michel and Charles Caramello, eds. *Performance in Postmodern Culture*. Milwaukee: Center for Twentieth-Century Studies, University of Wisconsin-Milwaukee, 1977.

Berner, Jeff, comp. *Aktual Art International*. Exh. cat. Stanford Art Book 8. Stanford, California: Department of Art and Architecture, Stanford University, 1987.

Bertozzi, Barbara, and Klaus Wolbert. *Gutai: Japanische Avantgarde 1954-1965*. Exh. cat. Darmstadt: Mathildenhöhe Darmstadt, 1991.

*Between Man and Matter: Tokyo Biennale '70*. Exh. cat. Tokyo: Tokyo Mainichi Newspapers and the Japan International Art Promotion Association, 1970.

*La Biennale di Venezia: ambiente, partecipazione, strutture culturali*. Vol. 2: "Attualità internazionali '72-76." Exh. cat. Venice, Italy: Venice Biennale, 1976.

Block, René. *Für Augen und Ohren: von der Spieluhr zum akustischen Environment: Objekte Installationen Performances*. Exh. cat. Berlin: Akademie der Kunst, 1980.

Block, René, ed. *Fluxus da Capo: 1962 Wiesbaden 1992*. Exh. cat. Wiesbaden: Nassauischer Kunstverein, Kulturamt der Landeshauptstadt Wiesbaden, and Harlekin Art/Fluxeum, 1992.

Block, René, ed. *1962 Wiesbaden Fluxus 1982: eine kleine Geschichte von Fluxus in drei Teilen*. Exh. cat. Wiesbaden: Harlekin Art and Berlin: Berliner Künstlerprogramm des DAAD, 1983.

Block, René, ed. *New York — Downtown Manhattan: Soho: Austellung, Theater, Musik, Performance, Video, Film*. Exh. cat. Berlin: Akademie der Künste and Berliner Festwochen, 1976.

Block, René, ed. *The Readymade Boomerang: Certain Relations in 20th Century Art*. Exh. cat. Sydney: Biennale of Sydney and Museum of Contemporary Art, 1990.

*Body Works*. Exh. cat. Chicago: Museum of Contemporary Art, 1975.

Bonito Oliva, Achille. *Europe/America: The Different Avant-Gardes*. Milan: Deco Press, 1976.

Bory, Jean-François. *Journal de l'art actuel, 1960-1985* (Journal of Contemporary Art, 1960-1985). Neuchâtel, France: Ides et Calendes, 1986.

*Breakthroughs: Avant-Garde Artists in Europe and America, 1950-1990*. Exh. cat. Columbus, Ohio: Wexner Center for the Arts in association with New York: Rizzoli, 1991.

Bronson, A. A., and Peggy Gale, eds. *Performance by Artists*. Toronto: Art Metropole, 1979.

Burnham, Jack. *Great Western Salt Works: Essays on the Meaning of Post-Formalist Art*. New York: George Braziller, 1974.

Carlson, Marvin. *Performance: A Critical Introduction*. New York: Routledge, 1996.

Carr, Cynthia. *On Edge: Performance at the End of the Twentieth Century*. Hanover, New Hampshire: University Press of New England, 1993.

Celant, Germano. *Pre-Cronistoria 1966-69: Minimal art, pittura sistemica, arte povera, land art, conceptual art, body art, arte ambientale e nouvi media*. Florence: Centro Di, 1976.

*Centre d'art contemporain, 1974-1979*. Exh. cat. Geneva: Centre d'art contemporain, 1979.

Champagne, Lenora, ed. *Out From Under: Texts by Women Performance Artists*. New York: Theatre Communications Group, 1990.

Cladders, Johannes. *The Avant-Garde in Europe 1955-70: The Collection of the Städtisches Museum, Monchengladbach*. Exh. cat. Edinburgh: Scottish National Gallery of Modern Art, 1981.

*Contemporanea*. Exh. cat. Rome: Parcheggio di Villa Borghese association with Florence: Centro Di, 1973.

*Contemporary Japanese Art: Fifth Japan Art Festival Exhibition*. Exh. cat. New York: The Solomon R. Guggenheim Museum, 1970.

*Dada in Japan: Japanische Avantgarde 1920-1970, eine Fotodocumentation*. Exh. cat. Düsseldorf: Kunstmuseum Düsseldorf, 1983.

Di Maggio, Gino. *Ubi Fluxus ibi motus 1990-1962*. Exh. cat. Milan: Nuove edizione Gabriele Mazzota, in association with the Venice Biennale, 1990.

Diamond, Elin, ed. *Performance and Cultural Politics*. New York: Routledge, 1996.

*Documenta V: Befragung der Realität, Bildwelten heute*. Exh. cat. 3 vols. Kassel: Neue Galerie and Museum Fridericianum in association with Documenta GmbH and C. Bertelsmann, 1972.

*Documenta VI: Malerei, Plastik, Performance*. Exh. cat. Kassel: Paul Dierichs KG and Co., 1977.

Dreyfus, Charles. *Fluxus/éléments d'information*. Exh. cat. Paris: ARC 2, Musée d'art moderne de la ville de Paris, 1974.

Dreyfus, Charles. *Happenings & Fluxus*. Exh. cat. Paris: Galerie 1900-2000, Galerie du Génie, Galerie de Poche, 1989.

Dupuy, Jean, ed. *Collective Consciousness: Art Performances in the Seventies*. New York: Performing Arts Journal Publications, 1980.

Elliott, David, and Kazu Kaido, eds. *Reconstructions: Avant-Garde Art in Japan 1945-1965*. Exh. cat. Oxford, England: Museum of Modern Art, 1985.

*Il encontro national de incercencao e performance*. Exh. cat. Amadora, Portugal: Associacao Poesia Viva, 1988.

*Encuentros 1972 Pamplona*. Exh. cat. Pamplona: Museo de Navarra in association with Madrid: Grupo Alea, 1972.

*English Art Today: 1960-76*. Exh. cat. Milan: Palazzo Reale, 1976.

Feminist Art Program, California Institute of the Arts. *Art: A Woman's Sensibility*. Exh. cat. Valencia, California: California Institute of the Arts, 1975.

*Fluxus Virus 1962-1992*. Exh. cat. Cologne: Galerie Schüppenhauer, and Munich: Aktionsforum Praterinsel, 1992.

Frank, Peter. *Theater of the Object: Reconstructions, Re-creations, Reconsiderations 1958-1972*. Exh. cat. New York: Alternative Museum, 1988.

Friedman, Ken, Peter Frank, and Elizabeth Brown. *Young Fluxus*. Exh. cat. New York: Committee for the Visual Arts and Artists Space, 1982.

*Giappone all'avanguardia: Il Gruppo Gutai negli anni Cinquanta*. Exh. cat. Milan: Galleria Nazionale d'Arte Moderna and Japan Foundation in association with Electa, 1990.

Glusberg, Jorge. *Art in Argentina*. Milan: Giancarlo Politi Editore, 1986.

Glusberg, Jorge. *El arte de la performance*. Buenos Aires: Ediciones de Arte Gaglianone, 1986.

Goldberg, Roselee. *Performance: Live Art 1909 to the Present*. New York, 1979. Revised edition published as *Performance Art from Futurism to the Present*. New York: Harry N. Abrams, 1988.

Gorsen, Peter. "Der spielbar gemachte Alltag oder die Rückkehr des Existentialismus in der Performance Art." In *Zur Definition eines neuen Kunstbegriffs*. Exh. cat. Innsbruck: Galerie Krinzinger, 1979.

Gray, John. *Action Art: A Bibliography of Artists' Performance from Futurism to Fluxus and Beyond*. Westport, Connecticut: Greenwood Press, 1993.

*Grupo Gutai: Pintura y Accion*. Exh. cat. Madrid: Museo Español de Arte Contemporaneo, 1985.

Grüterich, Marlis. "Performance, Musik, Demonstration: Kunst, die sich nach dem Evolutionsprinzip präsentiert." In *Kunst bleibt Kunst: Projekte '74: Aspekte internationaler Kunst am Anfang der 70er Jahre*. Exh. cat. Cologne: Kunsthalle and Wallraf-Richardtz Museum, 1974.

*Gutai and AU*. Nishinomiya, Japan: Art Space, 1982.

*Gutai bijutsu no 18-nen* (18 Years of Gutai). Exh. cat. Osaka: Osaka Fumin Center, 1976.

*Gutai: Koi to kaiga/Action and Painting*. Exh. cat. Kobe: The Hyogo Prefectural Museum of Modern Art, 1986.

*"Gutai": Mikan no zen'ei shudan — Hyogo Kindai Bijutsukan shozo sakuhin o chusin ni/The Unfinished Avant-Garde Group* (Focusing on the Collection of the Hyogo Prefectural Museum of Modern Art, Kobe). Exh. cat. Tokyo: The Shoto Museum of Art, 1990.

*Gutai 1955/56: Nihon gendai bijutsu no risutato chiten/A Restarting Point of Japanese Contemporary Art*. Tokyo: Penrose Institute of Contemporary Arts, 1993.

*Gutai-ten* (Gutai Exhibition). Exh. cat. in 3 parts. 1: 1954-1958; 2: 1959-1965; 3: 1965-1972. Ashiya, Japan: Ashiya City Museum of Art and History, 1992-1993.

Hansen, Al. *A Primer of Happening and Time/Space Art*. New York: Something Else Press, 1965.

Hapgood, Susan. *Neo-Dada: Redefining Art, 1958-62*. Exh. cat. New York: The American Federation of the Arts, 1994.

*Happening de Happenings, Y todos es happening*. Barcelona: Colección Granouers Happenings, 1979.

Hart, Lynda, and Peggy Phelan, eds. *Acting Out: Feminist Performances*. Ann Arbor: University of Michigan Press, 1993.

Haskell, Barbara. *Blam! The Explosion of Pop, Minimalism, and Performance 1958-1964*. Exh. cat. New York: Whitney Museum of American Art in association with W. W. Norton & Company, 1984.

Havens, Thomas R. H. *Artists and Patrons in Postwar Japan: Dance, Music, Theater and the Visual Arts, 1955-1980*. Princeton, New Jersey: Princeton University Press, 1982.

Hendricks, Jon, ed. *Fluxus, Etc*. Exh. cat. Bloomfield Hills, Michigan: Cranbrook Academy of Art Museum, 1981.

Hendricks, Jon. ed. *Fluxus etc./Addenda I: The Gilbert and Lila Silverman Collection*. Exh. cat. New York: Ink &, 1983.

Hendricks, Jon. ed. *Fluxus etc./Addenda II: The Gilbert and Lila Silverman Collection*. Exh. cat. Pasadena: Baxter Art Gallery, California Institute of Technology, 1983.

Hendricks, Jon. ed. *Fluxus Codex*. Detroit and New York: The Gilbert and Lila Silverman Fluxus Collection, in association with Harry N. Abrams, 1988.

Henri, Adrian. *Total Art: Environments, Happenings, and Performance*. New York: Praeger, 1974.

Higgins, Dick, ed. *Fluxus 25 Years*. Exh. cat. Williamstown, Massachusetts: Williams College Museum of Art, 1988.

Hindman, James. "Happening Theory and Methodology: Allan Kaprow, Claes Oldenburg, Ann Halprin 1959-1967." Ph.D. diss., University of Georgia, 1971.

Hoffmann, Justin. *Destruktionskunst: der Mythos der Zerstorung in der Kunst der fruhen sechziger Jahre* (Destruction Art: The Myth of Destruction in Art in the Early 1960s). Munich: Silke Schreiber, 1995.

*Hors Limites: l'art et la vie 1952-1994*. Exh. cat. Paris: Musée national d'art moderne, Centre Georges Pompidou, 1994.

Howell, Anthony, and Fiona Templeton. *Elements of Performance Art*. London: n.p., 1976.

Inga-Pin, Luciano, ed. *Performance: Happenings, Actions, Events, Activities, Installations*. Padua: Mastrogiacomo Editore, 1978.

*Italy Two: Art Around '70*. Exh. cat. Philadephia: Museum of the Philadephia Civic Center, 1973.

*Japon des Avant-Gardes 1910-1970*. Exh. cat. Paris: Musée national d'art moderne, Centre Georges Pompidou, 1986.

*Journées interdisciplicaires sur l'art corporel et performances* (Interdisciplinary Conferences on Body Art and Performance). Paris: Musée national d'art moderne, Centre Georges Pompidou, 1979.

Kaprow, Allan. *Assemblage, Environments and Happenings*. New York: Harry N. Abrams, 1966.

Kawakita, Michiaki. *Modern Currents in Japanese Art*. Trans. and adapted by Charles S. Terry. New York: John Weatherhill, and Tokyo: Heibonsha, 1974.

Kellein, Thomas. *Fluxus*. London: Thames and Hudson, 1995.

Kirby, Michael. *Happenings: An Illustrated Anthology*. New York: E. P. Dutton and Co., 1965.

Kirby, Michael. *The New Theatre: Performance Documentation*. New York: New York University Press, 1974. Reprint from the Drama Review Series.

Kostelanetz, Richard. *On Innovative Performance(s): Three Decades of Recollections on Alternative Theater*. Jefferson, North Carolina: McFarland & Company, 1994.

Kostelanetz, Richard. *The Theatre of Mixed Means: An Introduction to Happenings, Kinetic Environments, and Other Mixed-Means Performances*. New York: Dial Press, 1968.

Kriuchkova, Valentina Aleksandrovna. *Antiiskusstvo: Teoriia I Praktika Avangardistskikh dvizhenii*. Moscow: Izobrazitel 'noe iskusstvo, 1985.

Kultermann, Udo. *Art and Life*. Trans. John William Gabriel. New York: Praeger, 1971.

Kultermann, Udo. *Art-Events and Happenings*. London: Mathews Miller Dunbar, 1971.

*Kunst in Europa na '68*. Exh. cat. Ghent: Museum can Hedendaagse Kunst and Centrum voor Kunst en Cultur, 1980.

Lauf, Cornelia, and Susan Hapgood, eds. *Fluxattitudes*. Exh. cat. Ghent: Imshoot Uitgevres, 1991.

Lebel, Jean-Jacques. *Le Happening*. Paris: Denoël, 1966.

*Live Art: Australia and America: Performance Art, Reviews, Criticism, Feminist and Political Art Organizations, Art and Politics, Interviews with American Artists, Artist's Pages*. Adelaide, South Australia: A. Marsh and J. Kent, 1984.

Loeffler, Carl F., ed. *Performance Anthology, A Sourcebook for a Decade of California Performance Art*. San Fransisco: Contemporary Art Press, 1980.

Masotta, Oscar et al. *Happenings*. Buenos Aires: Editorial J. Alvarez, 1967.

Mayor, David, ed. *Fluxshoe*. Exh. cat. Cullompton, Devon, England: Beau Geste Press, 1972.

Mayor, David, and Felipe Ehrenberg, eds. *Fluxshoe Add End A*. Cullompton, Devon, England: Beau Geste Press, 1973.

Milman, Estera, ed. *Fluxus: A Conceptual Country*. Exh. cat. New York: Franklin Furnace et al., 1992. Special issue of *Visible Language* 26, no. 1-2 (Winter/Spring 1992).

Moore, Barbara. "New York Intermedia: Happenings and Fluxus in the 1960s." In *American Art in the 20th Century: Painting and Sculpture 1913-1993*. Edited by Christos M. Joachimedes and Norman Rosenthal. Munich: Prestel; New York: Neues Publishing Company, 1993.

Moore, Peter. *Peter Moore Photographs*. Exh. cat. Tokyo: Gallery 360•, 1989.

*Music, Sound, Language, Theater: John Cage, Tom Marioni, Robert Barry, Joan Jonas*. Exh. cat. Oakland: Crown Point Press, 1980.

Nöth, Winfried. *Strukuren des Happenings*. Hildesheim: Gerog Olms Verlag, 1972.

Nuttall, Jeff. *Performance Art*. London: J. Calder and Dallas: Riverrun Press, 1979.

O'Dell, Kathy. "Towards a Theory of Performance Art: An Investigation of Its Sites." Ph.D. diss., City University of New York, 1992.

*Outside the Frame: Performance and the Object: A Survey History of Performance Art in the USA Since 1950*. Exh. cat. Cleveland: Cleveland Center for Contemporary Art, 1994.

*Performance Art and Video Installation*. Exh. cat. London: Tate Gallery, 1985.

*Performance, eine andere Dimension: Gesprache mit den Kunstlern, Fotos von den Performances* (Performance, Another Dimension: Talks with the Artists, Photographs of the Performances). Berlin: Frolich & Kaufmann, 1983.

*Performance oggi* (Performance Today). Exh. cat. Bologna, Italy: Galleria comunale d'arte moderna, 1977.

*Persona*. Exh. cat. Belgrade: International Theatre Festival in association with Florence: Centro Di, 1971.

Peters, Ursula, and Georg F. Schwarzbauer, eds. *Fluxus — Aspekte eines Phänomens*. Exh. cat. Wuppertal: Kunst- und Museumverein Wuppertal, 1981.

Phelan, Peggy. *Unmarked: The Politics of Performance*. New York: Routledge, 1993.

Phillpot, Clive, and Jon Hendricks. *Fluxus: Selections from the Gilbert and Lila Silverman Fluxus Collection*. Exh. cat. New York: The Museum of Modern Art, 1988.

Pluchart, François. *L'art corporeal*. Paris: Limage 2, 1975.

Pontbriand, Chantal, ed. *Performance: Text(e)s and Documents, Multidisciplinary Aspects of Performance: Postmodernism*. Montreal: Parachute, 1981.

Popper, Frank. *Art — Action and Participation*. New York: New York University Press, 1975.

*ProspectRetrospect: Europa 1946-1976*. Exh. cat. Düsseldorf: Städtische Kunsthalle in association with Cologne: Buchhandlung Walther König, 1976.

Roth, Moira, ed. *The Amazing Decade: Women and Performance Art in America, 1970-1980*. Los Angeles: Astro Artz, 1983.

Ruhé, Harry. *Fluxus, the Most Radical and Experimental Art Movement of the Sixties*. Amsterdam: "A", 1979.

*Ryudo-suru bijutsu III: Neo-Dada no shashin/Art in Flux III: Neo-Dada Witnessed, Photo-Documents*. Exh. cat. Fukuoka, Japan: Fukuoka Art Museum, 1993.

*San Francisco Performance*. Exh. cat. Newport Beach, California: Newport Harbor Art Museum, 1972.

Sandford, Mariellen R., ed. *Happenings and Other Acts*. London: Routledge, 1974.

Sayre, Henry M. *The Object of Performance: The American Avant-Garde Since 1970*. Chicago: University of Chicago Press, 1989.

Schauer, Lucie. *Kunstübermittlungsformen: Vom Tafebild biz zum Happening: Die Meidem der bildenden Kunst* (Art Media: From Easel Painting to Happenings: The Media of Pictorial Art). Exh. cat. Berlin: Neuer Berliner Kunstverein, 1977.

Schilling, Jürgen. *Aktionskunst: Identität von Kunst und Leben*. Lucerne and Frankfurt: J. C. Bucher, 1978.

Schneider, Rebecca. *The Explicit Body in Performance*. New York: Routledge, 1997.

Schroeder, Johannes Lothar. *Identität, Überschreitung, Verwandlung: Happenings, Aktionen und Performances von bildenden Kunstlern*. Münster: Lit, 1990.

Shinohara, Ushio. *Zen'ei no michi* (The Avant-Garde Road). Tokyo: Bijutsu Shuppan-sha, 1968.

Sohm, Hans, and Harald Szeemann, eds. *Happenings & Fluxus*. Exh. cat. Cologne: Kölnischer Kunstverein, 1970.

Stellweg, Carla. "'Magnet — New York': Conceptual, Performance, Environmental, and Installation Art." In *The Latin American Spirit: Art and Artists in the United States, 1920-1970*. New York: The Bronx Museum of the Arts in association with Harry N. Abrams, 1988.

Stern, Carol Simpson. *Performance Studies: Texts and Contexts*. New York and London: Longman, 1993.

Stiles, Kristine. "Performance Art." In *Theories and Documents of Contemporary Art: A Sourcebook of Artists' Writings*. Edited by Kristine Stiles and Peter Selz. Berkeley: University of California Press, 1996.

Storck, Gerhard. *Wahrehmungen-Aufzeichnungen-Mitteilungen: die Erweiterung des Wirklichkeitsbegriffs in der Kunst der 60er und 70er Hahre* (Observations-Notes-Information: Extension of the Concept of Reality in the Art of the 1960s and 1970s). Exh. cat. Krefeld: Kaiser Wilhelm Museum, 1979.

Tapié, Michel, and Haga Toru. *Avant-Garde Art in Japan*. New York: Harry N. Abrams, 1962.

Tomioka, Taeko. *Koi to geijutsu: Ju-san-nin no sakka* (Action and Art: Thirteen Artists). Tokyo: Bijutsu Shuppan-sha, 1970.

Tucker, Marcia. *Choices: Making an Art of Everyday Life*. Exh. cat. New York: New Museum of Contemporary Art, 1986.

*25 Years of Performance Art in Australia*. Exh. cat. Paddington, Australia: Ivan Dougherty Gallery et al., 1994.

Ugwu, Catherine, ed. *Let's Get It On: The Politics of Black Performance*. Seattle: Bay Press, 1995.

Vautier, Ben, and Gino Di Maggio, eds. *Fluxus International & Co*. Exh. cat. Liège: Ville de Liège; Milan: Multhipla; and Nice: Direction des Musées de Nice Action Culturelle Muncipale, 1979.

Vergine, Lea. *Dall'informale alla body art: Dieci voci dell'arte contemporanea: 1960/1970*. Turin: Cooperativa Editorale Studio Forma, 1976.

Vergine, Lea. *Il Corpe come Linguaggio: La Body-Art e Storie Simili*. Milan: Gian Paolo Prearo, 1974.

*A View of a Decade, 1967-1977*. Exh. cat. Chicago: Museum of Contemporary Art, 1977.

Vostell, Wolf, ed. *Aktionen: Happenings und Demonstrationen Seit 1965*. Hamburg: Rowohlt, 1970.

Wick, Rainer. *Zur Soziologie Intermediärer Kunstpraxis: Happening, Fluxus, Aktionen*. Cologne, 1975.

*Weiner Aktionismus: Von der Aktionsmalerie zum Aktionismus, Wien 1960-1965/Viennese Actionism: From Action Painting to Actionism, Vienna 1960-1965*. Exh. cat. Vol 1: Klagenfurt, Austria: Ritter Verlag, 1988. Edited by Museum Fridericianum, Kassel; Kunstmuseum Winterthur; Scottish National Gallery of Modern Art, Edinburgh; and Österreichisches Museum für ange-wandte Kunst, Vienna.

*Weiner Aktionismus: Der zertrümmerte Spiegel, Wien 1960-1971/Viennese Actionism: The Shattered Mirror, Vienna 1960-1971*. Exh. cat. Vol. 2: Klagenfurt, Austria: Ritter Verlag, 1989. Edited by Hubert Klocker in cooperation with Graphische Sammlung Albertina, Vienna, and Museum Ludwig, Cologne.

Withers, Josephine. "Feminist Performance Art: Performing, Discovering, Transforming Ourselves." In Norma Broude and Mary D. Garrard, eds., *The Power of Feminist Art: The American Movement of the 1970s, History and Impact*. New York: Harry N. Abrams, 1994.

Yamaguchi, Katsuhiro, and Toru Shimizu. *Tsumetai pafomansu* (Cool Performances). Tokyo: Asahi Shuppan-sha, 1983.

Yoshida, Yoshie. *Kaitai-geki no maku orite: 60-nendai zen`ei bijutsu-shi* (The Curtain was Drawn on the Act of Dismantlement: The History of Avant-Garde Art in the Sixties). Tokyo: Zokei-sha, 1982.

*Yoshihara Jiro to "Gutai" 1954-1972/ Jiro Yoshihara and Gutai 1954-1972*. Exh. cat. Ashiya, Japan: Civic Gallery, 1985.

*Yoshihara Jiro to Gutai no sono go/Jiro Yoshihara and Today's Aspects of the Gutai*. Exh. cat. Kobe: The Hyogo Prefectural Museum of Modern Art, 1979.

Young, LaMonte, and Jackson MacLow, eds. *An Anthology*. New York: LaMonte Young and Jackson MacLow, 1963. New York: Heiner Friedrich, 1970. 2nd ed.

**Articles**

"Actions and Performances." *Art and Artists* (London) 7, no. 10 (January 1973): special issue.

Adams, Hugh. "Against a Definitive Statement on British Performance Art." *Studio International* (London) 192, no. 982 (July-August 1976): 3-9.

"Aktionismus." *Der Lowe* (Bern, Switzerland) 1, no. 31 (May 1974): special issue.

Almhofer, Edith. *Performance Art: die Kunst zu Leben.* Vienna: Hermann Böhlaus Nachf., 1986.

*Art Rite*, no. 10 (Fall 1975): special performance issue.

Ashton, Dore. "Happenings and Unhappenings." *Studio International* (London) 168, no. 859 (November 1964): 220-223.

*Avalanche* (New York), no. 1 (Fall 1971), no. 13 (Summer 1976).

Barber, Bruce. "The Terms: Limits to Performance?" *Centerfold* (Toronto) 2 (September 1978): 96-100.

Battcock, Gregory, ed. "L'art de performance." *Théorie et Critique* (Buenos Aires) 2 (December 1979): 13-79.

Blau, Herbert. "Les rhetoriques du corps et la guerre des nerfs." *Cahiers du Musée national d'art moderne* (Paris), no. 51 (Spring 1995): 18-31.

Bonito Oliva, Achille. "Process, Concept and Behavior in Italian Art." *Studio International* (London) 191, no. 979 (January-February 1976): 3-5.

Borden, Lizzie. "The New Dialectic." *Artforum* (New York) 12, no. 6 (March 1974): 44-51.

Boulanger, Chantel. "La performance: un art de l'ellipse?" *Vanguard* (Quebec) 13, no. 1 (February 1984): 26-33.

Burnham, Jack. "Towards a Working Ontology of Art." *Arts Magazine* (New York) 47, no. 3 (December-January 1973): 28-32.

Calas, Nicolas. "Bodyworks and Porpoises." *Artforum* (New York) 16, no. 5 (January 1978): 33-37.

Cavalcanti, Gilberto. "Apectos do ritual na arte contemporânea (Aspects of Ritual in Contemporary Art)." *Colóquio: Artes* (Lisbon) 22 (April 1975): 36-43.

Cirici, Alexandre. "L'art de la performance." *Théorie et Critique* (Buenos Aires) 2 (December 1979): 2-12.

"Danger in Art." *Flash Art* (Milan) no. 80-81 (February-April 1978): special issue.

Daniels, Dieter. "Fluxus Before Fluxus." *Kunstforum International* (Cologne), no. 115 (September-October 1991): 107-205.

Davis, Douglas. "The Size of Non-Size." *Artforum* (New York) 15, no. 4 (December 1976): 46-51.

Drucker, Johanna. "Collaboration without Object(s) in the Early Happenings." *Art Journal* (New York) 52, no. 4 (Winter 1993): 51-58.

Export, Valie, and Herbert Blau, eds. "Persona, Proto-Performance, Politics: A Preface." *Discourse: A Journal for Theoretical Studies in Media and Culture* (1992): special issue.

*Flash Art* (Milan), no. 84-85 (October-November 1978): special Fluxus issue.

"Fluxus." *Freibord: Zeitschrift für Literatur und Kunst* (Vienna) 73 (March 1990): special issue.

"Fluxus — Eine Nachruf zu Lebzeiten." *Kunstforum International* (Cologne) 115 (September-October 1991): special issue.

"Fluxus — 25 Years." *Freibord: Zeitschrift für Literatur und Kunst* (Vienna) 60 (1987): special issue.

Foote, Nancy. "Situation Esthetics: Impermanent Art and the Seventies Audience." *Artforum* (New York) 18, no. 5 (January 1980): 22-29.

Forge, Andrew. "Forces Against Object-Based Art." *Studio International* (London) 181, no. 929 (January 1971): 32-37.

Frank, Peter, and Ken Friedman. "Fluxus: A Post-Definitive History Where Response is the Heart of the Matter." *High Performance* (Los Angeles) 7, no. 3 (1984): 56-62.

"Free Fluxus Now." *Art and Artists* (London) 7, no. 7 (October 1972): special issue.

*Freibord: Zeitschrift für Literatur und Kunst* (Vienna) 64 (February 1988): special Fluxus issue.

Friedman, Ken, comp. "The Fluxus Performance Workbook." *El Djarida* (Trondheim, Norway) (1990): special issue.

Gaggi, Silvio. "Sculpture, Theater, and Art Performance: Notes on the Convergence of the Arts." *Leonardo* 19, no. 1 (1986): 45-52.

Goldberg, Roselee. "Performans: zolotoi vek" (Performance Art: The Golden Age). *Dekorativnoe Iskusstvo* (Russia), no. 5 (1991): 4-6.

Goldberg, Roselee. "Public Performance: Private Memory." *Studio International* (London) 192, no. 982 (July-August 1976): 19-23.

Goldberg, Roselee. "What Happened to Performance?" *Flash Art* (Milan), no. 116 (March 1984): 28-29.

Gorsen, Peter. "Theories of Performance: The Return of Existentialism in Performance Art." *Flash Art* (Milan), nos. 86-87 (January-February 1979): 51.

Graevenitz, Antje von. "Then and Now: Performance in Holland." *Studio International* (London) 192, no. 982 (July-August 1976): 49-53.

Groh, Klaus. "Performance Art: What is it?" *Leonardo* 14, no. 1 (Winter 1981): 37.

"Happening." *Bijutsu techō* (Japan), no. 301 (August 1968): special issue.

Hein, Hilde. "Performance as an Aesthetic Category." *The Journal of Aesthetics and Art Criticism* (Baltimore, Maryland) 28, no. 3 (Spring 1970): 381-386.

Heyd, Thomas. "Understanding Performance: Art Beyond Art." *British Journal of Aesthetics* (England) 31, no. 1 (January 1991): 68-73.

Higgins, Dick. "Something Else about Fluxus." *Art and Artists* (London) 7, no. 7 (October 1972): 16-21.

*High Performance* (Los Angeles) 1, no. 1 (1978) to the present.

Holborn, Mark. "Standing in the Shadow." *Artforum* (New York) 24, no. 9 (May 1986): 94-99.

*Interfunktionen* (Cologne), no. 1 (1968), no. 13 (1975).

Ishiko, Junzo. "Hai reddo senta ni miru no 'genzai.'" (The "Present" in the Case of Hi Red Center) *Bijutsu techō* (Japan), no. 345 (February 1971): 184-199.

Jappe, Georg. "Performance in Germany: An Introduction." *Studio International* (London) 192, no. 982 (July-August 1976): 59-61.

Johnston, Jill. "A Fluxus Funeral." *Art in America* (New York) 77, no. 3 (March 1989): 42-47.

Johnston, Jill. "'Happenings' on the New York Scene." *Encore* 9 (September-October 1962): 8-13.

Kaprow, Allan. "The Legacy of Jackson Pollock." *Art News* (New York) 57, no. 6 (October 1958): 24-26, 55-57.

Klüver, Billy. "Happenings." *Konstrevy* (Stockholm) 38, no. 2 (1962): 58-66.

Klüver, Billy. "Nine Evenings of Theatre and Engineering. Part 2. Notes by an Engineer." *Artforum* (New York) 5, no. 6 (February 1967): 31-33.

Kneubühler, Theo. "Das Happening: Geschichte, Theorie und Folgen" (The Happening: History, Theory and Consequences). *Werk* (Winterthur, Switzerland) 58, no. 2 (February 1971): 116-124.

Knížák, Milan. "Fluxus." *Kunstforum International* (Cologne), no. 115 (September-October 1991): 184-187.

Kontova, Helena. "The Unconscious History: Interview with Roselee Goldberg." *Flash Art* (Milan), no. 90-91 (June-July 1979): 30-36.

Kozloff, Max. "Pygmalion Reversed." *Artforum* (New York) 14, no. 3 (November 1975): 30-37.

Kunz, M. "The Development of the Physical Action into a Psychic Intensity of the Picture." *Flash Art* (Milan), no. 98-99 (Summer 1980): 12-14, 16-17, 24.

*La Mamelle Magazine: Art Contemporary* 1, no. 4 (Spring 1976): special issue on performance art.

Lamoureux, Johanne. "On Coverage: Performance, Seduction, Flatness." *Artscanada* (Canada) 38, no. 1 (March-April 1981): 25-27, 51.

Levy, Mark. "The Avant-Garde and the Open Work of Art: Traditionalism and Performance." *Art Com* 4, no. 4 (1982): 8-9, 43.

Lippard, Lucy R. "The Pains and Pleasure of Rebirth: Women's Body Art." *Art in America* (New York) 64, no. 3 (May-June 1976): 73-81.

Lippard, Lucy R. "Total Theater?" *Art International* (Lugano, Switzerland) 11, no. 1 (1967): 39-44.

Lischka, Gerhard Johann. "Performance und Performance Art: ein Bild-Zitate-Essay" (Performance and Performance Art: A Picture-Quotation-Essay). *Kunstforum International* (Cologne), no. 96 (August-October 1987): 65-193.

Marsh, Anne. "Performance Art in the 1970s." *Art and Australia* (Melbourne) 26, no. 3 (Autumn 1989): 412-418.

Mayer, Rosemary. "Performance and Experience." *Arts Magazine* (New York) 47, no. 3 (December-January 1973): 33-36.

McCoy, Ann. "Het bloed van de dichter: Medities over de rode mis." *Museumjournaal*, no. 1 (1986): 21-32.

McEvilley, Thomas. "Art in the Dark." *Artforum* (New York) 21, no. 10 (June 1983): 62-71.

Miller, Roland. "'All mad, drugged or drunk': Performance Art from the 70s and 80s." *Variant* (England), no. 4 (Winter 1987-Spring 1988): 8-12.

Moore, Peter. "Fluxus Focus." *Artforum* (New York) 21, no. 2 (October 1982): 33-37.

Morawski, Stefan. "Nurt główny aktualnych postaw anarachoartystycznych" (The Principal Curent of Actual Anarcho-Artistic Attitudes). *Rocznik historii szutki* (Poland), no. 12 (1981): 221-252.

Nemser, Cindy. "Subject-Object: Body Art." *Arts Magazine* (New York) 46, no. 1 (September 1971): 38-42.

Novick, Elizabeth. "Happenings in New York." *Studio International* (London) 172, no. 881 (September 1966): 154-159.

O'Dell, Kathy. "The Performance Artist as a Masochistic Woman." *Arts Magazine* (New York) 62, no. 10 (Summer 1988): 96-98.

Osborne, Harold. "Aesthetic Implications of Conceptual Art, Happenings, Etc." *British Journal of Aesthetics* (England) 20, no. 1 (Winter 1980): 6-22.

P-Orridge, Genesis, and Peter Christopherson. "Annihilating Reality." *Studio International* (London) 192, no. 982 (July-August 1976): 44-48.

"Performance Art." *Art & Design — Profile*, no. 38 (1994): special issue.

"Performance Art." *Studio International* (London) 192, no. 982 (July-August 1976): special issue.

"Performance at the Limits of Performance." *The Drama Review* (New York) (March 1972): special issue.

*Performance Magazine* (London) 1 (June 1979-the present).

Pijnappel, Johna, ed. "Fluxus Today and Yesterday." *Art & Design — Profile*, no. 28 (1993): special issue.

Pluchart, François. "L'art corporeal." *ArTitudes International*, no. 18-20 (January-March 1975): 49-96.

Poinsot, Marc. "Fluxus: Un art de l'événement." *Art Press* (Paris), no. 15 (December 1974-January 1975): 14-17.

"Politics and Performance." *TDR* (New Orleans) 13, no. 4 (Summer 1969): special issue.

Pontbriand, Chantal. "Notion(s) of Performance." *Parachute* (Montreal), no. 15 (Summer 1979): 25-32.

Raap, Jürgen. "Blutorden, oder, Die Wiedergeburt des Happenings (Order of the Blood, or, the Rebirth of Happenings." *Kunstforum International* (Cologne), no. 65 (September 1983): 199-200.

Restany, Pierre. "Une tentative américaine de synthèse de l'information artistique: les Happenings." *Domus* (Milan) 405, no. 8 (August 1963): 35-42.

Roberts, James. "Painting as Performance." *Art in America* (New York) 80, no. 5 (May 1992): 112-119.

Robbins, Eugenia S. "Performing Art." *Art in America* (New York) 54, no. 4 (July-August 1966): 107-111.

Roth, Moira. "Toward a History of California Performance: Part One." *Arts Magazine* (New York) 52, no. 6 (February 1978): 94-103; Part Two: 52, no. 10 (June 1978): 114-123.

Sabatini, Arthur J. "Terrorism and Performance." *Kunstforum International* (Cologne), no. 117 (1992): 147-151.

Schechner, Richard. "Happenings." *TDR* (New Orleans) 10, no. 2 (Winter 1965): 229-232.

Seckler, Dorothy Gees. "The Artist in America: The Audience is His Medium." *Art in America* (New York) 51, no. 2 (April 1963): 62-67.

Sharp, Willoughby. "Bodyworks: A Pre-Critical, Non-Definitive Survey of Very Recent Works Using the Human Body of Parts Thereof." *Avalanche* (New York), no. 1 (Fall 1970): 14-17.

Stiles, Kristine. "Sticks and Stones: The Destruction in Art Symposium." *Arts Magazine* (New York) 65, no. 5 (January 1989): 54-60.

*TDR* (New Orleans) 10, no. 2 (Winter 1965): special performance issue.

Tisdall, Caroline. "Performance Art in Italy." *Studio International* (London) 191, no. 979 (January-February 1976): 42-45.

Vergine, Lea. "Body Language." *Art and Artists* (London) 9, no. 6 (September 1974): 22-27.

*Vision* (Oakland, California), no. 1 (September 1975)-no. 3 (November 1976).

Von Graevenitz, Antje. "Then and Now: Performance Art in Holland." *Studio International* (London) 192, no. 982 (July-August 1976): 49-53.

Vostell, Wolf. "Fluxus." *Opus International* (Paris) 98 (Summer 1985): 10-17.

Whitman, Simone. "Nine Evenings of Theatre and Engineering. Part 1. Notes by a Participant." *Artforum* (New York) 5, no. 6 (February 1967): 26-30.

Wilson, Martha. "Women in Performance: 'best work of our time.'" *Women Artists News* 13, no. 3 (Fall 1988): 9-10.

Xerou, Efy. "Ap'ten action painting sto happening kai sten performance art" (From Action Painting to the Happening and to Performance Art). *Eikastika* (Greece), no. 53 (May 1986): 34-36, 38.

Zelevansky, Lynn. "Is There Life After Performance?" *Flash Art* (Milan), no. 105 (December 1981-January 1982): 38-42.

# ARTISTS' BIBLIOGRAPHIES

## Marina Abramović
Iles, Chrissie, ed. *Marina Abramović: Objects, Performance, Video, Sound*. Exh. cat. Oxford: Museum of Modern Art, 1995.

*Marina Abramović*. Exh. cat. Paris: Galerie des Beaux-Arts, 1991.

*Marina Abramović*. Exh. cat. Berlin: Neuen Nationalgalerie, in association with Stuttgart: Edition Cantz, 1993.

*Marina Abramović: Sur la Voie*. Exh. cat. Paris: Musée national d'art moderne, Centre Georges Pompidou, 1990.

## Marina Abramović and Ulay
Marina Abramović and Ulay. *Ulay/Marina Abramović: Relation Work and Detour*. Amsterdam: Idea Books, 1980.

Durland, Steve. "From Warriors and Saints to Lovers: Marina Abramović and Ulay." *High Performance* (Los Angeles) 9, no. 2 (1986): 50-55.

Iles, Chrissie, "The Shadow and the Reflection: The Relation Works of Marina Abramović and Ulay." In *Ulay/Abramović: Performances 1976-1990*. Exh. cat. Eindhoven, The Netherlands: Stedelijk Van Abbemuseum, 1997.

McEvilley, Thomas. "Marina Abramović/Ulay, Ulay/Marina Abramović." *Artforum* (New York) 22, no. 1 (September 1983): 52-55.

## Vito Acconci
*Avalanche* (New York), no. 6 (Fall 1972). Special issue: Vito Acconci.

Diacono, Mario. *Vito Acconci: dal testo-azione al corpo come testo*. New York: Out of London Press, 1975.

Kunz, Martin. "Interview with Vito Acconci about the Development of His Work Since 1966." In *Vito Acconci: Cultural Space Pieces 1974-1978*. Exh. cat. Lucerne: Kunstmuseum, 1978.

Linker, Kate. *Vito Acconci*. New York: Rizzoli, 1994.

*Vito Acconci: A Retrospective: 1969 to 1980*. Exh. cat. Chicago: Museum of Contemporary Art, 1980.

## Genpei Akasegawa
Akasegawa, Genpei. *Obuje o motta musan-sha* (A Propertyless Man with Objects). Tokyo: Gendai Shis-sha, 1970.

Akasegawa, Genpei. *Tokyo mikisā keikaku: Hai reddo sentā chokusetsu kōdō no kiroku* (Tokyo Mixer Plans: Documents of Hi Red Center's Direct Actions). Tokyo: PARCO Co., 1984.

"Mokei sen-en satsu jiken kōhan kiroku" (The Record of the One-Thousand-Yen-Note Trial). *Bijutsu techō*, no. 274 (November 1966): 137-168.

## Laurie Anderson
Anderson, Laurie. *Stories from the Nerve Bible: A Retrospective, 1972-1992*. New York: HarperPerennial, 1994.

Howell, John. *Laurie Anderson*. New York: Thunder's Mouth Press and Emeryville, California: Publishers Group West, 1992.

*Laurie Anderson: Works from 1969-1983*. Exh. cat. Philadelphia: Institute of Contemporary Art, University of Pennsylvania, 1983.

White, Robin. "Laurie Anderson." *View* (Oakland, California) 2, no. 8 (1980). Interview.

## Eleanor Antin
Bowen, Nancy. "On Art and Artists: Eleanor Antin." *Profile* (Chicago) 1, no. 4 (July 1981): 1-22. Interview.

*Eleanor Antin*. Exh. cat. Winston-Salem, North Carolina: Southeastern Center for Contemporary Art, 1996.

*Eleanor Antin: The Angel of Mercy*. Exh. cat. La Jolla, California: La Jolla Museum of Contemporary Art, 1977.

Nemser, Cindy. "Eleanor Antin." In *Art Talk: Conversations with 12 Women Artists*. New York: Charles Scribner's Sons, 1975.

Raven, Arlene and Deborah Marrow. "Eleanor Antin: What's Your Story?" *Chrysalis* (Los Angeles), no. 8 (Summer 1979): 43-51.

## Rasheed Araeen
Araeen, Rasheed. "Wer bin ich? Woher komme ich?" (Who am I? Where Do I Come from?) *Kunstforum International* (Cologne), no. 118 (1992): 233-35.

Hou Hanrou. "An Interview with Rasheed Araeen." *Art and AsiaPacific* (Australia) 2, no. 1 (January 1995): 102-107.

Overy, Paul, ed. *Rashed Araeen*. Exh. cat. London: South London Art Gallery, 1994.

Pivec, Helena. "I Had No Choice but to Deal with His Gaze which was Making Me Invisible: An Interview with Rasheed Araeen." *M'Ars* (Slovenia) 6, no. 1-4 (1994): 36-52.

*Rasheed Araeen: Making Myself Visible*. London: Kala Press, 1984.

## Mowry Baden
Bellerby, Greg. *Mowry Baden: Maquettes and Other Preparatory Work 1967-80*. Exh. cat. Victoria, Canada: Art Gallery of Greater Victoria, 1985.

Hicks, Mary. "Kinesthetic Aesthetics: The Structures of Mowry Baden." *Image and Issue* (Spring 1982): 62-63.

Jodoin, Andre. *Mowry Baden: Task-Oriented Sculptures*. Exh. cat. Toronto: Mercer Union, 1987.

*Mowry Baden: Sculpture*. Exh. cat. Calgary, Alberta: Alberta College of Art Gallery, 1987.

## Artur Barrio
*Barrio*. Exh. cat. Rio de Janiero: Edição FUNARTE, 1976.

*Barrio: texto do artista*. Exh. cat. Rio de Janeiro: Edição FUNARTE, 1978.

*Situações: Artur Barrio: Registro*. Exh. cat. Rio de Janiero: Centro Cultural Banco do Brasil, 1996.

## Joseph Beuys
*Joseph Beuys*. Exh. cat. New York: Solomon R. Guggenheim Museum, in association with London: Thames and Hudson, 1979.

*Joseph Beuys*. Exh. cat. Paris: Musée national d'art moderne, Centre Georges Pompidou, 1994.

*Joseph Beuys: Ideas and Actions*. Exh. cat. New York: Hirschl and Adler Modern, 1988.

Lindegren, Karin Bergqvist. *Joseph Beuys: Aktioner, Aktionen — Teckningar och Objekt 1937-1970 ur Samling van Grinten*. Exh. cat. Stockholm: Moderna Museet, 1971.

Schneede, Uwe M. *Joseph Beuys, die Aktionen: kommentiertes Werkverzeichnis mit fotografischen Dokumentationen*. Stuttgart, Germany: Ostfildern-Ruit, 1994.

Stachelhaus, Heiner. *Joseph Beuys*. Trans. David Britt. New York: Abbeville Press, 1987.

Tisdall, Caroline. *Joseph Beuys*. London: Thames and Hudson, 1988.

## Mark Boyle and Joan Hills
*Journey to the Surface of the Earth: An Exhibition to Launch an Earthprobe by Mark Boyle, The Sensual Laboratory & The Institute of Contemporary Archaeology*. Exh. cat. London: Institute of Contemporary Arts, 1969.

Locher, J. L. *Mark Boyle's Journey*. Stuttgart and London: Edition Hansjörg Mayer, 1978.

*Mark Boyle and Joan Hills' Reise um die Welt* (Mark Boyle and Joan Hills' Journey to the Surface of the Earth). Exh. cat. 3 vols. Lucerne: Kunstmuseum, 1978.

*Mark Boyle, British Pavilion, Venice Biennale 1978*. Exh. cat. London: British Council, in association with Idea Books, 1978.

## George Brecht
Daniels, Dieter, ed. *George Brecht — Notebooks*. Cologne: Walter König, 1991.

*Jenseits von Ereignissen: Texte zu einer Heterospektive von George Brecht*. Exh. cat. Bern: Kunsthalle, 1978.

Martin, Henry, ed. *An Introduction to George Brecht's Book of the Tumbler of Fire*. Milan: Multhipla Edizioni, 1978.

Nyman, Michael. "George Brecht: Interview." *Studio International* (London) 192, no. 984 (November-December 1976): 256-266.

*Sourdog Hex: George Brecht: Works 1957-1973*. Exh. cat. New York: Onnasch Gallery, 1974.

**Stuart Brisley**
Kent, Sarah. "Stuart Brisley." *Flash Art* (Milan), no. 80-81 (February-April 1978): 58-59. Interview.

Roberts, John. "Stuart Brisley Interviewed." *Art Monthly* (London), no. 46 (May 1981): 5-9.

*Stuart Brisley*. Exh. cat. London: Institute of Contemporary Arts, 1981.

Wegner, Nicholas. "Stuart Brisley: Actions and Installations." *CV: Journal of Arts and Crafts* (England) 3, no. 1 (March 1990): 22-27.

**Robert Delford Brown**
Coleman, A. D. "Introduction." In *Robert Delford Brown: First Class Portraits*. N.P.: The First National Church of the Exquisite Panic Press, 1973.

Juno, Andrea, and V. Vale, eds. "Pranks!" *Re/Search* (San Francisco), no. 11 (1987): 144-149.

Morgan, Robert C. "The Strange Case of Robert Delford Brown, Iconoclast." In *Robert Delford Brown: Icons of the First National Church of the Exquisite Panic*. Exh. cat. Verona: Ediziones and Archive Francesco Conz, 1992.

**Günter Brus**
*Brus: Malerei, Selbstbemalung, Selbstverstümmelung*. Vienna: Erich Felix Mautner, 1965.

*Günter Brus: Augensternstunden*. Exh. cat. Eindhoven: Stedelijk Van Abbemuseum, 1984.

*Günter Brus: Bild-Dichtungen*. Exh. cat. London: Whitechapel Art Gallery, 1980.

*Günter Brus: Limite du visible*. Exh. cat. Paris: Musée national d'art moderne, Centre Georges Pompidou, 1993.

**Chris Burden**
Béar, Liza and Willoughby Sharp. "Chris Burden: The Church of Human Energy." *Avalanche*, no. 8 (Summer-Fall 1973): 54-61.

Burden, Chris. *Chris Burden, 71-73*. Los Angeles: Chris Burden, 1974.

Burden, Chris. *Chris Burden, 74-77*. Los Angeles: Chris Burden, 1978.

*Chris Burden: A Twenty-Year Survey*. Exh. cat. Newport Beach: Newport Harbor Art Museum, 1988.

*Chris Burden: Jenseits der Grenzen* (Beyond the Limits). Exh. cat. Vienna: Öesterreichishes Museum für angewandte Kunst, 1996.

**James Lee Byars**
Byars, James Lee and Rudi Fuchs. *The Palace of Good Luck*. Exh. cat. Turin: Castello Rivoli, 1989.

Elliott, David, ed. *The Perfect Thought: Works by James Lee Byars*. Exh. cat. Berkeley: University Art Museum, University of California, and Houston: Contemporary Arts Museum, 1990.

*James Lee Byars*. Exh. cat. Bern: Kunsthalle, 1978.

Junker Howard. "James Lee Byars: Performance as Protective Coloration." *Art in America* (New York) 66, no. 6 (November 1978): 109-113.

**John Cage**
Fetterman, William. *John Cage's Theater Pieces: Notations and Performances*. Amsterdam: Harwood Academic Publishers, 1996.

*John Cage: Scores and Prints*. Exh. cat. New York: Whitney Museum of American Art, 1982.

Kirby, Michael and Richard Schechner. "An Interview with John Cage." *Tulane Drama Review* (New Orleans) 10, no. 2 (Winter 1965): 50-72.

Kostelanetz, Richard, ed. *John Cage*. New York: Praeger Publishers, 1970.

**Marc Camille Chaimowicz**
Kontova, Helena. "Interview with Marc Chaimowicz: Performance is Like a Perfect Day." *Flash Art* (Milan), no. 84-85 (October-November 1978): 13-14.

*Marc Camille Chaimowicz*. Exh. cat. London: Tate Gallery, 1981.

*Past Imperfect: Marc Camille Chaimowicz 1972-1982*. Exh. cat. Liverpool: Bluecoat Gallery; Londonderry: The Orchard Gallery; and Southampton: John Hansard Gallery, 1983.

Tisdall, Caroline. "Stuart Brisley and Marc Chaimowicz." *Studio International* (London) 192, no. 982 (July-August 1976): 16-18.

**Lygia Clark**
Bois, Yve-Alain et al. "Lygia Clark: Nostalgia of the Body." *October* (Cambridge, Massachusetts), no. 69 (Summer 1994): 85-109.

Brett, Guy. "Lygia Clark: The Borderline Between Art and Life." *Third Text* (London), no. 1 (Autumn 1987): 65-94.

Brett, Guy. "Lygia Clark: In Search of the Body." *Art in America* (New York) 82, no. 7 (July 1994): 57-63, 108.

Gullar, Ferreira, Mário Pedrosa, and Lygia Clark. *Lygia Clark*. Rio de Janeiro: Edição FUNARTE, 1980.

**Pinchas Cohen Gan**
Deitch, Jeffrey. "Pinchas Cohen Gan." *Arts Magazine* (New York) 50, no. 9 (May 1976): 12.

*Figure Form Formula: The Art of Pinchas Cohen Gan*. Exh. cat. Greensboro: The Weatherspoon Art Gallery, 1996.

*Pinchas Cohen Gan: Activities*. Exh. cat. Jerusalem: Israel Museum, 1974.

*Seven Artists in Israel 1948-1978*. Exh. cat. Los Angeles: Los Angeles County Museum of Art, 1978.

**Collective Action Group**
Brobinskaya, Ekaterina. "Kollektivnye poezdkiza..." (Collective Trips to...). *Dekorativnoe Iskusstvo* (Russia), no. 5 (1991): 15-17.

"Nikita Aleskeev, Goga Kizeval'ter, A. Monastyrskij and Co." *Flash Art* (Milan), no. 76-77 (July-August 1977): 16-17.

**Houston Conwill**
Jeffries, Rosalind Robinson. "Arthur Carraway and Houston Conwill: Ethnicity and Re-Africanization in American Art." Ph.D. Diss., Yale University, 1992.

Méo, Y. C. "Ritual as Art: The Work of Houston Conwill." *Black Art* 3, no. 3 (1979): 4-13.

Wilson, Judith. "Creating a Necesary Space: The Art of Houston Conwill, 1975-1983." *International Review of African American Art* 6, no. 1 (1985): 50-64.

**Paul Cotton**
Roth, Moira. "Toward a History of California Performance: Part One." *Arts Magazine* (New York) 52, no. 6 (February 1978): 94-103; Part Two: 52, no. 10 (June 1978): 114-123.

"Paul Cotton." In *Space Time Sound: Conceptual Art in The San Francisco Bay Area: The 70s*. Exh. cat. San Francisco: Museum of Modern Art, 1979.

**COUM Transmissions**
Ford, Simon. "Doing P-Orridge." *Art Monthly* (London), no. 197 (June 1996): 9-12.

Naylor, Colin. "Couming Along." *Art and Artists* (London) 10 , no. 9 (December 1975): 22-25. Interview.

Tutti, Cosey Fanni. "Prostitution: Sex Magazine Action Performance." *Curious* 46 (1976).

**Guy de Cointet**
Goldwater, Marge. "Guy de Cointet." In *Los Angeles in the Seventies*. Exh. cat. Fort Worth, Texas: Fort Worth Art Museum, 1977.

Hicks, Emily. "Guy de Cointet." In *Summer 1985*. Exh. cat. Los Angeles: The Museum of Contemporary Art, 1985. Interview.

*Guy de Cointet*. Exh. cat. Grenoble, France: Le Magasin, Centre national d'art contemporain, 1996.

"In Memoriam: Guy de Cointet." *Journal: A Contemporary Art Magazine* (Los Angeles) 37 (September-October 1983): 31-34. Obituary.

Miller-Keller, Andrea. *Guy de Cointet*. Exh. cat. Hartford, Connecticut: Wadsworth Atheneum, 1978.

**Jim Dine**
Brandt Corstius, Liesbeth. *Jim Dine: Schilderijen, Aquarellen, Objecten en het complete grafische Oeuvre*. Exh. cat. Rotterdam: Museum Boymans-van Beuningen, 1971.

Feinberg, Jean. *Jim Dine*. New York: Abbeville Press, 1995.

Gordon, John. *Jim Dine*. Exh. cat. New York: Whitney Museum of American Art, in association with Praeger, 1970.

*Jim Dine*. Exh. cat. Bordeaux: Centre d'art plastique contemporain, 1975.

Ruzicka, Joseph. "Jim Dine and Performance." In *American Art of the 1960s*. Exh. cat. New York: The Museum of Modern Art, 1991.

**John Duncan**
MacAdams, Lewis. "Sex with the Dead." *Wet* (Santa Monica, California) 5, no. 6 (March-April 1981): 60-61.

Duncan, John. "If Only We Could Tell You...." *High Performance* (Los Angeles) 3, no. 4 (Fall-Winter 1980): 34-35.

**Felipe Ehrenberg**
Gever, Martha. "Art is an Excuse: An Interview with Felipe Ehrenberg." *Afterimage* (New York) 10, no. 9 (April 1983): 12-18.

Krantz, Claire Wolf. "Felipe Ehrenberg: An Activist Artist Speaks out on Art, Politics, and Social Actions: Part I." *New Art Examiner* (Chicago) 12, no. 5 (February 1985): 38-43; Part II: 13, no. 6 (March 1985): 37-39. Interview.

*Muestra de instalaciones y performance de Felipe Ehrenberg, Helen Escobedo, Marcos Kurtycz*. Exh. cat. Mexico City: Instituto Nacional de Bellas Artes, 1993.

**Roberto Evangelista**
Brett, Guy. *Transcontinental: An Investigation of Reality*. Birmingham, England: Ikon Gallery and Manchester, England: Cornerhouse, in association with London and New York: Verso, 1990.

**Valie Export**
Eiblmayer, Silvia. "Valie Export's 'Feminist Actionism': In the Context of Performance and Body Art in the 1960s and 1970s." In *The Connected Body? An Interdisciplinary Approach to the Body and Performance*. Eds. Ric Allsopp and Scott deLahunta. Amsterdam: Amsterdam School of the Arts, 1996.

Kapke, Barry. "Body as Sign: Performance and Film Works of Valie Export." *High Performance* (Los Angeles) 12, no. 1 (Spring 1989): 34-37.

Prammer, Anita. *Valie Export: eine multimediale Künstlerin*. Vienna: Frauenverlag, 1988.

*Ulrike Rosenbach/Valie Export*. Exh. cat. Amsterdam: Stedelijk Museum, 1980.

*Valie Export*. Exh. cat. Linz, Austria: Oberösterreich Landesmuseum, 1992.

**Robert Filliou**
*Robert Filliou*. Exh. cat. Brussels, Hamburg, and Paris: Editions Lebeer Hossmann, 1990.

*Robert Fillliou*. Exh. cat. Paris: Musée d'art moderne, Centre Georges Pompidou, 1991.

*Robert Filliou: Das immerwährende Ereignis zeigt/ The Eternal Network/La fête permanente presente*. Exh. cat. Hannover, Germany: Sprengel-Museum; Paris: Musée d'art moderne de la Ville de Paris; Bern: Kunsthalle, 1984.

*Robert Filliou: From Political to Poetical Economy*. Exh. cat. Vancouver: Morris and Helen Belkin Art Gallery, University of British Columbia, 1995.

*Robert Filliou, 1926-1987: Zum Gedachtnis*. Exh. cat. Düsseldorf: Kunsthalle, 1988.

**Rose Finn-Kelcey**
*Rose Finn-Kelcey*. Exh. cat. London: Chisenhale Gallery and Birmingham: Ikon Gallery, 1992.

*7 aus London*. Exh. cat. Bern: Kunsthalle, 1973.

Tickner, Lisa. "One for Sorrow, Two for Mirth: The Performance Work of Rose Finn-Kelcey." *Oxford Art Journal* (England) 3, no. 1 (April 1980): 58-72.

**Sherman Fleming**
Fleming, Sherman. "Nigger as Anti-body." *WhiteWalls* 25 (Spring 1990): 54-56.

Fleming, Sherman. "RODFORCE and the Anti-Formalist Reclamation Organiztion." *High Performance* (Los Angeles) 5, no. 1 (Spring-Summer 1982): 143.

Stiles, Kristine. "RODFORCE: Thoughts on the Art of Sherman Fleming." *High Performance* (Los Angeles) 10, no. 2 (1987): 34-39.

**Lucio Fontana**
*Fontano e lo spazialismo*. Exh. cat. Lugano, Switzerland: Villa Malpensata Riva, in association with Edizioni Citta de Lugano, 1987.

*Lucio Fontana*. 2 vols. Brussels: La Connaissance, 1974.

*Lucio Fontana*. Exh. cat. Paris: Musée national d'art moderne, Centre Georges Pompidou, 1987.

*Lucio Fontana, 1899-1968*. Exh. cat. Barcelona: Centre Cultural de la Fundicio Caixa de Pensions, 1988.

*Lucio Fontana, 1899-1968: A Retrospective*. Exh. cat. New York: Solomon R. Guggenheim Museum, 1977.

**Terry Fox**
Marioni, Tom. "Terry Fox: Himself." *Art and Artists* (London) 7, no. 10 (January 1973): 38-41.

Sharp, Willoughby. "Elemental Gestures: Terry Fox." *Arts Magazine* (New York) 44, no. 7 (May 1970): 48-51.

*Terry Fox*. Exh. cat. Berkeley: University Art Museum, University of California, 1973.

*Terry Fox: "Articulations."* Exh. cat. Philadelphia: Goldie Paley Gallery, Levy Gallery for the Arts in Philadelphia, 1992.

*Terry Fox: Metaphorical Instruments*. Exh. cat. Essen, Germany: Museum Folkwang, in association with Berlin: Berliner Kunstlerprogramm des Deutschen Akademischen Austauschidienstes, 1982.

**Howard Fried**
Hopkins, Joel, Marsha Fox, and David Sherk. "Howard Fried: Interview." *Art and Artists* (London) 7, no. 10 (January 1973): 32-36.

*Howard Fried: Works from 1969 to 1983*. Exh. cat. Berkeley: University Art Museum, University of California, 1983.

Lewallen, Constance. "Howard Fried." Exh. brochure. *Matrix Berkeley 54*. Berkeley: University Art Museum, University of California, 1982.

Richardson, Brenda. "Howard Fried: The Paradox of Approach-Avoidance." *Arts Magazine* (New York) 45, no. 8 (Summer 1971): 30-33.

White, Robin. "Howard Fried." *View* (Oakland, California) 11, no. 7 (December 1979). Interview.

**Gideon Gechtman**
*Gideon Gechtman: Works 1971-1986*. Exh. cat. Tel Aviv: Stavit Editions, 1986.

*Makom: Zeitgenossische Kunst aus Israel*. Exh. cat. Vienna: Museum moderner Kunst Stiftung Ludwig, 1993.

**Gilbert & George**
*Gilbert & George 1968 to 1980*. Exh. cat. Eindhoven, The Netherlands: Municipal Van Abbemuseum, 1980.

Jahn, Wolf. *The Art of Gilbert & George, or An Aesthetic of Existence*. Trans. David Britt. New York: Thames and Hudson, 1989.

Ratcliff, Carter. *Gilbert & George: The Complete Pictures 1971-1985*. New York: Rizzoli, 1986.

Ratcliff, Carter, and Robert Rosenblum. *Gilbert & George: The Singing Sculpture*. New York: Anthony McCall, 1983.

Reise, Barbara. "Presenting Gilbert & George: The Living Sculptures." *Art News* (New York) 70, no. 7 (November 1971): 62-65, 91.

**Alberto Greco**
*Alberto Greco*. Exh. cat. Valencia, Spain: Centre Julio González and Madrid: Fundación Cultural MAPFRE Vida, 1992.

Glusberg, Jorge. "Alberto Greco." In *Art in Argentina*. Milan: Giancarlo Politi Editore, 1986.

Millares, Manolo. "El Happening." In *Alberto Greco*. Exh. cat. Valencia, Spain: Centre Julio González,

Noé, Luis Felipe. *Homenaje a Alberto Greco*. Exh. cat. Buenos Aires: Galería Carmen Waugh, Republished as *Alberto Greco*. Buenos Aires: Fundación San Telmo, 1987.

**Ion Grigorescu**
Koplos, Janet. "Of Walls and Wandering." *Art in America* 80, no. 7 (July 1992): 82-87.

Procopovici, Radu. "An Eye on the East: Romanian Art Today." *Flash Art* (Milan), no. 143 (November-December 1988): 83-85.

**Victor Grippo**
Brett, Guy. "Victor Grippo." In *Transcontinental: An Investigation of Reality* Birmingham, England: Ikon Gallery and Manchester, England: Cornerhouse, in association with London and New York: Verso, 1990.

Glusberg, Jorge. *Victor Grippo*. Exh. cat. Buenos Aires: Fundación San Telmo, 1980.

Glusberg, Jorge. *Victor Grippo: obras de 1965-1987*. Exh. cat. Buenos Aires: Seccion Argentian, Associación internacional de críticos de arte, 1988.

*Victor Grippo*. Exh. cat. Birmingham, England: Ikon Gallery and Brussels: Societé des Expositions du Palais des Beaux-Arts, 1995.

## Red Grooms

Cate, Phillip Dennis. *The Ruckus World of Red Grooms*. Exh. cat. Rutgers, New Jersey: Berkowitz Press for Rutgers University Art Gallery, 1973.

Ratcliff, Carter. *Red Grooms*. New York: Abbeville Press, 1984.

*Red Grooms: A Retrospective 1956-1984*. Exh. cat. Philadelphia: Pennsylvania Academy of the Fine Arts, 1985.

*Red Grooms: The Early Sixties*. Exh. cat. New York: Allan Frumkin Gallery, 1983.

## Guerrilla Art Action Group

Guerrilla Art Action Group. *GAAG: The Guerrilla Art Action Group, 1969-1976: A Selection*. New York: Printed Matter, 1978.

Battcock, Gregory. "Guerrilla Art Action — Toche and Hendricks Interviewed." *Art and Artists* (London) 6, no. 11 (February 1972): 22-25.

## David Hammons

Bey, David. "In the Spirit of Minkisi: The Art of David Hammons." *Third Text* (London), no. 27 (Summer 1994): 45-54.

Cameron, Dan. "David Hammons: Coming in from the Cold." *Flash Art* (Milan), no. 168 (January-February 1993): 68-71.

*David Hammons: Rousing the Rubble*. Exh. cat. New York: Institute for Contemporary Art, in association with Cambridge, Massachusetts: MIT Press, 1991.

Jones, Kellie. "David Hammons." *Real Life* (New York), no. 16 (Autumn 1986): 2-9. Interview.

Reid, Calvin. "Kinky Black Hair and Barbecue Bones: Street Life, Social History, and David Hammons." *Arts Magazine* (New York) 65, no. 8 (April 1991): 59-63.

## Al Hansen

"Hansen: Past/Present/Future Tense." *Lightworks*, no. 19 (Winter 1988-1989): 27-29.

Hansen, Al. *A Primer of Happening and Time/Space Art*. New York: Something Else Press, 1965.

Raap, Jürgen. "Kunstlerisches Ultimatum (Artistic Ultimatum)." *Kunstforum International* (Cologne), no. 117 (1992): 250-253.

## Maren Hassinger

James, Curtia. "Interview: Maren Hassinger." *Art Papers* (Atlanta, Georgia) 18 (January-February 1994): 6-8.

Berger, Maurice. *Maren Hassinger, 1972-1991*. Exh. cat. Brookville, New York: Hillwood Art Musum, Long Island Unversity, 1991.

Megerian, Maureen. "Entwined with Nature: The Sculpture of Maren Hassinger." *Woman's Art Journal* 17 (Fall 1996-Winter 1997): 21-25.

## Lynn Hershman

Jan, Alfred. "Lynn Hershman: Processes of Empowerment." *High Performance* (Los Angeles) 8, no. 4 (1985): 36-38.

*Lynn Hershman*. Exh. cat. Montbéliard Belfort, France: Edition du Centre international de création vidéo, 1992.

*Lynn Hershman is Not Roberta Breitmore, Roberta Breitmore is Not Lynn Hershman*. Exh. cat. San Francisco: M. H. de Young Memorial Museum, 1978.

Roth, Moira. "An Interview with Lynn Hershman." *Journal of the Los Angeles Institute of Contemporary Art*, no. 17 (January-February 1978): 18-24.

Tamblyn, Christine. "Lynn Hershman's Narrative Anti-Narratives." *Afterimage* (New York) 14, no. 1 (Summer 1986): 8-10.

## Dick Higgins

Af Klintberg, B. "Dick Higgins, Intermediakonstnar (Intermedia Artist)." *Kalejdskop* (Sweden), no. 3-4 (1977): 51-52.

*Dick Higgins*. Exh. cat. Oslo: Henie Onstad Art Center, 1995.

Higgins, Dick. *A Dialectic of Centuries: Notes Toward a Theory of the New Arts*. New York: Printed Editions, 1978.

Polkinhorn, Harry. *The Illusion of Reality: An Interview with Dick Higgins*. Oakland, California: SCORE Publications, 1987.

## Tatsumi Hijikata

"Bijutsu no Kijikata Tatsumi: Jikn ni egaku nikutai" (Tatsumi Hijikata as Art: Depicting with the Body in Time). *Bijutsu techō* , no. 561 (May 1986): special feature.

*Hijikata Tatsumi butō shashin-shū: Kiki ni tatsu niku-tai/Body on the Edge of Crisis*. Tokyo: PARCO, 1987.

*Hijikata Tatsumi but taikan: Kasabuta to kyarameru/Tetsumi Hijikata: Three Decades of Butoh Experiment*. Tokyo: Yushi-sha, 1993.

*Hijikata Tatsumi to sono shuhen-ten: Yami to hikari no ikonorojī/Exhibition: Works of Tatsumi Hijikata and People Influenced by Him — In Search of the Expression of Butoh and Art*. Exh. cat. Yokohama: Yokohama Citizen's Gallery, 1989.

## Susan Hiller

Fisher, Jean. *Susan Hiller: The Revenants of Time: An Essay*. Exh. cat. London: Matt's Gallery, Sheffield: Mappin Art Gallery, and Glasglow: Third Eye Centre, 1990.

*Susan Hiller*. Exh. cat. London: Institute of Contemporary Arts, 1986.

*Susan Hiller: 1973-1983: The Muse My Sister*. Exh. cat. Londonderry: Orchard Gallery, 1984.

*Susan Hiller: Recent Works*. Exh. cat. Cambridge, England: Kettle's Yard and Oxford, England: Museum of Modern Art, 1978.

## Rebecca Horn

*Rebecca Horn*. Exh. cat. Geneva: Centre d'art contemporain, 1983.

*Rebecca Horn*. Exh. cat. New York: Solomon R. Guggenheim Museum, in association with Rizzoli, 1993.

*Rebecca Horn: Zeichnungen, Objekte, Fotos, Video, Filme*. Exh. cat. Cologne: Kolnischer Kunstverein, 1977.

Roustayi, Mira. "Body Art: Rebecca Horn's Sensibility Machines." *Arts Magazine* 63, no. 9 (May 1989): 58-68.

## Tehching Hsieh

Siskin, Jonathan. "Still Doing Time." *High Performance* (Los Angeles) 5, no. 3 (Fall 1982): 76-77.

Ziolkowski, Thad. "The Implosive Quest of Tehching Hsieh." *New Observations*, no. 108 (September-October 1995): 10-11.

## Joan Jonas

De Jong, Constance. "Organic Honey's Visual Telepathy." *The Drama Review* (New York) 16, no. 2 (June 1972): 66-74.

*Joan Jonas: Scripts and Descriptions, 1968-1982*. Exh. cat. Berkeley: University Art Museum, University of California and Eindhoven: Stedelijk Van Abbemuseum, 1983.

*Joan Jonas: Works 1968-1994*. Exh. cat. Amsterdam: Stedelijk Museum, 1994.

Kaye, Nick. "Mask, Role, Narrative: An Interview with Joan Jonas." *Performance* (New York), no. 65-66 (Spring 1992): 48-59.

## Kim Jones

Hayt-Atkins, Elizabeth. "Kim Jones." *Art News* (New York) 88, no. 9 (November 1989): 188-189.

"Kim Jones." In *Unwinding the Vietnam War*. Ed. Reese Williams. Seattle: The Real Comet Press, 1987.

"Rat Book." *Dumb Ox* (Los Angeles), no. 4 (Spring 1977): 26.

## Michel Journiac

Labaume, Vincent. "Body of Evidence: Michel Journiac." *Blocnotes* (France), no. 6 (Summer 1994): 30-37, 135-139.

*Michel Journiac*. Exh. cat. Antwerp, Belgium: Internationaal Cultureel Centrum, 1980.

## Akira Kanayama

*Kanayama Akira dai 1-kai koten/Akira Kanayama*. Exh. cat. Osaka: Kuranuki Gallery, 1992.

*Kanayama Akira dai 1-kai-ten 1950/1992/Akira Kanayama: The 1st Individual Exhibition 1950/1992*. Exh. brochure. Nagoya: Gallery Takagi, 1993.

Yamamoto, Atsuo. "Kanayama Akira ni okeru toma-tizumu" (Kanayama Akira's Automatism). *Art Critique* (Kyoto), no. 21 (December 1992): 5.

## Tadeusz Kantor

Cieszkowski, Krzysztof Z. "Illusion and Repetition: Tadeusz Kantor Interviewed." *Art Monthly* (London), no. 42 (December 1980-January 1981): 6-8.

**Tadeusz Kantor** (continued)
Kobialka, Michal, ed. *A Journey Through Other Spaces: Essays and Manifestos, 1944-1990, Tadeusz Kantor*. Berkeley: University of California Press, 1993.

Marioni, Tom, ed. "Tadeusz Kantor." In *Visions* (Oakland, California), no. 2 (January 1976): 52-55.

*Tadeusz Kantor: Emballages, 1960-76*. Exh. cat. London: Whitechapel Art Gallery, 1976.

**Allan Kaprow**
*Allan Kaprow*. Exh. cat. Pasadena, California: Pasadena Art Museum, 1969.

*Allan Kaprow: Activity-Dokumente 1968-1976*. Exh. cat. Bremen, Germany: Kunsthalle, 1976.

*Allan Kaprow: Collagen, Environments, Videos, Broschuren, Geschichten, Happening-und Activity-Dokumente, 1956-1986*. Exh. cat. Dortmund, Germany: Museum am Ostwall, 1986.

Crary, Jonathan. "Allan Kaprow's Activities." *Arts Magazine* (New York) 51, no. 1 (September 1976): 78-81.

Giesler, Dan. "The Activity Art of Allan Kaprow and the Notion of Functional Sculpture." *Journal: A Contemporary Art Magazine* (Los Angeles) 32 (Spring 1982): 49-56.

Kaprow, Allan. *Essays on the Blurring of Art and Life*. Berkeley: University of California Press, 1993.

**Mike Kelley**
Kellein, Thomas. *Mike Kelley*. Exh. cat. Basel: Kunsthalle, Frankfurt: Portikus Gallery, and London: Institute of Contemporary Art, in association with Ostfildern: Edition Cantz, 1992.

Miller, John. *Mike Kelley*. Los Angeles: A.R.T. Press and New York: D.A.P., 1992. Interview.

Nesbitt, Lois E. "Not a Pretty Sight: Mike Kelley." *Artscribe International*, no. 83 (September-October 1990): 64-67.

Sussman, Elizabeth. *Mike Kelley: Catholic Tastes*. Exh. cat. New York: Whitney Museum of American Art, 1993.

**Jürgen Klauke**
*Jürgen Klauke: eine Ewigkeit ein Lacheln: Zeichnungen, Fotoarbeiten, Performances 1970/86* (Jürgen Klauke: An Eternal Smile: Drawings, Photographical Works, Performances 1970/86). Exh. cat. Karlsruhe, Germany: Badischer Kunstverein, in association with Cologne: Dumont Buchverlag, 1986.

*Jürgen Klauke: Formalisierung der Langeweile* (Formalization of Boredom). Exh. cat. Lucerne: Kunstmuseum, 1981.

Lischka, Gerhard Johann. "Du bist dem Ehenbild: Klauke ist sein Ebenbild" (You are Your Own Image: Klauke is His Own Image). *Kunstforum International* (Cologne), no. 88 (March-April 1987): 206-40.

Lischka, Gerhard Johann. "The Sequences." In *Jürgen Klauke: Fotosequenzen 1972-1980: Die Schwarz-Weiss Sequenzen*. Frankfurt am Main: Betzel-Verlag, 1982.

**Yves Klein**
Restany, Pierre. *Yves Klein*. Trans. John Shepley. New York: Harry N. Abrams, 1982.

Stich, Sidra. *Yves Klein*. Exh. cat. Cologne: Museum Ludwig, in association with Ostfildern: Cantz and New York: D.A.P., 1994.

*Yves Klein: 1928-1962*. Exh. cat. Paris: Musée national d'art moderne, Centre Georges Pompidou, 1983.

*Yves Klein, 1928-1962: A Retrospective*. Exh. cat. Houston: Institute for the Arts, Rice University, in association with New York: The Arts Publisher, 1982.

*Yves Klein, 1928-1962: Selected Writings*. Exh. cat. Trans. Barbara Wright. London: Tate Gallery, 1974.

**Milan Knížák**
AKTUAL Group. *AKTUAL Schmuck*. Cullompton, Devon, England: Beau Geste Press, 1974.

Fischer, Gunther. "Der Prague Provakateur: Milan Knížák." *Pan* (Germany), no. 2 (1992): 64-67.

Knížák, Milan. "Aktual in Czechoslovakia." *Art and Artists* (London), no. (October 1972).

*Milan Knížák: Action as a Lifestyle — Auswahl der Aktivitaten 1953-1985* (Selected Activities 1953-1985). Exh. cat. Hamburg: Kunsthalle and Bochum, Germany: Bochum Museum, 1986.

**Alison Knowles**
*The Four Suits: Benjamin Patterson, Philip Corner, Alison Knowles, Tomas Schmit*. New York: Something Else Press, 1965.

Knowles, Alison. *By Alison Knowles*. New York: Something Else Press, 1965.

Johnson, Tom. "New Music." *Musical America* (June 1974): 12-13.

Milman, Estera. "Road Shows, Street Events, and Fluxus People: A Conversation with Alison Knowles." *Visible Language* 26, no. 1-2 (1992): 97-107.

**Komar & Melamid**
*Komar & Melamid*. Exh. cat. Edinburgh: The Fruitmarket Gallery and Oxford, England: Museum of Modern Art, 1985.

Nathanson, Melvyn B. *Komar & Melamid: Two Soviet Dissident Artists*. Carbondale and Edwardsville: Southern Illinois University Press, 1979.

Ratcliff, Carter. *Komar & Melamid*. New York: Abbeville Press, 1988.

*Vitaly Komar and Aleksandr Melamid: A Retrospective*. Exh. cat. Wichita, Kansas: Edwin A. Ulrich Museum of Art, Wichita State University, 1980.

**Jannis Kounellis**
Celant, Germano. "The Collision and the Cry: Jannis Kounellis." *Artforum* (New York) 22, no. 2 (October 1983): 61-67.

*Jannis Kounellis*. Exh. cat. Eindhoven, The Netherlands: Stedelijk Van Abbemuseum, 1981.

*Jannis Kounellis*. Exh. cat. Chicago: Museum of Contemporary Art, 1986.

*Jannis Kounellis: Frammenti de memoria*. Exh. cat. Hannover: Kestner-Gesellschaft and Winterthur: Kunstmuseum, 1991.

**Shigeko Kubota**
Kubota, Shigeko. "Maruseru Dushan: Bannen no Dushan to chesu gemu" (Marcel Duchamp: His Last Years and Chess Game). *Bijutsu techō*, no. 319 (November 1969): 80-89.

Mellinger, Jean and D. L. Bean. "Shigeko Kubota." *Profile* (Chicago) 3, no. 6 (November 1983). Interview.

Roth, Moira. "The Voice of Shigeko Kubota: A Fusion of Art and Life, Asia and America." In *Shigeko Kubota: Video Sculptures*. Ed. Mary Jane Jacob. Astoria, New York: American Museum of the Moving Image, 1991.

**Tetsumi Kudō**
Jouffroy, Alain. "Rejisutansu: Kudō Tetsumi no, Kudō Tetsumi e no" (Resistance: On Tetsumi Kudō, to Tetsumi Kudō). *Bijutsu techō*, no. 381 (May 1974): 250-258.

*Kudō Tetsumi kaiko-ten* (Tetsumi Kudō Retrospective). Exh. cat. Osaka: The National Museum of Art, 1995.

Nakahara, Yusuke. "Kudō Tetsumi no sakuhin chūshaku" (Explanatory Notes on Works by Tetsumi Kudō). *Bijutsu techō*, no. 381 (May 1974): 221-249.

*Tetsumi Kudō*. Exh. cat. Amsterdam: Stedelijk Van Abbemuseum, 1972.

*Tetsumi Kudō: Cultivation by Radioactivity*. Exh. cat. Düsseldorf: Kunstverein für die Rheinlande und Westfalen, c. 1970.

**Yayoi Kusama**
"Kusama-Yayoi: Obusesshonaru to no shutsuji to tenkai" (Origins and Development of Obsessional Art). *Bijutsu techō*, no. 671 (June 1993): special feature.

*Kusama Yayoi-ten* (Yayoi Kusama Exhibition). Exh. cat. Kitakyushu, Japan: Kitakyushu Municipal Museum of Art, 1987.

*Love Forever: Yayoi Kusamai*. Exh. cat. Los Angeles: Los Angeles County Museum of Art, 1998.

*Yayoi Kusama: A Retrospective*. Exh. cat. New York: Center for International Contemporary Arts, 1989.

**Leslie Labowitz**
Labowitz, Leslie, and Suzanne Lacy. "Mass Media, Popular Culture, and Fine Art: Images of Violence Against Women." In *Social Works*. Ed. Nancy Buchanan. Los Angeles: Los Angeles Institute of Contemporary Art, 1979.

Labowitz, Leslie, and Suzanne Lacy. "Feminist Media Strategies for Political Performance." In *Cultures in Contention*. Eds. Douglas Kahn and Diane Neumaier. Seattle: The Real Comet Press, 1985.

Nabakowski, Gisland, and Petra Kipphoff. "Pro and Contra: 'Frauenkunst' gibtes die?" (Pro and Con: 'Women's Art,' Does it Exist?). *Art: Das Kunstmagazin* (Germany), no. 2 (February 1982): 68-71.

**Suzanne Lacy**
Askey, Ruth. "In Mourning and in Rage." *Artweek* 9, no. 2 (January 14, 1978).

Mifflin, M. "From a Whisper to a Shout: Suzanne Lacy Talks about Art as a Network for Women's Voices." *High Performance* (Los Angeles) 7, no. 2 (1984): 38-41, 83.

Newton, Richard. "Suzanne Lacy." *High Performance* (Los Angeles) 1, no. 1 (March 1978). Interview.

Roth, Moira. "Visions and Revisions: A Conversation with Suzanne Lacy." *Artforum* (New York) 19, no. 3 (November 1980): 42-45. Interview.

**John Latham**
*John Latham: Art After Physics*. Exh. cat. Oxford, England: Museum of Modern Art and Stuttgart: Staatsgalerie, in association with Edition Hansjörg Mayer, 1991.

*John Latham: Early Works 1954-1972*. Exh. cat. London: Lisson Gallery, 1987.

*John Latham: State of Mind*. Exh. cat. Düsseldorf: Städtische Kunsthalle, 1975.

Measham, Terry. *John Latham*. Exh. cat. London: Tate Gallery Publications, 1976.

Walker, John A. *John Latham: The Incidental Persona — His Art and Ideas*. London: Middlesex University Press, 1995.

**Jean-Jacques Lebel**
Blistène, Bernard. "Jean-Jacques Lebel: An Interview." *Flash Art* (Milan), no. 84-85 (October-November 1978): 57-63.

*Jean-Jacques Lebel: retour d'exil: peintures, dessins, collages 1954-1988*. Exh. cat. Paris: Galerie 1900-2000, 1988.

*Jean-Jacques Lebel: des années cinquante aux années quatre vingt-dix*. Paris: Galerie 1900-2000, in association with Milan: Mazzota, 1991.

Lebel, Jean-Jacques. *Entretiens avec le "Living Theatre."* Paris: Editions Pierre Belford, 1969.

**Lea Lublin**
Glusberg, Jorge. "Lea Lublin." In *Art in Argentina*. Milan: Giancarlo Politi Editore, 1986.

*Lea Lublin: présent suspendu*. Exh. cat. Paris: L'Hôtel des Arts and Toulouse: Centre régional d'art contemporain Midi Pyrénées, 1991.

**George Maciunas**
Moore, Barbara. "George Maciunas: A Finger in Fluxus." *Artforum* 21, no. 2 (October 1982): 38-45.

Knížák, Milan and Al Hansen. "George the Maciunas/How We Met." *Kunstforum International* (Cologne), no. 115 (September-October 1991): 112-123.

Restany, Pierre. "George Maciunas: L'archiviste et le catalyseur d'une situation, celle des années '60." *Domus* (Milan), no. 590 (January 1979): 51-54.

Smith, Owen F. "George Maciunas and a History of Fluxus; or, The Art Movement that Never Existed." Ph.D. diss, University of Washington, 1991.

Truck, Fred. *George Maciunas: Fluxus and the Face of Time*. 2 vols. Des Moines, Iowa: Electric Bank, 1984.

**Leopoldo Maler**
Glusberg, Jorge. *Maler*. New York: International Center for Advanced Studies in Art, New York University, 1987.

Klein, Ellen Lee. "The Magic of Leopoldo Maler." *Arts Magazine* (New York) 58, no. 2 (October 1983): 136-137.

*Leopoldo Maler: Mortal Issues — A Sanctuary with Flames and Figures*. Exh. cat. London: Whitechapel Art Gallery, 1976.

**Piero Manzoni**
Battino, Freddy. *Piero Manzoni: Catalogue Raisonné*. Milan: Vanni Scheiwiller, 1991.

*Mostra de Piero Manzoni*. Exh. cat. Rome: Galleria Nazionale d'Arte Moderna, 1971.

*Piero Manzoni*. Exh. cat. Paris: Musée national d'art moderne, Centres Georges Pompidou, 1991.

*Piero Manzoni: Paintings, Reliefs and Objects*. Exh. cat. London: Tate Gallery, 1974.

**Tom Marioni**
Futterman, Hilla. "Activity as Sculpture: Tom Marioni Discusses His Work with Hilla Futterman." *Art and Artists* 8 (August 1973): 18-21.

*The Sound of Flight: Tom Marioni*. San Francisco: M. H. De Young Memorial Museum, 1977.

*Tom Marioni: À la limite*. Exh. cat. Dijon: Bureau d'étude et de diffusion de l'art contemporain, 1984.

White, Robin. *View* (Oakland, California) 1, no. 5 (October 1978, updated January 1981). Interview.

**Georges Mathieu**
*George Mathieu: oeuvres anciennes, 1948-1960*. Exh. cat. Paris: Galerie Beaubourg, 1974.

Mathey, François. *George Mathieu*. Paris: Hachette-Fabbri, 1969.

*Mathieu*. Exh. cat. Rennes, France: Musée des Beaux-Arts, 1969.

Mathieu, Georges. *De la revolte à la Renaissance: au-dela du tachisme*. Paris: Gallimard, 1973.

Quignon-Fleuret, Dominique. *Mathieu*. Paris: Flammarion, 1973. English edition: Trans. Jeffrey Arsham. New York: Crown Publishers, 1977.

**Gordon Matta-Clark**
*Gordon Matta-Clark*. Exh. cat. Valencia, Spain: Centre Julio González and Marseille, France: Musée Cantini, 1983.

*Gordon Matta-Clark*. Exh. cat. San Francisco: Art Institute, 1978.

*Gordon Matta-Clark: A Retrospective*. Exh. cat. Chicago: Museum of Contemporary Art, 1985.

**Paul McCarthy**
Burnham, Linda. "Paul McCarthy: The Evolution of a Performance Artist." *High Performance* 8, no. 1 (1985): 37-43.

Rugoff, Ralph. "Deviations of a Theme: Paul McCarthy." *Artforum* (New York) 33, no. 3 (October 1994): 80-83, 118.

Rugoff, Ralph, Kristine Stiles, and Giacinto Di Pietrantonio. *Paul McCarthy*. London: Phaidon, 1996.

Schroder, Johannes Lothar. "Paul McCarthy: Alptraume Alpraume" (Nightmarish Visions, Nightmarish Spaces). *Kunstforum International* (Cologne), no. 129 (January-April 1995): 190-203.

**Bruce McLean**
*Bruce McLean*. Exh. cat. Edinburgh: Fruitmarket Gallery, 1980.

*Bruce McLean*. Exh. cat. Karlsruhe, Germany: Badischer Kunstverein, 1984.

*Bruce McLean*. Exh. cat. London: Whitechapel Art Gallery, 1981.

Gooding, Mel. *Bruce McLean*. Oxford, England and New York: Phaidon, 1989.

**David Medalla**
Araeen, Rasheed. "Conversation with David Medalla." *Black Phoenix* 3 (Spring 1979): 10-19.

Brett, Guy. *Exploding Galaxies: The Art of David Medalla*. London: Kala Press, 1996.

Brett, Guy. "Impromptus: David Medalla." *Art in America* 77, no. 11 (November 1989): 156-163.

MacIntosh, Alastair. "David Medalla: Art for Whom?" *Art and Artists* (London) 7, no. 10 (January 1973): 26-31. Interview.

**Cildo Meireles**
Brito Ronaldo and Eudoro Augusto Macieira de Souza. *Arte Brasileira Contemporânea: Cildo Meireles*. Rio de Janeiro: Edição FUNARTE, 1981.

*Cildo Meireles*. Exh. cat. Barcelona: Generalitat Valenciana and IVAM Centre del Carme, 1995.

De Zegher, Catherine et al. T*unga "Lezarts"/ Cildo Meireles "Through."* Exh. cat. Kortrijk, Belgium: Kunststichting-Kaanal-Art Foundation, 1989.

Zelevansky, Lynn. "Projects: Cildo Meireles." Exh. brochure. New York: The Museum of Modern Art, 1990.

**Ana Mendieta**
*Ana Mendieta*. Exh. cat. Barcelona: Fundació Antonio Tàpies, 1996.

*Ana Mendieta: A Retrospective*. Exh. cat. New York: The New Museum of Contemporary Art, 1987.

Clearwater, Bonnie, ed. *Ana Medieta: A Book of Works*. Miami Beach: Grassfield Press, 1993.

Jacob, Mary Jane. *Ana Mendieta: The Silhueta Series, 1973-1980*. Exh. cat. New York: Galerie Lelong, 1991.

Wooster, Ann-Sargent. "Ana Mendieta: Themes of Death and Resurrection." *High Performance* (Los Angeles) 11, no. 1-2 (Spring-Summer 1988): 80-83.

**Gustav Metzger**
Hoffman, Justin, ed. *Gustav Metzger: Manifeste und Schriften*. Munich: Verlag Silke Schreiber, 1987.

Metzger, George. *Auto-Destructive Art: Metzger at the AA*. London: Creation/Destruction, 1965.

Walker, John A. "Message fron the Margin." *Art Monthly* (London), no. 190 (October 1995): 14-17.

**Marta Minujín**
Barnitz, Jacqueline. "Marta Minujín: a Latin answer to pop" *Arts Magazine* (New York) 40, no. 8 (June 1966): 36-39

Glusberg, Jorge. *Marta Minujín Esculturas: hacia una invención de lo inextricable*. Exh. cat. Buenos Aires: Galería Rubbers, 1989.

Kirby, Michael. "Marta Minujín's Simultaneity in Simultaneity." *The Drama Review* (New York) 12, no. 3 (Spring 1968): 149-152.

Squires, Richard. "Eat Me, Read Me, Burn Me: The Ephemeral Art of Marta Minujín." *Performance* (England), no. 64 (Summer 1991): 18-27.

**Jan Mlčoch**
Cihakova-Noshiro, Vlasta. "Umeni zakazovat umeni" (The Art of Banning Art). *Vytvarne Umeni* (Czech Republic), no. 3-4 (1995): 124-133.

Marioni, Tom, ed. "Jan Mlčoch." In *Visions* (Oakland, California), no. 2 (January 1976): 44.

**Linda Montano**
Linda Montano. In *Space Time Sound: Conceptual Art in The San Francisco Bay Area: The 70s*. Exh. cat. San Francisco: Museum of Modern Art, 1979.

Montano, Linda. *Art in Everyday Life*. Los Angeles: Astro Artz and Barrytown, New York: Station Hill, 1981.

Montano, Linda. "Spirituality and Art." *Women Artists News* 10, no. 3 (Spring 1985): 8.

Roth, Moira. "Matters of Life and Death: Linda Montano Interviewed by Moira Roth." *High Performance* (Los Angeles) (December 1978).

**Robert Morris**
Morris, Robert. "Notes on Dance." *Tulane Drama Review* (New Orleans) 10, no. 2 (Winter 1965): 179-186.

*Robert Morris*. Exh. cat. Eindhoven, The Netherlands: Stedelijk Van Abbemuseum, 1968.

*Robert Morris*. Exh. cat. London: Tate Gallery, 1971.

*Robert Morris*. Exh. cat. New York: Whitney Museum of American Art, 1970.

*Robert Morris: The Mind/Body Problem*. Exh. cat. New York: The Solomon R. Guggenheim Foundation, 1994.

**Otto Muehl**
*Otto Muehl: Ausgewählte Arbeiten 1963-1986*. Vienna: Hubert Klocker, 1986.

Page, Robin. "Materialaktion und Materialaktionsfilme von Otto Muehl." *Die Schastrommel* (Bolzano) 2 (May 1970): unpaginated.

Schmölzer, Hilde. "Otto Muehl." In *Das böse Wien. Gespräche mit österreichischen Künstlern*. Munich: Nymphenburger Verlagshandlung, 1973. Interview.

**Saburō Murakami**
Kamperelic, Dobrica. "Art Identified." *Artefact* (Serbia) (1995): 30-33.

*Murakami*. Exh. cat. Osaka: Gutai Pinacotheca, 1963.

*Murakami Saburō-ten* (Saburō Murakami exhibition). Exh. cat. Ashiya, Japan: Ashiya City Museum of Art and History, 1996.

**Natsuyuki Nakanishi**
*Fünf Zeitgenossische Kunstler aus Japan*. Exh. cat. Düsseldorf: Stadtische Kunsthalle, 1983.

Hirai, Ryōichi. "Setten to shiteno kaiga: Nakanishi Natsuyuki no shinsaku" (Painting as a Point of Contact: New Works of Natsuyuki Nakanishi). *Bijutsu techō*, no. 458 (December 1979): 198-211.

Tanikawa, Koichi. "Keijijō-gaku to kaiga: Nakanishi Natsuyuki-ron" (Metaphysics and Painting: On Natsuyuki Nakanishi). *Bijutsu techō*, no. 369 (July 1973): 152-157.

**Bruce Nauman**
*Bruce Nauman*. Exh. cat. London: Whitechapel, 1986. Also published as *Bruce Nauman: Werken von 1965 bis 1986*. Basel: Kunsthalle, 1986.

*Bruce Nauman*. Exh. cat. and cat. raisonné. Minneapolis: Walker Art Center and Washington, D.C.: Hirshhorn Museum and Sculpture Garden, 1994.

*Bruce Nauman*. Exh. cat. New York: Leo Castelli Gallery, 1968.

*Bruce Nauman: Work from 1965 to 1972*. Exh. cat. Los Angeles: Los Angeles County Museum of Art, in association with New York: Praeger, 1972.

Sharp, Willoughby. "Bruce Nauman." *Avalanche*, no. 2 (Winter 1971): 22-35. Interview.

Van Bruggen, Coosje. *Bruce Nauman*. New York: Rizzoli, 1988.

**Paul Neagu**
*Gradually Going Tornado! Paul Neagu and His Generative Art Group*. Exh. cat. Sunderland, England: Sunderland Arts Center, 1975.

Neagu, Paul. "Gradually Going Ahead." *Artscribe International* 16 (February 1979): 48-50.

*Paul Neagu*. Exh. cat. Glasgow: Third Eye Center, 1979.

*Paul Neagu: A Generative Context, 1965-1981*. Exh. cat. Newcastle Upon Tyne: Coelfrith Press 64 and Sunderland Arts Center, 1981.

**Senga Nengudi**
Odita, O. Donald. "Temple." *Flash Art* (Milan) 30, no. 195 (Summer 1997): 123.

Odita, O. Donald. "The Unseen, Inside Out: the Life and Work of Senga Nengudi." *NKA Journal of Contemporary African Art* (New York), no. 6-7 (Summer-Fall 1997): 24-27.

Piper, Adrian. "Brenson on Quality." *Art Papers* 15, no.6 (November-December 1991).

Reid, Calvin. "Wet Night, Early Dawn, Scat-Chant, Pilgrim's Song." *Art in America* (New York) 85, no.2 (February 1997): 100-101.

"Senga Nengudi." in *Gumbo Ya-Ya: Anthology of African-American Women Artists*. New York: Midmarch Arts Press, 1995.

**Joshua Neustein**
*Joshua Neustein: Drawings 1970-1973*. Exh. cat. New York: Rina Gallery, 1973.

*Neustein*. Exh. cat. Tel Aviv: Museum, 1977.

*Seven Artists in Israel, 1948-1978*. Exh. cat. Los Angeles: Los Angeles County Museum of Art, 1978.

*Three Israeli Artists: Gross, Neustein, Kupferman*. Exh. cat. Worcester, Masschusetts: Art Museum, 1975.

**Hermann Nitsch**
*Hermann Nitsch: das orgien mysterien theater*. Exh. cat. Eindhoven, The Netherlands: Stedelijk Van Abbemuseum, 1983.

Stoert, Rudolf. "Hermann Nitsch: Uber sein O.M. Theater" (About His O.M. Theatre). *Kunstforum International* (Cologne), no. 111 (January-February 1991): 272-287.

Nitsch, Hermann. *Das orgien mysterien theater: die partituren aller aufgeführten aktionen 1960-1979*. Naples: Studio Morra, 1979.

Schmölzer, Hilde. "Hermann Nitsch." In *Das böse Wien. Gespräche mit österreichischen Künstlern*. Munich: Nymphenburger Verlagshandlung, 1973. Interview.

**Hélio Oiticica**
Brett, Guy. "Fait sur le corps: Le paragnole de Hélio Oiticica." *Cahiers du Musée national d'art moderne* (Paris), no. 51 (Spring 1995): 32-45.

Favaretto, Celso F. *A invencao de Hélio Oiticica*. São Paulo: FAPESP, 1992.

*Hélio Oiticica*. Exh. cat. London: Whitechapel Gallery, 1969.

*Hélio Oiticica*. Exh. cat. Rio de Janeiro: Projeto Hélio Oiticica, and Paris: Galerie Jeu de Paume et al., 1992.

**Claes Oldenburg**
Ashton, Dore. "Claes Oldenburg: 'The Store,' New York 1961." In *Die Kunst der Austellung*. Frankfurt: Insel Verlag, 1991.

*Claes Oldenburg*. Exh. cat. New York: The Museum of Modern Art, 1970.

*Claes Oldenburg: An Anthology*. Exh. cat. New York: The Solomon R. Guggenheim Foundation, 1995.

Haywood, Robert E. "Heretical Alliance: Claes Oldenburg and the Judson Memorial Church in the 1960s." *Art History* (Oxford, England and Cambridge, Massachusetts) 18, no. 2 (June 1995): 185-212.

Johnson, Ellen H. *Claes Oldenburg*. Harmondsworth, England and Baltimore: Penguin Books, 1971.

Oldenburg, Claes. *Store Days: Documents from The Store (1961) and Ray Gun Theater (1962)*. New York: Something Else Press, 1967.

**Yoko Ono**
*Les Films de Yoko Ono 1966-1982*. Exh. cat. Geneva: Centre d'art contemporain, 1991.

Haskell, Barbara and John G. Hanhardt. *Yoko Ono: Arias and Objects*. Salt Lake City: Gibbs Smith Publisher, 1991.

Hendricks, Jon. ed. *Instructions for Paintings by Yoko Ono: May 24, 1962*. Exh. cat. Budapest: Galeria 56, 1993.

Stiles, Kristine. "Unbosoming Lennon: The Politics of Yoko Ono's Experience." *Art Criticism* 7, no. 2 (1992): 21-52.

*Yoko Ono: This Is Not Here*. Exh. cat. Syracuse, New York: Everson Museum of Art, 1971.

**Orlan**
Ermacora, Beate. "Orlan." *European Photography* (Germany) 15, no. 2 (Fall 1994): 15-23.

Hirshhorn, Michelle. "Orlan: Artist in the Post-human Age of Mechanical Reincarnation." *Versus* (England), no. 3 (1994): 21-25.

Rose, Barbara. "Is it Art? Orlan and the Transgressive Act." *Art in America* (New York) 81, no. 2 (February 1993): 82-87, 125.

Stiles, Kristine. "Never Enough is Something Else: Feminist Performance Art, Probity, and the Avant-Garde." In *Avant-Garde Performance, Textuality and the Limits of Literary History*. Ed. James M. Harding. Madison: University of Wisconsin, forthcoming.

**Raphael Montañez Ortiz**
Carr, Cynthia. "An Artist Retreats from Rage: Raphael Montañez Ortiz." In *On Edge: Performance at the End of the Twentieth Century*. Hanover, New Hampshire: University Press of New England, 1993.

Picard, Lil. "Kill for Peace." *Arts Magazine* 41, no. 5 (March 1967): 15.

*Raphael Montañez Ortiz: Years of the Warrior 1960, Years of the Psyche 1988*. Exh. cat. New York: El Museo del Barrio, 1988.

**Lorenzo Pace**
Fox, Barbara. "Art View: African American Art." *U.S. 1* (Princeton, New Jersey), January 29, 1992.

*The Expanding Circle: A Selection of African American Art*. Exh. cat. Princeton, New Jersey: The Gallery at Bristol-Myers Squibb, 1992.

Raynor, Vivien. "Works that Follow a Family's History." *The New York Times*, July 18, 1993.

**Nam June Paik**
Herzogenrath, Wulf. *Nam June Paik: Fluxus — Video*. Munich: Selke Schreiber, 1983.

*Nam June Paik*. Exh. cat. New York: Whitney Museum of American Art, in association with W. W. Norton, 1982.

*Nam June Paik: Video Works 1963-1988*. Exh. cat. London: Hayward Gallery, 1988.

*Nam June Paik: Werke 1946-1976: Musik-Fluxus-Video*. Exh. cat. Cologne: Kunstverein, 1976.

**Gina Pane**
*Gina Pane: travails d'action*. Exh. cat. Paris: Galerie Isy Brachot, 1980.

Konterova, Helena. "The Wound as a Sign: An Encounter with Gina Pane." *Flash Art* (Milan), no. 92-93 (October-November 1979): 36-37.

Lawless, Catherine. "Entretien avec Gina Pane." *Les Cahiers du Musée d'Art Moderne* (Paris), no. 29 (Fall 1989): 97-104.

Oliveira, Emidio Rosa. "Gina Pane: Ou o corpo alusivo da dor" (Gina Pane: Or the Allusive Body of Pain). *Coloquio: Artes* (Lisbon), no. 39 (December 1978): 9-17.

Tronche, Anne. *Gina Pane: Actions*. Paris: Fall Editions, 1997.

**Lygia Pape**
Brett, Guy. "A Radical Leap." In *Art in Latin America: The Modern Period*. Ed. Dawn Ades, London: South Bank Centre, in association with New Haven, Connecticut: Yale University Press, 1989.

Herkenhoff, Paulo. *Lygia Pape*. Exh. cat. São Paulo: Galerie Camargo Vilaça, 1995.

*Lygia Pape*. Exh. cat. Rio de Janeiro: Edição FUNARTE, 1983.

**Giuseppe Pinot Gallizio**
Corgnati, Martina. *Pinot Gallizio*. Ravenna, Italy: Edizioni Essegi, 1992.

*Pinot Gallizio*. Exh. cat. Amsterdam: Stedelijk Museum, 1960.

*Pinot Gallizio e il laboratorio sperimentale d'Alba*. Exh. cat. Turin, Italy: Galleria Civica d'art Moderna, 1974.

*Pinot Gallizio: Immoralitè del perimetro*. Exh. cat. Torino, Italy: Galleria Civica d'Arte, in association with Milan: Mazzotta, 1994.

*Pinot Gallizio: Le situationnisme et la peinture*. Exh. cat. Paris: Galerie 1900-2000, 1989.

**Adrian Piper**
*Adrian Piper*. Exh. cat. Birmingham, England: Ikon Gallery; and Manchester, England: Cornerhouse, 1991.

*Adrian Piper, Reflections 1967-1987*. Exh. cat. New York: Alternative Museum, 1987.

Cottingham, Laura. "Adrian Piper." *Journal of Contemporary Art* (New York) 5, no. 1 (Spring 1992): 88-136. Interview.

Lippard, Lucy R. "Catalysis: An Interview with Adrian Piper." *The Drama Review* (New York) 16, no. 1 (March 1972): 76-78. Reprinted in *From the Center: Feminist Essays on Women's Art*. New York: E. P. Dutton and Co., 1976.

Piper, Adrian. *Out of Order, Out of Sight*. 2 vols. Cambridge, Massachusetts: The MIT Press, 1996.

**Michelangelo Pistoletto**
Celant, Germano. *Pistoletto*. Trans. Joachim Neugroschel. New York: Rizzoli, 1989.

*Michelangelo Pistoletto*. Exh. cat. Florence: Forte de Belvedere, in association with Electa, 1984.

*Michelangelo Pistoletto*. Exh. cat. Hannover, Germany: Kestner-Gesellschaft, 1973.

*Pistoletto*. Exh. cat. Venice: Palazzo Grassi, 1976.

**Jackson Pollock**
*Jackson Pollock*. Exh. cat. Paris: Musée national d'art moderne, Centre Georges Pompidou, 1982.

Kaprow, Allan. "The Legacy of Jackson Pollock." *Art News* (New York) 57, no. 6 (October 1958): 24-26, 55-57.

Namuth, Hans. *L'atelier de Jackson Pollock*. Exh. cat. Paris: Pierre Brochet, 1978. Also published as *Pollock Painting*. New York: Agrinde Publications, 1980.

O'Connor, Francis V., and Eugene V. Thaw, eds. *Jackson Pollock: A Catalogue Raisonné of Paintings, Drawings, and Other Works*. New Haven, Connecticut: Yale University Press, 1978.

Ratcliff, Carter. *The Fate of a Gesture: Jackson Pollock and Post-War American Art*. New York: Farrar, Straus, Giroux, 1996.

Tono, Yoshiaki. *Gendai bijutsu Porokku igo* (After Pollock). Tokyo: Bijutsu Shuppan-sha, 1965.

**William Pope L.**
Morgan, Robert C. "Performance and Spectacle." *Tema Celeste* (Italy), no. 40 (Spring 1993): 62-65.

Sims, Lowery Stokes. "William Pope L." *High Performance* (Los Angeles) 15, no. 4 (Winter 1992): 46-47.

**Robert Rauschenberg**
Hopps, Walter. *Rauschenberg: The Early 1950s*. Exh. cat. Houston: The Menil Collection, in association with Houston Fine Art Press, 1990.

Kotz, Mary Lynn. *Rauschenberg: Art and Life*. New York: Harry N. Abrams, 1990.

*Rauschenberg/Performance 1954-1984*. Exh. cat. New York: Arthur A. Haughton Gallery, Cooper Union for the Advancement of Science and Art and Cleveland: Cleveland Center for the Arts, 1983.

*Robert Rauschenberg*. Exh. cat. Washington, D.C.: National Gallery of Fine Arts, Smithsonian Institution, 1977.

*Robert Rauschenberg: A Retrospective*. Exh. cat. New York: The Solomon R. Guggenheim Foundation, 1997.

**Carlyle Reedy**
Brett, Guy. "Carlyle Reedy." *Art Monthly* (London), no. 93 (February 1996).

Reedy, Carlyle. "Dream — Reality." *And: Journal of Art and Art Education* (England), no. 25 (1991): 7-13.

Reedy, Carlyle. *Obituaries and Celebrations*. London: Words Worth Books, 1995.

**Klaus Rinke**
*Ex-Hi-Bi-Tion: Klaus Rinke*. Exh. cat. Oxford, England: Museum of Modern Art, 1976.

*Klaus Rinke: 1954-1991, Retro-Activ*. Exh. cat. Düsseldorf: Kunsthalle, in association with Richter Verlag, 1992.

*Klaus Rinke: Travaux 1969/1976*. Exh. cat. Paris: ARC Musée d'art moderne de la ville de Paris, 1976.

*Rinke-Hand-Zeichner: die autonomen Werke von 1957-1980* (Rinke-Hand-Draftsman: The Autonomist Works from 1957-1980). Exh. cat. Stuttgart: Staatsgalerie and Düsseldorf: Kunstmuseum, 1981.

Weiss, Evelyn. "Phenomenology of a Time-Space System." *Studio International* (London) 187, no. 965 (April 1974): 174-180.

**Ulrike Rosenbach**
*Ulrike Rosenbach: Foto, Video, Aktion*. Exh. cat. Aachen, Germany: Neue Galerie-Sammlung Ludwig, 1977.

*Ulrike Rosenbach/Valie Export*. Exh. cat. Amsterdam: Stedelijk Museum, 1980.

*Ulrike Rosenbach: Video and Performance Art*. Exh. cat. Boston: Institute of Contemporary Art, 1983.

*Ulrike Rosenbach: Video, Performance, Installation 1972-1989*. Downsview, Canada: Art Gallery, York University, 1989.

*Ulrike Rosenbach: Videokunst, Foto, Aktion/Performance, feministische Kunst*. Frankfurt am Main: U. Rosenbach, 1982.

**Dieter Roth**
*Dieter Roth*. Exh. cat. Chicago: Museum of Contemporary Art, 1984.

*Dieter Roth: Bilder, Zeichnungen, Objekte, Bucher, Druchgraphik, Postkarten*. Exh. cat. Braunschweig, Germany: Kunstverein, 1973.

*Dieter Roth: Gesammelte Werke* (Collected Works). Exh. cat. Stuttgart: H. Mayer, 1969.

*Dieter Roth: Originale 1946-1974*. Exh. cat. Hamburg: Kunstverein, 1974.

**Zorka Ságlová**
Jirousova, Vera. "Velky malychralik Zorky Saglove (The Big Little Rabbit of Zorka Ságlová). *Vytvarne Umeni* (Czechoslovakia), no. 1 (1993): 22-31.

*Zorka Ságlová: Obrazy* (Pictures). Exh. cat. Prague: Ustredni Kulturni Dum, 1990.

*Zorka Ságlová: 1965-1995*. Exh. cat. Prague: Galerie Vytvarného Umeni, 1995.

**Niki de Saint Phalle**
Hulten, Pontus. *Niki de Saint Phalle*. Exh. cat. Stuttgart: Kunst und Ausstellungshalle der Bundesrepublik Deutschland, 1992; Glasgow: McLellan Galleries; and Paris: Musée national d'art moderne de la ville de Paris, 1993.

*Niki de Saint Phalle*. Exh. cat. Düsseldorf: Kunstverein, 1968.

*Niki de Saint Phalle*. Exh. cat. Stockholm: Moderna Museet, 1981.

*Niki de Saint Phalle: exhibition retrospective*. Exh. cat. Paris: Musée national d'art moderne, Centre Georges Pompidou, 1980.

**Alfons Schilling**
*Alfons Schilling: binoculare Zeichnungen: traghare Instrumente (die Emotionalisierung)*. Zurich: Kunsthaus, 1979.

*Alfons Schilling: Sehmaschinen*. Exh. cat. Vienna: Österreichisches Museum für angewandte Kunst, 1987.

Federspiel, Jürg. "Alfons Schilling: ein Künstler des Raumschiffs gennant Erde." *Tages-Anzeiger Magazin* (Zurich), no. 21 (1977): 15-21.

Reder, Christian. "Mit dem Kopf durch die Leinwant. Im Gespräch mit Alfons Schilling." *Falter* (Vienna) 20 (October 1985): 19-20. Interview.

**Tomas Schmit**
*The Four Suits: Benjamin Patterson, Philip Corner, Alison Knowles, Tomas Schmit*. New York: Something Else Press, 1965.

*Tomas Schmit: Fishing for Nets*. Exh. cat. New York and Cologne: Michael Werner Gallery, 1994.

**Carolee Schneemann**
Cameron, Dan. "Object vs. Persona: The Early Work of Carolee Schneemann." *Arts Magazine* (New York) 57, no. 9 (May 1983): 122-125.

Castle, Ted. "Carolee Schneemann: The Woman Who Uses Her Body as Her Art." *Artforum* (New York) 19, no. 3 (November 1980): 64-70.

Kultermann, Udo. "Die Performance-Art von Carolee Schneemann." *Idea: Jahrbuch der Hamburger Kunsthalle* 6 (1987): 141-151.

McPherson, Bruce, ed. *Carolee Schneemann: More than Meat Joy: Complete Performance Works and Selected Writings, 1963-1978*. New Paltz, New York: Documentext, 1979.

**Rudolf Schwarzkogler**
Badura, Trisha Eva. *Rudolf Schwarzkogler: Leben und Werk*. Vienna: Museum moderner Kunst Stiftung Ludwig, 1992.

Klocker, Hubert. "Rudolf Schwarzkogler: Action Photography." *Camera Austria*, no. 42 (1993): 3-14.

*Rudolf Schwarzkogler*. Exh. cat. Innsbruck: Galerie Krinzinger, 1976.

*Rudolf Schwarzkogler*. Exh. cat. Vancouver: University of British Columbia, 1993.

*Schwarzkogler 1940-1969*. Exh. cat. Vienna: Galerie nächst St. Stephan, 1970.

**Bonnie Sherk**
Burnham, Linda. "Between the Diaspore and the Crinoline." *High Performance* (Los Angeles) 4, no. 3 (Fall 1981): 49-71. Interview.

Lambie, Alec. "Things are Not as They Seem." *Artweek* (Oakland, California) 3, March 25, 1972, 3.

Roth, Moira. "Toward a History of California Performance: Part One." *Arts Magazine* (New York) 52, no. 6 (February 1978): 94-103.

Tarshis, Jerome. "Portable Park Project 1-3." *Artforum* (New York) 9, no. 2 (October 1970): 84.

**Shōzō Shimamoto**
Shimamoto, Shōzō. *Geijutsu towa hito o odorokasu koto de aru* (Art is to Surprise People). Tokyo: The Mainshi Shimbun, 1994.

Shimamoto, Shōzō. *Jibun mo shiranai jibun no e* (My Pictures That Even I Did Not Know). Nishinomiya, Japan: Art Space, 1977.

*Shōzō Shimamoto Networking*. Nishinomiya, Japan: Art Space, 1990.

**Ushio Shinohara**
*Shinohara*. Exh. cat. New York: Japan House Gallery, 1982.

Shinohara, Ushio. "Jikken-shitsu: Fukusei kaiga no koko-romi" (Laboratory: An Experiment of Imitation Paintings). *Bijutsu techō*, no. 232 (February 1964): 62-67.

*Shinohara Ushio-ten/Ushio Shinohara*. Exh. cat. Hiroshima: City Museum of Contemporary Art et al., 1992.

**Kazuo Shiraga**
Shiraga, Kazuo. "Kōdō no yaju" (A Beast of Action). *Bijutsu techō*, no. 219 (April 1963): 65-68.

Shiraga, Kazuo. "Bōken no kiroku: Episōdo de tsuzuru Gutai gurūpu no 12-nen" (The Document of Adventure: Twelve Years of the Gutai Group). Parts 1-6. *Bijutsu techō*, nos. 285-289, 291 (July-December 1967).

*Shiraga Kazuo no sekai-ten* (The World of Shiraga Kazuo). Exh. cat. Kyoto: Gallery Be-Art, 1985.

*Shiraga Kazuo-ten/Kazuo Shiraga*. Exh. cat. Amagasaki, Japan: Cultural Center, 1989.

*Ugoki to koi no kiseki: Shiraga Kazuo, 1960-ten* (Movement and Action: Kazuo Shiraga, 1960). Exh. cat. Tokyo: The Contemporary Art Gallery, 1989.

**Barbara T. Smith**
Askey, Ruth. "Meal Time Catharsis." *Artweek* (Oakland, California), May 31, 1980.

Clothier, Peter. "Barbara Smith in Search of Identity." *Artweek* (Oakland, California), February 11, 1977.

Roth, Moira, ed. *Barbara Smith*. Exh. cat. La Jolla: Mandeville Gallery, University of California, San Diego, 1974.

Smith, Barbara T. "Birthdaze." *High Performance* (Los Angeles) 4, no. 3 (Fall 1981): 19-24.

Wortz, Melinda. "Barbara Smith's Dimensions." *Artweek* (Oakland, California), September 14, 1974.

**Daniel Spoerri**
*Daniel Spoerri*. Exh. cat. Paris: Centre national
d'art contemporain, 1972.

*Daniel Spoerri*. Exh. cat. Zurich: Helmhaus, 1972.

Hahn, Otto. *Daniel Spoerri*. Paris: Flammarion, 1990.

*Petit lexique sentimental autour de Daniel Spoerri.*
Exh. cat. Paris: Musée national d'art moderne,
Centre Georges Pompidou, 1990.

**Petr Štembera**
Marioni, Tom, ed. "Petr Štembera." In *Visions*
(Oakland, California), no. 2 (January 1976): 41-43.

Miller, Roland. "The Curtain Rises II." *Variant*
(England), no. 12 (Summer-Fall 1992): 18-21.

Štembera, Petr. "Petr Štembera." In *Oosteuropese
Conceptuel Fotografie*. Exh. cat. Eindhoven,
The Netherlands: Technische Hogeschool, 1977.

**Wolfgang Stoerchle**
*Harry Shunk: Projects — Pier 18*. Exh. cat. Nice:
Musée d'art moderne and de contemporain, 1992.

*Wolfgang Stoerchle*. Exh. cat. Grenoble, France:
Le Magasin, Centre national d'art contemporain, 1996.

"Wolfgang Stoerchle." *Studio International* (London)
(April 1972).

**Jirō Takamatsu**
*Gendai no sakka 2: Takamatsu Jirō/Artists Today 2:
Jirō Takamatsu*. Exh. cat. Osaka: The National Museum
of Art, 1980.

Lee, Fan U. "Takamatsu Jirō: Hyōshō-sagyō kara deai
no dekai e" (From Representation to Encounter).
*Bijutsu techō*, no. 320 (December 1969): 140-165.

Ōoka, Makoto. "Diarōgu 14: Takamatsu Jirō" (Dialogue
No. 14: Takamats Jirō). *Mizue*, no. 793 (February 1971):
44-55. Interview.

*Takamatsu Jirō-ten* (Takamatsu Jirō Exhibition).
Exh. cat. Tokyo: Tokyo Gallery, 1982.

Tani, Arata. "Seido-ron, sono go 1: Takamatsu Jirō —
aruiwa hy gen no kōzō ni tsuite" (After "Concerning the
'Institution,'" Part 1: Origins of Takamatsu Jirō — or,
On the Structure of Expression). *Bijutsu techō*, no. 375
(December 1973): 105-123.

Tono, Yoshiaki. "Japan." *Artforum* (New York): 5,
no. 8 (April 1967): 71-74.

**Atsuko Tanaka**
*Tanaka Atsuko koten* (Solo Exhibition of Tanaka Atsuko).
Exh. cat. Osaka: Gutai Pinacotheca, 1963.

*Tanaka Atsuko 1960: Ten to sen no uzumaki*
(Tanaka Atsuko 1960: The Votex of Points and Lines).
Exh. cat. Tokyo: The Contemporary Art Gallery, 1985.

*Tanaka Atsuko-ten* (Tanaka Atsuko Exhibition).
Exh. cat. Osaka: Gallery Kuranuki, 1991.

**Mark Thompson**
Brooks, Liz. "Seven Obsessions." *Performance*
(London), no. 62 (November 1990): 9-16.

"Mark Thompson." In *Animal Art Steirischer Herbst '87*.
Exh. cat. Graz, Austria: Steirischer Herbst, 1987.

"Mark Thompson." In *Performance-Ritual-Process*.
Ed. Elizabeth Jappe. New York and Munich: Prestel-
Verlag, 1993.

Thompson, Mark. "Lining the Wild Bee." In *Fire
Over Water*. Ed. Reese Williams. New York: Tanam
Press, 1986.

**Jean Tinguely**
Hulten, Pontus. *Meta: Jean Tinguely*. Boston:
New York Graphic Society, 1975.

*Jean Tinguely: Catalogue raisonné, sculptures and
reliefs, 1954-1968*. Zurich: Galerie Bischofberger, 1982.

*Jean Tinguely — Meta-Maschinen*. Exh. cat. Duisberg,
Germany: Wilhelm Lembruck Museum der Stadt, 1978.

*Machines de Tinguely*. Exh. cat. Paris:
Centre national d'art contemporain, 1971.

*Museum Jean Tinguely Basel: The Collection.*
Berne: Bentaly, 1996.

*Tinguely*. Exh. cat. Paris: Musée national d'art
moderne, 1988.

**Rāsa Todosijević**
Malsch, Friedmann. "Rāsa Dragoljub Todosijević."
*Kunstforum International* (Cologne), no. 117 (1992):
200-206. Interview.

Marioni, Tom, ed. "Rāsa Todosijević." In *Visions*
(Oakland, California), no. 2 (January 1976): 31-36.

*Rāsa Todosijević*. Exh. cat. Zagreb: Galerija
Suvremene Umjetnosti, 1982.

**Kerry Trengove**
*Kerry Trengove (1946-1991)*. Exh. cat.
London: Chisenhale Gallery, 1992.

*Kerry Trengove: Points of Defence*. Exh. cat.
Londonderry, Northern Ireland: Orchard Gallery, 1985.

*Kerry Trengove: Portail du Territoire*. Exh. cat.
Lyon, France: Musée du Rhone, 1981.

**Ulay**
McEvilley, Thomas. *Der Erste Akt* (The First Act).
Stuttgart: Edition Cantz, 1994.

*Ulay: Instant Fotografie*. Exh. cat.
Amsterdam: Stedelijk Museum, 1981.

*Ulay: Fototot*. Exh. cat. Zagreb:
Galerija Suvremene Umjetnosti, 1977.

**Ben Vautier**
*Art Ben*. Exh. cat. Amsterdam: Stedelijk Museum, 1973.

*Ben Libre*. Exh. cat. Saint Etienne, France:
Musée d'art et d'industrie, 1981.

*Ben, pour ou contre: une retrospective*. Exh. cat.
Marseilles: MAC, Galeries contemporaines des musées
and Paris: Réunion des musées nationaux, 1995.

*Ben Vautier*. Exh. cat. Valencia, Spain:
Institució Valenciana d'estudio i investigació, 1986.

**Wolf Vostell**
Schilling, Jürgen. *Wolf Vostell: Dé-coll/agen,
Verwischungen, Schichtenbilder, Bleibilder,
Objektbilder, 1955-1979*. Exh. cat. Braunschweig:
Kunstverein, 1980.

*Vostell*. Exh. cat. Berlin: Neuer Berliner
Kunstverein, 1975.

Vostell, Wolf. *Dé-coll/age Happenings*. Trans.
Laura P. Williams. New York: Something Else Press,
1966.

Vostell, Wolf. *40 10 Happening Konzepte 1954 to 1973*.
Milan: Multhipla Edizione, 1976.

Vostell, Wolf. *Happening und Leben*. Neuwid
and Berlin: Hermann Luchterhand Verlag, 1970.

**Franz Erhard Walther**
*Franz Erhard Walther*. Eindhoven, The Netherlands:
Stedelijk Van Abbemuseum, 1972.

Lange, Susanne. *Der 1. Werksatz (1963-1969) von
Franz Erhard Walther*. Exh. cat. Frankfurt am Main:
Museum für Moderne Kunst, 1991.

Lingner, Michael, ed. *Das Haus in dem ich wohne: die
Theorie zum Werkentwurf von Franz Erhard Walther*
(The House in Which I Live: The Theoretical Basis of the
Work of Franz Erhard Walther). Klagenfurt, Austria:
Ritter, 1990.

**Peter Weibel**
Dreher, Thomas. "Valie Export/Peter Weibel:
Multimedia Feminist Art." *Artefactum* (Belgium) 10,
no. 46 (December 1992-February 1993): 17-20.

Lischka, Gerhard Johann. "Peter Weibel." *Kunstforum
International* (Cologne), no. 108 (June-July 1990):
137-142. Interview.

*Peter Weibel: Malerei, Zwischen Anarchie und
Forschung*. Exh. cat. Graz, Austira: Neue Galerie am
Landesmuseum Joanneum, 1992.

Weibel, Peter. *Kritik der Kunst, Kunst der Kritik. Er Says
and I Say*. Vienna and Munich: Jugend and Volk, 1973.

**Franz West**
Fleck, Robert. "Franz West: Masterfully Unmasterly."
*Art Press* (Paris), no. 187 (January 1994): 16-22, E1-6.

"Franz West." *Parkett* (Switzerland), no. 37 (September
1993): special issue.

*Franz West*. Exh. cat. Ljubljana: Moderna Galerija, 1993.

*Franz West: Ansicht*. Exh. cat. Bern: Kunsthalle, 1988.

*Franz West: Investigations of American Art*. Exh. cat.
Warsaw: Galerie Foksal and New York: David Zwirner,
1992.

**Hannah Wilke**
*Hannah Wilke: A Retrospective*. Exh. cat.
Columbia: University of Missouri Press, 1989.

Savitt, Mark. "Hannah Wilke: The Pleasure Principle."
*Arts Magazine* (New York) 50, no. 1 (September 1975):
56-57.

Sims, Lowery. "Body Politics: Hannah Wilke and
Kaylynn Sullivan." In *Art & Ideology*. Exh. cat. New York:
The New Museum of Contemporary Art, 1984.

Wooster, Ann-Sargent. "Hannah Wilke." *Artforum*
(New York) 14, no. 4 (December 1975): 73-75.


**Emmett Williams**
Williams, Emmett. *My Life in Flux — and Vice Versa*.
Stuttgart: Edition Hansjörg Mayer, 1991.

Williams, Emmett. "Die Leiden der jungen Emmetts"
(The Suffering of the Young Emmett). *Kunstforum
International* (Cologne), no. 115 (September-October
1991): 197-205.

Williams, Emmett. *Schemes & Variations*. Stuttgart
and London: Edition Hansjörg Mayer, 1981.


**Zaj**
*A Zaj Sampler: Works by the Zaj Group of Madrid*.
Trans. Peter Besas. New York: Something Else Press,
1967.

Ferrer, Esther. "Fluxus and Zaj. " *Zehar* (Spain), no. 28
(December 1994-February 1995): 22-29.

*Juan Hidalgo — Zajy la generación del 51*.
Exh. cat. Las Palmas, Spain: Centro insular de cultura,
1990.

Hernández, Sol and Montse Ramírez. "Hidalgo and
Marchetti." *Flash Art* (Milan), no. 44-45 (April 1974).

*Zaj*. Exh. cat. Madrid: Museo national centro de arte
Reina Sofia, 1996.

**LENDERS TO THE
EXHIBITION'S READING ROOM:**

Vito Acconci, Eleanor Antin, John Baldessari,
Collezione Angelo Calamarini, Francesco Conz,
Bill Gaglione, Barbara Gladstone Gallery,
Jon Hendricks, Jean-Noël Herlin, Joan Jonas,
Allan Kaprow, Mike Kelley, Komar & Melamid,
Steven Lieber, Jean-Jacques Lebel, Archivio Piero
Manzoni, Marta Minujin, The National Museum of Art-
Osaka, Claes Oldenburg and Coosje van Bruggen,
Archivio Giuseppe Pinot Gallizio, Adrian Piper,
Carolee Schneemann, The Gilbert and Lila Silverman
Collection, Staatsgalerie Stuttgart, Magdalena Stumpf.

Special thanks to: Linda Bunting at the Getty Institute
of Research for Arts and Humanities, Jon Hendricks,
Jean-Noël Herlin, Allan Kaprow, Mike Kelley,
Steven Lieber, John Bowlt and Nicoletta Misler at the
Institute of Modern Russian Culture at USC.